London's 'Golden Mile'
*The Great Houses of the Strand
1550–1650*

Manolo Guerci

LONDON'S 'GOLDEN MILE'

THE GREAT HOUSES OF THE STRAND 1550–1650

Paul Mellon Centre
for Studies in British Art
Distributed by Yale University Press
New Haven and London

To my wife, Eleonora

First published in 2021 by the Paul Mellon Centre for Studies in British Art
16 Bedford Square, London, WC1B 3JA
paul-mellon-centre.ac.uk

Copyright © 2021 by Manolo Guerci

All rights reserved. This book may not be reproduced or transmitted in any form or by any means, electronic or mechanical, including photocopy, recording or any other information storage and retrieval system, without prior permission in writing from the publisher.

ISBN 978-1-913107-23-9 HB
Library of Congress Control Number: 2021935716

British Library Cataloguing-in-Publication Data
A catalogue record for this book is available from the British Library

Designed and typeset in Fontanova Indigo by Dalrymple
Origination by DL Imaging
Printed in China through World Print Ltd

Endpapers Details of John Norden, *Civitas Londini*, 1600.
National Library of Sweden

Frontispiece Canaletto, *The City of London*, c.1750, seen from the garden of Somerset House. Royal Collection Trust (detail of fig. 74)

Right Daniel Mytens, *Thomas Howard, Earl of Arundel*, ?1616, in the sculpture gallery at Arundel House. National Portrait Gallery, London (detail of fig. 42)

Contents

Acknowledgements vii

Abbreviations xii

Preface xiii

Introduction 1

1 ESSEX HOUSE 17

2 ARUNDEL HOUSE 33

3 SOMERSET HOUSE 55

4 THE SAVOY 77

5 BURGHLEY HOUSE 89

6 BEDFORD HOUSE 105

7 WORCESTER HOUSE 127

8 SALISBURY HOUSE 137

9 DURHAM HOUSE 159

10 YORK HOUSE 175

11 NORTHUMBERLAND HOUSE 195

Conclusion 219

Notes 226

Bibliography 247

Index 256

Acknowledgements

I BEGAN LOOKING AT THE ARCHITECTURAL history of London in 1998 when, as an Erasmus student at University College London, I attended an MPhil course, 'Eighteenth- and Nineteenth-century London', run by Adrian Forty. I remember how puzzling I found the eclecticism of some buildings such as Edmund Street's Law Courts, and how reassured I felt when looking at Charles Barry's Reform Club. I then moved on to studying the Roman Baroque through an enigmatic palace of the mid-seventeenth century, the Palazzo Mancini, born out of the cultural interchanges of the Roman and French courts: not only was it conceived by Cardinal Jules Mazarin, or Giulio Mazzarino, for his Italian family but it also eventually became the seat of the French Academy of Rome, from 1725 to 1804. This research set me on the move, first to Paris and eventually to London, by which time I had developed an interest in comparative studies of domestic architecture. In 2003 I moved to St John's College, Cambridge, where my archival experience and an eye for reconstruction drawings gained from working on the restoration of French monuments were put into practice on an MPhil and a PhD. Their subject turned out to be the so-called Strand palaces in London, eleven major houses which once stood along the Strand in London, all long gone but promising in terms of archival sources. This research required the investigation of a crucial area of the capital, surprisingly, if conveniently for me, understudied, given its importance first as the medieval setting of the power houses of the clergy, then as the headquarters of the greatest Tudor and Jacobean magnates. They turned it into the centre of architectural conspicuous consumption from about the 1550s to the 1650s. My PhD concentrated on Salisbury House and Northumberland House, the only palaces built at the beginning of the seventeenth century. Through later research at both St Catharine's College, Cambridge, and the Paul Mellon Centre for Studies in British Art, London, I expanded and concluded the study of Northumberland House, which became a leading workshop of British architectural practice and was the only Strand palace to reach the nineteenth century. Then I decided to analyse all eleven houses, as a book on the whole group had never been written.

Covering a journey begun some two decades ago, the list of acknowledgements is vast and I am grateful to many people over the course of my research. Here I should like to thank those directly involved with the creation of this book, beginning with the many scholars who have given generously of their time and expertise: Simon Adams, Jennifer Alexander, Elizabeth Angelicoussis, Patricia Croot, Matthew Dimmock, Dianne Duggan, Thomas Duggan, Anthony Geraghty, Dorian Gerhold, Elizabeth Goldring, Ruth Guilding, John Harris, Karen Hearn, Paula Henderson, Maurice Howard, Jill Husselby, Andrew Lawler, Philip McEvansoneya, Kathryn Morrison, Ann Saunders, Tracey Wedge and Jeremy Wood. Special thanks go to Gordon Higgott and Mark Girouard, who have followed and mentored my work since the beginning, have read and commented on most chapters and whose willingness to share what is a unique knowledge of the period has been both rare and inspiring. Equally, Maurice Howard has supported me and the development of the book with many important suggestions. The late David Watkin, who supervised my PhD, has also been a constant source of support, as well as the initiator of this prolific research, while Deborah Howard has been there for me each time I needed help. A particular mention must also be made of Gillian Malpass, longstanding and much-loved editor at Yale University Press in London, without whom this book would simply not exist.

The following owners of private archives have generously granted access to their documents, while their custodians have unfailingly supported this project: the Duke of Bedford, Ann Mitchell, Nicola Allen, Andrew Mitchell and

J. M. W. Turner, *York House Water-Gate, Westminster, with York Buildings Waterworks*, 1794–5 (detail of fig. 198)

Natasha Kikas at Woburn Abbey; Kate Harris at Longleat House; the Duke of Norfolk, John Martin Robinson, Heather Worne and Margaret Richards at Arundel Castle; the Duke of Northumberland, Christopher Hunwick, Claire Baxter, Lisa Little and the whole team at Alnwick Castle; the Burghley House Preservation Trust, Miranda Rock (house director), Jon Culverhouse (curator), Tim Halliday and Rosemary Canadine; the Marquess of Salisbury, Robin Harcourt-Williams (to whom go my warmest thanks) and Sarah Whale at Hatfield House; Elaine Milsom at Badminton House. Of those in charge of public repositories, I wish to acknowledge the archivists of the Paget Archives, Folger Shakespeare Library, Washington, DC; the London Metropolitan Archives; the Historic England Archives; Pamela Birch at the Bedfordshire Archives and Records Office; Claire Brown at Lambeth Palace; Steven Hobbs and Gill Neal at the Wiltshire and Swindon Archives; Andrew George at the Staffordshire Record Office; Diane Ludlow at the West Sussex Record Office; and Andrew Parry at the Gloucestershire Archives. As for the many librarians who facilitated my work, I thank the staff at the Courtauld Institute of Art and the British Library, London, as well as those at Cambridge University Library, particularly Colin Clarkson, for his kind assistance over many a palaeographical query. My gratitude also goes to Emma Atwood at Boston College; Mark Bainbridge and Renée Prud'Homme at Worcester College, Oxford; Julia Gardner at the University of Chicago Library; Charles Hind and Jonathan Makepeace at the RIBA Drawing Collection, London; Mark Nicholls at St John's College, Cambridge; Susan Palmer and Frances Sands at the Sir John Soane's Museum Library, London; Mary L. Robertson at the Huntington Library, San Marino, California; the staff at Sotheby's Research Department; Kate Higgins at the Mercers' Company, London; and A.C. Cooper Ltd. Those mentioned in this paragraph, as well as the institutions indicated in the image captions, also provided invaluable assistance and, where possible, free or reduced fees for the publication of images in their care. In a book so heavily illustrated, this made for a significant contribution and I am very grateful to them all. Equally, I wish to thank the Marc Fitch Fund, the Society of Architectural Historians of Great Britain, and the Division of Arts and Humanities of the University of Kent for their generous support with image costs.

Research for this book has been supported by the British Academy, the Kent School of Architecture and Planning, the Isaac Newton Trust and the Paul Mellon Centre for Studies in British Art. The Mellon has indeed been behind every step of it, and I am very grateful to Brian Allen, Mark Hallett, Martin Postle, Sarah Turner, Mary Smith, Emily Lees, Katharine Ridler and Tom Powell. As editors, Emily and Katharine were incredibly helpful throughout the publication process. The anonymous peer reviewers, alongside comments from the Paul Mellon Centre's Publications Committee, have also much improved the book, while any remaining errors or inaccuracies are obviously my own.

Don Gray, Gerald Adler and Natalie Conetta, together with my colleagues at CREAte (the Centre for Research in European Architecture) of the Kent School of Architecture and Planning at the University of Kent, have been an invaluable source of support. Among my friends – you know who you are and I love you all – I should like to mention Claudia Conforti and the late Paolo Avarello, splendid hosts each time I happened to be in Rome. An eminent scholar of the history of Italian architecture (and more), Claudia has been a constant source of encouragement and is a very dear friend.

After completing the first draft of this book in March 2018, I had a serious skiing accident in the Alps. My gratitude goes to everyone who assisted me, from the first aid carabinieri to the medic and paramedic of the air ambulance who brought me to Brixen's hospital, where I was treated. Michael Rauter, the surgeon who twice operated on me, alongside the doctors and nurses there, was truly excellent. Addenbrooke's Hospital in Cambridge took over my care, while the physiotherapists Martin Callingham at the Cambridge Physiotherapy Clinic, Hannah Burlinson at Brooksfield Hospital Campus's Dynamic Health and Stefano Lombardi at the Wellness Centre, Cambridge, literally made me walk again. The surgeons Claudio Pizzi, Francesco Boni and Luigi Mossa, as well as the neurologist Paul Watts, friends of the family, have provided unfailing and constant support. To Peter Passler, whom I met while in hospital and has since become a friend, helping me at every opportunity during the long process of recovery, including hospitality and assistance at Brixen, go heartfelt thanks. To my brother Dario, with whom I was skiing, and my mother, Alba, who nursed me for several weeks, I give my grateful love. I also want to thank my mother and my father, Luciano, for being a rock in my life, and my parents-in-law, Maddalena and Filippo, for all their support and for being such nice people. Over many a conversation, including on the complexities related to living in two countries with a young family, and with parents coming and going, Gillian Malpass once told me that one would have to thank them for having splendidly delayed this book, at which we both laughed, but it is hard to imagine how I would have coped without their presence. To my wife, Eleonora, who has shared every burden by looking after our children, Angelica and Giulio, during countless research trips and extended periods of writing, and has been *there* throughout, I dedicate this book.

following pages William Morgan, *London and Westminster*, *c.*1682. By permission of the Pepys Library, Magdalene College, Cambridge ('London and Westminster', I, 2972, 38–39)

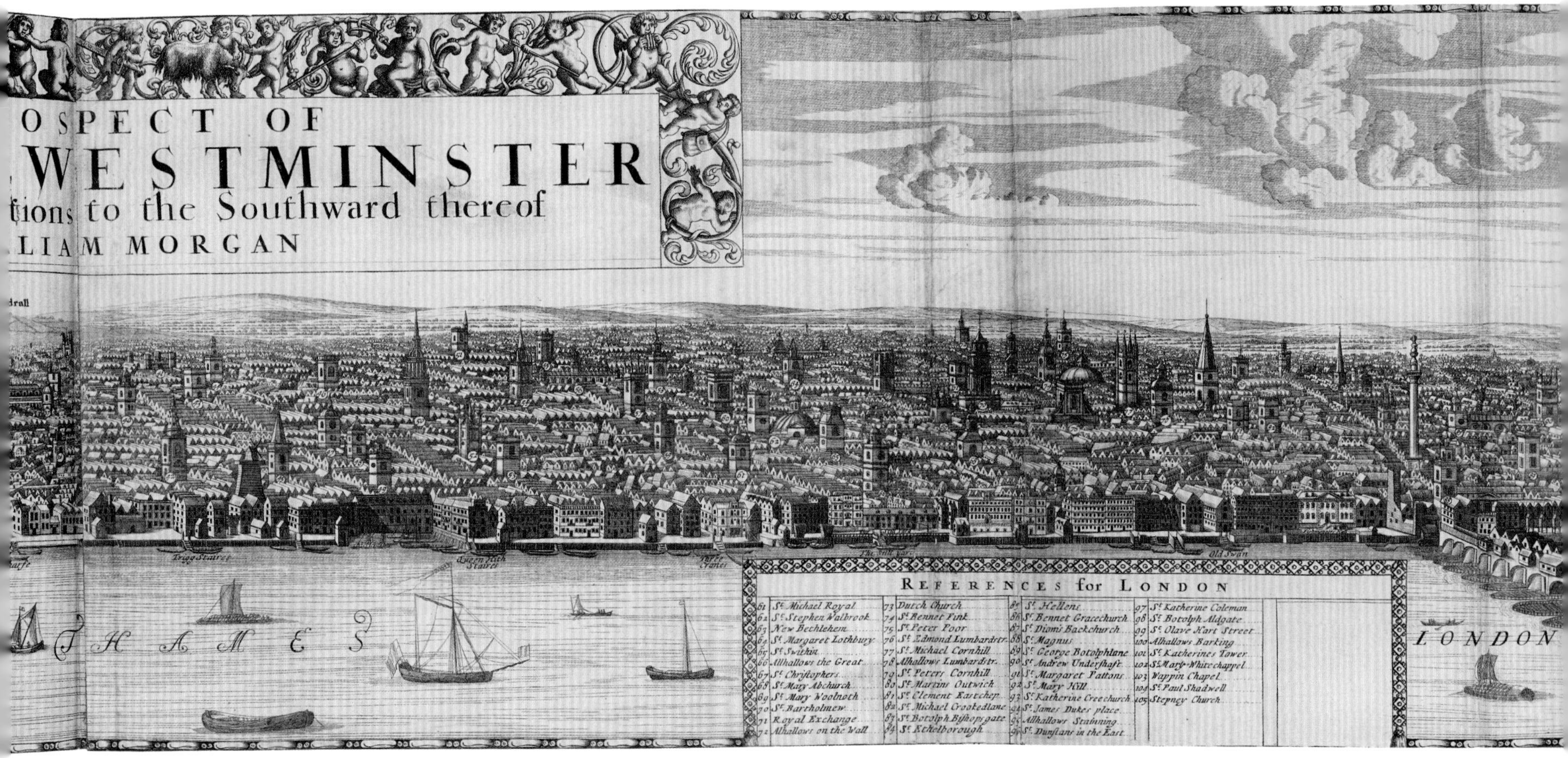

OSPECT OF WESTMINSTER
tions to the Southward thereof
LIAM MORGAN

REFERENCES for LONDON

61 St. Michael Royal	73 Dutch Church	85 St. Hellens	97 St. Katherine Colemun
62 St. Stephen Walbrook	74 St. Bennet Fink	86 St. Bennet Gracechurch	98 St. Botolph Aldgate
63 New Bechlehem	75 St. Peter Poor	87 St. Dionis Backchurch	99 St. Olave Hart Street
64 St. Margaret Lothbury	76 St. Edmund Lumbardstr.	88 St. Magnus	100 Alhallows Barking
65 St. Swithin	77 St. Michael Cornhill	89 St. George Botolphlane	101 St. Katherines Tower
66 Alhallows the Great	78 Alhallows Lumbardstr.	90 St. Andrew Undershaft	102 St. Mary-Whitechappel
67 St. Chrystophers	79 St. Peters Cornhill	91 St. Margaret Pattons	103 Wappin Chapel
68 St. Mary Abchurch	80 St. Martins Outwich	92 St. Mary Hill	104 St. Paul Shadwell
69 St. Mary Woolnoth	81 St. Clement Eastcheap	93 St. Katherine Creechurch	105 Stepney Church
70 St. Bartholmew	82 St. Michael Crookedlane	94 St. James Dukes place	
71 Royal Exchange	83 St. Botolph Bishopsgate	95 Alhallows Staininge	
72 Alhallows on the Wall	84 St. Ethelborough	96 St. Dunstans in the East	

THAMES

LONDON

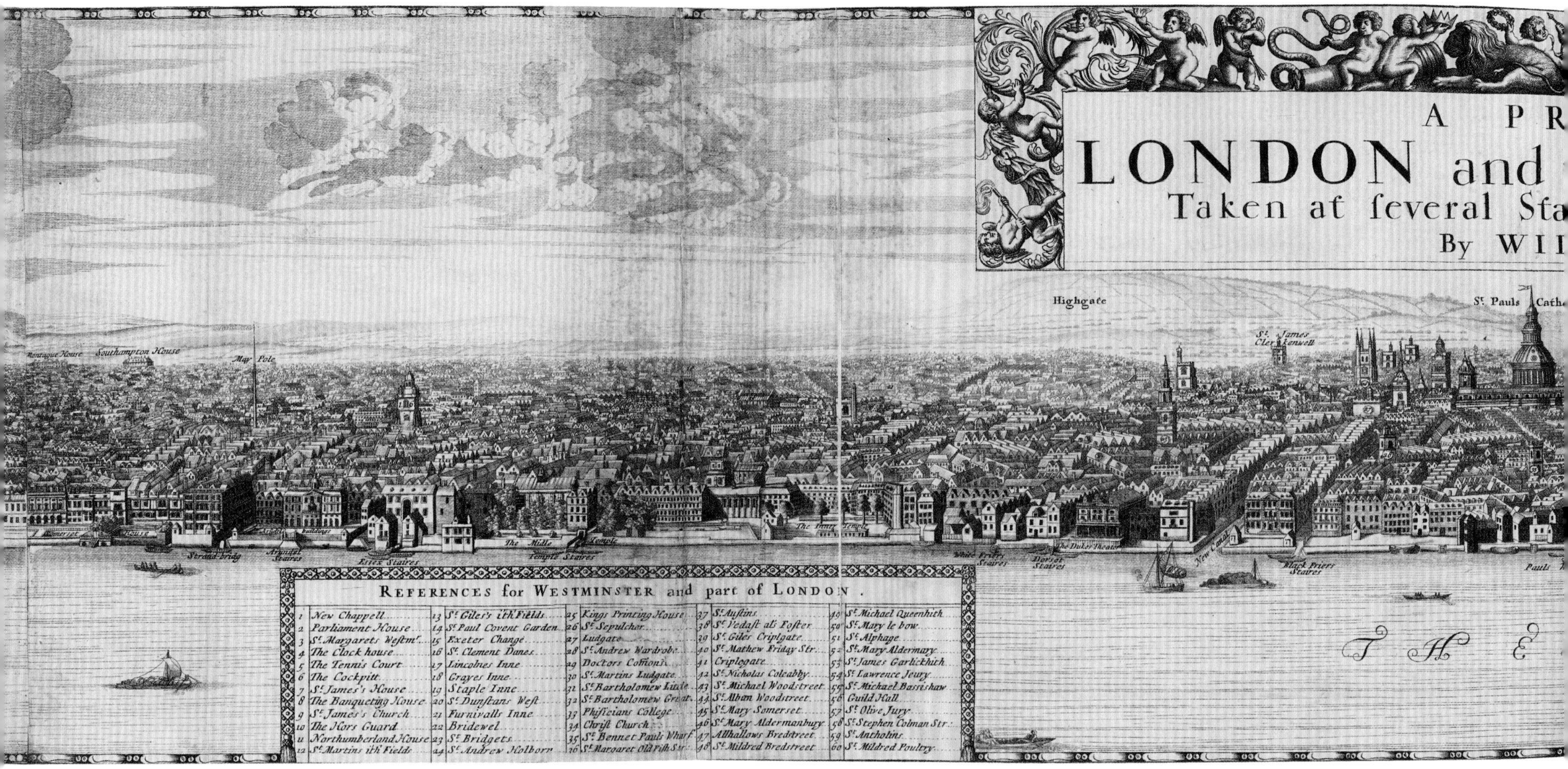

A PR[OSPECT of the Cities of]
LONDON and [WESTMINSTER]
Taken at several Sta[tions...]
By WI[LLIAM...]

REFERENCES for WESTMINSTER and part of LONDON.

#		#		#		#	
1	New Chappell	13	St Giles's ith Fields	25	Kings Printing House	37	St Austins	49	St Michael Queenhith
2	Parliament House	14	St Paul Covent Garden	26	St Sepulcher	38	St Vedast ali Foster	50	St Mary le bow
3	St Margarets Westmr	15	Exeter Change	27	Ludgate	39	St Giles Criplgate	51	St Alphage
4	The Clock house	16	St Clement Danes	28	St Andrew Wardrobe	40	St Mathew Friday Str	52	St Mary Aldermary
5	The Tennis Court	17	Lincolns Inne	29	Doctors Commons	41	Criplgate	53	St James Garlickhith
6	The Cockpitt	18	Grayes Inne	30	St Martins Ludgate	42	St Nicholas Coleabby	54	St Lawrence Jewry
7	St James's House	19	Staple Inne	31	St Bartholomew Little	43	St Michael Woodstreet	55	St Michael Bassishaw
8	The Banqueting House	20	St Dunstans West	32	St Bartholomew Great	44	St Alban Woodstreet	56	Guild Hall
9	St James's Church	21	Furnivalls Inne	33	Physicians College	45	St Mary Somerset	57	St Olive Jury
10	The Hors Guard	22	Bridewel	34	Christ Church	46	St Mary Aldermanbury	58	St Stephen Colman Str
11	Northumberland House	23	St Bridgets	35	St Bennet Pauls Wharf	47	Alhallows Bredstreet	59	St Ancholins
12	St Martins ith Fields	24	St Andrew Holborn	36	St Margaret Old Fish Str	48	St Mildred Bredstreet	60	St Mildred Poultry

Abbreviations

ACA	Alnwick Castle Archives
AC	Arundel Castle Archives
AT	Anthony Taussig's Private Archives
BH	Burghley House Archives
BHA	Badminton House Archives
BL	British Library, London
BOD	Bodleian Library, Oxford
CP	Cecil Papers, Hatfield House Archives
CKS	Centre for Kentish Studies, Canterbury
CSP	Calendar of State Papers
EP	Estate Papers, Hatfield House Archives
EPM	Estate & Private Manuscripts, Hatfield House Archives
FP	Family Papers, Hatfield House Archives
FPS	Family Papers Supplement, Hatfield House Archives
FP2S	Family Papers 2nd Supplement, Hatfield House Archives
HE	Historic England Archives, Swindon
HH	Hatfield House Archives
HL	Huntington Library, San Marino, California
HMC	Historical Manuscripts Commission
IHR	Institute of Historical Research, London
LH	Longleat House Archives
LMA	London Metropolitan Archives
LP	Lambeth Palace Library, London
NPG	National Portrait Gallery, London
OED	Oxford English Dictionary
ODNB	Oxford Dictionary of National Biography
PHA	Petworth House Archives (West Sussex Record Office)
RIBA	Royal Institute of British Architects, London
SM	Sir John Soane's Museum, London
SP	State Papers, The National Archives
TNA	The National Archives, Kew
WA	Woburn Abbey Archives
WC	Worcester College Library, Oxford
WSHC	Wiltshire and Swindon History Centre

Preface

ORIGINATING FROM MY CAMBRIDGE doctorate, 'The Strand Palaces of the Early Seventeenth Century: Salisbury House and Northumberland House' (2007), which concentrated on two of the eleven great houses which once stood along the Strand, this book illustrates a crucial yet much neglected chapter of London's history. Neglected, no doubt, because none of these houses survived that frenzy of redevelopment that has long characterised the capital, of which the Strand as a strategic thoroughfare remains a poignant reminder. The site of Arundel House, for instance, has been recently redeveloped once more, while most if not all the buildings which replaced the Strand palaces from the late seventeenth century onwards have themselves been long superseded. If the Strand, and the centre of London in general, is made of many different layers from particular ages and fashions, its golden age falls within the hundred-odd years between the 1550s and the 1650s. This coincides with the apex of those magnates, old and new, who flourished during the Tudor and Jacobean era, arguably the most fascinating period of English history.

Since the beginning of this project, I have asked myself how to approach the subject, as a book on the whole of the Strand palaces was clearly a daunting task. Not only was it because this is a history of reconstruction based exclusively on records which are widely scattered, uneven in scale per case study and rarely of the most directly helpful kind such as plans and drawings. The main question, in fact, was whether to produce a house-by-house analysis or one which would cross-reference them through thematic discussions. The latter structure had a certain appeal as, after many years of collecting and processing documents on these houses, I was perhaps more inclined to draw conclusions than set the scene. This presented, however, a fundamental problem, for without setting that scene there could be no theme-based argument, while a book which attempted both scopes seemed to me too ambitious and unmanageable: what I was confronted with was in fact the first step, from scratch, towards bringing the great Strand houses and their largely unwritten histories back to the fore of scholarly debate. I therefore conceived this book as a sort of compendium in which each house, arranged in topographical order from east to west, is chronologically analysed with its builders, inhabitants, contents and subsequent histories roughly within the timeframe just mentioned, and with short introductory sections on their origins and summaries of their subsequent histories, following traditional historical descriptions of London's architecture. The conclusion, however, highlights parallels according to themes, so as to instigate future discussion.

While every attempt has been made to reconsider each house afresh, the scale and scope of the chapters vary according to what could be found and the accessibility of the sources, not always straightforward when dealing with private archives.

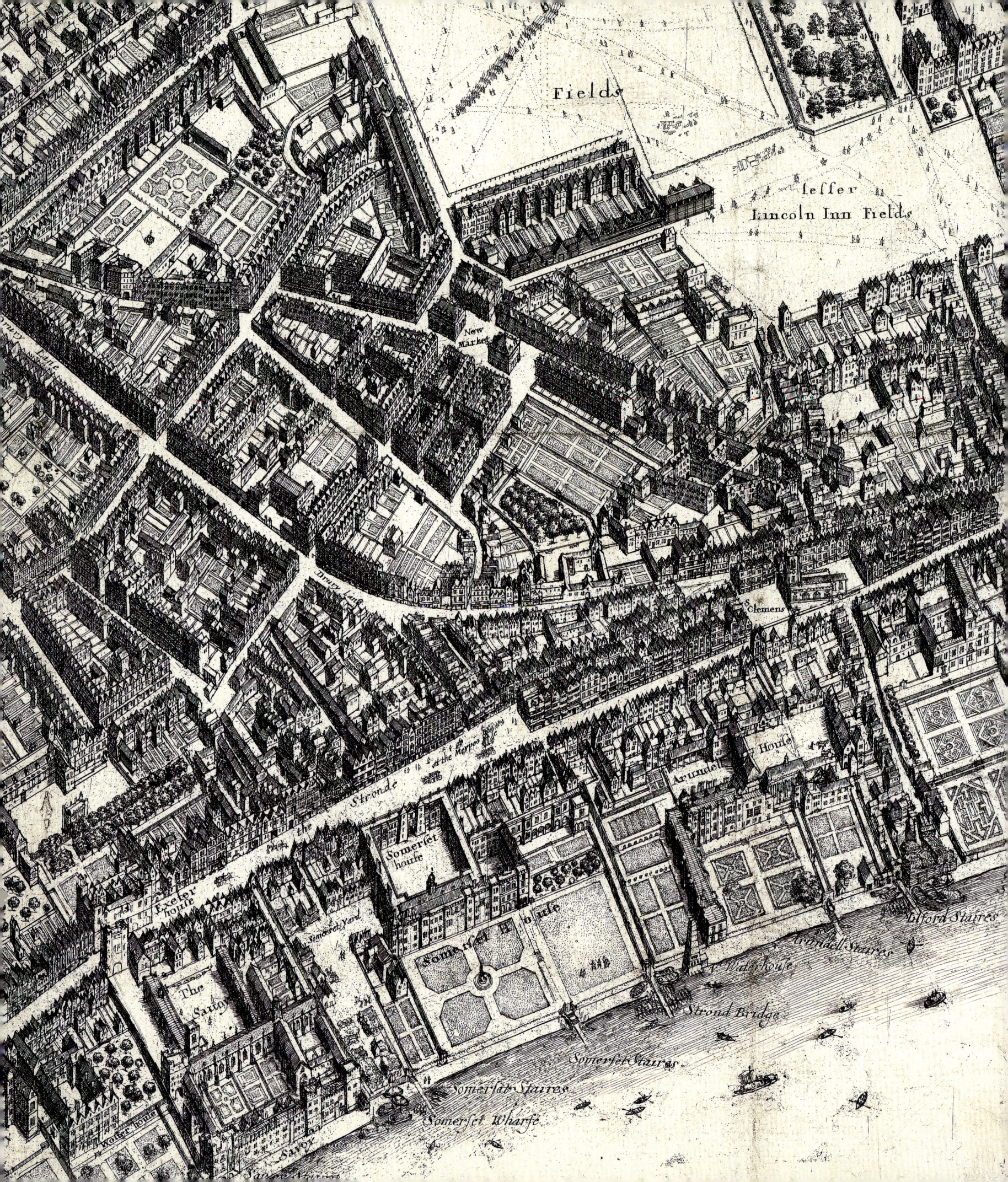

INTRODUCTION

IN BRITISH POPULAR CULTURE, THE TERM 'Golden Mile' refers to the stretch of amusement arcades on the seafront at Blackpool, with the Tower and its Ballroom, the rides and fortune tellers, the phrenologists and oyster bars, or indeed the many slot machines which may have triggered the nickname.¹ In recent times it has been more widely appropriated as a synonym of bounty; indeed, *mutatis mutandis*, the term perfectly captures the uniqueness of the Strand in London, and the galaxy of power and prestige broadcast to the Early Modern world via an unprecedented level of architectural conspicuous consumption.² As this book will show, the protagonists are the so-called 'Strand palaces', eleven great houses built from the mid-sixteenth century along the Strand, hence their name. All but two faced the River Thames. Neither 'Strand' nor 'palace' has ever been part of their individual names, which stem from their most famous builders or occupants and, customarily for this country (and, consequently, in the title of this book), avoid anything grander than 'house' for non-royal residences. Both words, however, perfectly describe what we are dealing with. The location identifies a historically crucial thoroughfare, of which more shortly, while 'palace' refers to the way these houses were perceived, given the civic role they performed within a city which had not quite seen the like before. For the Strand palaces created a virtually uninterrupted line of majestic riverside mansions, embodying the same sense of prestige discussed in theoretical literature on urban architecture from Alberti onwards and rooted in the palazzi that beautified many great cities on the Continent, not least because of their function in international diplomacy. A 'palace', as David Pearce explained in his *London's Mansions* (1986),

> *is not just a big house, nor in this context a royal or Episcopal house, nor even necessarily the residence of an aristocrat – it is a house designed for ceremony, a house of parade, self-consciously formal. It is lifted above the ordinary by its scale, drama and, perhaps, beauty. Such a mansion is to be approached, entered and traversed in a pre-ordained sequence ...*³

Developed to represent the state as de facto substitutes for Whitehall by the Post-Reformation political class, this palatial type grew out of the necessity for their occupants to be in London once a permanent court had been established at Whitehall. The majority of the Strand palaces

1 Wenceslaus Hollar, bird's-eye view of the 'West Central District' (detail of fig. 8)

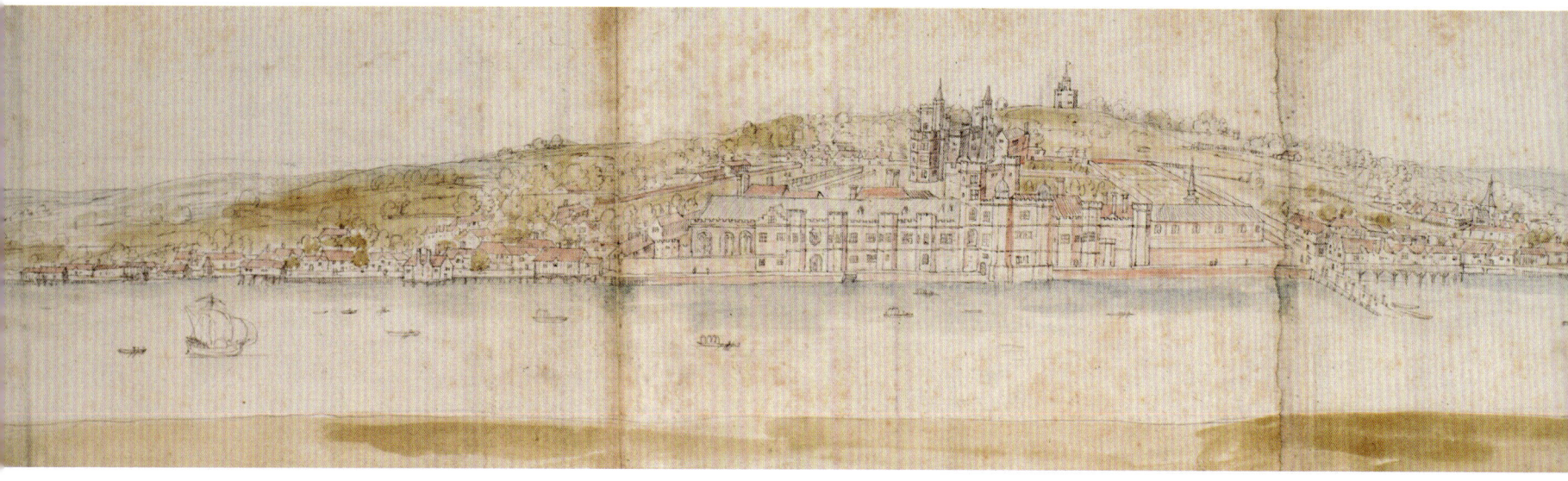

differed from their European counterparts in a fundamental way: they lacked an urban appearance, for they hid from the street and instead opened towards the Thames, recreating a *rus in urbe* at a time of increasing development – one could think of a parallel with the Italian *villa suburbana*. They were, according to how one approached them, completely secluded. There could indeed be no greater contrast between the urban and the riverside, for the impression one got from the Strand, in spite of several rather imposing gatehouses, would give little or no idea of what a visitor would be confronted with once inside. The reason for this is that at least five of the nine Strand palaces overlooking the Thames could be approached from the river, often via ornate water gates which gave access to elaborate gardens, deep enough to allow the right sense of perspective and even grandeur to the approach itself. In these instances, the water front acted as the main entrance.[4] Accounting records are full of expenses for travelling along the Thames, while Pepys's diary offers many insights into the busy riverine environment. Described by Stow in 1598 as 'more than 60 miles in length, to the great commodity of Travellers, by which all kinde of merchandites are easily convaied to London, the principal Store-house, and staple of all commodities', the Thames was twice as wide as it is currently, and deep enough for the fleet to lie anchored close to buildings.[5] It was also well stocked with 'the fat and sweet salmon, daily taken in the streams, and that in such plenty as no river in Europe is able to excel it', as William Harrison reported in his *Description of England* of 1577.[6] It is therefore unsurprising that the river should have acted as a magnet for prime residential property, be it episcopal, aristocratic, or indeed royal palaces.

Perhaps the first of the riverine typology relevant here was Greenwich Palace (fig. 2), a Crown property from the mid-fifteenth century conveniently close to Eltham Palace, the hunting lodge of Henry VIII.[7] As a staging post between Dover and London, Greenwich would have been the first mansion anyone would have seen. Equally, given its position on rising ground, and the bend of the Thames, views from it would have been far-reaching to both east and west. This is another trait observable in the Strand palaces, the rooftops of which (and towers, 'surveying houses' or, in one instance, a major portico by the river) would have commanded ample views. Greenwich was of course the most easterly of a series of royal palaces along the river, followed, in a westward direction, by Whitehall, Richmond and Hampton Court. In the middle of and facing this royal route, like the royal box of a theatre, the Strand itself extended from Temple Bar to Charing Cross, acting as the 'big channel of communication' between the City and the Inns of Court to the east and the Court and Parliament to the west, respectively the economic, judicial and political sancta of the kingdom (fig. 3). River and highway were therefore two sides of the same coin when it came to access, representation, significance and land value, hence to the establishment of the Strand as London's 'Golden Mile'.

The role of the Thames and the relative status of those sites which faced it and those which did not – we could speak of the nine riverside palaces versus the two on the north side of the

2 Anthonis van den Wyngaerde, view of Greenwich Palace from the river, 1558–62. © Ashmolean Museum, University of Oxford

3 Georg Braun and Franz Hogenberg, 'London' in *Civitates Orbis Terrarum*, 1572, derived from the lost 'Copperplate Map of London' of 1553–9. University Library, Heidelberg. Wikipedia, Public Domain

The Strand is shown on the bend of the Thames down river from Westminster.

Strand – raise a number of points discussed in the following chapters. These include water gates (as opposed to gatehouses) and gardens, 'surveying houses' from which views of the river could be enjoyed, or indeed riverside promenades or roof walks, and how important these were for the design and appearance of each complex. The question as to whether the riverside palaces were more prestigious than those on the north side of the Strand is an interesting one, for, despite all the advantages described, what also mattered was the capacity for self-sufficiency provided by fields and orchards and the possibility they afforded for further expansion and speculation, an aspect which proved crucial in the subsequent history of the Strand palaces. Indeed, the large area of Covent Garden, thus named as originally the garden of the Convent of Westminster, is linked to the most important of the riverside palaces. It eventually formed the core, with Friars Pyes and Long Acre, of what is still one of the largest private holdings in London, the Bedford Estates. Equally, prominent Strand magnates whose palaces were limited in size and capacity to expand strove to amass land in the area and attempted or managed to purchase or control more than one site. Besides, in the small pond of Tudor and Jacobean politics most of these patrons were related to one another in some way. Indeed, by the time the Strand had reached full capacity in the mid-seventeenth century, marriage was expressly being used to gain ownership of a palace there, as in the case of Northumberland House (see Chapter Eleven).

To go back to what we might describe as the dichotomy, perhaps quintessentially English, between 'outward' and 'inward', and to get an idea of the impact of those Strand palaces which did have a proper urban front, let us turn again to Harrison's 1577 *Description of England*:

This also hath beene common in England, contrarie to the customes of all other nations, and yet to be seene (for example in most streets of London), that many of our greatest houses have outwardlie beene verie simple and plaine to sight, which inwardlie have beene able to receive a duke with his whole traine, and lodge them at their ease. Hereby moreover it is come to passe, that the front of our streets have not beene so uniforme and orderlie builded as those of forreine cities.[8]

In the Strand, aspects of uniformity and order would be picked up by some of the most civic-minded patrons according to the Albertian recommendation that the planning of a house should be reflected in the decorum of the overall city. But the dichotomy between exterior and interior, as well as the differences between sites among the eleven palaces, are also a sign of where most of them came from. For they nearly all originated, to varying degrees, from the so-called Bishops' Inns, the power-houses of the high clergy built from the thirteenth century onwards, most of them outside the City itself in the open spaces along the Strand, a village which simply took its name from being located on the shore or 'strand' of the Thames.[9] As self-sustaining estates, the inns relied on the 'rents', tenements with shops at ground level along the street front, which customarily formed part of their precincts, thereby hiding the main house. Being too valuable to be disposed of, they determined the commercial viability of these properties, a factor in the eventual downfall of the Strand palaces. It is after the break with Rome, and the consequent Dissolution of the monasteries from 1536, that the inns were gradually taken over, remodelled or rebuilt by those who had risen to prominence under the Tudors and later the early Stuarts. This had famously included the confiscation of Cardinal Wolsey's own palace at Whitehall, where Henry VIII then based his court and where, one might say, it had all begun (fig. 4).

The climax of our story came between roughly the 1550s and 1650s, starting with the construction of Somerset House from 1547 and ending with the Civil Wars of 1642–51, by which time some of the great houses had begun to decline. It is a century which saw the entrenchment of conspicuous consumption in architecture as well as the notion of a permanent satellite court, whereby a number of these seats were either treated as extensions to Whitehall or became royal property. This does not mean that those sites closest to Whitehall had a higher status (certainly in the first part of the period), for what mattered was size, whether existing buildings were habitable or could be repurposed, their status according to the bishopric they had represented and, as mentioned, access to and prominence from the river, alongside self-sufficiency and potential for development. Those properties physically closer to the Court did indeed rise in importance towards the second part of the period but this was more to do with the availability of plots than a real shift in the way these palaces were appreciated. As we shall see, it is Somerset House, about halfway along the Strand, that marked a seismic shift in terms of self-representation and the establishment of a secular palatial type. It is also the palace that became the main residence of queens, starting from Elizabeth I, thereby creating a royal outpost between the City and Whitehall, as well as adding another stop, as it were, on the riverine path which connected all royal palaces.

Prior to what one might call the Strand palace phenomenon, the need to spend more time in the capital in order to pass the Henrician legislative programme had already seen leading courtiers establish permanent and often grand seats in London. Some of these were in the City, such as Thomas Cromwell's at Austin Friars or Sir Edward North's at the Charterhouse, which not only still stands but also went from monastic to secular occupancy (fig. 5).[10] Indeed, after it had passed in 1565 to Thomas Howard, 4th Duke of Norfolk, this house was known as Howard House, where another Thomas Howard, 1st Earl of Suffolk, lived before inheriting his uncle's Northampton (later Northumberland) House in the Strand. And the Strand is where the first bishops' inns passed into the hands of other (perhaps higher) courtiers from the 1530s. In effect, it is the availability of these episcopal properties that not only allowed closer proximity to the Court but stepped up the game altogether. In parallel to the Dissolution of the religious houses, this edging out of bishops from their old seats, whether along the Strand or elsewhere in London, was used by the Henrician government to provide an expanded and radicalised court with new domestic outposts.[11]

While this secularisation established a type of grand house across London and the country, the Strand was top of the list for any ambitious courtier. Still relatively undeveloped in the early to mid-1500s, especially on the northern side, its great ecclesiastical estates provided much space for

4 Anthonis van den Wyngaerde, view of Whitehall Palace from the river, *c*.1544. Bodleian Libraries, University of Oxford. Wikipedia, Public Domain

5 Bird's-eye view of the Charterhouse, 1786. Wellcome Collection, London. Wikimedia Commons, licensed under Creative Commons Attribution 4.0 International

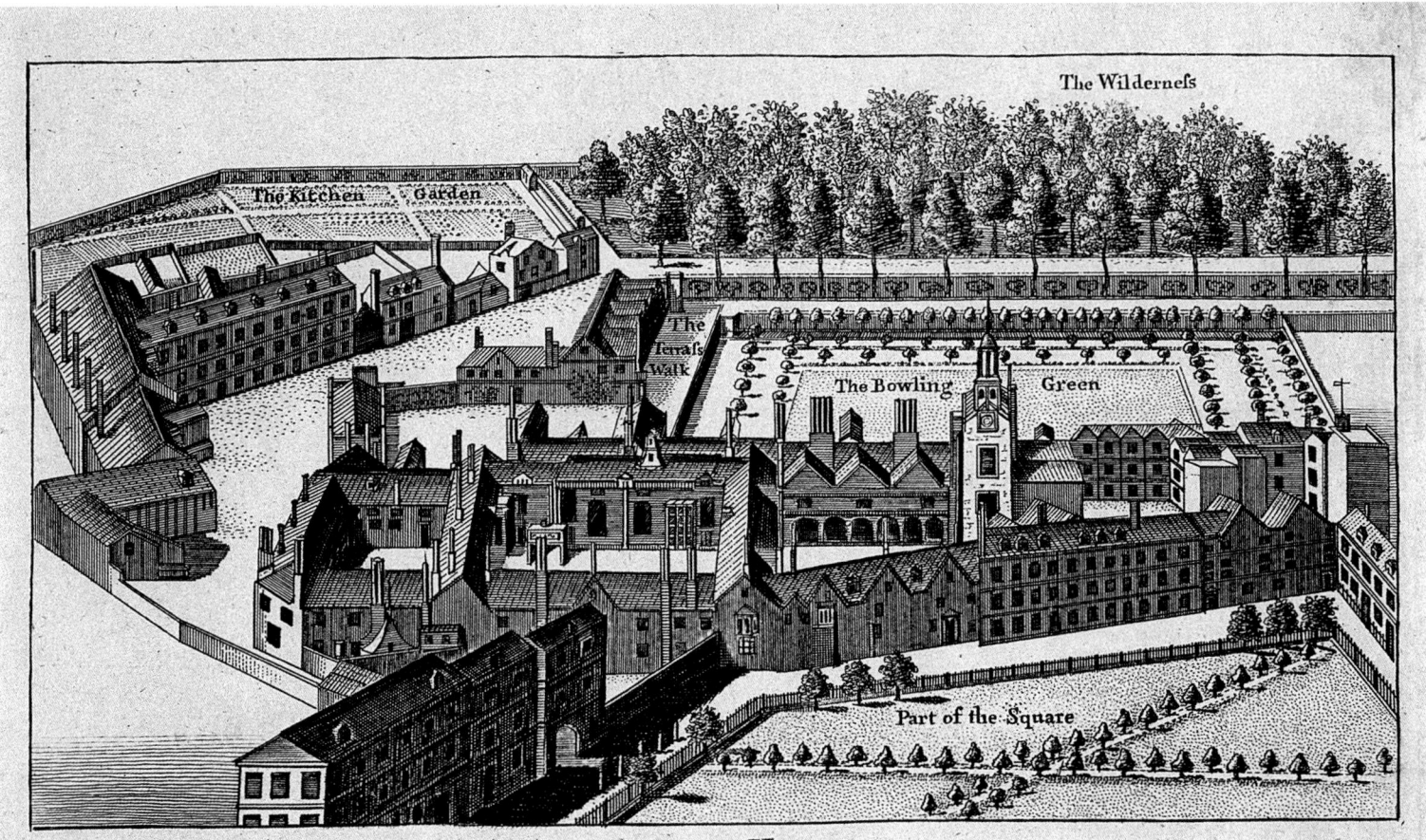

THE CHARTER HOUSE

6 Magdalena de Passe, or Willem de Passe, *Edward Seymour, 1st Duke of Somerset*, 1620. © National Portrait Gallery, London (D23465)

development and houses on the river side would have been prominently situated. There ensued a war for the last plot between old and nouveaux courtiers and magnates, with bricks and mortar as the sharpest of weapons.

The protagonists cover the whole spectrum of the Tudor and Jacobean ruling elite, from those who emerged with Henry VIII, chief among them Edward Seymour, Lord Protector Somerset (fig. 6), who built Somerset House, to Elizabeth I's favourites, Leicester and Essex, closely associated with Essex House.[12] Then there were William and Robert Cecil, both Secretary of State under Elizabeth's long reign and 'rulers' of what has been described as the 'Regnum Cecilianum', who in turn erected Burghley House and Salisbury House. As Master of the Court of Wards and High Steward of Westminster, William not only controlled the patrimony of noblemen minor, quite a few of whom had possessions in the Strand, but also virtually the whole area, where he and Robert amassed major holdings. With another pillar of the Strand, Henry Howard, 1st Earl of Northampton (who went on to build Northampton House), Robert also secured the succession of James I (fig. 7). There were the Bacons, Sir Nicholas and Sir Francis, as well as Sir Thomas Egerton, the Baron Ellesmere of the famous household ordinances produced for York House, where all three had lived as keepers of the Privy Seal. Among the Stuart favourites were George Villiers, 1st Duke of Buckingham, and Philip Herbert, 4th Earl of Pembroke, who both earned a substantial piece of the Strand, the first ousting Francis Bacon from York House under James I, the second acquiring one of the most sizeable and historically important episcopal palaces, Durham House, under James's successor, Charles I. During Elizabeth's reign, the latter house had been the residence of Sir Walter Ralegh, a notorious casualty of the change from the last Tudor to the first Stuart. The seventeenth century brought other famous residents such as the Earl Collector Thomas Howard, 14th Earl of Arundel, of Arundel House, and Algernon Percy, 10th Earl of Northumberland, who turned Northampton House (or Suffolk House, renamed after another Thomas, James I's notorious Lord Treasurer) into the long-lasting London seat of the Percys. Alongside the Cecils at Burghley House on the north side of the Strand lived the Russells at Bedford House, who were later involved with the development of Covent Garden and are still in control of the Bedford Estates. Old and new, these resonant names, and four generations of queens at Somerset House, were coupled with royal embassies and visiting dignitaries from foreign courts, as well as with writers, poets, artists and architects such as Chaucer, Spenser, Hollar, Rubens, Orazio Gentileschi, Ben Jonson and Inigo Jones, or Balthasar Gerbier, a mere illustrious few of the creative minds along the Strand. Altogether, patrons, artists and foreign dignitaries give us a sense of how much these grand houses represented what has been described as a 'multinational, polyglot constellation of potency and influence' and 'an unparalleled site for the privileged enjoyment of the hospitality and general largesse of the early modern elite'.[13]

All in all, the Strand palaces are a varied lot, as were their builders' and occupants' stances on architecture. Yet, while leading figures were sometimes highly instrumental in building at these sites, just as many simply lodged in them and we do not know what if anything they contributed. That said, never before or after this period was the Strand such a focus for experiment and display. Nor was its architecture ever again so influential, for its patrons also erected remarkable country seats with the same competitive drive, often employing the same architects and craftsmen. Apart from this town

7 Unknown artist, *The Somerset House Conference*, 1604. © National Portrait Gallery, London (665)

Robert Cecil and Henry Howard sit prominently to the right, at the head of the English delegation.

and country mutual influence, discussed in the Conclusion, the Strand houses played a pivotal role in introducing new motifs and fashions in style, arrangement and display. Because of their relative accessibility, it was possible for anyone important to visit them, whereas country houses were remote and difficult to reach and there were no images in circulation.[14] It is indeed because of their influence that one might even suggest that the Strand palaces are key to the shaping of an English architectural identity.

By the mid-seventeenth century, the whole area around the Strand had been filled and transformed beyond recognition, with nine of the eleven great houses dominating the river or south side, while the other two on the north side impinged on Covent Garden, no longer the garden of the Convent of Westminster but a fully developed and fashionable part of London. This is chiefly illustrated by Wenceslaus Hollar's celebrated view of the so-called 'West Central District' (fig. 8), the only surviving impression

INTRODUCTION | 7

Lincoln Inn
Fields
Lesser Lincoln Inn Fields
S. Giles Fields
S. Giles
Piazza
in Coventgarden

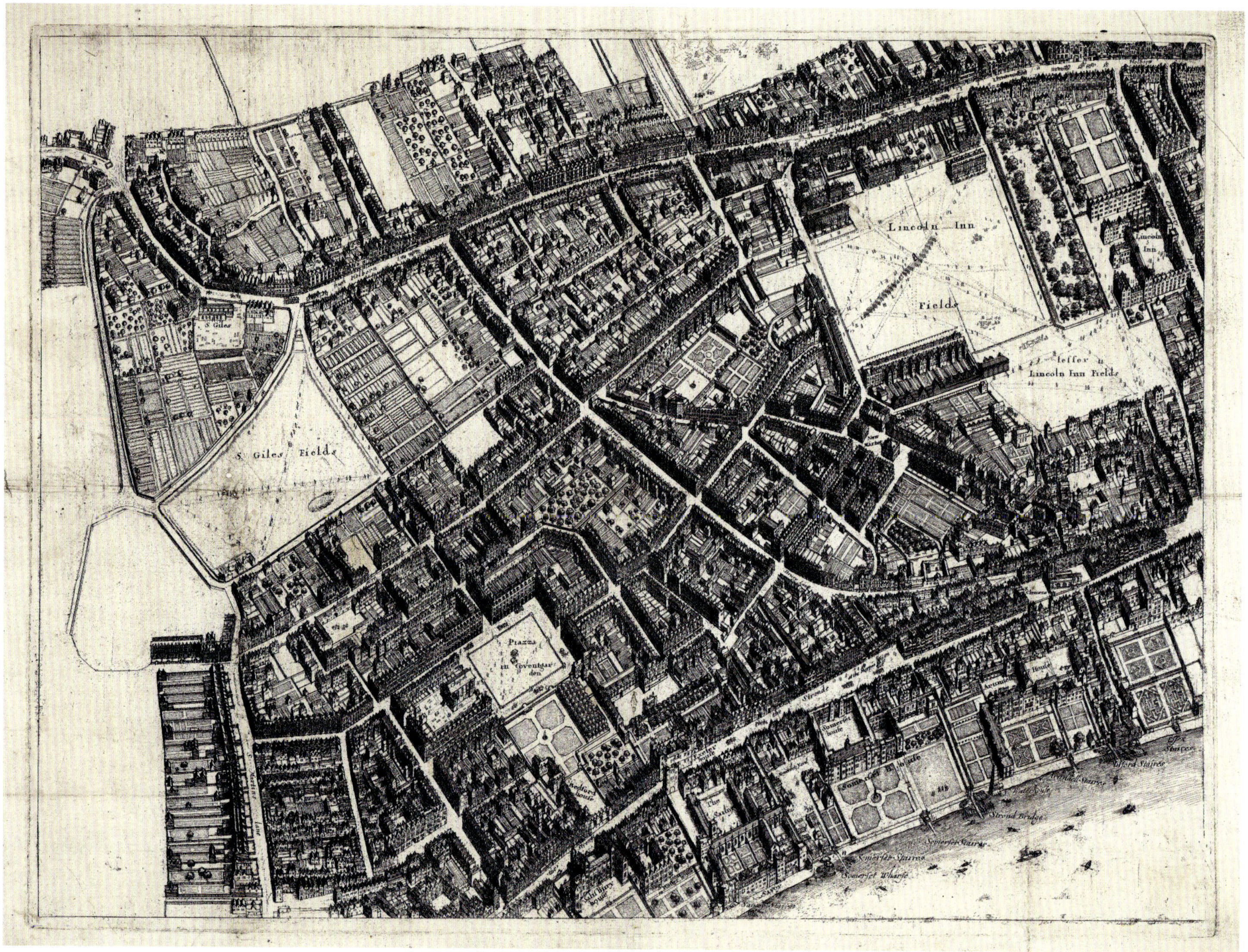

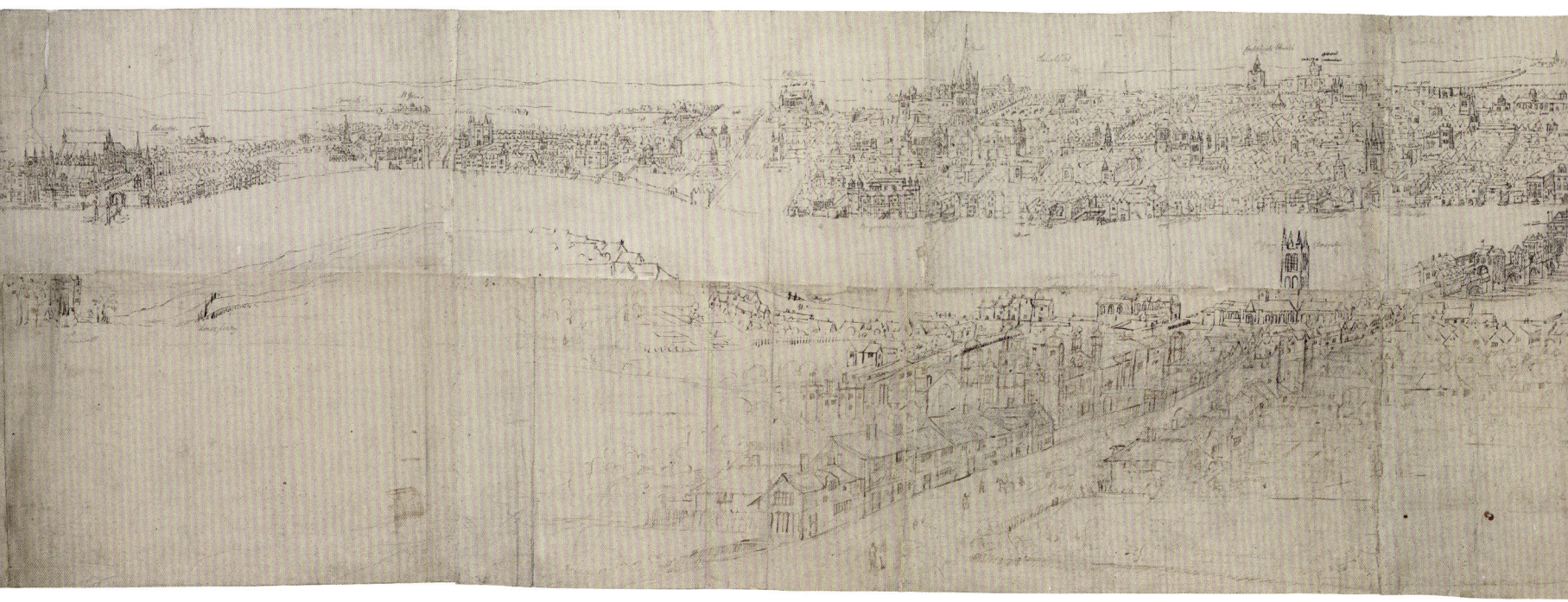

8 Wenceslaus Hollar, bird's-eye view of the 'West Central District', before 1666. Folger Shakespeare Library, Washington DC. Licensed under Creative Commons Attribution-ShareAlike 4.0 International

9 Anthonis van den Wyngaerde, *Panorama of London from the River*, c.1544. © Ashmolean Museum, University of Oxford

The Strand is to the left of London Bridge along the bend in the river.

of his Great Map of London prepared before the Great Fire of 1666. Precise and crucial to this study though it is, the view is not free from artistic licence.[15] The same is true for early topographical prints, beginning with Anthonis van den Wyngaerde's *Panorama of London from the River*, now dated to about 1544, which includes the earliest insights into the area and on the Strand more generally (fig. 9).[16]

A succession of diverse views provides key sources, to be interpreted in the light of detailed documentary evidence. They include *The Woodcut Map of London* of 1561–70, otherwise known as 'Agas' from a spurious attribution to the surveyor Ralph Agas (c.1540–1621), as well as Georg Braun and Frans Hogenberg's 'London' in *Civitates Orbis Terrarum* of 1572, both derived from the lost 'Copperplate Map of London' of 1553–9, others by Hollar, John Norden's *Speculum Britanniae* of 1593, all the way down to John Ogilby and William Morgan's map of London of 1677.[17] The art of London's topography, rooted in the Northern European tradition of these artists, developed alongside the Strand palaces, so much so that Hollar is reputed to have drawn his views from surveys made from the top of Arundel House. Yet hardly ever do records easily match topographical evidence. One is therefore left with an intricate jigsaw of a great variety and number of documents, accounts and inventories in particular. Drawings and plans that are directly relevant to architectural reconstruction are rare survivors. The reliability of this body of evidence, much of which is either presented here for the first time or re-examined afresh, is then in itself a challenge; equally, the absence of the buildings themselves has obviously worked against the near-archaeological reconstruction of both interiors and exteriors attempted in each chapter. While this makes for a contrast with my studies on the Italian and French contexts where buildings generally survive, the resulting picture is one in which each house fills a particular part of the overall story.

Working from east to west, the most easterly of these mansions, hence nearest to the City and adjacent to Gray's Inn, was Essex House. It was a compound, rather than a single structure, which maintained the medieval pattern of a courtyard entered through a gatehouse. Begun for the Bishop of Exeter in about 1324 and later granted to William Lord Paget, Secretary of State to Henry VIII, in 1569 it passed to Robert Dudley, Earl of Leicester and Elizabeth's chief favourite, who added to and improved it. In 1588 the house was inherited by Leicester's stepson, Robert Devereux, 2nd Earl of Essex, who also gained a special place in the queen's heart. But in 1600 the house was besieged by the queen's forces, for Essex's adherents gathered there to confront queen and government. Essex House was at the centre of political as well as, perhaps in consequence of, private affairs: Elizabeth had travelled back and forth many times via the river

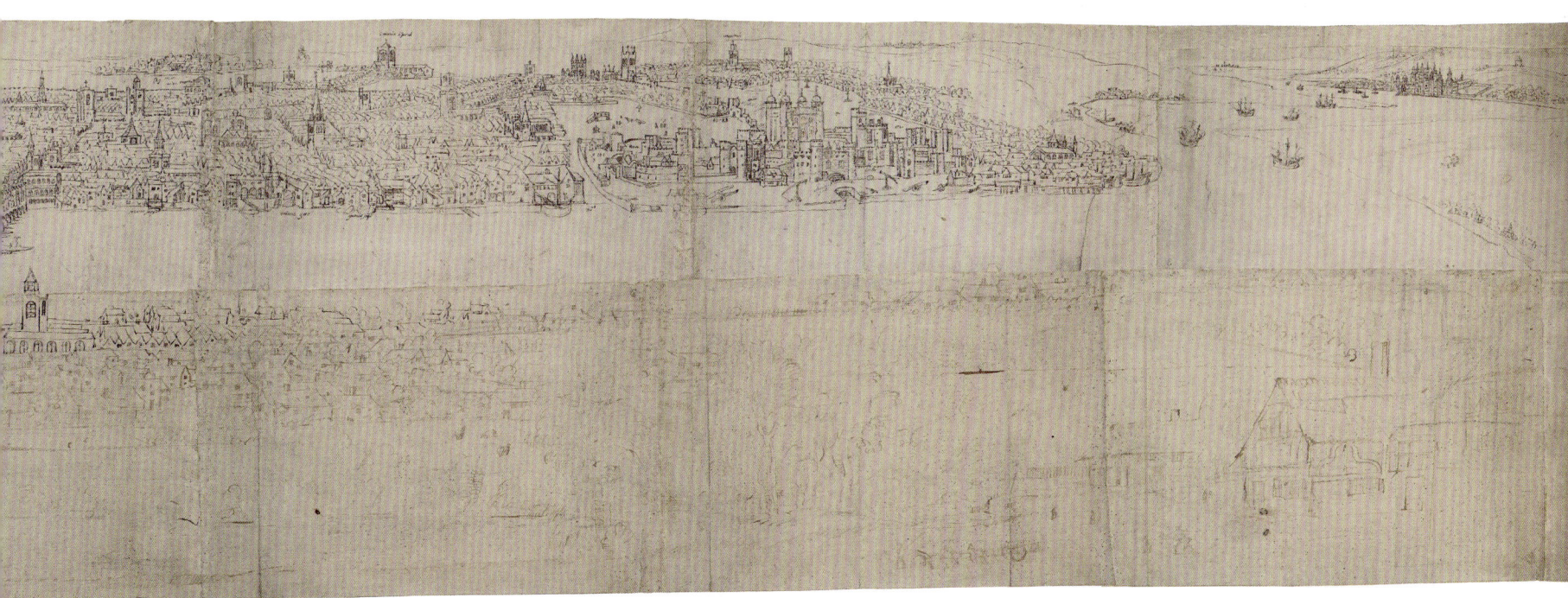

from Whitehall to Essex House (underlining the role of the Thames in the status of the Strand palaces). The house is also interesting for its early galleries, in their arrangement, number and contents. Perhaps the first top-storey gallery appeared here.

By contrast, the next mansion on the riverside going west stands out for its virtuoso relationship between architecture and collections. This is Arundel House (fig. 10). It too was a compound which occupied an impressive site of three and a half acres, granted in 1545 to Thomas Seymour, brother of the Protector, and the former residence of the Bishop of Bath and Wells. After Seymour's execution in 1549, the house was

his galleries. Jones also rearranged the gardens to display some of the Arundel sculptures, thereby creating what is credited as England's first 'garden of antiquities', again a fashion initiated by Julius II. As we shall see, however, antique statues may have decorated the garden of Burghley House well before and Burghley himself preceded Arundel as the 'Nestor of Britain' (see Chapter Five).

English architecture of this period has at times been regarded as insular or backward in comparison with Jones's Italianate style. But the reality, as will be observed throughout this book, is far more interesting and nuanced. As the Surveyor of the King's Works from 1615 to 1643 and

10 Wenceslaus Hollar, riverfront view of Arundel House, *c.*1630. Royal Collection Trust, RCIN 913268. © Her Majesty Queen Elizabeth II 2021

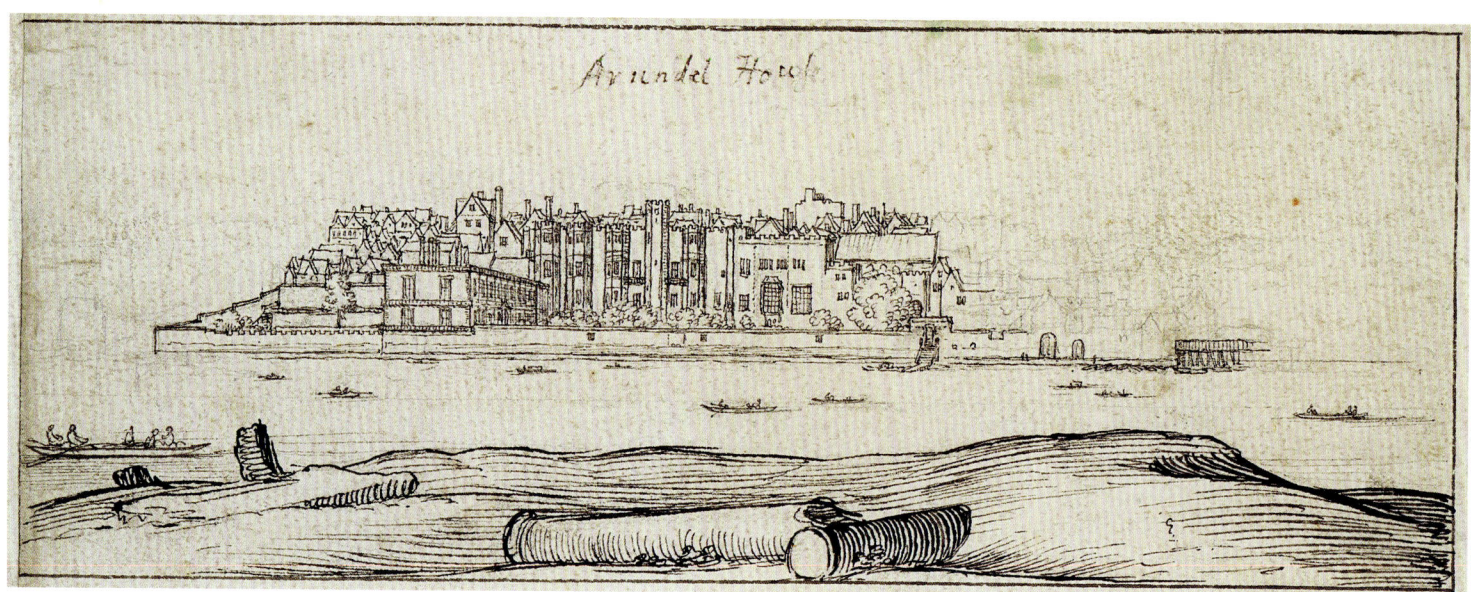

sold to Henry Fitzalan, 12th Earl of Arundel, and in 1607 it passed to Thomas Howard, 2nd Earl of Arundel of the new creation (14th of the old line). This is the earl who would be styled the 'Father of Virtue in England' for his reputation as an art collector, and it is precisely for his collection that Howard recreated two *all'antica* galleries in a range running down to the river, turning Arundel House into the setting of the then largest collection of antiquities on English soil. His galleries, where marbles and paintings were separately displayed, echoed the Sala Grande of the celebrated Palazzo Farnese, as well as Pope Julius II's Cortile del Belvedere, which Arundel would have seen during his time in Rome. Inigo Jones, Arundel's friend and protégé who more than anyone else is responsible for bringing classicism into England, had accompanied him there and probably modified

earlier as a talented masque-designer and architect in embryo, Jones is the *eminence grise* behind many of the houses discussed here. Since his role is not always clearly identifiable, this adds to the difficulties of reconstructing the histories of these houses. The other artist in Arundel's entourage was Hollar, the Bohemian etcher who came to England in 1636 and produced those crucial depictions of seventeenth-century London, reputedly from the top of Arundel House.

Next to the west was Somerset House, the quintessentially great Strand mansion, even prototype, built from 1547 to 1552 by Edward Seymour, Jane Seymour's brother and de facto ruler as Lord Protector during Edward VI's minority (fig. 11). This was the first house to include Covent Garden in its premises as a way to support and maintain Somerset's new ducal rank. John Summerson described it as 'the first

11 Wenceslaus Hollar, riverfront view of Somerset House, *c*.1658. By permission of the Pepys Library, Magdalene College, Cambridge ('London and Westminster', I, 2972, 237f)

12 Wenceslaus Hollar, riverfront view of the Savoy, 1652–1677. By permission of the Pepys Library, Magdalene College, Cambridge ('London and Westminster', I, 2972, 237d)

deliberate attempt to build in England a house composed altogether in the classical taste'.[18] This alone made it superior to all others but it was also the only palace on the south (river) side of the Strand with a grand street facade for about fifty years (until the construction of Salisbury House and Northampton House in the early seventeenth century).[19] Somerset House proved immensely influential both architecturally and socially: it was the initiator of a visual style that emphasised the authority, and in some cases invented the history, of a new political elite.[20] As the headquarters of a subject with royal power and aspirations, the house became a substitute for Whitehall as the centre of government administration: 'all solicitation and resort are at the Protector's [maison] where the Council meet and all business is despatched', noted the Holy Roman Empire's ambassador, François van der Delft.[21] The house had indeed been conceived as 'an aristocratic palace of monarchical intent', a distinction that shaped many of its later counterparts on the Strand and beyond.[22]

In contrast to Essex and Arundel whose houses, grand though they were, consisted of a patchwork of different edifices, Edward Seymour was able to build largely according to his plan, by demolishing the inns of the Bishops of Worcester, Chester and Llandaff, as well as the church of St Mary-le-Strand. This is an important distinction because it indicates both the status of its builder and the state of the art of aristocratic and royal building.

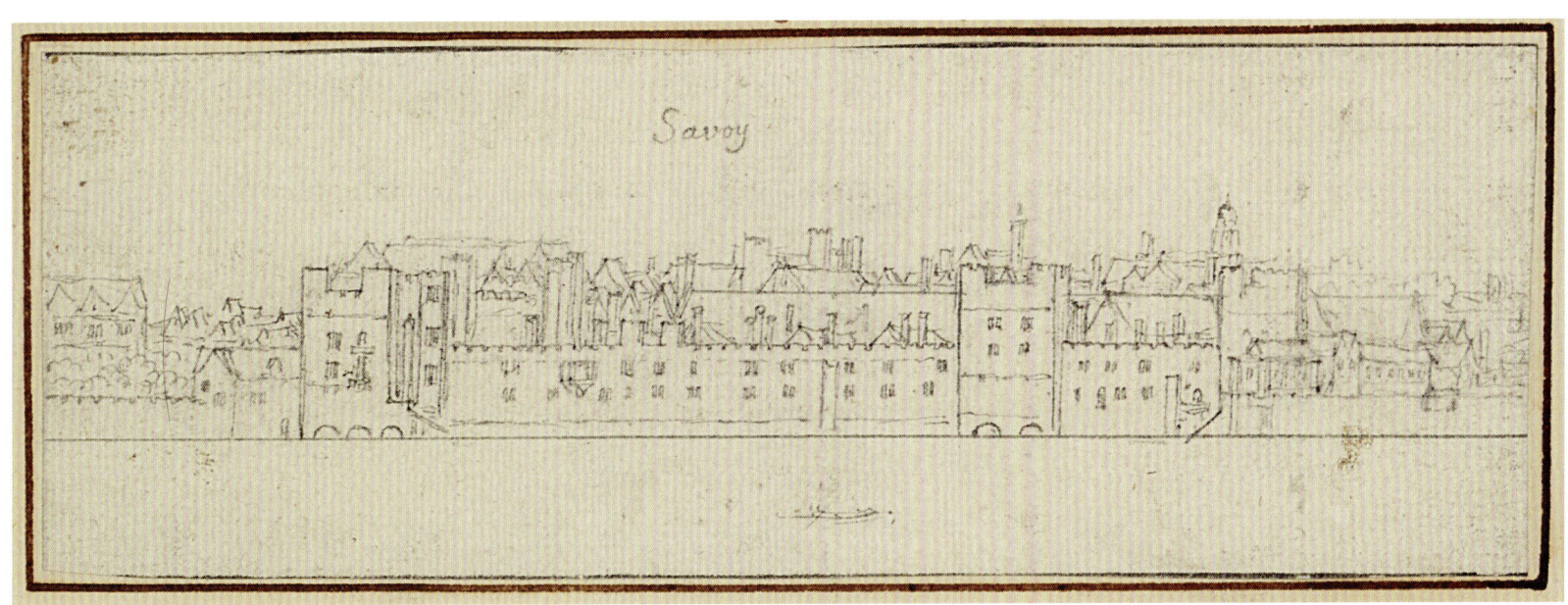

INTRODUCTION | 11

Next to Somerset House stood the thirteenth-century Savoy Palace, the oldest of the Strand houses, transformed from the early 1500s into a hospital and refuge for indigents (fig. 12). It took its name from Peter Count of Savoy, the uncle by marriage of Henry III, who built and occupied the palace until his death in 1268. In about 1366 Geoffrey Chaucer was married in the chapel (dedicated to St John the Baptist, rebuilt in the sixteenth century and still standing), as he was effectively a member of the household of John of Gaunt, 1st Duke of Lancaster, who had inherited the palace. And it is here that another Lancaster apparently planted roses from Provence, which came to be the cognisance of that family. As the Savoy's secular history largely predates the period covered here, the house does not strictly meet the criteria of a Strand palace but it was a place of lodging and reception, as were several of the royal houses in central London. The Savoy also offers useful insights into the development of the area up to the mid-1500s, including the rise of all the neighbouring bishops' inns.

Opposite the Savoy and next west, on the north side of the Strand stood the great pile erected by William Cecil, Lord Burghley, Elizabeth I's most trusted and long-standing minister as well as the leading architectural patron of the time (see fig. 8). It had an annexe called Cecil House, purposely built for his younger son, Robert, on a site originally occupied by the rectory of St Clement Danes. Like Somerset House, Burghley (later Exeter) House had an imposing facade which stood directly on the street and perhaps featured a frontispiece with a tower of the orders. Either way, it majestically dwarfed its surroundings, as a castle would a village. Well known as a college for boarders, where noblemen minor would be placed under Burghley's care in his role as Master of the Court of Wards, it was a traditional if massive complex of two courtyards with corner towers, a central hall with rooms and services at either end and a loggia facing a formal garden to the north. Featuring a great variety of different planting arrangements, as well as one of the earliest garden grottos, the garden included a Roman inscription from the remains at Chichester. It may also have displayed the statues of the twelve Roman emperors, sent from Venice in 1561, thereby setting a precedent not just for the museum garden of Lord Arundel, as previously remarked, but for those of Buckingham or indeed Charles I (see Chapters Two and Ten).

To the west of Burghley House stood Bedford House, erected in 1585 by Edward Russell, 3rd Earl of Bedford, to replace the family mansion on the opposite side of the Strand. Its large garden extended as far north as Covent Garden, where Inigo Jones built the celebrated piazza with surrounding buildings for the 4th Earl in 1631–7 (see fig. 8). Besides this important development of London, Bedford House illustrates self-sufficiency well, pointing to how each of the Strand palaces supported themselves in their different ways. By contrast, its predecessor back on the river side, known as Worcester House (fig. 13), the former inn of the Bishop of Carlisle, provides insights into sequestration, the searching for goods of malefactors and the overall impact on these palaces of the Civil Wars. Worcester House also vividly reveals the Russell family as key players of the area, but when it comes to the history of the building itself, and what it was actually like, we are hindered by the uneven availability of documentary sources. As explained in the Preface, research in private archives is not always straightforward. Yet Salisbury House, the next to the

13 Wenceslaus Hollar, riverfront view of Durham House, Salisbury House and Worcester House, c.1630. By permission of the Pepys Library, Magdalene College, Cambridge ('London and Westminster', I, 2972, 237c)

14 Inigo Jones, elevation for the New Exchange in the Strand, London, 1608. Worcester College, Oxford, H&T 9. The Provost and Fellows of Worcester College, Oxford

west, is exceptional in its architectural evidence (and its availability), which associates it with Burghley House and no doubt is related to the celebrated architectural patronage of the Cecils.

Salisbury House had been built from 1599 to 1613 as two attached houses, known as Great Salisbury House and Little Salisbury House, by Robert Cecil, 1st Earl of Salisbury, the man who ruled the country as Secretary of State to both Elizabeth I and James I (see fig. 13). This complex clearly reveals the extent to which architectural display had become part of the keeping of state. Its garden would have featured a portico overlooking the Thames of unprecedented classical sophistication and may have established a pattern of 'Roman' loggias along the river, as part of James I's neo-Augustan project to transform London into the capital of 'Magna Britannia'. The portico was conceived and drawn by John Osborne, the Remembrancer of Cecil's Exchequer and clearly part of that lively group of amateur, sometimes skilled architects who converged with artists and patrons to 'make' the Strand.

Durham House, a property of that See until 1641, when Charles I granted it to the 4th Earl of Pembroke, stood next to the west (see fig. 13). It has much to tell about its times, from its ecclesiastical history, to political manoeuvring in order to control occupancy (chiefly the notorious eviction of Walter Ralegh), to collections and movables, but less about the buildings themselves, once again for lack of archival evidence. The exception is John Webb's grandiose designs for its rebuilding, one of several highly ambitious and well documented though largely unexecuted projects for reconstructing the royal palaces of Somerset House, Whitehall and Greenwich. Earlier in the century, part of the Durham House site had also been acquired by Robert Cecil for his New Exchange venture, for which Jones had produced one of his earliest architectural drawings (fig. 14). The Exchange, the first competitor of its royal counterpart in the City, was part of Robert's attempt at controlling surrounding properties, as had his father before him.

After Durham House came York House, originally built in about 1237 for the bishops of Norwich and at first known as Norwich Place (fig. 15). Associated from 1555 to 1625 with one of the highest officers in the land, the Lord Keeper of the Great Seal, this is the house where aspects of keeping of state and ritual come to the fore, given

INTRODUCTION | 13

the significance of the household ordinances of Thomas Egerton, 1st Baron Ellesmere. As noted, he held office between Nicholas and Francis Bacon. York House was indeed the scene of the philosopher's 'gayest hours', as well as of his 'sharpest griefs' when it finally passed to James I's favourite, George Villiers, 1st Duke of Buckingham, in 1622. But the Duke quickly turned it into a magnificent palace, complete with a new water gate devised as a triumphal arch, which has survived in the gardens of the Victoria Embankment: this is the sole indicator of the scale and lustre of the complex to which it once gave access. It has been regarded as only one part of a projected palace of colossal proportions, of which it would have defined the central axis. The new front as seen in contemporary topography is dismissed as a short-term measure before these major works would have begun (see Chapter Ten). As will be seen, this was not the case. Works at York House are mainly associated with Balthasar Gerbier, the courtier, diplomatist, miniature painter, architect and writer. He also supplied to Villiers an unprecedented collection of old masters including Titian's *Ecce Homo*, which sent Inigo Jones down on his knees and occasioned an unheard-of offer from Arundel.[23] Indeed, if the earlier history of this house brings ritual to a secular climax, the latter sees the apex of architectural conspicuous consumption, just at the time when such courtly excess led to not only Buckingham's assassination in 1628 but also the unrest which gave rise to the Civil Wars and the beheading of the king.

Oddly enough, the motto of this most extravagant of courtiers was the severe *Fidei Coticula Crux*, 'the cross is the touchstone of faith'.

From 1642 to 1647, York House was rented by Algernon Percy, the 'proud' 10th Earl of Northumberland, while he transformed his newly acquired palace in the Strand, its neighbour to the west. The last of the series, and indeed the nearest to Whitehall, Northampton (later Northumberland) House had been built over 1605–14 by Henry Howard, the mighty 1st Earl of Northampton, as an enormous courtyard house (fig. 16). That courtyard alone could have contained the whole of Salisbury House, the only other palace built at the same time, by Robert Cecil. Howard and Cecil together orchestrated James VI of Scotland's accession to the throne of England in 1603, hence the unification of the two crowns. This stands as an almost incredible achievement, not only given the well-known complexities of the case – from an unmarried Protestant queen to the son of her Catholic cousin who had once claimed Elizabeth's throne – but also because there was no love lost between the two men, as Howard had long been kept in the shade while the Cecils thrived. Indeed, he usually described Robert Cecil, famously short and humpbacked, as the 'little lord' or 'little man', even once 'the little one itself'. Following Cecil's death in 1612, Howard wrote to Viscount Rochester that 'so many rejoice, and so few seem to be sorry … [He] is near his mistress [Elizabeth I] … if any one can love so ugly and deformed a fellow'.[24] These feelings are clearly reflected in

15 Wenceslaus Hollar, riverfront view of York House, c.1630. By permission of the Pepys Library, Magdalene College, Cambridge ('London and Westminster', I, 2972, 237b)

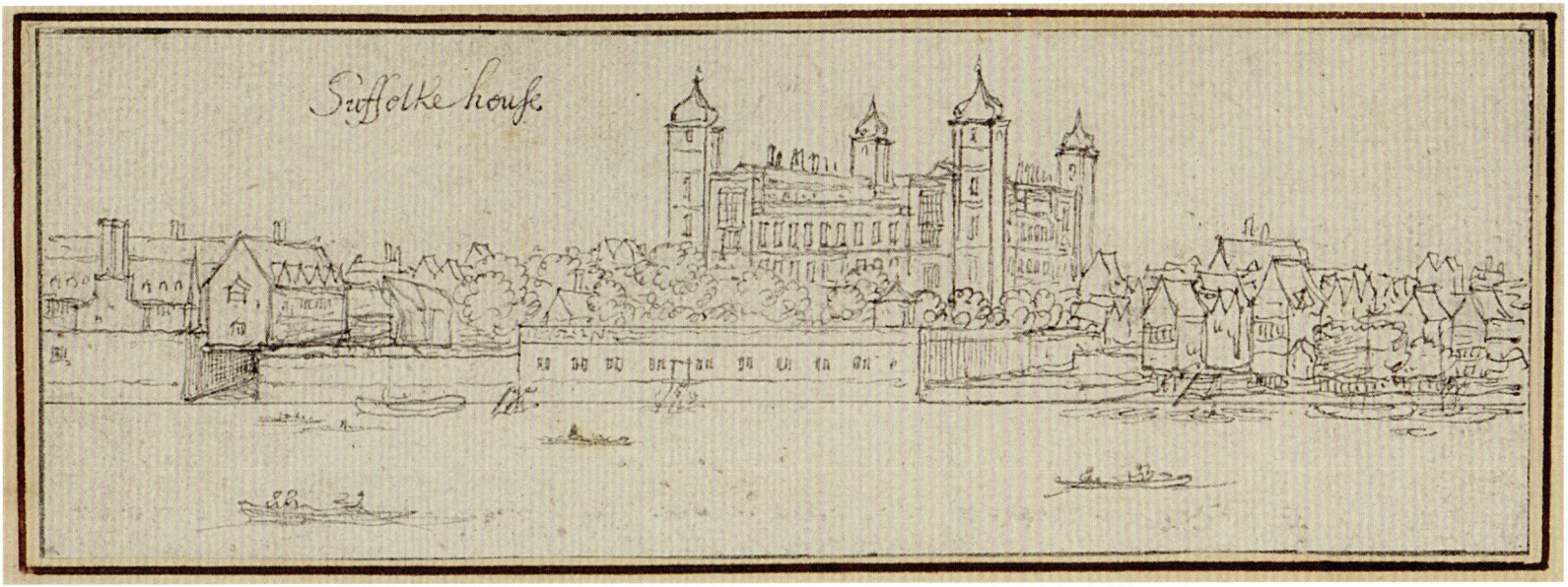

16 Wenceslaus Hollar, riverfront view of Northumberland House, first engraved 1647. By permission of the Pepys Library, Magdalene College, Cambridge ('London and Westminster', I, 297, 237a)

the competition between their Strand palaces, a notable instance of the war of bricks and mortar. For, like Hardwick Hall in Derbyshire, Northampton House was a celebration of its owner in old age, and of somebody obsessed with self-representation and lineage in an era increasingly dominated by the newly rich (like the Cecils), when Howard had finally regained political prominence. Without a proper country seat, Howard had devolved most of his resources to London and, fittingly, his Strand palace became the grandest of them all.

From the time of the Restoration of the Monarchy in 1660, the plan for which was first mooted there, right down to the Reform Bill of 1832, Northumberland House remained at the core of political and social history and became the epitome of British architecture. The last of the Strand palaces, this house survived until 1874 as the stronghold of a celebrated family of patrons who defied that frenzy of redevelopment and shift to the west which pushed the Strand into oblivion.

All but a few of the Strand palaces were demolished within the seventeenth century and their history has been neglected. For more than a century after its publication in 1908, Edwin Beresford Chancellor's *The Private Palaces of London: Past and Present* was still the main, but by no means comprehensive, reference on the subject. The first proper account of London architecture, the *Survey of London* (1900–), includes brief (and now outdated) analysis of only those houses in the parishes covered by the series: as it happens, almost half the Strand is not dealt with. The same is true for the various publications on London houses and London more generally which – celebrated though some are, like the surveys of John Stow (1598) and John Strype (1720) – have dealt with the Strand palaces as a marginal topic.[25] Three of those palaces have been studied individually in antiquarian books or articles, of great value but now dated.[26] Between the 1980s and the early 2000s, a few more have been examined at the Courtauld Institute of Art, London, under the supervision of John Newman.[27] Useful though these studies are, most give limited attention to the actual Strand palaces, as the analysis is almost invariably concentrated on the wider patronage of their builders in a selected period. More recent studies, including my own on Salisbury House (2006, 2007, 2010) and Northumberland House (2007, 2008, 2010, 2014, 2016, 2019), Simon Thurley's monograph on Somerset House (2009), as well as Paula Henderson and Jill Husselby's seminal article on Burghley House (2002), have since appeared (see the respective chapters). The topic, one might say, has gathered momentum, but a book on them all remained to be written, especially as it became clear during my research that London is unique in the English context. Indeed, one cannot understand the development of the English country house – and the establishment of a truly English style in response to the earthquake of the Reformation – without the Strand palaces. As we shall see, they form the 'dialogue around them and beyond them'.[28]

17 The complex of Essex House bounded by Middle Temple on the east (right) and Milford Lane on the west (left) (detail of fig. 8)

1 · ESSEX HOUSE

ESSEX HOUSE LAY BETWEEN MIDDLE Temple on the east and Arundel House on the west (more precisely, a row of dwellings along Milford Lane, the boundary between the two palaces, leading to Milford Stairs). As the most easterly, it would have been the first of the Strand palaces to be seen by anyone entering London by river. With its imposing facades and elaborate gardens, chiefly depicted in Hollar's 'West Central District' view, prepared before the Great Fire of 1666, it would also have provided a fair idea of the continuous arc of palatial residences which followed (fig. 17). However, like the majority of these houses with episcopal origins, it would not have been visible from the Strand, for the 'rents' (tenements with shops along the street front), which customarily formed part of the precincts of the bishops' inns, completely hid it. Indeed, there could be no greater contrast between the impression one got from the river and that from the highway.

Beyond the period 1569–88 when Robert Dudley, 1st Earl of Leicester, was associated with the house, its history is characterised by almost continuous changes of occupants, with consequent scattered archival sources, in themselves not particularly revealing since key evidence is missing (on which more shortly). Moreover, as in most instances of the great Strand patrons, the relatively ample literature on its famous owner, chiefly Elizabeth Goldring's *Robert Dudley, Earl of Leicester, and the World of Elizabethan Art* (2014), largely focuses on matters other than architecture. An attempt at dealing with the building was made by Jane Clark in 1981, in one of those pioneering Courtauld dissertations led by John Newnam.[1] As previously observed, these are mainly concerned with the wider patronage of each courtier and Essex House is no exception. The most comprehensive reference on the subject was Charles Kingsford's meticulous *Archaeologia* article of 1923, published a year after his study on Arundel House.[2]

The Inn of the Bishops of Exeter: 1324–1539

The first record of the bishops of Exeter's inn goes back to 1324, when Walter de Stapledon (or Stapeldon), the head of that see from 1308 to his death in 1326, seemingly began building on site.[3] Originally, the area had probably belonged to the Knights Templar, to whom Henry II granted the church of St Clement Danes in 1173. The advowson of St Clement's, with some tenements opposite the church, then passed to the Canons of the Holy Sepulchre at Warwick, whose properties were held of the Honour of Leicester, so that, when in 1280 the Inn of the Canons opposite St Clement's was granted for life to William de Breuse, Bishop of Llandaff, it was with the assent of Edmund 'Crouchback', 1st Earl of Leicester and Lancaster. Both figures will be encountered again in Chapters Three and Four on Somerset House and the Savoy respectively.

Bishop Stapledon's main acquisition consisted of five messuages owned by the priory of St Sepulchre, including one held by William de Beresford, the Chief Justice of the Common Bench, to whom it had been demised for life. By the time of this purchase in 1324, Stapledon had probably also obtained a plot of land between the tenements and the Thames that measured 100 feet on the west side, about 140 feet on both the east and river sides and about 130 feet on the north. Possession of this plot – which had passed first to the Knights of St John on the Templars' dissolution in 1312 – appeared controversial, for an inquisition in 1327 found that the Bishop of Exeter had usurped it under a concession made by Aymer de Valence, Earl of Pembroke, who had owned it intermittently until his death in 1324. The plot also covered only a portion of a new garden, adding to an already seemingly large site where Stapledon is said to have carried out great building works, including a 'fair tower' by the river, using stone from the Church of the Holy Innocents.

Given Stapledon's role as the second funder of the rebuilding of Exeter Cathedral, one assumes that he revelled in these works; he did not, however, see them completed for, as one of Edward II's most unpopular ministers, he was murdered by the mob in Cheapside on 15 October 1326 during the fighting between parties loyal to the king or to Queen Isabella.[4] His hostel in Eldedenes Lane in the City, which was looted and burnt down, was probably Stapledon's own house, as the See of Exeter did not have a permanent London inn before his time. The incident shows that by 1326 Exeter Inn was not yet habitable, which appears to be confirmed by another (gruesome) story of the bishop's headless corpse being taken to St Clement Danes and buried without reverence in a heap of sand outside the house he was building there.

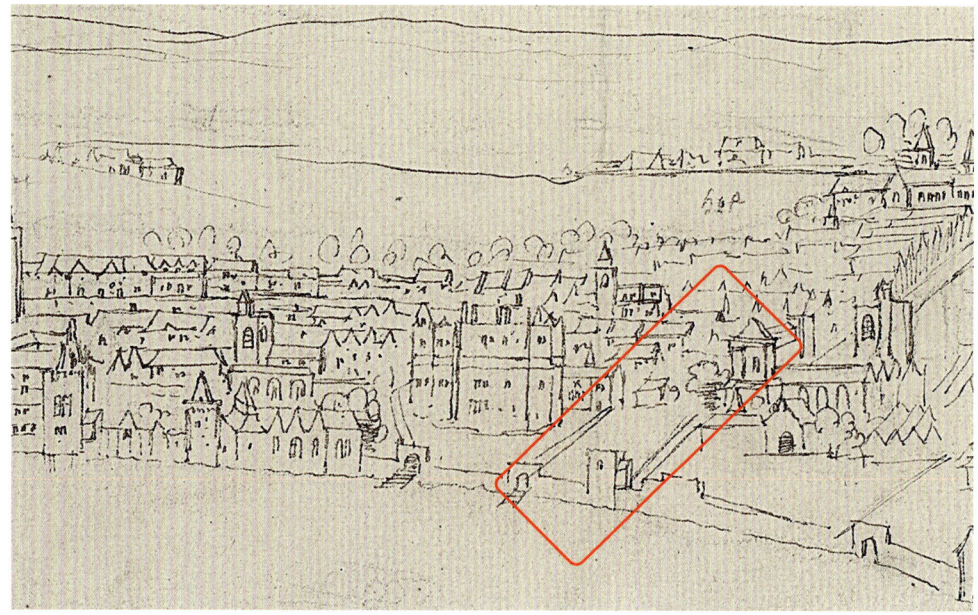

Walter Stapledon was succeeded by James Berkeley (d. 1327) for merely three months, and then, even more briefly, by John Godeley, whose election was quashed. The first to occupy Exeter Inn was therefore John Grandison, the great builder of Exeter Cathedral, left incomplete by Stapledon, and of the collegiate church of Ottery St Mary, who remained in charge until his death in 1369.[5] In 1338 Bishop Grandison granted to John of St Paul (or Pol), the King's Clerk and later Archbishop of Dublin, the property previously acquired by Stapledon from William de Beresford, together with the annexed chapel of St Thomas. Stretching from the Strand to the Thames, and extending westward to the boundary of the Bishop of Bath and Wells's land, this property must have formed a substantial part of the complex of Exeter Inn, so much so that Grandison had reserved to himself some houses, shops and small gardens, including the use of the chapel. What the inn actually consisted of is difficult to ascertain, for there is more, though scattered, information about its ancillary tenements than on the main episcopal residence. It is known, for instance, that one of the lesser messuages which formed part of the property let to John of St Paul was eventually held by none other than Edward, the Duke of York killed at Agincourt in 1415. In 1362, when Archbishop St Paul died, his tenement was described as a messuage with an adjoining garden and seven shops. Then there is a reference to the hall 'within the Inn of the bishop of Exeter without Temple Bar' in a deed of 1376, and Stow relates that Edmund Lacy,

18 Anthonis van den Wyngaerde, *Panorama of London from the River*, c.1544 (detail of fig. 9). © Ashmolean Museum, University of Oxford

Detail showing the site of Exeter House, squeezed between Bath Inn, later Arundel House (left), and Temple Church (right).

18 | LONDON'S 'GOLDEN MILE'

the bishop from 1420 to 1455, rebuilt the great hall.⁶ Construction on site continued and by the 1530s more than eleven extra houses or shops within the property were let by Bishop John Vesey (?1462–1554). But it was not to last, as the cloud of the Dissolution soon covered all episcopal properties on the Strand: as early as 1539, three years after that controversial Act, Exeter Inn was granted to Thomas Howard, 3rd Duke of Norfolk (1473–1554), who relinquished his previous grant of the Nun's Priory at Clerkenwell in exchange for the Strand property. As will be seen throughout this book, while episcopal properties may not have been strictly speaking dissolved, these 'exchanges' were almost invariably to the detriment of the incumbent, and became the leitmotif of the period.

The 3rd Duke of Norfolk and Sir William Paget: 1538–1563

Norfolk was the uncle of two of Henry VIII's wives, Anne Boleyn and Catherine Howard, hence part of the king's inner circle. He was certainly occupying Exeter Inn during 1541–2 and may have retained it as a tenant until his fall in 1546, while waiting or, rather, 'praying that Bath Place might light on him', as 'he had no place of his own in London'.⁷ Three years later, in 1549, Bath Place was instead sold to Henry Fitzalan, 12th Earl of Arundel, whose grandson and heir, Philip Howard, was Norfolk's grandson too (see Chapter Two). It is unsurprising in the small pond of Tudor dynasties that Norfolk was also the grandfather of another notorious Strand magnate, Henry Howard, 1st Earl of Northampton, the builder of Northampton House (see Chapter Eleven).⁸

The earliest insights into the area and the Strand in general are provided by Wyngaerde's *Panorama of London from the River* of about 1544, produced during Norfolk's occupancy (fig. 18). In it we can clearly distinguish Bath Inn, as well as St Clement Danes and Temple Church, but the site of Exeter Inn, marked by a passage known as Milford Lane⁹ on the west and another passage along the boundary of the Temple on the east, appears squeezed in, probably because of or partly due to the view's angle. Moreover, what stood along the Strand near St Clement Danes is barely discernible because dwarfed by the surrounding bigger structures. By contrast, a tower or banqueting house by the river, perhaps the 'fair tower' built by Bishop Stapledon in the early fourteenth century, stands prominently in the south-east corner.

Norfolk's fall in 1546 cleared the way for one of his enemies, William Paget (1505/6–1563), among those formidable new men in the fast-changing landscape of Tudor politics who had managed to become one of Henry VIII's closest advisers. Paget secured several high roles, from one of two Secretary of State positions in 1543, to Comptroller of the Royal Household and Chancellor of the Duchy of Lancaster in 1547.¹⁰ While the last role alone would have justified, indeed eased the search for a Strand palace, in addition royal letters were sent in February 1548 on Paget's behalf to Bishop Vesey of Exeter and to the dean and chapter, still the nominal proprietors of Exeter Inn. Sure enough, by July that year letters patent had confirmed Paget as the new owner of 'all that capital messuage and mansion vulgarly called Exetour Place, situated in the parish of St. Clement Danes, together with all cellars, solars, houses, stables, curtilages, gardens, etc., thereto belonging, and all messuages, houses, gardens, wharves, rents and services whatsoever in the said parish'.¹¹ Henry also granted Paget a parcel of land from the garden of Middle Temple about seventy feet wide and stretching 130 feet southwards from Exeter Rents, essential to enlarge a seemingly narrow site, as shown by Wyngaerde (see fig. 18). This is likely to have been followed by new building, as the next available view of the site, the 'Agas' *Woodcut Map of London* of 1561–70, shows additions to the east including a tower not previously known and overall a distinctive complex with a gatehouse and a formal garden marked as 'Paget Place' (fig. 19). By contrast, the Banqueting House depicted by Wyngaerde and the passage leading to it, which represented the eastern boundary, are no longer there, probably a casualty of the eastward expansion. Yet a pitched-roof riverside building appears in the western corner of the property. These characteristics are generally confirmed by Braun and Hogenberg's nearly contemporary 'London' in *Civitates Orbis Terrarum* of 1572, but derived, as the Agas map, from the lost 'Copperplate Map of London' of 1553–9 (fig. 20).¹² In Braun and Hogenberg's depiction, however, the Essex House site still includes the passage on the east side, demarcating it from the Temple's precincts, and lacks the building adjoining the new tower: it thus appears narrower than that shown in the Agas

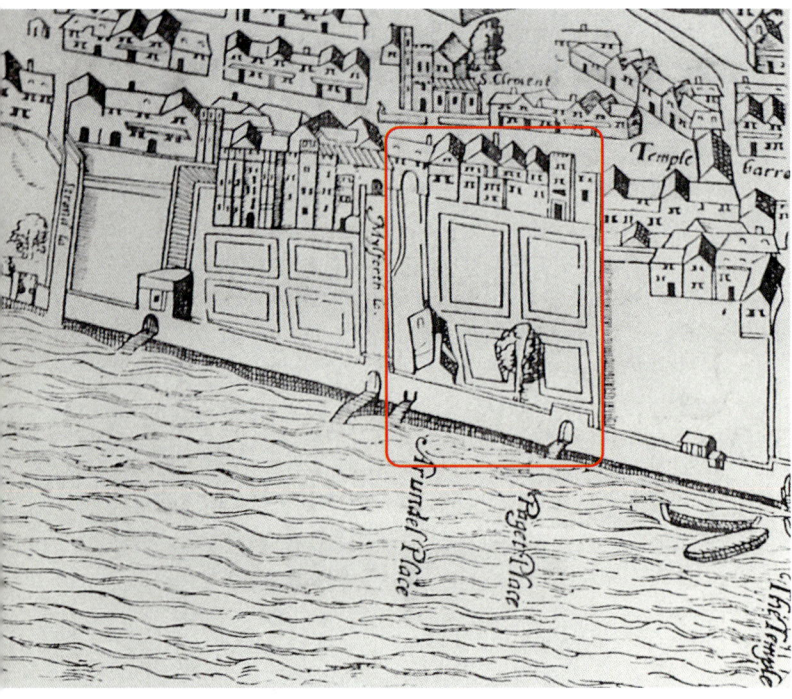
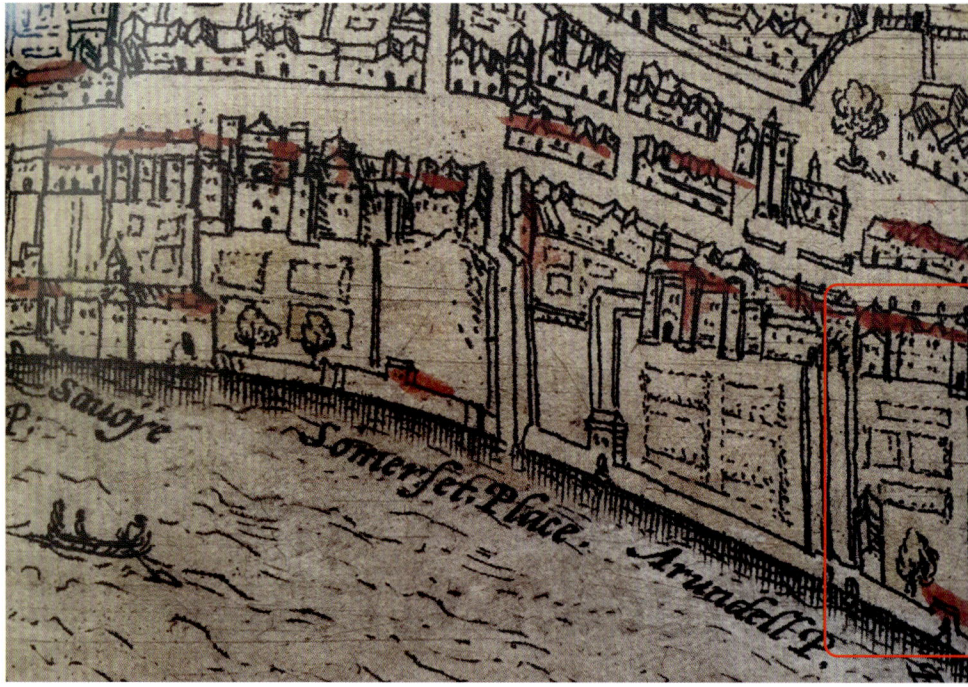

map. In effect, while both depictions are marked as Paget Place, one wonders whether they represent two slightly different stages.

On William Paget's death in 1563, after nearly twenty years of ownership, Paget Place passed to his son Henry, who died without male issue in 1568, having transferred the palace to feoffees to be sold within two years. So it was that the Spanish ambassador, lodging there in 1569, had to vacate the complex when it was sold to Robert Dudley, 1st Earl of Leicester, for £2500.[13] By that time, however, the site was no longer as William Paget had assembled it, for a house and garden, built in 1556 in Milford Lane, had already changed hands (it later became the rectory of St Clement Danes), while other premises on that side, possibly including the building by the river, were transferred in 1568. Four further messuages next to Milford Lane, occupied by labourers and craftsmen, were separately held from 1569.

The House of Robert Dudley, 1st Earl of Leicester: 1569–1588

As Elizabeth I's chief favourite, or 'the chick that sytteth next the hen', as one source put it,[14] the figure of Robert Dudley has reached an almost mythological place in the Tudor court. Born around 1532, the first part of his life had been marked by the fall of his family after his father's abortive attempt to establish Lady Jane Grey on the English throne instead of the Catholic Mary, in 1553.[15] Despite being condemned to death for treason, Robert did not, unlike his father, go to the scaffold; however, by the time he was restored in blood in 1557, he was destitute. Then, with the accession of his childhood friend as Elizabeth I in 1558, Dudley's fortunes took a dramatic twist, as honours were bestowed on him, leading to membership of the Privy Council in 1562 and elevation as Baron Denbigh and Earl of Leicester in 1564. This followed highly conspicuous acquisitions of land and property, including the grant of Kenilworth Castle in Warwickshire in 1563 and the purchase of Wanstead Manor on the Essex bank of the River Lea in 1578, in addition to that of Paget Place on the Strand some eight years prior.[16]

Soon renamed Leicester House, the Strand palace represented the culmination of Dudley's position in the inner sanctum of Tudor magnates, for his immediate neighbours included not only Philip Howard, 13th Earl of Arundel, but the queen herself at Somerset House, although she rarely used that palace (see Chapters Two and Three). Further west, on the north side of the Strand, William Cecil, 1st Baron Burghley and Elizabeth's chief minister, had also by then rebuilt a house acquired in 1559 (see Chapter Five), while other resounding names soon followed. Kenilworth, Wanstead and Leicester House provided Dudley with at least three residences throughout the year in which to entertain or be close to the monarch.[17]

19 Paget Place, detail of the *Woodcut Map of London*, 1561–70 ('Agas'), reprinted 1633, derived from the lost 'Copperplate Map of London', 1553–9. Mitton 1908. Wikimedia Commons Public Domain

20 Paget Place, detail of Georg Braun and Frans Hogenberg, 'London' in *Civitates Orbis Terrarum*, 1572, derived from the lost 'Copperplate Map of London', 1553–9. University Library, Heidelberg. Wikipedia, Public Domain

As Simon Adams observed, this epitomised the 'successful Elizabethan courtier', well grounded in the Renaissance tradition of what a courtier should be, as Baldassare Castiglione wrote in his influential treatise *Il Cortegiano* (1513–28).[18] And such success was especially notable when the courtier was having to start all over again or was new to the game.

Well acquainted with such thought, Dudley belonged in the first category, for his association with the Strand had started at an early stage, while his 'ascent' to Leicester House had moved east through two other palaces with direct royal connections. The first was Durham House, left to Princess Elizabeth by Henry VIII, on which Dudley's father, John, the ill-fated Duke of Northumberland, had set his sights; the second was Somerset House, given to Elizabeth in exchange for that residence. Robert had lived in the first in the early 1550s and again between 1565 and 1568, where he had entertained the queen (see Chapter Nine). In the second, Dudley had been the keeper until the fall of his father in 1553, hence possibly in charge of the works to prepare the house for Elizabeth following the swap, and from the 1570s onwards he kept a room there (see Chapter Three). It is therefore unsurprising that, as soon as a property became available, the newly elevated peer snatched it. This is particularly the case with Dudley since Leicester House was close to Somerset House. As has been suggested, another reason may have been Leicester House's association with Warwick, Kenilworth and the Honour of Leicester dating back to Edmund Crouchback.[19] In this way, Dudley could be seen as the ideal courtier in securing that network of ancestral estates, while also putting himself in a position to marry the queen should the opportunity ever become reality. However controversial, the death of his first wife, Amy Robsart, in 1560 enabled him to pursue that chance and he did not remarry for eighteen years. His secret wedding with Lettice Knollys, Countess of Essex, caused Elizabeth's displeasure and the banishment of the new Countess of Leicester from court. But, as Dudley himself put it quoting a Latin adage on the changes that the passage of time brings, 'Tempora mutantur et nos mutamur in illis'.[20]

The question as to what Leicester House looked like, and what Robert Dudley did to it, primarily rests on the study of topographical and contextual evidence, as no other architectural record is known to have survived. As for written sources related to building within the period, these are scarce and scattered. By contrast, an exceptional number of inventories, fourteen in total, distinguishes Dudley's tenure as one of the best documented in this respect in the entire Elizabethan period.[21]

Early depictions of the palace (see figs 18–20), while clearly indicating a development of both buildings and precincts, are fairly vague and relatively unilluminating. So would be the next available view, produced by John Norden for his *Speculum Britanniae* in 1593, some twenty years after Braun and Hogenberg's, were it not for the angle which allows one to confirm and visualise what was to be expected (fig. 21). That is, the complex of Leicester House, like the majority of former episcopal palaces, developed around a courtyard, where the Strand front was characterised by tenements of different sizes – twenty in 1590 along 350 feet[22] – while the main apartments faced the garden and the river. The plot was irregularly shaped and remained so throughout its history, which suggests that by the 1590s the extent of the complex had reached its definitive size: it was approximately 600 feet long and of variable widths, from a minimum of about 200 feet by the riverside, to the approximately 350 feet along the Strand with the additions prior to Dudley's time. Through Norden we can also begin to distinguish some of the principal parts

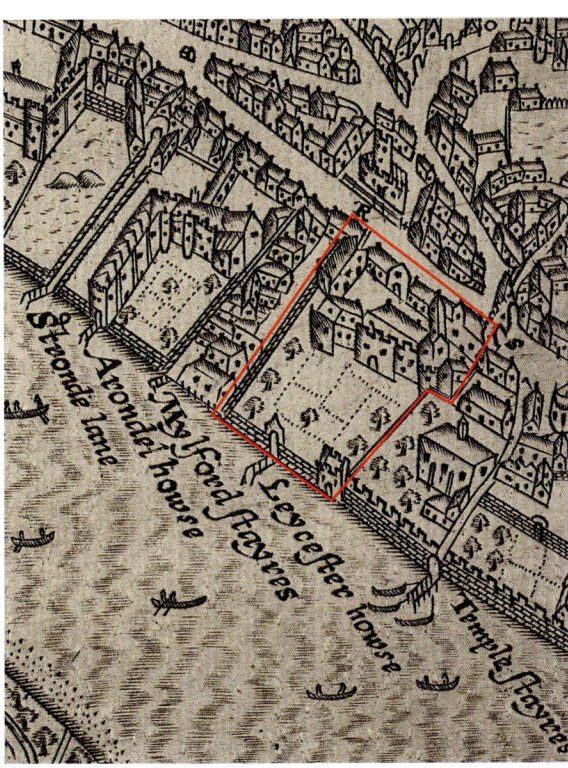

21 The complex of Leicester (later Essex) House, detail of John Norden, *Speculum Britanniae*, 1593. Folger Shakespeare Library, Washington DC. Licensed under Creative Commons Attribution-ShareAlike 4.0 International

of Leicester House, which includes a castellated, full-height building in the centre of the garden range, likely to represent the great hall erected by Edmund Lacy in the first half of the fifteenth century. Norden also noted that the chapel of the Bishop of Exeter, located at the outer gate 'apperteyning to S. Clementes Danes' in the Strand, had been turned into a porters' lodge, though whether by Paget or Dudley we are not told.[23] Both of them were credited in John Stow's *Survay of London* of 1598 for having, respectively, 'enlarged' the house and 'of late new builded there'.[24] The poet Edmund Spenser, part of Dudley's literary circle in the 1570s and 1580s, described the property in his *Prothalamion* of 1596:

> ... *there stands a stately place,*
> *Where oft I gained gifts and goodly grace*
> *Of that great lord, which therein wont to dwell,*
> *Whose want too well now feels my friendless case*
> ...
> *From those high towers this noble lord issuing,*
> *Like radiant Hesper, when his golden hair*
> *In th'Ocean billows he hath bathed fair,*
> *Descended to the river's open viewing,*
> *With a great train ensuing.*[25]

Indeed, the 'river's open viewing' had a designated place on the Thames, where a crenellated banqueting house – first seen in Wyngaerde's view but unrecorded in either the 'Agas' map or Braun and Hegenberg's – is clearly depicted by Norden in the south-east corner of the complex (see figs 18–21). Whether or not a similar structure existed before Leicester, a reference to a stone banqueting house appears in a letter he wrote to Lord Burghley on 17 May 1575:

> *I have to thank your L. also very hartely, perceiving by Hen. Hawthorn that your L. is plesed to help me that I may have some stone toward the making a lytle banquett-house in my garden. Yf yt please your L. to let him know your further mynde touching the same, the pleasure wil be great you doe me, and I wyll [be] reddy [to] the best of my power to requite.*[26]

This is part of a correspondence between the two peers related to the celebrated visit of the queen to Kenilworth that summer, where a similar structure to a banqueting house, probably of timber or even canvas (and probably not 'lytle'), had previously been considered.[27] It seems that the building now attached to the gatehouse at Kenilworth might have been a banqueting house.

However, Leicester's buildings there are all in the local sandstone, apart from a single alabaster fireplace now in the gatehouse, nor is there any trace of anything built of a different stone; this would exclude a connection with Burghley's stone, for that would have to have been limestone, of which he had a quarry nearby.[28] There is a reference from 1600 linking Dudley to the erection of a banqueting house 'neare the water syde', which clearly points to the one in London, while a source in 1676 confirms that that building was indeed made of stone.[29] If Dudley's letter refers to London, it is one of the few potential clues to a building chronology. It also shows a degree of architectural patronage shared with the most renowned architectural connoisseur at court, who had clearly recommended Henry Hawthorne, a former Purveyor to the Royal Works previously employed at Theobalds and possibly at Burghley's own house in the Strand (see Chapter Five).[30]

There appears, indeed, to have been an architectural dialogue between the two magnates, for in an earlier letter, of 10 August 1571, Burghley had asked Leicester to 'lett me staye amongst my dusty laborors' while stressing that 'being in the middest to be fyneshed forceth me to assure your Lordship to hasten to get it covered'; this could be achieved

> *wholly and only with borrowyng here in the Cite whereby as I take plesure in my fond humor of buyldyng, so have I a stay and stopp from much rejoysyng whan I behold the cost to be doone by borrowyng, and so had I rather doo my Lord and leave my heyre less land to repaye it then by bribery in an office.*[31]

Written 'From my house in Westminster', that is, Burghley's own Strand palace, the letter gives no clue about the building but it is perhaps more probable that it concerned London rather than Stamford or Theobalds (see Chapter Five). Burghley's accounts for 1578 show a payment to 'the serjeant painter' 'for my Lord of Leicester's arms over the chimney', listed right after works by the same 'upon the gallery'.[32] Leicester was then a crucial political ally, though his reputation as an influential patron of the arts and fellow builder may have played a role. After all, he was credited by Camden with having 'built much for his pleasure' at Wanstead, while he had also, apparently, conceived the 'platt' for the vast pavilion erected en route to Kenilworth before Queen Elizabeth's progress of 1575.[33] His father's legacy as one of the leading architectural patrons of the late Henrician and Edwardian courts had also credited him with the introduction of a wealth of Renaissance motifs at Kenilworth, including a loggia as early as 1569. John Shute's *First and Chief Groundes of Architecture*, which appeared in London in 1563, was equally bound up with the Dudleys' patronage and possibly published at Leicester's request.[34]

In the absence of Leicester's accounts and disbursement books for the whole of the 1570s and most of the 1580s, it is difficult to assess the extent and nature of his works at Leicester House.[35] Fragmentary financial records from the latter decade do not indicate any sizeable building activity, with the exception of the garden, to which I shall return. Perhaps this was due to the fact that the earl had spent vast sums at Kenilworth and was being cautious in London.[36] The circumstantial evidence gathered here none the less points to some activity concentrated in the first part of the 1570s. This is plausible given that Leicester had purchased the property in 1569 and seems to have begun improvements soon after, alongside the major works at Kenilworth. Of the latter we know slightly more, including the names of some of those who may have been involved. These include Robert Coxe, the chief mason from 1552 until at least 1571; the Italian engineer Giulio Spinelli, documented at the castle in 1570; the mason William Spicer, formerly employed by Sir John Thynne at Longleat, who acted as the surveyor of the earl's works and went on to become the Surveyor of the Royal Works in London; or the artisan Robert Trunquet or Trunckey, a Flemish joiner in the so-called 'Nonsuch-Bellin-Revels circle', who had contributed to some of Henry VIII's ephemeral creations as well as to the pavilion that Leicester erected on the road to Kenilworth.[37] Henry Hawthorne may have been involved too and one wonders whether the same craftsmen were re-employed at Leicester House, where works were generally intended, as will be seen, for 'show and pleasure'.[38] After all, between 1573 and 1585, the queen had been a visitor to the house (and to Leicester's other abodes) with a frequency seldom matched by any other courtier in the kingdom, while it is well known that the Strand palace played an influential role as the setting of an important collection and as a literary and artistic centre. It was here that Sir Philip Sidney, Leicester's nephew, worked on his *Defence of Poetry*, the first formal treatise on English vernacular literature, and 'Old' *Arcadia*, an exploration of the theories expounded in the *Defence*, while the so-called Areopagus society, which included Edmund Spenser, Edward Dyer and Gabriel Harvey, regularly met at the house to discuss how ancient and continental Renaissance poetic forms could be adapted for English usage.[39]

Of the fourteen inventories of Leicester House produced during Dudley's lifetime and thereafter, six are arranged by rooms: of those, four are relevant here.[40] The first two are closely related probate inventories, compiled by crown officials after the earl's death on 4 September 1588.[41] The third was made on 3 April 1590 by the Queen's Commissioners and Sheriffs of Middlesex following the seizure of the house and its contents in part satisfaction of a debt of £10,000, for which Leicester had been bound to the queen in 1581.[42] The fourth was compiled on 21 November 1590 for Leicester's widow, Lettice Knollys.[43] The main probate inventory of 1588 and the one following the seizure of April 1590 were transcribed by Kingsford, with the lease of part of the house in 1639, another key source which provides clues to the location of rooms.[44] As there do not seem to have been significant alterations after Dudley's tenure, these three documents can be cross-referenced with later topographical sources for Leicester House, namely Hollar's pre-1666 (see fig. 17), and John Ogilby and William Morgan's 1677 map of London (fig. 22). All combined, the

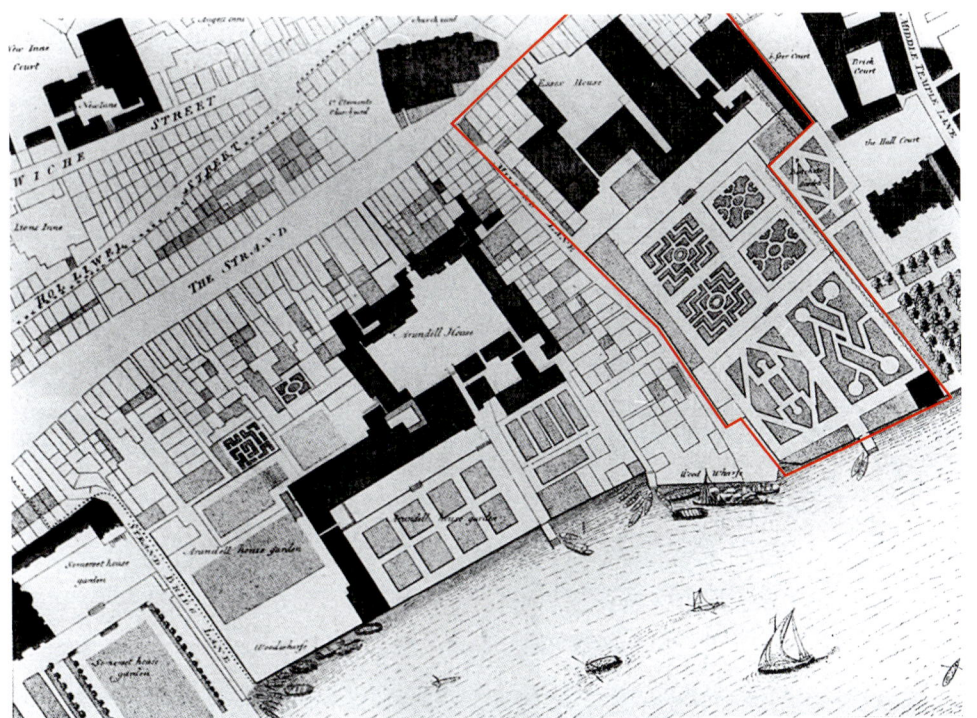

22 Plan of the complex of Essex House, detail of John Ogilby and William Morgan, *Map of London*, 1677. Mitton 1908. Wikimedia Commons Public Domain

inventories allowed Kingsford a comprehensive reconstruction of the interiors, including a conjectural plan of the house as it may have been in 1640 (fig. 23).[45] These sources have been re-examined afresh in the light of new unpublished evidence from 'A Booke of Computations of buildings' of c.1615–25, produced for the 9th Earl of Northumberland, who had lived at the house from 1600 to 1605. It provides the measurements of what must have been the most important rooms at Leicester House, as well as further information on its interiors.[46] Although a proper reconstruction drawing cannot be achieved here (with no historical plan of some sort to go by), we still gain new, precious insights into the arrangement of Leicester House.

The 1588 probate inventory appears to have started on the first, upper floor of the garden wing, as one of the first rooms to be appraised is the 'Greate Chamber over the hall'.[47] As seen in Norden's 1593 view (see fig. 21), the Hall stood in the middle of that range; back then, it stood out as a seemingly double-height room with a crenellated top. By the time of Hollar's pre-1666 depiction (see fig. 17), however, it appears embedded within the two-storey section of the garden front bounded by the tower, which stood out asymmetrically towards the eastern end of the garden front. From the Booke of Computations one learns that the Hall was 45 feet long, 24 feet wide and 18 feet high, which made it reasonably tall for a double height. But if the Great Chamber was on top of the Hall, that range could not have been an average two storeys high, as we have to assume that the Hall alone was that height.[48] While this may initially appear to contrast with Hollar's single row of windows as well as with the presence of a seemingly average door on the garden front (more or less coinciding with the one represented by Norden; see fig. 21), a closer look reveals how these two floors actually corresponded to three in the middle wing just behind. One should also consider the sloping nature of the site, which in the majority of the Strand palaces overlooking the river meant a difference of about one level between the street and garden ranges, so that two storeys on the former meant three on the latter.[49] In addition, notwithstanding Hollar's unparalleled accomplishment in London topography, his reliability must be treated with care.[50]

The 'Greate Chamber over the hall' featured five 'large peeces of hangings wth the Queenes Armes in the border, very ould', furniture of

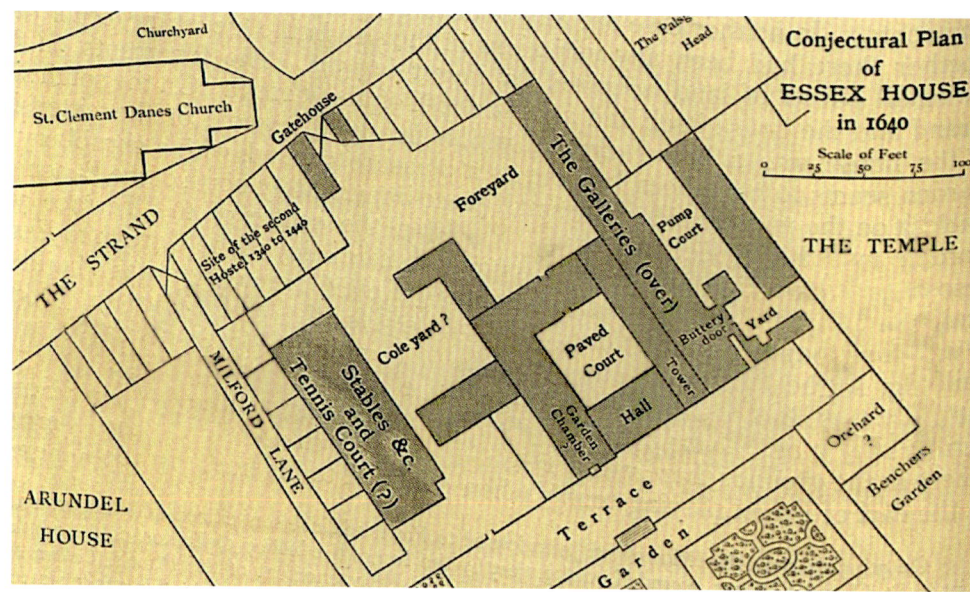

various kinds, as well as an 'Instrument wth sundry stopes in it wth a frame of beache' and 'a map of the world'.[51] This Great Chamber ought to be the one marked as 'of the South side' in the Booke of Computations, which measured 51′ 4″ by 23′ 7″ and 15′ 3″ high. Nearly identical to the Hall in width, it was about 6½ feet longer and may also have covered part of the western range overlooking a walled courtyard (fig. 23 and see fig. 17).[52] As the 1639 lease describes, it was connected to the ground floor by 'those staircase and stairs leading and assending [sic] out of and from the northward side of the great Hall', which faced the 'square paved court', that is, the second court from the Strand seen in Hollar, referred to in the Booke of Computations as 'The Courte paved', which measured 60 by 48 feet (see fig. 23).[53] Adjoined to the east was the 'Wthdrawing Chamber next the greate Chamber over the Hall', which occupied the remainder of the garden front including part of the tower.[54] In 1588 it included 'v peeces of ould hangings of course pillos', several pieces of furniture and 'three little Mapps and a latten Candlesticke'.[55]

The next entry in the 1588 inventory is the 'greate Gallerye', seemingly the most important of what appear to be three galleries, rather than the two known to scholars. The evidence for a third gallery comes from the inventory produced for Leicester's widow in November 1590, which, alongside a Low and High Gallery, includes an 'Armory galyre'.[56] None of the other sources cited here includes a third gallery. One gallery can be firmly located, while the other two compete to be identified as the only other gallery mentioned in the 1639 lease.

23 Charles L. Kingsford, 'Conjectural Plan of Essex House in 1640'. Kingsford 1923, p. 20

The Great Gallery is assumed to have been what the two 1590 inventories call the 'High Gallery'. In this case the lease of 1639, on which any identification relies, is not immediately decipherable.[57] The lease includes a 'Long Gallery lyeing and being upon the third floore over the said cellars' (revealing that Leicester House did have a basement or cellars, probably occasioned by the slope of the site) and a 'gallery lyeing over the same foure chambers'.[58] The two are different, for the cellars below the Long Gallery were 'lyeing adioyning to the eastward side of the foreyard belonging to the said capital messuage', that is, were in the first courtyard from the Strand seen in both Hollar and Ogilby and Morgan (see figs 17 and 22). By contrast, the 'foure chambers' under the other gallery were 'lyeing upon one floore upon the eastward side of the square paved court', that is, in the second courtyard, albeit still along the east of the house. As these four rooms were themselves 'upwards' of the 'Wthdrawing Chamber next the greate Chamber over the Hall', this other gallery must have been on the fourth floor. If the Great Gallery (as in both the probate inventory of 1588 and Booke of Computations) does coincide with the 'High Gallery' (as in the 1590 inventories), then it was indeed the room described in the lease as the 'gallery lyeing over the same foure chambers' on the fourth or top floor as it appears in Hollar ('High' referring to its position rather than to the ceiling). It ran south towards the garden, which it overlooked through a pair of double windows to the east of the tower, specified in the lease as 'at the southwest end of the same gallery' (see fig. 17). From the 'Wthdrawing Chamber next the greate Chamber over the Hall', the appraisers had therefore gone up one floor via the 'stair case and stayres leading from the said eastward dore of the said wthdrawing chamber upwards unto the foure chambers' previously mentioned and from those to the gallery.

Listed in the Booke of Computations as 106 feet long and 20 feet wide by '10 foote hiegh to the compass of the roofe wch is also 6 foote', this barrel-vaulted gallery would have been an impressive room, with far-reaching views over the garden and across the Thames (see Conclusion). Furnished with a 'high Chaire' and a number of stools 'all covered wth greene velvet, ould and much worne', a 'square table' and a 'paire of latten aundirons', as well as a 'long foote Turquoy carpett', it displayed twenty-eight pictures and eight maps. Next to it, the lease recites, were the 'waynscotted chamber and the little roome called the Stayrehead Chamber att the top of the saide staire case, being wthout the said gallery', while from the gallery itself one could descend to the leads 'there neare', probably on top of the Great Chamber, as shown by Hollar (see fig. 17).[59]

After the Great Gallery, the 1588 inventory lists five rooms occupied by members of the household, followed by the 'Chappell Closett' and the 'Chappell' itself.[60] The positon of the Chapel is difficult to confirm but it was probably on the ground floor under the north part of the Great Gallery and was possibly of double height. Some eleven rooms further on,[61] there then appears the 'lowe Gallerie', included in the Booke of Computations as 88 feet long, 19 wide and 10 high. It featured, besides the usual furniture comprising chairs, stools and a table, 'xii ould guilte leather hanginges', a 'paire of latten andirons embossed' and a 'verie ould mappe in a frame'. As the name suggests, this room would have been at a lower level than the Great or High Gallery. And indeed, the first gallery described in the 1639 lease (located, as noted, on the third floor of the east wing in the foreyard of Leicester House) was one storey lower than the Great Gallery and ran north towards the Strand. The assumption that this gallery was the 'lowe Gallerie' may therefore seem justified, yet the lease clearly defined the room as a 'Long Gallery', not Low, which is what the other gallery is called in all three inventories.[62] Could a truly long gallery equate to the longest of the three?

Contents, scope and perhaps location of the third gallery are clarified by the inventory of November 1590 for Lettice Knollys, where the 'Armory galyre' is listed immediately after the 'High galerye'.[63] Interestingly, the 1588 inventory lists a conspicuous amount of armour as an individual entry valued at £436, accounting for about an eighth of the total value of the contents at Leicester House, £3198. In addition, the Queen's Commissioners' inventory of April 1590 lists a room called 'in the Armory' albeit devoid of its original contents, located near the Chapel. The latter, as noted, was in the east wing, probably under the north part of the Great Gallery, while the 'Armory galyre' was sufficiently near it to be listed immediately after that top-floor room. The Long Gallery as described in the lease and the 'Armory galyre' may therefore have been the same room. If so, the other gallery, referred to in all the documents as the Low Gallery, remains unidentified unless one reconsiders the connotation of 'low', perhaps indicating a room on a much lower level, possibly the ground floor. This interpretation finds a parallel in the 1509 inventory of the London house of Edmund Dudley, Leicester's grandfather, which lists a 'Lowe Galarye by the Gardeyn', presumably located on the ground floor.[64] At Leicester House, such a 'low' gallery would have featured alongside other public rooms such as the 'Dininge Chamber', followed by the 'greate Chamber next the Garden', which contained 'iiijor peeces of old hangings of the storye of Moyses founde in a basket' and different musical instruments.[65] These rooms were probably in the south-west range and likely to have been in sequence with the Hall. The ground floor also included at least one of the apartments for family members, generally composed of a chamber and closet preceded by a withdrawing chamber, as well as the usual set of service rooms associated with the kitchen, located near the Hall on the south-east corner of the house around a small yard called Pump Court (see fig. 23).[66] The inventories list the Banqueting House, perhaps that discussed with Burghley in 1575, a two-storey structure at the south-east corner of the garden overlooking the river, clearly depicted by Hollar and by Ogilby and Morgan (see figs 17 and 22). This would have been the third such structure on the site, after the 'fair tower' by the river built by Stapledon in the early fourteenth century and the Banqueting House featured in Wyngaerde's c.1544 view during the tenure of the 3rd Duke of Norfolk (see fig. 18).

Within this square building with bay windows on its west side, as drawn by Hollar, the banqueting room proper would have been on the upper floor so as to command views, while the 'lower rome' and 'Gardeners Chamber' were located under it.[67] Both the probate and Commissioners' inventories only record furniture spread among the three rooms, but the inventory of November 1590, under the heading of 'the Banquetyng howse', begins with 'ii sets of very fine hangings'.[68] It is indeed here, as will be seen, that some of Leicester's most precious tapestries were displayed.

Overall, the inventories specify about fifty rooms, spread over three to four floors.[69] Among the most important public rooms were no less than three great chambers, one on the ground floor next to the Hall and two on the first floor.

The Great Chamber over the hall 'of the South side' was followed by the Withdrawing Chamber and faced the garden, while the Great Chamber 'of the North side' overlooked the foreyard towards the Strand. The Booke of Computations measured the latter at 42 by 23 feet and 12 feet high 'with a compass roof some 18 inches more'.[70] But it is the number, position and perhaps size of the galleries, which occupied every level of the eastern wing of Leicester House, probably one per floor, that were both exceptional and innovative.

Whether or not Robert Dudley was responsible for the construction of his galleries we cannot be certain, for, as noted earlier, evidence of his building is scant and circumstantial – with the possible exception of the Banqueting House. Plans for a long gallery at Kenilworth never materialised either.[71] Nevertheless, it is unlikely that a gallery as grand as the High Gallery existed before he took over: indeed, building one such room on top of an existing structure may well have started here with him: it may have been the showpiece of a programme of improvements which the earl certainly made soon after obtaining the palace in 1569, in order to display his growing collections.[72] From Goldring's extensive studies on the subject one learns that the picture collection alone was not just larger than those at Kenilworth and Wanstead but was also the only one to be expanded before Leicester's death.[73] In terms of content and display, it is equally considered a forerunner of the great aristocratic picture collections of seventeenth-century London, of which the Strand was the embodiment.

By the time of Dudley's death in September 1588, the quantity of works of art at Leicester House was conspicuous. The exact number is difficult to ascertain because items were moved around between various properties, as reflected in the inventories. In this respect, the most complete is the household inventory of 17 December 1588, which lists some 124 pictures and 58 maps.[74] But it is to the probate inventory that one must return for a sense of how the collections were divided. It is clear, for instance, that hangings, 131 pieces predominantly 'ould', far outweighed pictures, recorded as eighty-one, for almost every room of some standing had tapestries on display. Apart from those with the 'storye of Moyses founde in a basket' in the 'Great Chamber next the Garden', with 'the Queenes Armes in the border' in the 'Great Chamber over the hall' or with 'my Lordes

24 Marcus Gheeraerts the Elder, *Elizabeth I*, c.1578. Private collection. This painting may have been displayed at both Leicester House and Wanstead. Goldring 2014, fig. 98

25 William Segar, *Robert Dudley, Earl of Leicester, with the Lord Steward's Staff*, c.1587. Private collection. Displayed at Leicester House prior to c.1590. Goldring 2014, fig. 10

Armes' stored in a wardrobe, they are described as featuring 'fflemmish ells fille', 'flowers and leaves' and 'Imagerye'. Twelve 'ould guilt leather hanginges' were then on the walls in the Low Gallery on the ground floor, where, similarly, no or few pictures are recorded.

While tapestries were still the most expensive form of wall decoration, Leicester's interest in paintings, and what can be deduced of his thought and care for their display, might be seen to mark the beginning of a gradual shift in the relative status of tapestry versus painting, which played out over the seventeenth century, as will be seen throughout this book.[75] Indeed, in contrast to the rooms just listed, the Great or High Gallery on the top floor featured 28 pictures and 8 maps, by far the highest concentration in the whole house, excluding the 50-odd paintings and 17 maps (out of a total of 36) contained in the wardrobe. Mostly portraits, pictures in the Great Gallery included three of Leicester and one of Queen Elizabeth (figs 24 and 25), alongside those of continental notables and members of the earl's immediate family (such as, apparently, Veronese's celebrated portrait of Sir Philip Sydney[76]). Whether either of the two sculpture busts of the 'Quenes Majestie and my Lord cut in alabaster' recorded at the house in the late 1570s and early 1580s ever featured in this gallery remains unclear.[77]

In spite of the Great or High Gallery's treasures, it was the Long Gallery or Armoury below it that scored the highest number, with some 1348 pistols, muskets and other military items, including five complete sets of armour, one of which was 'graven and gilte', another partly so and one 'for a horseman'. We know from the 1588 inventory that Leicester had commissioned a suit of armour from the celebrated Antwerp-born engraver Eliseus Libaerts (fl. 1560s), and that he was a leading patron of the Greenwich armoury, while the famous works assumed to be a pair of the queen and an armour-clad Dudley, perhaps by Federico Zuccaro, of 1575, show him in a suit of russet steel with gilt engravings.[78] Such a gallery – epitomising chivalric pride and symbolising Leicester's political dominance as a quasi-royal husband in waiting – would have provided military gravitas to the earl, demonstrating a

perfect balance between the two aspects of a learned Elizabethan courtier, whose 220 books 'great and small' were also, remarkably, included in the probate inventory.[79] Equally, one finds a room called 'The Embroderers prentise', which must have been used by somebody learning the craft that is well represented in the house, not only through its many precious hangings but also its carpets, covers and embroidered blankets of the finest sorts. Indeed, Leicester has been linked to Richard Hickes, the head weaver of the Sheldon tapestry manufactory at Barcheston in Warwickshire and employed at Court in the Queen's Great Wardrobe from the mid-1580s, whose documented patrons included Bess of Hardwick. Through Hickes the earl ordered the 'ii sets of very fine hangings' recorded in the Banqueting House in November 1590, which must be the 'ij peeces of fyne hanginges w[i]th my Lordes Armes' listed in the wardrobe in the 1588 probate inventory (at which point the Banqueting House only featured walnut and marble-inlaid tables). These were in fact part of the series of four tapestries 'with my Lo Armes in the middell thereof verie large & faire: made for the banqueting howse' in the mid-1580s and adapted from two sets of well-known plates by Jan Vredeman de Vries (figs 26 and 27).[80] De Vries was also a major influence on the 'Porticus' at Salisbury House erected by Robert Cecil between 1605 and 1610 (see Chapter Eight).

Leicester, once again like Burghley, had some interest in gardens, so much so that in 1584 he was prepared to offer about £33 plus meat and drink to 'a perfect gardener' and his men for Wanstead.[81] While his first efforts appear to have been made at Kenilworth, where the garden was decorated with spheres of painted sandstone, obelisks and bears following royal heraldic models at Hampton Court and Nonsuch, it was the garden in London that was the most modern.[82] There a broad terrace across the whole south front led down to an entirely formal garden of two geometrical parterres on a central axis straight to a water gate, a design which provided regularity to an irregular complex (see figs 17 and

26 Tapestry for the Banqueting House at Leicester House, c.1585. Wool and silk, 284 × 476 cm. Victoria and Albert Museum, London

The arms and motto of Robert Dudley ('Droit et Loyal') are surmounted by the Dudley bear and rugged staff.

28 | LONDON'S 'GOLDEN MILE'

27 Tapestry for the Banqueting House at Leicester House with Dudley's arms, c.1585. Wool and silk, 292 × 263 cm. Glasgow Museums Collection. Licensed under Creative Commons Attribution 4.0 International

22). To the west, a line of trees hid the dwellings along Milford Lane, while stables might have occupied the north-west of the property, together with a tennis court perhaps to be identified with the tall building depicted there by Hollar (see figs 17 and 23).[83] On the south-east corner stood the Banqueting House, while the only orchard seems to have been confined to a small plot opposite the Kitchen, in between the easternmost part of the house and the Temple's Benchers Garden. The garden of Leicester House also featured a sundial made in 1584 by 'young Adams', perhaps the Robert Adams (later the Surveyor of Works) responsible for the new dial at Whitehall two years before.[84] As a member of the Inner Temple since 1561, Leicester had also created a small formal garden there for his own use in 1576 (later known as the Alienation Office Garden).[85]

The layout of Leicester's garden in the Strand has been compared to that of the French royal architect Philibert de l'Orme's at the Château d'Anet (1547–52, as known from the site plan engraved by Jacques Androuet du Cerceau). De l'Orme's work was a model for the great garden at Wollaton, Nottinghamshire, in the 1580s. Equally, it has been related to an anonymous Elizabethan 'plott' for a terraced waterside garden which bears interesting similarities to the garden of Leicester House (fig. 28).[86] Despite being rather strictly rectangular, as opposed to the slightly angled shape of the Strand site seen in Hollar and confirmed by Ogilby and Morgan (see figs 17 and 22), it is indeed possible that this plan was meant for the earl. It shows a terrace followed by two parterres, leading, through arbour tunnels, to an elaborate water gate flanked by a battlemented wall, with a couple of obelisks along the side boundaries, not seen in the others.[87]

The 2nd and 3rd Earls of Essex: Early 1590s–1646

The death of Robert Dudley on 4 September 1588 led to a complicated and lengthy settlement of his estate, which lasted for more than fifty years.[88] In his will of 1587, Leicester House had been bequeathed to Lettice Knollys for life, with the remainder to his illegitimate son, also named Robert, with the proviso that if he died without issue the property would pass to Robert Devereux (1565–1601), Leicester's step- and godson or even, according to widely publicised rumours, his actual son.[89] By 1593, following the seizure of Leicester House in 1590 and the subsequent renegotiation of its lease (with that of Wanstead) by Devereux himself as the 2nd Earl of Essex, the Strand palace had become his, and for the last time changed its name, to Essex House.

Like that of his stepfather, Essex's relationship with Elizabeth as her new (rather younger) favourite attracted considerable attention, while its tumultuous nature and drastic epilogue at the turn of the century characterise the peak of Devereux's relatively brief tenure of Essex House, and virtually all we know of it. Moreover, he does not seem to have built anything anywhere, for he had very little money.[90] Following the Essex Rebellion of 1600–01, an increasingly embattled Essex, who had transformed the palace into a centre for disaffected aristocrats (the 'Essex House Cabal'), unemployed army officers and noisy Puritan preaching, unsuccessfully tried to rally the City to his cause, so as to pre-empt his enemies and denounce them to the queen. The earl was executed for high treason on 25 February 1601, and the house passed to his son Robert, 3rd Earl

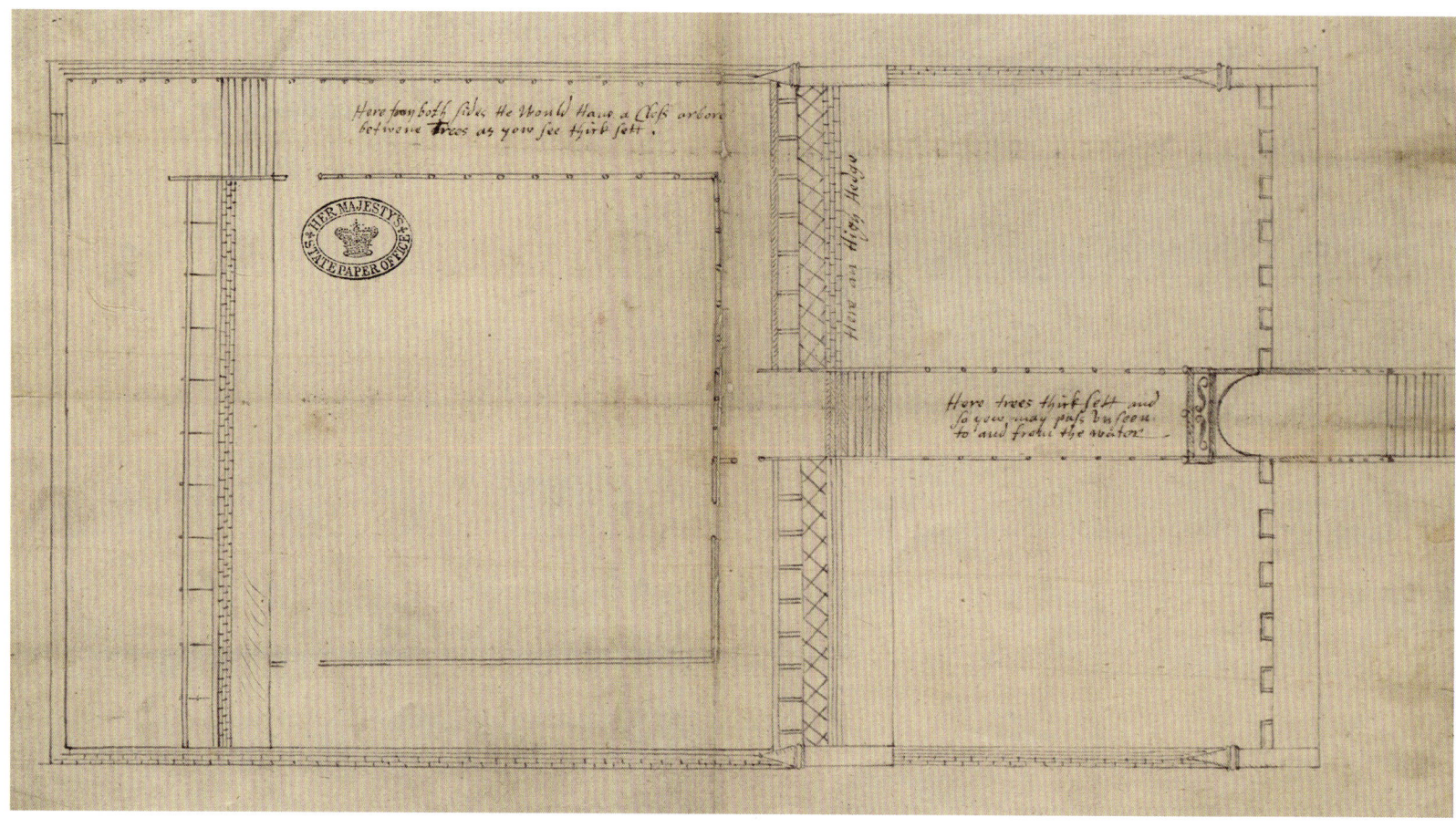

of Essex (1591–1646), who lived elsewhere until his coming of age, apparently preferring to stay with his grandmother Lettice.[91] The latter, who lived into old age until 1634, had married as her third husband Sir Christopher Blount, one of Robert Dudley's gentlemen. Meanwhile, Essex's own widow, Frances Walsingham (1567–1633), the Principal Secretary's daughter first married to Philip Sidney, continued to live at Essex House, which seems at the time to have been under the control of the Earl of Nottingham, the Lord Admiral.[92]

Born at Essex House, the 3rd Earl of Essex was married aged thirteen to Frances Howard, herself only eight months his senior, in 1606.[93] She was the daughter of Thomas Howard, 1st Earl of Suffolk, and great-niece of Henry Howard, 1st Earl of Northampton of that house at the opposite end of the Strand (see Chapter Eleven). It was Northampton, in the hope of furthering ties with James I's favourite, Robert Carr, who seven years later engineered Frances' notorious divorce in 1613. But it was Essex who eventually had the better of it, as he sat as a juror in the trial of his former wife and her new husband, accused of and executed for the murder of Sir Thomas Overbury, who had opposed the match. There began a time of multiple occupation of Essex House, as Sir Josceline and Sir Allan Percy, brothers-in-law of Essex's aunt, the Countess of Northumberland, were resident in 1605–6. The Percy link came via the marriage of the 2nd Earl of Essex's sister, Dorothy Devereux, to the 9th Earl of Northumberland; they too were resident at Essex House, for their son Algernon, the future 10th Earl of Northumberland, was born there in 1602. Essex House was then the designated abode, briefly, of the Elector Palatine when he came to London to marry Princess Elizabeth in 1612, while James Hay, 1st Earl of Carlisle, who had married Lucy Percy, Essex's cousin, was also often there. Carlisle's secretary, Sir Francis Nethersole, equally used the house between 1620 and 1624, and from December 1627 to March 1628 it was occupied by Robert and Dorothy Sidney, 2nd Earl and Countess of Leicester. She was the sister of the Countess of Carlisle, while he was the great-nephew of Robert Dudley (after whom the title had become extinct), and went on to build the new Leicester House in the homonymous square in the 1630s. Further occupants of Essex House include Elizabeth Pawlett, the

28 Plan of an unidentified garden leading down to a river [Eliz. I]. National Archives, Kew, SP 12/288

29 The redeveloped Essex House site, detail from John Strype, *A Survey of the Cities of London and Westminster*, vol. 4, p. 116, 1720 (detail of fig. 83). Folger Shakespeare Library, Washington DC. Licensed under Creative Commons Attribution-ShareAlike 4.0 International

daughter of Sir William Pawlett of Edington, Wiltshire, the second wife of the 3rd Earl of Essex (from whom he had also separated in 1631); she lived there till the outbreak of the Civil War. The earl largely continued to live elsewhere: the fact that Cavalier songs called the house 'Cuckolds Hall' after his first wife accused him of impotence may have played a role. It is in these circumstances that in 1639 the eastern part of Essex House, as noted earlier from the lease, was let for £1100 to the earl's sister Frances (1599–1674) and her husband, William Seymour, 1st Marquess of Hertford and 2nd Duke of Somerset (1587–1660), for ninety-nine years.

Subsequent Years: 1646–mid-1670s

The 3rd Earl of Essex died at Essex House on 15 September 1646 with no surviving issue, leaving the palace to his sister Frances for life, after which it was to go to Sir Charles Shirley, the elder son of his other sister, Dorothy, with a remainder to his brother Robert. This was contested by Lady Frances, but an agreement was reached whereby the house was divided between her and the Shirleys. Like all its neighbours, Essex House was used for quartering soldiers during the Civil War, though the Hertfords continued to live there. After the Great Fire of 1666, the house was used for a time by the lawyers of Doctors' Commons and the Court of Arches, while part of it had been let since 1651 to Sir Orlando Bridgeman, who lived there as Lord Keeper from 1667 to 1672. In 1673, Lady Frances' granddaughter and namesake, and her husband, Thomas Thinne, had an apartment there too.[94]

What happened to Essex House during all these years is unclear. Samuel Pepys, who on 24 January 1669 attended a meeting there of naval officers in the king's presence, found it 'large but ugly'.[95] Comparison of Hollar's view of the mid-1600s with Ogilby and Morgan's plan of 1676 (see figs 17 and 22) reveals the square Paved Court almost totally filled in, as well as an apparently broader east wing, suggesting additions to increase accommodation given the presence of multiple households. It is known from correspondence following Lady Frances' death on 24 April 1674, after which Essex House was to be sold, that its value was about £7000. But, as Arthur Capel, 1st Earl of Essex of the new creation and Lord Lieutenant of Ireland, wrote on 16 May 1674, 'my Lady Dutchess was careless enough in her business, & therefore I suspect ye Timber & other things, if they come to be searched, will be found very faulty', so much so that 'Twill cost a man any thing extraordinary to sett it right'. Nevertheless, he thought that 'this being a Noted House it will not be difficult to let it to some Ambassador'.[96] While Capel – 'being necessary for me to have a House in London, & I am sure, take all circumstances, none can be so fit for me as this will be' – was trying to buy the property, and Charles II was prepared to agree to a sale for £12,000 in reward for Capel's services in Ireland, speculative builders such as Nicholas Barbon soon had the better of it. Without waiting for a formal conveyance Barbon had entered the garden of Essex House, 'which he hath absolutely destroyed and layed thoro' it the foundation of that street which he designes'.[97] By the late 1670s, probably shortly after the 1677 publication of Ogilby and Morgan's plan, the site had been converted into 'houses and tenements for taverns, alehouses, cookshops and woodmongers'. Part of the site along the eastern boundary was acquired by the Middle Temple, while the portion of the house let to Bridgeman since 1651 was still inhabited by his wife in the early 1680s and survived until the mid-1770s, hosting the Cotton Library from 1712 to 1730 (fig. 29).[98]

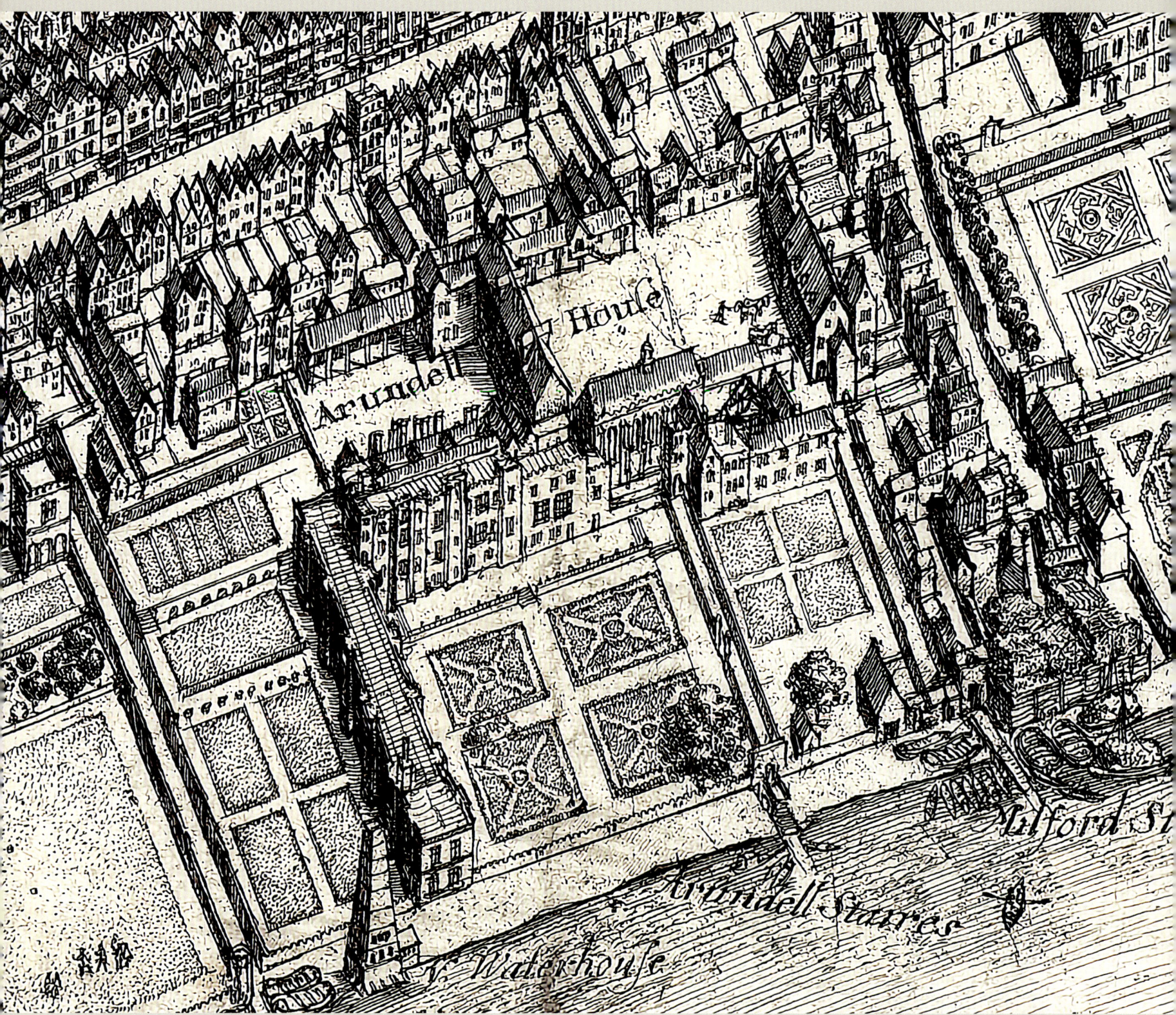

30 The complex of Arundel House bounded by dwellings along Milford Lane on the east (right) and Strand Bridge Lane and Somerset House on the west (left) (detail of fig. 8)

2 · ARUNDEL HOUSE

ARUNDEL HOUSE LAY BETWEEN SOMERSET House on the west and Essex House on the east (more precisely, a series of dwellings along Milford Lane, which divided the two palaces, leading to Milford Stairs to the east and Strand Bridge Lane next to Somerset House to the west; fig. 30). It was the former inn of the Bishop of Bath and Wells known as Bath Inn or Place, and its site, with more than 500 feet of river frontage and 400 feet deep back to the street, was the biggest among the episcopal palaces along the Strand. If less architecturally prominent than other great inns such as Durham House, Arundel House changed drastically when it became the chief residence of Thomas Howard, the famous Collector Earl, in 1607 (fig. 31). But, as with the Duke of Buckingham's collection at York House, studies on his collection were not matched by analysis of the settings, for which scholars still relied on Kingsford's 1922 extensive article 'Bath Inn or Arundel House' – one of the useful if dated accounts of some of the Strand palaces published in *Archaeologia*.[1]

The Inn of the Bishops of Bath and Wells: 1228–1539

The history of the Arundel House site can be traced back to the early thirteenth century, when Eustace de Fauconberg, Bishop of London from 1221, was granted the land in the parish of St Clement Danes. On his death in 1228 this passed to Jocelyn, the Bishop of Bath and Wells credited with the construction of both Wells Cathedral and its London residence.[2] When Bishop Jocelyn died in 1242, Bath Place was granted by Henry III to his queen's uncle, Peter of Savoy, who held it during the vacancy of the bishopric, probably until securing the grant of the site where he built his own Savoy Palace, around 1246 (see Chapter Four).

By the beginning of the fifteenth century the complex of Bath Place must have been highly regarded, for the Drapers Company appears to have considered it a model when building its new hall in St Swithin's Lane.[3] Bath Place at this time consisted of a hospice, or main house, and twenty annexed small tenements, the 'Rents' of which represented the main source of income. Two such tenements towards the west end of the Strand frontage were called 'le Cardinallis Hatt' and 'le Tabard', and seem to have been reserved for the bishops' use, which makes one wonder about the actual use of the main house, termed 'hospicium' (as were other episcopal palaces).[4] Either way,

the Cardinal's Hat probably owed its name to the Italian Cardinal Adriano da Castello (or Castellesi), Bishop of Bath and Wells from 1504 to 1518, when he was succeeded by Cardinal Wolsey, who thus became entitled to Bath Place. This was the third property on the Strand to which Wolsey had access for, as Archbishop of York from 1514 and Lord Chancellor from 1515, he could also use York House, even if he seems to have preferred Durham House (where he lived intermittently in 1516–18, and again in 1528 while his own York Place at Whitehall was being completed). By 1528, Wolsey had exchanged the See of Bath for that of Durham (see Chapter Nine). It was at Bath Place under Bishop John Clerk that Cardinal Lorenzo Campeggio, last cardinal protector of England, resided for the negotiations in 1528 with Henry VIII over his wish to divorce Katherine of Aragon, and throughout her trial. This episode reminds us how the episcopal palaces acted as satellite buildings to accommodate royal and state guests, and perform various state functions, all of which shaped their very raison d'être after the Reformation.

William Fitzwilliam, 1st Earl of Southampton, and Thomas Seymour, 1st Baron Seymour of Sudeley: 1539–1549

The first secular owner of Bath Place was William Fitzwilliam, 1st Earl of Southampton and Henry VIII's High Admiral, to whom 'the chief mansion place or capital messuage called the Bishop of Bathe's place with all and singular houses, edifices, buildings, courts, orchards, &c' was granted in 1539. In exchange for Bath Place, briefly known as Hampton Place, Bishop Clerk had to accept an inferior dwelling called the Minories in the east of the city.[5] Southampton died without issue in 1542 and the property reverted to the Crown. Then in 1545 it passed to Thomas Seymour, the brother of the more famous Edward who had been amassing neighbouring properties for the construction of Somerset House since 1537 (see Chapter Three). The sale of Bath or Hampton Place amounted to £700 and included seventeen of the original twenty tenements along the Strand.[6] Alongside the bookbinder, haberdasher and a variety of other craftsmen, the tenants recorded

31 Attributed (by the author) to Wenceslaus Hollar, engraving showing Lord Arundel as the antiquarian art collector 'Father of Vertu', late 1630s–early 1640s. © National Portrait Gallery, London (D26506)

32 Bath Inn, detail from Anthonis van den Wyngaerde, *Panorama of London from the River*, c.1544 (detail of fig. 9). © Ashmolean Museum, University of Oxford

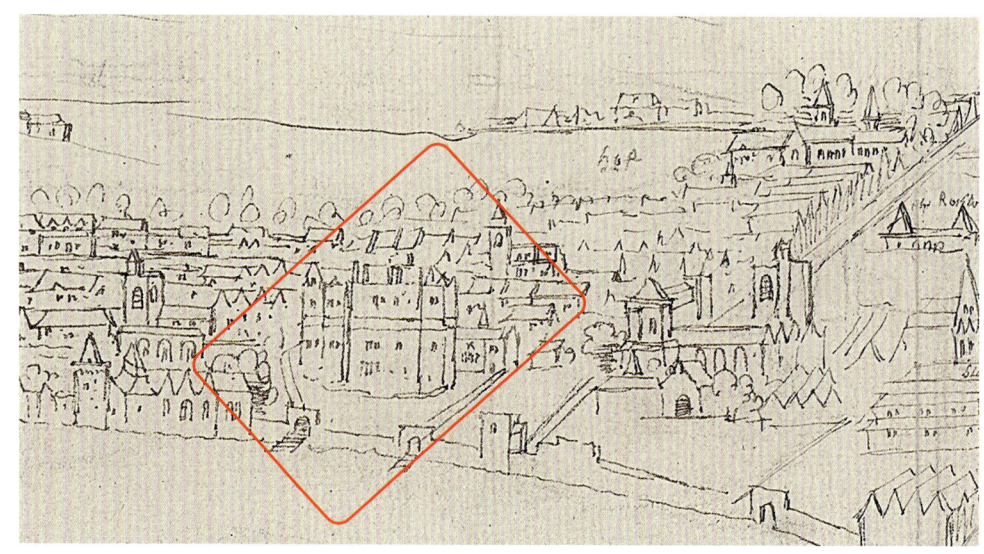

34 | LONDON'S 'GOLDEN MILE'

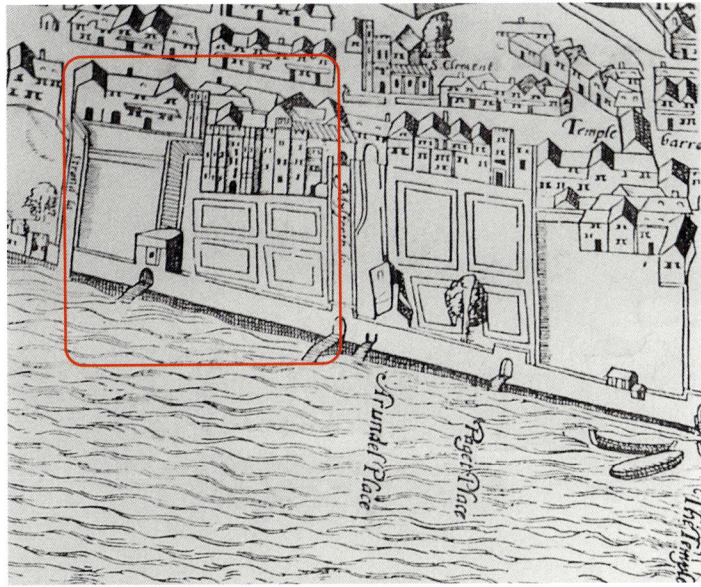 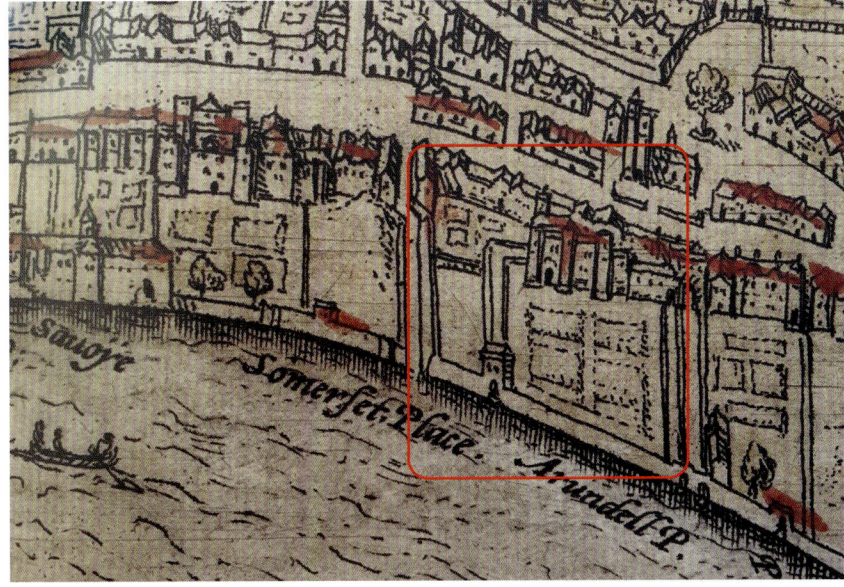

33 Arundel Place, detail of the *Woodcut Map of London*, 1561–70 ('Agas'), reprinted 1633, derived from the lost 'Copperplate Map of London', 1553–9. Mitton, 1908. Wikimedia Commons Public Domain

34 Arundel Place, detail of Georg Braun and Frans Hogenberg, 'London' in *Civitates Orbis Terrarum*, 1572, derived from the lost 'Copperplate Map of London', 1553–9. University Library, Heidelberg. Wikipedia, Public Domain

in the letters patent include the 'Keper' and 'Surveyour', another instance of such dwellings' twofold function of providing an income and accommodating retainers.

According to John Stow, Thomas Seymour rebuilt the greater part of what had been renamed Seymour Place, a view passed down in chronicles in the seventeenth and eighteenth centuries.[7] It is difficult to establish this, however, since the first view of the site, Wyngaerde's, is generally dated around 1544 and would therefore predate any work Seymour may have done (fig. 32). The next available views, the 'Agas' and that by Braun and Hogenberg (figs 33 and 34), were produced some ten to twenty years later, when the property had passed to another more likely builder, not least given his much longer tenure. In the mid-1540s, the complex was primarily characterised by a distinctive range with polygonal bays and tower, flanked by a series of lower buildings among which we can perhaps recognise the lantern of the old Hall, depicted by Hollar in 1646. That view is part of two engravings showing the outer or main courtyard from both south and north ends, which, though about a century later, largely illustrate its medieval state (figs 35 and 36). It is known that Thomas Seymour acquired part of the garden of Strand Inn to the west of Bath Place (the rest of which was purchased by his brother Edward in 1547), and created a new lane from the Strand to the river, probably Strand Bridge Lane, which formed the boundary between Arundel House and Somerset House (fig. 37 and see figs 33 and 34).[8] Thomas may also have added to the existing building on this side of the complex, but his attainder and execution in 1549 make it unlikely that he did anything more conspicuous. The question here is who was behind the extension stretching down to the Thames from the western end of the main range, which became a celebrated part of the house during the Collector Earl's tenure (see fig. 10). Both the Agas and Braun and Hogenberg maps show the extension so crudely than one wonders whether it was complete, or even in existence, by the end of the 1540s. By contrast, in 1593 Norden depicted it clearly as a long tall wing (see fig. 37), though by then two successive owners had held it.

Henry Fitzalan and Philip Howard, 12th and 13th Earls of Arundel: 1549–1590

The more likely builder of the new wing, who succeeded Thomas Seymour, is Henry Fitzalan, 12th Earl of Arundel (1512–1580), who purchased the complex, thus renamed Arundel House, in 1549 for a nominal sum of £41 6s 6d.[9] Fitzalan is likely not simply because of his long tenure of some thirty years, but also because of an intriguing entry in the Customs Accounts in the National Archives for '1 galarye of stone for my Lord of Arundell c[on]t[a]yn[ing] other stone for … makynge of hys galarye & gate', apparently in the summer of 1565.[10] This 'galarye' was coming from Antwerp on the order of Thomas Gresham, who in the same years also provided building material for his patron William Cecil's Theobalds in Hertfordshire, Burghley House at Stamford in

35 Wenceslaus Hollar, forecourt of Arundel House looking south towards the Thames with the Hall to the right, 1646. Thomas Fisher Rare Book Library, University of Toronto. Wikimedia Commons Public Domain

36 Wenceslaus Hollar, forecourt of Arundel House looking north towards the Strand, 1646. Thomas Fisher Rare Book Library, University of Toronto. Wikimedia Commons Public Domain

The large window over the barn on the east side (right) may belong to a room which Hollar is said to have used as a studio.

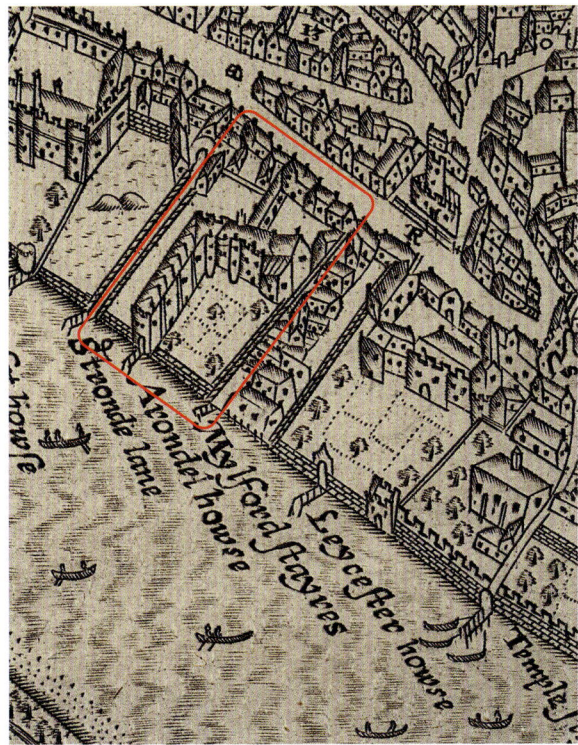

37 Arundel House, detail of John Norden, *Speculum Britanniae*, 1593. Folger Shakespeare Library, Washington DC. Licensed under Creative Commons Attribution-ShareAlike 4.0 International

Lincolnshire and possibly Burghley's own Strand palace too (see Chapter Five).[11] Could this have been for Arundel House, namely the seemingly Doric stone gallery or loggia, attached to the west front of the Collector Earl's galleries, seen in Cornelis Bol's view of c.1640 (fig. 38)? And, even more intriguingly, could the '1 galerye of stone' effectively be a disassembled gallery from somewhere in the Low Countries, extended and adapted in London?[12]

One of six peers appointed to attend the young Edward VI, then a member of Mary's Privy Council and even a rumoured husband for Elizabeth I, Fitzalan was abroad in 1566–67, ostensibly to treat his gout in Padua but also passing through the Spanish Netherlands and the Rhineland.[13] The stone gallery might, of course, have been for Arundel Castle, or indeed the palace of Nonsuch, which Mary had granted the earl in 1556, seemingly at his own request to save it from demolition, in exchange for four manors in Norfolk and a payment of £486.[14] He then set to, dealing with Nonsuch's 'buildings, reparations, paviments, and gardens, in as ample and perfit sorte as by the first intente and meaning of the said Kinge [Henry VIII] his olde maister, the same should have bene performed, and so it is nowe evident to be beholden of all strangers, and others, for the honour of this Realme, as a pearle thereof'.[15] Against this background, whichever building the imported stone was for, Fitzalan's engagement with Arundel House seems quite logical.

38 The gallery at Arundel House, detail of Cornelis Bol's view of the Thames with Arundel House, c.1640. Private collection. Photograph © A. C. Cooper Ltd, London

Upon his death in 1580 Henry Fitzalan was succeeded by his grandson and heir Philip Howard, 13th Earl of Arundel (1557–1595), the son of his daughter Mary, who had married the 4th Duke of Norfolk. The succession to the title, as Kingsford put it, had none the less taken place 'under a cloud'. The family's devout Romanism, reinforced by the union of two of the most powerful Catholic names in the realm, eventually told against the new earl, who was arrested in 1585 and sent to the Tower for the remainder of his life. There he carved the famous inscription 'quanto plus afflictionis pro Christo in hoc saeculo, tanto plus gloriae cum Christo in futuro' ('the more affliction we endure for Christ in this world, the more glory we shall obtain with Christ in the next'). This proved prophetic, as he was beatified by Pius XI in 1929 and canonised by Paul VI in 1970 as a witness of Christ and an example of the Roman Catholic faith.[16] At the time of his arrest, Philip's wife and children, who had been allowed to live at Arundel House from time to time and only by special permission, had to vacate the site whenever Elizabeth I was at Somerset House.[17] After the Earl's attainder in 1589, his estates were declared forfeit and an inquiry into the Strand palace followed. The resulting survey, dated 1590, provides detailed information as to the various parts of the complex, described as 'Unum messuagium sive domus mancionalis vocatus Arrundell house, cum uno atrio in primo introit, duobus gardinis, uno pomario, diversis ambulatoribus, uno le bowling alley, necnon diversis pulchris edificiis cum horreo, stabulis. Cum omnibus et singulis pertinenciis' ('a messuage or mansion house called Arundel House, with a courtyard, two gardens, an orchard, different passages, one [named] the Bowling Alley, as well as a variety of beautiful buildings, with a barn, stables and all related appurtenances').[18] Clearly seen in Norden's 1593 view (see fig. 37), the 'atrio in primo' was the Great Court right behind the tenements along the Strand, composed, as the survey indicates, of the 'Storehouse upon the right hand coming in towards the Hall', followed by an old and new 'Barne with the Stables adjoyning', the 'old Backhouses and Colehouse raynging from the end of th' old stable to the porch of the hall' and 'One long Storehouse on the West syde of the said Court'. These buildings can be seen in Hollar's 1646 depictions of the north and south ends of the court and, partially, in his view of the 'West Central District' (see figs 35, 36 and 30). Each building has also been identified through Ogilby and Morgan's plan of 1677 (fig. 39).[19]

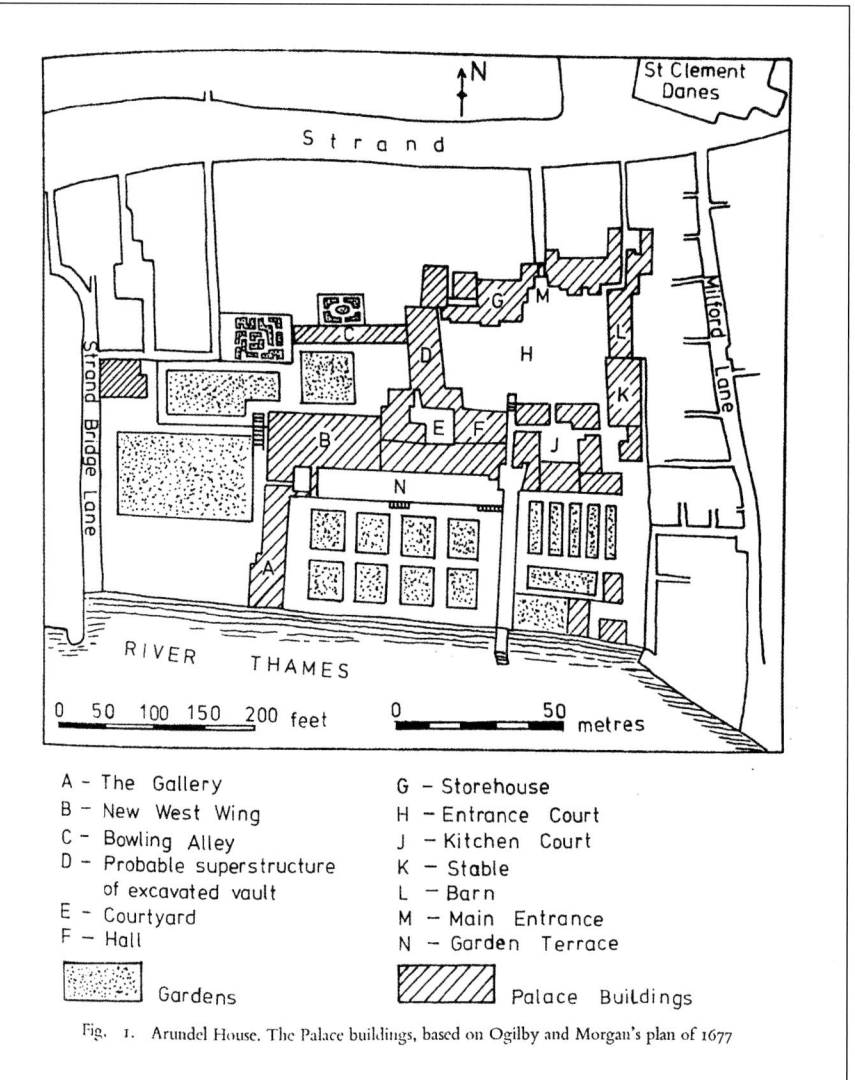

Fig. 1. Arundel House. The Palace buildings, based on Ogilby and Morgan's plan of 1677

39 Reconstruction of the complex of Arundel House based on Ogilby and Morgan's plan of 1677. Hammerson 1975, fig. 1

Next in the 1590 survey's list is the 'Kechyn Court and other places'. The first, as one would expect, lay next to the Hall towards the east, and comprised 'One house of divers offices', 'Two Kechyns, 'Three roomes […] belonging to the hott-house nere the privy kechin', A pastery and divers lodgings', and 'One pale from the said Lodginges to the Themmes […] Clxv foote in length, which pale devideth the kechine garden, and the passage to the Slaughter house and pryvye'. The 'Comon Bridg to the Slaughter house', that is, the river gate used for deliveries known as Milford Stairs, is also recorded. Chief among the 'other places' were 'The great brick house and galleryes', clearly the mansion house in existence by Thomas Seymour's time and its extension towards the river which acted as long galleries, completed if not conceived by Henry Fitzalan. As such, the extension would have been the most recent part of the complex, but it too was in need of repairs involving 'plummers, playsterers, tyler and carpenter' for a total of £30, equal to a year's rent from the tenements in the Strand. The point of the survey was in fact to enlist all 'needfull Reparacions', which amounted to some £370, but, as virtually none of the fabrics was exempt from repairs, one gets a fairly comprehensive picture.

Between 1589 and the beginning of the new century, Arundel House was inhabited and owned by diverse figures. The Lord Chamberlain Henry Carey, Lord Hudson, was granted its lease in 1590 but Anne Dacre, the struggling 13th Earl's countess and mother of the future Earl Collector, was allowed the use of 'three ground rooms, three rooms over them, three lobbies and the roof on the west side of the great court'.[20] The arbiter behind these arrangements was Robert Cecil, by then Secretary of State, whose name is also connected to garden expenses there in 1600.[21] As such, Countess Anne wrote to him, as did Charles Howard, 1st Earl of Nottingham and Lord High Admiral. The latter had a double connection with the house as Hudson's son-in-law and cousin of the attained Earl of Arundel, who had died in the Tower in 1595. Nottingham had indeed set his sights on the Strand palace, which was granted to him by James I in August 1603, shortly after ascending to the English throne.[22] This probably reflected the high esteem in which he was held by both the new king and his predecessor.[23] But his tenure was short-lived: by 1607 Arundel House had been restored to Thomas Howard, 14th Earl of Arundel, with his title and part of the estates.[24] Yet he had to make a payment of £4000 to Nottingham, whom Arundel deemed 'dammed' for it – but one instance of a series of rapacious manoeuvres to profit from the earl's inheritance by other Howards.[25] This included his powerful great-uncle, Henry Howard, 1st Earl of Northampton, at the time busy building Northampton House, and his step-uncle and namesake Thomas Howard, 1st Earl of Suffolk and future Lord Treasurer, as well as Northampton's principal heir and favourite (see Chapter Eleven).[26] That said, competition over Arundel House could hardly have been surprising, since it was considered so desirable that the French ambassador, Maximilien de Béthune, Duke of Sully, who lodged there in 1603, described it as 'one of the most beautiful and convenient lodgings with the most numerous rooms on one floor and all of one suite that I have ever seen'.[27]

The House of Thomas Howard, 14th Earl of Arundel: 1607–1646

Born penniless in a cottage at Romford in Essex in 1585, and brought up in straitened circumstances by his mother, Thomas was determined, from an early age, to reinstate the family to its ancient lustre as the holder of the premier earldom in England. In 1605, aged twenty, he was restored in blood as Earl of Arundel and Surrey and granted Arundel Castle with the remaining Norfolk estates. The following year he was introduced to court and married Aletheia Talbot (d. 1654), Bess of Hardwick's granddaughter and the heiress of Gilbert, 7th Earl of Shrewsbury.[28] With an estimated income of 60,000 crowns a year, and both spirit and intellect matching that of her husband's, Aletheia was the ideal match for the ambitious earl.[29]

One of the earliest references to Arundel House comes in a letter Thomas wrote thence to his father-in-law on 17 November 1607:

Old Southampton, I am sure you hear, is dead, and hath left the best part of her stuff to her son, and the greatest part to her husband, the most of which I think will be sold, and dispersed into the hands of many men, of which number I would be one if the Admiral [Nottingham] were not damned for making me pay £4000 for this house, as well as Sir Thomas Heneage is for that stuff … [30]

'Old Southampton' was Mary Wriothesley, Countess of Southampton from her first marriage to Henry, 2nd Earl; she had remarried twice, to Sir Thomas Heneage and Sir William Hervey. Heneage had procured the 'stuff' mentioned in the letter, from which it can be deduced that Arundel, as soon as he had regained official possession of the Strand palace, was looking at sales to furnish what may have been somewhat bare interiors. This is also an early hint of the start of his career as collector, which eventually earned him the title of England's 'Father of Vertue'.[31] Crucial to Arundel's emergence as such was an extended visit to Italy in 1613–14 in the company of Inigo Jones, for whom the experience was a determining factor too, both for his leading role as royal surveyor and in the development of Arundel House.[32]

Early signs of Thomas and Aletheia's passion for, indeed partnership in, building can be seen in their transformation of a house in Highgate, north London, acquired in 1610 from Sir William Cornwallis and subsequently turned into an Italianate villa with a casino or banqueting house in the garden.[33] In 1615, soon after their return from Italy, Jones's name is associated with a 'walke and business' there, overseen by Aletheia but with her husband's heart 'very much upon it'.[34] The other property in the couple's minds was Greenwich Lodge, which Thomas had inherited from Henry Howard in 1614: the relationship with his great-uncle and fellow scholar had improved over the years and by the end of Henry's life they were on affectionate terms. It was in fact Arundel who commissioned Northampton's tomb from Nicholas Stone and Isaac James, which included sculpted representations of the cardinal virtues that may have been influenced by the Roman statues Arundel had brought back from Italy.[35] While Greenwich, Highgate and, as will seen, Arundel House were being transformed at the same time, the construction of a further lodge at Gowbarrow Park in the Lake District, a place which reminded the countess of Italy, was also being contemplated: 'there is not such another to be seen', she emphatically wrote to the Earl, 'And for a Lodge I hope you will let me be the architect when we are upon the place.'[36] While nothing seems to have developed out of this project, Aletheia received detailed instructions about the fitting of Greenwich's interiors, which are again associated with the presence of Inigo Jones: 'I forgotte to leave order wth Dixe, aboute the wainscottinge, the bottome of the romes at Greenwich', wrote Thomas from Theobalds on 24 April 1615. This was to be 'halfe a yarde deepe, & fitting the gilte leather unto them, I thinke it were fitte, that the gilt leather for all the romes were made up of one depth because they may serve together any where etc, & they in lesse romes may be hanged soe much the higher'. He concluded by hoping that 'Mr Jones' would 'sette the wainscott particion in hand for the lowe Gallery, and let the organne be removed into the lower dininge Chamber'.[37]

Contrary to Highgate – sold and replaced in the 1630s by Albury in Surrey, where the earl could entertain his intellectual circle – and Tart Hall in St James's Park for the countess and her Catholic friends, Greenwich Lodge burned down in January 1617: God's punishment, wags claimed, given Arundel's conversion to Anglicanism at Christmas 1616.[38] Whether or not divine, this was indeed a punishment, as Thomas and Aletheia had filled it with treasures brought back from Italy. The loss, however, meant that the couple then had only one London residence to concentrate on, and so it was that Arundel House became the focus of their efforts, for which they again turned to Inigo Jones.

As evidenced by a few, precious lines in their correspondence, works seem to have started by 1616 and continued until at least 1619. The first reference comes in an undated letter probably written around 1615/16, in which Thomas exhorts his wife to speed up progress, much in the same gentle but firm way as he instructed her on the other houses: 'I desire the works shoulde goe on at Arundell House apace, for the terme drawce apace'.[39] The second reference is found in 1618, when the earl's 'deerest Hart' (as each exchange began) was asked to

take order that the mattes, & all the stuffe be taken out of the rooms towardes the water at Arundell House for on Monday I have given order they goe in hande, to deale wth the roomes, & I pray bidde Wilson make very greate haste for nowe is the only spare time & I desire exceedingely to see things done ...[40]

One wonders whether 'Wilson' was Thomas Wilson (d. 1629), one of Burghley's former retainers and Keeper of the State Papers, who lived in Durham Rents and had been in charge of extensions at Salisbury House in 1609 (see Chapter Eight). In 1619, while Arundel was at Royston with a recovering king, we then hear of the 'many things I should have donne in London', clearly hampered by James's health: 'but this desire to see the kinge well puttes all out of my heade'.[41] In October that year, however, he wrote again to his wife from Theobalds to 'further our workes at Arundell House, as much as you may', while also providing instructions about the 'picture of Charles the fifte' (probably, the Holy Roman Emperor, Charles V): 'let it be hanged up in the gallery-ende chamber, before I come on Monday'.[42] These references evidently relate to modifications and/or improvements made to the southward extension of Arundel House, completed, as previously noted, by Henry Fitzalan, Thomas's grandfather, in the second half of the sixteenth century. This, as noted, included galleries. One can only speculate on their original

40 Inigo Jones, elevation for the 'Italyan' gate along the garden wall to the west, 1618. RIBA Collections (12957)

41 John Smythson, Arundel House, 1618, plan of the garden (top); elevation of the balcony overlooking the river (middle left); window of the gallery (left); western garden gate (right). RIBA Collections (29201)

arrangement, and the result of Arundel's adaptations is equally shrouded in mystery because the chief evidence of these interiors, Daniel Mytens's famous double portraits of the earl and countess, tentatively dated 1616, have been proved to be a *capriccio* (figs 42 and 43).[43]

Jones's presence, while 'intimately connected with all that went on at Arundel House', also seems to have produced fewer results than one would expect, considering that architect and patron were then closer than they would ever be.[44] This, however, is because what happened to the Strand palace, contrary to the expectations surrounding the myth of the Earl Collector, was probably little more than a make-over, and one which concentrated mainly on the galleries and garden.[45] What is known for certain is that Jones was asked to make changes to the windows of the Gallery wing – to which the letter of 1618 referring to emptying the river end of the rooms may relate – and to two gates in the garden, and that much later, in the 1630s, he created a 'room for designes', supervised by Arundel's eldest son, Lord Maltravers.[46] Of those changes, only one design by Jones for the 'newe Italyan gate' of 1618 exists (fig. 40), while the rest is known through John Smythson, who recorded them during his visit to London in 1618–19. His drawings include one showing 'the plateforme of the garden at Arendell house'; 'The Italyan grate over the watter', that is, a balcony overlooking the Thames; 'A newe Italyan wyndowe [of] the gallerye at arrundell: house'; and the 'newe Italyan: gate at Arundell house in the garden there', located, as shown in the plan of the garden, in the centre of the western (right-hand) wall (fig. 41). Considering that this side of the garden was bordered by the eastern side of the galleries, as can be seen in Hollar's pre-1666 view (see fig. 30), the new gate must have opened directly onto it. Indeed, a pedimented gateway is clearly seen in the centre of the gallery wing in Hollar's *c.*1630 riverfront view of Arundel House (fig. 44 and see fig. 10), while Esselens's 1660s depiction of the

42 Daniel Mytens, *Thomas Howard, Earl of Arundel*, ?1616, in the sculpture gallery at Arundel House. © National Portrait Gallery, London (5292)

43 Daniel Mytens, *Aletheia Talbot, Countess of Arundel*, ?1616, in the portrait gallery at Arundel House. © National Portrait Gallery, London (5293)

south-east corner of the gallery shows an equally pedimented structure but with double doorways (see fig. 49). Back to Smythson's drawings, the series continues with 'An Italyan gate in my Lo: of Arundelles garden: at London: at Arundell house' (fig. 45), which shows the opposite gate in the eastern (left-hand) wall, it too designed by Jones and depicted in a painting of Thomas Howard of about 1627 (see figs 51 and 52). And a 'chymney peece at Arundalle House' together with 'The upright draughte' and 'grounde plate' of 'the Italyan wyndowe' there (figs 46 and 47). At Smythson's request, Thomas Ashby also recorded another chimneypiece at Arundel House, similar to the previous one, but the exact location and indeed authorship of both of which remain uncertain (fig. 48). Nevertheless, their association with what would have been the novelties introduced by Jones in the galleries may suggest, as for the balcony over the river, who was actually behind them.[47] A 'carver and tombemaker', Ashby may have carved the chimneypiece, and indeed he provided an estimate for making a replica of it.[48]

Alongside the scale of Arundel's architectural changes in London, a parallel 'deconstructive' argument has also been made in relation to his

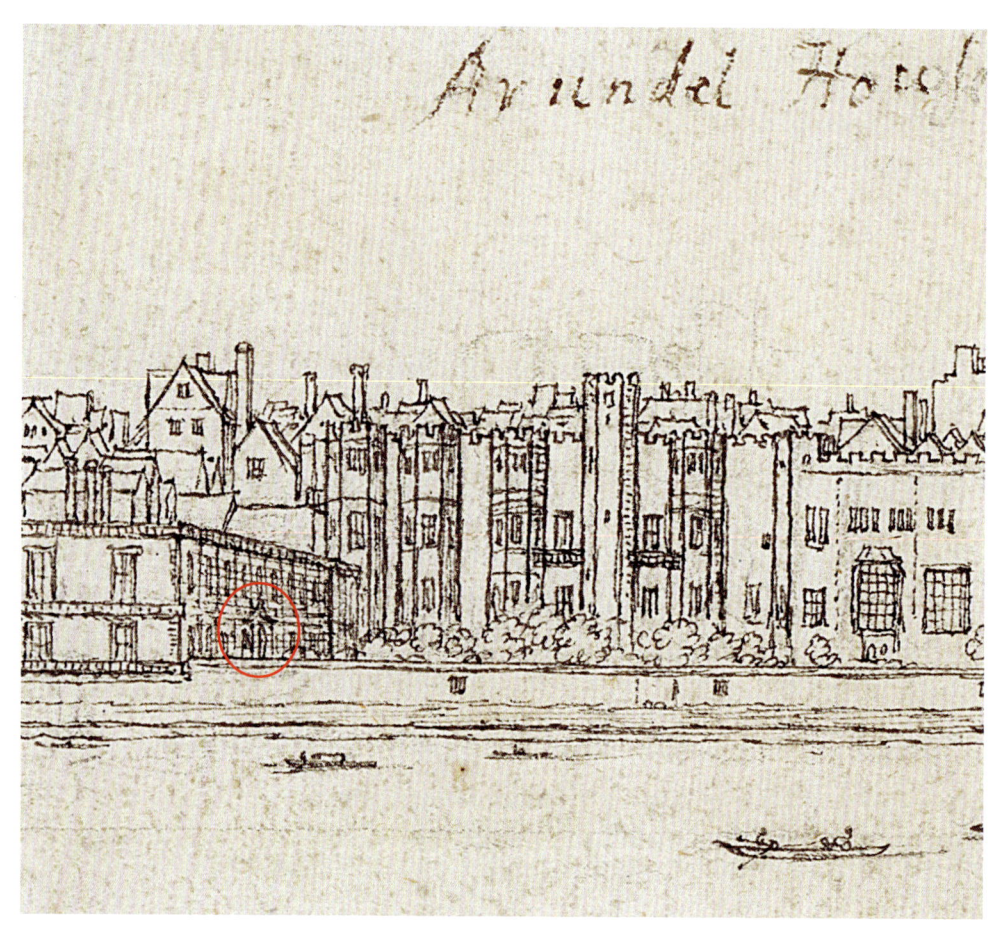

44 | LONDON'S 'GOLDEN MILE'

44 *opposite* Wenceslaus Hollar's riverfront view of Arundel House, *c*.1630, with highlight showing central pedimented entrance (detail of fig. 10). Royal Collection Trust. © Her Majesty Queen Elizabeth II 2021

45 *opposite, left* John Smythson, elevation of the 'Italyan' gate along the garden wall to the east, 1618. RIBA Collections (29204)

46 *opposite, middle* John Smythson, elevation of a chimneypiece at Arundel House, 1618/19. RIBA Collections (29203)

47 *opposite, right* John Smythson, elevation window, with its plan, at Arundel House, 1618/19. RIBA Collections (29202)

48 *right* Thomas Ashby, elevation of a fireplace at Arundel House, with estimate for a replica, 1618. RIBA Collections

collection of statues, it too shrouded in myth.⁴⁹ It is therefore necessary to reassess the evidence, unfortunately limited to little more than these references in the correspondence, as no relevant accounts or inventories have survived for this period. The first room-by-room inventory, discovered around 2015 by John Martin Robinson at the end of another inventory of the 6th Duke of Norfolk's Weybridge House, is in fact not only dated 1684, hence during the redevelopment of the site, but is also, perhaps consequently, largely incomplete, as will be seen at the end of this chapter (while the inventory of 1655 exclusively lists works of art). As well as Mytens's portraits, however, a number of relevant views can be studied.

Arundel's apparent restraint from the mainstream display of lavish buildings, the main sport of the day (described by Evelyn as the discrepancy between reputation and action), may have been the lesson learnt from his disgraced father and was also perhaps in tune with a sense of aristocratic gravitas free of the unnecessary: he was, after all, the country's premier earl. The impact of whatever he did or was reputed to have done, and indeed of his vast collection, was greatly felt. And it is by analysing Mytens's 'vision' that one begins to understand the reasons, for there lies the atmosphere intended by both patron and architect. This analysis must also take into account the following: Hollar's *c*.1630 depiction of the south-western elevations in a general view of the complex from across the river (see fig. 10); Cornelis Bol's painting of the south-eastern sides of the gallery wing, dated to the 1640s (see fig. 38); and Jacob Esselens's view of 1659–69 showing its south-western corner (fig. 49). Hollar too, as previously remarked, was among Arundel's famous protégés, reputed to have drawn his chief view of London's 'West Central District' from the very top of Arundel House.⁵⁰ By comparing these complementary and in the main mutually confirming views with Mytens's portraits (see figs 42 and 43), one begins to see where the invention lies.⁵¹ First of all the Earl's Sculpture Gallery, if indeed located, as suggested by the artist, towards the river end of the wing, should have had two windows facing the Thames, as opposed to a single arched doorway (onto a balcony).⁵² Equally, this part of the building clearly had windows on both sides, rather than merely on the east. Bol's painting also shows that the last three bays of the river end of the gallery wing were taller and larger, features partly confirmed by Esselens but totally missing in the Mytens. Windows and shape notwithstanding, a barrel-vaulted room generally implies double height, hence the use of both floors.⁵³ This, in turn, would have meant the levelling of the site, which sloped steeply down to the Thames, an aspect which appears to be confirmed by both Hollar and Bol, for the former shows high containing walls to the east of the building while the latter depicts a Doric loggia along the whole ground floor. But if the Sculpture Gallery occupied the whole height of the river end of that wing, how did it relate to the Painting Gallery located at its opposite end, with a seemingly lower ceiling and clearly even with a courtyard garden towards the Strand, hence at first-floor level from the river? Was the room between the two galleries, where Mytens positioned the Earl and Countess, on split levels? This is indeed how it appears in a reconstruction in D. Sturdy and A. Brueggeman's article on British gardens and the origins of the museum between 1590 and 1740, which suggests how the gallery wing might have appeared after Inigo Jones's

ARUNDEL HOUSE | 45

alterations (fig. 50).⁵⁴ Tantalising though this is, however, the drawing is almost literally based on Mytens.⁵⁵

In spite of a fair degree of artistic licence, Mytens gives a flavour of the sort of classical interiors Arundel and Jones sought.⁵⁶ Exemplified by the separation between paintings and sculptures, these would have been in tune with the Earl's emulation of great Italian models such as the celebrated Sala Grande in the Palazzo Farnese in Rome or Julius II's Cortile del Belvedere at the Vatican. This powerful link was further emphasised by the decision to continue the display of statues, inscriptions and architectural carvings in the garden, which created a museum *al fresco*, emulated by other Strand patrons such as Buckingham at York House, Northumberland at his palace or indeed Charles I at St James's Palace and Henrietta Maria at Somerset House (see Chapters Ten, Eleven and Three).⁵⁷ As will be seen, antique statues may have decorated the garden of Burghley House well before all others, while Burghley certainly preceded Arundel as the 'Nestor of Britain' (see Chapter Five). Be that as it may, a glimpse into what is reputed to be England's first garden of antiquities is provided by a portrait of the Earl of Arundel of *c*.1627, which shows a section of the garden terrace with Jones's eastern gate in the background (figs 51 and 52).

Despite numerous studies on the Arundel collection, information concerning its size remains ambiguous, not least because of its chequered subsequent history. According to

49 Abraham Rademaker (fl. 1691–1735) after Jacob Esselens, south-east corner of the gallery at Arundel House. RKD Netherlands Institute for Art History

50 Conjectural reconstruction of the Gallery at Arundel House 'after Jones' alterations', from Sturdy and Brueggeman 1997, fig. 9

51 [Paul Van Somer], portrait of Thomas Howard (detail), c.1627. Portland Collection. Harley Gallery, Welbeck Estate / Bridgeman Images

Detail of fig. 52 showing the garden of Arundel House with Inigo Jones's eastern gate in the background.

one source, it comprised 37 statues, 128 busts and 250 inscriptions, as well as a large number of sarcophagi, altars and fragments.[58] In terms of paintings, the 1655 inventory of pictures and other objects drawn up after Lady Arundel's death the previous year in Amsterdam (where the larger part of the collection had been moved in 1641), listed 598 entries including 43 attributed to Holbein, 37 to Titian, 26 to Parmigianino, 17 to Giorgione, 16 to Dürer, 13 to Raphael and Brueghel and decreasing numbers to Van Dyck, Rubens, Giulio Romano, Mantegna, Bassano, Bronzino as well as almost any other great master one can think of.[59] Notwithstanding the gap between the original number and the amount brought to Holland – part of the collection had stayed behind while another portion would have followed the Earl in Italy – and accounting for false attributions and occasional repetitions, this figure alone and the variety of the works far outnumbered even the largest estimate of the other great collector and rival in the Strand, the Duke of Buckingham, who may have owned more than 400 paintings. We do not, of course, know whether all the Howard collection was displayed at Arundel House but it is most likely, especially after the loss of Greenwich, that the majority would have been kept in London, which undoubtedly was the main focus of the couple. Whatever the competition between Arundel and Buckingham, one single work in the latter's possession – so sought after by the Earl that he offered an unheard-of £7000 for it, and so exceptional that it sent Inigo Jones down on his knees when he saw it at York House in December 1624 – had not made it to Arundel House. This was Titian's *Ecce Homo*, which Gerbier had secured for his patron for £275 (see fig. 197).[60]

While paintings must have been hung almost everywhere at Arundel House, the Hall may also have been decorated with panelling including the controversial portrait now at Arundel Castle associated with Inigo Jones and traditionally believed to represent Henry Howard, Earl of Surrey, an identification recently confirmed by Charlotte Bolland at the National Portrait Gallery (fig. 53).[61] Then there were drawings, including some two hundred books of them by Michelangelo, Leonardo, Raphael and other famous masters, for which a purposely built room, certainly the first of its kind among the Strand palaces, was created by Jones.[62] And of course the famous library, furnished with globes and

ARUNDEL HOUSE | 47

52 [Paul Van Somer], portrait of Thomas Howard, *c.*1627. Portland Collection. Harley Gallery, Welbeck Estate / Bridgeman Images

53 After William Scrots and Inigo Jones, *Henry Howard, Earl of Surrey*, c.1607. © National Portrait Gallery, London (5291). On permanent loan to Arundel Castle

marble busts of Greek and Roman philosophers, contained an impressive accumulation of books and manuscripts, some acquired from family members such as his great-uncle Northampton (for whose entire library he paid £529 and transferred to Arundel House in 1615) and from Willibald Pirckheimer's descendant (whose library he bought in 1636), others presented to him, like the Vitruvius which Robert Cecil gave 'to my Lo[rd] of Arondell' (see Chapters Eight and Eleven).[63] There were also prints, especially historic sets of Dürer's woodcuts and Italian topographical and architectural engravings. Chief among the several engravers called in by the earl to etch the works of art in the collection was Hollar, brought back from Cologne in 1636 and who had eventually married a lady-in-waiting to the Countess of Arundel.[64]

While prints and drawings were exhibited to the public in what the earl's librarian Francis Junius described as the 'Academie at Arundell house', the palace was clearly on the must-see list of a wide range of people. The German painter Joachim von Sandrart, for instance, after several visits in 1627 recorded in his *Life* the splendour of the house, reserving his highest praise for the antique sculptures in the garden; he was also impressed by the Holbeins, which 'held the master's place' in the Gallery.[65] A couple of years later, Abram Booth, a high-ranking delegate from the Dutch East India Company, described it as 'worth seeing before all others', a distinction likely to have been shared by Charles I and Henrietta Maria, who were received at least twice in the galleries.[66] The king had processed through all the rooms to see the collection.[67]

The painting and sculpture galleries and the gardens were clearly the highlights of Arundel House, for the rest had probably remained largely unchanged since the works initiated by Thomas Seymour in the 1550s and completed by Henry Fitzalan in the following decades. These had resulted in an eclectic mixture of different buildings, where the medieval Hall and adjoining mid-sixteenth-century turreted west wing happily coexisted with the elaborate Italianate gallery wing running down to the Thames. Into this we get clear insight in Hollar's 'West Central District' view (see fig. 30), perhaps depicted around the time of Arundel's death, in Padua in 1646.[68] By then, the earl and his wife had parted company, one in voluntary exile in Italy, the other in Holland, while title and estates had passed to their eldest surviving son, Henry Frederick Howard (1608–1652), who embarked on a long litigation with Countess Aletheia over the inheritance.[69]

Subsequent Years: 1646–1689

During and after the Civil War, like most of its aristocratic neighbours, Arundel House became a commodity of Parliament. Despite its strong connection to both Catholicism and the Royalist cause, this proto-museum was so highly esteemed that even Edmund Ludlow (the parliamentarian best known as one of the judges who signed the warrant for the execution of Charles I), recommended that 'his Lordship shall have consideration for the use of it, and that care should be taken to preserve the house in as good order as may be' while it was transformed into a garrison in October 1650.[70] Repeatedly seized by the government, on 15 September 1656 the Discovery Commissioners reported that 151 pictures and 103 statues 'of great value' were to be found at Arundel House and that following an inspection, and 'detailed inventory thereof', they had been moved into one room and locked up.[71] If these paintings are added to the total recorded in the 1655 inventory, they reach a staggering 749, a figure which would have been unrivalled, even though they may not all have been kept in the Strand. It is especially remarkable because this was just a portion of a much wider collection, including antique statues and all sorts of memorabilia, alongside books and prints.

The 15th Earl of Arundel survived his father only six years. Title and estates passed to his eldest son, another Thomas (1627–1677) but with a different reputation: it arose from his alleged 'irredeemable lunacy' caused by a fever caught in Padua, where he had followed his grandfather, which had damaged his brain.[72] Thomas never returned to England and his brother Henry (1628–1684) became the de facto head of the family. In 1652 Henry married Lady Anne Somerset (1631–1662), the daughter of Edward Somerset, 2nd Marquess of Worcester, of Worcester House in the Strand (see Chapter Seven). Then in 1660, within months of Charles II's restoration, Henry succeeded in restoring the Howards to the dukedom of Norfolk, a long-awaited move ironically bestowed on his absentee brother, who became the 5th Duke. On the latter's death in 1677, however, titles and estates officially became Henry's.[73]

Like his collector grandfather, the 6th Duke of Norfolk was a friend of John Evelyn, who thought he had 'great abilities and a smooth tongue, but little judgement'. The diarist was also critical of his building works, as the £10,000 spent at Weybridge was but on a 'miserable sandy site', while three times that amount was spent on the duke's palace in Norwich, which he called a 'dunghole place', too cramped and close to the river, so that the cellars flooded.[74] Evelyn had also assisted the duke in the improvement of Albury in Surrey, the villa created by the 14th Earl where Norfolk had quietly lived during the Commonwealth. There he had designed the 'Great Room', the canal and a grotto or 'crypta thro' the mountaine in the park', and supervised the laying of a vineyard.[75]

After the Great Fire in 1666, Norfolk granted the Royal Society the use of some rooms at Arundel House, and both Evelyn and Pepys recorded attending a meeting there. The latter had been at the house in 1661, when he commented on the flowers in the garden and the fine statues in the Gallery, 'a brave sight' – confirmation that the majority of the least movable objects had not been removed from their original location. This is presumably the reason why 103 statues 'of great value' were recorded there in 1656.[76] Pepys and Evelyn were also part of the discussion related to the potential construction of a building to house the Society permanently in the grounds of Arundel House. And again, through Evelyn's well-known salvage operation, the Arundel Library was donated in 1667 to that society, for 'this gentleman [the duke] had so little inclination to books that it was the preservation of them from embezzlement'. Remarking how the 'precious monuments were miserably neglected and scattered up and down about the gardens and other parts of the house, and how exceedingly the common air of London impaired them', Evelyn then persuaded the duke to bestow the sculptures on the University of Oxford, following a selection he himself had put together.[77] This resulted in the celebrated *Marmora Oxoniensia Ex Arundellianis*, edited by Humphrey Prideaux and presented by Evelyn to Norfolk at Arundel House on 28 April 1676.

By the early 1670s, Arundel House was 'in decay and very ruinous', after neglect and modifications during the Civil War. For the only known refurbishment programme, seemingly largely confined to the gallery wing, had taken place some fifty years earlier under the Earl Collector. Consequently, in 1671 the 6th duke secured an Act of Parliament for 'Building Arundell House and

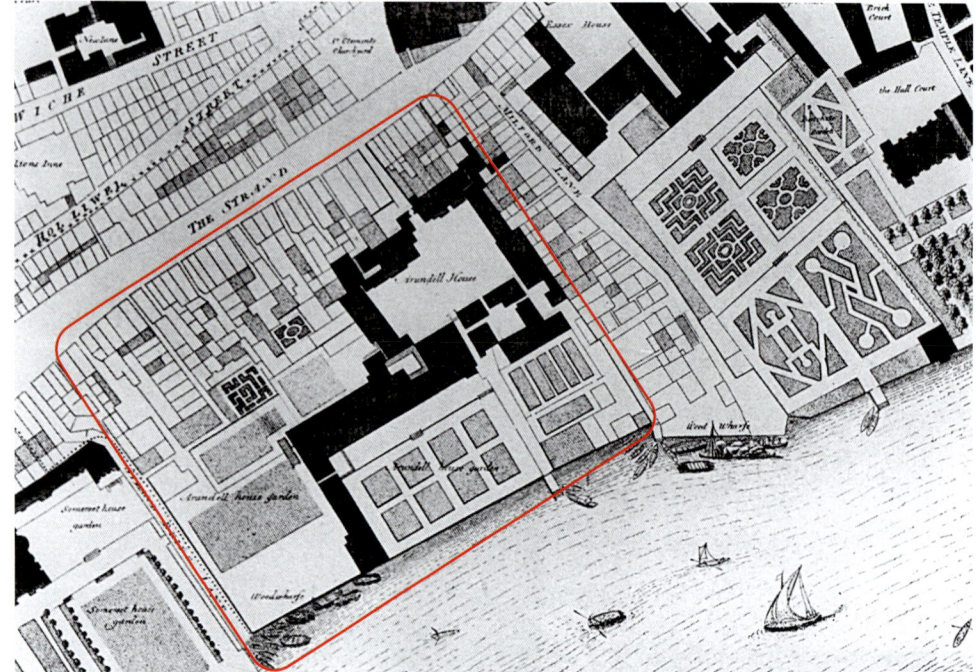

54 Plan of the complex of Arundel House, detail of John Ogilby and William Morgan, *Map of London*, 1677. Mitton 1908. Wikimedia Commons Public Domain

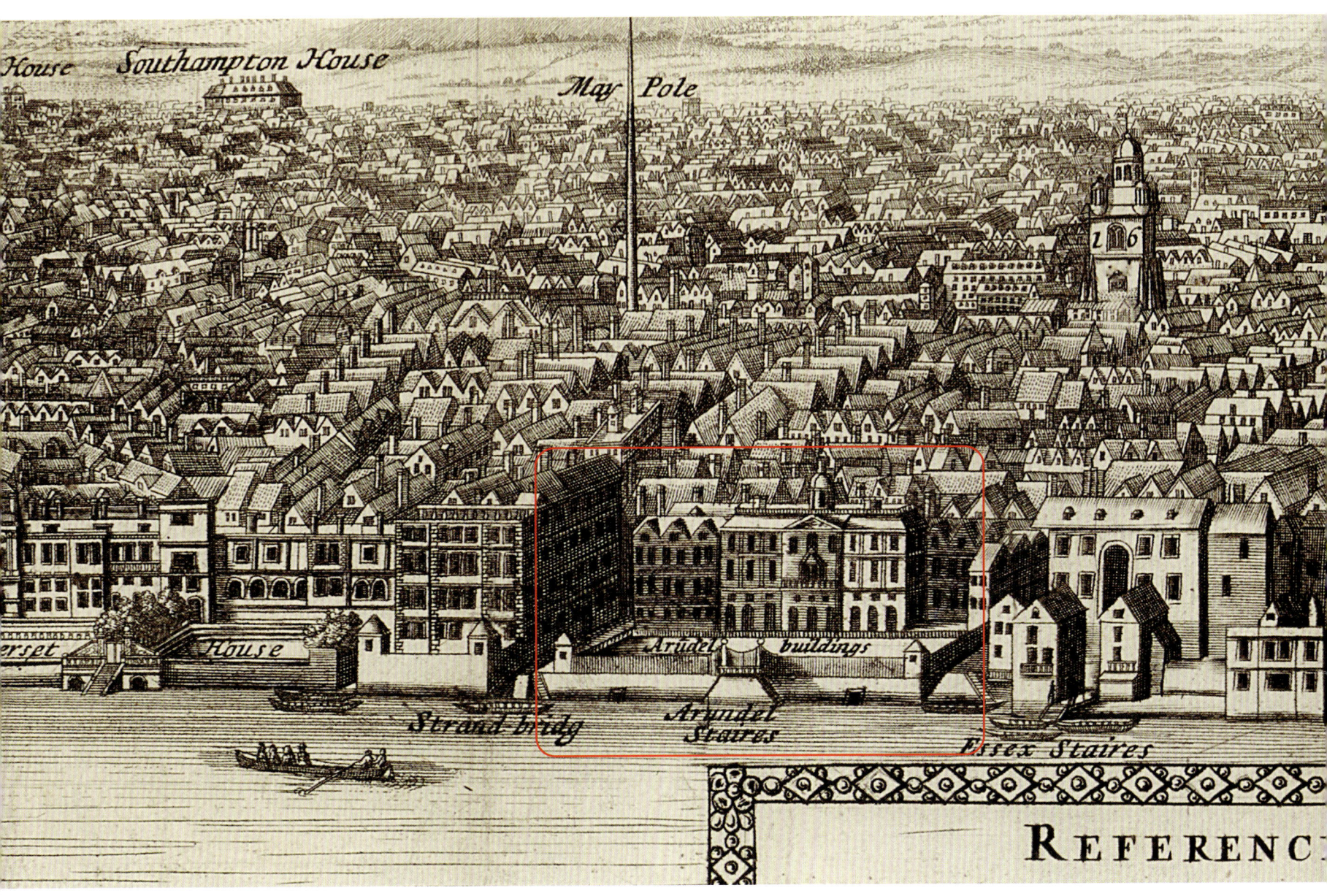

55 Arundel buildings, detail of William Morgan, *London and Westminster*, c.1682 (detail of images on pp. x and xi). By permission of the Pepys Library, Magdalene College, Cambridge ('London and Westminster', I, 2972, 38–39)

tenements thereunto belonging', which allowed him to redevelop the whole site and to erect a new house for himself facing the river.[78] Then, in 1676, he was granted a strip of reclaimed land forty feet deep from Strand Bridge Lane to Milford Stairs 'for beautifying the said buildings by bringing them to a more just symmetry and proportion all along the river, as for enlarging the garden of the House'.[79] A year later, Ogilby and Morgan published the general plan of the complex, still largely unchanged since Henry Fitzalan's time (fig. 54). William Morgan's view of London and Westminster of c.1682 (fig. 55), however, shows a new nine-bay house with somewhat Palladian features, two storeys high over an arcaded ground-floor loggia, surrounded by tenement buildings on three sides. The design for a new Arundel House, which Evelyn had seen as early as 1659, is variously associated with Robert Hooke, the famous scientist, gentleman architect and fellow member of the Royal Society, or with his friend and co-founder of the society, Sir Christopher Wren, in charge of the Royal Office of Works since 1669.[80] But the design was ultimately abandoned, as the £480 a year reserved from the new rents in order to rebuild the house had been 'swallowed up' in the construction of Surrey Street.[81]

As in all the other redevelopments of Strand palaces, the street's name derived from one of the titles traditionally linked to the historical owner of the site. In 1682, as Morden and Lea's map shows, there was still a vacuum marked 'The Ground for Arundel house' (fig. 56), which suggests that Morgan's nearly contemporary

ARUNDEL HOUSE | 51

view did not represent reality. Six years later, in 1689, the 7th Duke, another Henry, who had succeeded his father in 1684, was empowered by a new act to grant leases of that very area, and two further new streets bearing the other titles of the family, Arundel and Norfolk, were laid. The site as completely redeveloped is shown on a map in Strype's *Survey* of 1720 (fig. 57). But the demolition of the old Strand palace must have been gradual, for in 1684, when the 6th Duke died, an inventory of the 'House at London' was taken.[82] As previously remarked, this is partial as only a handful of rooms, predominantly subsidiary, are included, probably those still standing or furbished. The document is, however, illuminating in that it provides unpublished information, particularly on which statues were still there.

The appraisers (named Stephen Galloway and Robert Drake) began the inventory with the 'Rome two pair of Stairs towards the water Side', which included 'one Japan tree table, eight Cain bottom Chairs, four pictures and one Drawing box of Olive Wood'. It was followed by the 'Anti Chamber upon the same floor', with two chests of drawers, stands, one cabinet and 'severall peces of Dutch carthen ward' (woven coarse cloth), as well as 'two peces of tapestry hangings and 13 pictures'. Then came the 'Waldrob', filled with several items including 'Six Beds of Bruxels hangings' and, apparently, a 'bag with Gold'. The next entry was the 'Rome next the Street 2 pair of Stairs', an indication that the appraisers were still on the same level but had reached the opposite side from where they started. This contained, like the wardrobe, bedroom items, including 'four peces of tapestry hangings', while four more were recorded in the next two rooms, occupied by members of the household. These preceded the only two entries of any standing in the inventory, the 'biggest Parlour' and the Little Parlour', even if their content is unremarkable. Next came the Kitchen, followed by 'An Account of the Linen', and some eight chambers seemingly in the stables, as they are all listed under that heading. As seen, the stables lay to the east of the Hall in the Great Court and may have been part of Jones's rebuilding (see fig. 35). By the 1680s, given the presence of so many chambers, they had clearly been converted, perhaps to accommodate different uses during the Commonwealth. What follows, however, is of greater interest, as it comprises the earliest information on what statues were still at Arundel House. This long list,

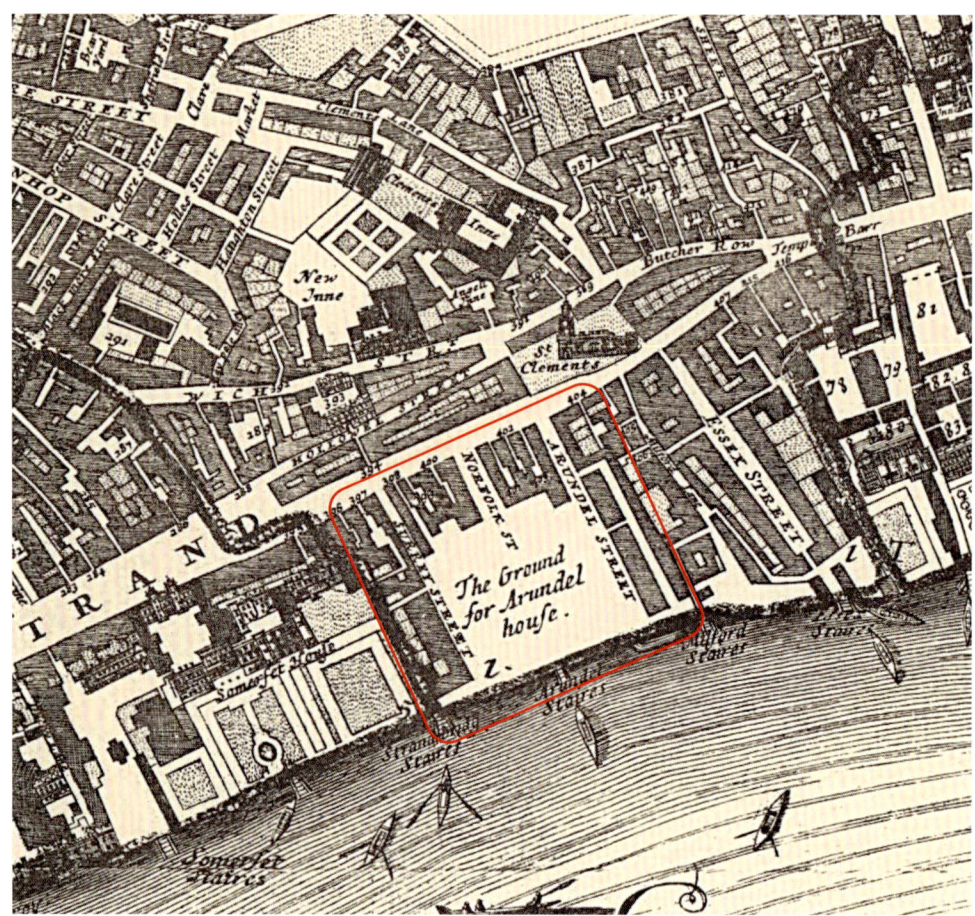

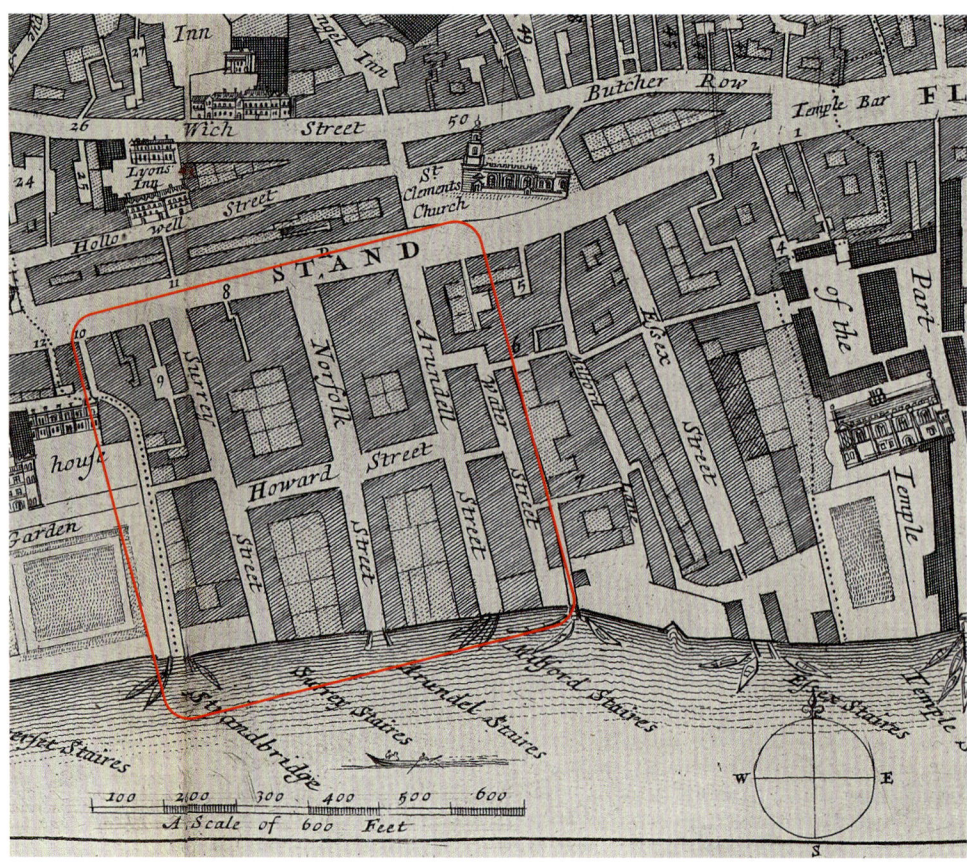

56 The partially redeveloped site of Arundel House as it appears in Robert Morden and Philip Lea's map of London, 1682. U.S. Library of Congress Map Collections, published by London Topographical Society, 1904. Wikimedia Commons

57 The redeveloped Arundel House site, from John Strype, *A Survey of the Cities of London and Westminster*, vol. 4, p. 116, 1720 (detail of fig. 83). Folger Shakespeare Library, Washington DC. Licensed under Creative Commons Attribution-ShareAlike 4.0 International

headed 'In the Yard or Garden severall Statues', is therefore worth quoting in full:

> *one Jupiter one Senator one other Senator, one Mars two Sibils, five small Statutes the Body of a Hermophred halfe life, one Diana, a Bachus in Small figures; one flora two Anticks woemen fugures as big as the Life, two of a lesser Statue two Sitting Woemen Antique one Ledia Herodias and a Roman Souldier small fugures an Atick term, a Pallas and a Mercury much broken; two Cerefs bigger than the life Antique, a Body in Drapery of a small Statute a Prophet Antique; one Senator not finished two Woemen figures Antick bigger than the life, a figure in Drapery without a head, the Body of a Gretian Venus in peces, a Moderass Statute in Woeman habit; a Cicero, Romg [sic], a large Antique figure, a great Pallas and a Donis four Bodys without heads or arms, seven truncks without heads arms or feet, two Sphinxes and a broken Lyon, nineteen Bustards or heads nine brocken heads and four bustards, fourteen broken small bodys fifteen broken Rel[ie]ves and the broken Ciphers with Rel[ie]ves and severall other broken pieces of Statues with two peces of Collumbs, five broken tables and a grave Stone of Marble, two marble Stands of foot for a table Inlayd with my Lords Armes and one large Iron Chest*

In addition, 'At Mr Foxes House' (one of the houses in the complex) were 'one Great Cupitt at Length one little Cupitt in the Balcony, 3 broken heads one the Rails, a Little Stone Child with out Legs two or three small defeased [? defaced] heads In the paved yard and other partes of the house Sett for Ornament, 12 or 11 Poeggars [? Beggars] to the Life, half way also a broken eurn'. Lastly, all this was followed by Thomas and Aletheia 'Earle and Countesse of Arondals in their Effigies half way'. The total valuation for both Weybridge and London amounted to some £10,350, only about £1,619 of which related to Arundel House. By far the highest value in the whole of the inventory after jewellery and gold plate, however, came from these statues, which amounted to £1,250.

It is not the purpose of this chapter to dwell further on the collection, which has been studied by others. None the less it is clear that a substantial part of the statues had not been transferred to Oxford, and it is perhaps because of this that experts have described those that were as 'the mere residue of the hoard'.[83] That hoard will have to be reassessed in the light of Robinson's discovery and my analysis.

ARUNDEL HOUSE | 53

58 The complex of Somerset House between Strand Bridge Lane and Arundel House on the east (right) and Dutchy Lane and the Savoy on the west (left) (detail of fig. 8)

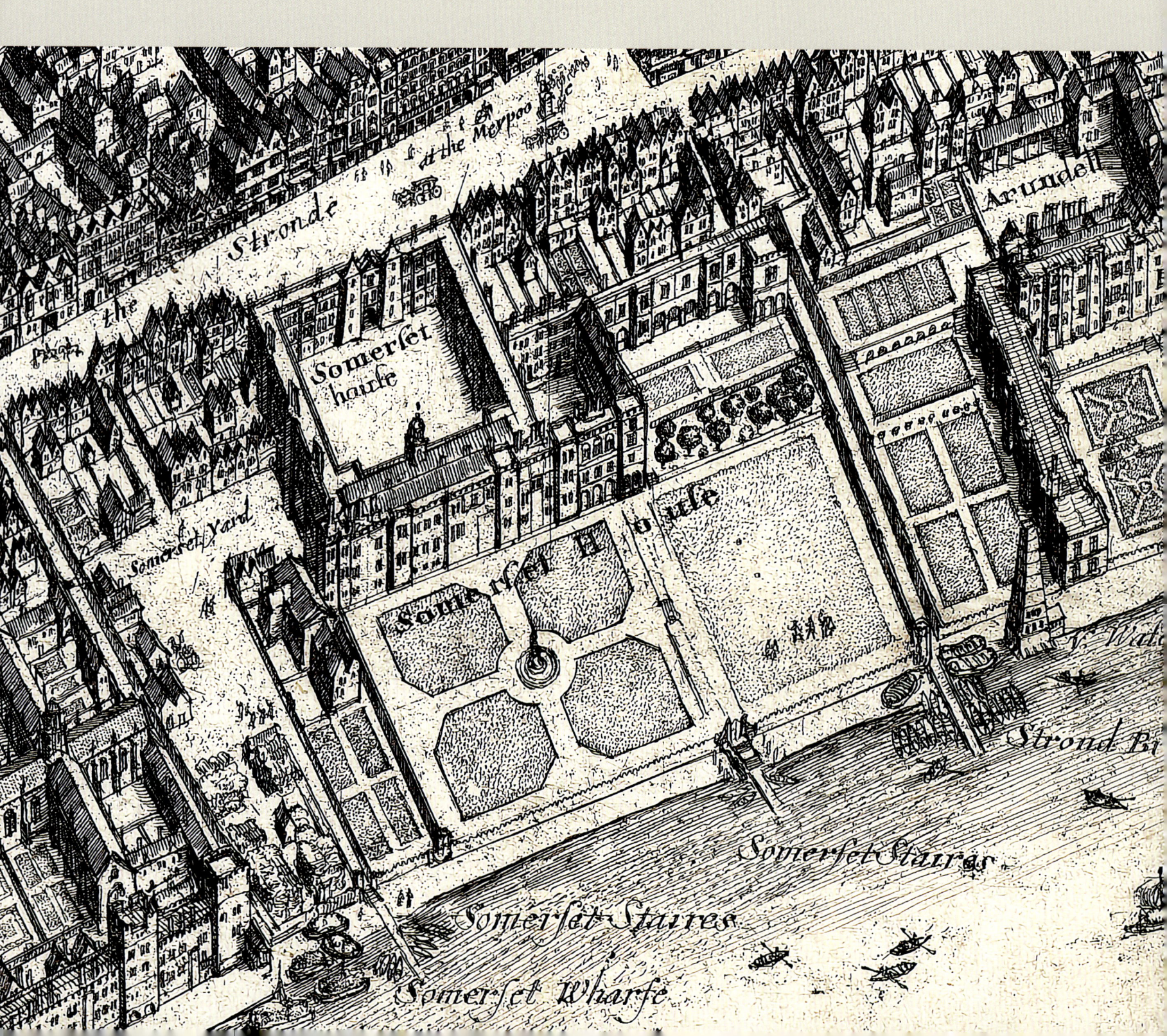

3 · SOMERSET HOUSE

SOMERSET HOUSE LAY BETWEEN THE SAVOY on the west and Arundel House on the east (fig. 58). Conceived as 'an aristocratic palace of monarchical intent'[1] by Edward Seymour (*c*.1500–1552), Lord Protector Somerset and hence England's de facto ruler for a short period after Henry VIII's death in 1547, Somerset House was, arguably, the most influential of all the Strand palaces. It set the pace chronologically, stylistically and typologically for a number of other mansions, from the near-contemporary Burghley House to the early seventeenth-century Northampton (later Northumberland) House, and to several country seats built by members of Somerset's inner circle. It was also the most influential because it almost immediately became a royal residence occupied by four consecutive queens. Consequently, Somerset House has attracted attention not just in the traditional London histories but within scholarship on royal building, namely Howard Colvin's monumental *History of the King's Works* (1963–82). This status also earned it two monographic studies: Raymond Needham and Alexander Webster's *Somerset House Past and Present*, of 1905, followed a century later by Simon Thurley's *Somerset House: The Palace of England's Queens 1551–1692*, which appeared in 2009.[2] What follows is a critical reassessment of all sources related to Somerset House in the light of the broader perspective of the whole series of the Strand palaces.

The site of Somerset House originally consisted of five individual properties east of the Savoy, acquired piecemeal by Seymour from 1537.[3] This was barely a year since his sister Jane had married Henry VIII, an event which propelled him into the stratosphere of Tudor politics.[4] Seymour's first acquisition was Chester Inn, as the site belonging to the bishopric of Coventry, Lichfield and Chester was known, sandwiched between Worcester Inn on the west and the parish church and churchyard of St Mary of Strand (not to be confused with St Mary-le-Strand) on the east.[5] The first reference to a property of that see dates to the late thirteenth century, when Walter Langton, Treasurer of England from 1295 to 1307 and Bishop of Coventry until his death in 1321, took up residence there. By 1535 the complex consisted of the 'capital messuage called Chester Place, with gardens, orchards, courts and other buildings, and also thirteen tenements called Chester Rents', customarily located along the Strand. Seymour's occupation of the inn may have started before 1537, as a tenant of the current bishop, Rowland Lee, but it soon turned into ownership, for by April of that year he had secured the freehold, confirmed by Act of Parliament in 1539. This was another enforced 'exchange', whereby Lee was given a Seymour property at Kew. The next two properties to be added to Seymour's portfolio, Worcester Inn and St Mary of Strand, both of which bounded his first purchase, were similarly forcibly swapped by Henry VIII with the See of Worcester, in whose possession or control they had been since the thirteenth century. Worcester Inn consisted of a principal messuage with a gatehouse to the Strand, eight houses and various plots and the usual 'rents' along the Strand (seven tenements in total) together with the church and its compound, on which the bishopric held the advowson. (Henry, 1st Duke of Lancaster, of the neighbouring Savoy Palace had granted a plot to enlarge its churchyard in 1355; see Chapter Four.) By 1546, the whole lot had been granted to Seymour.

The last two properties to be secured lay in the way of eastward expansion, as they bounded St Mary on the east. They consisted of two small inns within a relatively narrow plot: a public one called the Goat, on the Strand, and an inn of Chancery right behind it called the Strand, with a garden extending towards the river. The latter is more often called Llandaff Inn[6] because it had belonged to the bishopric of Llandaff since the 1280s, before the lawyers took it over at the start of the sixteenth century. Like the neighbouring St Mary's, the construction of this episcopal residence had relied on the favour of two other prominent residents of the Savoy, Edmund 'Crouchback' and Thomas, respectively 1st and 2nd Earls of Leicester and Lancaster, who had granted the land. As for the Goat Inn, it had been a property held on the honour of Leicester (granted by Henry le Waleys, Mayor of London, to Combe Abbey in 1293) and eventually reverted to the Crown on the Dissolution. Edward Seymour acquired the Strand Inn around 1547, while the Goat, which had previously been sold to various parties, was conveyed to him in 1550 in exchange for property he had purchased on the north side of the Strand. Within about ten years, Seymour had thus managed to secure the whole area, approximately 500 by 400 feet, between the Savoy and Bath Inn (itself granted in 1545 to Edward's brother, Sir Thomas Seymour,

c.1508–1549). Consequently, by the time Edward had reached the pinnacle of his career in 1547 as the Protector to his nephew Edward VI, then aged nine, and declared himself Duke of Somerset, the Seymour brothers controlled an enormous part of the Strand. This included Covent Garden (as noted earlier, formerly possessed by Westminster Abbey), granted to Edward in the same year to support his new ducal rank.[7]

What Somerset retained of this series of buildings is not altogether clear. According to John Stow they were all demolished but it is more likely that the majority of the tenements on the Strand side, except for those within the Chester Inn site, as well as some of the main chambers including the hall of that inn, were retained, for the Protector continued to live in and run the government from Chester Inn between 1547 and 1549. The Goat Inn was also preserved, while the rest, including St Mary's, was demolished to make way for the first largely new mansion in the Strand. The process did not go unnoticed, especially as in digging the new foundations 'the bones of many who had been buried there', as Somerset's attainder recorded, 'were dug up and carried into the fields'. This was repeated in the cloisters on the north side of St Paul's Cathedral and the Charnel House, with all chapels and tombs therein demolished, together with the steeple and most of the Church of St John of Jerusalem in Clerkenwell, all to provide Somerset with building material.[8]

The House of Edward Seymour, 1st Duke of Somerset: 1547–1552

A rough idea of the 'before and after' can be gained by comparing Wyngaerde's depiction of the area taken around 1544 with the 'Agas' map of 1561–70 and Braun and Hogenberg's of 1572 (figs 59–61), the last two originating from the lost Copperplate Map of London of 1553–9. Wyngaerde shows a series of scattered edifices among which one can clearly distinguish the church of St Mary with its tower, as well as a riverfront building with pitched roof and turrets. No doubt erected piecemeal, they stand in stark contrast with the neighbouring Bath Inn: one wonders why that property was granted to Thomas instead of Edward, given the Protector's dominance and the seemingly large difference between the two properties. This is if the tall range with polygonal bays and towers of

59 Estimated area of the future Somerset House, bounded on the right by Bath Inn, later Arundel House. Detail of Anthonis van den Wyngaerde, *Panorama of London from the River*, c.1544 (detail of fig. 9). © Ashmolean Museum, University of Oxford

60 The complex of Somerset House, detail of the *Woodcut Map of London*, 1561–70 ('Agas'), reprinted 1633, derived from the lost 'Copperplate Map of London', 1553–9. Mitton 1908. Wikimedia Commons Public Domain

61 The complex of Somerset House, detail of Georg Braun and Frans Hogenberg, 'London' in *Civitates Orbis Terrarum*, 1572, derived from the lost 'Copperplate Map of London', 1553–9. University Library, Heidelberg. Wikipedia, Public Domain

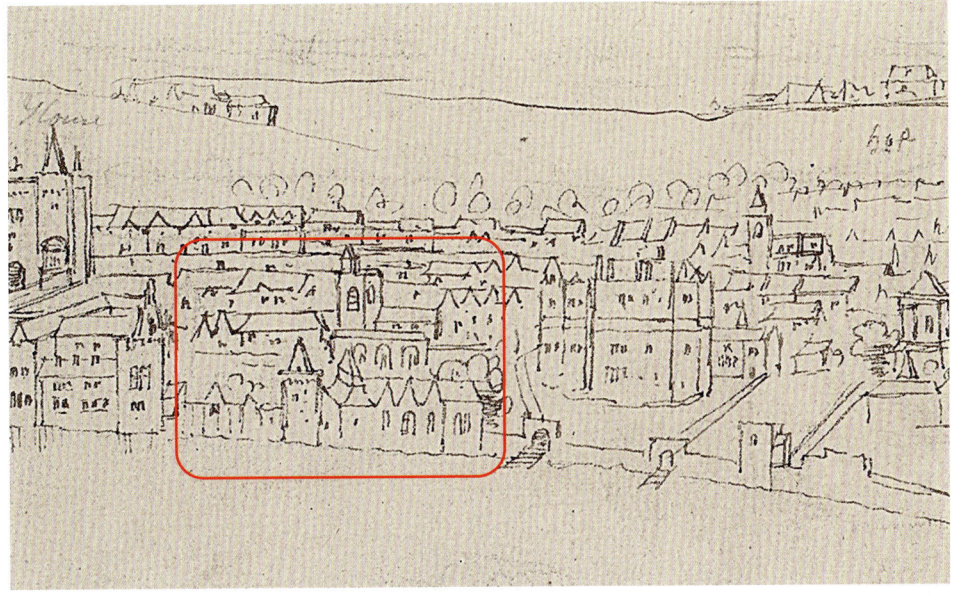

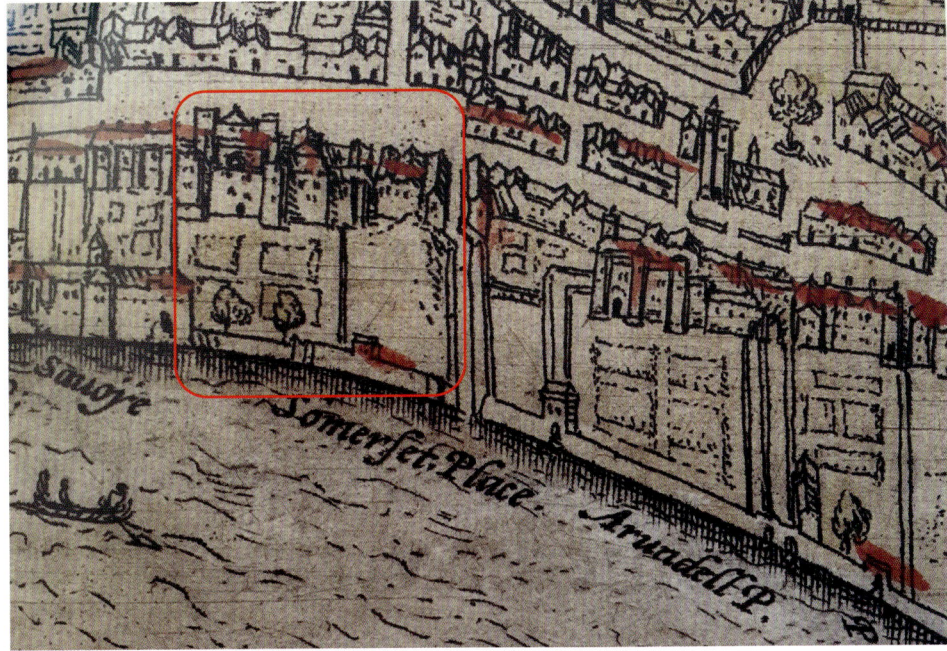

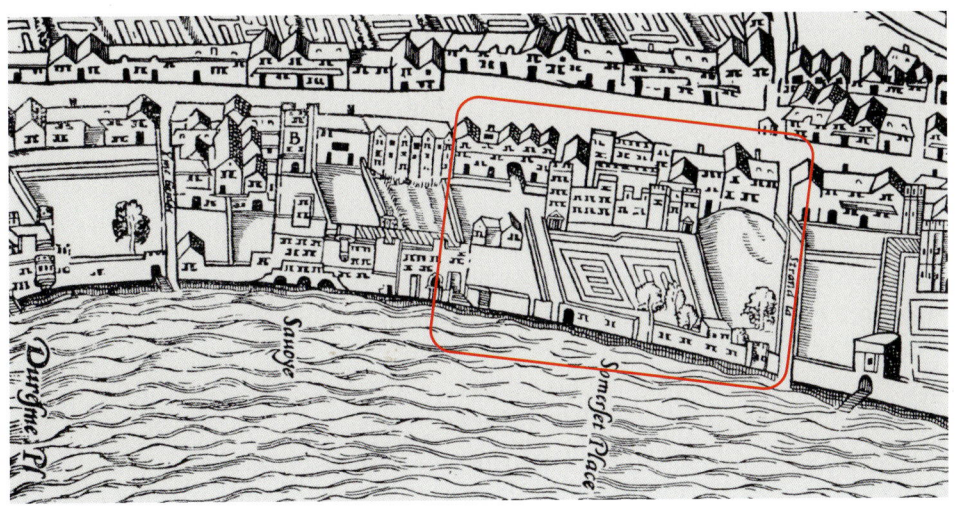

Bath Place was in place before Thomas obtained the site (see Chapter Two). However, these circumstances must be contextualised within the Protector's fancy of building mainly from scratch, which may have determined the selection of a comparatively more modest site. Somerset could thus create a palace which would mark his role while also satisfying his passion for architecture. In any event, the difference between Edward's and Thomas's sites would soon be gone, given that by the time of the Agas and Braun and Hogenberg views the main body of Somerset House with formal gardens had replaced most of the random buildings. That said, works were possibly still in progress: remarkably, a mound of rubble was depicted on the right of the site, probably coming from demolition and denoting incompleteness.

Although it is barely distinguishable in either the Agas or Braun and Hogenberg view, Somerset House developed around a courtyard, as amply confirmed by other sources discussed later, with a facade directly on the Strand, flanked by the usual rents. The front seems to have had some sort of central pediment with two higher ends and might have been battlemented, though this particular feature is only seen in Agas. By contrast, the river frontage, again especially in Agas, appears less regular, with several different buildings (see fig. 60).

The progress of Somerset's works in general can be ascertained through the accounts of John Pikarell, the duke's cofferer, which cover the period 1 April 1548 to 7 October 1551.[9] His total expenditure amounted to about £10,000, some £4000 of which went to skilled craftsmen while £2000 was paid to labourers and gardeners. The rest mainly paid for building material, a great deal of which, as previously stated, came from the demolition of buildings on site and elsewhere. Of those native craftsmen mentioned in the accounts – John Revell, Lewis Stockett, Humphrey Lovell, William Cure and John Puncherdown – many went on to achieve high positions in the Elizabethan Office of Works.[10] Foreign names include those of Nicola Bellini of Modena and Giles Gering, who had produced the stucco panels at Nonsuch.[11]

What Somerset achieved in the space of at most five years, from 1547 to his death in 1552, is not altogether clear. As of January 1550, following his arrest the previous October, he had been deposed as Lord Protector and deprived for a time of his income and properties. By mid-year his position

SOMERSET HOUSE | 57

had been restored but in October 1551 he was arrested again, tried and eventually executed for felony in January 1552. An 'apparent judgment from Heaven', wrote Howell in 1657, 'fell upon him', as that 'large and goodly House, call'd now Somerset House … rose out of the ruins of the Church', pointing, in no uncertain terms, at the controversial demolition of St Mary.[12] The manuscript copy of Norden's *Speculum Britanniae* (c.1580) describes the palace as 'not fully finished', a state confirmed by Stow, while Walpole in the eighteenth century related that only the walls were complete when the duke was led to the scaffold.[13] It is likely, however, that three sides of the quadrangle, the south, east and north, were habitable enough, given that part of Chester Inn, where Somerset lived prior to 1547 and during construction, may well have been incorporated into the new fabric. This is corroborated by both the Agas and Braun and Hogenberg views, where the river frontage appears to be composed of different buildings (see figs 60 and 61). A better glimpse into the state of Somerset House is provided by Norden in 1593 (fig. 62): he reveals how the main quadrangle still had wings of different heights, with a tall, crenellated river facade and east wing, and a much lower and clearly incomplete west wing. The Strand front, in contrast, does seem finished.[14]

The Strand elevation is perhaps one of the most quoted in English architectural history and certainly the most famous part of the house. Yet its appearance in 1552 has become controversial, for Simon Thurley has challenged the established view among scholars that John Thorpe's well known and earliest depiction of it shows the original front (fig. 63): Thurley re-dates it to c.1610–11 as opposed to the c.1603 previously suggested by John Summerson.[15] What is at stake here is whether the palimpsest of the Strand front, with its eclectic mixture of native and foreign influences best epitomised by the triumphal-arch motif of the gatehouse and the semi-circular projecting windows within it, was the first of its kind or one of the last. Typical of the English Renaissance, this front is generally cited as a model for other houses, not least those built by Somerset's inner circle such as Sir John Thynne's Longleat House in Wiltshire, Sir Thomas Smith's Hill Hall in Essex or Cecil's Burghley House in Northamptonshire.

Thurley's tantalising suggestion is based on an estimate of work dated 16 March 1610 for

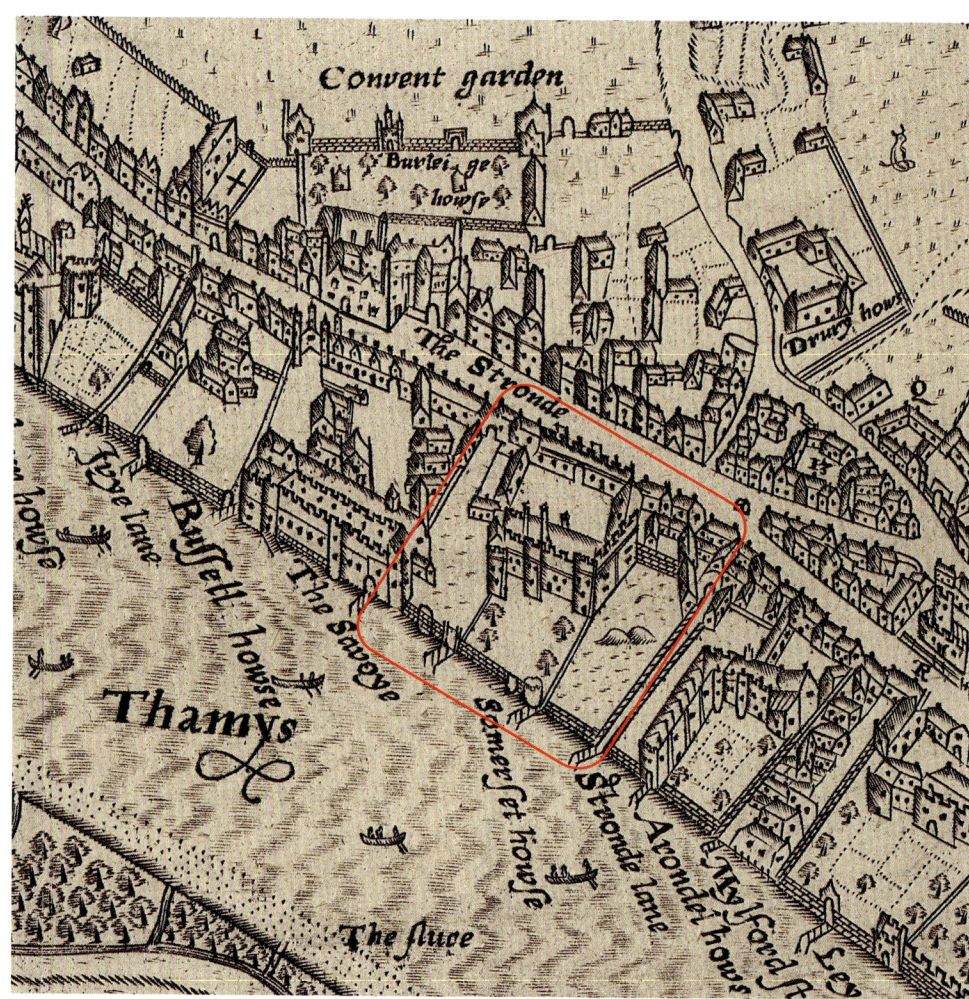

'the charges of such worcks as are intended to be don on the first court', which included raising the 'north side towards the streete … with ashlar cornish, railes and ballesters', as well as the 'square windows towards the streete … with ashlar and other open worcks, pedestals, architrave, freize and cornice'. The 'fore front', that is, the frontispiece, was 'to be clensed and the railes and ballesters amended'.[16] The other evidence he quotes is a mason's bill of 1611 for £500 worth of works including 'railes and ballisters'.[17]

First of all, these are details, though certainly significant. The question, then, is twofold: did the estimate translate into action and, if so, how do we know that the architectural details it mentions were not already in existence? Surely, after more than half a century, whatever had been introduced by Somerset would need attention, as indeed the line about 'clensing' the frontispiece suggests, while also confirming the existence pre-1610 of 'railes and ballisters'. It is also known, as discussed later, that from 1609 the house underwent substantial work for James I's queen,

62 The complex of Somerset House, detail of John Norden, *Speculum Britanniae*, 1593. Folger Shakespeare Library, Washington DC. Licensed under Creative Commons Attribution-ShareAlike 4.0 International

63 John Thorpe, elevation of the Strand front and partial ground-plan of the first court of Somerset House, c.1603 and 1610–11. © Sir John Soane's Museum, London (vol. 101, fols 87–8)

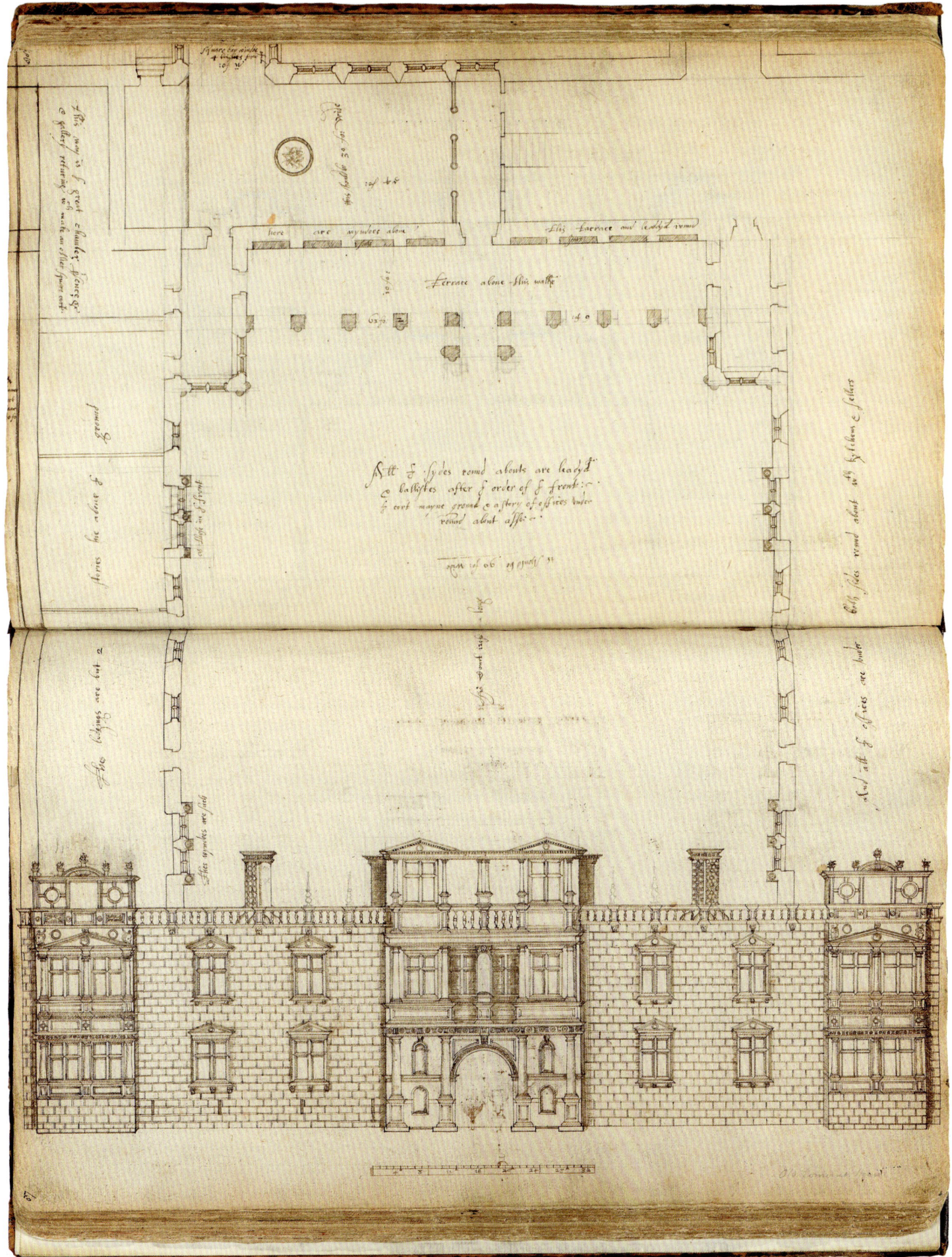

which included the cleaning and restoration of the Strand front. According to Thurley, however, Thorpe's drawing 'shows neither Protector Somerset's House nor the house as altered by Anne of Denmark', for the first would have lacked, at the least, the decorative pattern shown along the roofline, was possibly crenellated (as vaguely depicted in the Agas map) and would have had chimneys as the principal roofline element, while the second, as later evidence suggests, did not resemble Thorpe's elevation in all its details.[18] But if that elevation, as previously believed, is not a record of what Somerset erected, what was its scope? In *The Book of Architecture of John Thorpe* (1964–6), Summerson suggested that it might show a proposal not necessarily by Thorpe carried out from 1609 – referring, however, to the plan attached to the elevation. And the latter, he maintained, 'almost certainly belongs' to Somerset's time, a view confirmed by Colvin in 1982.[19] Thurley, instead, considers the elevation to be part of the proposal, pointing at Simon or Edward Basil, respectively the Surveyor of the King's Works and his brother, then clerk of works at Somerset House, as those for whom Thorpe may have produced a presentation drawing.[20]

In the absence of conclusive evidence, one is left with stylistic analysis, on which the established view has essentially been based so far. In his monumental *Elizabethan Architecture* (2009), Mark Girouard revisits the whole palimpsest of this facade, reaffirming how it unequivocally derives from Serlio in almost all its parts even if 'it is easy enough to pierce the classical disguise and see the traditional Tudor entrance façade behind it'.[21] Behind this kind of exercise, as every scholar dealing with the subject (Thurley included) has argued, ought to be Somerset, the well-known architectural patron, together with his fellow amateur architects Thynne and Burghley. After all, the point of erecting an elevation along the Strand, itself unusual because it was at the expense of valuable letting properties (only four other palaces had such a feature), was to make a grand and novel gesture, as Somerset is credited with having done. For the origins of this facade it therefore seems inconceivable to imagine otherwise. When it comes to specific details such as the top stage of the bay windows on either side of the facade, which would have raised the 'north side towards the streete … with ashlar cornish, railes and ballesters', as in the 1610 estimate, Thurley might none the less be right. Probably part of the much needed repairs and modifications for Queen Anne, the square with an inscribed circle motif which frames both top stages remained a favourite device of the early seventeenth century, for instance in the woodwork of the Hall and Chapel at Hatfield (supervised by Basil). In contrast, the flaming grenades on the very top, not seen before the 1560s and definitely derived from Serlio's Book IV (1537), had gone out of fashion in the early seventeenth century.[22] But if one assumes replacement, the grenades would have been in keeping with what was there before. In fact, this whole top-stage apparatus at Somerset House is identical to the courtyard roofline built in 1575–8 at Burghley House in the country: if Edward Seymour was not the first in the chain, whoever reworked his facade in the early 1600s must have copied it from Burghley House.[23] This is peculiar, and in a way brings us back to where we started, for it is much more plausible that the latter house was inspired by the former, not vice versa.

In 1553 Somerset House became the official residence of Princess Elizabeth. This initiated a tradition and two subsequent queens made the house their main abode. For Elizabeth it was the result of a swap engineered by John Dudley, 1st Duke of Northumberland, who had taken Somerset's role as Lord Protector from 1550. He had set his sights on Durham House, which Edward VI had granted Elizabeth in fulfilment of their father's will: as the former residence of that powerful northern bishopric it was pivotal to Dudley's ambitions of assembling large landholdings based on great northern estates.[24] For the next five years Elizabeth used Somerset House whenever she came to London and it was there that she lodged after her ascent to the throne in 1558. During her reign, however, even if she held court at the house for short periods, it never became a principal royal residence; like many neighbouring palaces, it was used to accommodate various embassies such as the Duc de Montmorency's in 1572, that of John Casimir, son of the Elector Palatine, in 1578–9, and the Prince Dauphin of France and his retinue for the queen's proposed marriage to the Duke of Anjou in 1581.[25] Those parties occupied the principal rooms, while other apartments would be used as favour lodgings for Elizabeth's closest courtiers, such as Robert Dudley, the 1st Earl, who had a room there from 1570, or Henry Carey, Lord

Hudson and Chamberlain of the Household from 1583, who lived within the site until 1585.[26]

Elizabeth's surrender of Durham House was probably on the understanding that Somerset House would be made good for her use. Indeed, Dudley's son Robert was the keeper of the house until the fall of his family following Jane Gray's abortive reign and later a resident, as noted. He seems to have been in charge of the works, which amounted to a total of £893. While more was spent between 1558 and 1565, in 1567–70, 1575 and again in 1584–5, most of it appears to have rendered the house habitable or repaired it, since parts were collapsing, as highlighted by a report issued soon after Elizabeth's accession. A 'gallery before the hall', that is some kind of covered shelter perhaps alluding to the loggia seen in Thorpe's plan, replaced a previous makeshift version on the south front of the courtyard (see fig. 63).[27] Repaired in 1597, and featuring tiles, this 'gallery' anticipated the arcade built there from 1611. In 1585 the queen spent Lent at Somerset House and a new 'preaching place' was built, even if her own private services were held in the neighbouring Savoy Chapel.[28] This may be all that was done during her tenure, but one question concerning the completion of the west wing remains to be answered.

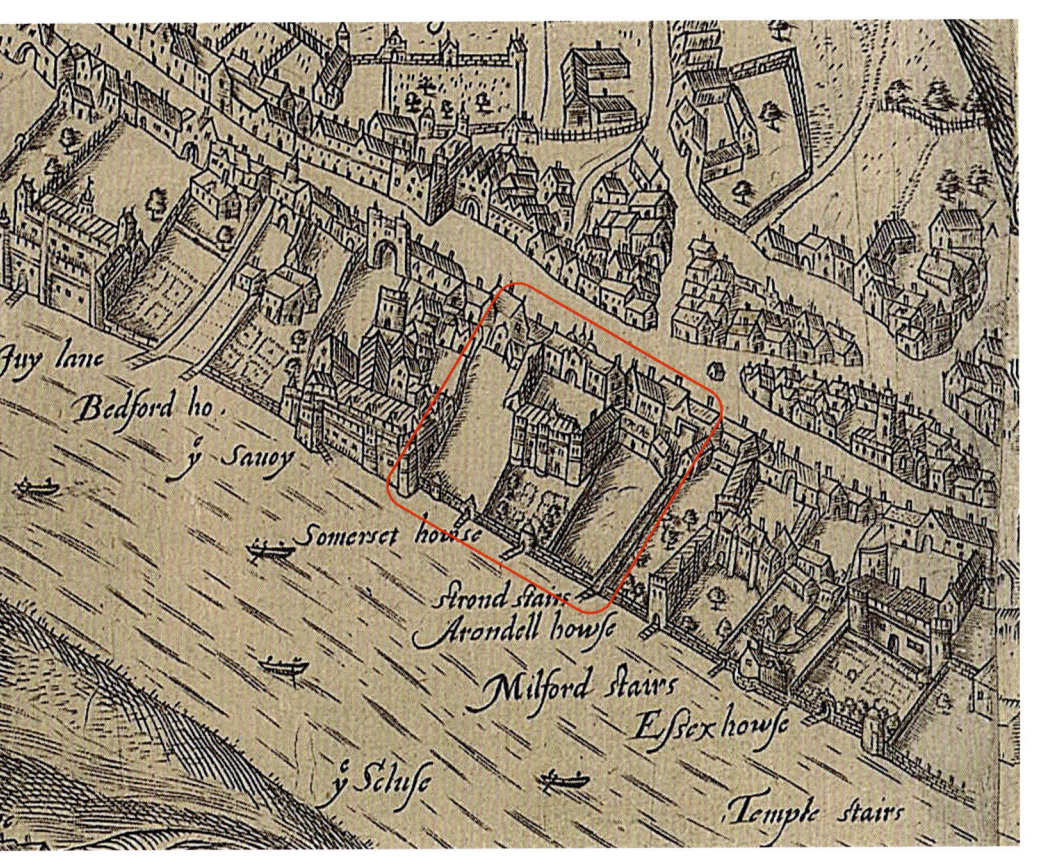

64 The complex of Somerset House, detail of John Norden, *Civitas Londini*, 1600. National Library of Sweden

The House of Anne of Denmark: 1603–1619

Somerset House became Anne of Denmark's official residence after her husband's accession to the English throne in 1603. And it stood out once again, compared with both its neighbours (more numerous and more conspicuous than in the 1550s) and perhaps all the other royal houses. As in the instance of Elizabeth I, however, the choice of this complex had been a matter of contingency, since no other Tudor queen's residence in London was available. Behind the decision was Robert Cecil, the keeper of the house and High Steward of the queen's courts since 1603.[29] In effect, given its perennial state of repair, Somerset House may initially have seemed unappealing, which is perhaps one reason why nothing of relevance happened to the house before 1609, nor did Anne use it before its full refurbishment. This is the background against which one should appraise the enormous sums spent over the next four to five years for its reconstruction and furnishing, amounting to a staggering £45,000, unparalleled since Henry VIII and certainly one of the most ruinous enterprises of James I.[30] Before then, Somerset or Denmark House, as it was formally renamed in 1617 to mark its independence from the king's household at Whitehall,[31] had continued to accommodate state guests. These included the Spanish and Dutch delegations gathered there in 1604 for the negotiations of the Treaty of London, more commonly known as the Somerset House Conference, which concluded the nineteen-year Anglo-Spanish War. This occasioned the well-known painting in the National Portrait Gallery (see fig. 7), which provides the only known view of an interior of the palace, identified as the Council Chamber in the east wing of the main quadrangle.[32] This was hung with precious tapestries and had a large four-light casement window, the backdrop to the delegation table where sit Robert Cecil and Henry Howard, both of whom were in the midst of building or expanding their own Strand palaces. If the identification is correct, what is seen through the window is the elevation of the west wing, with plain transom windows on the main floor and dormer windows along the garrets. The painting is generally understood as a contemporary record of the conference.[33] Therefore in 1604 the west wing was no longer incomplete, as Norden showed it in 1593 and indeed in the 1600 reprint (of uncertain reliability; see figs 62 and 64).

SOMERSET HOUSE | 61

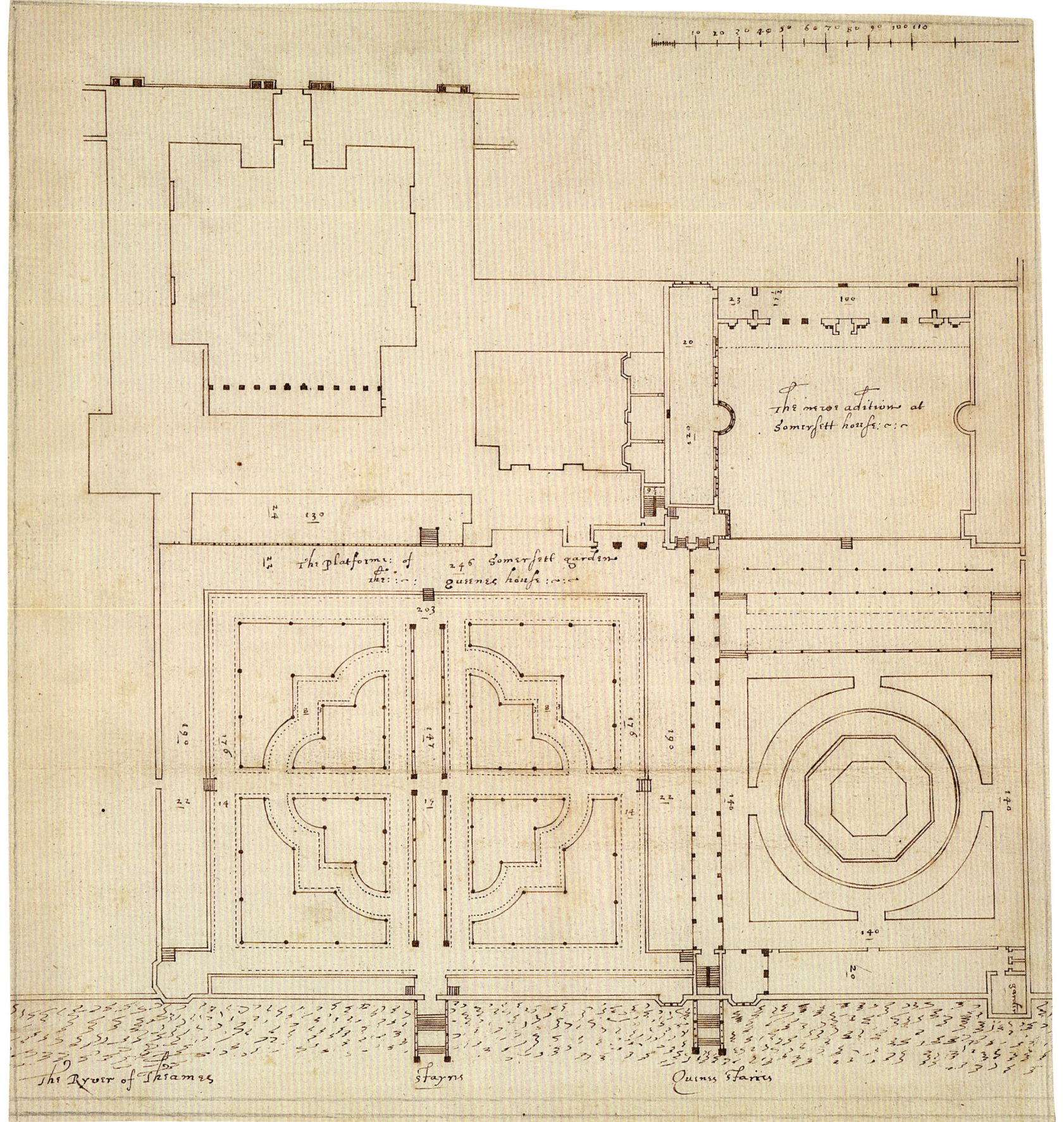

65 Robert Smythson, ground-plan of Somerset House and gardens, 1609 or *c*.1611. RIBA Collections (29111)

Unless, that is, what we see in the painting is not a range matching the others in height but a lower one. Yet, the position of the Council Chamber seems higher than a mere ground floor, while the opposite wing, seen in perspective, seems to match that height. The shadow cast from the south wing, which we know was as tall as the east range, seems to confirm this interpretation, and a re-examination of two plans including Thorpe's provides further elucidation, as will be seen.

If Somerset House may have initially been unfit for a queen, it was still considered by no less than the Venetian ambassador 'the most splendid house in London after the royal palace',[34] an interesting remark considering how royal it soon became. Given the importance of the view of these palaces from the river, it is not surprising that the first sign of activity was the creation of a new Privy Garden to the east of the house, the area previously covered by a mound of rubble, as seen in the Agas map and Braun and Hogenberg's view (see figs 60 and 61). This was still somehow in place in 1593, when Norden depicted the area (see fig. 62), and by the early 1600s rearrangement must have become a priority, especially in the process of turning the house into Anne's chief residence. So it was that in 1609 William Goodrowse, one of the king's sergeant surgeons, was paid £400 for 'building … raising and levelling the ground and garden', which seems to imply that the state of the ground had indeed remained unchanged since the 1560s. In 1611, Goodrowse relinquished to the Crown a property he owned in the north-east corner of the complex, so that expansion in that direction could be achieved. This was part of a series of transactions whereby ownership of the site was consolidated, which also involved the regularisation of leases, especially those relating to tenements in the north-west part. Among those is a lease dated 1630[35] bearing the name of John Villiers, Viscount Purbeck and elder brother of Charles, 1st Duke of Buckingham, the king's notorious favourite who had recently gained ownership of York House (see Chapter Ten).

The remodelled garden, the layout of the existing building and what was being proposed are shown in Robert Smythson's well-known plan of Somerset House, variably dated 1609 or *c*.1611 (fig. 65).[36] This shows the existence, only marginally discernible in Norden, of a second inner (or lower) courtyard to the east of the main quadrangle, against which a new, three-sided addition open towards the Privy Garden was being considered. The latter was centred on an octagonal feature representing the rock grotto known as Parnassus, designed by Isaac de Caus, who built another more intimate grotto at Bedford House in the early 1630s.[37]

Of the new intended courtyard for Somerset House, only the north and west ranges were eventually carried out. The former impinged on Goodrowse's previous property and consisted of a two-storey brick building with stone arches supported on Doric columns on the ground floor and a projecting 'square window', it too in stone, in the centre. While the first floor of this range was mainly occupied by a Cross Gallery, the west range included a Privy Gallery, 120 feet long and 20 feet wide, adjoined, along the side facing the inner court, by a series of three small rooms destined as Privy Lodgings. A direct connection between the Privy Gallery and the existing state rooms on the south front of the inner courtyard was also provided.[38] Accounting for the slope of the site, and a projecting room on top of the south end of the Privy Gallery, the river front of the west range looked like a tower, even if it featured only two main storeys, like the north range. Responsibility for these works lay with the royal Office of Works, headed by Simon Basil. The only 'plott' mentioned in relation to the house was in fact made by his brother Edward 'against her Majs coming thither', for which a payment of 40 shillings is registered in the accounts of 1610–11.[39] This may well have been a presentation plan not too dissimilar from the one produced by Smythson.[40]

While the eastern part of the complex was given new shape by two galleries and a wholesale remodelling of the Privy Lodgings, the garden was rearranged with terraces and paths laid with black and white stones; the boundary walls to the east and south – respectively along Arundel House and the Thames – were also reinforced. In 1612 attention switched back to the main quadrangle. In spite of what was done during the Elizabethan period, this presumably remained in essence as Lord Protector Somerset had conceived it. Knowledge of its internal layout comes from two sources: a plan of *c*.1608–11 of the first floor of the Strand range (fig. 66) and the ground-plan, which includes the Strand elevation but not the Strand range, by John Thorpe (see fig. 63). The first was produced following the 1605–6 rearrangement of the state rooms on the first floor overlooking the Strand, transformed into a lodging for Robert

SOMERSET HOUSE | 63

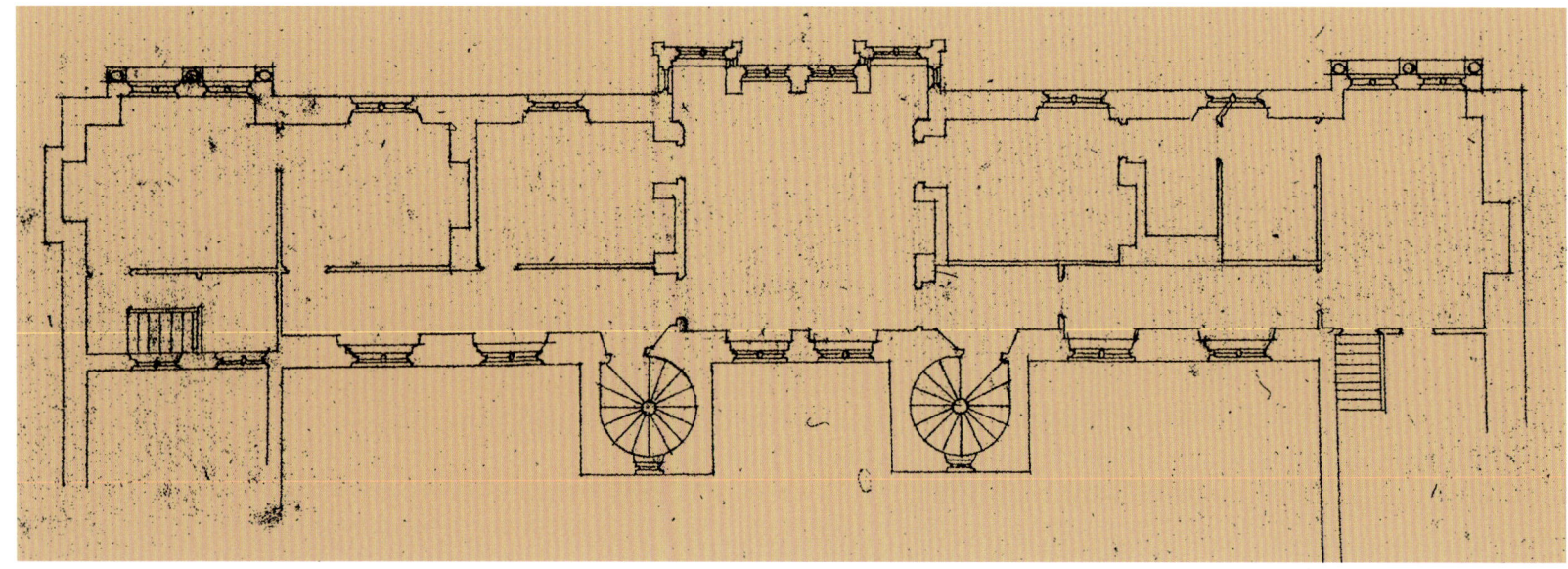

66 First-floor plan of the Strand range of Somerset House, c.1608–11. Hatfield House Archives, CPM II 56. Reproduced with permission of the Marquess of Salisbury, Hatfield House

Cecil, keeper of the house since 1603. If one disregards the thin partitions, the majority of which must have been introduced at the time, one can picture how this level acted as the original *piano nobile*: a Long Gallery opening onto the Strand, occupying most of the east wing, possibly up to the Council Chamber discussed earlier; then some five rooms overlooking the Strand, the central one over the whole of the gatehouse, with a slightly larger room at the west end. Accessed by two spiral staircases in the turrets, and with a virtually all-glazed front, this central room must have hosted public events; it was majestically doubled by a much bigger open-air version on the roof.[41] That the first-floor *piano nobile* of Somerset's house was on the top floor we learn by cross-referencing this plan with Thorpe's elevation (see fig. 63). This set a precedent for other palaces with a direct view over the Strand, such as Northampton House: its top-floor state rooms were even more remarkable because a middle (first) floor resulted in a second-floor *piano nobile* (see Chapter Eleven). In the country, such an extraordinary arrangement came to define the splendour of Hardwick Hall.

As for Thorpe's plan, apart from the elevation (which does not fully agree with the plan of c.1608–11 as the latter does not include the projecting, semi-circular windows in the centre nor the niche in between), it also gives some idea of what the house would originally have been like.[42] First of all we get a confirmation of the sheer scale of the main quadrangle as recorded by Smythson, the two sides of which measured 100 feet across by 120 feet.[43] Equally confirmed by Thorpe's notes is the vertical layout of the house, as one would have guessed from the evidence considered thus far and from the topography of the site: that is, two storeys at the Strand and three at the riverside, counting the partly underground basement below the east, south and west wings. Thorpe's plan shows the ground floor of the house but includes, as was typical of him, information about more than one floor. The Hall, no doubt double-height, is on the left-hand side of the south wing, probably followed, at least in the original arrangement, by a big kitchen. By the time of Thorpe's plan, however, kitchens had been moved to the basement, probably closer to the Hall.[44] This is, again, exactly what pertained at Northampton House. Thorpe's notes also inform us of the original arrangement of the inner court on the east of the main quadrangle: this was composed of a suite of state rooms including the Great Chamber, Presence Chamber and Gallery, which must have complemented those on the Strand, at least until the *piano nobile* on the Strand front was partitioned. As for the architectural language of the main courtyard, it was, Thorpe writes, 'after' that of the Strand elevation.

To what extent Thorpe's drawing is a survey as opposed to a proposal is difficult to establish, for the plan is a peculiar if not unusual mixture of both. The new arcade or loggia between the two square returns on the south front, for instance, is a faithful record of what was realised in 1611–13. By contrast, the east and west wings were reconstructed in stone to a height of three storeys, rather than the two indicated in the plan: 'Thes

Lodgings are but 2 stories hie above ye ground'.[45] As can be ascertained from later drawings, however, this does not seem to have increased the overall height of the quadrangle.[46]

Notwithstanding the limits of Thorpe's plans, which are often working surveys with information about more than one floor on a single sheet (see, for instance, fig. 204), this point about levels is relevant here. Unquestionably, Somerset House had a set of state rooms, likely to be the Protector's original, on the first floor of the main quadrangle, certainly along the east and Strand ranges. These rooms were complemented by a further suite in the inner courtyard facing the river, which would have been on the same level as the Hall, that is, the ground floor on the courtyard (street) side or first floor from the garden, given the slope down to the river. The issue is to which of those two sets the Council Chamber where the Somerset House Conference took place belonged. If it was among those on the first floor, the west wing must have been completed by then and Thorpe's is definitely a survey in so far as the two side wings are concerned. If, however, that chamber was part of the other set of state rooms, or on the same level, it would have to be located on the ground floor, in which case the view in the painting (see fig. 7) no longer makes sense. One is therefore inclined to conclude that the main quadrangle had indeed been completed during Elizabeth I's tenure.[47]

Alongside work on the main courtyard, which was largely concentrated on changes related to the side wings (from two to three storeys so as to increase lodging capacity), attention was focused on the garden front, which still maintained a battlemented and rather disjointed appearance. It was therefore rendered with false masonry joints marked with a trowel and frescoed to look like stone. The Strand front too, as previously mentioned in relation to its controversial dating, was cleaned and restored and rain gutters introduced, as evidenced by an eighteenth-century drawing which shows rain-water heads dated 1612.[48] Then, in 1613–14 there came the turn of the Hall, the front of which was refaced with stone while the interior was given a large black and white chimneypiece. Another prominent chimneypiece was also installed in the room at the east end of the Cross Gallery, as part of a decorative programme for this new part of the house, Privy Lodgings included, until 1617. By then, Inigo Jones had succeeded Basil in the Surveyorship, though his participation at Somerset House is first recognised in 1617–18 when a new lantern was erected over the Hall.[49] Jones's indebtedness to the patronage of Anne of Denmark is well known when it comes to the masques she commissioned.[50] His architectural role among the Strand palaces is none the less much harder to tackle, and Somerset House is no exception during Anne's phase. This changed, as will be seen, with Henrietta Maria.

Her new palace, greatly transformed by this long campaign of refurbishment and enlargement, was enjoyed by the queen for only a short time. For, while a sort of house-warming party had been given in 1614 when works were not fully finished, she did not take up residence until 1617, when the house's name officially changed to Denmark House, a title it retained until the Commonwealth. Two years later she was dead.[51] James I, who had rarely visited the palace, granted it to Charles, Prince of Wales, while its keepership went to his favourite, Villiers, who took up lodgings there with his wife (York House was not gained until 1622; see Chapter Ten). In addition, Villiers's brother John (already mentioned as leasing a dwelling in the complex), was assigned the rents from twenty-four tenements for life. Prince Charles lived at St James's Palace, so Denmark House went back to its former use as lodgings for diplomats and state guests. In 1623, for instance, when preparations were being made to receive the Infanta following Charles and Villiers's (by then Buckingham) marriage expedition to Spain, it was inspected alongside Durham House and St James's Palace as a potential residence for the new queen. It was Durham House that was judged 'the fittest for the grandees': St James's was deemed not grand enough for the occasion.[52] None of this came to fruition, as the Spanish match was abandoned. King James died in 1625 and Charles married another (very) Catholic princess, Henrietta Maria, the daughter of Henry IV of France and Marie de' Medici, to whom Denmark House was granted as part of her jointure in 1626.

The House of Henrietta Maria: 1626–1641; 1660–1669

While Anne's court had essentially been private and independent from James's, Charles and Henrietta were more closely entwined, which affected the scope of the Strand palace. Anne's

Catholicism had been equally reserved, another trait in sharp contrast with Henrietta's controversial display of hers. The new queen also brought the French fashion she had grown up with (and was again exposed to while in exile during the Civil Wars), in both etiquette and interior decoration. In effect, Henrietta's foreign taste accounted for Denmark House's unique combination of Englis classicism and the mature Baroque style of the Continent. Had it not been for the Commonwealth interlude, hers would have been the longest tenure of the house by far.

Henrietta's first phase of residence over the fifteen years up to 1641 is primarily marked by the construction of a chapel between 1630 and 1635, which finally provided what had been thought of since at least 1623, when the anticipated arrival of the Infanta triggered Inigo Jones's first plan for it (alongside that for St James's Palace). This was not simply a private chapel, but a friary church to accommodate the Capuchins, on whose order Charles and Henrietta had finally settled after the twelve priests who had accompanied her to

67 Inigo Jones, sketch elevation for the Chapel niche at Somerset House, c.1632. RIBA Collections (22793)

68 Inigo Jones, plan and elevation for the Chapel window at Somerset House, 1632. RIBA Collections (22797)

69 Inigo Jones, elevation of a tabernacle frame with figure holding an orb for the exterior of the Chapel at Somerset House, c.1632. RIBA Collections (22738)

70 *opposite, below right* Fragment of a Roman entablature from Asia Minor, 2nd century AD, from Lord Arundel's collection. Museum of London. Angelicoussis, 2004, fig. 12

71 *above* Engraving of the Somerset House chapel screen made for *Isaac Ware's Designs of Inigo Jones and others*, c.1731, pl. 30. RIBA Collections (46139)

London were expelled following ostentatious celebrations of the Mass. Whether or not Jones's solution bore any similarity to that previous plan, it brilliantly resolved the limits imposed by the site to the west of the house formerly occupied by the tennis court, long and narrow on a north–south axis. By positioning the main access on the chapel's west transept, possibly marked by an imposing niche for which a design exists alongside those for a window and a tabernacle, Jones in fact gave the illusion of a correct orientation (figs 67–9).[53] Internally, one of the highlights would have been the double-storey screen to the royal closet with its frieze combining carved heads and consoles, which Jones had modelled on an antique fragment at the neighbouring Arundel House (figs 71 and 70).[54]

Before any of these projects took place, Jones had also overseen and designed a number of other works both in and outside the house, for which, remarkably, some drawings survive. Thus this is the best-documented period as far as the Surveyor is concerned, not just at Denmark House but for the Strand palaces overall. First, the queen's

SOMERSET HOUSE | 67

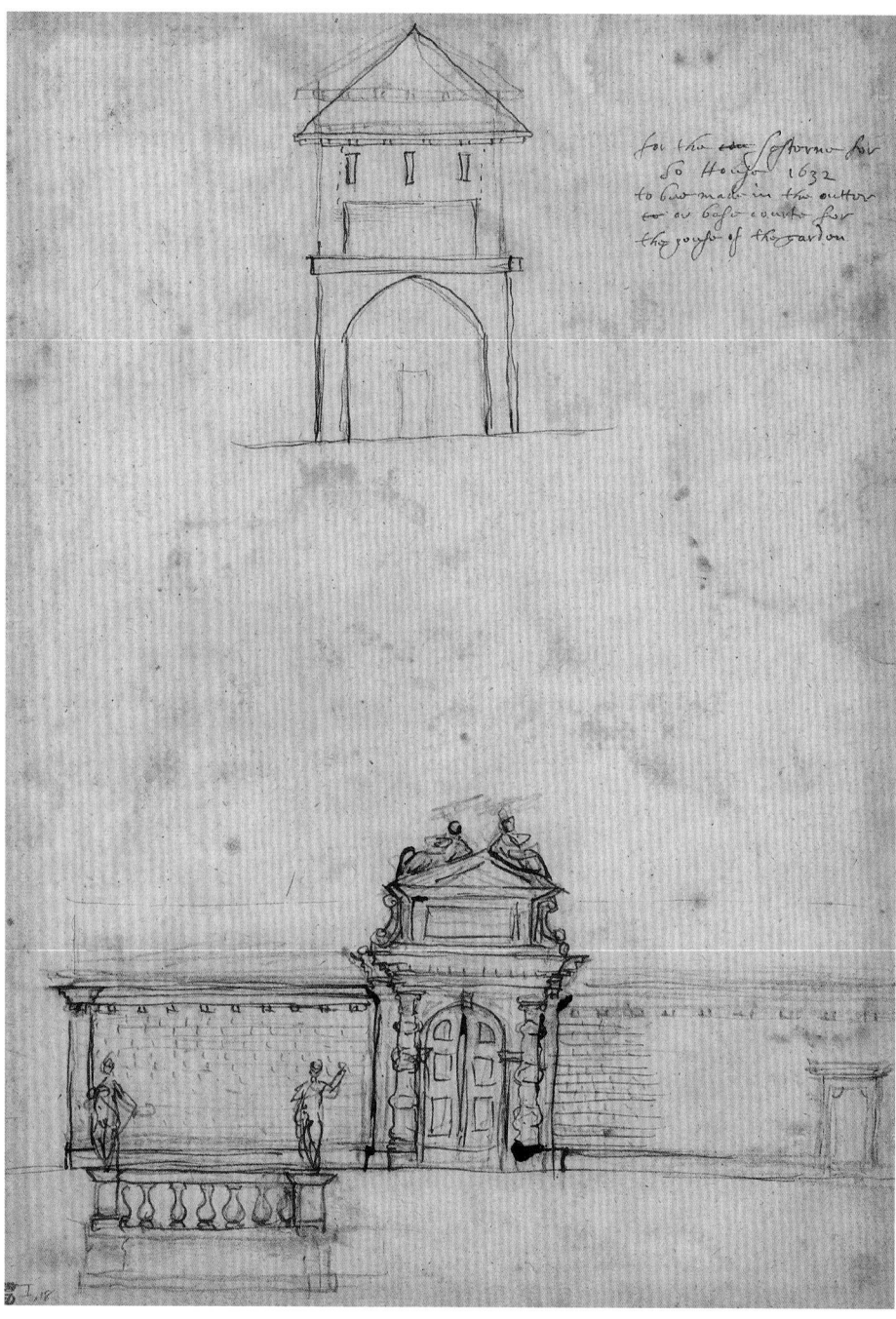

Chapel and Closet, probably no more than a domestic oratory and anteroom used by Anne of Denmark, were redecorated in 1626–7 and then from 1628 an elaborate programme of refurbishment of her inner rooms began. This included a new Cabinet Room, effectively her private office, on the upper floor at the east end of the Cross Gallery (not the old one situated over the south end of the Privy Gallery), for which we have a design for doorways together with two splendid drawings for carved or painted panels bearing the insignia of Henrietta Maria and attesting to her introduction of the French style of interior decoration (fig. 72).[55] As well as the new Cabinet Room, these panels have also been associated with the Bedchamber which the queen again in French fashion had turned into a chief public room with a magnificent *lit de parade*, probably gifted by France.[56] Outside, a new water gate was constructed on axis with the Privy Gallery, for which another of Jones's sketch designs, probably related to it, survives (fig. 73).[57] What was actually built – the much depicted balustraded platform accessed via a pair of gates between ornamental piers – was a simpler version, probably by Inigo's then very

72 Inigo Jones, elevation for doorways in the new Cabinet Room at Somerset House, 1628–30. RIBA Collections (22796)

73 Inigo Jones, designs for a cistern house at Somerset House (top) and for a water gate, probably for Somerset House too, 1628–32. RIBA Collections (22798)

68 | LONDON'S 'GOLDEN MILE'

74 Canaletto, detail from *The City of London*, c.1750, seen from the garden of Somerset House, with Inigo Jones's water gate. Royal Collection Trust, RCIN 400504. © Her Majesty Queen Elizabeth II 2021

young pupil, John Webb (fig. 74 and see figs 49, 58 and 11).[58] Jones's water gate appears on the same sheet as his rough sketch for a cistern house, built in 1632 to supply water to the garden of Denmark House, though its form as built was also different. In 1635 attention switched back to the Cross Gallery, which was remodelled and given a new overmantel for the Jacobean chimneypiece there, as evidenced by another Jones design (fig. 75).[59]

A new tennis court was also built, while the garden was given a new fountain, set up in 1637 by Hubert Le Sueur in collaboration with the Surveyor, who had produced a drawing for it three years earlier (fig. 76).[60] By then, the garden had been enriched with some of the statues purchased by Charles I from the Duke of Mantua between 1628 and 1632, part of a collection which also included numerous paintings.[61] Jones's sketch

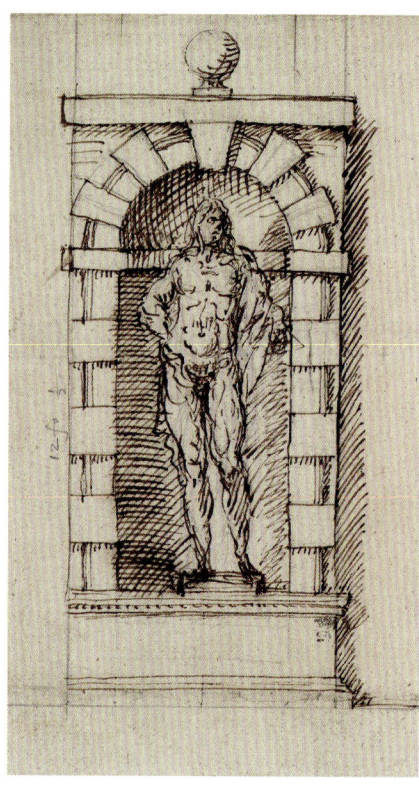

for a niche containing a statue may refer to this (fig. 77).⁶²

Thus, Henrietta's improvements were concentrated on the river side of the palace, while what her predecessor had done along its Strand front was limited to the restoration and cleaning of Somerset's facade. That is, the urban side of Denmark House had remained largely untouched since its first construction: by the late 1630s it not only required attention but was also probably judged as fundamentally superseded, especially against Jones's latest additions. It is possibly in this context that two designs dated 1638 were produced in the hand of John Webb but 'authentically Jonesian', for a grandiose reconstruction of the Strand side, which would have involved the demolition of both Somerset's elevation and the tenements that flanked it.⁶³ The first version, with two imposing *piani nobili* over a tall ground-floor podium, in the mould of Palladio's town palaces (especially his design for the Doge's Palace in Venice) but over-stretched, is unsurprisingly marked as 'not taken' (fig. 78). The second, more in tune with the proportions of the area, where tenements would have been about three storeys high, was clearly a direct adaptation to the site and little more than a new facade (fig. 79). This too, however, came to nothing, for these drawings lay among the series of unexecuted and possibly speculative plans for royal or near-royal palaces including Whitehall and Durham House (for which Webb produced another series, in the 1640s, for the 4th Earl of Pembroke; see Chapter Nine).

As one would expect, Inigo Jones's role at Denmark House did not end with architecture, for soon after Henrietta had been granted the palace he designed a theatre for the pastoral *Artenice*, erected in the upper part of the Hall. In 1633 he then built a room in the lower court for the performance of another pastoral, *The Shepherd's Paradise*, while in 1638 the Hall was again adapted for *The Passionate Lovers*.⁶⁴

Henrietta Maria left London in January 1642 and was absent for the next eighteen years. During the Commonwealth, Denmark House, renamed after its original builder perhaps in an attempt to obscure the strong Catholic association to these foreign queens, fell into general disrepair while parts of it, such as the Chapel, were considerably damaged. Its quintessentially royal standing also seems to have hindered any specific use by Parliament, which seems to have concentrated more on debating its fate. After all, a number of apartments had been rendered uninhabitable following the notorious sale of the king's goods which took place at the palace. This is how some of the statues made their

75 Inigo Jones, designs for a Jacobean chimneypiece with a new overmantel in the Cross Gallery at Somerset House, 1636. RIBA Collections (22801)

76 Inigo Jones, perspective with two sketch plans for a fountain in the garden of Somerset House, *c.*1633. Chatsworth. Image © The Courtauld, Conway Library

77 Inigo Jones, sketch elevation for a niche with a voussoired architrave surround containing a statue, mid-to-late 1630s. RIBA Collections (22739)

78 *opposite, above* John Webb, design 'not taken' by Inigo Jones for a new Strand frontage of Somerset House, 1638. The Provost and Fellows of Worcester College, Oxford

79 *opposite, below* John Webb, plan and elevation by Inigo Jones for a new Strand frontage of Somerset House, 1638. The Provost and Fellows of Worcester College, Oxford

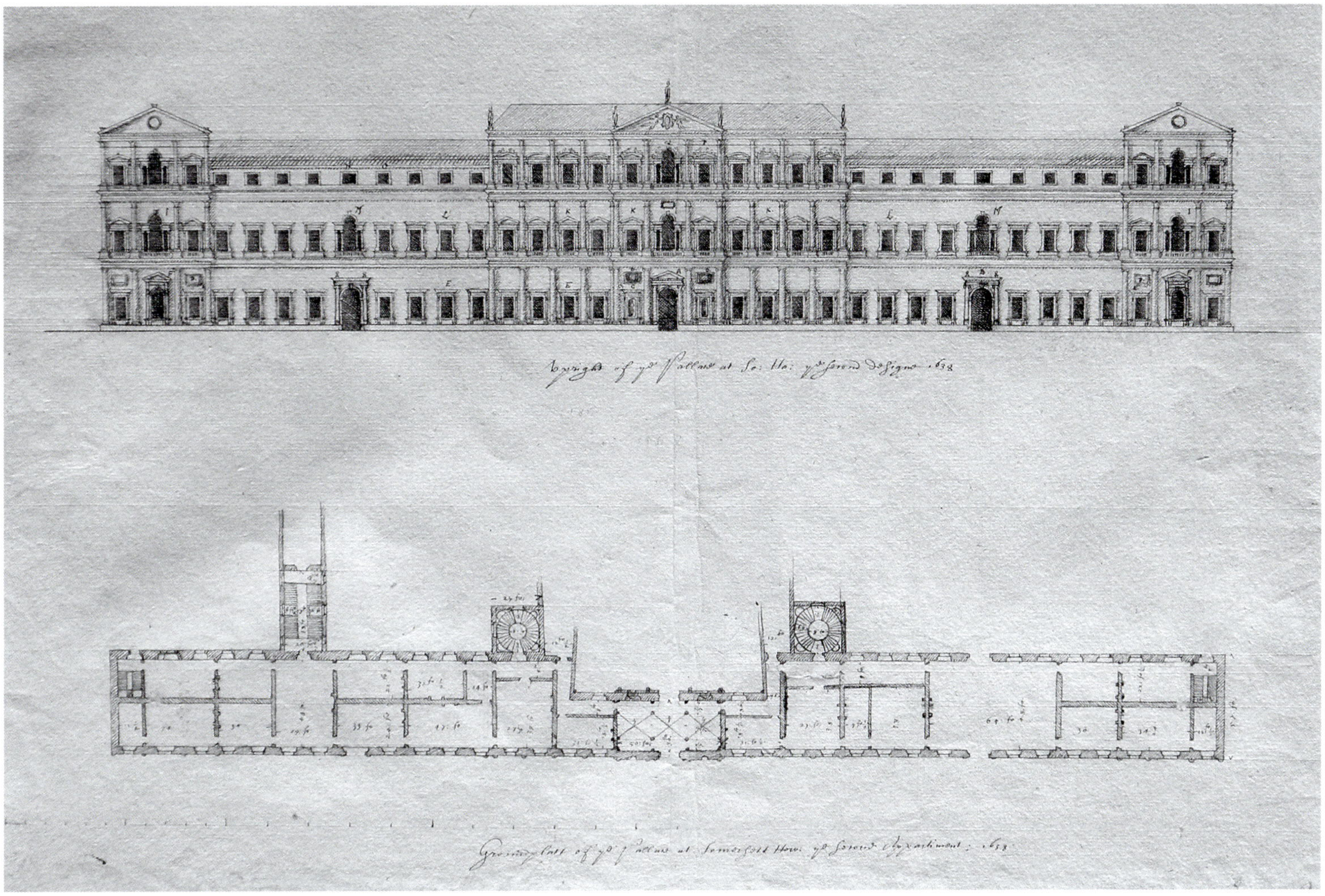

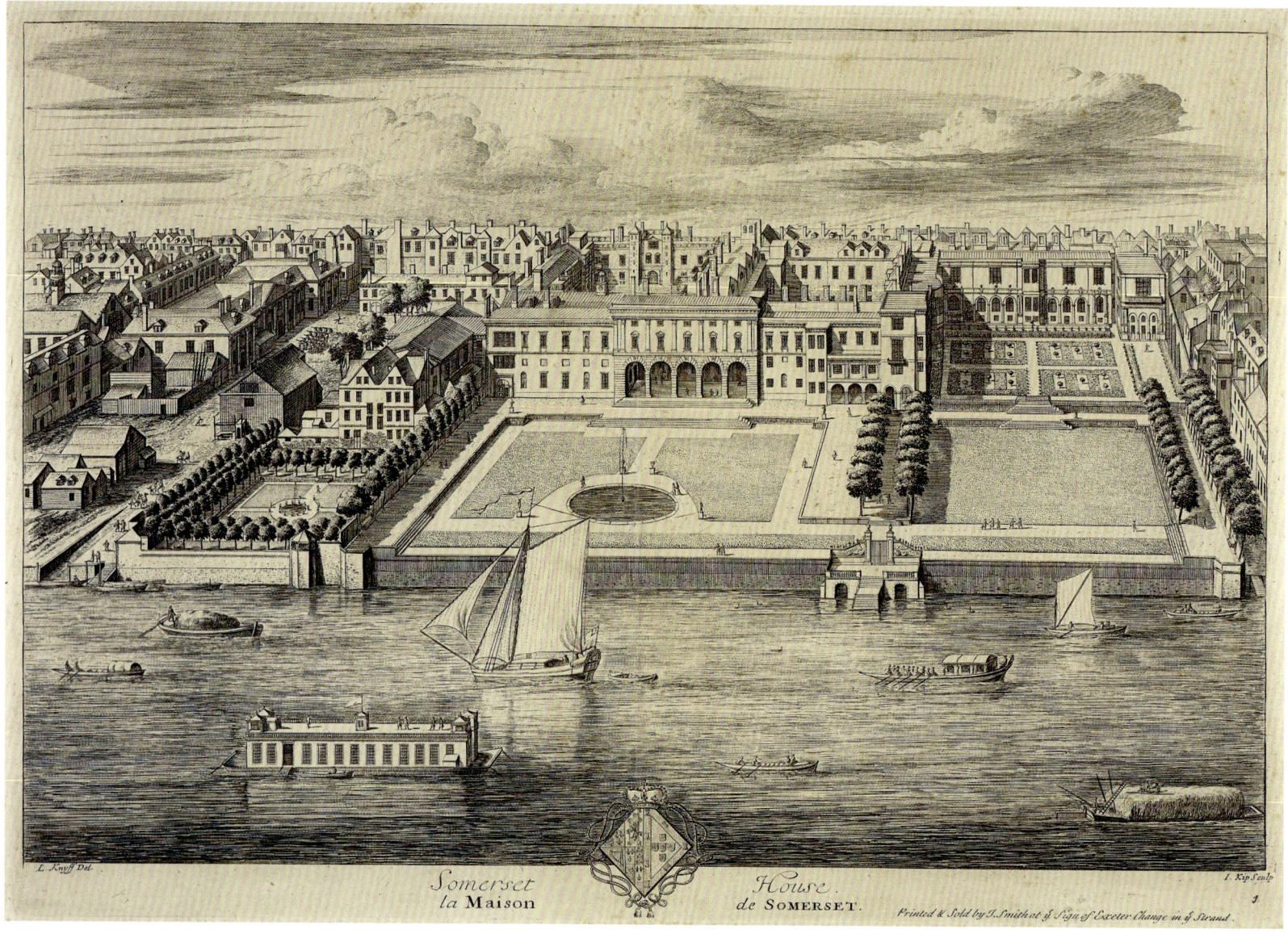

way further up the Strand to the garden of Northumberland House (see Chapter Eleven). Among the occupants of Somerset House had been the army, who transformed its interiors into their headquarters, partitioning rooms, removing panels, adding privies and so forth. Its state was therefore lamentable, and by the time the then dowager Queen Mother came back in November 1660, repairs had already begun.[65] These and a number of alterations were still under way in July 1662, when Henrietta Maria, after a long sojourn in France, was forced to stay at Greenwich. The palace was not fully ready for two more years and then was only briefly enjoyed: the aging dowager, blaming deteriorating health on the English climate, as Continentals do, decided to cross the Channel one last time in spring 1665.[66]

As we have seen, towards the end of her first phase of residence in the late 1630s, Henrietta had contemplated a complete reconstruction of the Strand front. That project, too onerous at the time and then perhaps too grand for a dower house, was definitely abandoned but attention switched back, after some fifty years, to the river side. An additional set of state rooms was built against the original south front of the main quadrangle, providing a new Great Staircase, Presence Chamber and Privy Chamber. The old Hall thus became a large antechamber for Henrietta's so-called 'Circle', a key royal event she had introduced in the 1630s, whereby courtiers and selected guests were received in her presence.[67] Perhaps more importantly, the new block occasioned the unification of the facade, with a carefully composed arcaded frontispiece based on

80 Somerset House, detail of Leonard Knyff and Jan Kip, *Britannia Illustrata or Views of Several of the Queen's Palaces also of the Principal Seats of the Nobility and Gentry of Great Britain*, 1707. © The Trustees of the British Museum (1880,1113.1421)

72 | LONDON'S 'GOLDEN MILE'

the Palazzo Magnani in Bologna or the Palazzo Guastaverza in Verona, but ultimately derived from Serlio (fig. 80). As for who designed this, Webb seems to be the most likely, having been acquainted with the queen through Jones since at least the 1620s. As in other instances, he may have worked under the Surveyor's supervision, which would explain why Colen Campbell stated that the front 'was taken from a Design of Inigo Jones, but conducted by another Hand', a view shared by another source which clearly points at such partnership. There were also Hugh May, the Paymaster of the Works, who figures in the accounts of 1661–2, and the Surveyor himself, Sir John Denham, whose roles remain uncertain.[68]

As well as allowing access from the garden, hence from the water gate, to the new suite, for the first time the Great Staircase connected the queen's apartments directly to the Chapel. This had been reinstated as a Catholic friary church on her return, when its French congregation had been removed to the Savoy Chapel next door. Its state, however, in spite of some preparations made, must have been unsatisfactory, as it too was entirely refitted. The house that had replaced the original friary was then refurbished back for that use, while a new block of lodgings was added against the Cross Gallery on the south-east of the palace, so as to accommodate the queen's household. Protected by a tall wall, it lay between that gallery and the back of the tenements along the Strand. The garden was also refashioned with new plinths for statues in front of Webb's facade.

The House of Catherine of Braganza: 1669–1705

Queen Henrietta Maria died on 10 September 1669 and Somerset House was granted to Catherine of Braganza, Charles II's wife. Unlike her predecessors, however, she preferred Whitehall and did not reside there until 1685, when she too became a widow. Catherine's tenure is therefore architecturally uneventful beyond a further restructuring of the Chapel, where galleries were added and the friary enlarged, and the construction of a vast stable block for fifty-six horses, probably designed by Robert Hooke, on the west of the house.[69] The stable yard can be seen in William Morgan's 1682 view of the complex and in plan in that by Morden and Lea of the following year (figs 81 and 82). In one thing, however, the queen was perfectly in tune with the previous occupant and that was the intense use of the palace for Catholic liturgy, which resulted in allegations of conspiracy around the Popish Plot of 1678. Catherine was seen as complicit in the plan for the assassination of Charles II that

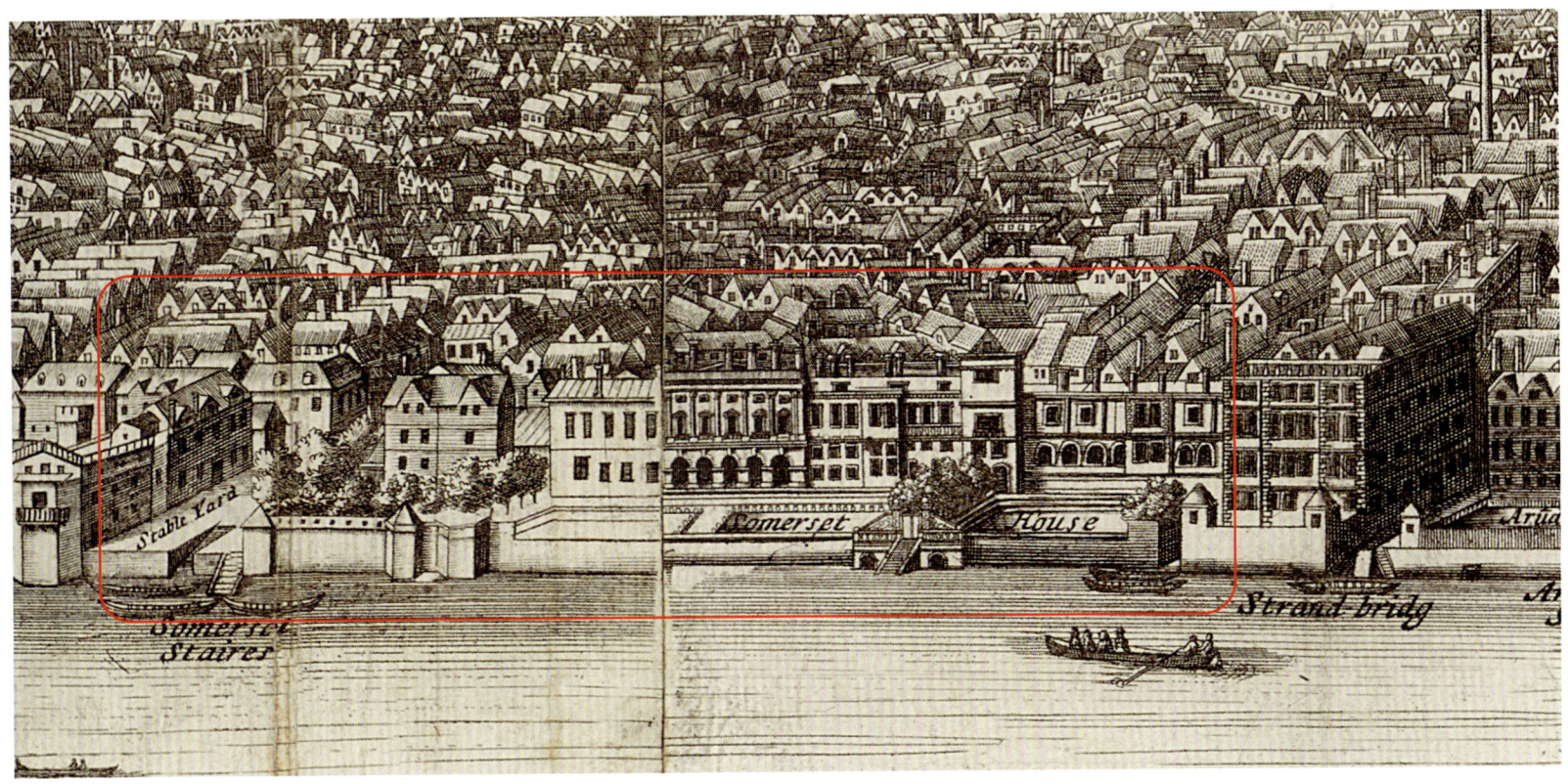

81 The complex of Somerset House with the stable yard on the left, detail of William Morgan, *London and Westminster*, c.1682 (detail of images on pp. x and xi). By permission of the Pepys Library, Magdalene College, Cambridge ('London and Westminster', I, 2972 38–39)

SOMERSET HOUSE | 73

would have cleared the way for the accession of his Catholic brother James, Duke of York. The Somerset House Chapel was therefore shut and the one at St James's Palace, where she had worshipped in the early years of her reign, reinstated. This coincided with the appointment as Catherine's Treasurer and Receiver General of Henry Hyde, 2nd Earl of Clarendon and brother-in-law of the Duke of York (whose father, the 1st Earl Lord Chancellor, had lived at Worcester House; see Chapter Seven), for whom the friary was converted back to a house. But all this did little to placate the opposition and the crisis erupted during the reign of James II himself, who had ascended to the throne in 1685. When he escaped to France with his second wife, Mary of Modena, and their son in 1688, Catherine of Braganza's house had to be protected against the mob, and Somerset House was effectively turned into a place of confinement for the isolated dowager. As the situation did not improve with William III, she eventually returned to Portugal in 1692, effectively marking the end of what was by then a century-old tradition of queen consorts residing at Somerset House. The following two queens, Anne and Caroline, were indeed granted the house but they chose not to inhabit it. The reasons were various. First of all, by the early eighteenth century, when Strype depicted the palace in his 1720 edition of the *Survey* (fig. 83), it must have been in serious disrepair, considering that since Catherine's time little had been done and then only to prevent collapse.[70] Secondly, and perhaps more significantly, the Strand had lost its prominence as the place to be several decades earlier, with all but a couple of the eleven great houses which once 'made' the area no longer extant. In their stead, new houses for the middle classes and a number of commercial ventures had been speedily erected, some of which, like the one put up by the Cecils, were short-lived. In this context, the dilapidated Somerset House became increasingly more incongruous and isolated, though it still sporadically hosted diplomatic parties and royal embassies, which occasioned the odd repairs. By 1761, the Strand front was 'much defaced by time and the smoke of the city', while the passage to the garden through the palace was 'extremely disagreeable, the broken staircase, the appearance of the walls, the darkness, and the filth, render it like the descent into a prison', as emphatically reported by the Dodsleys.[71] In 1771 George III handed over the

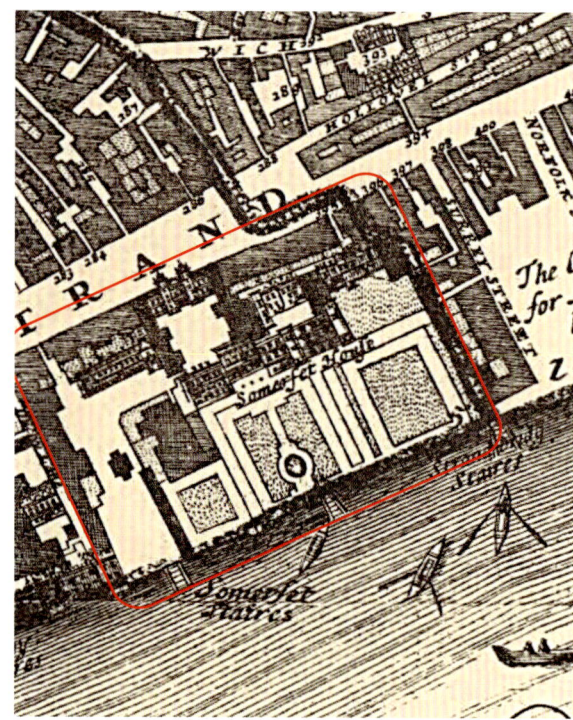

royal apartments to the newly established Royal Academy, a brief gift as merely three years later he agreed that the whole palace should be pulled down for the construction of public offices and that Buckingham House should instead become the queen's official dower house. So it was that the former, after being at the core of politics and architecture for more than two centuries, made way for Chambers's new Somerset House, while the latter was eventually transformed into the main London residence of British sovereigns.[72]

82 *above* The complex of Somerset House in Morden and Lea's map of London, 1682. U.S. Library of Congress Map Collections, published by London Topographical Society, 1904. Wikimedia Commons

83 *opposite* The complex of Somerset House in John Strype, *A Survey of the Cities of London and Westminster*, vol. 4, p. 116, 1720. Folger Shakespeare Library, Washington DC. Licensed under Creative Commons Attribution-ShareAlike 4.0 International

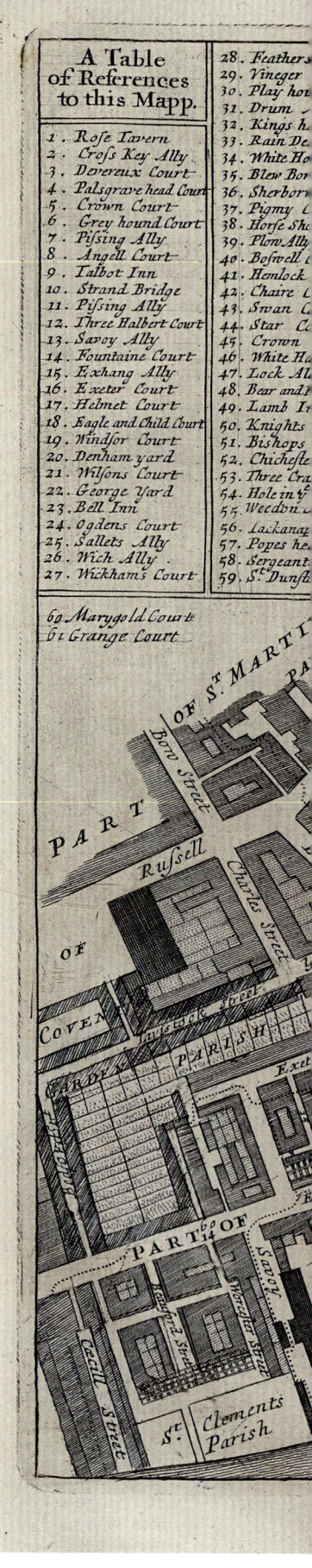

84 The Savoy complex between Dutchy Lane and Somerset House on the east (right) and Worcester House on the west (left) (detail of fig. 8)

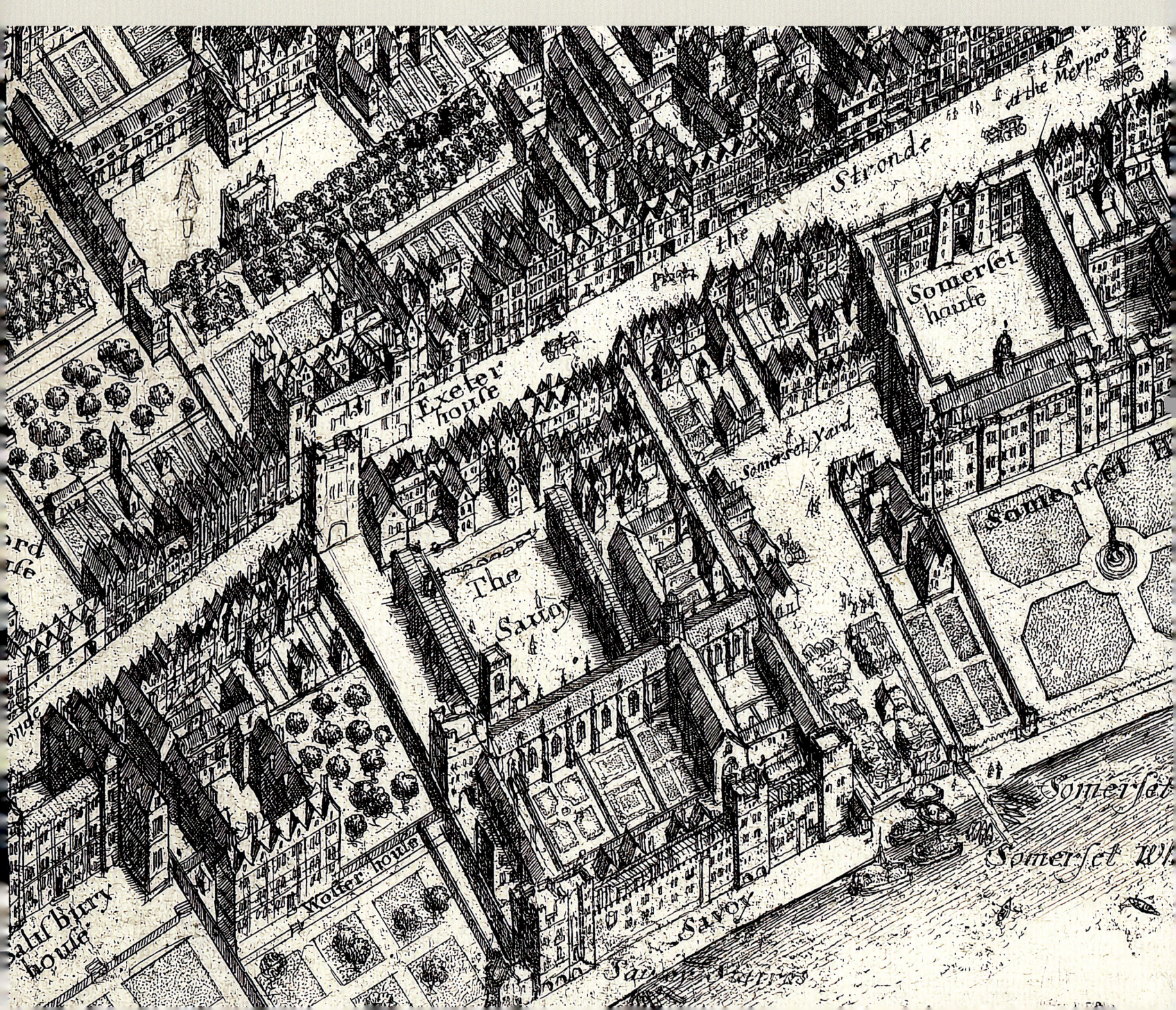

4 · THE SAVOY

LOCATED BETWEEN SOMERSET HOUSE AND Worcester House, the Savoy, or Savoy and Lancaster Palace, is different from the other Strand houses because its secular history largely predates the period covered here; in the sixteenth and seventeenth centuries it mainly served as a hospital, as well as other institutional purposes (fig. 84). The Savoy has been included in this book for historical and topographical continuity, and for useful insights into the development of the Strand up to the sixteenth century, which saw the rise of all the neighbouring bishops' inns. What follows, however, can only be a summary of its long history, drawn from the wide (if mostly repetitive) literature on London and the one monographic study by the Reverend William John Loftie published in 1878, still a unique though clearly dated contribution to the subject.[1] In fact the Savoy was never scrutinised by the Survey of London series (1900–), as it falls in the Parish of St Clement Danes, yet to be covered, while the extant archival evidence is extremely scattered.[2]

Private palace, then hospital, school, refugees' house, military barracks and prison, by the time of its demolition in the late eighteenth century the Savoy had long assumed its familiar appearance of a fortified complex right on the riverside, as depicted by John Norden in 1593 (fig. 85). The first available view is, however, in Wyngaerde's 1544 *Panorama some fifty years prior, which offers a comparable and fuller scene* (fig. 86). As well as the massive gatehouse in the top western corner – perhaps more isolated than in 1593 but for a couple of houses to the east – one sees the main body with three towers, two directly on the river's edge, together with the other wings forming the traditional cross-shaped hospital part of the complex.

The House of Peter, Count of Savoy: 1246–1268

According to Norden, the Savoy was first built by Peter, Count of Savoy (1203?–1268) and the uncle of Eleanor of Provence (d. 1296), who had married Henry III (1207–1272) in 1236.[3] By 1246, this illustrious representative of the 'Queen's poor relations crowding into England to see what they could obtain'[4] had received a grant of what became the nucleus of the complex. From this time date the earliest references to most of the neighbouring bishops' inns, an indication that by the 1250s the Strand was already scattered with major abodes. Such a description must also apply to the Savoy, though nothing except its magniloquent name attests to what Count Peter actually built. Henry's grant to his 'beloved uncle', for which an annual rent of 'three barbed arrows' was to be paid at Michaelmas, included 'all those Houses upon the Thames, which pertained to Brian Lisle, or de Insula, in the way, or the street, called the Strand'.[5] Two additions followed: the first, obtained from the Hospital of St James, was an area towards the south 'opposite the church of the Innocents' (what became St Mary-le-Strand), demolished by Protector Somerset to make way for his own palace (as seen in Chapter Three); the second, acquired from Bartholomew de Venyt, included the remaining parcels of ground on the west pertaining to Brian Lisle, together with land of the Bishop of Carlisle, whose neighbouring inn was the embryo of Worcester House (see Chapter Seven). This is about all we know of the Savoy's origins. In 1268, after a life spent between England and Savoy on a number of diplomatic missions, Peter died, leaving the palace to the monks of St Bernard the Great.[6]

The House of the Earls and Dukes of Lancaster: 1284–1399

The monks only briefly enjoyed ownership of the Savoy, as barely two years later Queen Eleanor acquired it for her son Edmund 'Crouchback', 1st Earl of Leicester and Lancaster (1245–1296), who later appears in full possession of it.[7] As with all the contemporary episcopal palaces, the Savoy must have been large enough to accommodate several households, so that what became known as the Queen's House provided not just for Edmund but for his older brother, the future Edward I (1239–1307), who lodged there with his wife Eleanor of Castile on bringing her back to England in 1265. It must have been in good repair too, as this second Queen Eleanor made it her town residence whenever she came to London. In 1279 the palace was then occupied by Alexander III, King of Scotland and Edward I's brother-in-law, known to have lodged between the 'courts' of the Bishop of Chichester, who must have resided within the complex, and the Earl of Lancaster, who with his wife Blanche probably continued to occupy part of his mother's house.

Eleanor of Provence's grant to 'her most dear son' Edmund, dated 24 February 1284, included the 'Domos, gardinum, placeas et redditus cum

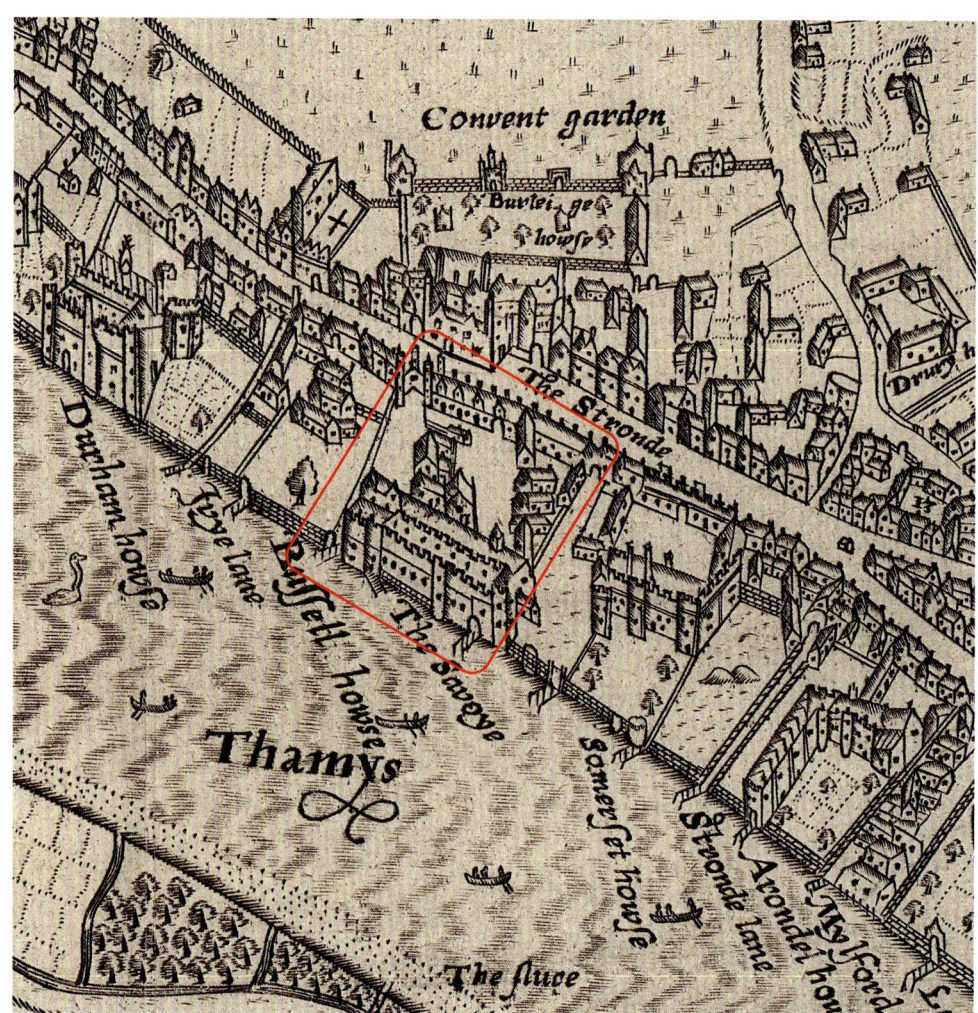

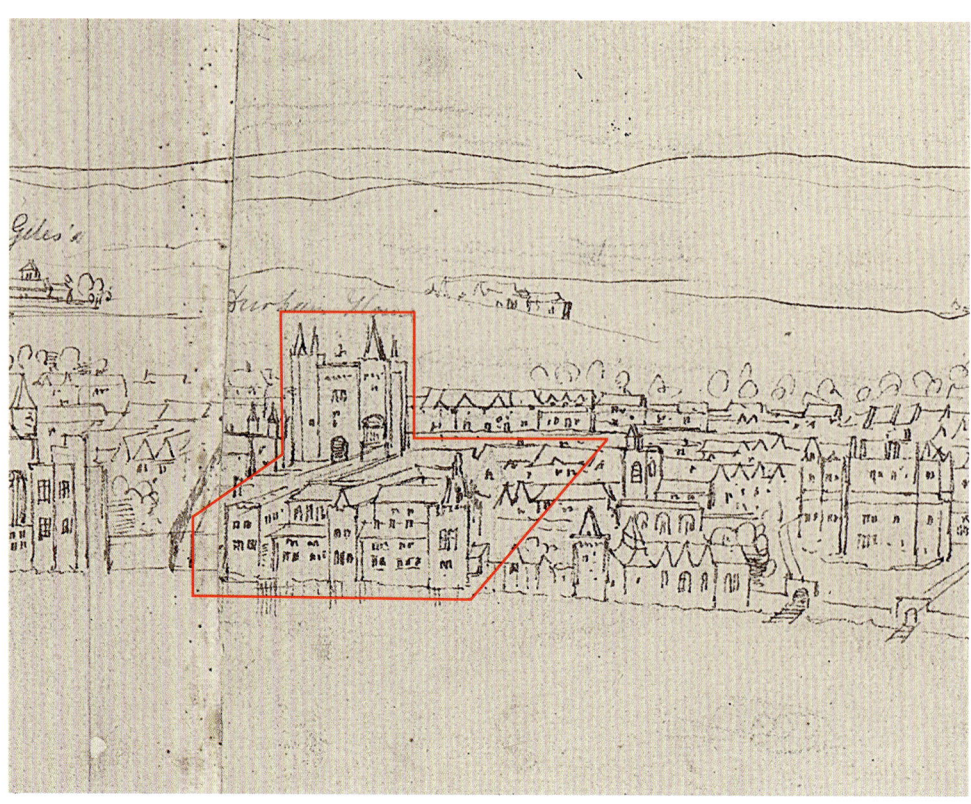

85 The Savoy complex, detail of John Norden, *Speculum Britanniae*, 1593. Folger Shakespeare Library, Washington DC. Licensed under Creative Commons Attribution-ShareAlike 4.0 International

86 The Savoy complex, detail of Anthonis van den Wyngaerde, *Panorama of London from the River*, c.1544 (detail of fig. 9). © Ashmolean Museum, University of Oxford

pertinentis suis' – a complex with a number of different buildings, some surely along the Strand, as well as orchards, from which rent could be drawn.[8] The specification of a 'gardinum' also points to a fairly formal space where the Earl of Lancaster is asserted to have conveyed some plants of the famous red rose from Provence that became the emblem of his dynasty.[9] While the garden may have preserved rare species, the main house was licensed in 1293 to crenellate or fortify the complex, thus to be surrounded by a wall 'de petra et calce' (stone and mortar).[10] This may well have coincided with further aggrandisement and gave the Savoy the defensive aspect with which it eventually became associated, even if Vertue's image of 1736 (fig. 87) has little in common with its thirteenth-century status, as will be shown.

87 George Vertue, 'A View of the Savoy from the River Thames', 1736, from *Vetusta Monumenta*, 1789, vol. 2. © The Trustees of the British Museum (1880,1113.1397)

After Earl Edmund's death in 1296, the Savoy passed to his eldest son, Thomas, 2nd Earl of Lancaster (c.1278–1322),[11] of whose tenure we know next to nothing except that he added to a grant of land to the Bishop of Llandaff first made by his father in 1280, later absorbed by the construction of Somerset House (see Chapter Three). In 1315 Edward II (1284–1327) signed an ordinance, apparently triggered by the 2nd Earl, for the paving of the Strand, still in perilous condition despite its much increased commercial importance.[12] Many such acts are recorded over the long history of the thoroughfare, notably during the period of both William and Robert Cecil, among the most prominent and civically engaged residents of the area (see Chapters Five and Eight).

As far as the ownership of the Savoy is concerned, Thomas's turbulent role in the political events eventually cost him his head and the palace was granted to Edward, Earl of Chester and Edward II's eldest son, soon after it had been sequestered in 1322. But in 1324 it was restored in an uneventful succession to the 3rd Earl of Lancaster, Thomas's brother Henry (c.1280–1345).[13] It was instead the tenure of Henry, 4th Earl and later 1st Duke of Lancaster (c.1310–1361),[14] that marked a considerable expansion of the Savoy's grounds, which then reached their final size. Acquisitions, concentrated in the second half of the 1340s, included all the land and houses belonging to Sir Henry le Scrop, or Scrope, in the parishes of St Mary-le-Strand and St Clement Danes.[15] This probably coincided with the process of enlargement and beautification costing 52,000 marks reported by Walter Harrison in 1776, according to whom it had started in 1328 and had rendered the palace 'so superb ... as to exceed in magnificence every other structure in the kingdom'.[16] This extravagant expenditure was rumoured to have been supported by Henry's greatest achievement on the field, the 1345 victory against the French whereby the Agenais and much of Périgord and Quercy were regained, in addition to ransoms amounting to £50,000.[17]

Following Henry's elevation to the dukedom in 1351, the Savoy became the headquarters of the great Duchy Palatine of Lancaster, with the right to exercise all liberties belonging to the County Palatine, formerly enjoyed by the Earl of Chester. The Chapel of St John's, the only surviving part of the original complex, thus became a 'Chapel Royal'.[18] In 1353, and again in 1359 and 1361, there was more paving of the Strand, which was so deep and muddy from the constant passage of carts and carriages bringing goods to the market at Westminster that a toll had to be levied. Another sign of the increasing urbanisation of the area is afforded by a grant made by the duke in 1355 of a parcel of his Savoy land for the enlargement of the cemetery of the church of St Mary-le-Strand (later yet another casualty of the Protector's building works). On and off from 1357, as the 'fairest Manor of England' the Savoy became the enforced residence of John, King of France, captured at the Battle of Poitiers.[19]

The 1st Duke of Lancaster died without male issue and was succeeded by his daughters, Matilda or Maud and Blanche, respectively Countess and Duchess of Lancaster. Matilda died with no heirs in 1362, so Blanche inherited the entire estate with her husband, John of Gaunt (1340–1399;

THE SAVOY | 79

they married in 1359), who became 1st Duke of Lancaster of the new creation. He was the fourth son of Edward III and the father of the future Henry IV.[20] It is at this point in his history that Loftie attempts a description of the complex by way of merging miscellaneous sources, including verses from Geoffrey Chaucer, a protégé of the Duke and Duchess of Lancaster who considered the palace 'a constant resort of his' and married a member of the household in the chapel.[21] Such an attempt can only be made by comparing the Savoy with other contemporary structures such as the episcopal Durham House, about which more can be deduced as it survived seemingly unaltered into the age of maps. Yet this is an appropriate moment in the Savoy's history for a description since the palace was shortly afterwards destroyed.

The house of John of Gaunt, as it was then referred to, probably consisted of a principal courtyard building surrounded by ancillary structures, probably located nearer the river than the Strand, for both practical and aesthetic reasons. Access would have been either via the traditional water gate, possibly a simple passage through the river wall, or via a much more prominent gatehouse along the street, which acted as the main and most formal access to the complex, as in most bishops' inns. It is known that since 1293 the palace was protected by stone walls, while its overall appearance, again as customary, was one of fortification. This did not, however, mean lack of decoration, for the architecture seems to have abounded in typically medieval elements such as vanes of different colours and shapes. Of this characteristic mixture we may get some glimpses in Chaucer's 'Dream', which Loftie convincingly linked to the Savoy as it is an allegory related to the union of John and Blanche, whose marriage was supposed to have been one of love (though short-lived for she died in 1368):

> *Within an isle methought I was,*
> *Where wall and gate was of glass*
> *And so was closed round about*
> *That leave less none come in nor out,*
> *Uncouth and strange to behold*
> *For every gate of fine gold,*
> *A thousand vanes, aye turning,*
> *Entuned had and birds singing*
> *Diverse: and on each vane a pair,*
> *With open mouths against the air.*
> *And of a suite were all the towers,*
> *Subtly carven after flowers*

> *Of uncouth colours, during aye,*
> *That never been none seen in May,*
> *With many a small turret high.*[22]

Loftie also called on Chaucer's poem 'The Boke of the Duchesse, or the Dethe of Blanche', since its description of her rich chamber as 'well depainted, and with glass' is again believed to refer to the Savoy. And so it goes on, for a number of other verses include references to both interiors and exteriors which, if not expressly related to the Strand palace, may well, as Loftie wrote, 'suit our purpose'.[23] At the same time, we do know that the garden, which may have surrounded the palace on more than one side, was well kept, as information about the wages of the Duke's gardener has survived.[24] Equally clear is that the Savoy under John of Gaunt must have reached its golden age as the seat of a royal court, with a licence from 1377 for a chancery of the duchy. That office was filled by a number of later residents of the Strand such as the formidable William and Robert Cecil, the latter even keeping a set of rooms in the palace.

The increase in magnificence of the Savoy seems to have been paralleled (as not infrequently in history) by the growing unpopularity of its owner, whose power had risen to a dangerous peak. So much so that in 1381 an angry mob of the 'Rebels of Kent and Essex, did most barbarously burn this House, with many Vessels of Gold and Silver, which they threw onto the River; all of which they did out of popular malice to John of Gaunt'.[25] Other sources report on the lavishness of its interiors, for which five carts 'would hardly have carried all the silver and jewels, not to mention the pure gold and gilt plate'. Loftie also relates how the insurgents, attracted by the fine spirits kept in the cellars, managed to trap themselves and 'perished in wine', or how they mistook barrels of gunpowder for gold and silver, cast them into the fire and 'blew up the Hall, destroyed the houses, and almost themselves'.[26] At all events, the Savoy seems to have been largely dismantled and lay as a source of building materials, such as lead, for the next sixteen years until the duke's death on 2 February 1399. John of Gaunt was succeeded by his son, Henry of Bolingbroke (1367–1413), who a fortnight before had become King of England and who annexed the palace to the Crown, together with the whole of the Lancaster estates. In the following years miscellaneous documents attest to considerable building works probably concentrated on the houses along the Strand, though some refer to repairs to the tower called 'Symeon Toure' and to both the street and water gates. One of these buildings may have been used as the gaol, as a couple of references attest to the existence of one. Another entry mentions a house called the 'Hertishorne' located between the 'Floure de lise' and the garden of the Prior of St John's, who had probably retained a garden by the river when he resigned the stewardship of the Savoy. These references are interesting as they became part of later transactions: both the Hartshorne and the Fleur de Lis were granted to William Cecil, while the latter's site eventually became part of his estate (see Chapter Five).[27] As for the palace itself, we can only assume that it survived in its dilapidated form well into the early years of the Tudor dynasty, when Henry VII decreed that it should be turned into a hospital. This decision is mentioned in his will of 1509, which attests to some building activity being in progress 'after the maner, fourme and fashion of a plat which is devised for the same, and signed with our hande'. Endowed with lands and tenements, it was to provide 'oon hundredth beds garnished, to receive and lodge nightly oon hundredth pouer folks, as also a certain number of Preists, and other ministers and servitours, men and women'. These were granted 'boks, chalices, vestments, aultre clothes, aultre tables, and other implementes', while a master was to be appointed.[28] Master and brethren were apparently to take turns at the main gate to take and feed any person deemed 'an object of charity'. A traveller was to be lodged for one night and provided with a letter of recommendation and sufficient money to reach the next hospital.[29]

The Hospital: 1509–1702

The new hospital was not actually opened until 1517, since much activity was required for its foundation. Not least was the clearing and rebuilding of the site, which must have concentrated on the area formerly occupied by the main house. What was granted to the king's executors was in fact only the 'scitum maneri nostri de Savoy', where the palace had stood, described as between the properties of the Bishop of Worcester on the east and of the Bishop of Carlisle on the west, while the rest of the complex evidently remained part of the Crown estates. In 1512 the executors were given licence to found the hospital, by which time works must have progressed for in November 1514 Cardinal Wolsey, then Archbishop of York and as such resident of York House (see Chapter Eleven), held two councils at the Savoy. Humphrey Cook, Henry VIII's Master Carpenter, is credited with the work by an inscription in the Chapel, where he was buried in 1530, while the priest William Holgil supervised the construction.[30] The latter became the first master of the new hospital, the statutes of which were confirmed in 1524. There were two priests who assisted a matron and a woman under her, a doctor and a surgeon, a baker, a cook and sub-cook, as well as a gardener and porter.[31] Henry VII's establishment 'for the reliefe of 100 poore people … performed by the most famous Hen.[ry] 8 his sonne, and sufficiently furnished with lande, and revenues, for the maintenance thereof', as Norden recalls, thus begun to function.[32] While the earliest available depiction of the complex, as previously stated, dates from around the 1540s (see fig. 86), contemporary evidence suggests that it attracted attention from foreign visitors, including three French gentlemen who 'desired among other things to see the Hospital of Savoy' and were shown 'notable th[ings in] the said hospital'.[33] This is not surprising, as the hospital was among the first to be established in the capital. It also appears to have grown fairly quickly, as by 1535 what had not been included in the initial grant, namely 'divers houses within the precinct' of the Savoy, as well as gardens and orchards, were endowed to the establishment.[34]

Within the next couple of decades, the Savoy Hospital was suppressed and funded again by Edward VI, who had succeeded his father in 1547, and Queen Mary, who succeeded after her half-brother's death in 1553. During this period of uncertainty, the Savoy attracted a different sort of attention, from William Cecil, who was in the process of building his own Strand palace right opposite the Savoy and was seeking any opportunity for expansion (see Chapter Five).[35] Although Cecil did not succeed in securing the hospital's land, his position as Secretary of State allowed him to control its future, which was once again threatened by a change of ruler, as Elizabeth I had succeeded Mary after her death in 1558. It was indeed the Secretary who in 1574 reappointed one of the hospital's most controversial masters, Thomas Thurland, first elected in 1559 and then removed because he had 'embezelled the Revenues exceedingly, made many Leases and Sales privately without the Knowledge and

Consent of the Chaplains' and 'sold away divers Chantries (settled perhaps by Queen Mary upon the Hospital) to the Sum of 53l. per Annum'.[36] In these circumstances, one would expect the Savoy to have fallen into disrepair. Yet, some building activity may have been carried out, as the second available view of the hospital, in the so-called 'Agas' map of London of 1561–70 (fig. 88), seems to show a more developed site than in the 1540s, when Wyngaerde first depicted it (see fig. 86). The fortified appearance of the wing along the river, for instance, is much more prominent, while previously unseen dwellings appear next to the Strand gatehouse. As this is comparable with Norden's view of 1593 (see fig. 85), we can assume that most of the enlargement of the Savoy Hospital was in fact carried out between the 1540s and the 1560s, when it is generally believed to have been neglected.

Thomas Thurland was succeeded by William Mount in 1575, during whose mastership the Savoy was first used as barracks for the troops who came to protect Cecil (or Burghley) and, later, Exeter House against the abortive rebellion of the Earl of Essex. Mount died in 1602, by which time further buildings seem to have been added to the main complex, as can be seen in Norden's updated map reprinted two years before (fig. 89). He was succeeded by Richard Neale, yet another of Cecil's creatures as his former domestic chaplain. In 1603, Queen Elizabeth died and a new era in the history of the hospital began. Following Neale's nomination as the Dean of Westminster in 1605, George Montaigne

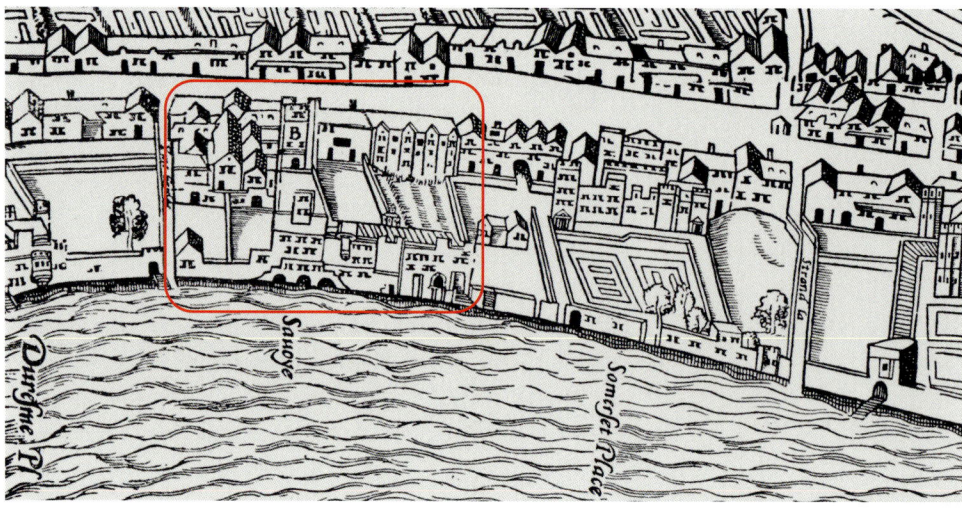

became the new master, leaving an interesting account which covers the revenues of the Savoy for a full year. We thus learn (or perhaps have confirmed given the prominence of the site) that the 'Tenements within the Savoy gates' were in fact lucratively let to persons of office and high rank, who competed with each other to secure a dwelling in the Strand. Much as with any of the other palaces studied in this book, such practices had long been followed (including under Thurland's tenure) and endured until the troubles in the reign of Charles I.

The list of tenants in Montaigne's account also reveals the various premises which adjoined the main hospital. Sir David Murray, for instance, occupied the 'innermost tower near the chapel door with other rooms', for a yearly rent of £4. 'The great Tower or Gatehouse' was let for £6 a

88 The Savoy complex, detail of the *Woodcut Map of London*, 1561–70 ('Agas'), reprinted 1633, derived from the lost 'Copperplate Map of London', 1553–9. Mitton 1908. Wikimedia Commons Public Domain

89 The Savoy complex, detail of John Norden, *Civitas Londini*, 1600. National Library of Sweden

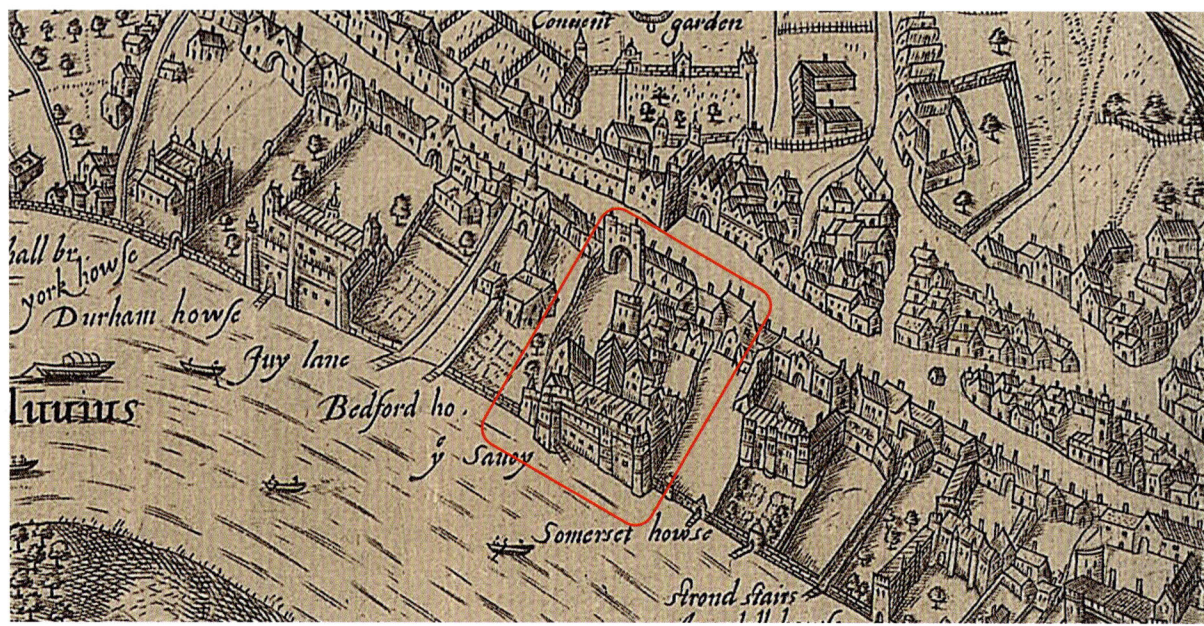

year to George, Lord Carew, who seems to have continued to live there while Master General of the Ordnance and after he was elevated to the Earldom of 'Totness' in 1626. The lodgings of Sir George Manners (who succeeded his brother as 7th Earl of Rutland in 1632 and whose niece had married George Villiers, 1st Duke of Buckingham) were by the 'Common Water Gate' and must have been simpler given the rent of £1 a year. Equally priced were the rooms formerly of a member of the same family: a Mr Roger Manners had lived 'over the Poor Gate', then occupied by Sir Francis Fane. Yet another Manners, Lady Elizabeth (a first cousin of Sir George), who had married Thomas Cecil, 1st Earl of Exeter, had also kept a lodging there for £2 a year, and there are letters dated from the Savoy by the earls of Huntingdon, Cumberland and Northampton (not the Henry Howard of Northampton House on the Strand). According to Pennant, Cumberland and Northampton had lived and died in 1605 and 1630 respectively at the 'Dutchy House', part of those tenements formerly belonging to the Duchy of Lancaster, 'the claim to which', as Harrison reported, 'has been so long dormant, that the tenants in possession have supported an exclusive title to the premises, and have constantly lived in them without paying any rent, besides the common parish taxes'.[37] But at least in one case this was an exaggeration, as Northampton appears to have been charged £4 a year in Montaigne's list. In 1609, all the rents amounted to more than £32 of annual income, which clearly added financial appeal to the Mastership of the Savoy. Lord Carew described the income in a letter, after Montaigne too moved to the Deanery of Westminster in 1617, as one 'of no great worth, yet somewhat hath some favour'.[38]

After the brief tenure of one Walter Balcanquall, the position fell to the Archbishop of Split, Marco Antonio de Dominis, who held it from 1618 to 1621. Nothing seems to be known of the connection with the Savoy of this controversial priest, 'a man for many masters' who seems to have taken either Protestant or Catholic side on personal convenience and eventually died a heretic in Rome in 1624.[39] Perhaps because of his position, however, the Savoy Chapel was put forward for the Infanta's use in 1623, when the Spanish match was still being negotiated. In 1626, when Durham House was being investigated in relation to gatherings of Catholics, attention was also called to the Hospital 'where masse is usually sayd and much resort of people to it'. As a result, Balcanquall, reappointed after de Dominis, was required to seize 'all the Popish books and Massinge stuffe that shall be found there'.[40]

Beginning from Wyngaerde's 1544 view, the various depictions of the Savoy Hospital have offered an idea of how it developed into an articulated complex predominantly by the river but with additional parts towards the Strand. By far its best representation, however, is in Hollar's bird's-eye view of the 'West Central District', executed no later than 1666 (see fig. 84). In addition to the wing by the Thames (seen in almost all previous views), one can clearly distinguish a neat cruciform structure right behind it, which forms a series of courtyards including three elaborate gardens. Along the western boundary with Worcester House stands the prominent gatehouse, aligned with two further towers towards the river. Adjacent to the middle tower rises the Chapel's bell-tower, which sits at the south end of a long nave. The bell-tower and the hospital wings appear battlemented, as typical of the period, with high ogival windows, while a lantern sits prominently on top of the crossing. This particular feature can be distinguished in Agas's depiction of the 1560s and again in Norden's views, especially that of 1593 (see figs 85 and 88), though only Wyngaerde and Hollar illustrate the cruciform structure. Pennant, however, while clearly stating that the hospital was indeed 'in form of a cross', remarks how its 'walls ... are entire to this time', referring to Henry VII's original foundation.[41] Although pre-Hollar views are partial, modern understanding of the hospital's development by the 1560s depends on them. Hollar's depiction, by contrast, is generally confirmed by Richard Newcourt's in 1658 (fig. 90), rough though it is, and by George Vertue's drawings made in 1732 (figs 92 and 91 and see fig. 87).

Balcanquall's death in 1645 coincided with the civil commotion that marked the end of Charles I's reign. During most of the Interregnum the Savoy was headed by John Bond and apparently turned into a refuge for foreigners and Roman Catholics. By contrast, after the Restoration in 1660, it became the venue for the celebrated Savoy Conference in 1661, hosted by Gilbert Sheldon, the Bishop of London and new Master. Aiming to revise the Book of Common Prayer, this was a meeting between the restored Anglicans and the Presbyterians, which led to the Act of Uniformity in 1662, the 'Clarendon Code', named after one of its principal creators, Edward Hyde, 1st Earl of Clarendon and Charles II's Lord Chancellor (conveniently, he lived next door in Worcester House; see Chapter Seven). This was the last notable event in the history of the Savoy, for thereafter it entered a period of slow but irreversible decline both in significance and use and consequently in the actual fabric of the building. The next few years were marked by a petition against a French congregation being established on the premises: a certain 'Mr. d'Espagne' had erected there 'a new church without any authority of licence', thereby upsetting a rival congregation in the City.[42] The church was none the less granted letters patent in March 1661 and remained in place until at least the 1750s, when Vertue's 1736 plan of the complex was published: it clearly includes the 'French Church' on the east side (fig. 91).

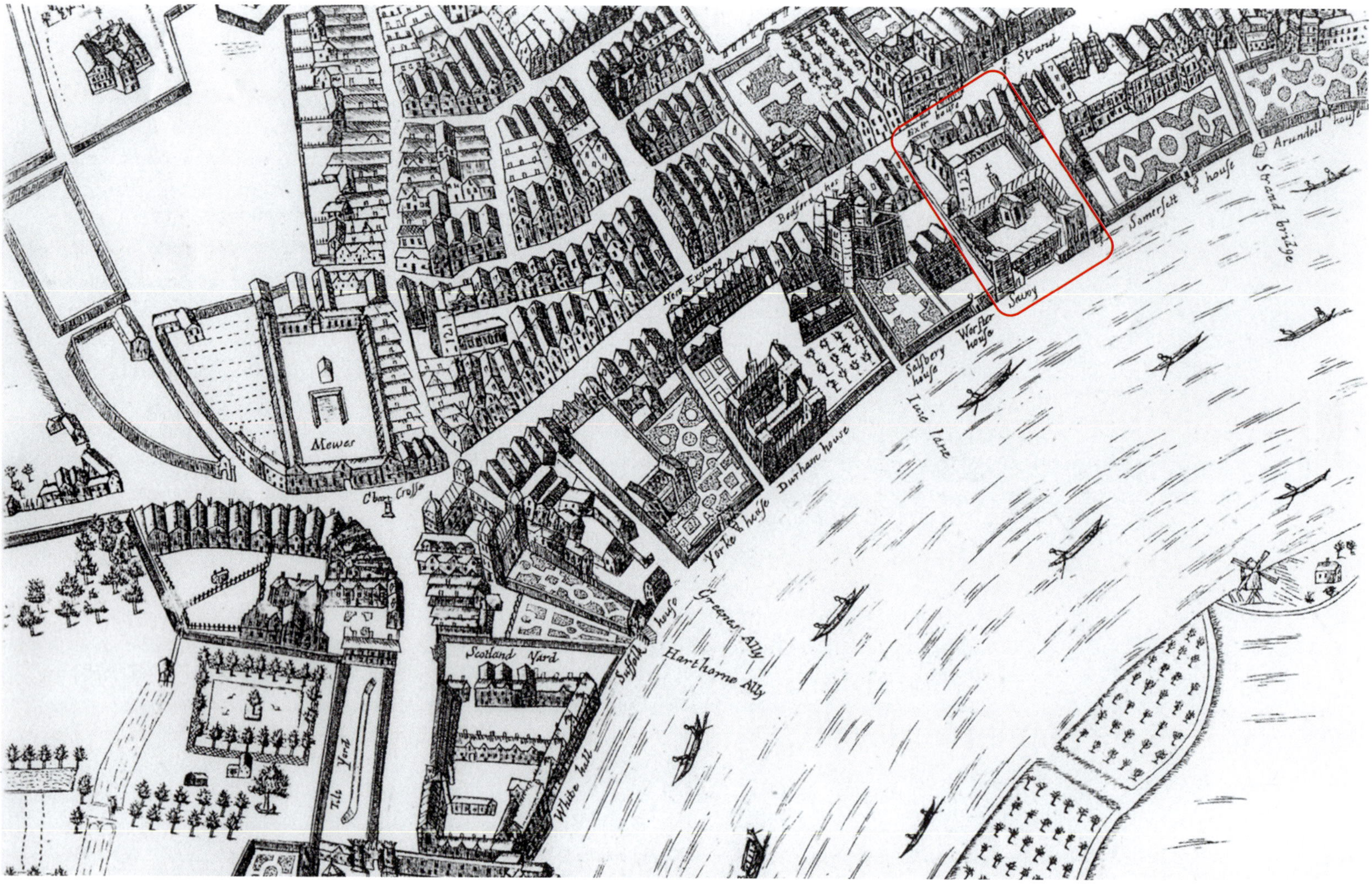

Just as Worcester House was searched for 'hidden treasure' by the Council of State in May 1660, so too was the Savoy in 1661 when a

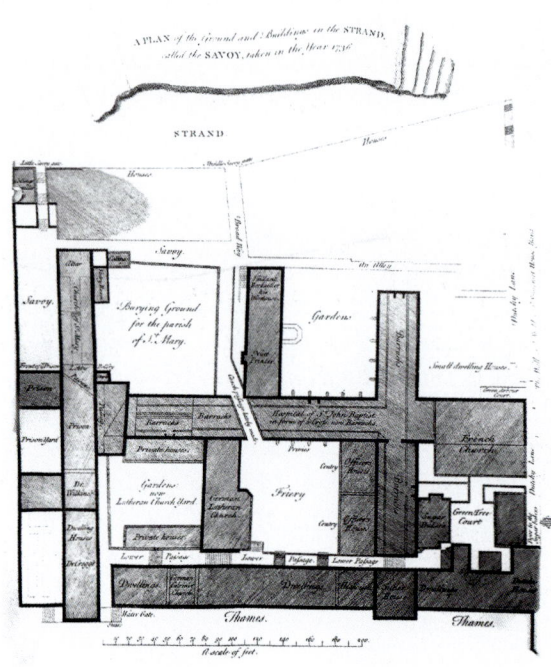

90 The Savoy complex, detail of Richard Newcourt and William Faithorne, 'An exact delineation of the City of London and Westminster', 1658. By kind permission of the Syndics of Cambridge University Library (Map Room, Maps BB.77.90.14)

91 George Vertue, plan of the Savoy Hospital, 1736. *Vetusta Monumenta*, 1789, vol. 2, pl. XIV

92 *opposite* George Vertue, views of the Savoy Hospital, 1753: on the left the entrance to the prison and on the right part of the chapel. *Vetusta Monumenta*, 1789, vol. 2, pl. XII. © The Trustees of the British Museum (1880,0911.1295)

84 | LONDON'S 'GOLDEN MILE'

The SAVOY HOSPITAL in the STRAND.   Vol. II. Plate XII.

AN historical account of the Savoy, so called from Peter earl of Savoy, who built a palace there, has been given already in Plate V of this Volume. But that palace being destroyed by the rebels of Kent and Essex, this hospital was erected there by K. Henry VII. In memory whereof the date of its foundation, with the two following Latin verses written in the manner of those times, were placed over the gate towards the street.

1505
HOSPITIVM HOC INOPI TVRBE SAVOIA VOCATVM
SEPTIMVS HENRICVS FVNDAVIT AB IMO SOLO.

That inscription remained till the building was burnt down, not long after the great fire of London in 1666, as Newcourt relates, Repertor. Vol. I. pag. 696.

The CHAPEL of the HOSPITAL.

THIS chapel now serveth as a parish church to the tenements near adjoining, and others in the neighbourhood; and is reckoned in the bills of mortality, as one of the seven parishes in the city and liberties of Westminster, by the name of St. Mary Savoy.

G. Vertue delin. et sculp.   Sumptu Societ. Ant. Lond. 1753.

Published according to Act of Parliament. Nov. 29. 1753.

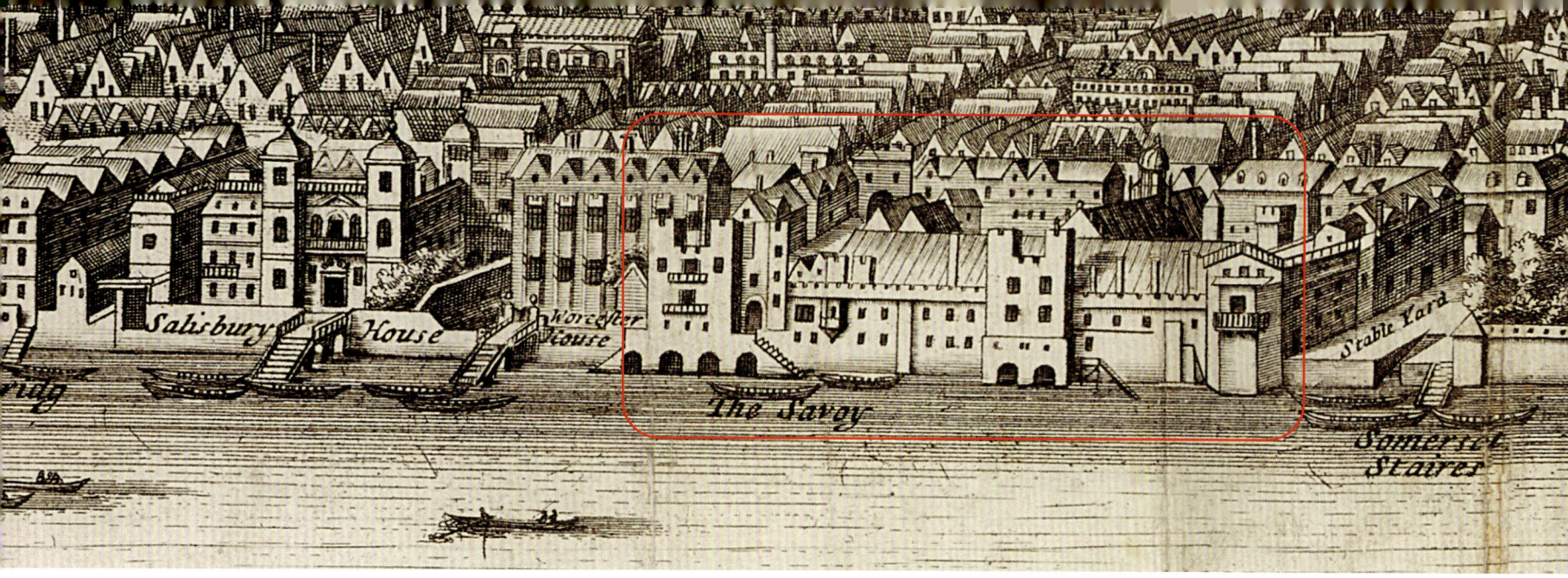

warrant was granted to search for goods belonging to the late king, Cromwell and other figures excepted from the Act of Oblivion. That year a fire also destroyed the houses of the chaplains, and then in 1670 Parliament granted permission to lease part of the premises for forty years, whereby new houses were built within the site. In the meantime, Henry Killigrew, the younger brother of Thomas (the well-known dramatist and a Groom of the Bedchamber to Charles II), had been appointed the new master.[43] Henry Killigrew's long tenure, from 1663 to 1697, saw the removal of the king's printers from the Savoy, its partial transformation into military barracks and the erection of a church and school for the Jesuits, founded by James II in 1686. In 1682 the palace appeared in William Morgan's *View of London and Westminster* (fig. 93). However unlikely a Jesuit school might have seemed from the site's history, 'it was not improbable that the new academy in the Savoy', as Macaulay reported in 1848, 'might, under royal patronage, prove a formidable rival to the great foundations of Eton, Westminster and Winchester'. But, he continues, 'the populace, which is always more moved by what impresses the senses than by what is addressed to the reason ... saw with dismay and indignation a Jesuit college rising on the banks of the Thames, friars in hoods and gowns walking in the Strand', ignoring the fact that such scenes had been commonplace before the Dissolution, when the area was scattered with convents.[44] In any event, the Jesuits' attempt was short-lived, as the school was dissolved immediately on the deposition of James in 1688, merely two years after its foundations.

With the accession of William and Mary, the status of the Savoy declined further. In 1697, a bill was passed for abolishing its privileges of sanctuary, whereby those 'bad characters' who had been lodged there escaped 'to Ireland, to France, to the colonies, to vaults and garrets in less notorious parts of the capital'.[45] The hospital was officially dissolved in July 1702, two years after the death of Henry Killigrew, its last master. By then, the whole complex had been leased as tenements apart from the main cruciform building, which was divided between barracks and military hospital, and the master's house and chapel. The chaplains' lodgings, burnt some forty years previously, had never been rebuilt and lay in ruins.

The condition of the Savoy in the early eighteenth century was described by Strype in 1720, whose account and view of the complex (fig. 94) provide precious glimpses:

> *This Savoy House is very great and at this present a very ruinous Building. In the midst of its Buildings, is a very spacious Hall, the Walls three Foot broad at least, of Stone without, and Brick and Stone inward. The Ceiling is very curiously built with Wood, and having Knobs in due Places hanging down, and Images of Angels holding before their Breasts Coats of Arms, but hardly discoverable. On one is a cross Gules between four stars, or else Mullets. It is covered with Lead, but in divers Places perished, where it lies open to the Weather. This large Hall is now divided into several Apartments. A Cooper hath a Part of it for the stowing of his Hoops, and for his Work. Other Parts of it serve for two Marshalseas for keeping Prisoners, as Deserters, Men prest for military Service, Dutch*

93 The Savoy, detail of William Morgan, *View of London and Westminster*, c.1682 (detail of images on pp. x and xi). By permission of the Pepys Library, Magdalene College, Cambridge ('London and Westminster', I, 2972, 38–39)

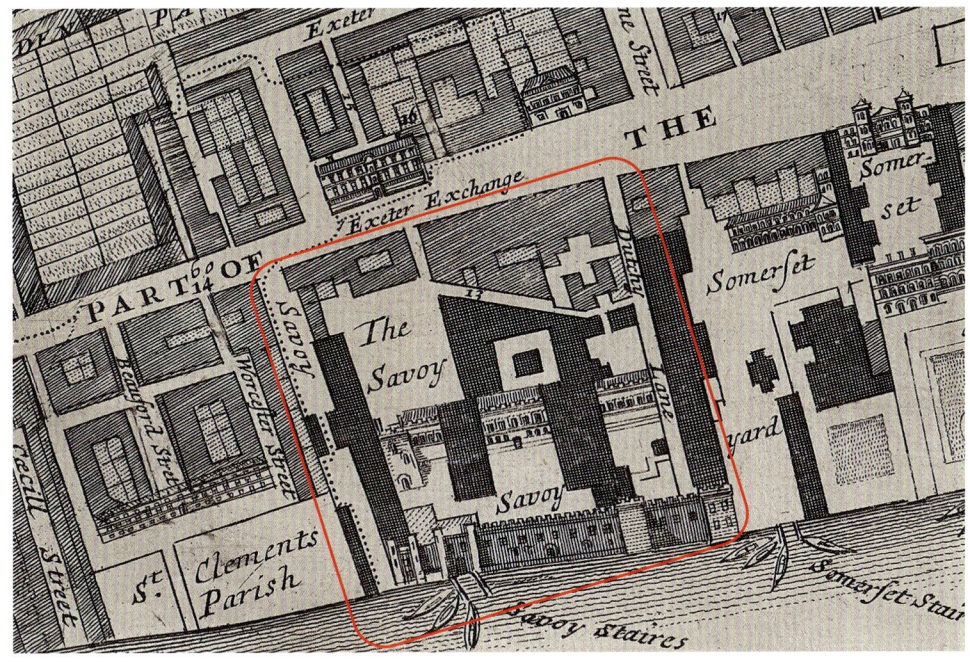

94 The Savoy complex in John Strype, *A Survey of the Cities of London and Westminster*, 1720, vol. 6, p. 87, 1720 (detail of fig. 83). Folger Shakespeare Library, Washington DC. Licensed under Creative Commons Attribution-ShareAlike 4.0 International

95 W. Deeble, a view of the Savoy Hospital in ruin. Hughson 1817, vol. 1, p. 207

Recruits, &c. Towards the East End of this Hall is a fair Cupolo with Glass Windows, but all broken, which makes it probable the Hall was as long again; since Cupoloes [sic] are wont to be built about the middle of great Halls … [46]

When the hospital was dissolved, a number of the many leases granted by Killigrew still had several years to run and, while rents appear to have been improved in 1715, in 1739 enquiries were made as it was found that some of the tenants were refusing to pay. They had bought keys and gained possession of several houses, apparently disregarding the legality of their holdings. Vertue's drawings illustrate the complex not long afterwards (see figs 87, 92 and 91). If their neatness perhaps conceals the actual state of affairs, their reliability is confirmed by Strype, whose record of the complex largely echoes the arrangement of Vertue's plan of the 'Grounds and Buildings' (see fig. 91). In 'this Savoy', as Strype continues after his earlier, somewhat romantic description, 'how ruinous soever is, are divers good Houses. First, the King's Printing Press for Proclamations, Acts of Parliaments, Gazets, and such like publick Papers', evidently re-established after its suppression during Killingrew's mastership. 'Next a Prison. Thirdly, a Parish Church, and three or four other Churches and Places for Religious Assemblies; viz. For the French, for Dutch, for High Germans, and Lutherans, and Lastly, for the Protestant Dissenters.'[47]

The decline of the Savoy can be followed through subsequent chronicles, which provide eye-witness accounts of some poignancy. In 1761, Robert and James Dodsley reported that 'nothing here is to be seen, but the ruins of the ancient edifice built with free-stone and flint, among which is still remaining part of a great building', while in 1776 Harrison mentioned a fire which destroyed the barracks, that is, most of the original part of the hospital (see fig. 91).[48] What remained of these was still somehow in use in 1791, as remarked by Pennant, who also noted how the prison at the Savoy had become 'scandalous infectious'.[49] But the most vivid and detailed account of the end is given by David Hughson in 1817, by which time the building of Waterloo Bridge had led to the destruction of whatever had survived. Reporting a description of September 1816, he observes how the Savoy had become 'the rendezvous for curious persons, who appear anxious to inspect the ancient walls of the once royal palace', deemed an 'object worthy the inspection of the antiquary' (fig. 95). While he wrote, those very walls were being pulled down, not without some difficulty since 'in several parts the thickness is eight or ten feet', hence 'one hard mass, almost immovable'.[50] The construction of Chambers's Somerset House (1776–1801), whose west front occupies part of the Savoy precincts, the approaches of the new bridge and, lastly, the construction of the Victoria Embankment from 1864, gave the site its final *coup de grace*. The Chapel is the only, incongruous, remnant of it all.

THE SAVOY | 87

96 Burghley (later Exeter) House on the north side of the Strand, opposite the Savoy (detail of fig. 8)

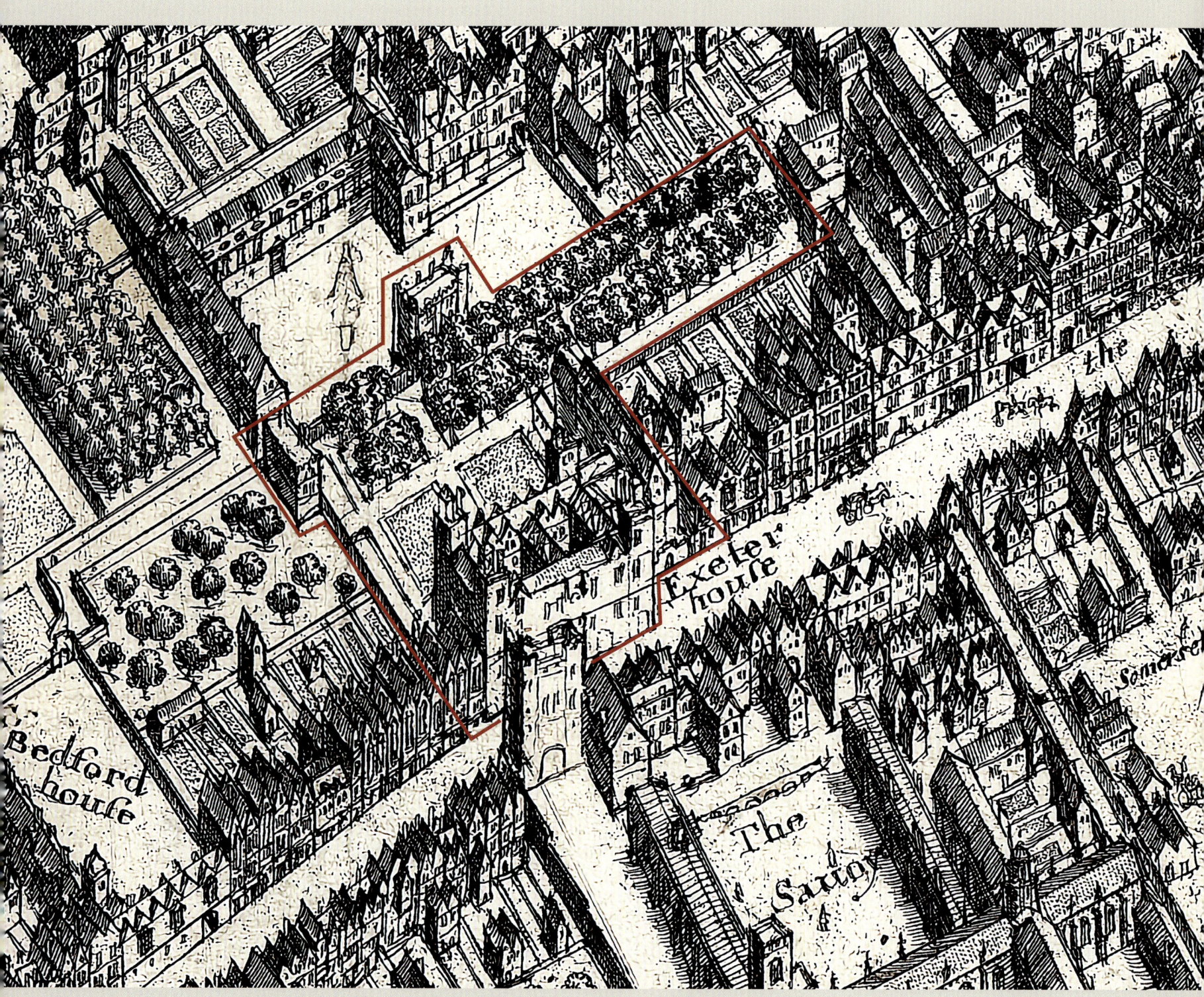

5 · BURGHLEY HOUSE

BURGHLEY HOUSE, OTHERWISE KNOWN AS Cecil or Exeter House and chiefly depicted in Hollar's bird's-eye view of the 'West Central District' as turreted and with two courtyards, lay on the north side of the Strand opposite the Savoy (fig. 96). Like Somerset House (see Chapter Three) but for different reasons, its imposing facade stood directly on the street and was flanked on the west by a row of tenements (part of the Bedford Estate) which separated it from the neighbouring Bedford House, the only other palace on this side of the Strand. On the east, the house projected out at a point where the road widened into a broad thoroughfare. Enhanced by the simplicity of its surroundings, in stark contrast with the almost continuous sequence of palatial residences on the river side, Burghley House reflected the prominent status of its builder, William Cecil (1520/1–1598), 1st Baron Burghley, Queen Elizabeth's Principal Secretary and her most trusted and long-standing minister, as well as the leading architectural patron of the period.

If Burghley the statesman and patron has received considerable attention, his London house, demolished in 1676, was perhaps the least known of the Strand palaces.[1] This changed in 2002, when Jill Husselby and Paula Henderson published a seminal article on the remarkable and then newly discovered plan of Burghley House (fig. 97), which represents most of what had been known on the history of this house.[2] The development of the site can be closely followed, as numerous deeds and some relevant accounts survive, primarily at Burghley's ancestral seat in Lincolnshire, also called Burghley House, and to a much lesser extent, at his son Robert Cecil's Hatfield House. Yet knowledge of the interiors remains limited, since the plan only shows the ground floor while no inventory is known to exist of either this house or any other Cecil (Exeter) residences at the time.[3] This chapter reconsiders all the evidence afresh.

The House of William Cecil, 1st Baron Burghley: 1559–1598

On 23 November 1559, barely a year after Queen Elizabeth's succession, William Cecil obtained the lease of a house belonging to St Clement Danes's parsonage described as

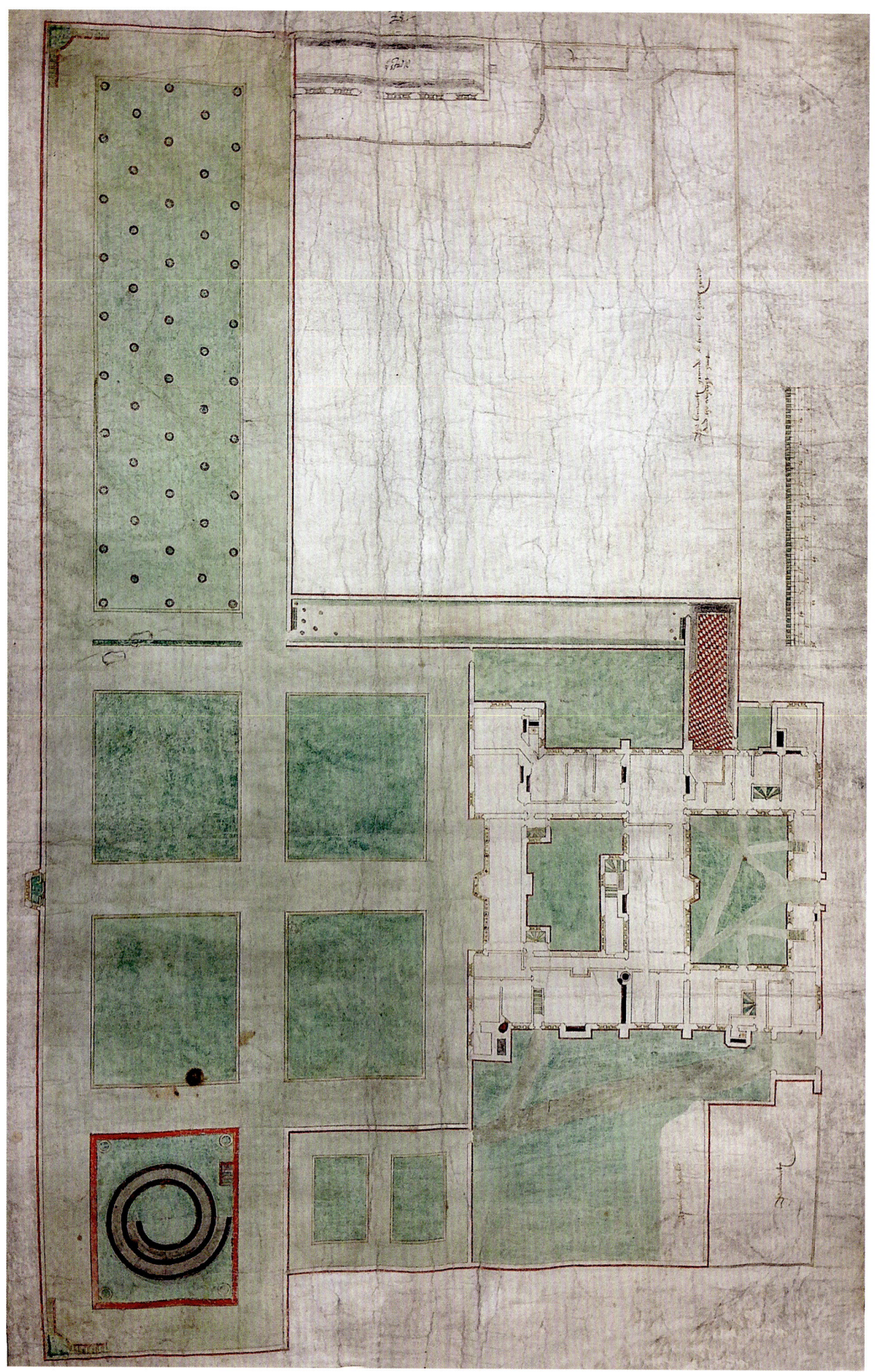

97 *opposite* Plan of Burghley (later Exeter) House, *c.*1562–7, oriented east (top) west (bottom), Strand (south) on the right. Burghley House Collection, Ex Map 358

98 Palmer House opposite the Savoy, detail of the *Woodcut Map of London*, 1561–70 ('Agas'), reprinted 1633, derived from the lost 'Copperplate Map of London', 1553–9. Mitton 1908. Wikimedia Commons Public Domain

99 The area occupied by Palmer House (north side) and the adjacent houses to the east, opposite the Savoy, detail of Georg Braun and Frans Hogenberg, 'London' in *Civitates Orbis Terrarum*, 1572, derived from the lost 'Copperplate Map of London' 1553–9. University Library, Heidelberg. Wikipedia, Public Domain

all that mesuage curtilage and garden with th appurtynence sytuate and beinge over against the hospitall of the Savoy ... latelie ... in the Tenure of sr Thomas Palmer Knight And which mesuage was latelie buylded by the same sr Thomas Except onelie one howse with th appurtynence called the p[ar]sonage howse wherein one Francis Nicholas then dwelled ...[4]

A henchman of Edward Seymour, Duke of Somerset, and a supporter of Lady Jane Grey, Palmer had obtained the site in the reign of Edward VI (1547–53), when he pulled down the old building and 'began to builde the same of Bricke, and Timber, very large and spatious', as Stow's 1598 Survay relates.[5] Palmer was executed for high treason with John Dudley, Leicester's ill-fated father, in August 1553, scarcely a month after the succession of the Catholic Mary, and the property then reverted to the Crown. The following year it was leased by Job Rixman, then the Rector of St Clement, to James Basset, for the term of eighty years at forty shillings per annum, but the change of ruler in 1558 once again transformed the political scene, this time in favour of the rising Secretary. In return for the property, Cecil was licensed to give William Harward, who had succeeded Rixman, lands worth £4 per annum.[6]

An idea of what Palmer's house looked like is provided by the 'Agas' map of 1561–70, and by Braun and Hogenberg's map of 1572, both deriving from the lost 'Copperplate Map' of London of 1553–9, hence predating Cecil's tenure. In the Agas map (fig. 98), the house appears to be composed of three two-storeyed pitched (or gabled) units, where the easternmost one is perpendicular to the other two. The building clearly stands out among its neighbours. At the back, a garden either formal or laid out with planting allotments, like all its neighbours, extends as far as the wall of Covent Garden, which had been granted to the 1st Duke of Somerset in 1547 and to the 1st Earl of Bedford in 1552 (see Chapters Three and Six). Palmer's house is less prominently identified by Braun and Hogenberg (fig. 99), where little attempt appears to have been made to distinguish it from the adjacent row of houses: indeed, those to the east, depicted in the Agas map as three further units up to where the Strand widened, here appear to be part of the same complex. As in the previous depiction, a large garden follows to the north. Both views seem to agree on the absence of side wings or indeed a proper courtyard arrangement, even if what might be a detached building in the garden behind the eastern side of the main house in Braun and Hogenberg may have occasioned a part enclosure. The 'curtilage' mentioned in the lease was perhaps in this area of the complex.

As well as securing surrounding properties, Cecil appears to have immediately set about enlarging the complex and improving the house: by February 1560 a conveyance with Lord Paget (of Paget Place, shortly the Strand palace of Robert Dudley; see Chapter One) and Philip Cockeram provided him with 'a piece of ground on which the east end of Sir William Cecil's brick house is built', together with 'the Hartshorne, a house on the west, 2 stables on the west, [and] a cottage on the corner'.[7] Further information

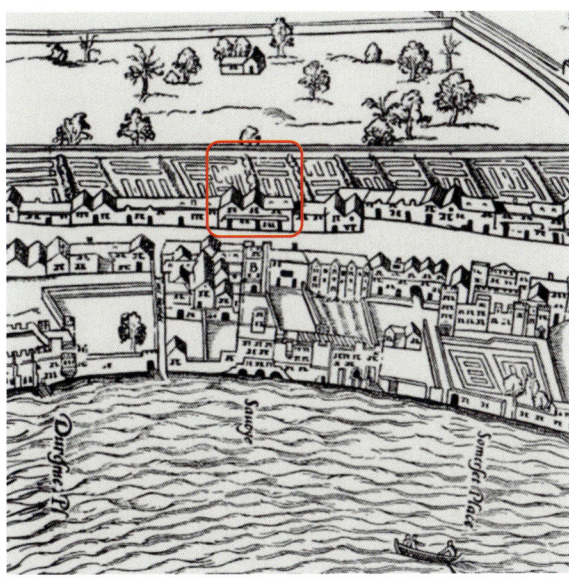

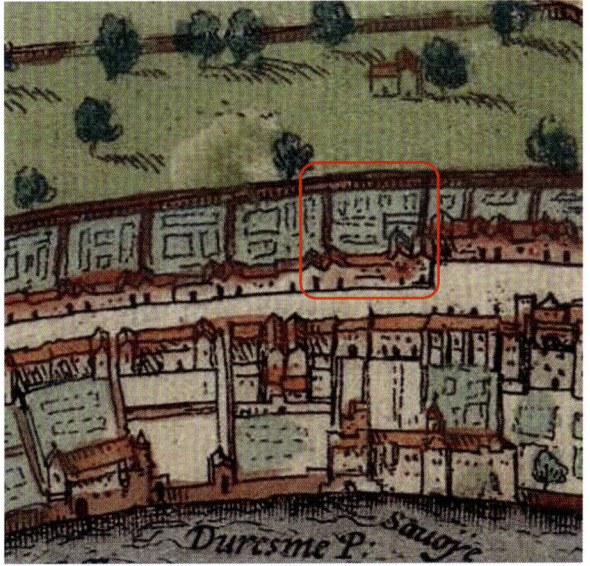

on the building works' progress is provided by a letter of 17 June 1560, where Nicholas Bacon, Cecil's brother-in-law and Lord Keeper (as such the resident of York House; see Chapter Ten), remarked that he had visited the house and that 'all things go well forward', even if he did not appreciate 'ye prvye in ye west end', as it was 'to nere ye logyng, to nere an hoven and to nere a lytle lardre', concluding that it should have better 'offendyd yor eye outward then your nose inward'.[8]

The Hartshorne (or 'Hertishorne') mentioned in the deed was located next to a tenement called 'le Flower de Luice' – both formerly part of the Savoy precincts (see Chapter Four) – to be granted to the Secretary with 'four cottages with gardens in the parishes of St Mary at Strand & of St Clements outside the bar of the New Temple' by the queen on 20 February 1561.[9] This followed another grant by Francis, 2nd Earl of Bedford, of 24 January, which is quoted at length as it provides important information:

> *all that pece of pasture grounde beyng partt of one greate pasture lately called the Covent Garden … is nowe staked out divided and bounded from residue … [and] lyeth on the South side of pt of the said greate pasture and pt of the South side thereof adjoyneth to the garden of the capital messuage or mansion house of the same Sir Willm whyche … is newly buylded by the same … and contayneth … in breath at the Est end thereof threscore and eighten fote [78 ft] of assise and in breath at the West end thereof threscore and eighten fote of assise and it contayneth in length from the Est to the West foure hundred fourescore and one fote [481 ft] of assise and the uttermost pt of the North side thereof directly against the est [corner] of the new building of the said capital messuage is distant from the foundation of the brick work of the north side of the said new building one hundreth fifty and eighten fote of assise wherein is also one sittyeng or bowying place for a baye wyndowe to be cast out of a brick wall the space of five fote towards the north entended to be made there by the said Sir William together with lib[er]ty to make and to have one dore or gate to enter into and walk within the grounde te[ne]ment adjoynyng next of the same Pile and as nede shall requyre … to enclose and fence in With brick or otherwise the said pece of pasture … And … all those foure messuage[s] … together with all gardens … towards the West and to the said capital messuage … towards the East and upon the high strete towards the South …* [10]

This document is mainly related to Cecil's enlargement of the garden, which was to include a section of Covent Garden measuring 481 by 78 feet, and to the creation of one of what would eventually be three banqueting houses. It clearly refers to a newly built mansion house and to the foundation on the north side 'of the new building of the said capital messuage', which on the one hand suggests that that part of the fabric was still under construction (hence the foundations) while on the other that the new building was part of an existing capital messuage. On 25 May 1561 Florence Diaceto, one of the queen's agents and later secretary to Paul de Foix, the French Ambassador in London, wrote to Cecil that since he was 'building both in London and in the country' he might be interested to know 'that a quarry of marble equal to that of Rome has been discovered in the Pyrenees'. Diaceto was a friend of the owner and, 'on looking at the sketches which he has sent to Mr. Killigrew' (the dramatist Thomas Killigrew), Cecil's protégé, he would have obtained marbles for chimneypieces, doors or windows 'very cheaply'. The sketches were to be shown to the queen too as a further potential beneficiary of the same marble.[11] Two months later, on 14 July 1561, Cecil himself noted in his diary that the house was not 'fully finished', still being, as he subsequently reported to Nicholas Throckmorton, a 'rude cottage'.[12] But it was good enough to host Elizabeth for supper.

The year 1561 had been important for William Cecil: he had secured and mostly rebuilt a mansion in the Strand and had become Master of the Court of Wards and High Steward of Westminster. These posts allowed him to control the patrimony of noblemen minor, quite a few of whom had possessions in the Strand (see, for instance, Chapter Seven), and to control almost the whole area, where he later amassed major holdings.[13] Together with a house in Milford Lane (the passage leading to the river between Essex House and Arundel House), he purchased that year the parsonage house previously excluded from the lease of 1559 and a house adjoining it.[14] At the start of 1563 Richard Clough, a member of the so-called 'House of Gresham', named after Sir Thomas Gresham (1519–1579, the well-known merchant, financier and agent in the Low Countries in the Secretary's service since 1562), wrote to Cecil that he was involved with his gallery, *had spoken with the mason, and sends back the old pattern for Cecil to confer with his mason at home, so he may show the whole ground how the gallery shall stand. The mason's advice is that the pillars should be made of one stone, and the arches accordingly, either antique or modern. As he hears from Cecil so he will proceed therein.*[15]

A previous letter from Gresham himself of August 1561 had informed Cecil that 'your pillars of marbell be aryved in saftie' from Flanders, and items imported from Antwerp, including '16 little pillars of marbill for the gallery' at a pound each, had been billed in December.[16] As well as pointing to Cecil's direct involvement with this gallery – in itself unsurprising as he is widely regarded as the architect of all his houses – these exchanges may equally relate to Burghley House at Stamford, under construction since 1558, also with loggias. But it would fit nicely with the loggia depicted in the plan of the Strand palace, as will be seen (see fig. 97).

In December 1563 a house in the Strand on the west of Cecil's mansion was then granted, once again, by the Earl of Bedford, while in November 1564 came the 'finding of the jury as to the encroachment of Mr. Secretary Cecil's house upon the highway'.[17] This suggests that Cecil had either rebuilt or modified the Strand front, for there would otherwise be no reason for infringement. Could this relate to the couple of columns either side of the main entrance seen in the plan of Burghley House, discussed later, the date of which would tally with the early 1560s (see fig. 97)? They clearly encroached on the highway and may have been the first stage of a gateway devised as a tower of the orders.[18] Hollar is unrevealing in this respect, though one can perhaps distinguish some kind of decoration on the top stage of the frontispiece which may relate to this (see fig. 96). Be that as it may, on 14 November 1565 Bedford provided three further plots of Covent Garden for the 'enlarginge of the Garden and Orcharde', namely two matching areas fifteen feet long and twelve feet wide at either corner of the garden wall and one, fifteen feet long and thirty-two feet wide, in the middle of it, 'where there ys already made and buylded a house with baye or jettye sett oute of the right range of the said garden walle into the said covent garden'. This was the Banqueting House erected after the grant of 24 January 1561, which was to be 'enlarged' and, together with the new corner plots, 'make certen roomes for the more ease and commoditie of his said garden and orcharde'.[19] Two contemporaneous sketches by Cecil show the extent of the changes; one of them, including measurements, indicates slightly larger additions than were agreed (figs 100 and 101). By 1568 these garden houses had been erected, for a fine, registered soon after the sale of 1565, was levied on Cecil and Bedford, who must have again contravened the regulations against buildings encroaching onto open spaces.[20] In 1570, a 'piece of Covent Garden near the White Hart Inn in the Strand' was also obtained, one more time, from the Earl of Bedford.[21] It was bounded 'on the east by a fence lying next the highway which runs from the Strand to St. Giles; on the west by the orchard adjoining the house of Sir William Cecil; on the south by the gardens of the White Hart'.[22]

While 1570 saw the last purchase related to Cecil's house, the following year the newly elevated Baron Burghley, which occasioned the palace's change in name from Cecil to Burghley House or Place, was still (happily) 'amongst my dusty laborors'. This comes from a letter 'From my house in Westminster' which Burghley wrote to the Earl of Leicester, regarding works that needed 'to be fyneshed' and 'covered' in a hurry. They somehow concerned Leicester, who had recently obtained Paget Place, and began an architectural dialogue between the two (see Chapter One). The earl was in fact reassured that whatever work Burghley was undertaking, it could be achieved by 'wholly and only with borrowyng here in the Cite whereby as I take plesure in my fond humor of buyldyng, so have I a stay and stopp from much rejoysyng whan I behold the cost to be doone by borrowyng, and so had I rather doo my Lord and leave my heyre less land to repaye it then by bribery in an office.'[23] That last remark reminds us how a building and an office of state were often one and the same thing, which had and continued to characterise the most prominently political Strand palaces, such as Salisbury House, built by Burghley's younger son and political heir (see Chapter Eight).

During 1567–72 William Cecil spent some £750 on his London house.[24] From 1577 there is an estimate for the 'fyneshinge of the house and seates in the garden', with the stable, barn and fence wall, while in 1578 a payment was made to 'the serjeant painter upon the gallery', followed by one 'to him for my Lord of Leicester's arms over the chimney, colouring rails in the garden, with the four posts about the fountain for pipes from

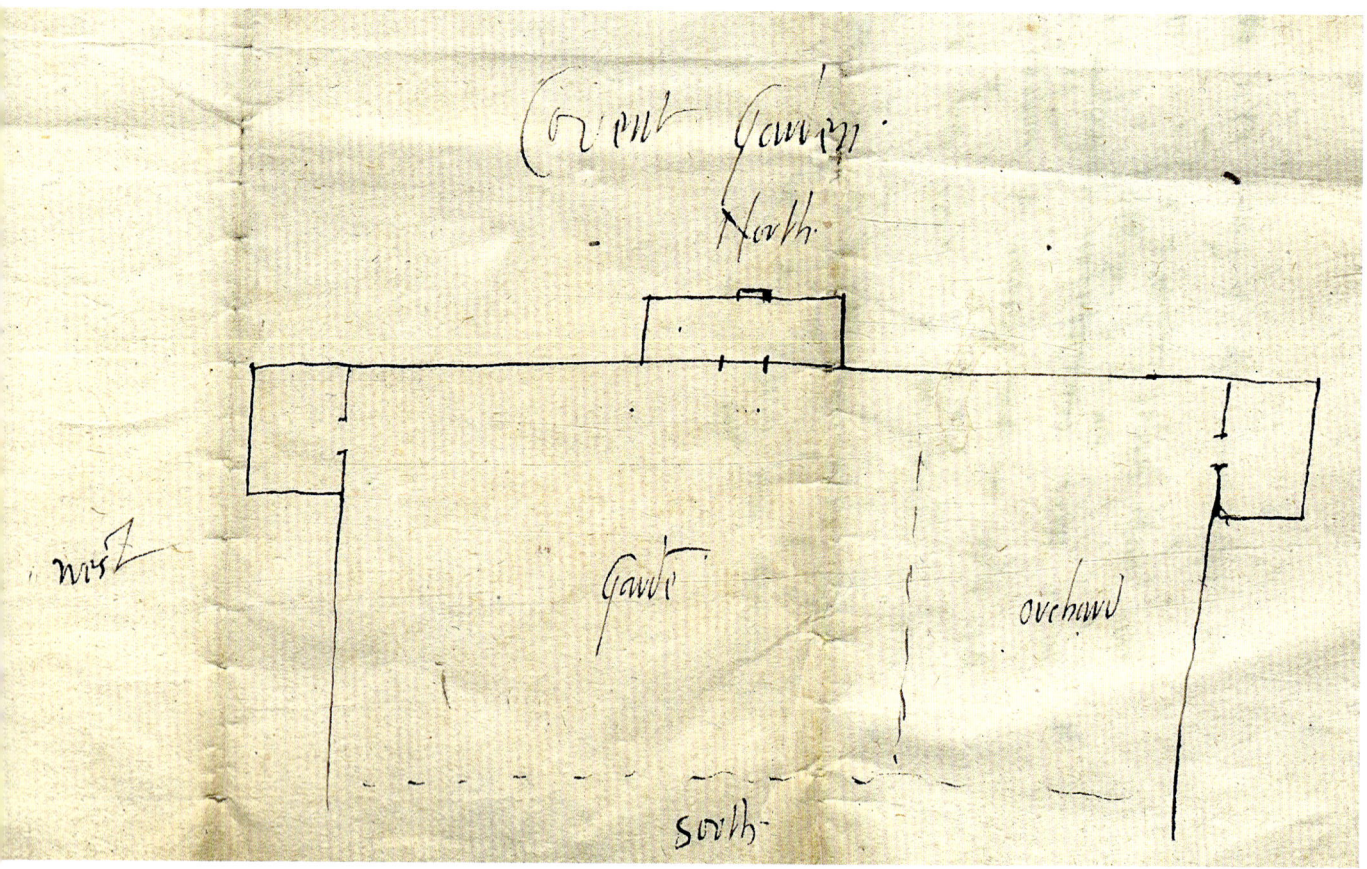

100 William Cecil, sketch of the layout of the garden of Burghley House with the new banqueting houses along the edge of Covent Garden, 1565. Burghley House Collection, Ex H5/33

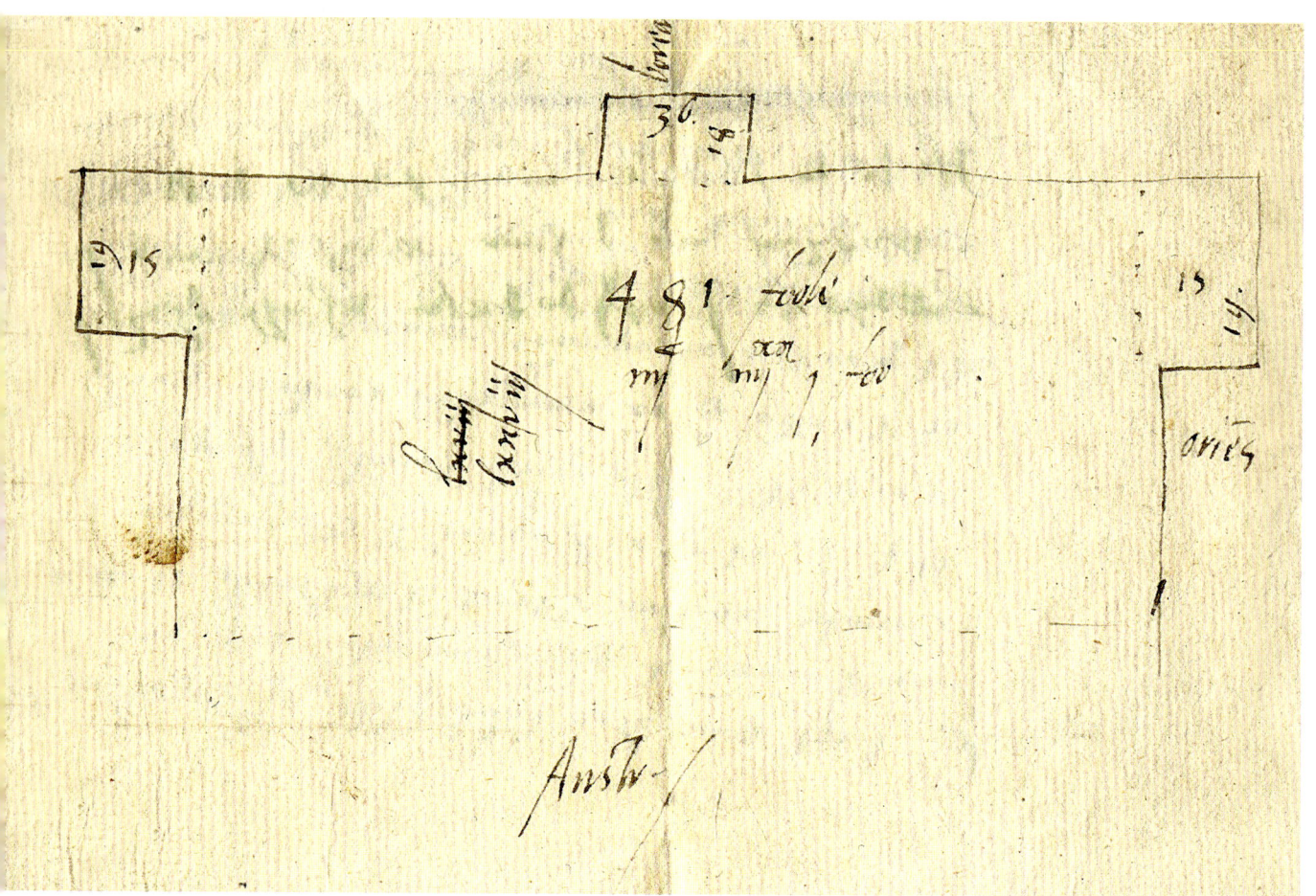

101 William Cecil, sketch with measurements of the layout of the garden of Burghley House with the new banqueting houses along the edge of Covent Garden, 1565. Burghley House Collection, Ex H5/33

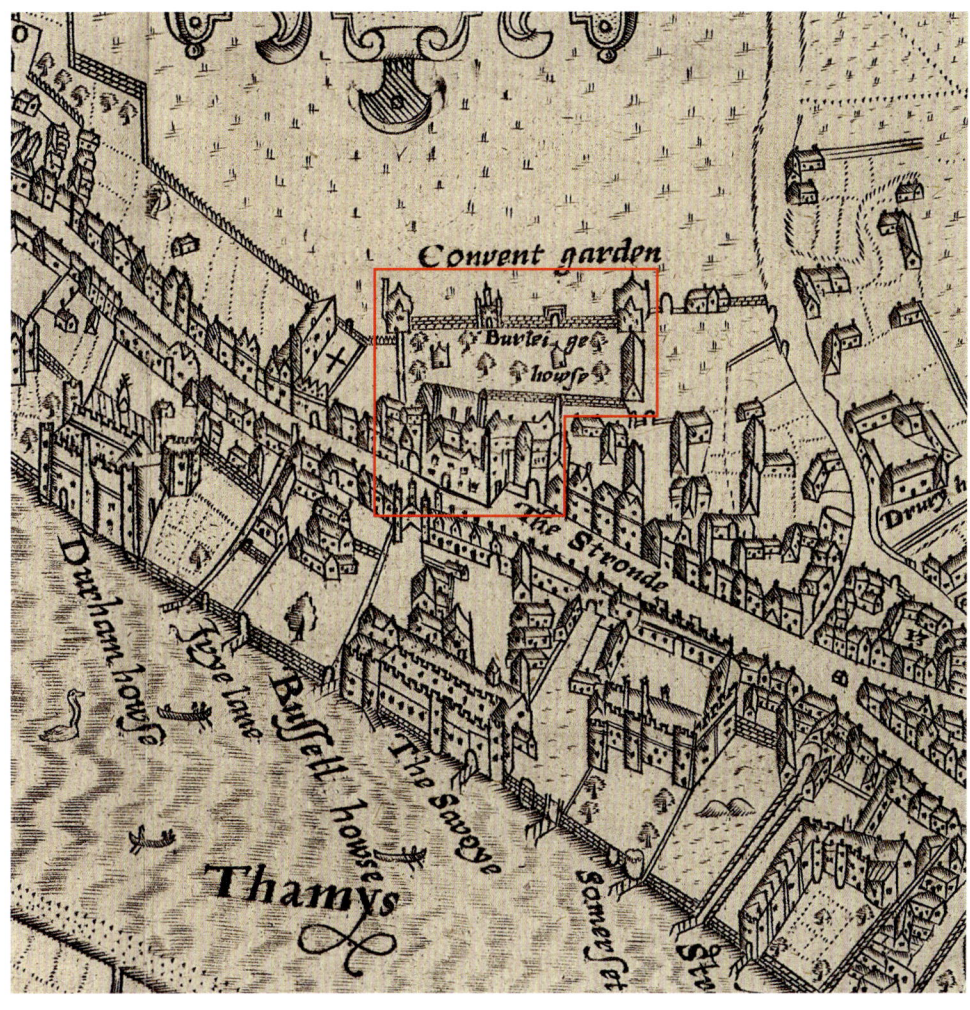

102 Burghley House, detail from John Norden, *Speculum Britanniae*, 1593. Folger Shakespeare Library, Washington DC. Licensed under Creative Commons Attribution-ShareAlike 4.0 International

the moor'.²⁵ While neither bills nor estimate can be clearly pinned down, one wonders whether works in the gallery and garden may be associated with the same space discussed with Richard Clough in 1563.

In the 1580s an annexe to the east of the main house was built to accommodate Robert Cecil, by then in his twenties. Norden's *Speculum Britanniae* of 1593 describes it as 'a proper howse', and between 1596 and 1603 it appears in leases by Burghley to Robert, and then by Robert to others and vice versa, from which we learn that the 'tenement builded by Lord Burghley … near adjoining the great mansion house' had since been enlarged by Robert Cecil.²⁶

Other than these auxiliary buildings, not much seems to have happened to the main house beyond the 1570s.²⁷ Cecil claimed that it had cost him the hefty sum of 'the sale of lands worth £100 by year', while Norden, one of his protégés, described it as 'a verie fayre howse raysed with bricks, proportionablie adorned with four turrets placed at the four quarters of the howse' and depicted it as such (fig. 102).²⁸ In this view, the Strand front bears some similarity to that of Palmer's house as recorded by both Agas and Braun and Hogenberg (see figs 98 and 99), for one clearly sees the steep pitches (more identifiable as gables here) at either corner of what is a similarly elongated elevation, where the number of floors seems comparable. By contrast, a series of buildings do appear at the back, ostensibly creating a courtyard arrangement only possibly indicated before. The garden is also prominently depicted, with the three elaborate Banqueting Houses built by 1567, the gate into Covent Garden mentioned in 1565, two smaller structures, perhaps fountains, at either side, one of which could be related to the 1578 payment mentioned earlier, and a long-pitched building, probably the stables, along the eastern part of the wall. Despite the obvious difference in sophistication, this representation is not too dissimilar from Hollar's mid-seventeenth-century view, which still shows a primarily elongated and seemingly not particularly wide building, with an imposing and fortified appearance (see fig. 96).

While two courtyards along an east–west axis can be distinguished in Hollar, their actual size is in no way comparable to that of the majority of the riverside palaces shown by him, beginning from the near contemporary Somerset House. Interestingly, Burghley himself thought of his London house as old by 1585, a remark which could not have referred to the actual age of the 'new building', built at most some twenty-five years prior, but was probably a matter of style.²⁹ Unless, that is, he was specifically referring to that part of Burghley House which still belonged to Palmer's time. Here too comments made by the Secretary (Lord Treasurer from 1572) about the house being built 'of necessity' and being 'but convenient', support the idea of a relatively inconspicuous complex, and one that had resulted from accretions.³⁰ After all, Burghley's well-known and cherished depiction of himself riding a mule in his garden speaks eloquently about the sort of person he was (fig. 103). Neither Norden's nor Hollar's depictions, however, tally altogether with the plan of Burghley House, which shows a considerably larger building, not least because the two courtyards are oriented along the north–south axis, not east–west, a feature that doubles its depth (see figs 96, 97, 102). But if one only considered the first half of the plan, the resulting courtyard house would tally more with

BURGHLEY HOUSE | 95

the views, and one wonders whether this is what was actually depicted by Hollar, not least as his reliability, as remarked elsewhere in this book, has proved controversial.[31] That said, he appears not to have cut the building but to have turned it ninety degrees, while maintaining its relatively narrow and elongated silhouette. The point about the two courtyards and their orientation is important here, as the north–south axis of the plan allows the interpretation of the northward courtyard as the part added by Burghley, instead of the one facing the Strand, which in itself would coincide, at least in embryo, with Palmer's house. That the structure of the first half of the house existed is also supported by the presence in the plan of buttresses either side of the central wing, added, as Husselby and Henderson suggested, for the addition of extra storeys.[32] After all, such an arrangement, which allowed Cecil to live in one side of the house while the rest was being built – this is probably what he meant by 'rude cottage' when the queen supped there in 1562 – would hardly make sense if one were building from scratch. The need for two small courtyards at the expense of a grander arrangement seems otherwise unjustified.

While construction, as noted, was well under way by February 1560, the plan of Burghley House must have been drawn in the first half of that decade, as it includes the part of the garden acquired by Cecil from Bedford in January 1561, as well as a bay projecting from the north side of the garden wall, built by November 1565, but not the three banqueting houses in place by 1568. Given Cecil's well-known interest in maps and more generally in architecture, the plan may have been produced for show or as a collectable item, similarly to the 'porticus' drawing made for his son Robert at the beginning of the seventeenth century, probably for one of James I's visits (see fig. 154). Or perhaps it had a legal purpose. As for its authorship, two names have been put forward. The first and most likely is Lawrence Bradshaw, Surveyor of the Royal Works from 1547 to 1560, and the second is Henry Hawthorne, Purveyor to the Queen's Works from 1562.[33] The latter was also employed at Theobalds, while his name is associated with a Banqueting House possibly at Essex House, built by Robert Dudley with Cecil's help in about 1575 (see Chapter One).

The plan of Burghley House is also of crucial importance when it comes to its internal arrangement, as it is virtually the only source we have, beyond brief references in William Cecil's will and the few words by Norden who stated that 'within it is curiouslye beautified with rare devices, and especially the oratory placed in an angle of the great chamber'.[34] One entered the first court through a gateway flanked by columns, perhaps part of a frontispiece devised as a tower of the orders, as previously suggested, in the middle of an otherwise rather forbidding Strand front. That front's sheer scale, extending over 150 feet, marked the boundary with the busy thoroughfare and distinguished it from the modest tenements on either side. This contrast was highlighted by the Marquess of Winchester in 1560, as well as more generally by Harrison's Description of England of 1577, where London streets are described as not 'so uniforme and orderlie builded as those of forreine cities'.[35] On the east, west and south sides the first court was flanked by offices

103 Attributed to Marcus Gheeraerts the younger, *William Cecil, 1st Baron Burghley and Lord High Treasurer of England*, 1587?. Bodleian Libraries, University of Oxford

and staff rooms partly catering for Burghley's substantial household, estimated at between fifty and eighty, while the north side, marked by a bow window on axis with the gate, was almost entirely occupied by the Great Hall (see fig. 97).[36] Located, as usual, next to the service quarters in the north-west corner of the house, it 'was ever well furnished with Men, served with Meate, & kept in good Ordre. For his Steward kept a standing Table for Gentlemen. Besydes two other long Tables (manie Tymes twice sett.) One for the Clerk of the Kitchin, the other for Yeomen.'[37] It no longer functioned, however, as the main space for dining, which had increasingly taken place in the Parlour for the family, or in the Great Chamber for more official occasions. Measuring 42 by 20 feet, the Hall was not in fact particularly large, though it seems to have been of a fairly standard size for the city: the nearby Hall at Essex House, at 45 by 24 feet, was only marginally bigger (see Chapter One). Interestingly, both halls probably predate their famous owners, which suggests that the importance and size of these rooms had been diminishing steadily since the mid-1500s. By the turn of the century, they had indeed become quasi-lobbies, as the first series of plans for Salisbury House indicates (see Chapter Eight). In the light of this development, it is likely that the little room to the right of the Hall was a sort of guard chamber, one of those 'chambers used for suitors' mentioned in the will where the many daily petitioners Burghley dealt with 'as he went to the hall', as his biographer wrote, could be accommodated.[38] This was especially the case since his own set of rooms – described in the will as 'my bedchamber ... and in my two closetts, and any chambers thereto adjoyneing, and extending to the lodgings of ... Robert Cecill', or the shorter 'my bedchamber and two studies' – appears to coincide with the adjacent north-east range of the second courtyard.[39] The only issue with this interpretation might be the absence in the plan of the principal stairs, for the stairs leading off the north side of the Hall only reach a mid-height gallery, which appears to be the equivalent of the tribune generally located along the short side of halls. But this side of the plan may well have been reworked, as a sketch by William Cecil himself of 1562/3 includes a stair and a small lobby towards the western end of the Hall that are not shown here (fig. 104). A great staircase could indeed have been positioned in lieu of the two small rooms to the west of the Hall; equally, however, it could have been where the supposed Guard Room is. If the big room to the east of the Hall was indeed a Parlour, as suggested by Husselby and Henderson, such a staircase would have sat in between them, which is exactly what happens in the first series of plans for Salisbury House (see fig. 139).[40] Either way, that Parlour, with three doors, one of which opened onto the first courtyard, would have inevitably acted as a room of passage, which is somewhat unusual.

While the ground floor, beyond Cecil's own set, was primarily dedicated to staff and service rooms, the first floor, of which there is no plan, would have contained the main rooms of state. These probably began with a Great Chamber, which could potentially have sat on either of the side wings along the second court, assuming that the height of the Kitchen was not in the way, or indeed above the Hall, if the latter, once again, was not double-height. This is conceivable not just because of its lesser role but because a double chimneybreast along its north wall suggests the presence of a room, either above or below it. (This in itself does not preclude the presence of a double-height hall with a room on top, a third floor.) A Great Chamber over the Kitchen would have been warm and directly connected to each other by the staircase in the north-west corner

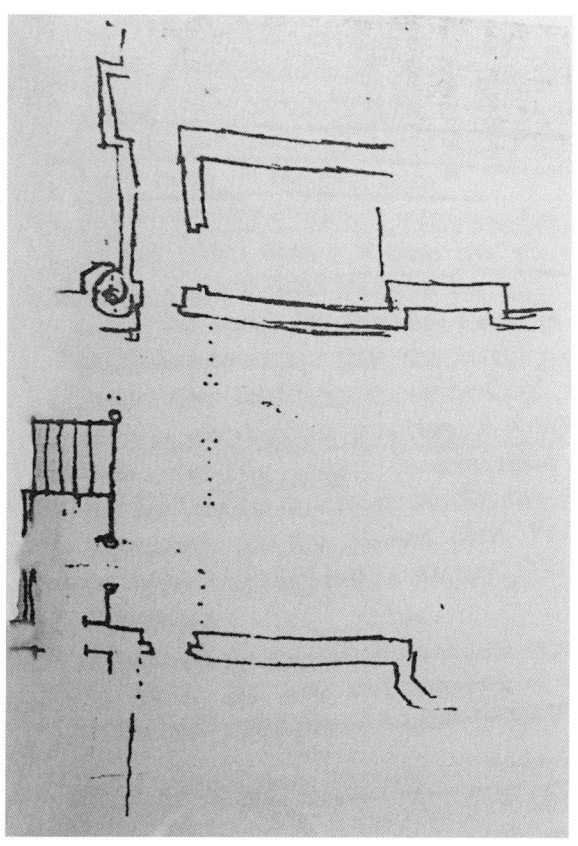

104 William Cecil, sketch showing the western end of the Hall and parts of the kitchen range, 1562/3. National Archives, Kew, SP 12/27/54

and by the adjacent one in the internal turret – important in a house where state entertainment was both frequent and on a grand scale. The Privy Council often met (and dined) there, while after the first visit to the 'rude cottage' in 1562 the queen had returned five more times, mainly towards the end of Cecil's life. In 1591, the day of his departure from London, Essex (another of Burghley's former boarders) mustered his cavalry for her in the garden of Burghley House, a parade she must have witnessed from one of the Banqueting Houses. In 1595 she stayed from 30 January to 1 February, following the marriage of Burghley's daughter Elizabeth, of whom she was godmother, to the Earl of Derby. But back in 1581 it had been the magnificent state dinner for the French delegation that possibly saw the apex of Burghley's entertainment in London (three days after a similar event at Essex House; see Chapter One), when hopes of a marriage for the queen were still alive.[41] Costing a staggering £362, it gathered the entire Privy Council with highly distinguished courtiers being served by Cecil's elder son Thomas and his nephew Francis Bacon alongside eighty-three named gentlemen and yeomen. The most important guests were seated along the north and south sides of the Great Chamber, information which supports the above-the-Hall hypothesis, while others sat in the 'garden gallery' and in the garden itself. This 'garden gallery' may well refer to a long first-floor gallery running along the north side of the house overlooking the garden – as in the west front of Burghley House at Stanford or the south wing at Hatfield – or to the loggia below it seen in the plan (see fig. 97). That was an open gallery, not too dissimilar from the loggia at either of those houses or indeed at Theobalds, of which some drawings exist (figs 105 and 106).[42] Fifteen balusters are shown in the Strand plan (as small circles along the loggia), a detail which is tantalisingly close to the '16 little pillars of marble' imported from Antwerp in 1561. If the Great Chamber, which included an oratory particularly praised by Norden, was on the west side of the second court and the Long Gallery overlooking the garden followed in the north wing, the east side of the house, right above Burghley's apartment, could have been occupied by the mighty Mildred (1526–1589), his second wife, whom he married in 1545.[43] Other rooms, either on the first or second floors among the apparently three levels visible in Hollar and confirmed by references in the will, included the upper Library situated 'over his great chamber', which implied another library on a lower floor, and a further 'study over the porche' probably above the main entrance from the Strand.[44] This and the two studies next to the Bedchamber on the ground floor were the Secretary's inner sanctum, as they housed his precious collections including books, gold plates and 'all evidences and rolls belonging to his pedigrees' plus 'all writings concerning the Queen', the latter of which, unsurprisingly, were to be

105 'Upright of a Gallery [in the] garden' [as the drawing is called] at Theobalds, endorsed by William Cecil [the notes on the drawings are in WC's hand], 1572–3. Hatfield House Archives, Cecil Papers 143/41, 42. Reproduced with permission of the Marquess of Salisbury, Hatfield House

passed to his son Robert.⁴⁵ It is also there that Cecil retired to read 'if he had no busynes (which was seldom)', as his biographer relates once more, while his antiquarian collection included 'many coins and very rare ancient monuments', as William Camden wrote to the scholar and cartographer Ortellius in 1577.⁴⁶ Camden went as far as calling Cecil the 'Nestor of Britain', noting that his London gardens featured an inscription from the Roman remains at Chichester.

Rather like the Thames for the riverside palaces, it was indeed the garden, some 178 feet at its deepest by 481 feet from east to west, that provided Burghley House with its best vantage point. This is no doubt the reason why there were two garden gates into Covent Garden, as well as not one but three banqueting houses strategically placed along the edge of what in the 1590s was still open pasture: they provided not just perspective but the very idea of *rus in urbe*.⁴⁷ By contrast with the Strand front, the garden range was therefore open and architecturally more articulated. At least once, the queen had indeed come 'by the Felds from Christ Church', rather than from the Strand, while Cecil himself used that route 'for nearness' to Theobalds.⁴⁸

While practicality may have been paramount to Burghley, intrinsically a humble man on his mule (hence his comments about the shortness of the journey), this northern approach also became part of his civic concerns: he took upon himself the overall decorum of Covent Garden, as he had with the Strand. In a letter of 18 May 1593 to the officers of the 2nd Earl of Bedford, he lamented how

> *the same grownde is much spoyled, and suche commoditie as the sayd Erle and his freindes might enioye by takeinge the Ayre greatly interrupted, the moste parte wheareof growth by multytudes of Barke [back] Doares not well suffexxed, and by the sclenderrness of the fence agaynste the howses and gardeyns bordering therevpon … wch I maye not … see vnreformed …*

He thus demanded that 'the sayd fences to bee sufficientel made and also to restreyne all those barke Doares from henceforward that the same grownde bee not made so Common', while admonishing that, 'yf any shall offende, I require yow to geve me knowledge of them to the ende I maye take order for redresse and for punishment … whereof I chardge yow not to fayle'.⁴⁹

As for the richness of his own garden, it was certainly a matter of personal pleasure for someone whose many enthusiasms included horticulture. Hence the presence in the plan of almost all types of gardens that one would expect in a large country estate, such as a utilitarian kitchen garden to the north of the service court on the west, an orchard in the north-east, perhaps a privy garden in the L-shaped compartment to the east bounded by a tennis court and bowling alley,

106 Elevation of the inner side of the gatehouse at Theobalds, endorsed by William Cecil: 'The inwd. Syde of the gatehouse. voyd' and 'second plat of my gatehouse and gallery. voyd', date unknown. Hatfield House Archives, Cecil Papers 143/50. Reproduced with permission of the Marquess of Salisbury, Hatfield House

two unique features among the Strand palaces and related to the fact that Burghley House, as previously remarked, acted as a college for young noblemen.[50] But most important of all was a large, quadripartite pleasure garden, aligned with the house itself. In the north-west corner there was also a garden mount, a medieval feature that continued to be popular during the Tudor and early Stuart period, such as those surviving at Lyveden New Bield in Northamptonshire, the lodge of Sir Thomas Tresham. The point was to provide yet another elevated viewing platform, a crucial aspect, as we have seen, on the north, river-less side of the Strand. One even wonders whether Norden's small building surrounded by four trees (see fig. 102), like those around the mount in the plan, could actually be a banqueting house sitting on top of the mount (like that of Henry VIII at Hampton Court), rather than one of two fountains, as previously suggested. The plan contains no evidence of any of the incidental ornaments or indeed exotic features reported at Cecil's other gardens, such as columns, obelisks, a grotto – one of the first in England – with coloured stones, crystals and corals, or even the giochi d'acqua at Theobalds. But this does not imply their absence, not least because the stones and architectural features imported from Antwerp may well have landed here, as previously discussed, with perhaps the statues of the twelve Roman emperors sent to Burghley from Venice in 1561. Either way, the inscription from the Roman remains at Chichester in itself would have provided some precedent for the museum gardens of Arundel, Buckingham or indeed Charles I (see Chapters Two and Ten).

Subsequent Years: 1598–1676

William Cecil died at Burghley House in London on 4 August 1598. In line with the relative frugality that had governed his personal affairs, his body was to be carried to Stanford 'without anie pompe … in some coache covered with blacke, accompanied onelie with twelve personnes and noe more … for avoiding of an unnecessary charge in a longe carriage of a deade carcasse'. These sobering remarks come at the beginning of Burghley's will, whereby the Strand palace, together with 'all my householde stuffe and furniture … excepting what otherways bequeathed', went to his first son Thomas (1542–1623), who soon renamed it Exeter House after his elevation to that earldom in 1605.[51] The annexed Cecil House, leased to Robert in 1596 and still apparently under his control in 1603, was renamed Wimbledon House in 1625 when Edward Cecil (d. 1638), Exeter's third son, was created Viscount Wimbledon. Described by Strype as 'a very handsome house', this is the building for which Inigo Jones designed the entrance with 'pergular' in about 1618, depicted by John Smythson around the same time (fig. 107) and probably derived from an engraving in Fracart's *Premier livre d'architecture*, published in Brussels in 1616. Mid-sixteenth-century examples of this type of entrance can be found at several of the palaces in the Via Giulia in Rome.[52]

Thomas Cecil, as well as his son Edward, appear to have used their respective residences only intermittently, for in 1617 the main house was occupied by Exeter's daughter Elizabeth, the widow of Sir William Hatton (the nephew of the queen's 'Dancing Chancellor'); there she entertained James I and Anne of Denmark.[53]

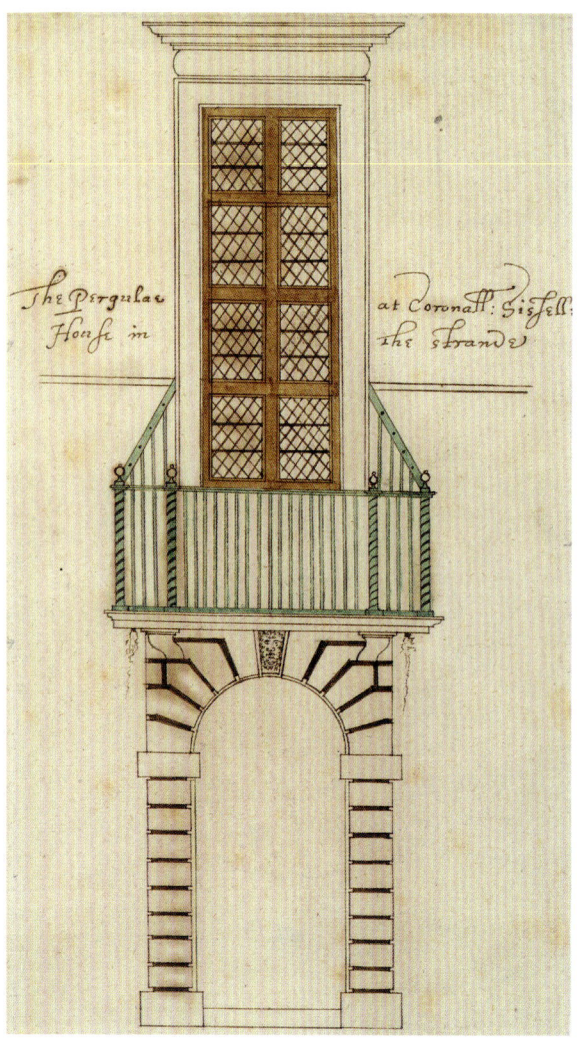

107 John Smythson, record drawing of Inigo Jones's design for the 'Pergular at Coronall, Sissell's House in the Strande', c.1618. RIBA Collections (12952)

100 | LONDON'S 'GOLDEN MILE'

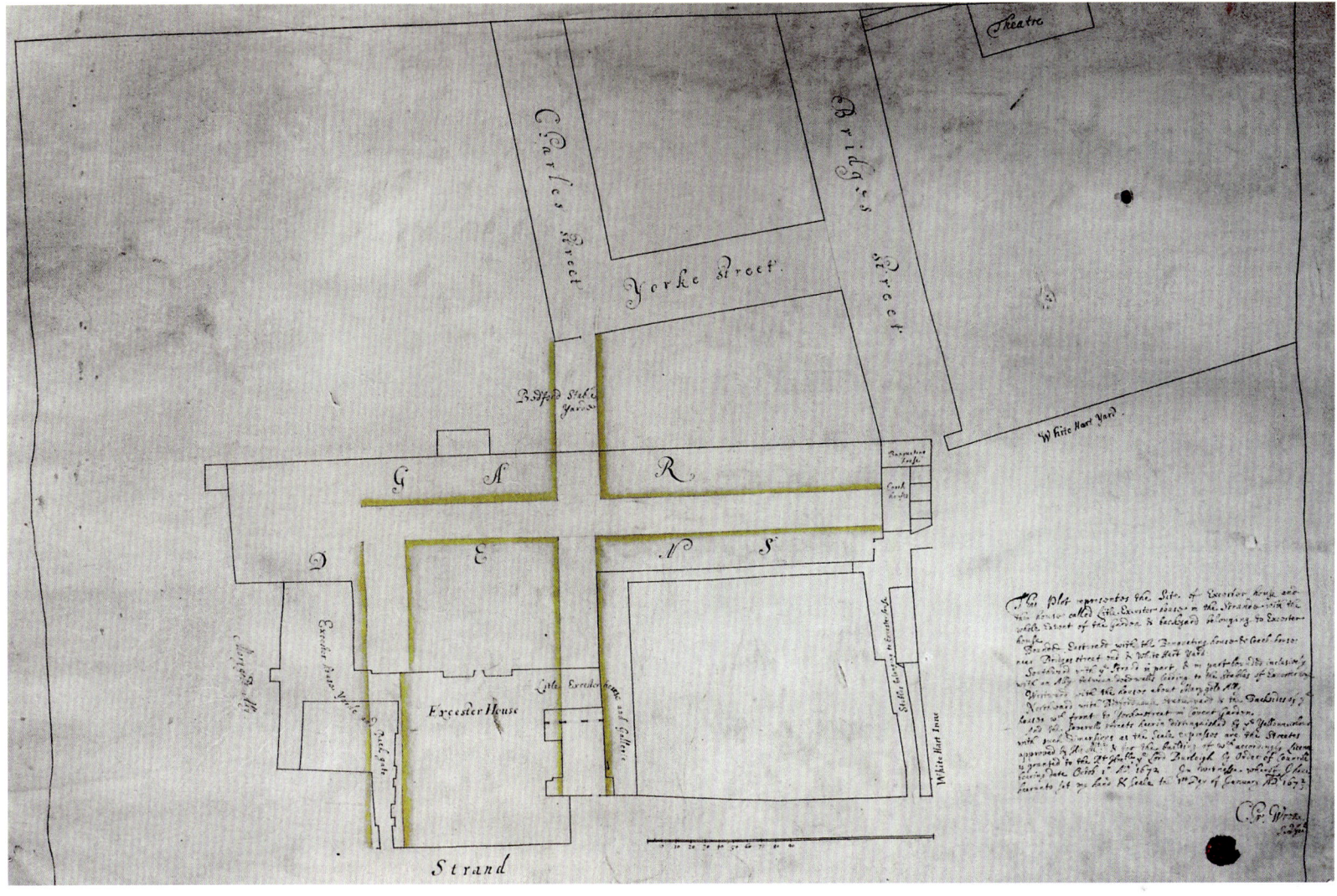

108 Christopher Wren, proposed changes to the site of Exeter (former Burghley) House in the Strand, 1 January 1673. Burghley House Collection, Ex H13/1

The annexe was let to Sir Thomas Edmonds, the Treasurer of the King's Household. In 1623, when the Spanish match between Prince Charles and the Infanta was still regarded as a possibility, Exeter House accommodated the Spanish Ambassador Extraordinary, for whom it was richly furnished and decorated. Its availability, however, seems to have been controversial: it came after several other aborted options, including St James's Palace and both Durham House and Somerset House, and William (1566–1640), the 2nd Earl of Exeter, who had succeeded his father in February, affirmed that 'he could not find it in his heart to bid those in it begone, especially Lord Denny'. This of course indicates that the house had been let throughout.

Meanwhile, railings had been erected round the central Banqueting House to protect it from cattle in 1607 and in 1622 the grant allowing right of access to Covent Garden, first established between Burghley and the 2nd Earl of Bedford in 1561, was renewed.[54] The new Russell in charge was Francis, the future 4th Earl of Bedford who soon created the Covent Garden piazza and built the office and stable blocks opposite the garden of Exeter House. That changed the area in earnest and, incidentally, rendered the renewed agreement void (see Chapter Six). In 1627, a fire destroyed part of the building, including Wimbledon House, while by 1657 the chapel attached to it had been fitted up for Catholic worship, apparently for the use of Henrietta Maria. This is inferred from Evelyn, who on Christmas Day that year attended Mass in the chapel, only to be detained by Puritan soldiers on the grounds that none should any longer observe the superstitious festival of the Nativity. But after being examined in a room at Exeter House and dismissed 'with much pity for his ignorance', he was released. This is virtually all we know about the house during the Commonwealth, after which it was occupied by Frances Howard, Duchess of

BURGHLEY HOUSE | 101

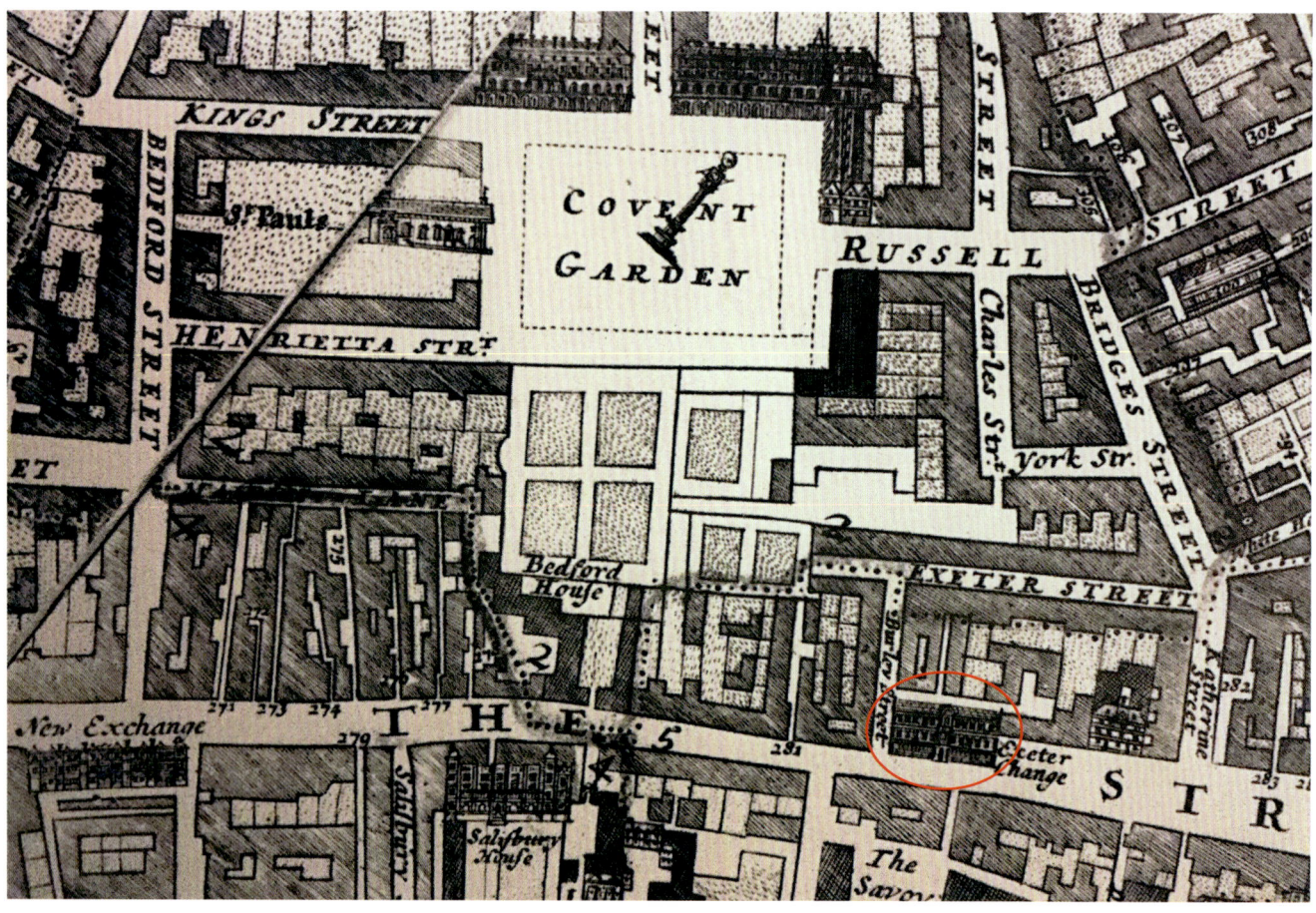

109 Elevations of the Exeter Change, detail from Ogilby and Morgan, *Map of London*, 1681–2. Sheppard 1970, pl. 5

The Covent Garden piazza houses, Great Salisbury House and the New Exchange can also be seen.

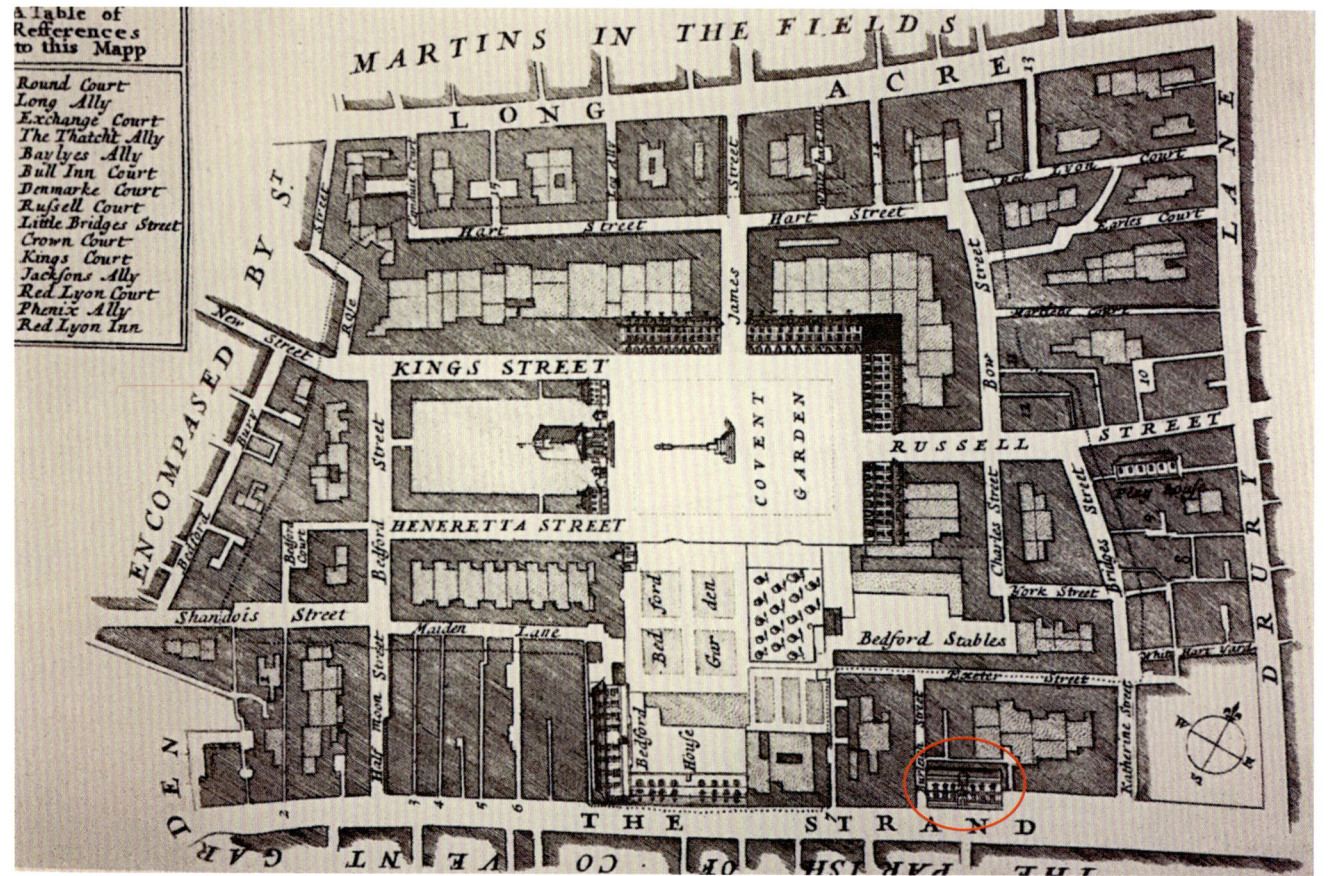

110 Richard Blome, elevation of the Exeter Change, detail of the 'Map' of the Parish of St Paul, Covent Garden, c.1686. Sheppard 1970, pl. 6

The Covent Garden piazza houses and Bedford House can also be seen.

Richmond. Following the Great Fire of 1666 it was rented by the government for the accommodation of the Court of Arches and Prerogative Courts, which had no place of their own after the destruction of Doctors' Commons. Later still, the 1st Earl of Shaftesbury and his second wife, Francis Cecil, the daughter of the 3rd Earl of Exeter (c.1600–1643), were living there, during which time the philosopher John Locke, who was the tutor to Shaftesbury's son and physician to the household, worked on his celebrated *Essay Concerning Human Understanding*.

Shaftesbury's tenure ended in 1676, when he took up residence at Thanet House in the City; in that year Exeter House was demolished. Decline had started at the turn of the decade, when John,

111 George Cooke, view of the menagerie at the Exeter Change, 1826, showing the left-hand side of the Change's original facade. © The Trustees of the British Museum (1880,1113.2859)

4th Earl of Exeter (1628–1678), had requested a licence to build over the site of 'Excester house and the house called Little Excester house in the Strande', as recited in a survey drawing produced by the then Surveyor General, Christopher Wren, on 1 January 1673 (fig. 108). This source not only shows the approved changes but also visualises the extent of the property at the time, fairly similar to that in the plan of 1562–7 (see fig. 97). It is perhaps somewhat chilling too, as one wonders what Wren, requested 'to view the ground & consider how this might best be done for the public convenience', would have made of the disappearance of such an important building, alongside many of the Strand palaces. One is indeed tempted to detect some hesitancy in Wren's actual report, ordered on 1 October 1671, where he stated that 'without the concurrence of the 5th Earle of Bedford', whose nearby stables would have been affected, 'I do not conceive that any considerable advantages will acrew either to the publique or ye Pet[itio]n[er] &c.'[55] But the new scheme, which partitioned the site into several plots around two north–south axes and one east–west parallel to the Strand, was indeed licensed in October 1672, approved by Wren the following 1 January and finally signed off by Charles II on 24 January.[56]

Of the new streets, the one running east–west was built and named Exeter Street, while of the other two, meant to link the Strand with the Charles Street indicated in the survey (coinciding with the current southern part of Burghley Street), only one was realised at the time, due to Bedford's resistance. Of the new buildings, the most important was the Exeter Change, erected right after demolition in 1676, depicted in both Ogilby and Morgan's map of 1681–2 and in Richard Blome's of c.1686 (figs 109 and 110), and described by Strype as consisting of 'two Walks below stairs, and as many above, with Shops on each side for Semsters, Milenners, Hosiers, &c.' However, as Strype continues, 'it received a check in its Infancy, I suppose by those of the New Exchange', the first of its kind in the Strand, built by Robert Cecil at the beginning of the century (see Chapter Eight). By the 1720s it had become 'worse and worse; insomuch that the shops in the first Walk next the street can hardly meet with Tenants, those backwards lying useless, and those above converted to other uses'.[57] These other uses included a menagerie, eventually acquired by the Italian Stefano Polito in 1810, who renamed it 'The Royal Menagerie' (fig. 111). On show were 'a nest of wild beasts' including elephants, two rhinoceroses, a pair of kangaroos, a 'gigantic male ostrich', a Bengal tiger and a pair of lions, who somehow all cohabited within the confines of the place and most definitely attracted attention. Lord Byron was impressed by a performing elephant and wished 'he was his butler', and Jane Austen mentions the menagerie in *Sense and Sensibility* (1811).[58]

In 1829, when improvements to the Strand were undertaken, the axe fell on the Exeter Change too, though the area remained in the family until 1855, when the Marquis of Exeter sold it for about £50,000.

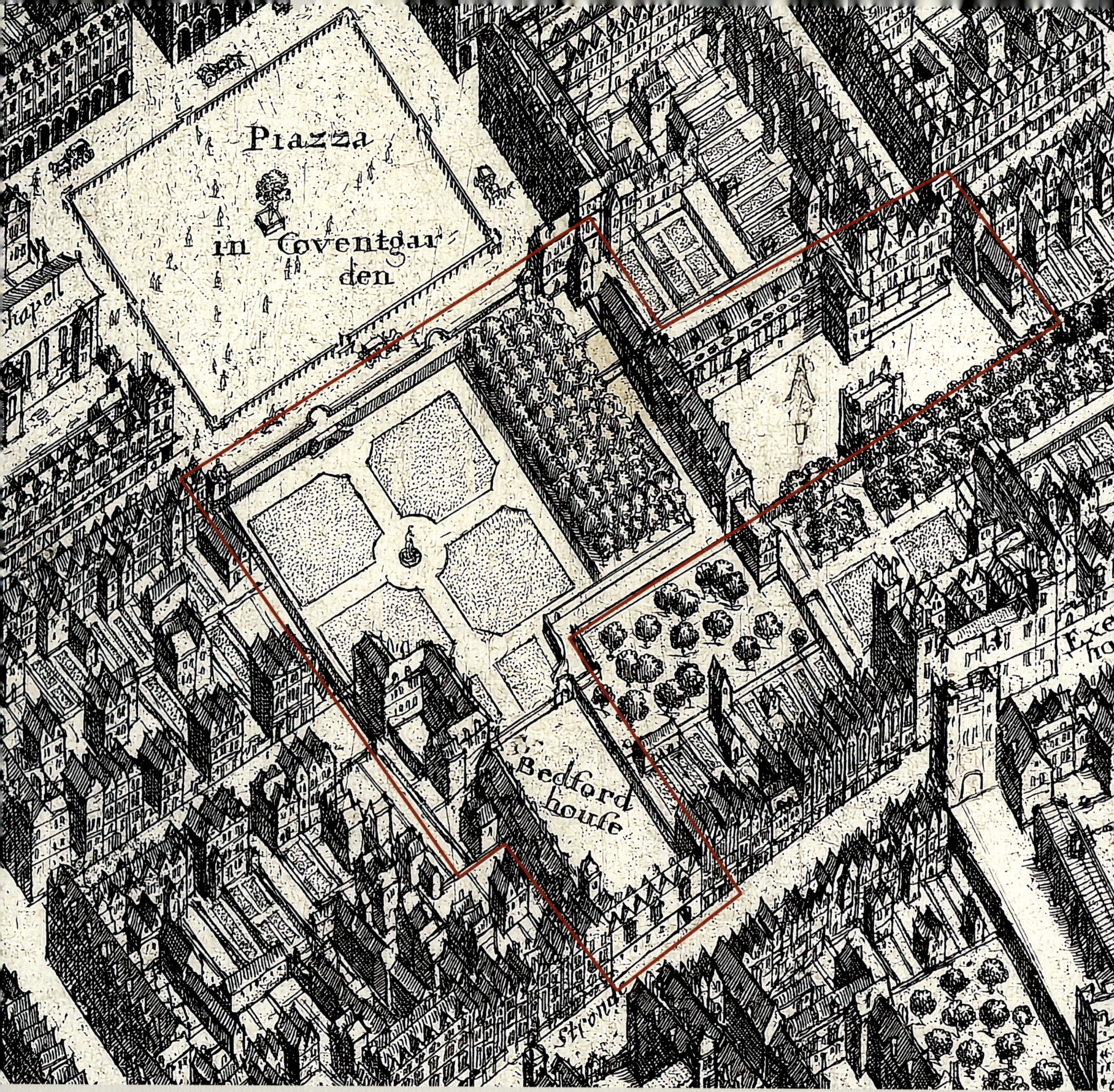

112 The complex of Bedford House with the stables compound to the east (right), at the heart of the Bedford Estate (detail of fig. 8)

6 · BEDFORD HOUSE

BEDFORD HOUSE WAS THE ONLY OTHER palace to lie on the north side of the Strand (alongside Burghley House), with the main facade directly opening onto it, amid rows of tenements. As Hollar's 'West Central District' view of the mid-seventeenth century attests, along with such sources as John Lacy's remarkable map of Covent Garden of 1673,[1] Bedford House was a seemingly simpler, piecemeal and incomplete affair which made for a somewhat irregular L-shaped complex (figs 112 and 113). By contrast, the garden extending to the north onto Covent Garden was elaborate, with a grotto, a grove of trees to the east, a 'halfe round banqueting house' to the west and a terrace with garden pavilions overlooking the piazza created by Inigo Jones.[2] Similarly to Burghley House, the garden side was indeed its best but it had a rather less imposing Strand front. This was two storeys high and prominently gabled, but fairly shallow, perhaps because it derived from the multiplication of a single dwelling (like the first plans for Salisbury House; see Chapter Eight). It was flanked by a tower followed by an orthogonal wing to the west of similar height but twice its width, itself continued by a taller addition towards the northern end. This taller part was composed of four ranges of which three formed a court open to the west, while the fourth projected north to the garden's corner. Instead of matching wings on the north and east sides, a mere wall screened the tenements' back gardens and an orchard, while enclosing a large forecourt. From the Strand, this was accessed through a gateway in the east end of the front, while another gateway in the north-east corner of the forecourt led to a walled carriageway connected to the large stable court to the east. This court had ranges of impressive stables and offices on its west, north and part of the east side, all facing the garden of Burghley House and also accessible from a gatehouse in the north-east corner. It was via two ornate gates that the forecourt of Bedford House was linked to its garden, which faced Jones's piazza.

It is perhaps due to the resonance of Jones's celebrated development and its rich subsequent history, as opposed to the seemingly unremarkable architecture of Bedford House – described by Beresford Chancellor as not 'on that scale of grandeur which characterised the other noble houses in the Strand'[3] – that this complex is less known among its counterparts and seldom cited. In effect, the comparatively rich studies on Covent Garden, with a dedicated volume of the Survey of London

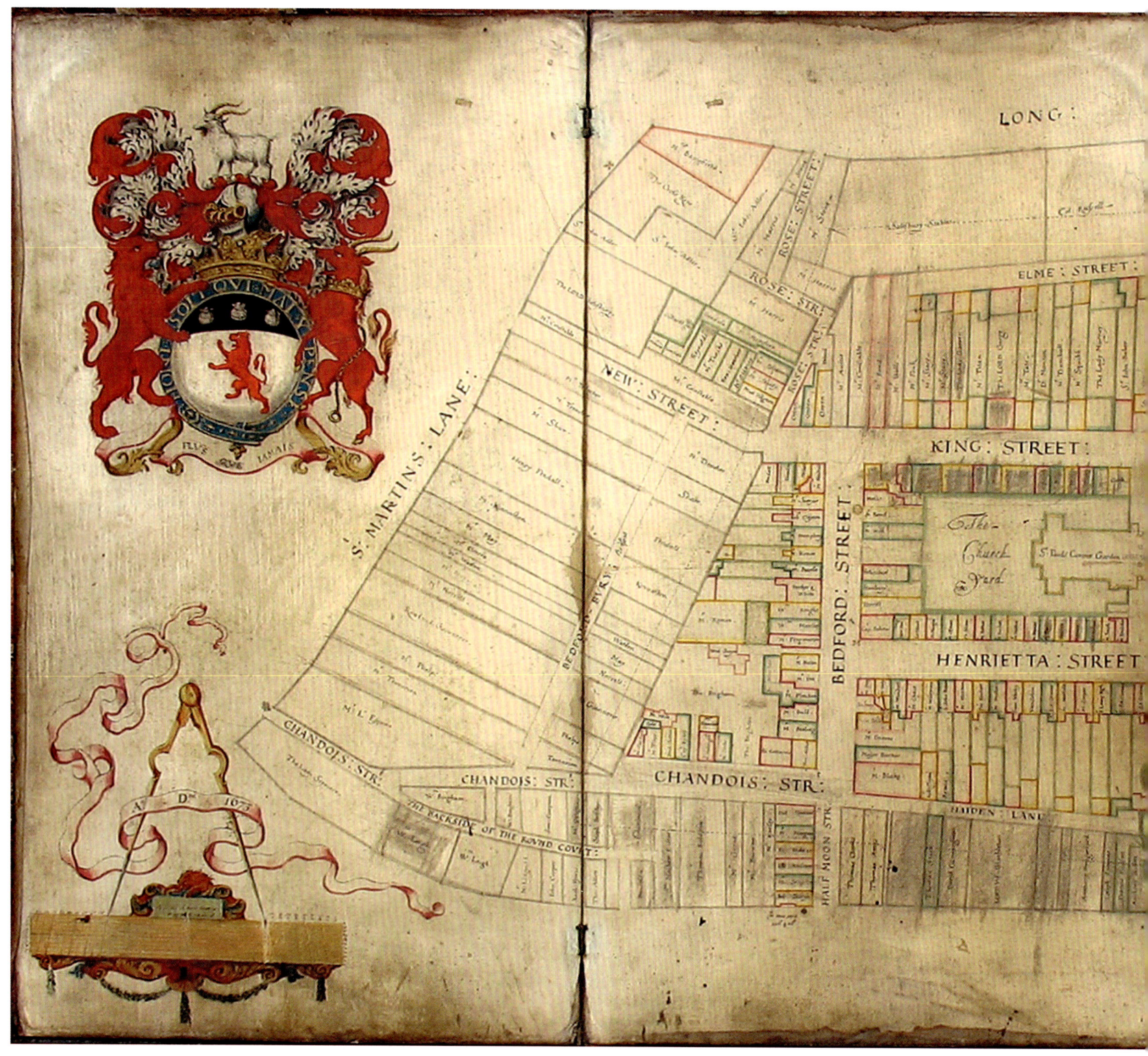

(1970), a doctoral dissertation by Diane Duggan (2001) on the architectural patronage of 4th Earl of Bedford, the man behind Jones's creation, and a number of subsequent articles by her, only partially deal with the house, especially when it comes to its early history.[4] The same is true of the pioneering studies by Gladys Scott-Thomson, the archivist at Woburn Abbey, the Bedfords' ancestral seat in Bedfordshire, from the 1930s to the 1950s. Yet her many unpublished notes on the two Strand palaces of the family's, Bedford House and Worcester House (see Chapter Seven), are still of great value.[5] Bedford House is in fact relatively well documented, with papers from the London office of the Bedford Estate transferred to the archives at Woburn, while those relating

113a–d John Lacy, map of Covent Garden, 1673. Woburn Abbey Collection

106 | LONDON'S 'GOLDEN MILE'

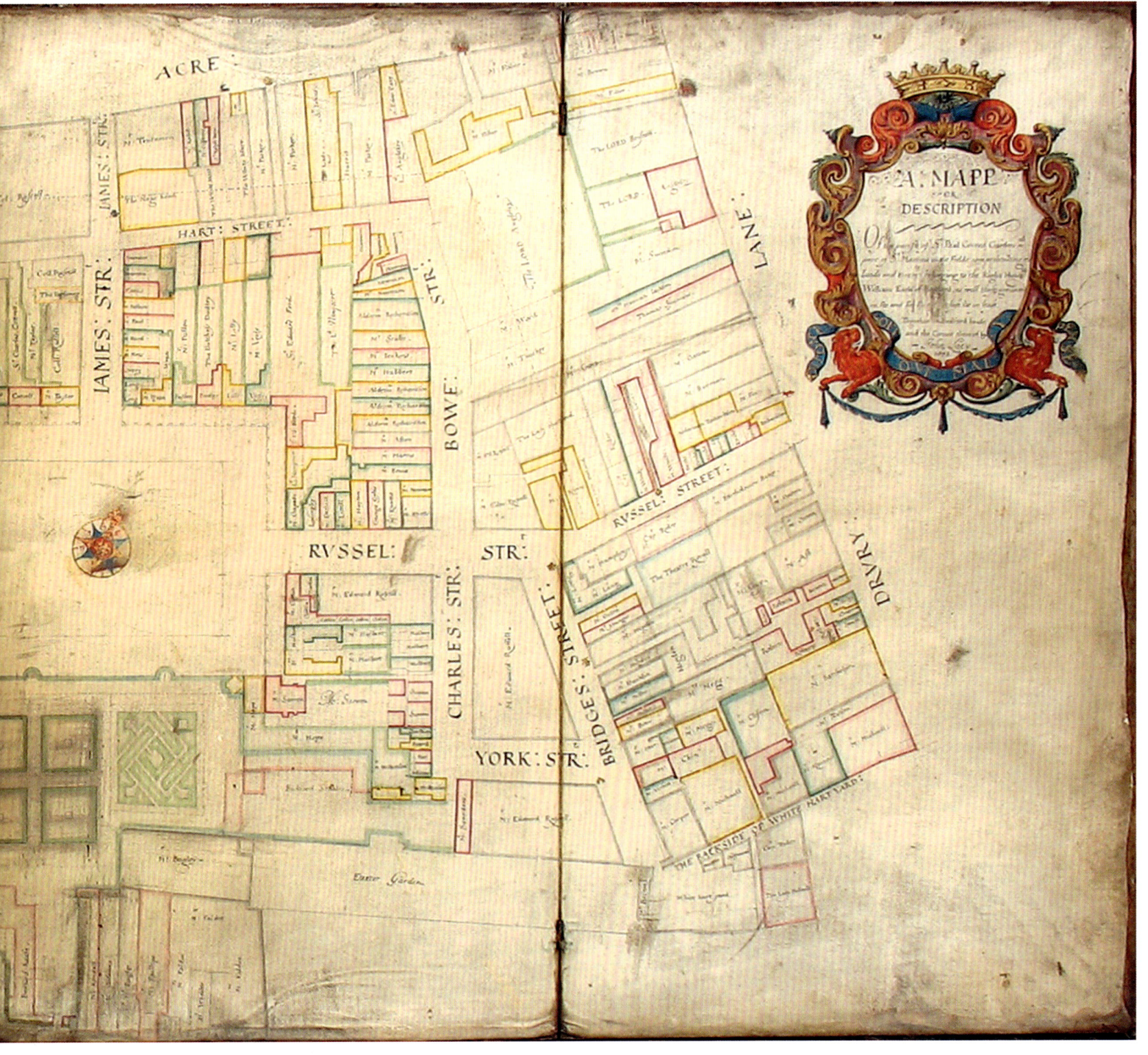

to Covent Garden mainly went to the London Metropolitan Archives in the early 1990s, when the office was disbanded.[6] A note dated June 1970 accompanying a bundle of the Covent Garden papers of 1593 to 1686 indicates how they had been seen and listed by John Summerson 'some years ago' but not by the Survey of London staff, hence were not in their volume.[7] Alnwick Castle has some material too, since an acrimonious dispute in 1639 between Francis Russell, 4th Earl of Bedford, and his agent Robert Scawen resulted in some of the papers being removed (or stolen) by the latter when defecting to the 10th Earl of Northumberland, of that house further down the Strand (see Chapter Eleven).[8] This chapter examines all the evidence afresh.

BEDFORD HOUSE | 107

The House of Edward Russell, 3rd Earl of Bedford: 1585–1627

A house of the Earls of Bedford generally known as Russell House had existed on the opposite side of the Strand since 1539, when the former inn of the Bishop of Carlisle passed to John Russell, afterwards 1st Earl of Bedford (c.1485–1555), Henry VIII's Comptroller of the Household. Following the death of Francis, 2nd Earl of Bedford, on 28 July 1585, a day after the death of his third but eldest surviving son, Francis, Russell House descended to the female line and was subsequently sold to the Worcesters, whereby it became Worcester House (see Chapter Seven). The contents of Russell House, the Bedford title and the estate in Covent Garden were inherited instead by Edward (1572–1627), Lord Russell, the only grandson of the 2nd Earl, then a minor.[9]

Originally owned by the Abbot and Convent of Westminster, the land forming the so-called Bedford Estate had come into the possession of the 1st Earl of Bedford through two separate grants, in 1541 and 1552, by Henry VIII and Edward VI respectively, and remained in the family for four hundred years. The first grant

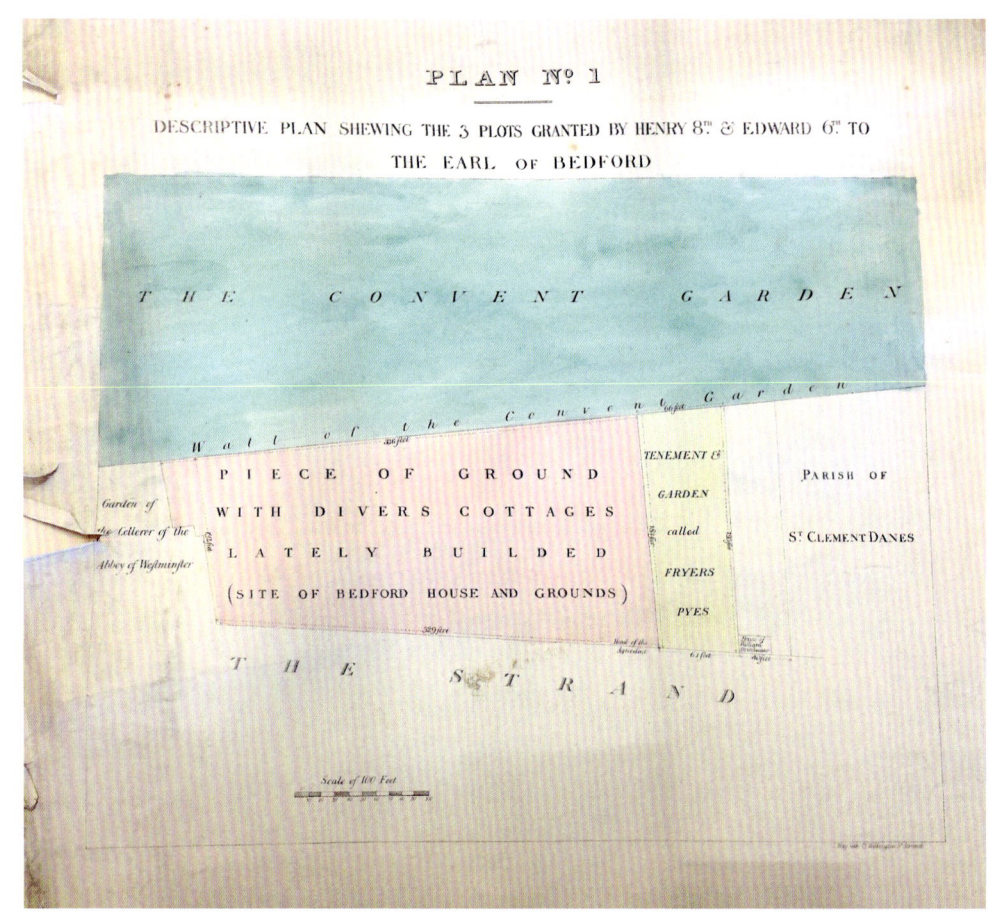

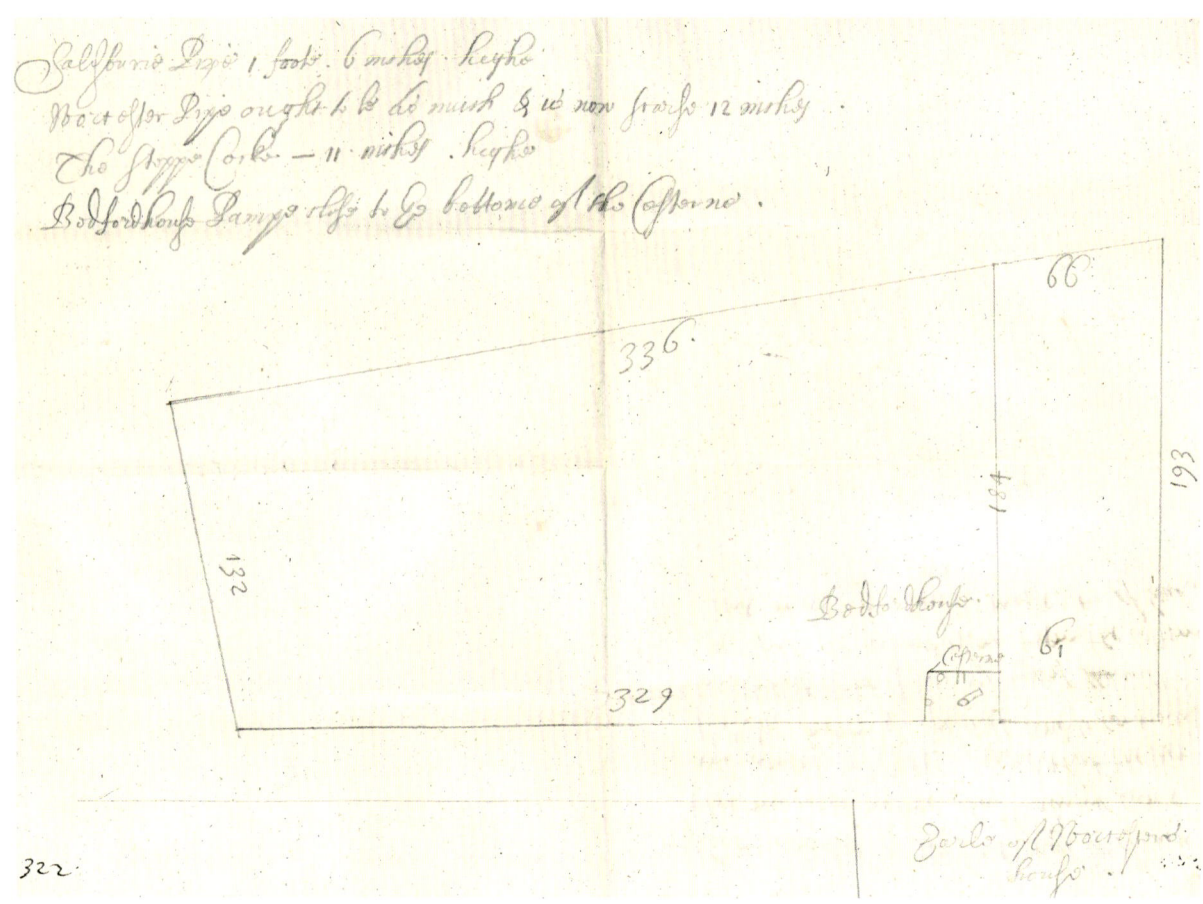

114 'Descriptive Plan Shewing the 3 Plots Granted by Henry 8th & Edward 6th to the Earl of Bedford', from 5th Report of HM Commissioners of Woods, for the scheme to widen the Strand, 1826. London Metropolitan Archives

115 Plan of the area occupied by Bedford House and partly by Worcester House opposite, produced over a dispute for a water pipe, 1630s. Alnwick Castle, Sy:Y.III.2/5/13. Collection of the Duke of Northumberland

108 | LONDON'S 'GOLDEN MILE'

116 Conjectured site of Bedford House (in the red circle) in relation to Palmer House (in the red rectangle), detail of the *Woodcut Map of London*, 1561–70 ('Agas'), reprinted 1633, derived from the lost 'Copperplate Map of London'. Mitton, 1908. Wikimedia Commons Public Domain

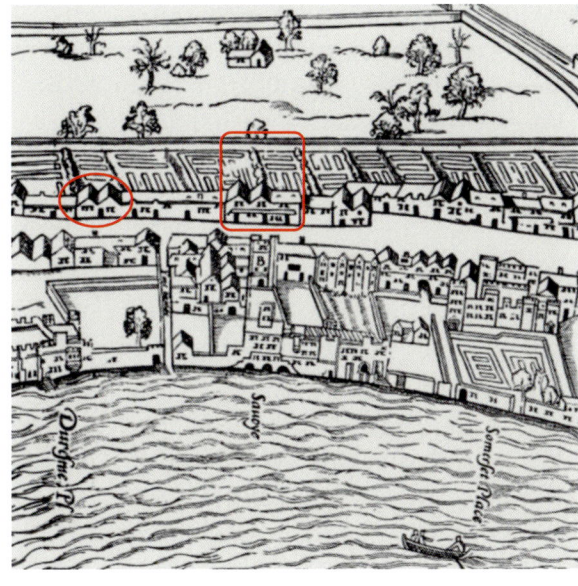

117 Bedford House, detail of John Norden, *Speculum Britanniae*, 1593. Folger Shakespeare Library, Washington DC. Licensed under Creative Commons Attribution-ShareAlike 4.0 International

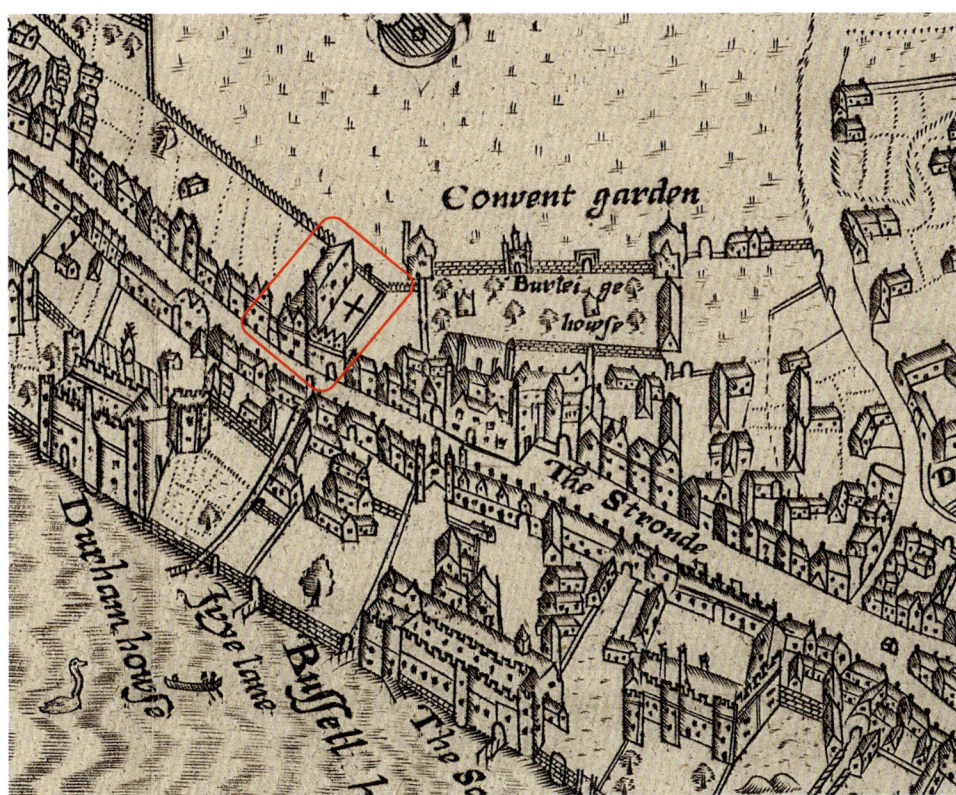

consisted of two pieces of land later called Friars Pyes, abutting the Strand and almost directly opposite Russell House, and the second included Covent Garden (the garden of the Convent of Westminster), which adjoined Friars Pyes to the north, and a further seven acres called Long Acre, themselves adjoining the garden to the north. After Westminster's confiscation by Henry VIII, it had formed part of the enormous grant made to Edward Seymour, Duke of Somerset, which was parcelled out in different directions by Edward VI.[10] Mainly pasture land, Bedford's acquisition was primarily intended to extend the limits of the main residence (later Worcester House) on the south side of the Strand, fully developed by then, as a means of providing for his household. This is a reminder that the Strand palaces, and the episcopal inns before them, were meant to be self-sufficient.

A 'Descriptive Plan Shewing the 3 Plots Granted by Henry 8th & Edward 6th to the Earl of Bedford' (fig. 114) shows the extent of the estate and the site of the new 'Bedford House and Grounds', an irregular plot formerly part of Friars Pyes right opposite Russell House, since occupied by 'divers cottages lately builded' and measuring 329 feet along the Strand, between the 'tenement & garden called Fryers Pyes' on the east and the 'Garden of the Cellerer of the Abbey of Westminster' on the west; 184 feet deep on the east and 132 feet deep on the west; and 336 feet along the 'Wall of the Convent Garden' on the north side. These measurements are confirmed by a rough ground-plan of Bedford House of the 1630s (fig. 115).[11] Wyngaerde's earliest depiction of the area (see fig. 86), produced in *c.*1544, only a few years after the first grant of Friars Pyes in 1541, has an unfavourable viewpoint and does not show the site; it does, however, confirm that there was hardly anything built beyond the line of tenements along the north side of the Strand, for the corresponding pastureland was still largely undeveloped and remained so for almost another century, until about the 1630s.

The next topographical source is the Agas map of 1561–70 (fig. 116), which derives from the lost 'Copperplate' map of 1553–9 and is therefore almost contemporaneous with the second grant of Covent Garden and Long Acre in 1552. As a bird's-eye view, it is more illuminating but only in that it shows the extent of the whole estate, for the precise location of the Bedford plot can hardly be discerned among a fairly nondescript row of buildings and back gardens. However, if one takes as a reference the parsonage of St Clement Danes, acquired by William Cecil in 1559 (see Chapter Five) and clearly seen right opposite the Savoy before the corner houses where the Strand widened, one is tempted to identify the two gables to the left of that parsonage as belonging to the site of Bedford House. A similar scenario is depicted by Braun and Hogenberg's map in 1572 (see fig. 99), also derived from the Copperplate map. The next view in John Norden's 1593 map clearly shows the new complex as composed of the main gabled body along the Strand and the side wing extending northwards to the wall of Covent Garden on the west, with the tall tower in between and the large, enclosed forecourt (fig. 117).[12] Apart from the kind of C-plan building to the north of the side wing, as well as the garden and stable buildings extending into Covent Garden, what appears in 1593 ties in with Hollar's depiction of the main complex in the mid-seventeenth century (see fig. 112). The year 1593 can therefore be considered as the *terminus ante quem* for completion of the main stage of construction. It also marks the coming of age of Edward Russell, 3rd Earl of Bedford, who had inherited the title and estate aged twelve after the death of his grandfather in 1585. This date in turn ought to provide the *terminus post quem*, for a new Bedford House became a necessity only after the title had become detached from the original Russell House.[13]

Edward's trustees were his aunt Anne Russell, Countess of Warwick, and his uncle William, Lord Russell of Thornhaugh (*c*.1553–1613), the 2nd Earl's fourth and only surviving son.[14] As a ward of the Crown, Edward's affairs would have been managed by Lord Burghley, Master of the Court of Wards and High Steward of Westminster since 1561 (as noted in Chapter Five). This was just as well, for the two were distantly related: Elizabeth Cooke, one of Mildred Cecil's four sisters, had married John Russell (d. 1584), Edward's uncle.[15] In 1586 the wardenship was then granted to Anne Russell and her husband Ambrose Dudley, Earl of Warwick, but Burghley remained in charge throughout the minority.[16] The extent of the Secretary's control was in effect almost limitless, as may be read in a letter related to Elizabeth I's visit to Woburn Abbey, written to him on 16 July 1572 by the 2nd Earl:

> *I am now going to prepare for her Majesties coming to Woborne, which shall be done in the best and most hastiest manner that I can. I trust your Lordship will have in remembrance to provide helpe that her Majesties tarrieng be not above two nights and a daye, for so long tyme do I prepare. I pray God, the Rowmes and Lodgings there may be to her Majesties contentacion for the tyme.*[17]

Alongside the Warwicks, the construction of Bedford House would consequently have seen Burghley involved – given also the proximity to his own Strand palace, let alone his reputation in matters architectural. At least partially, the house must have been a new build, for the first available reference, from the 3rd Earl's revenues of Michaelmas 1586, describes it as the 'Capitall messuage called Bedford house newly buylded & letten during my Lo. mynoryty'.[18] The next reference follows his coming of age in 1593, when Anne Russell released to her nephew 'all manner of ymplementes, seelinges, portalles, and other household stuffe and furniture of myne whatsoever, nowe remayninge and being in … Bedford howse'.[19] The house must have been habitable by at least 1590, for the Earl of Warwick died there that year.[20] Building must therefore have occurred within *c*.1585–90, plenty of time for a new house – bigger constructions like Burghley's, or indeed Somerset House, were largely completed within a similar time-frame (see Chapters Three and Five).

As in these other palaces, the question of pre-existence is an important one, particularly as the seemingly unremarkable Strand front of Bedford House may well, as previously mentioned, have been adapted from former dwellings, such as the two gabled houses seen in the Agas map of 1561–70 (see fig. 116); these are tantalisingly similar to those seen at the Strand head of the west wing in Norden's view (see fig. 117). When Friars Pyes had been granted to the 1st Earl in 1552, the area was indeed occupied by 'divers cottages lately builded', while somewhere within the site that earl had subsequently (no later than 1555, the year of his death) put up a 'wooden mansion', 'less pretentious' than Russell House, which both he and the 2nd Earl had seldom if at all used.[21] By 1564 stables had also been built along the Strand front of Friars Pyes, to provide, once again, for the Bedfords' main abode on the opposite, south side.[22] These were large and had haylofts above.[23] When the 3rd Earl inherited the site, it was therefore fairly built up, certainly on its street front. Yet, whatever the wooden mansion – possibly a sizeable timber-framed building – or any of the ancillary structures, there was no large house, as a description of Friars Pyes contained in the 'inquisition' taken after the 2nd Earl's death in 1585 testifies.[24]

While the Strand range of Bedford House, referred to in later payments as the 'old timber house', may well have incorporated pre-existing structures, the wing to the west extending north to the wall of Covent Garden, and the tower in between, were certainly new, as neither appears in any of the topographical views prior to Norden's in 1593.[25] In its probable mixture of old and new, the complex was in no way unusual among the Strand palaces. Less usual, perhaps, was the way it developed – it 'runneth backwards', as John Stow put it[26] – but only if compared to more prominent courtyard houses such as Somerset's or Burghley's, which reflected the grandeur of their political roles, far exceeding that of the young Bedford. Indeed, if one compares the site of Bedford House and grounds in the descriptive plan of the Bedford Estate with later plans of the complex (see figs 114 and 113b and c), one realises that the part with the main house, the Strand range of which was about 100 feet long of the 329 potentially available, occupied a third of it and was concentrated in the south-west corner. This confirms the relatively utilitarian nature of the enterprise: valuable rent from existing properties to the east up to Burghley House was to be retained, if not prioritised (another common trait among the Strand palaces). That said, Bedford House still caught the attention of Stow, who, after describing Burghley House in his *Survay of London* of 1598, continued that 'From thence is now a continuall new building of divers fayre houses, even up to the Earle of Bedfordes house, which is a goodly house, lately builded nigh to Ivy Bridge, over against the olde Bedforde house'.[27] Indeed, the complex was neither inconspicuous nor small, as a subsequent edition of the *Survay* specifies:

Bedford House – in the Strand, but runneth backwards; being a large but old built house, having a great Yard before it For the reception of coaches; with a spacious garden having a Terrace walk adjoining the Brick wall next the garden; and from there receives the Prospect thereof. Behind this garden are the coach houses and stables; and for the Conveniency thereof there is a passage into Charles St. shut up by a large gate.[28]

The last part of this description concerning the garden, coach houses and stables must indeed refer to the period related to the 4th Earl of Bedford and to his improvements of the 1630s, discussed shortly. For, before then Bedford House had virtually no garden beyond a small area to the north of the forecourt, about ninety feet at its widest, derived from an adjustment of the boundary with Covent Garden in 1612, occasioned by the erection of a brick wall in lieu of the old wooden fence seen in Norden (see fig. 117). As shown in a contemporary plan (fig. 118), this was to enclose the remaining twenty-acre 'great pasture' area of Covent Garden, around which

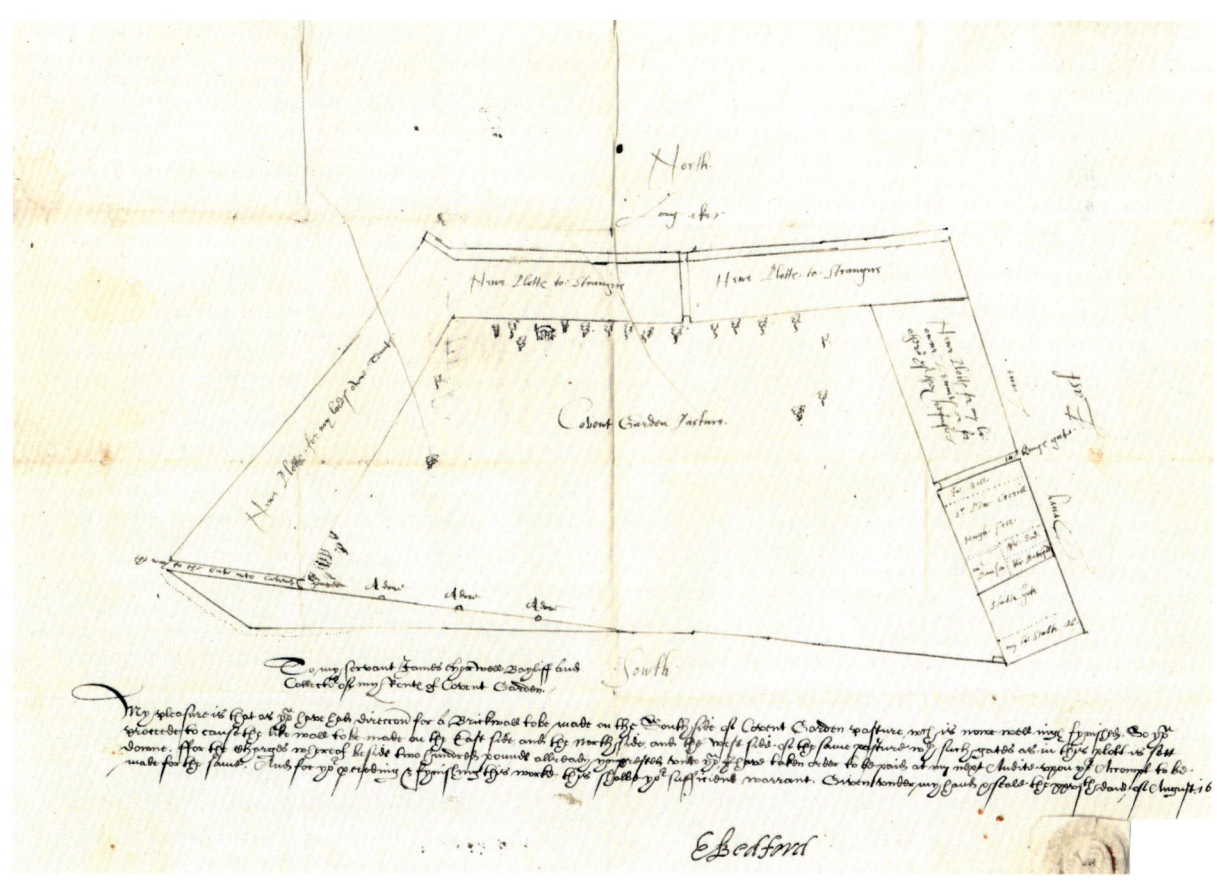

118 Plan for the enclosure of Covent Garden Pasture, 1612. Alnwick Castle, Sy:Y. III.2/1/3/3/2. Collection of the Duke of Northumberland

BEDFORD HOUSE | 111

plots were to be leased off for building, so as to put part of the estate to profit. The first development took place in 1615 on the north side, when Long Acre was laid out in collaboration with the lessee of the Mercers' Company land, and by 1618 leases had been granted to a number of tenants.[29]

The adjustment to the garden is virtually all we know about, and may be all that happened to Bedford House during the tenure of the 3rd Earl, for neither he nor his wife, Lucy Harington (1581–1627), whom he had married in 1594, seem to have lived there for any length of time. The earl seems to have had a preference for country life, especially after a serious fall from a horse in 1613 turned him into an invalid and he reportedly became a recluse. The countess when in town mostly used her own family residence in London, Harington House in Bishopsgate. Otherwise she resided at Twickenham Park from 1608 to 1617 and then at Moor Park near Rickmansworth in Hertfordshire, granted to the Bedfords by James I in 1617.[30] At these two houses the countess created celebrated gardens, part of her leading role as a patron of the arts.[31] She was a kinswoman of Sir Philip and Mary Sidney through her maternal grandmother and namesake Lucy, and of John Harington of Kelston, the poet and translator of Ariosto, as well as being closely associated with such poets, playwrights and translators as Michael Drayton, John Florio, Samuel Daniel and Ben Jonson, and John Donne who wrote several poems to and for her. The countess's reputation has eclipsed the substantial debts and political misfortunes of her husband, despite whom, rather than because of, she gained eminence.[32] Indeed, as Queen Anne's favourite Lady of the Bedchamber, she had considerable influence at court while her determination was renowned, if somewhat grudgingly acknowledged: 'if she hathe not more resembled her sex in loving her owne will', wrote Robert Cecil of her sponsoring her brother as a potential husband for Cecil's daughter.[33] Yet all efforts were compounded by constant financial problems, for the Harington estate, of which she later inherited a substantial part, was encumbered with debts of £40,000, while her husband's notorious mismanagement of the Bedford inheritance placed considerable extra strain on that estate. This reached a new peak following the 3rd Earl's disastrous involvement in the Essex Rebellion of 1601 (see Chapter One), for which he was initially confined to Bedford House, then exiled from court and fined £20,000, later reduced to half. In the circumstances, two plots of land at the northern end of St Martin's Lane were sold to Robert Cecil in 1609 (see Chapter Eight), who indeed coveted the whole of Covent Garden and Long Acre and had begun to put pressure on both Bedford and the Lord Chancellor, Ellesmere, to grant an Order in Chancery in 1606 for their sale. But the 3rd Earl's former trustees, Anne and particularly William Russell (heir apparent in the absence of issue), intervened. The 2nd Earl and Countess had in fact failed to produce an heir, since both their son and daughter, born in 1602 and 1610, had died soon after birth. It was William's son, Francis Russell (1587–1641), following his father's death in 1613, who obtained control of the whole estate, which eventually became his own in 1619. This came on condition of a yearly maintenance of £1695 to the 2nd Earl and Countess and of the right to live at Bedford House, leased back for the remainder of their lives.[34] In the early 1620s, it was none the less let to the Earl and Countess of Rutland, who were probably its last residents until the house and earldom passed to Francis, for Edward and Lucy died within a few weeks of each other in May 1627.[35] The 3rd Earl of Bedford has gone down in history for the wrong reasons, in spite of the fact that the development of Coven Garden had begun under his auspices and that some of his wife's patronage had been sponsored by him.

The House of Francis Russell, 4th Earl of Bedford: 1627–1641

The 4th Earl is regarded as perhaps the most earnest of the family, a man 'in advance of his time altogether', as well as someone who 'seems to have had the ability, highly unusual among the peerage, to reduce expenditure when under financial pressure'.[36] Indeed, the rebuilding of Woburn Abbey, the draining of the Fens and, of course, the development of Covent Garden, alongside an active career at court which eventually brought him the position of Lord Treasurer, provided subsequent generations of Russells with wealth and restored political dominance.[37] Although Francis continued to live in the old Russell of Thornhaugh's house in Chiswick after officially succeeding to the title in 1627, his centre soon switched to Bedford House to meet the demands of politics and of the Covent Garden development.

It is perhaps surprising, given the quantity of documents produced for the latter, that the only evidence concerning the Strand palace is a relatively short bill from a stonemason of 9 August 1628, 'In primis for a figgure of an oulde woman w.th a catt in her lapp', which nevertheless yields a number of important points.[38] First, it is authorised by Edward Carter (d. 1663), Jones's deputy at St Paul's Cathedral from 1633 and later employed at Northumberland House (see Chapter Eleven), then clearly acting as Bedford's surveyor.[39] The mason, however, is a certain Meller, possibly identifiable as Hans Weller, the chief workman on the three funeral monuments commissioned by Francis Russell in about 1618.[40] The statue of an old woman with a cat (on which more later) was worth £10, the same amount it was priced in the bill and the most expensive item there, as certified by another document, signed by Nicholas Stone (c.1586–1647) and others.[41] Stone was Jones's master mason at the Banqueting House (1619–22), as well as his co-architect for the York House water gate in the mid-1620s (see Chapter Ten); he too became involved with the earl's works at Covent Garden, having worked for him at Woburn Abbey in the 1620s.[42] Secondly, the bill refers to works in 'several roomes about the house' including 'oulde stone squared and sett in the passage to the Parlor', as well as 'lockstones hookestones and boultstones in all the newe buildings', where 'two newe chimney peeces' (as well as reworking two old ones), were also set up. Other items include much paving, 'stone squared and sett on the wash house' and 'within two dores [in] the garden', and 'newe stone laid in … the courtyard'. These indicate overall general repairs and upgrading, in progress by 1628 and possibly much needed, for the complex seems to have received little if any attention since the early 1590s. The household was also considerably different from that of the 3rd Earl, as Francis Russell and his wife Catherine (d. 1657), the daughter of Giles Bridges, 3rd Baron Chandos, had ten children, eight of whom survived to adulthood.

The 'newe buildings' must be contemporaneous with the northern extension of the garden or, rather, the creation of a garden, which acted as the 'forth side' to the Covent Garden piazza, in progress by the early 1630s.[43] This included the new St Paul's, a temple-style church surrounded by porticoed houses on the east and north sides of the square, triggered in the mid- to late 1620s by the need to provide an increasing number of parishioners with a new place of worship. The concept of the piazza was born, as John Summerson put it, out of the 'happy conjunction' of three men: 'Charles I, with his fine taste and would-be autocratic control of London's architecture; Jones with his perfectly mature understanding of Italian design; and the Earl of Bedford with his business-like aptitude for speculative building.'[44] Francis does not appear to have been directly interested in gardens, for there is no reference to them in his personal papers or in the Commonplace Books, the hand-written miscellanea compiled by and for himself, in themselves remarkable and indeed a testament to his stature. In the first volume, for instance, under 'home' one finds a reference to Serlio, while under 'dwelling' one learns about the correct orientation of houses according to climate, as discussed by Palladio among others.[45] There are also fascinating fragments of political gossip, such as the remark attributed to Henry Howard, 1st Earl of Northampton (the builder of Northumberland House; see Chapter Eleven), that 'King Jeamses hope of the commonwelth wase like top [to] be cast away upon Edwin Sandys instead of Goodwin Sands'.[46]

The point here, as remarked by Duggan, is not whether Bedford was genuinely interested in gardens, or architecture for that matter, but that the creation of an elaborate garden surrounded by equally elaborate houses was the only way to ennoble his Strand palace. For it not only had no proper garden, unlike all his neighbouring grandees' houses, but was also old-fashioned and piecemeal, as previously pointed out.[47] Leaving the fourth side unbuilt also allowed space for new stables, until then located at a distance at the south-east end of Drury Lane (see fig. 118). Thus the classicism of the new north range, and of the piazza overall, would have appealed to the earl as a prestigious project: he would change from the one with perhaps the least attractive Strand palace to the promoter of the very last word in architecture. Furthermore, the inclusion of a church (an aspect that seems to have gone unremarked so far) would transform Bedford House into that complex of palace and church promoted in the Renaissance and much emulated in the seventeenth century. This was a contrast with the other palaces, apart from Somerset House, the Savoy and Durham House, and the last two did not really count because they were virtually unchanged since medieval times. Italian examples of a church acting as a public and family chapel (or at any rate a celebration of the family's patronage) span San Lorenzo for the Palazzo Medici in Florence or the Duomo for the Palazzo Piccolomini in Pienza, both early to mid-1400s, to Santa Maria in Via Lata for the Palazzo Chigi-Odescalchi in Rome some two centuries later.[48] Those families needed to establish themselves, much like Francis Russell did (albeit for different reasons). Invariably, this implied a palace in town, the bigger and/or more elaborate the better, and a seat in the country, on both of which the earl concentrated.

Evidence of the new layout of the Bedford House complex and of the whole estate is provided by a series of plans, the first two of which are ground-plan surveys, one little more than a sketch, the other annotated and scribbled over (figs 119 and 120).[49] The latter plan has been dated to 1628–30 and attributed to Isaac de Caus (c.1590–1648), the garden designer, architect and hydraulic engineer responsible for the grottoes at the Banqueting House (1623), Somerset House (1630–33) and Woburn Abbey (1633–4). De Caus not only joined Carter as surveyors of Jones's work at Covent Garden but also appears to have been responsible for the other elaborate grotto at Bedford House, together with most if not all of the garden design.[50] Like Carter and Stone, he too lived within the estate.[51] His plan may sketch water collection or disposal for the new piazza, and/or water features at Bedford House but it shows the outline of two apse-shaped viewing platforms projecting out of the terrace wall, which formed the boundary of the garden (fig. 120).[52] The western platform and the north-west corner of the complex can be seen in a painting of Covent Garden of c.1649–56, sometimes called the 'Earliest View' as it is the first known depiction of the area and indeed the only non-topographical source to date (fig. 122).[53] It is therefore a precious view, even if only the furthest north-western side of Bedford House is included. To the left of the platform, but on

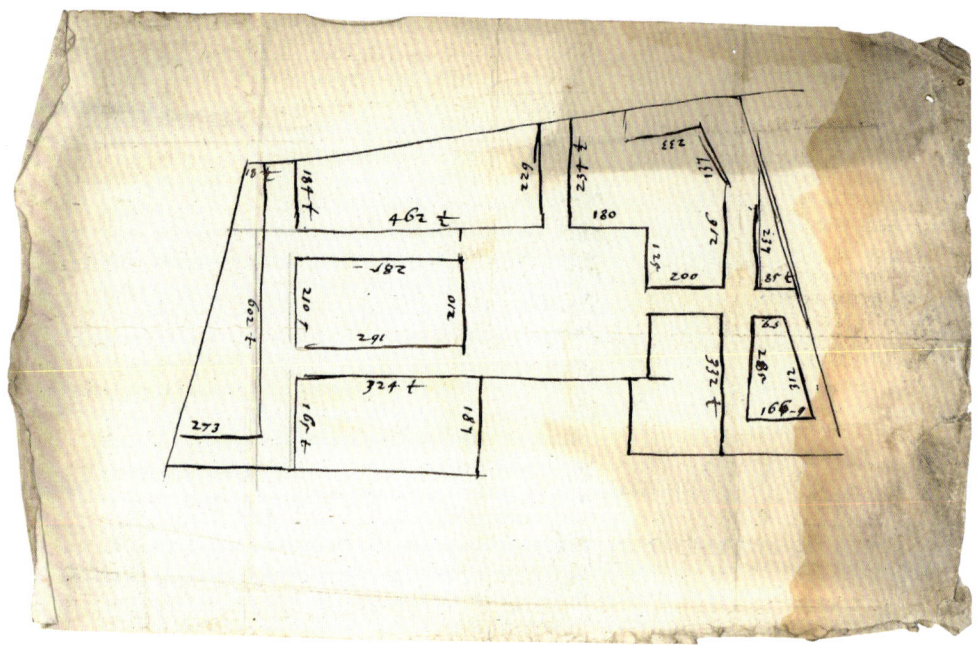

119 Sketch plan of Covent Garden, early 17th century. Alnwick Castle, Sy:Y. III.2/1/3/3/6. Collection of the Duke of Northumberland

120 Isaac de Caus, scaled plan of Covent Garden, 1628–30. Alnwick Castle, Sy:Y. III.2/1/3/3/5. Collection of the Duke of Northumberland

121 Thomas Colepeper, plan of the grotto in Bedford House's garden, 1705, redrawn by Diane Duggan. Duggan 2001, fig. 43

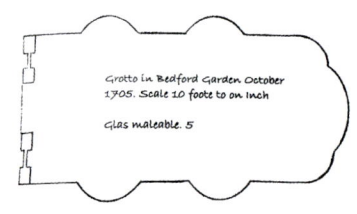

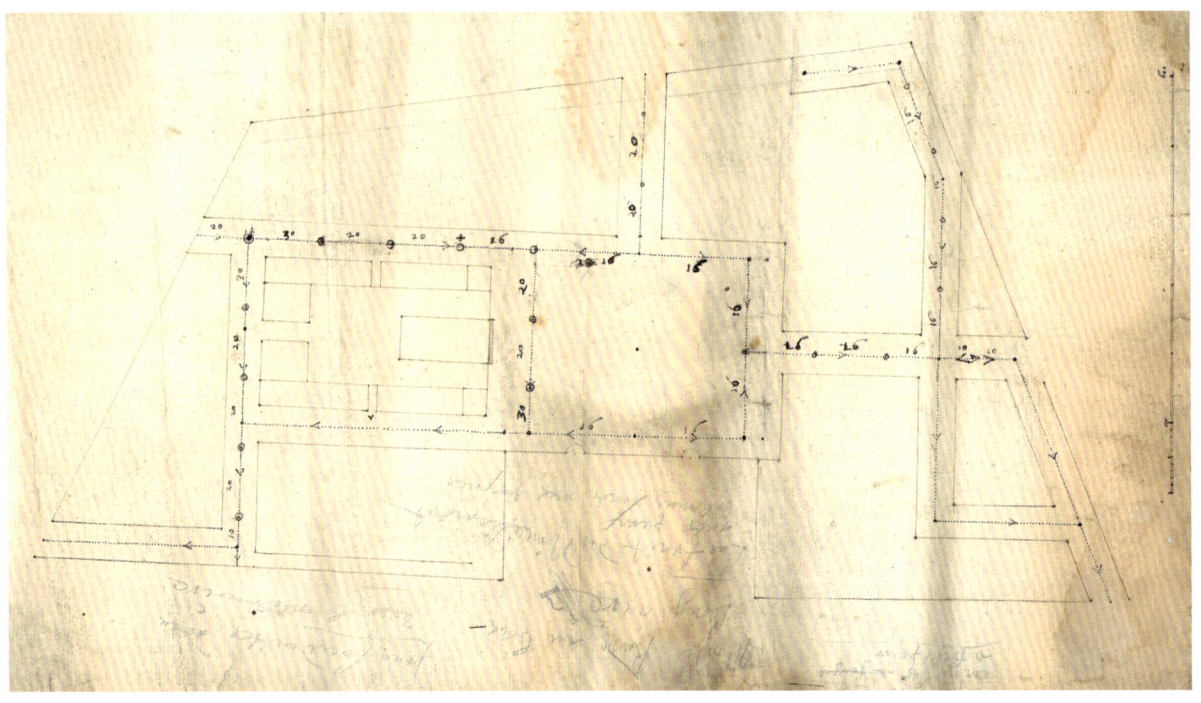

122 *opposite, above* English School, *London, a View of the Piazza, Covent Garden*, 1649–56. Sotheby's

123 *opposite, below* Attributed to Isaac de Caus, design for a fantastic grotto. Victoria and Albert Museum, London

114 | LONDON'S 'GOLDEN MILE'

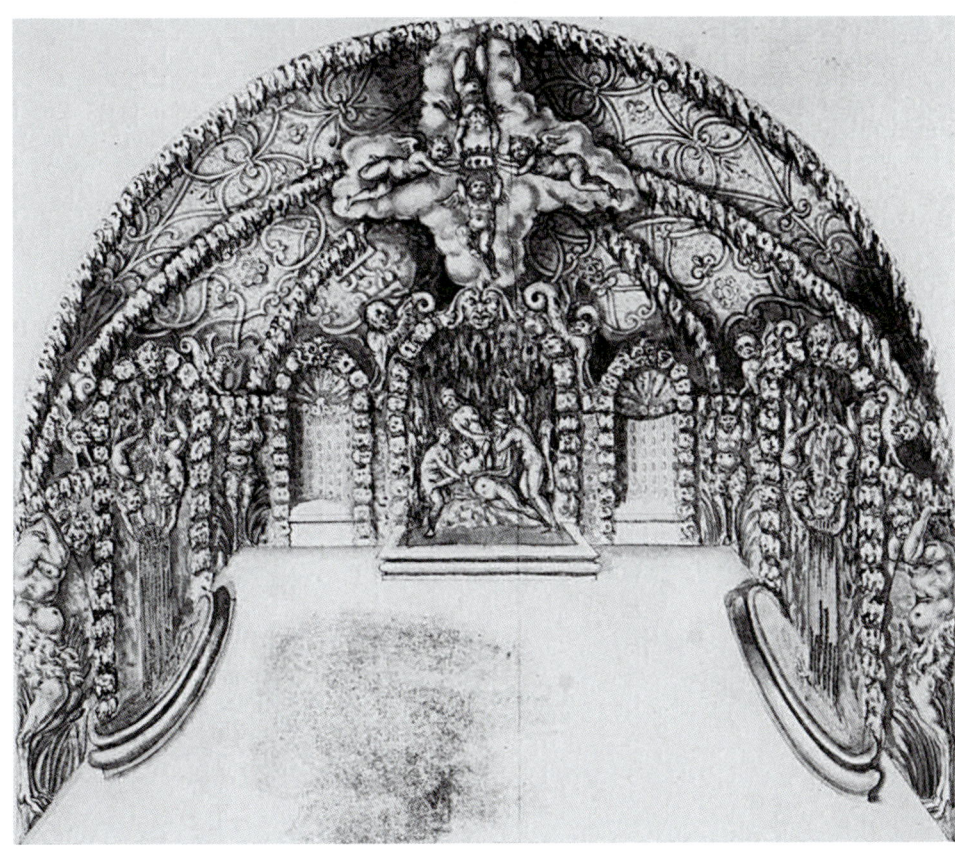

axis with it when one allows for the perspective's angle, as also confirmed by Hollar and later plans, is a triple-arched gateway surmounted by stone balls. This was no doubt on top of the double staircase leading to the terrace, again shown by Hollar and others as on axis with the central alley (see figs 112 and 113c) and, seemingly, with a window in the north elevation of the west wing (see fig. 125). De Caus's grotto, as Duggan has convincingly suggested, would have occupied the corresponding area underneath the double staircase, terrace and platform for some forty feet in length. That is comparable to a survey plan by Thomas Colepeper of the 'Grotto in Bedford Garden' of October 1705, which also shows a large central niche, apparently corresponding to the viewing platform above, and two smaller niches either side (fig. 121). What it may have looked like inside may also be suggested by one of three grotto designs attributed to de Caus with a theme based on Diana and Callisto, similar in style to Woburn's grotto (fig. 123). Equally, a drawing of a wall fountain in a niche, likewise attributed to de Caus but in relation to the grotto he designed at

BEDFORD HOUSE | 115

Wilton House (1635/6), may instead be linked to the Bedford House one (fig. 124).[54]

Associated with the grotto were two banqueting houses at either end of the terrace, the western one of which appears in the 'Earliest View', while their plans and dimensions are evidenced by John Lacy's map of 1673 (see figs 122 and 113c). With a Greek-cross plan some twenty feet across, pedimented aediculed transepts and prominent domed roofs, these garden pleasure buildings were the width of the terrace, hence about thirty square feet. In terms of size and arrangement they could therefore not compete with those at the neighbouring Burghley/Exeter House, built some sixty years earlier on a grander scale (see Chapter Five). In terms of style, however, they embodied the latest Jonesian fashion, which is unsurprising given the architect's background presence and his close relationship with de Caus, who presumably designed them. Indeed, it has even been suggested that the domed summerhouses at The Vyne in Hampshire of c.1632 may have been by the same hand.[55]

Probably inspired by a well-known engraving by Jacques Callot of 'le Grand Parterre de Nancy' (1625), the elaborate garden layout and the architectural features of the viewing terrace (see Chapter Eight for the 'porticus' at Salisbury House) made for some witty contrast with the primitivism of St Paul's and, to a lesser extent, with the astylar rigour of the building seen on the west side of Bedford House and which was clearly in tune with the rest of the square (see fig. 122). Three-bayed, two-storeyed with gables and a central balcony, this was the Evidence House where the muniments of the whole of the Bedford estates were kept, for the London house was the centre of administration, as with most Strand palaces.[56] The footprint of this building can be seen in Lacy's and subsequent maps – Ogilby and Morgan's of 1681–2 and Crowle's plan of Covent Garden of c.1690 – as detached and projecting into Maiden Lane; conversely, Hollar's mid-seventeenth-century view shows it within the garden, the tail end of the house (see figs 112 and 113b, 125 and 109). Hollar's reliability has been questioned elsewhere in this book – the precise dates of the 'West Central District' view are not known, other than that it was the only surviving impression of his Great Map of London prepared before the Great Fire of 1666. Nevertheless, the link between the Evidence House and the 4th Earl's 'newe buildings' (in progress by 1628 as known from the stonemason's bill) can be strengthened by the fact that Francis was the absolute 'keeper' of the Bedford Estate, as testified by an inventory for him of 1635 of 'all such Deeds writings and evidences'.[57] Moreover, the architecture of this building is reminiscent of the two houses either side of the church (fig. 126), which fit well with the astylar gravitas of Edward Carter, who authorised the 1628 bill for Bedford House and was no doubt closely associated with de Caus in the design of its garden, as they later were when surveying the piazza houses. Duggan has even suggested that a drawing on the verso of the de Caus wall-fountain design which she associates with the earl's grotto in London (see fig. 124) may be an initial sketch for the Evidence House.[58] With Carter and de Caus, Nicholas Stone may have had a direct role. He was involved with the evaluation of the statue of an old woman with a cat, and with works at Covent Garden, as well as with Woburn Abbey and de Caus's previous grotto, as discussed earlier. The triple-arched gateway on top of the garden stairs is in fact reminiscent of his York House water gate of c.1626 (see fig. 192).

Next to the Evidence House was another garden building described in a bill of 1660 as the 'halfe round banqueting house', with a

124 Attributed to Isaac de Caus, 'Design for a wall fountain'. The Provost and Fellows of Worcester College, Oxford (H&T 123)

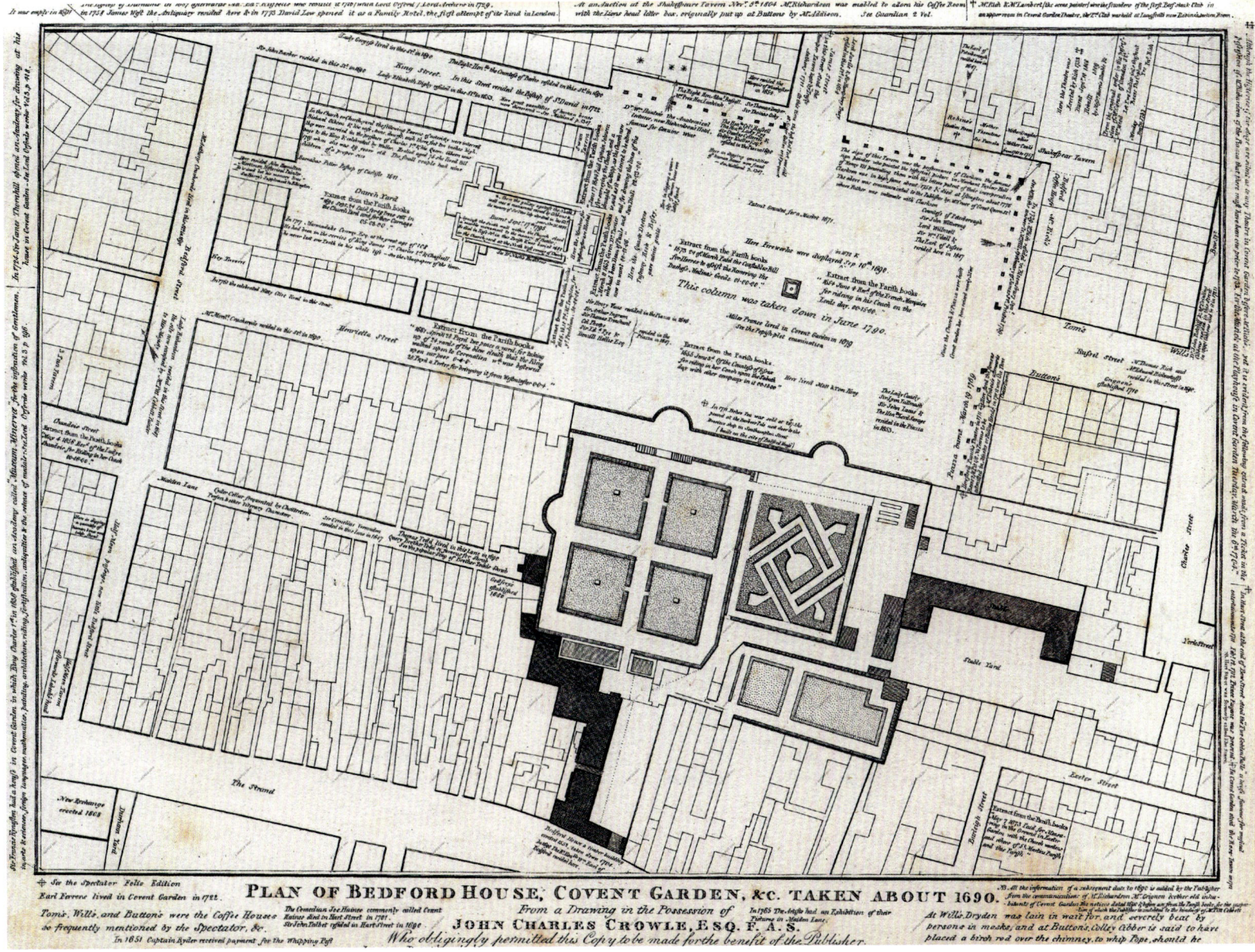

125 Crowle's 'Plan of Bedford House, Covent Garden', c.1690, reprinted L. J. T. Smith, 1809. Wikimedia Commons Public Domain

rusticated triple-arched facade along the west wall (see fig. 122). Its extent can be seen in Lacy's and subsequent maps, while it appears to have been open to the garden and perhaps flanked by two rooms. Four geometrical parterres characterised the main part of the garden, at the centre of which was a feature seen in Hollar, probably a fountain and possibly incorporating the statue of an old woman with a cat. It was probably made for Lord William Russell, Francis's son and heir, in Portland stone and was the costliest item in the 1628 bill, as previously observed. This kind of genre statuary was not uncommon in Renaissance gardens, especially after 'comic' or 'inferior' work had come to the fore in such celebrated gardens as the Villa Medici at Pratolino (1569–81) by Buontalenti. Indeed, Lord Russell as the 5th Earl later commissioned a similar figure for the garden at Woburn, representing an old woman employed there for weeding.[59] That a fountain existed is supported by de Caus's 1628–30 ground-plan of the Bedford Estate, where the annotations appear to concern a study of water flow (see fig. 120). Water was in fact an issue, for the new piazza development still lacked a proper water supply, even though it was yielding £1000 a year by 1641. The earl's first attempt at tackling the matter had ended in Chancery, with an unsuccessful lawsuit against the Bishop of Durham, as water at Durham House came from a spring in Covent Garden, granted to the see 'from time immemorial' (see Chapter Nine).[60] As Bedford and the former Russell houses shared a water cistern (see fig. 115 and Chapter Seven), the dispute

over supply lasted from about 1617 till 1635, around which date a poignant letter was written to Francis, Earl of Bedford, by the Countess of Worcester, who alleged that 'water which heere we have swallowed & druncke was poysoned, by a dead, stinking, rotten, & wee feare poysoned Ratte', further remarking that 'for your Lo: to blame your servants after we are deade, will be of little amendes to us.'[61]

As for the interiors of Bedford House, what we know derives mainly from a largely unpublished inventory taken on 12 September 1643 by the Parliamentary commissioners John Jackson and George Crompton, only two years after the earl's death, close enough to how he would have left them, certainly in terms of arrangement but perhaps not contents.[62] The document had in fact been triggered by the sequestration of the house, together with the Bedford estates, as a consequence of the 5th Earl's removal to Oxford to join Charles I and his court. His goods and chattels in the Strand, which were seized in order to meet the payment of £800 imposed on him as a 'delinquent', may have been dealt with beforehand. Indeed, the appraisers found neither gold nor much silver plate and virtually no paintings on which to lay their hands. But the fine furniture and wall-hangings were still there in large numbers. In 1643 Bedford House was occupied by Sir William Waller (c.1597–1668), a prominent Parliamentarian, and his household, though names and titles of the Bedfords still predominate in the inventory by rooms. The inventory must have started from the more private part of the complex along the western range and potentially from its northern end southward, for the first rooms to be appraised are bedchambers, beginning with the 'Nursery': as noted earlier, the Bedfords had had ten children. Richly furnished, the Nursery featured '4 peeces of tapestry hangings & 1 window curtaine of Red kersey' valued at £9, '1 large bedstead curtained and wallancd of tawny Cloath', bedsteads, blankets, stools, an elbow chair, one table and a Turkey carpet. It was followed by 'Lady Wallers Chamber', which had '5 peeces of old tapestry hangings', '1 little table', an 'old turkey worke carpett' and '1 Screene of Red Cloath', worth altogether about £6. The 'Maides Chamber adjoyining' including 'old vardas [? arras] hangings About the roome' came next, while the following 'Mr Russells Chamber under the garret on the north side' suggests

126 Wenceslaus Hollar, view of Covent Garden piazza facing west, 1630s. The Metropolitan Museum of Art, New York, Harris Brisbane Dick Fund, 1917. Public Domain under CC 1.0

that the appraisers had climbed up a level. Both wings of Bedford House, we may remember, were two storeys high, that is ground and first floor, with garrets, roughly (and partially) depicted by Richard Blome in c.1686 (see fig. 110).

Notwithstanding its garret location, 'Mr Russels Chamber' was richly furnished with such items as '1 bed steade with Red velvet vallancd and Damaske curtaines 1 feather bed 2 feather boulsters 1 guilt 3 blankets 1 taffety guilt', as well as '4 peeces of tapistry hangings', worth £6 and £6 10s respectively, together with '1 table with turkey carpet [and] 1 cushion of the same'. The next in the list was 'My Lords Chamber', probably located alongside the other rooms on the main floor below the garrets. It included '1 peece of tapistry hangings' valued at £2, one bed, bolster and 'Red rug' at £3, '5 chairs of Red cloath' and '1 window curtaine of the same' and was adjoined by 'Mr Grisles Chamber' with 'hangings About the Roome of stript [striped] Stuff' and '1 window and curtaine and carpett of the same', and by the 'Closett adjoyning', which contained various items such as a 'child bed'. Then came 'the Lord Russells Chamber', with '1 peece of tapistry hangings' alongside the usual bedroom items, followed by a 'Mr Raphells Chamber', the 'house keepers lodging Chamber', and the 'Drawing Parlor', which featured '2 peeces of tapistry hangings', '18 greene brancht [branched] velvet chaires', 1 table' and '1 greene bwade cloath carpet', for a total value of £10. The Drawing Parlour was adjoined by a closet, which contained various pieces of furniture as well as '2 pictures', the only to appear in the inventory, for a total figure of £4. The next entry, probably an addendum as it is written on the verso of the previous page in a different hand, is 'the dyning Parlor', with '1 Screen of green cloth 2 tables with carpets of green broad cloth 10 chaires of guilt lether & 6 stooles of the same sort', overall valued £7. It was followed by a 'Mr Crawlyes Chamber', a closet, and 'one Roome at the end of the Gallery in Mr Edward Chamb[e]r' which included '5 peeces of tapistry hangings' and little else, valued at £20, one of the highest figures overall. 'William Grotts Chamber', a 'roome completely hanged with old tapistry', came next.

While the presence of parlours indicates a gradual shift between the private and public sides of Bedford House, the following entries, the 'Gallery towards the Streete' and the 'great Chamber', which must have occupied the whole of the main floor of the Strand front for a total length of about 100 feet, clearly marked the boundary. The Gallery would have occupied the narrow, gabled range seen in Hollar, about 60–70 feet long by some 15 feet across with three tall windows projecting onto the street, potentially matched by an equal number facing the court, as suggested by a later inventory discussed shortly. The Great Chamber might have been the room immediately adjoining in the west wing, its width perhaps spanning its two gabled ends on the Strand, about 25–30 feet across.[63]

The 'Gallery towards the Streete' must have belonged to the house as built for the 3rd Earl of Bedford, or perhaps even to the wooden mansion erected by the 1st Earl, assuming that that structure occupied the Strand front.[64] Either way, while not quite comparable in size to other near contemporary galleries such as Leicester's or Burghley's, its appearance with full-height windows on both sides would have been prominent and unique, for the palaces with street facades – Somerset House, Burghley House, Salisbury House and Northumberland House – all featured galleries perpendicular to the Strand, with at best only one window onto it. By contrast, at least two, Somerset House and Northumberland House, had Great Chambers entirely facing the thoroughfare.

The Gallery at Bedford House was 'hanged About with greene cloathe guilt leather hangings' worth £7 and included '1 Elbow chaire & 9 back chaires, with '1 stooles [and] 6 high stooles of crimson velvett'. The Great Chamber, in contrast, had '9 peeces of tapistry hangings', '1 drawing table & 2 carpetts of turkey worke' with '24 back chairs of blew kersey 2 standard', for a total of about £24, the highest value of all rooms in the whole inventory. The next two entries are the 'Waiting Roome' and the 'Suite Roome', the former elaborately furnished with '5 peeces of tapistry hangings', seemingly located on the same first floor of the west wing, just off the Great Chamber. Some ten chambers of household members, including butler and footmen, came next and were perhaps partly on the lower, ground level towards the north of that wing, for they are followed by the Kitchen, Scullery and 'one Garrett Northward'. Then came two more chambers, the first of a certain 'Mr Whiteing' with 'leather hangings About the Roome', the second where 'the old Lord dyed In', which included '6 peeces of Tapistry hangings 1 elbow chaire of Red Cloath inbrodered 1 other Elbow chaire of Red velvett', as well as '1 bedstead curtaines & vallancd of damask 1 feather bed 1 boulster A pillow 1 blankett & a green Rugg'. Next appeared the 'Terrett Roome', evidently in the tower between the two ranges of Bedford House and possibly sizeable since it was filled with a number of elaborate items such as '10 high stooles of figured satten with silver lace', 'elbow' and 'high back' chairs of 'red velvet lace', '1 greene couch flowered with gould' and '8 foulding stools of the same', with '1 square table' and '10 guilt candlesticks', as well as '1 seller of glasses wth 39 glasses & silver screwes & A case for it'.[65] In a house which had no other views of the river and the surrounding city, such a high chamber must have been an important one.[66]

By reaching the tower, the appraisers had evidently moved back from the northern end of the west wing, where servants' chambers and possibly the kitchen and related services were located, towards the Strand range, for the next two entries are the 'Porters Lodge' and the 'Lodge on the same floare', which must have been at street level near the main gate in the east of the facade. Nearby were the 'still house' and 'Hall', the latter merely furnished with '2 tables 3 formes 1 side table'. The inventory continues with a few more servants' chambers and auxiliary spaces, such as the 'Wash House', a fairly sizeable building with garrets and at least two additional rooms, mentioned in the 1628 bill. While the Wash House was against the eastern boundary wall near the stables, as ascertained through payments from 1660 and the inventory of 1700, neither the stables nor the Evidence House feature in the 1643 inventory. Both, however, may well have been part of 'all the newe buildings' put up by Carter for the 4th Earl, for which 'lock-stone hookestones and boultstone … beinge 66 stones' were billed in 1628.

As well as room contents, the inventory of 1643 lists a number of trunks, one of which contained 91 books bound and unbound, a 'Deade box' with some 44 books and several cabinets including one with 40 books in it, worth £1 4s.[67] As seen in other chapters, books were unappraised, as in this trunk at Bedford House, separately listed when of considerable importance to their owners, as at Salisbury House, or disregarded completely given their comparatively low value (as at Northumberland House).

Bedford House's contents totalled £765 18s 9d and were distributed over forty-five rooms, twenty-three of which had fireplaces; they included a Drawing and a Dining Parlour, at least one Gallery, a Great Chamber, a Waiting Room, Suite Room and a prominent Turret Room, all richly furnished with tapestries – some sixty-six in total, including those in trunks where three sets valued between £40 and £60 were stored – gilt leather hangings, Turkish carpets and other precious objects but no gold and virtually no silver plate or paintings (probably removed before seizure). Among it all, the hangings were the most conspicuous loss, so much so that the 5th Earl's father-in-law, the Earl of Somerset, alleged that the deprived owners compensated themselves by instigating the seizure of his own house, this time by Royalists rather than Parliamentarians, who had removed the very tapestries on which Bedford and his wife 'had long since cast envious eyes … even pretending that they were originally Russell property'.[68] Be that as it may, most of the important rooms of Bedford House had indeed no place for pictures, which may also explain their apparent lack, while fine tapestries continued to be the preferred mode of decoration, for nearly all the interiors were still tapestry-hung in 1700.[69]

The House of William Russell, 5th Earl and 1st Duke of Bedford: 1641–1700

The 4th Earl of Bedford died unexpectedly of smallpox on 9 May 1641 and was succeeded by William (1616–1700), the eldest of his four sons. Known 'to be one of the middle party of peers' and apparently keeping to the family disapproval 'at one and the same time of the character of the Stuarts and the politics of Cromwell', the 5th Earl, from 1694 the 1st Duke, was first and foremost a country gentleman whose primary interest was the advancement of the Bedford estates.[70] A year after the sequestration in 1643, these had been restored to him and put back to profit with new investments including further development of Covent Garden; his control and ownership of that lasted far longer than any other Russell's before or since. The chief events related to the London estate were the creation of the parish in 1646, the building of Drury Lane Theatre in 1662–3 and the founding of the market in 1670. All these eventually proved fatal to the future of Bedford House, despite the many restrictions aimed at maintaining a certain level of tenancy, such as those forbidding sublets to any person carrying on the trade of smith, farrier, soap-boiler, butcher or any other 'noysome' or public trades of inns or victualling houses.[71] Throughout this period, Bedford House remained the centre of gravity of all business, as well as the 5th Earl's chief residence in London, repaired, added to and overall improved at a pace unseen even during the 4th Earl's tenure, according to the existing documents – the last of these had been for work in 1628. Indeed, the highest number of available bills, covering the years 1657–61, 1669, 1671, 1678, 1680–82, 1685–90 and 1692–3, falls within this period.[72] Altogether, they amount to some £1017 worth of works and are most informative.

Once his mind finally became set on Bedford House, the 5th Earl begun to add to it, albeit some fifteen years after inheriting it. Perhaps this gap was because of the Interregnum (though he played no important role in it) but it is more likely that his father's massive fen drainage project consumed his attention and money. Indeed, alongside general repairs, the first bill of 1657 includes the 'taking up of the garrett floore in the new building next the garden & laying it again'. This is likely to be an addition to the north of the house, rather than another such building referred to in later bills, put up in 1680–81, as will be seen.[73] We also learn that the complex had cellars, for the following payment in 1658 records 'staires going down into the Beare Cellar', while wine cellars feature in other bills. Neither was inventoried in 1643. The floor of the western Banqueting House was also being repaired, while a 'Balcony Case & dores' were added to it. Neither Lacy's (1673) nor Blome's (c.1686) map, which respectively show a plan and elevation of the Banqueting House, includes a balcony (see figs 113c and 110); it could however have faced the garden (one of a few, as we shall see) or indeed the piazza, acting as a sort of tribune. The offices on the east of the complex feature prominently too in repairs undertaken in 1658, together with mending at the 'bolting mill' (a mill or machine for sifting meal from flour), a reminder of the recently rural nature of the area and indeed the self-sufficiency of the Strand palaces. If these repairs might have been part of turning the complex into *rus in urbe*, another entry for 'making a house for the gardiner to sett his fflores in standing in ye wilderness' confirms that a wilderness existed by then. The house replaced an old shed pulled down the previous year and afforded some classical details such as a cornice and moulding. This wilderness was an elaborate garden feature, first seen in Lacy's map but absent in Hollar's view: it consisted of groups of trees and bushes cut into particular shapes to form narrow alleys akin to mazes, with seats in between.[74] These early carpenter's bills confirm the existence of the stables, with expenditure on them totalling £137 – among the highest, although they were probably built by the 4th Earl, as previously observed.[75] The carpenter was the younger Richard Rider (or Ryder, d. 1683), the son of the London master carpenter employed on Robert Cecil's stables to the west of Covent Garden in 1609 (see Chapter Eight), who like others in the Bedfords' entourage lived nearby, in the house first occupied by de Caus in Russell Street (see fig. 113d). In 1638–9 Rider had worked on the partial reconstruction of the New Exchange and in 1655 he was involved with the construction of the garden staircase at Northumberland House (see Chapters Eight and Eleven). Although himself an active speculative builder, it was under the supervision of John Davenport, the 5th Earl's surveyor and Master Carpenter in the Office of Works, whose name appears in the early bills, that Rider initially worked at Bedford House and Covent Garden, eventually replacing Davenport in both the earl's service and at the Works.[76]

Regardless of their original extent, the stables were substantially rearranged in 1669 by Thomas Morton, as a bill 'ffor taking downe ye wall And putting In ye windows off ye stables next to Captaine wiledens' garden' attests. Amounting to a total of £36 18s, works included 'digging ye foundation off ye New house', evidently an addition to the existing stables, to be erected 'Next ye garden', perhaps the one belonging to a 'Mr Wilkinson' (rather than the fairly unclear 'wiledens' or 'wiledins'), whose garden, as Lacy's 1673 map confirms, bounded the east corner of the Bedford stables (see fig. 113c).[77] In 1671, '267 yards in the Cantiliver eaves and outward dores' of both stables and coach house were twice coated by the painter Richard Heath, along with their '72 lights of windows', 'postes and Rayles in the Court yard before the house', as well as a number of the earl's private rooms such as 'my Lords Bed Chamber', his Closet and the 'Roome over them'. The chimneypieces in both Bed Chamber and Great Chamber were also painted (the wainscot in the Great Gallery had been dealt with earlier), together with '24 Buckettes with my lords Armes', at an overall cost of £17. Most of the interiors mentioned so far, as well as others including the Kitchen and related services, had also received considerable attention from the glazier Thomas Joyner in 1659, while the pavier John Jolly had provided 290 yards of 'paving worke' in 1669. They received, respectively, £6 and £12.

The next building in need of repair was the Evidence House, where two iron bars twenty-two feet long were introduced in 1671 'to bond the walls' by Edward Gillet the smith, at a cost of £4 15s 4d.[78] In the same year, the carpenter John Channell, who had erected scaffolding, made an 'oaken planke 4 inches thick for ye fastening the iron bolts to for ye securing ye butments of ye arch of the evidence house' and provided 'a planke with a braise' to secure its corner 'next the halfe moon' Banqueting House. He was also 'taking downe the outside of the old timber house backward', no doubt part of the 3rd Earl's house of 1585–90 and perhaps of the 1st Earl of Bedford's wooden mansion, in place by 1555. Channell then rebuilt it, made 'new framing for the side' and windows with 'whether boards', made good its roof and floors and covered the outside 'backward' with '52 foot of fur timber'. Overall, this cost £64. Alongside floor repairs in several places, including the 'gallerye, & of the Chambers by it', we then learn of the presence of the 'privye in ye drying yard' as well as of 'putting up the hangings', an indication that the house was also being re-hung with tapestries, substantially if not totally curtailed in 1643.

A clear distinction between the two parts of Bedford House appears in the next available bill of 1678, when the plasterer John Parsones was paid £7 for '35 yards of laithing & plaistering in the old house' and for '663 yards of whashing stoping whiteing ciseing and blacking' which included the 'front of ye old house' as well as 'the back stairs and passage in the new building' (the addition referred to in 1657) alongside some thirteen chimneys in among various chambers such as the 'Auditors Roome'. Another item mentioned in a bill of 1680 from Parsones was the staircase in 'the high building', perhaps that part of the old house rebuilt by John Channell in 1671.[79]

Whatever the extent, scope and indeed location of 'the new building next the garden' of 1657, in 1680–81 Venterus Mandey (1645–1701), a bricklayer to Lincoln's Inn from 1667, received some £154 to erect a 'New Building for the Right Hon:ble the Earle of Bedforde In his Garden at Bedford House', which contained a 'ground chamber', the earl's new Bed Chamber, Closet and 'stoole room' on the first floor, and a new wardrobe in the garrets.[80] This new building was linked to the northern end of the old house (where those private rooms of the earl previously refurbished were located) by a passage that cut through the chimney of his former chamber, the front of which was also taken down. The passage had a bell with a 'rope and pulleys', probably connected to the service rooms nearby, as the kitchen range had to be altered to accommodate this new addition. It is also clear from the bills that a second gallery, unrecorded or not recorded as such in 1643, featured in this part of the complex: Channell, paid £162 in 1681 for overall carpentry works, put a post under the corner of the passage 'next the gallery to secure the floor over the bakehouse', a further indication that the earl's new set of rooms was not far from such services. A distinction between the 'gallery next ye Courte' and the 'gallery and closet next the Strand' is then made by William Oram, a most useful source for room names and locations, in his plasterwork bill of 1687, which amounted to £14.[81] Potentially the 'Gallery goeing out of the oulde buildings into the new', as Oram described it in a bill of 1688, this other gallery may have been located towards the far end of the west wing, as seen in a nineteenth-century print of Crowle's plan of Bedford House of c.1690 (see fig. 125), with a tall window projecting out of its northern elevation, on axis with the central garden alley (as remarked earlier). The new 'brick house', thus distinguished from the 'old timber house' in later payments, could have followed to the left. These bills also inform us of the presence of a 'little Hall', as opposed to the main, wainscoted one, as well as of the great staircase, which must have been located near the Great Chamber. Equally, we become acquainted with such issues as a bug infestation in 1687, for which Channell was asked to whitewash the 'gardiners roome' and the 'porters Chamber over the lodge' to 'kill the bugs'. Then Bedford House had 'new Lights before the front' (that is, on the Strand) by 1689, costing 10s for half a year's rent.

The 5th Earl's three new rooms were wainscotted by the joiner William Cleare in a manner appropriate to their importance and size. Totalling £120, the expenditure too was proportionate. The panels in the Bed Chamber were framed with a 'stone molding' three inches wide, the base and sub-based ones being raised.

The walls were also decorated with a wainscot cornice eleven inches deep, while the mantel had a cornice-shelf. There were two doorways with again a 'stone molding' six inches wide and two sash windows. The panel in the adjoining Closet was framed by large bolection mouldings, those of the base and sub-base being also raised, while the rest was as in the previous room, including the decoration of the one doorway and window. By contrast, the wainscot of the 'stoole Room' was simply 'mitred with a bead', the base and sub-based panels being raised once again. The cornice was only six inches deep while the door case had a five-inch architrave. Externally, the new building was faced with stock bricks and finished with a wooden cornice, painted by John Pinke in 1692 with the three pediments which framed the sash windows. Two lucarne windows with ornaments featured in the roof. Pinke's bill is important (and costly, at £97), for it provides much valuable information. Not only does it include the gilding of two balconies, a reminder that these feature prominently at Bedford House – in the Evidence House, the western Banqueting House, in the garden, over the stables' door as well as 'foreward to the street' – but it also attests to the presence of four painted 'ffigures in ye garden & ye pedistalls thay stand upon', three painted and gilded 'Dyalls in ye Garden In ye Ould Building', as well as of a 'Draggons Head' painted in green. Together, they adorned what must have been an eclectic mixture of old and new, where the original part of the house – the Strand front and the majority of the west wing, timber-framed and largely unaltered if substantially repaired – contrasted sharply with the latest additions, no doubt in tune with the Jonesian style of Covent Garden as interpreted by Davenport and Rider, and indeed with what was an elaborate garden with a grotto and three banqueting houses, perhaps the chief attraction of the whole complex. Even before these latest additions, Bedford House had caught the attention of Samuel de Sorbière, the French physician and man of letters who included it in his *Voyage en Angleterre* of 1666 with the high-sounding title of 'Palais de Bethfordt'.[82] While this may contrast with the lower architectural status of this house compared to other Strand palaces, it points to what must have become an interesting complex by this date. (For the use of the word 'palace' and foreigners' perceptions of these great houses see the Introduction and Conclusion.)

Evidence of the layout of Bedford House in the early 1690s is provided by Ogilby and Morgan's map of 1681–2 and Crowle's plan of Covent Garden of c.1690 (see figs 109 and 125). As far as its northern parts are concerned, what they show does not tally with either Hollar's view (understandably given the different date and controversial reliability) or with Blome's map of c.1686, the only other source to show the elevations of the house, which does not distinguish between old and new (see figs 112 and 110).[83] As for the interiors, we can rely on another unpublished inventory of 6 October 1700, taken after the death of the 5th Earl almost exactly a month earlier.[84]

This inventory begins with the stables, followed by a series of rooms for household staff such as the groom and coachman's chambers, as well as auxiliary buildings like the 'wash house' and 'Laundry Roome'. The garden, with '3 stone Roles 5 wainscot seats 1 leaden cistern & a stone table', and the 'Gardiners Roome' with '1 Bedstead 1 feather bed & bolster one rug & one blankett' also feature in the first part of the document, followed by the 'Woodhouse', the 'Porters Lodge', the 'Stewards Hall', the 'Dry and wett Larder', the 'Pantrey', the 'Cole hole', the 'Pastrey', the 'Kitchin', the 'Scullery' and the 'Oate cake Roome'. With the exception of the porter's lodge next to the main gate and a few others, these rooms would have been located towards the northern end of the west wing, where the Kitchen and related services stood. Two chambers of household members, including 'Mrs Russells Womans Roome', came next and mark the boundary with the formal side of Bedford House, given that the next six entries cover most of the public rooms, located in the old part of the complex. Even after all the additions, this still constituted the majority of the palace. The first of these rooms was the 'Lower Parlor', followed by the 'Gilt leather Roome', so named after its 'gold guilt leather hangings', alongside '1 Bedstead & curtaines 1 feather bed & boulster 1 rug 3 blankets' and a 'cane couch 2 chairs 1 table & a close stoole'. One wonders whether these hangings had anything to do with the 'guilt leather hangings' which featured in the 'Gallery towards the streete' in 1643, the only room at the time with such items. And was the 'Gilt leather Roome' actually the 'gallery next ye Courte', that is, along the west wing, as evidenced by the bills but unaccounted for in either inventory? As will be seen, this room is one of two potential contenders. The next entry is the 'Drawing

Room 1 p[ai]r of staires', an indication that the appraisers had changed level. It included '5 old p[iece]s of Tapestry hangings 1 camblet couch 13 cane chaires & cushins 1 window curtaine' and was followed by the 'Gallery', clearly the main one along the Strand, as its contents include '6 white [?] window curtaines', belonging to the three windows on either side of this room. Its '6 p[iece]s of stript hangings' must have hung in between them, while '11 cane chairs' and '1 table stand & glass' furnished the room. The 'great Chamber', exactly as in 1643, came next, with '6 p[iece]s of Tapestry hangings 24 cane chairs 2 stands 3 green Serge window curtaines and rods 2 tables 1 turkey worke Carpitt 1 large Japan screen 2 wicker sckreens 4 damask cushions', amounting to about £25, the second highest after the earl's Bed Chamber in the whole house. Indeed, a Japanese screen must have been a rarity at the time.[85] As argued earlier, the Great Chamber was located in the south-west corner of the complex, with at least two windows along the Strand.

Next in the inventory came the 'Withdrawing Roome', hung with 'ffour old p[iece]s of Damask hangings' and containing '2 white window curtaines & rod 7 damask cushins 7 dutch chaires'. From this room at the southern end of the west wing, the appraisers went north through a series of auxiliary rooms occupied by household members, including a 'Mr Potters Roome', hung with 'old guilt leathers' – the only other place to feature such items – the 'housekeepers Roome', the 'Linnen Roome', the 'Cooks Roome', a 'Mr Whale's Roome', and 'My Lords Apparell', containing a range of elaborate clothes worth some £47. After one more chamber, they then reached the 'Passage', no doubt the link between the old timber house and the new brick building, which contained a 'clock & case & glass lanthorne'. This led to the 'Groom of ye Chamb.rs Rooms' followed by 'my Lords Drawing Roome' – perhaps the 'ground chamber' mentioned in the bills – which featured '4 p[iece]s of tapestry hangings 2 window curtaines 1 guilt lether screen a walnutt tree table stand & glass 8 cane chairs & cushins a table bedsted a fether bed and bolster 1 rug 2 blankett 1 turky Carpitt 1 black Cabinett', as well as '3 maps 1 picture', the very first recorded in the inventory. The next entry is a Closet, probably one of those described as 'under my Lords Chamber' in a bill of 1687, which

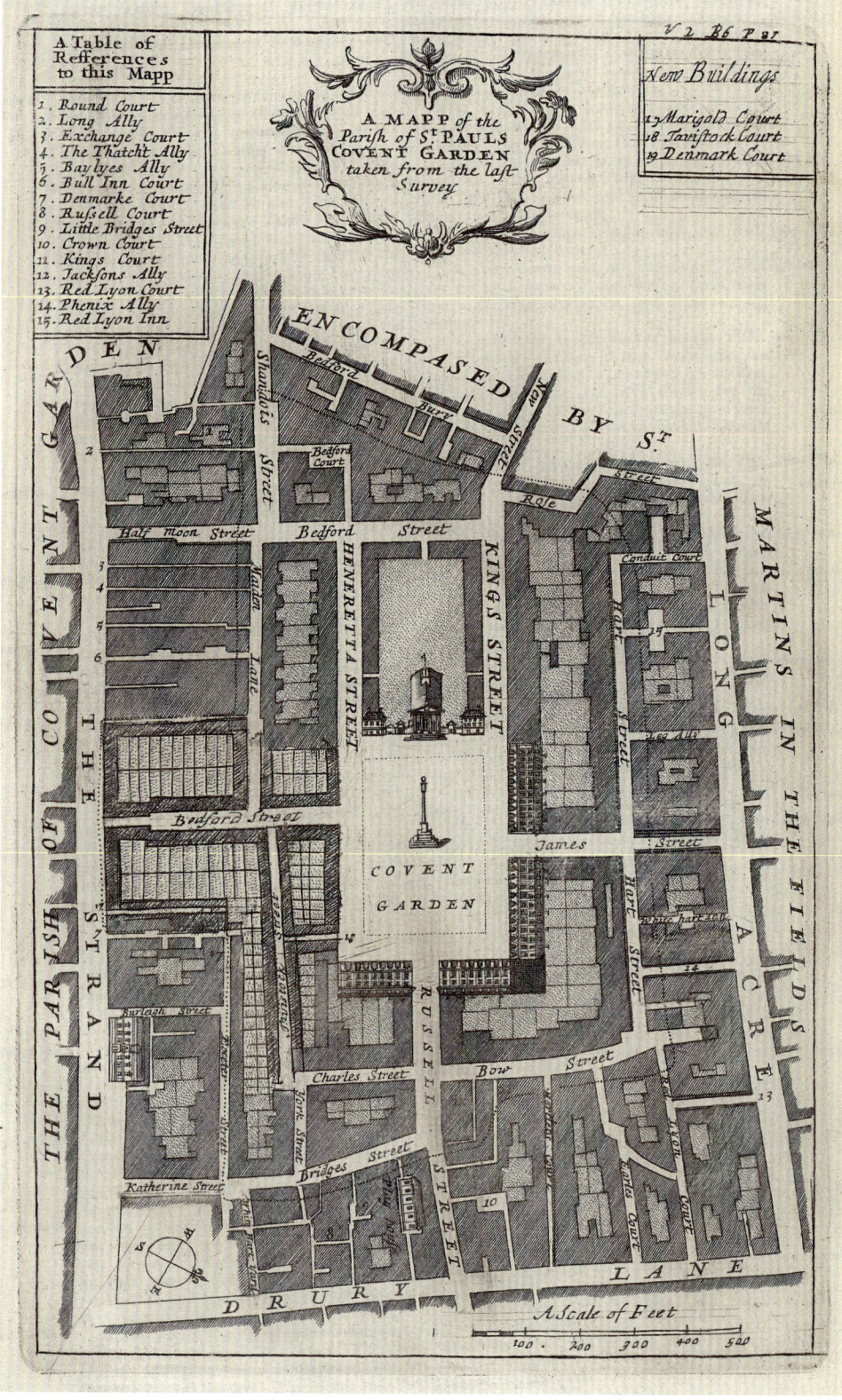

preceded the earl's new Bed Chamber and Closet above, erected in the early 1680s. Appraised at £58 13s and including '1 Damask bed Compleat with 8 chairs & hangings of ye same 2 wind: Curtaines & rods Table stands & glass', the Bed Chamber had by far the most valuable contents

127 Richard Blome, 'Map of the Parish of St Paul', c.1686, updated 1720, from John Strype, *A Survey of the Cities of London and Westminster*, vol. 6, p. 87, 1720. Folger Shakespeare Library, Washington DC. Licensed under Creative Commons Attribution-ShareAlike 4.0 International

in the house. After the Closet came 'my old Lords Study', which had clearly belonged to the recently deceased earl, and his other private rooms, where a second picture was found.

A 'Mr Upton Roome', containing among other things a 'Coffee Mill', was listed next, followed by the 'Great Roome 1 p[ai]r of staires' with '3 p[iece]s of old Tapestry hang[ings]'. This room, somewhere to the north of the house between the earl's and countess's chambers (the next entry is 'my Lady Bedfords Roome') could be the second contender for the 'gallery next ye Courte'. The remaining entries are all on chambers of household members, while the Wardrobe (the last but one room to be appraised) was possibly the new wardrobe on top of the new brick building; it was clearly spacious enough for the many items listed there. Seven pictures are noted there, which amounts to nine overall, against more than seventy tapestries, which had definitely remained the preferred though outdated mode of decoration at Bedford House. At about £705, the value of its contents in 1700 was also similar to the £765 of 1643, except that this time a considerable amount of plate, valued at £384 12s 6d, brought the total to well over £1000. The overall number of rooms had also risen from 45 in 1643 (23 with fireplaces), to 65 in 1700, all but 5 with hearths.[86] As previously noted, however, the first inventory did not include the stable range or cellars.

Subsequent Years: 1700–1707

The 5th Earl was succeeded by his grandson, Wriothesley Russell (1680–1711), the son and heir of William, who had been executed after becoming ensnared in the Rye House Plot in 1683. Contrary to his grandfather, whose fondness for Bedford House had kept it at the centre of the family's enterprises, the 2nd Duke almost immediately parted with the Strand palace,

as he preferred to live at his mother's house in Bloomsbury, Southampton House. Built for Thomas Wriothesley, 4th Earl of Southampton, this had passed to the Bedfords via marriage and was soon renamed Bedford House.[87]

While the development afforded by the Covent Garden Estate had saved Bedford House until 1700, as opposed to almost all its counterparts along the Strand including its neighbour, Burghley House, demolished in the 1670s, the commercial nature of the area had greatly increased. A scheme was therefore prepared for speculators to build over its capacious site and for the consequent expansion of the market. The 2nd Duke's proposal required a 'great street' 50 feet wide from the piazza to the Strand, a linking street 30 feet wide westwards to Maiden Lane and another, 20 feet wide, eastwards to Charles Street. The building plots in between were to be devised to provide an annual rent of £1100, the whole undertaking largely complete by 1707. The duke also proposed to let the existing fruit and vegetable market in the piazza for seven years at an annual rent of £300, while he undertook to add a fish market in lieu of the stables, which eventually came to nothing. But in all other respects the proposal was carried through, with the new Southampton and Tavistock Streets (named respectively after the family of the duke's mother and the Russells' marquisate) and the eponymous rows and courts of houses, described as 'very noble' in 1714 (fig. 127). These names merely hint at what had been one of the last bastions of the golden age of the Strand.[88] Only a few years previously, it had been the scene of entertainment for King William III, but was now yet another theatre of 'housebreakers', whose many bills included one for 'Pulling down the Grotto', the centrepiece of one of the Strand's most spectacular gardens, as well as 'for removing the Evidence House', where the entirety of the Bedford Estate papers had been kept till then.[89]

128 The complex of Worcester House between the Savoy to the east (right) and Salisbury House to the west (left) (detail of fig. 8)

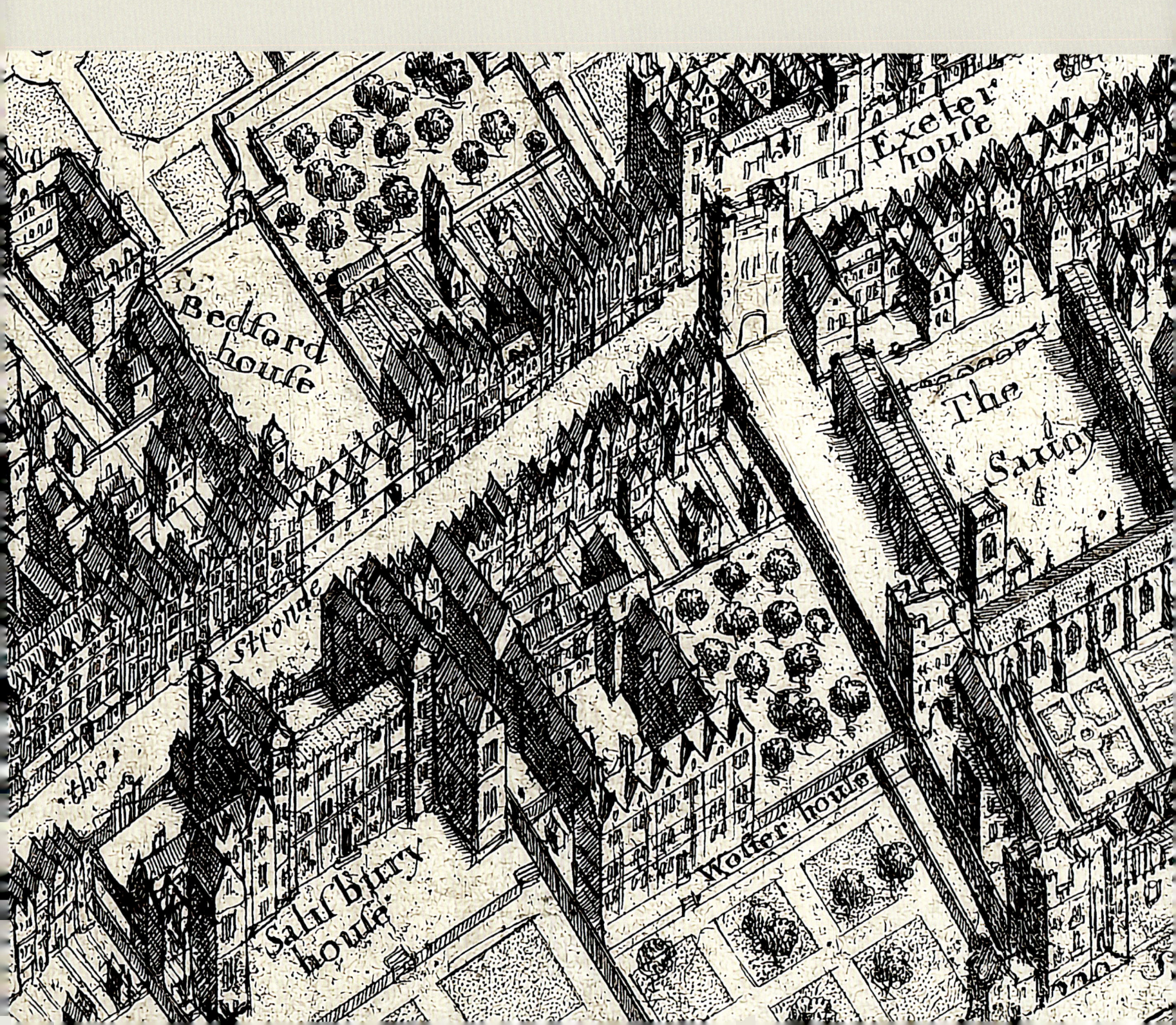

7 · WORCESTER HOUSE

WORCESTER HOUSE LAY BETWEEN THE Savoy on the east and Salisbury House on the west (fig. 128). This former residence of the See of Carlisle was known as Carlisle Inn or Place in pre-Reformation times and then successively as Russell or Bedford House, Herbert or Worcester House and Beaufort House and Buildings once it passed to secular ownership in the Tudor period. The earliest available view of the area by Wyngaerde in the 1540s hardly shows the site, while in the Agas map of 1561–70 (fig. 129; as noted, derived from the lost 'Copperplate' map of 1553–9), one sees a cluster of buildings facing two separate gardens in between the Savoy and Ivy Bridge Lane (Salisbury House on the western side was not built until 1599). A relatively sizeable house, partly developed round a courtyard and with a substantial riverfront garden, first appears in Norden's map of 1593 (fig. 130). As usual, it was accessed both by water and by a gatehouse on the Strand, flanked by tenements. These were known as Carlisle Rents, granted in the early 1400s to John, Julien and William Boteler of London at varying rents for a term of forty years. Carlisle Rents were much sought after and income from them amounted to six per cent of the 'temporalities' of the see in pre-Reformation times. The Boteler indentures are interesting in that they illustrate how this part of the property was developed, hence what a typical Strand tenement was like. Among the stipulations dictated by Bishop William Strickland were that the lessees should erect

> *(1) shops along the Strand frontage, on ground at least 15 ft. wide, with solars of oak timber covered with tiles; (2) buildings along the whole of the stable frontage and 'la lane' (Ivy Lane), extending back 16ft. at least from the highway, with an entrance door, solars and cellars, oak timber and a covering of tiles; (3) a stew for fish in the garden of Carlisle Place and a latrine along the stone wall; (4) a 'mud-wall' of sufficient height to enclose the two plots and separate them from the bishop's garden on the south and west and the lane on the west as well ...* [1]

The Botelers were also permitted to erect additional houses 'at pleasure' and to re-use the old timber from the 'the old house there called "le yhethous" with the stables annexed'. Thomas, 2nd Lord Dacre, built a house within Carlisle Rents too, during the reign of Henry VIII, on which his successor, William, 3rd Lord Dacre, obtained a lease from Bishop Kyte in 1527.[2]

The secular history of Worcester House is primarily associated with two families, the Russells and the Worcesters. For the former the house was their main residence in London from 1539 to 1600, for a time alongside Bedford House; the latter owned it thereafter until its demolition in 1682. Its history shows the Russells as key players of the area, while providing particular insights into sequestration, searching for the goods of malefactors and the overall impact of the Civil Wars on the Strand palaces. However, when it comes to the building itself, historians are hindered by limited access to key documentary sources, as noted in the Introduction.[3] To date, Sidney J. Madge's 1945 'Worcester House in the Strand', part of the pioneering *Archaeologia* articles, has represented

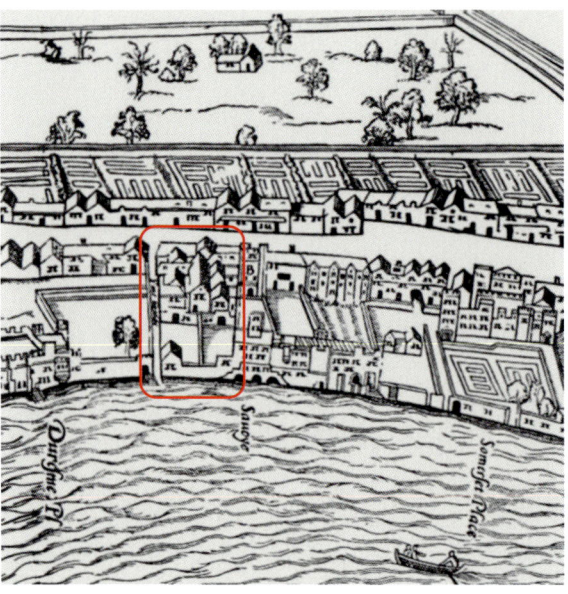

129 The area originally occupied by Carlisle Place between the Savoy and Ivy Bridge Lane, detail of the *Woodcut Map of London*, 1561–70 ('Agas'), reprinted 1633, derived from the lost 'Copperplate Map of London', 1553–9. Mitton 1908. Wikimedia Commons Public Domain

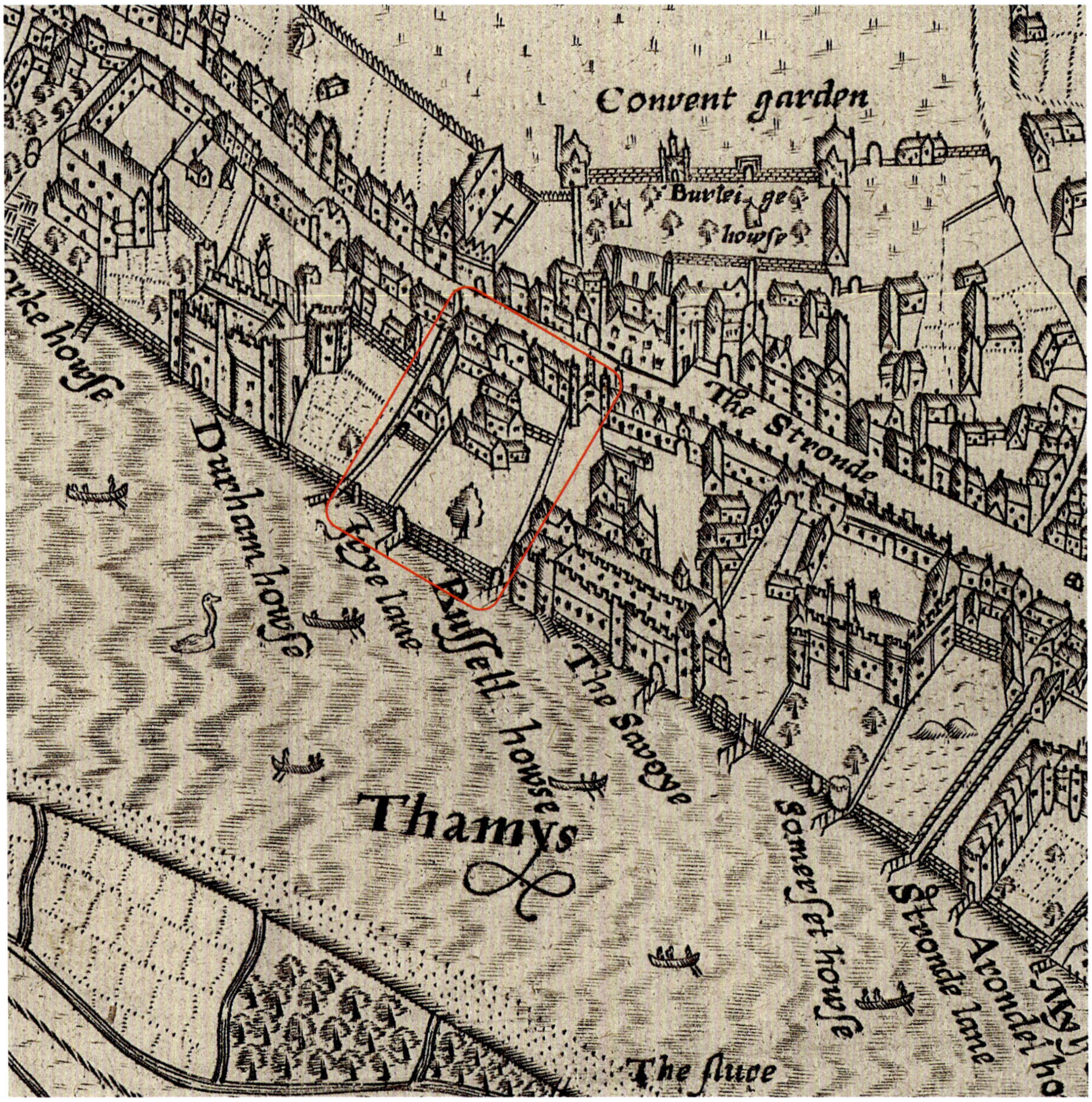

130 The complex of Russell (later Worcester) House in between the Savoy and Ivy (Bridge) Lane, detail of John Norden, *Speculum Britanniae*, 1593. Folger Shakespeare Library, Washington DC. Licensed under Creative Commons Attribution-ShareAlike 4.0 International

the most comprehensive account; it includes a full transcription of what appears to be the only room by room inventory of the palace (of which more shortly). The *Survey of London* series does not cover the parish of St Clement Danes, within which Worcester House falls. What follows has benefited from the comprehensive analysis of the Russell sources made for the previous chapter, including the relationship with neighbouring Strand palaces, and from a close investigation of the London views, alongside a fresh appraisal of all the available evidence. All this has enabled a new reading of the inventory so that the various rooms may be identified, giving as close as possible a picture of the interiors of Worcester House.

The Inn of the Bishops of Carlisle: 1238–1539

The history of Worcester House can be traced back to 1238, when it is mentioned in connection with a penitential procession recounted by the historian Thomas Fuller (1608–1661): 'When they came to the bishop of Carlisle's (now Worcester) House the scholars went the rest of the way barefoot, *sine capita et mantellis*' ('without hoods and mantles') 'and thus the great legate [the papal legate] at last was really reconciled to them' (see Chapter Nine).[4] The bishop at the time was Walter Mauclerk, the King's Treasurer, while other notable episcopal owners include Thomas de Appleby, in residence between 1363 and 1369, Thomas Merks, the executor of Richard II's will, from 1397 to 1400 and Edward Story, who headed the see from 1468 to 1477 and continued to reside in 'the Bysshop of Carlelles place apud le Stronde' even when translated to Chichester in 1477. Worcester House is also associated with Henry VIII's divorce from Katherine of Aragon, Anne Boleyn's coronation and Cardinal Wolsey's downfall during the episcopacy of Bishop Kyte (1521–37). Kyte was succeeded by Robert Aldrich, whose residency at Carlisle Place lasted only a year, for in 1539 it passed to John Russell, afterwards 1st Earl of Bedford, the King's Comptroller of the Household (see Chapter Six). This handover involved complicated arrangements whereby Aldrich, who was to be paid £16 per annum by Russell, moved to Rochester House in Lambeth Marsh and renamed it Carlisle House, while the Bishop of Rochester gained possession of Russell House at Chiswick.[5]

The House of the Earls of Bedford: 1539–1600

Beginning with a relatively modest estate inherited in Dorset and Somerset, John Russell had risen to the Tudor aristocracy as 1st Earl of Bedford in 1550 and possessed considerable wealth by the time of his death in March 1555. This came through a succession of lucrative offices, from Lord High Admiral to Lord Privy Seal, the result of carefully cultivated and long-lasting relationships with both Henry VIII and Edward VI.[6] With lands from the former abbeys of Tavistock, Woburn and Thorney, secured between 1539 and 1551, Russell's holdings in London expanded beyond the south side of the Strand into the so-called Bedford Estate in Covent Garden, granted in 1541 and 1552 by Kings Henry and Edward respectively. At least part of this estate was probably acquired to supplement the garden and grazing facility for his household at Russell House, since all the southern frontage of the Strand was already occupied with no room for expansion. By 1564, for instance, a large stable block had been built on the north side and some sort of 'wooden mansion' as probably an annexe to the main abode (see Chapter Six).

Like his father, Francis, 2nd Earl of Bedford, thought of the house as the family's primary residence in London, by then renamed after the new owners: 'my mansion house wherein I dwell comonlie called Russell House situate & being in the parish of S. Clement Danes'.[7] As was customary for the Strand palaces, the house continued to accommodate state entertainments, such as the one for the French embassy in 1561, until the 2nd Earl's death on 28 July 1585. Since three of the 2nd Earl's sons had predeceased him with no male issue, his grandson, Edward Russell, at twelve years old inherited the title and the Bedford estate, where Bedford House would soon be built (see Chapter Six).[8] Apart from its contents (left to Edward and sold[9]), Russell House went to Bridget, Dowager Countess of Bedford, for her lifetime: the 2nd Earl was her third husband after Sir Richard Morrison and Henry Manners, 2nd Earl of Rutland. However, she seldom if ever used it, as she appears to have retired to another property, in the precincts of White Friars in Fleet Street, bequeathed to her by her first husband.[10] Instead, Russell House was leased for a time to the Earl of Derby, whose correspondence is dated thence in 1595–6.[11]

After Bridget's death in January 1601, it then became vested in Anne Russell (1578–1639), the 2nd Earl's granddaughter and sole surviving heir of his son John; in June 1600 she had married Henry Somerset, Lord Herbert (1577–1646), later 5th Earl and 1st Marquess of Worcester.[12] The property, however, is recorded in the possession of Lord Herbert's father, Edward, 4th Earl of Worcester (1550–1628), who might have bought it as part of the marriage settlement and certainly used it as his main London residence, while the newly wedded couple probably lived in one of the attached houses.[13]

The House of the Earls of Worcester: 1600–1682

A view of the property at this time is provided by Norden's map of Westminster as reprinted in 1600 (fig. 131, where it is labelled 'Bedford House'). By contrast with the 1593 version, the complex has been divided in two, as its western part had been bought by Robert Cecil in 1599 (see Chapter Eight). In that area stood Dacre House and its grounds, occupied in 1598 by Cecil's step-brother Thomas, Lord Burghley, afterwards 1st Earl of Exeter.[14] It had been rebuilt by Lord William Howard, who had married the granddaughter of the 3rd Lord Dacre in 1577 and used it as their primary London residence.[15] By the end of the century, however, the freehold of this house must have reverted to the Bedford estate, as Cecil was dealing with the Dowager Lady Elizabeth Russell (1528–1609), the wife of John, one of the sons of the 2nd Earl of Bedford, and Anne's mother, on whom Russell House had been vested. Née Cooke, Lady Russell was also Cecil's aunt as his mother's sister. Two letters of September 1599 reveal that the sale had caused controversy despite the family link for it had almost been enforced (just as Ralegh was ruthlessly pushed out of Durham House in 1603; see Chapter Nine). Dacre House was 'new built, and fair to the street, well watered with conduit water, no small commodity, a garden the length of the house, a private water gate, of small cost of maintenance, of more receipt by the lodgings in the garden than the other is of, a stable which the other wanteth', as the Dowager Lady Russell was at pains to stress, but it was the 'other', that is, Russell House, that Cecil had set his heart on.[16] At the time, this was occupied by Lady Derby, who herself had an interest in purchasing it. Neither she nor, remarkably, Sir Robert had their way, as Lady Russell, with a frankness rarely seen in the correspondence with so powerful a figure, was adamant 'that none should have my consent to buy it while I breathe, whereby my dead husband's name should be rooted out of Russell House'.[17] As has been seen, this indeed ensued but only in consequence of her daughter's marriage into the Herberts, which it could be argued kept the property within the family.

By the early 1600s, Russell, Bedford or as it was soon renamed Worcester House was more than three centuries old, no doubt needing attention, while the change of ownership must have triggered a series of repairs and alterations.[18]

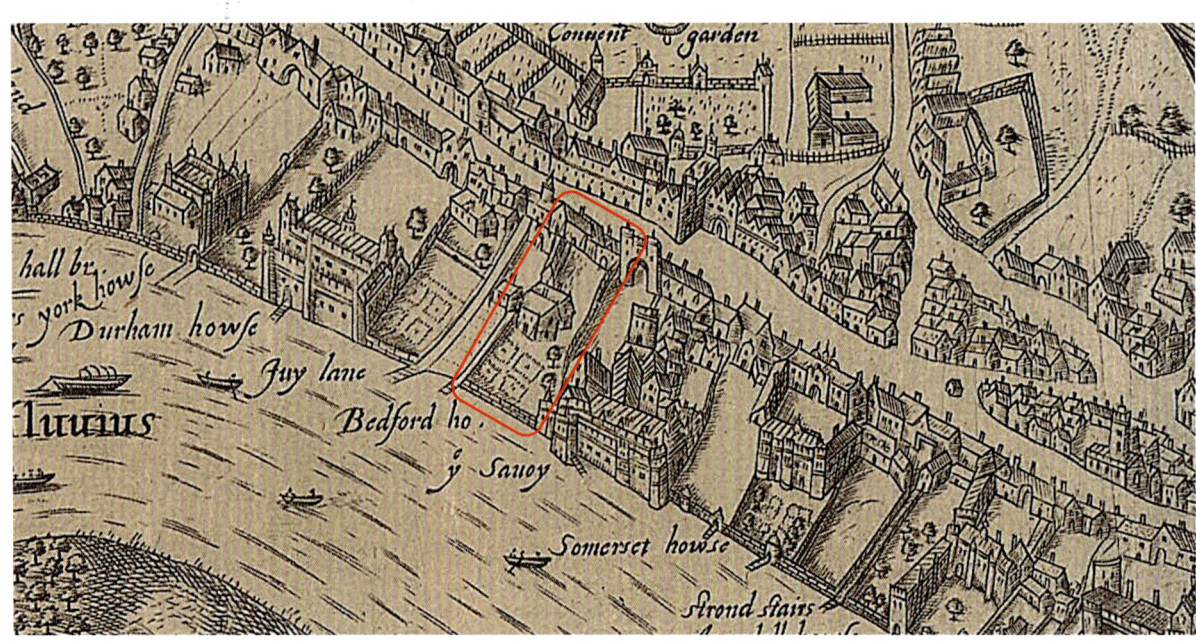

131 Worcester House, detail of John Norden, *Civitas Londini*, 1600. National Library of Sweden

After quoting Stow's 1603 account of Cecil's new mansion, the chronicler James Howell in 1657 reported the well-known story of the walnut tree 'which much hindered the prospect of Salisbury House Eastward': £100 was offered to remove it only to cause 'a new Brick building to be there erected, where the Tree stood'.[19] The story refers to the 4th Earl of Worcester, who was probably adding to the old house, for a letter to Cecil of August 1603 relates that

> there is in Worcester House many carpenters and other kind of labourers lodged (I doubt not but is is without the Earl's knowledge) they having 'howsen' and household within the city, whiter they usually resort, and so return hither again; by which means some of them have died in his house of pestilence, and been conveyed through the garden unto the Savoy [Hospital].

The information concerns the spread of pestilence, which had come and gone during the sixteenth century, and how to limit contagion, as Worcester House was next to Cecil's.[20] The 4th Earl is again referred to in 1608, when a London upholsterer was charged with stealing his lordship's property (as in similar incidents at Durham House and Burghley House), namely 'a chaire-cushin of clothe of tissue lined with yellowe satten and fringed and tasselled with silke and gold worth £10, and two couche-bedd cushins of carnation cullered velvett' of the same value.[21] The 4th Earl's ownership of Worcester House is then further and unequivocally confirmed by a deed executed on his death in 1628 that settled the Strand house and other assets on his son Henry, Lord Herbert, for life.[22] Carlisle Rents, by then composed of sixteen messuages, were instead entailed on Edward, Lord Herbert's son, as part of his marriage settlements with Elizabeth Dormer, sister of Robert, 1st Earl of Carnarvon.[23]

At about this time, the house appears in Hollar's Thames-side view of Durham House, Salisbury House and Worcester House with a six-bay, gabled riverfront characterised by mullioned windows framed by some kind of giant pilasters (see fig. 13). Hollar also depicted it in his 'West Central District' plan (see fig. 128) as a sizeable courtyard house over two storeys on the Strand side and three towards the river, with a formal garden preceded by a terrace towards the Thames and an enclosed orchard to the east. While Worcester House lay behind Carlisle Rents, depicted along the street front, its western wing appears to have continued up to the Strand. This may have been an extension of the former gatehouse, as no such building can be seen in the view, nor is there any other visible entrance from the street. By contrast, a water gate clearly featured in the middle of the river wall, with a small building on its eastern edge, perhaps a version of the 'Surveying Place' to be found in a similar position at Salisbury House or Leicester House.

Any alteration made to Worcester House is likely to have been carried out by the 4th Earl, for the house entered its final phase with Lord Herbert, who succeeded as 5th Earl of Worcester in 1628. It is from this period, however, that we get the most information about it. This is partly due to the survival of a series of documents related to a dispute of the 5th Earl and his wife with Francis Russell, 4th Earl of Bedford, over a shared cistern between Bedford House and Worcester House, which includes a rough sketch of the boundaries of the two properties (see fig. 115). But the primary information comes from the two searches and inventories after the complex became entangled in the Civil Wars.[24] In 1639, the 5th Earl had pledged himself and his heir fully to support the king against the Scots and Parliament thereafter. This earned him the title of 1st Marquess in 1642 but in 1646, after being forced to surrender his ancestral seat, Raglan Castle, to the forces of Sir Thomas Morgan, he was taken into custody by the Parliamentary forces and died at Covent Garden, in a 'mean dwelling' not far from Worcester House.[25] In these circumstances Worcester House was searched on 16 November 1641 by Sir John Hippesley and on 21 April 1643 by William Parker and Richard Milner. Parker testified to hidden goods and sumptuous objects worth £2000 but grossly undervalued, as Parliament only got £600. The contents of the house, including iron and timber, were seized and sold too, according to 'An Inventory of the goods of the Earle of Woster A delinquent', taken on 21 July 1643, soon after the second search.[26] This is the first, and to my knowledge only, such document on this house arranged by room: the previous inventory, taken after the death of Countess Elizabeth, the 5th Earl's mother, in 1622, is arranged by subject.[27] It therefore offers unique insights into Worcester House, which had more than fifty rooms divided between the 'old building' and the 'new building', a clear reference to what had been added by the 4th Earl of Worcester at the beginning of the century. The appraisers, John Cole, John Westcott and Humphrey Seale, appear to have started from the street front, possibly that extension of the west wing which, as previously argued, may have incorporated the gatehouse, where a series of service rooms are recorded. This included the 'Taylers Room up 3 p[ai]rs of Stayres', which may well be the upper-floor lodging above the tailor's shop, flanked by 'A litl garrett next the taylors Roome on the same floare' and another room still marked as 'Up 3 pr of staires'. The appraisers then listed 'An other Roome up 6 staires higher' with 'Roomes on the same floare', all fitted with beds and related furniture as in the previous ones. The distinction 'higher' suggests a further level, though '6 staires' may well be a synonym of '3 pr of staires'. The following three entries are recorded as 'upp[e]r Roome' in the 'new building' (or 'New buildings'), indicating that the earlier unclassified rooms and the new fabric were connected at an upper level, for no change is registered in this respect. From those, they moved to 'A lite Roome next below', then in the 'Long garrett' and into two further rooms on the same level, all 'in the old building'. These too were fitted up with seemingly modest furniture.

At this point there appears to be a shift from the simple rooms listed thus far and the main apartments, for the following entries are named after members of the family and their contents are definitely more sumptuous. The next room, located at a lower level, probably the first floor, was the 'Chamber up one p'r of staires' occupied by Thomas Somerset, one of the 5th Earl's sons, which included '7 peeces of old tapestry hangings' among a range of bedroom furniture. It was followed by two more rooms on the same floor, still presumably in the old part of the house as the next entry, 'A lite Matted Room' packed with tapestry and furniture, is the first back in the 'New building'. A 'Matted Roome on the same flower next the Thames side' came next, an indication that the appraisers had reached the garden front. This was followed by the chamber of 'M'is Watsons', a member of the household, '2 lite Roomes next to' it, another room on 'the same flore Matted' and lavishly furbished with '4 peeces of tapestry hangings', and the 'Gallery', which must have been located on the first floor, as all the others listed after Thomas Somerset's Chamber, for no level change is recorded. On the garden side this was of course the second floor, because of the slope between the Strand and the Thames.

The Gallery too must have at least partly faced the river, for no change in orientation is recorded there. As it was still part of the new building, one wonders whether the Gallery was in one of the two side wings, as in other contemporary examples such as Salisbury House or Northumberland House (see Chapters Eight and Eleven). This room contained '21 pictures in frames', '1 Mapp', '28 pictures w'thout frames', '1 litle Couch of Cloath of silver', '1 Elbow Chaire & 8 stoole of silver fugureed googaraine', '1 Elbow Chaire 2 low stooles of Cloath of silver', '1 Elbow Chaire 2 back Chairs', '3 stools & A foote stoole' and '1 pr of Organs'. The 'Organs' have been associated with William Byrd, the 'Father of Musick', who lived at Worcester House under the patronage of the 4th Earl.[28] Adjacent to the Gallery was a 'litle Matted Roome' which included three more pictures (no other room had any more).

The first floor must have ended here, as the next entry is marked 'At the staires head goeing downe out of the Gallery', where a marble table stood. The appraisers had therefore reached the ground floor (at Strand level), where a 'litle Roome under the gallery Matted', 'A litle Roome next below [? the gallery]', as well as 'The Lord Harberts Chamber', 'the greate Chamber' and 'the Hall' are recorded. Lord Herbert's Chamber was the bedroom of Edward Somerset, the 5th Earl's heir, styled as Lord Herbert from 1628 to 1644. It was lavishly decorated with '5 peeces of tapestry hangings', the same number as but smaller than those in the Great Chamber, the only room where the tapestries are described as 'large'. The Great Chamber was furbished with '2 Drawing tables', '2 square tables' and '2 Court Cubberds', while the Hall featured '1 old Drawing table 1 other old table 3 formes & A Court Cubberd'. The appraisers then descended into the basement (ground floor at garden level), which accommodated other members of the household as well as the usual suite of service rooms – Kitchen, Larder, Scullery, Pantry and cellars.[29]

The last rooms to be inventoried were 'A Matted Roome next the strete' and 'the Porters Roome', both clearly on the Strand front, followed by 'the Stable', 'the upp'r long garrett Claymed by Mr. Cruff the uphouster at chering crose' and the housekeeper's bedroom. The inventory also listed '10,000 foot of oaken Inch board' and 'Certaine oaken planks And scaffolding poles & boards', sold and delivered to the Surveyor of the Fortifications 'for the use of the State', with '1 Chaldron of Coles' and 'halfe a Chaldron of Coles'. Overall, the contents were valued at about £276 and sold for less than £260, another gross undervaluation considering the fifty-two paintings and forty-one tapestries scattered around the house, and nowhere near the estimated value of the earl's possessions of £10,000. In effect, what the appraisers saw were probably the 'leftovers', as searches for the concealed goods of the 5th Earl were still continuing in 1647–9, for beds, carpets, hangings, plates, a travelling coach worth £6, hatbands set with diamonds, various jewels and sets of pearls, 320 bunches of coined gold in canvas covers estimated at £2000 and the enamelled gold chain with fifty links which Elizabeth, Lady Montagu, had claimed as her own.[30] She was alleged to have taken for her own use 'the gold, jewellery, plate, clothing etc. belonging to the late Marquess'; her accuser was Dr Thomas Bayly, who was entrusted with the earl's 'most secret councils and especially employed by him in his affairs of greatest concernment even to the time of his death'.[31]

Emptied of its content and some of its fixtures, Worcester House was taken over by Parliament, the Scottish Commissioners being the first to arrive in August 1643. The following year, the Committee of Both Kingdoms was also established there. Its members included Algernon Percy, 10th Earl of Northumberland, who had recently acquired the former Northampton House in the Strand. The Committee of Accounts came next in 1645, while Parliament prepared to sell the Herbert estates and to assign an income of £4 per week to Margaret, Countess of Worcester (d. 1681), the daughter of the 5th Earl of Thomond and the second wife of Edward Somerset. Although the house was initially reserved from the sale, William Cecil, 2nd Earl of Salisbury (1591–1668), succeeded in getting the officials concerned to include 'the mansion-house situate and being in the Strand, commonly called Worcester House, together with the Gate House, being next the Street, and the other tenements, situate and lying between the said Gate and Salisbury House'.[32] Cecil was clearly retracing his father's footsteps but what followed is of great relevance here, for the property was surveyed on 23 March 1648. This reveals that the main house consisted of 'Threescore Roomes great & small, the greater p'te whereof are of an ancient Structure, ye rest of a later to w'ch doeth belong a stable w'ch will contain eight horses, & two coach howses', while the

> *Garden abutting upon ye River of Thames from Salisbury Howse garden unto a Passage lately sett out, and now belonging unto divers Tenements in the Strond from ye River up to ye Howse at ye west side [is] 107 foote, and in breadth at ye East end 137 foote or thereabout: And one other Garden plot lying betweene ye before menc'oned garden and ye Tenements on the streete side containing in lengh from East to West 90 foote or thereabouts And in breadth from North to South 82 foote or thereabouts, with a Passage from ye Howse betweene ye said gardens towards ye Savoy …*

There was also 'an ancient Howse in the Streete w'ch hath allwais belonged to Worcester Howse, containing thirty-five roomes, leading into ye great Howse', which has been linked to the Gate House and the buildings of Carlisle Rents in the early fifteenth century and must refer to that western part of the fabric connected to the Strand.[33] The Cecils' second attempt at securing this complex came to nothing, however, as Parliament decided first to include it in their gifts to Thomas, 3rd Lord Fairfax, for his many successes in the field, then to substitute for this York House and finally, in August 1649, to retain it for administration purposes. The question of 'retention, gift or sale' of those sequestered Strand mansions, which included Durham House and Somerset House, had in fact been settled by an Act of Parliament passed earlier that year. As a result, by 1656 more than a dozen committees of the Council of State, including that 'for removing obstructions in the sale of the Honours, Manors and Lands of the late King, Queen and Prince', were installed at Worcester House. Instead, the Gate House and Carlisle Rents were sold.

After the death of the 5th Earl and 1st Marquess of Worcester in 1646, the title had passed to Edward, 2nd Marquess (1602/3–1667), who was banished in 1649 for his active support of the Royalist cause. On his return from France in 1653, he was charged with high treason and sent to the Tower but released a year later, after which he retired from political life. It was Margaret, his second wife, who first petitioned for the return of Worcester House on 3 October 1653, a process that took the rest of the decade to complete.[34] When she eventually took possession in May 1660, the Council of State was still searching 'for hidden treasure', thereby 'endangering the foundations of Worcester House', which had been used since at least 1650 as a depot for riches seized by Parliament.[35] Further action had to be taken before 'Anne Tisser, who holds the gatehouse, part of Worcester House, and other tenants who hold adjoining houses called Carlisle Rents', would surrender these premises.[36]

The countess eventually succeeded in regaining control of the whole property, which had been settled on trustees for her use during her husband's lifetime. Then in 1660 Edward Hyde, 1st Earl of Clarendon and Lord Chancellor, moved in while his own Clarendon House in Piccadilly was being built. It thus became the Chancellery of England, of which Pepys mentions the Great Hall where Clarendon was installed as Chancellor of the University of Oxford.[37] It was here that James, Duke of York and then King James II, married Anne, Clarendon's daughter, on 3 September 1660, causing much gossip since marriage to a commoner was, as Evelyn put it, a 'strange change'.[38] Members of the royal family felt none the less at their ease in this house, for a year later Charles II arrived 'in a plain and common riding-suit and velvet cap, in which he seemed', as Pepys recorded, 'a very ordinary man to one that had not known him'.[39]

After years of apparent neglect and adaptation to other uses, Worcester House was 'not in so good reparation' but still 'far more commodious for your Lordship than where you now are', as the 2nd Marquess described it to Lord Clarendon in a letter of 9 June 1660, when the Chancellor was about to move in. It was therefore offered to him 'without requiring … one penny of rent', something Clarendon must have rejected, willingly or otherwise, as he eventually paid a hefty £500 a year for it.[40] His occupancy lasted until 1666, when he moved to Berkshire House, St James's, and then to his newly built Clarendon House. Worcester House seems to have been rarely used thereafter and merely for some public functions – for which its Great Hall was clearly well adapted – such as the installation of the Duke of Ormond as Chancellor of the University of Cambridge in 1669 or that of the Duke of Monmouth to the same office five years later. At around this time Hollar published his 'View of London extending eastwards from Peterborough House to Somerset House', which includes another, essentially unchanged depiction of the river front of Worcester House, with its gabled six-bay facade (fig. 132).

After the death of the 2nd Marquess in 1667, the house was inherited by Henry Somerset (1629–1700), 3rd Marquess and 1st Duke of Beaufort from 1682. This occasioned a further change in name, to Beaufort House. There is some confusion about what happened thereafter, as Pennant in 1791 states that the house was demolished by the 1st Duke but Thornbury says that it was burnt down in 1695.[41] The most illustrative account of the period is offered by John Strype (1643–1737) in 1720, who must have witnessed the development with his own eyes:

his Grace finding it crazy, and by its Antiquity grown very ruinous, and altho[gether] large, yet not after the modern Way of Building, thought it better to let out the Ground to Undertakers, than to build a new House thereon, the Steepness of the Descent to

the Thames rendring it not proper for great Courts, nor easy for Coaches, if the house were built at such a distance from the Street, as would have been proper: And having at the same time, bought Buckingham House at Chelsey, in an Air he thought much healthier, and near enough to the Town for Business. However his Grace caused a lesser House to be there built for himself, to dispatch Business in, at the End of a large Street leading to it, and having the conveniency of a Prospect over the Thames. On both sides are now very fair and good Houses built, well inhabited, generally by Gentry, especially in the Part next the Thames, which is much broader, than at its entrance out of the Strand. The front Houses in the Strand, which are lofty and well built, are inhabited by

132 Worcester House, detail of Wenceslaus Hollar, 'view of London extending eastwards from Peterborough House to Somerset House', early 1670s. By permission of the Pepys Library, Magdalene College, Cambridge ('London and Westminster', I, 2972, 34–35)

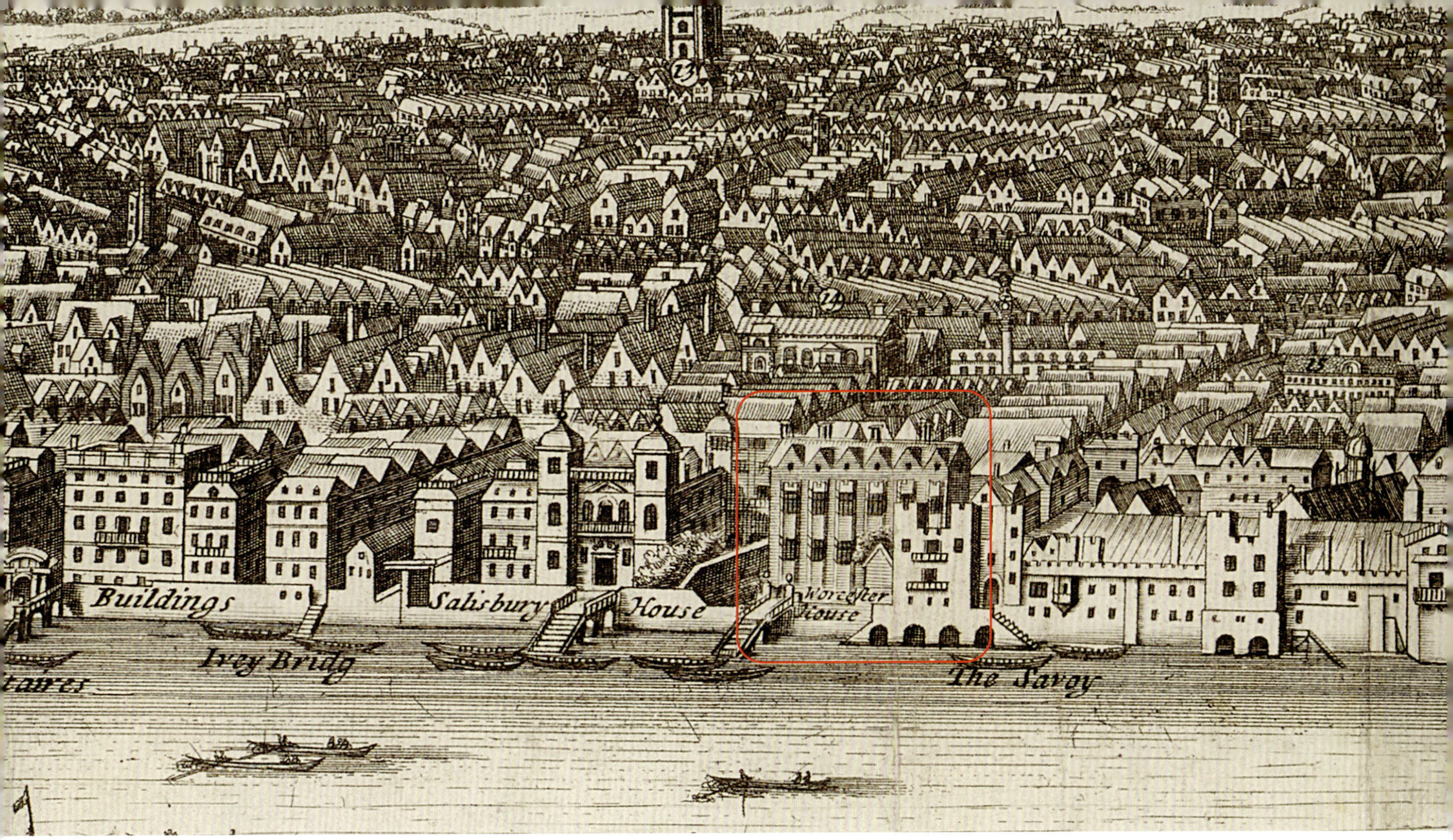

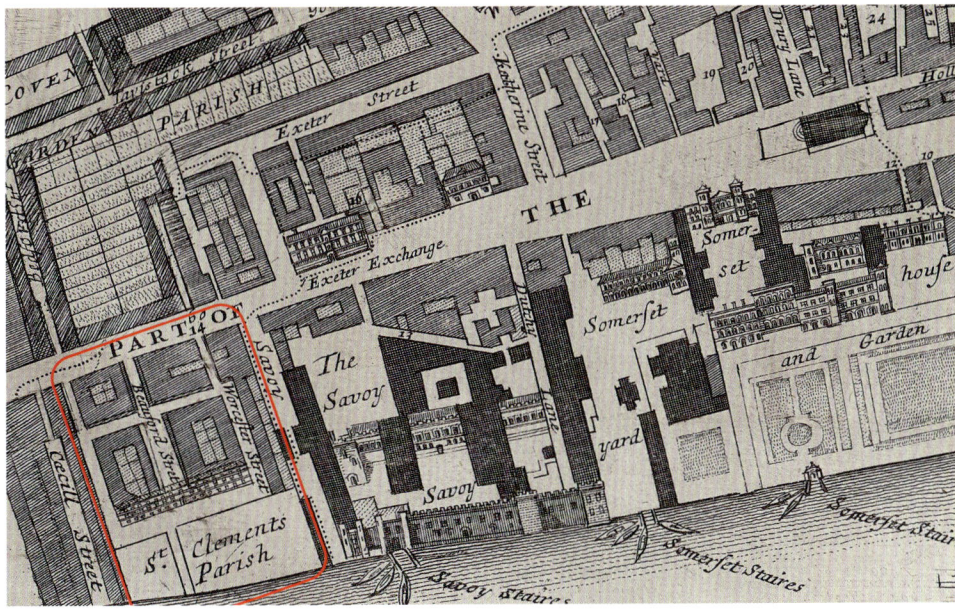

133 Beaufort (former Worcester) House, detail of William Morgan, *View of London and Westminster*, c.1682 (detail of images on pp. x and xi). By permission of the Pepys Library, Magdalene College, Cambridge ('London and Westminster', I, 2972, 38–39).

134 Area occupied by Beaufort Buildings, detail of John Strype, *A Survey of the Cities of London and Westminster*, vol. 4, p. 116, 1720 (detail of fig. 83). Folger Shakespeare Library, Washington DC. Licensed under Creative Commons Attribution-ShareAlike 4.0 International

Tradesmen; with one very fine Tavern ... close by this Tavern is an Alley that leadeth to Fountain Court, a very handsome Place with ... good Buildings which are well inhabited. Out of this Court is a Passage into the Street, where the Dukes House stood, which gave the name to Beauford Buildings. This House of the Dukes, with some others, was lately burnt down ...[42]

Whether the conflagration relates to the old Beaufort House or the lesser house which apparently replaced it, the fire probably served as a pretext for redevelopment, as Beresford Chancellor in 1908 remarks.[43] Either way, documentary sources attests to the demolition of the main house in about 1682, the year the 1st Duke had purchased the Chelsea house.[44] The contemporaneous *View of London and Westminster* by William Morgan still includes the river front of Beaufort House but it was for the very last time (fig. 133). The new Beaufort Buildings, seen in a map of London in Strype's 1720 edition of the *Survey* (fig. 134), were themselves wiped out some hundred years later, when the Savoy Theatre was built in their stead, 'leaving neither name nor stone' to recall the ancient house which had stood there for five centuries.[45]

135 The complex of Salisbury House, composed of Great Salisbury House (right) and Little Salisbury House (left), between Worcester House to the east (right) and Durham Rents and New Exchange to the west (left). Durham House, which would have stood behind the Exchange and extended towards the river (see fig. 180), is not seen as Hollar's view is cut here (detail of fig. 8)

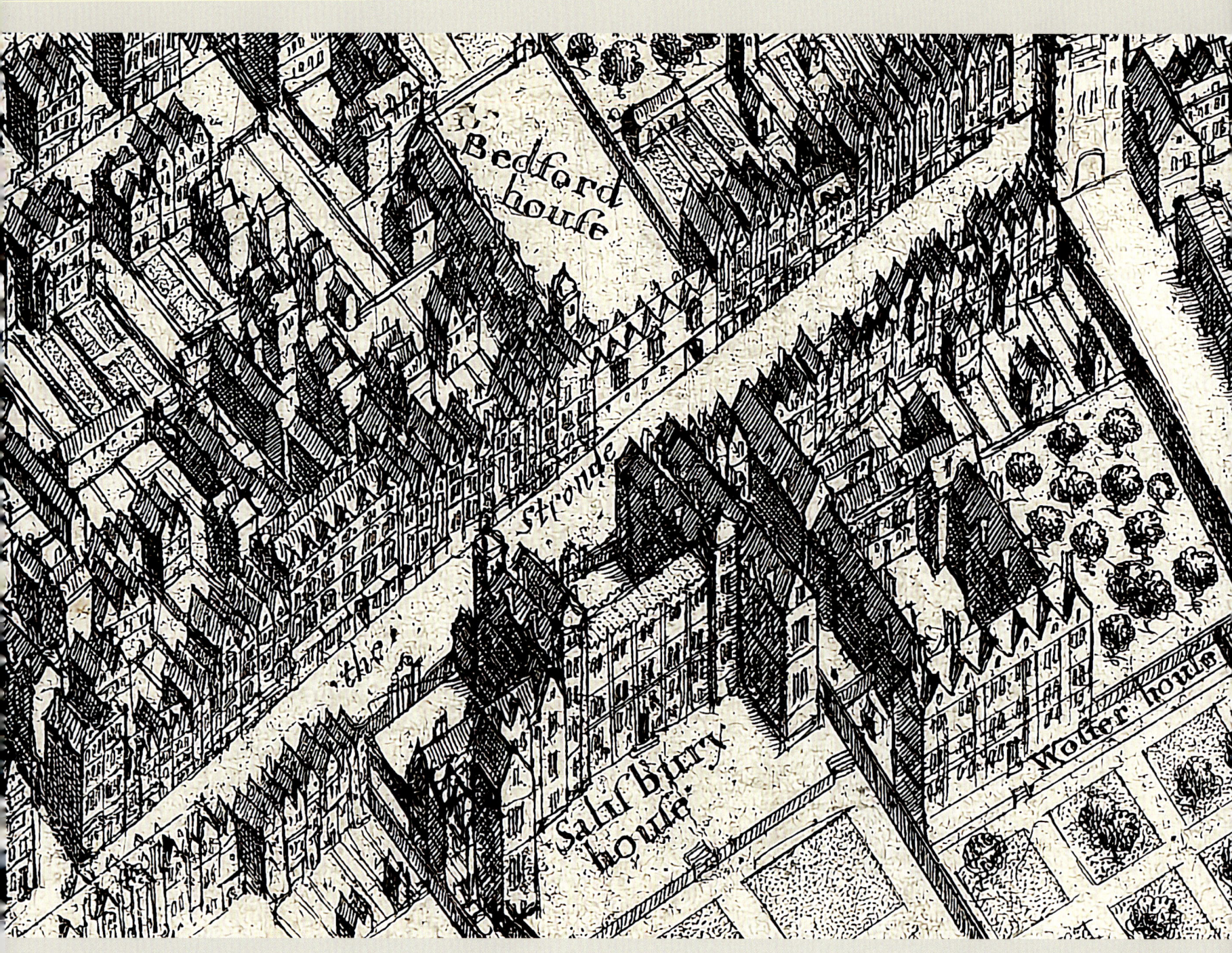

8 · SALISBURY HOUSE

SALISBURY HOUSE IS THE ONLY STRAND palace to have been built *de novo* in the early seventeenth century, apart from Northumberland House. Born out of the remarkable outpouring of architectural patronage initiated by Lord Burghley, it was effectively a complex of two attached houses known as 'Great Salisbury House' and 'Little Salisbury House', erected by his son Robert, 1st Earl of Salisbury, from 1599 (fig. 135). Its history has been illustrated extensively by several recent publications.[1] This chapter enlarges on these and contextualises the house according to this book's rationale.

The House of Robert Cecil, 1st Earl of Salisbury: 1599–1613

Born on 1 June 1563 at Burghley House – 'short, crookbacked but with noble countenance and features'[2] – Robert Cecil became his father's worthy successor as Secretary of State from 1596 and indeed the new head of what has been described as a 'Regnum Cecilianum' (fig. 136).[3] 'Sero sed Serio', 'late but in earnest', his motto poignantly recites: he ascended to the title of 1st Earl of Salisbury in 1605, becoming in 1608 the holder of the most powerful and lucrative of the Crown offices, that of Lord Treasurer of England.

During his father's lifetime, Robert had lived in the annexe of Burghley House (see Chapter Five). His nomination as Chancellor to the Duchy of Lancaster in 1597 had also temporarily provided him with its house, the Savoy Palace (see Chapter Four). When both places were lost in 1599, the first because of Burghley's death, the second after Cecil's resignation from the chancellorship in order to take up the new office of Master of the Wards, he immediately secured Dacre House and grounds from his aunt, Lady Elizabeth Russell, which lay 'between the highe Streete on the North and the Ryver of Thames on the Southe and the messuage … called Russell house … on the East … [and] Ivey lane on the weste'.[4] As Norden's map of 1593 shows (fig. 137), the site was small but the house was 'new built, and fair to the street, well watered with conduit water … the garden the length of the house, [and] a private water gate', as Lady Russell was at pain to stress, for her nephew had originally set his sights on the main Russell House (see Chapter Seven).[5] From November 1600, Richard Percival, Cecil's de facto private secretary and himself 'addicted to building and gardening', had then acquired numerous

properties west of the original site, most of which came from William Fortescue, the owner of the so-called Durham Rents.[6] These were twenty-two dwellings with gardens lying between Durham House and Ivy Lane along the Strand, granted to Fortescue's father, Sir Nicholas, the Groom Porter of Henry VIII, in 1544. Meanwhile, clearing and rebuilding had swiftly advanced, for Simon Basil, the Controller and later Surveyor of the King's Works – indeed a creature of both Secretaries – had given it undivided attention: 'I will from 6 to 6 give my daily attendance', he promised Cecil in 1601.[7] Between 1601 and 1602, Cecil had received detailed reports from Basil almost four times a month, while the site's daily progress was monitored by a special 'Clercke to take notesse of all such matterialls and Mens Laboure, that shalbe there ymployed'.[8] This was to enlighten the Secretary on the smallest architectural detail, in which he notably took great interest, and to control costs and building material, a large quantity of which had come from the Crown, the Bishop of London and Lady Sidney.[9]

136 Lord Burghley with his son Robert Cecil, both wearing the blue ribbon of the Order of the Garter, painted after Burghley's death in 1598. Cranborne Manor. Reproduced with permission of the Marquess of Salisbury, Hatfield House

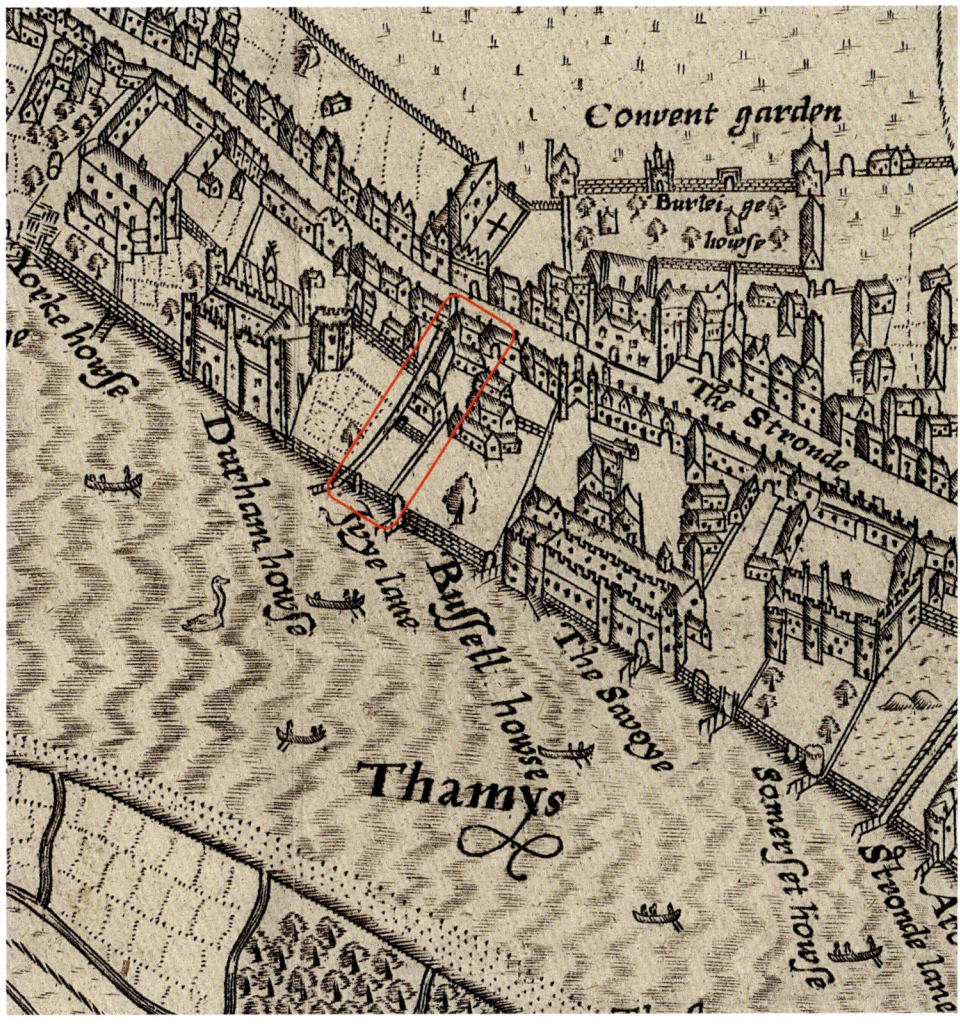

137 Dacre House and grounds in between Russell House on the east (right) and Ivy (Bridge) Lane to the west (left), detail of John Norden, *Speculum Britanniae*, 1593. Folger Shakespeare Library, Washington DC. Licensed under Creative Commons Attribution-ShareAlike 4.0 International

With such organisation, the main structure of the house was up by August 1601, while Basil was dealing with a 'new addition' on the west, for which two tenements had been bought and demolished but for their vaulted basements, and Ivy Lane was altered.[10] The result was promising: Walter Cope, a long-standing member of Cecil's entourage, had seen the front of the house and liked 'very well of it, if so be that the new addition in the court were correspondent'. He suggested that 'that side [of the new addition] next the court may be coloured like into bricks, and being done at such time as the plaster is green, it will retain its colour very well'. Then, referring to the main front of the house, he proposed 'two fair returns of square windows, the one proportionable to the brea[d]th of your gallery [west] and the other answerable next to my Lord Herbert's house [east]'.[11] In September 1601, Cope 'had spoken for the hastening of your house and street'.[12] The following January the 'wall towards my Lord's court' was under construction,[13] while in September Percival reported that 'the bedchamber is wainscoted, the chamber next it will not be finished these eight day, your cabinet will be all ended this day; but I do not believe that the chamber which they say you intend to make your bedchamber will be fit for you to lie in yet these three months, the walls, though covered with wainscot, are so moist and musty'.[14] Cecil had also been sent a 'homely present … worth gold and silver', that is, one of the first water closets invented by Sir John Harrington.[15] By 6 December 1602 building must have been completed enough to receive Queen Elizabeth at what is described as the 'warming of Master Secretaries new house', for which extraordinary celebrations, excellently described in Matthew Dimmock's *Elizabethan Globalism* (2019), were put in place.[16] This ends the first stage of construction, urged on by the advanced age of the queen, who died three months later. According to Stow, it was 'a large and stately house of brick and timber', for which Cecil had 'also levelled and paved the highway near adjoining, to the great beautifying of that street and commodity of passengers'.[17] The 'hall was well furnished with choice weapons, which her Majestie took special care of', as the barrister John Manningham recorded, while the gallery in the west wing was known for its vast extent, such that Walter Cope had struggled to find appropriate hangings for it.[18] The interiors clearly stood up well, as on 1 January 1603 the poet and courtier Sir Arthur Gorges told Cecil that 'A fitter place than your new house I know none, where it may sort with some, though hardly second many, of your delicacies'.[19]

Evidence of the house at this stage is provided by two sets of drawings by Simon Basil, the first an interim design dated 1600, hence before the westward expansion, the second for its probable actual state in 1602.[20] The first series consists of four plans and two elevations of a small but elaborate courtyard house (see figs 138–43), obtained by multiplying a 'unit house', a conventional urban type since early Tudor times, which must have characterised many of the old tenements along the Strand.[21] The scheme was adapted to Cecil's original site as acquired in 1599, which was sixty feet wide. Given the slope on the river side, the basement features three cellars, a large Kitchen opening onto the courtyard, two Larders and a Pantry (fig. 138). A terrace the width of the house, accessed from a central corridor linked to the upper floor via a couple of spiral stairs,

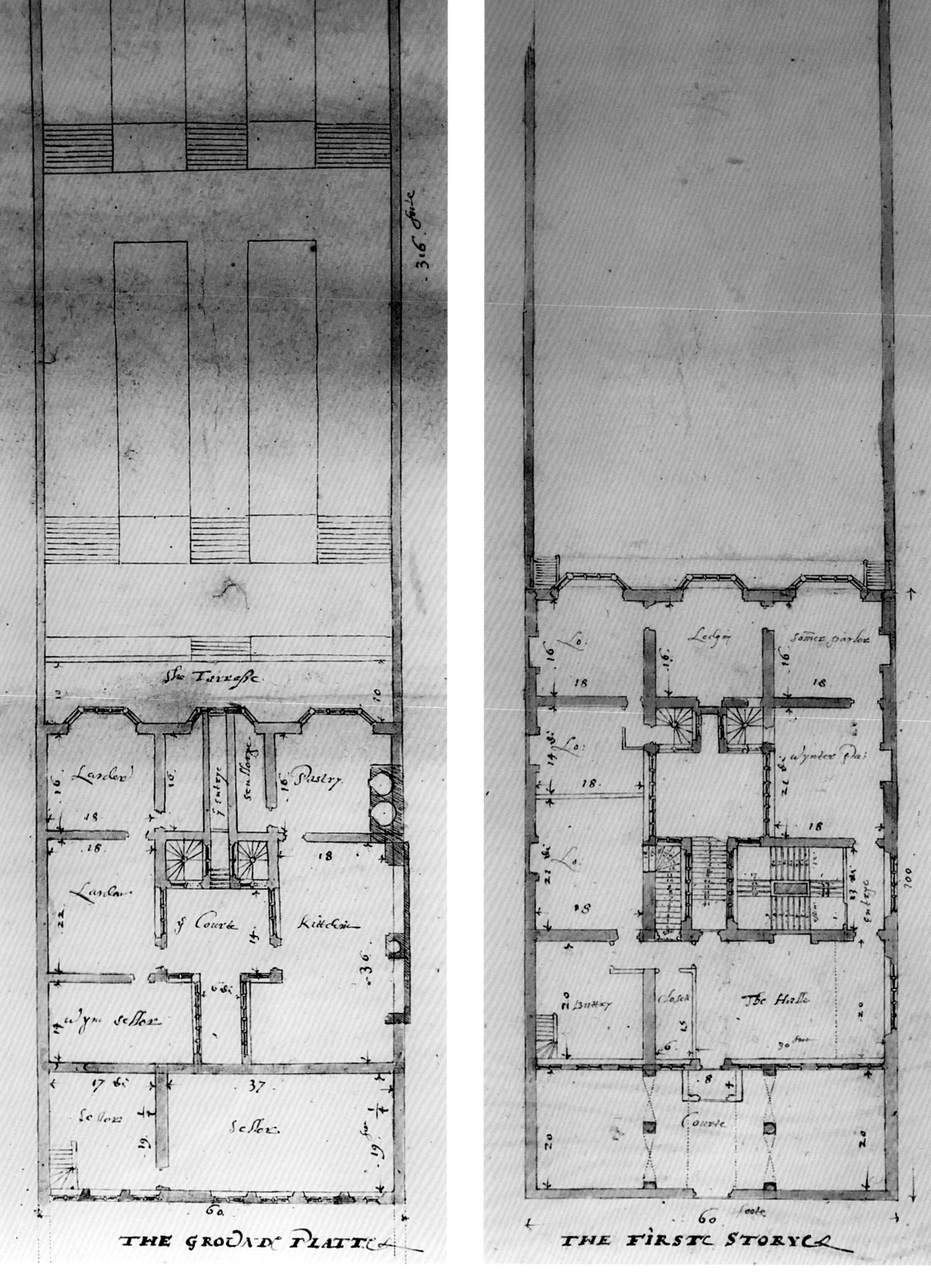

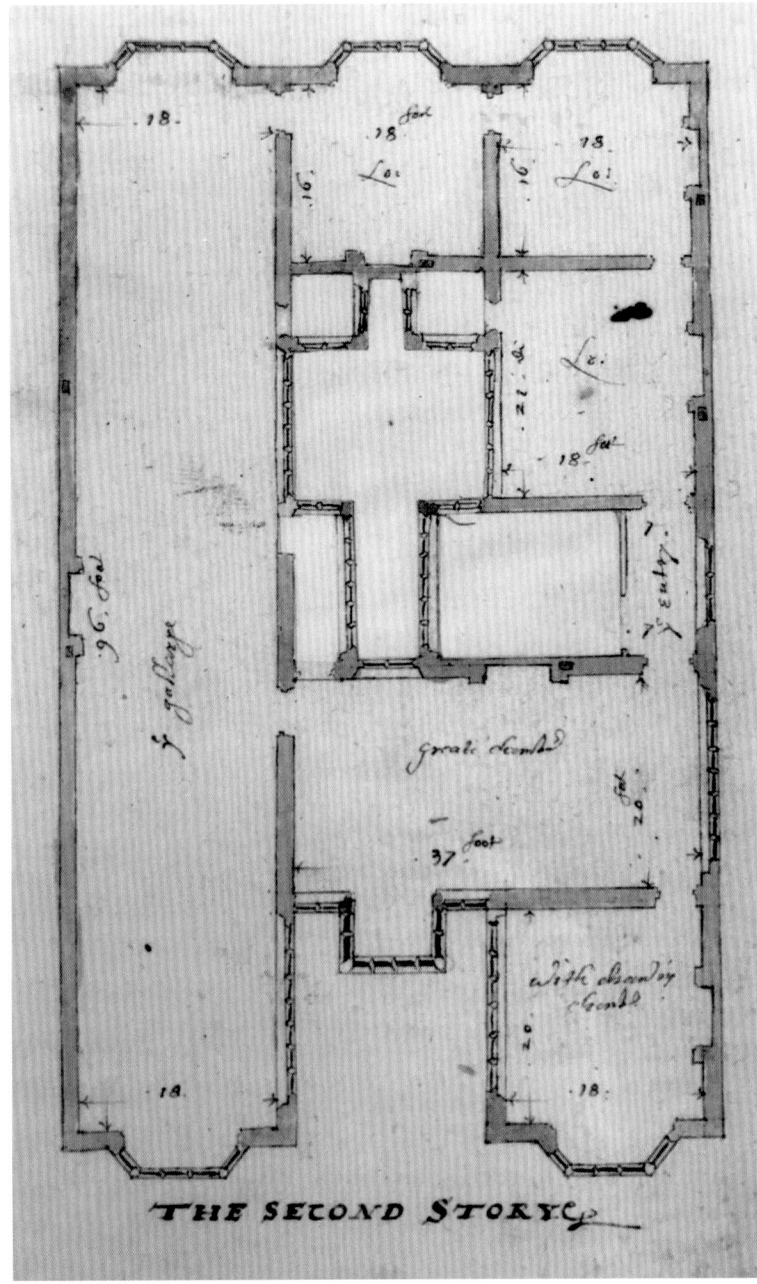
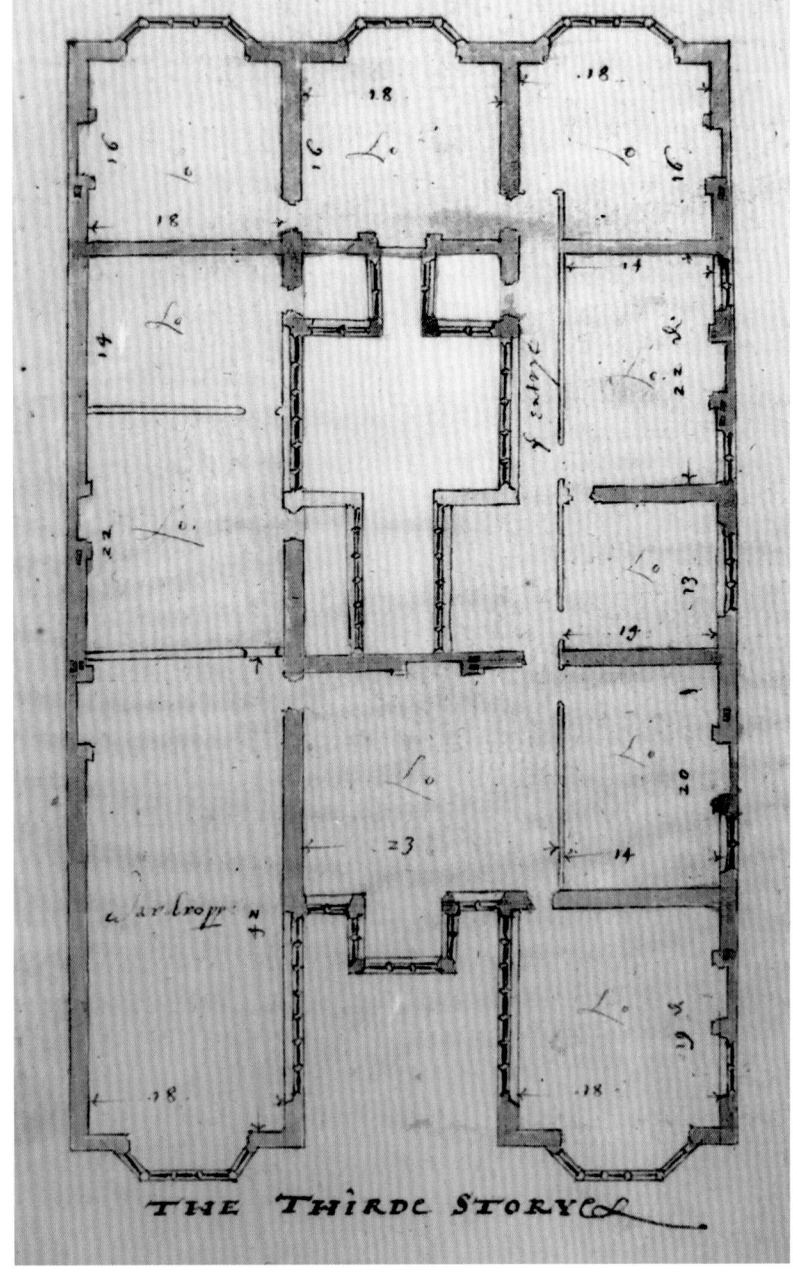

138 *opposite, left* Simon Basil, basement plan for Salisbury House, 1600 (Strand bottom). Bodleian Libraries, University of Oxford, Gough Drawings, A3 fol. 72r. Creative Commons Licence CC-BY-NC-4.0

139 *opposite, right* Simon Basil, ground-floor plan for Salisbury House, 1600 (Strand bottom). Bodleian Libraries, University of Oxford, Gough Drawings, A3 fol. 73r. Creative Commons Licence CC-BY-NC-4.0

140 Simon Basil, first-floor plan for Salisbury House, 1600 (Strand bottom). Bodleian Libraries, University of Oxford, Gough Drawings, A3 fol. 74r. Creative Commons Licence CC-BY-NC-4.0

141 Simon Basil, second-floor plan for Salisbury House, 1600 (Strand bottom). Bodleian Libraries, University of Oxford, Gough Drawings, A3 fol. 75r. Creative Commons Licence CC-BY-NC-4.0

precedes a formal garden on several levels running down to the Thames. The ground floor (first floor from the garden; fig. 139) has a courtyard on the Strand side which gives access to the Hall, joined by the Buttery on its east side, and conventionally linked to a Winter Parlour, followed by a second, Summer Parlour, a Lobby and what appears to be the main lodging on the garden side. Innovatively for a town house of this period, the garden is directly linked to the Summer Parlour and the main lodging by external staircases either side of the house (see fig. 143). The first floor (fig. 140) includes the standard sequence of public rooms with a Great Chamber leading into the

SALISBURY HOUSE | 141

Withdrawing Chamber (which, however, does not lead into a state bedchamber). A Long Gallery of ninety-six feet runs the entire length of the house, while the lodgings are in its south-west corner, whence there is access to the upper level of the house (fig. 141) which contains ten more chambers and a large wardrobe. The elevations are fairly simple (figs 142 and 143), despite the attempt to create a three-sided plan by suggesting the projection of the two front wings, mainly by the bow windows and curved gables with scrolled sides, while the decoration is limited to string courses.

The second series of plans differs little from the first apart from the presence of the westward addition (see figs 144–8). At basement level (fig. 144) this includes a large Kitchen and a vaulted Cellar, while the main body of the house, still revolving round a courtyard, features the usual service rooms. The garden, accessed at an axial point from the Loggia as before, equals the width of the main house, still sixty feet wide, and runs down to the river. The ground floor (first from the garden; fig. 145) is accessed from a large side courtyard open to the Strand. The Hall, flanked by the great staircase (accessed at its south end), is followed by the usual set of rooms, the Parlour, Withdrawing Room and Bed Chamber, on the garden side. The Parlour is also linked to a large Chapel, while the rooms on the Strand side are for household members: two of them are even marked 'Mr Percyvalls roomes'. Over the Hall, on the first floor (fig. 146), there is the Great Chamber, followed by the Long Gallery of eighty-four feet (shorter than the earlier plan's of ninety-six feet) and a series of lodgings. The second floor (fig. 147) provides further rooms and large wardrobes, while the garret storey (fig. 148) is to be found only over the main body of the house. My reconstructed elevations for these plans (figs 149 and 150) show equally simple facades, though more imposing than the 1600 elevations given the extended length of the site.

The second stage of construction of Salisbury House began in 1605, when it was decided to extend it eastwards with a new wing. This was well under way by the time the king and his entourage had dined there on 27 May but not finished: on 9 August Thomas Wilson remarked that 'everything by the view represents to the fantasy an idea of what it will be, a building apt to give the eye contentment'.[22] Wilson was another of Burghley's former retainers, Keeper of the State Papers, himself a resident of the Strand at

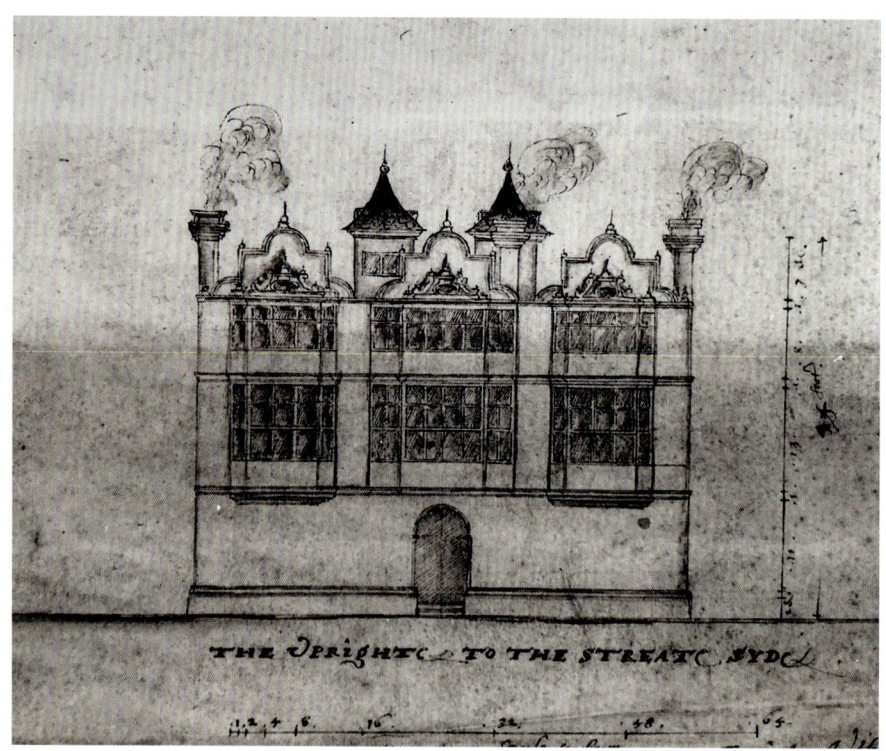

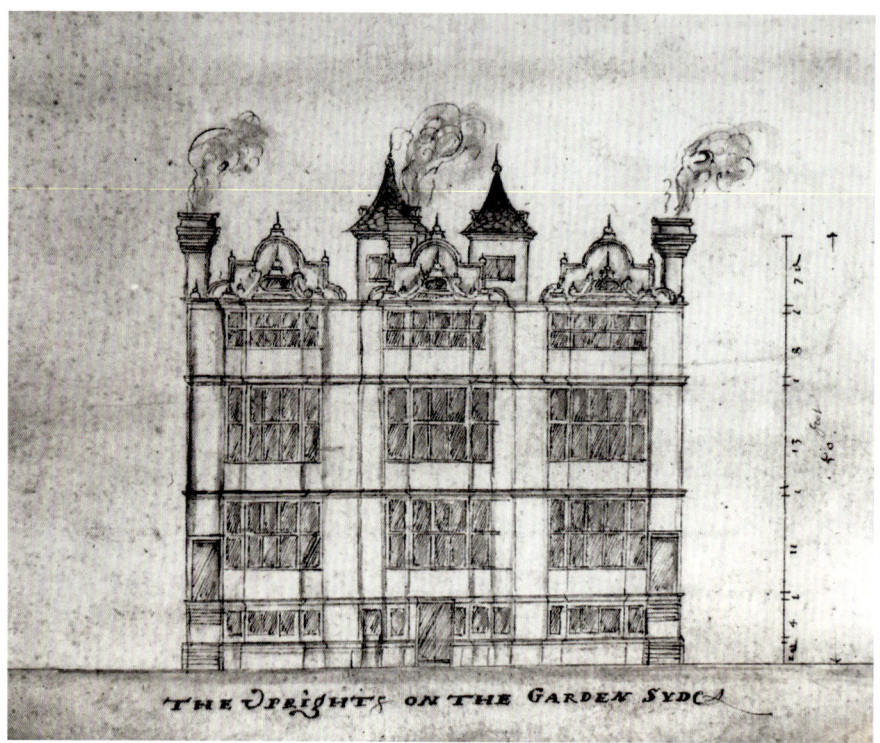

142 Simon Basil, Strand front for Salisbury House, 1600 (Strand bottom). Bodleian Libraries, University of Oxford, Gough Drawings, A3 fol. 81r. Creative Commons Licence CC-BY-NC-4.0

143 Simon Basil, garden front for Salisbury House, 1600 (Strand bottom). Bodleian Libraries, University of Oxford, Gough Drawings, A3 fol. 81r. Creative Commons Licence CC-BY-NC-4.0

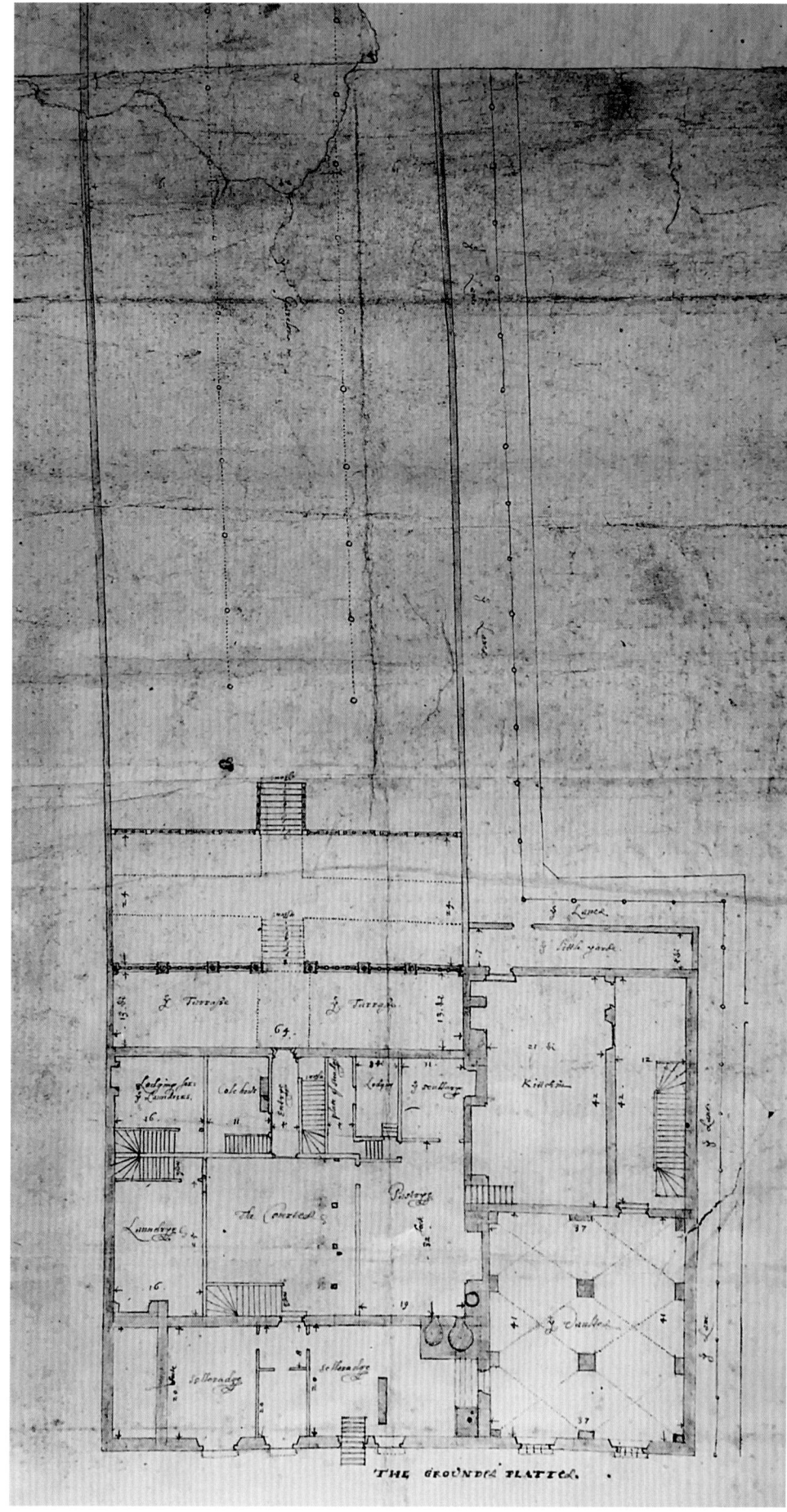

one of Durham Rents and possibly also involved with Arundel House in 1618 (see Chapter Two). It appears that the garden side of the new wing had an open loggia at ground level, probably connected with the arcaded loggia which had been previously built in this part of the house (fig. 150 and see fig. 144). A layout of the property in the 1690s (fig. 151) reveals that the new wing was a rectangular block sixteen feet wide by c.110 feet long projecting at right angles to the great house, though possibly lower and different in style, as suggested by Hollar (see fig. 135). As for its function, it was mainly occupied by the 'newe library', which was decorated under Wilson's instructions, 'my Lord willing me to let the Library be adorned in such sort I thought fit'.[23] It was here that the king and queen were entertained in 1608 to celebrate Cecil's appointment as Lord Treasurer with a masque by Ben Jonson and Inigo Jones, whose design for a rocky mound and a fine classical archway can be connected to the masque.[24] This and a design of c.1608–9 for a similar arch constitute the first evidence of Jones's use of architecture in his drawings for masques (figs 152 and 153).[25] The 1605 addition may also have contained a new gallery, of c.120 feet (considerably longer than the previous one of 84 feet), which would have kept pace with the 160-foot Long Gallery at Northumberland House, under construction at the same time (see Chapter Eleven).[26]

Major remodelling of both the inside and outside of the house took place from the spring of 1607 to improve what had been hurried for the reception of Queen Elizabeth in 1602. A new floor was added to the western, lower part of the building, in conjunction with a 'flat forme over the great chamber and steares wch will be seene to the street … to be made with arches of french termes and wth beastes standing upon pedestals', and executed by the carpenter William Wood under the supervision of Robert Liminge (d. 1628).[27] The latter, himself a carpenter, was the surveyor of Hatfield House, Cecil's new country seat built from 1607 to replace Theobalds, which he had inherited but exchanged with the king. At the time, Liminge also worked under Basil in the Strand, as the various 'agreements' between the two indicate.[28] There was also a new 'open

144 Simon Basil, basement plan of Salisbury House, 1600–02 (Strand bottom). Bodleian Libraries, University of Oxford, Gough Drawings, A3 fol. 80r. Creative Commons Licence CC-BY-NC-4.0

SALISBURY HOUSE | 143

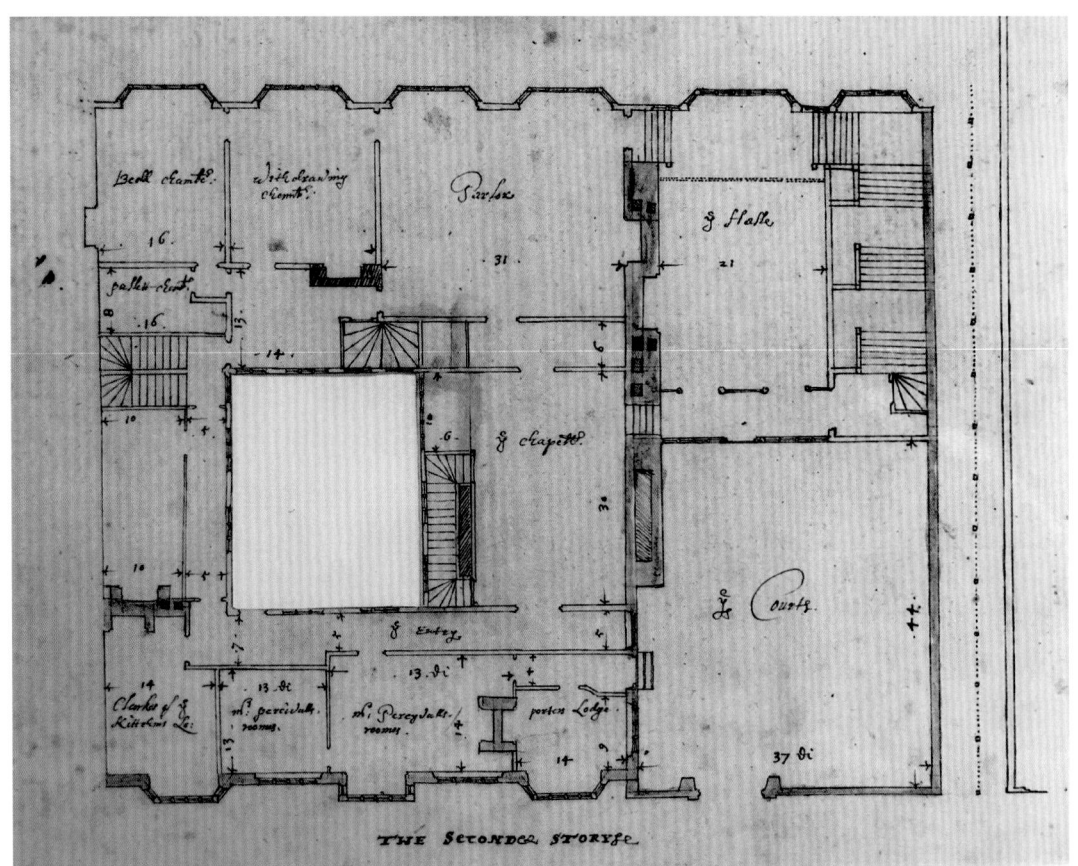

145 Simon Basil, ground-floor plan of Salisbury House, 1600–02 (Strand bottom). Bodleian Libraries, University of Oxford, Gough Drawings, A3 fol. 79r. Creative Commons Licence CC-BY-NC-4.0

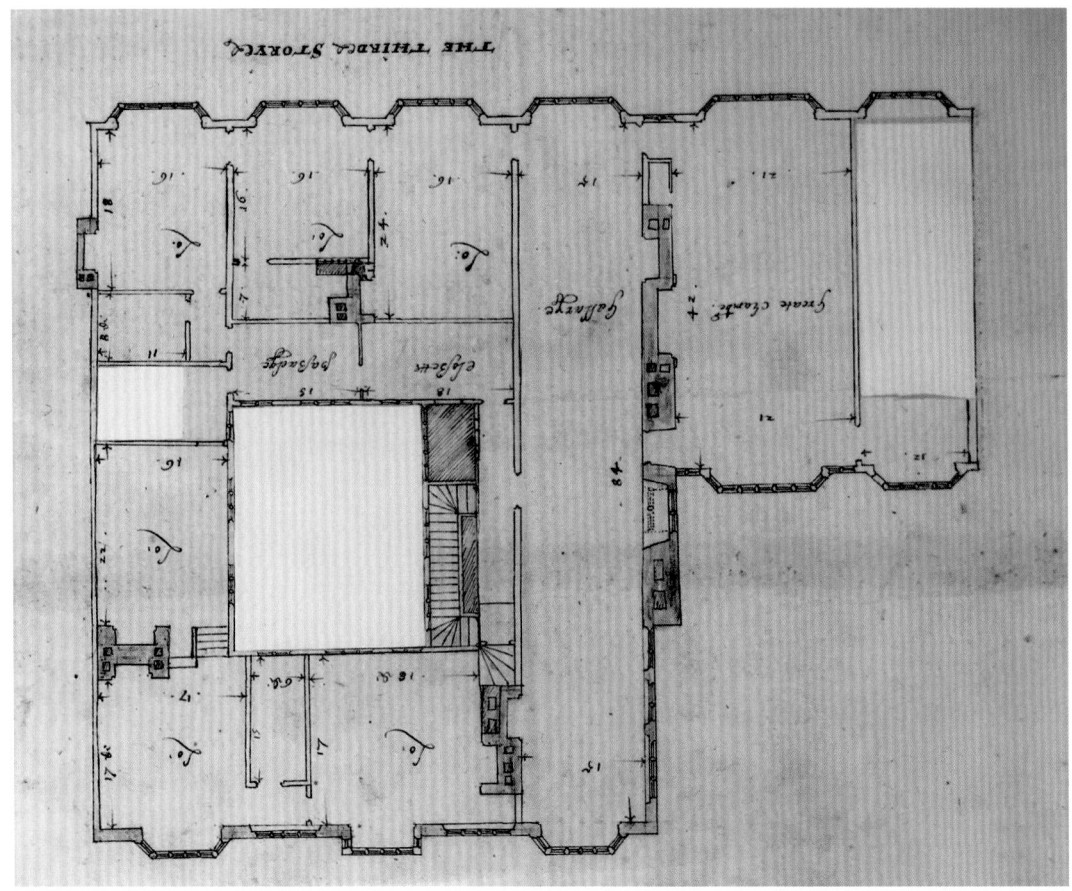

146 Simon Basil, first-floor plan of Salisbury House, 1600–02 (Strand bottom). Bodleian Library, University of Oxford, Gough Drawings, A3 fol. 78r. Creative Commons Licence CC-BY-NC-4.0

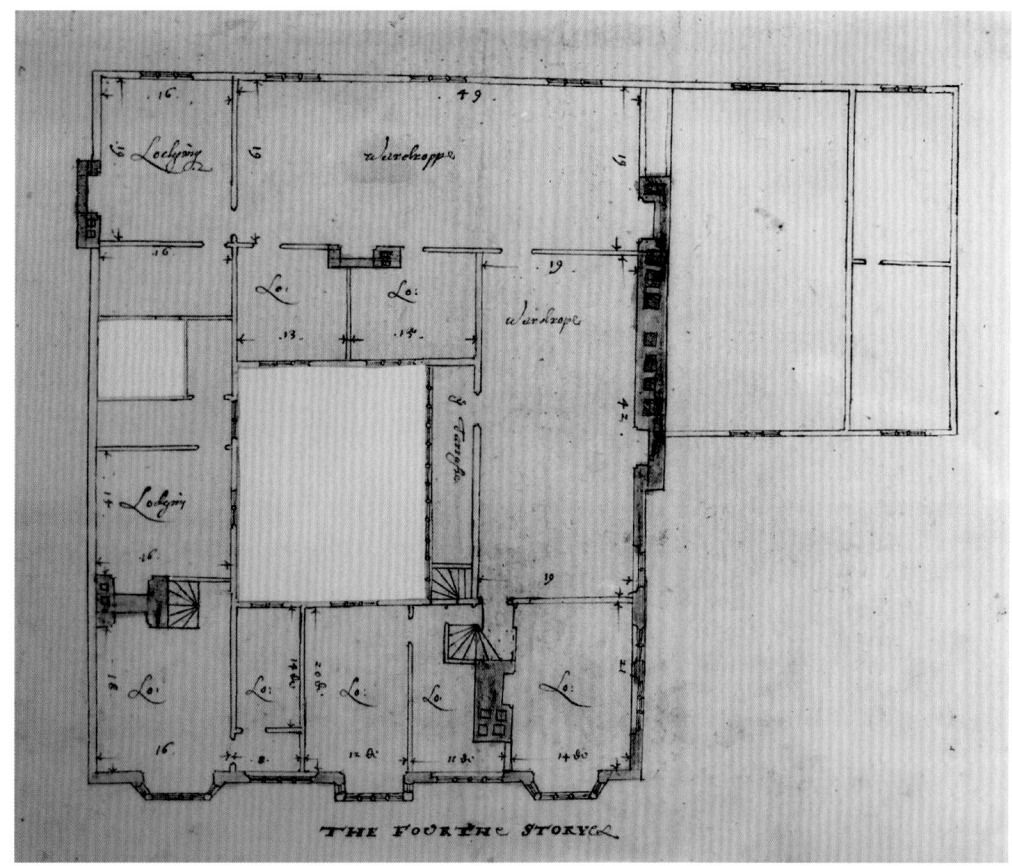

147 Simon Basil, second-floor plan of Salisbury House, 1600–02 (Strand bottom). Bodleian Libraries, University of Oxford, Gough Drawings, A3 fol. 77r. Creative Commons Licence CC-BY-NC-4.0

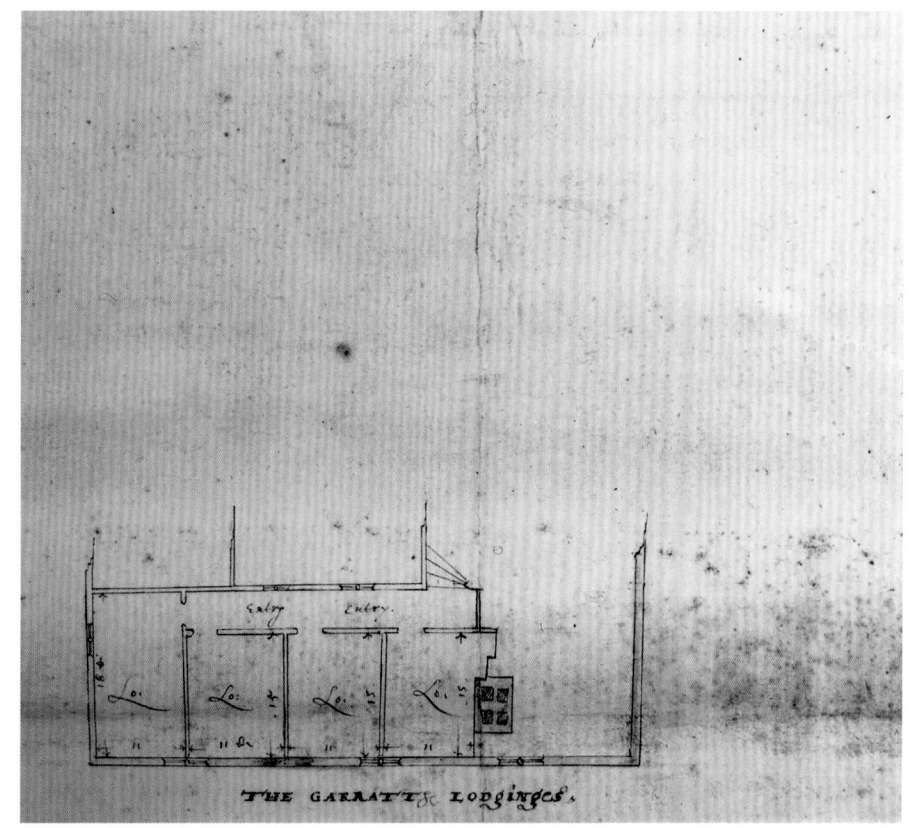

148 Simon Basil, third-floor plan of Salisbury House, 1600–02 (Strand bottom). Bodleian Libraries, University of Oxford, Gough Drawings, A3 fol. 76r. Creative Commons Licence CC-BY-NC-4.0

gallery towards the street', while all the windows were decorated between 1607 and 1608 with stone tafferels carved by one John de Buck, and twelve heraldic beasts ornamented the gable ends of both fronts.[29] In addition, Rowland Buckett painted and gilded two unicorns, two dragons, two griffins and four lions, 'all of stone that are to stand on the top of the leads to the garden wards, to be wrought into oil'. The same craftsman was paid to paint 'the parsonage [personage] that stands in the small arches towards the gardene on the outside of the house', possibly a series of moulded figures which decorated the arcaded loggia onto the garden.[30]

Salisbury House's skyline was considerably improved by turrets, in place since at least 1607.[31] According to Hollar, the two on the garden side were placed on the corners and stood out from the main body (see fig. 135). This is confirmed by the c.1690 layout of the property (see fig. 151); the turrets contained spiral stairs which connected all levels of the building. The turrets on the street front, though, were probably simple projections from the roof. Works carried out in this period included the 'great lanthorne', possibly the clock tower, described as being 'on the tope of the House … laide into oyle Cullers and the walls thereof painted like glasse'. Around it stood six heraldic lions bearing Salisbury's 'Coates and Creastes'. There were also '3 great Vaines' distributed on the top, decorated with the full blazon of Salisbury's arms.[32]

The records of these years inform us of considerable improvements to the garden. By

149 Reconstruction of the Strand elevation and section of (Great) Salisbury House as it stood in 1602, based on the plans by Simon Basil, 1600–02. © Manolo Guerci, 2004

150 Reconstruction of the garden elevation and section of (Great) Salisbury House as it stood in 1602, based on the plans by Simon Basil, 1600–02. © Manolo Guerci, 2004

151 Layout of Great Salisbury House with the new extension, c.1690. Reproduced with permission of the Marquess of Salisbury, Hatfield House (Hatfield House MSS, Drawer 11/18)

152 Inigo Jones, design for a 'rock' and an archway, perhaps for Lord Salisbury's entertainment of May 1608, 1608–09. Chatsworth. Image © The Courtauld, Conway Library

153 Inigo Jones, design for an archway for an unidentified entertainment, 1608–09. Chatsworth. Image © The Courtauld, Conway Library

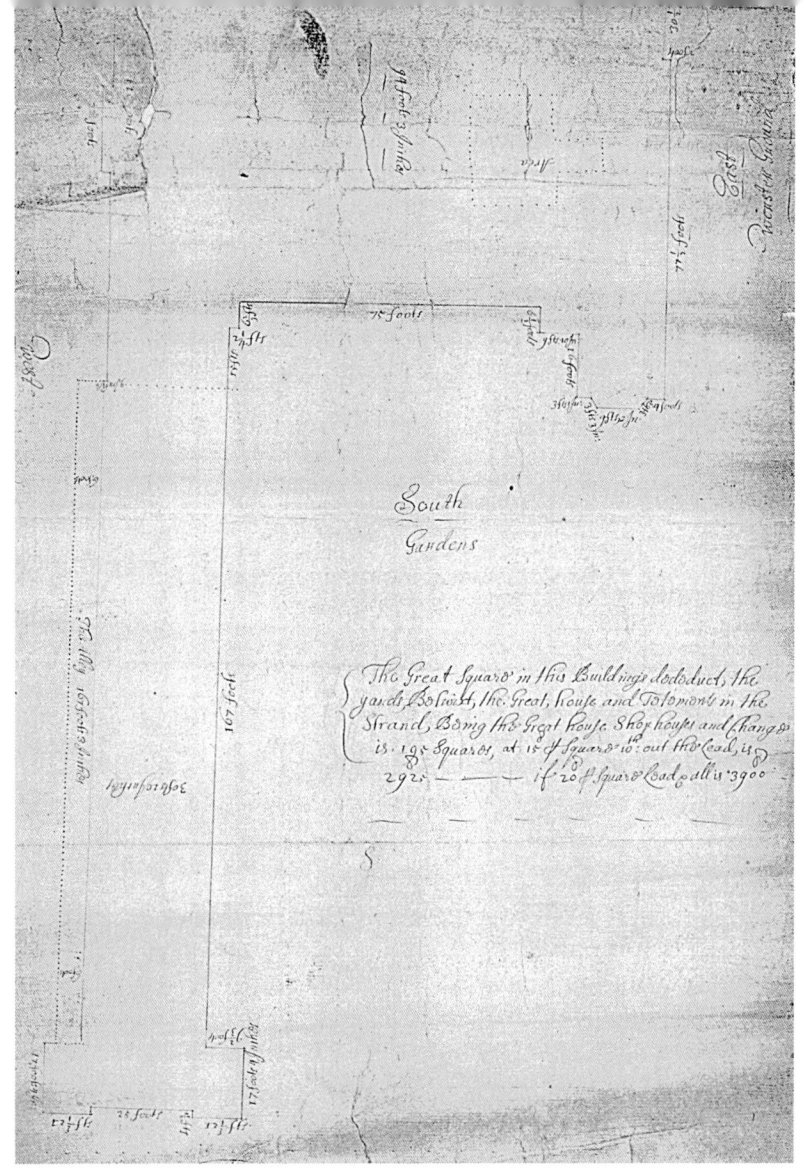

August 1609, Jenever the joiner had worked 'about the seat in the garden', as had 'Poole the Plumber', probably creating a fountain, while John the gardener was paid for keeping pheasants there, perhaps a charming attempt at creating *rus in urbe*.[33] By far the greatest improvement to the garden would have been the 'Porticus', an extraordinary, but unexecuted, two-storey loggia for its river end (figs 154–7), designed between 1605 and 1610 by John Osborne, Remembrancer of the Exchequer as well as an amateur architect responsible for some of the earliest manifestations of academic classicism in England.[34] It represents the peak of Cecil's sophisticated patronage and was possibly conceived for one of James's visits. In effect, it would have established a pattern of 'Roman' loggias along the Thames as part of the king's neo-Augustan project to find London built of wood and leave it of stone, as the capital of Magna Britannia.[35]

The construction of the western addition in 1602, together with the first altering of Ivy Lane, had been an ambitious development requiring the acquisition of further properties. In April 1603 Cecil had been informed by Percival that a 'great personage' wanted the lease of Durham House and that he should speedily secure it considering that 'the very form and shape of your own house, must need you to desire'.[36] Durham Rents lay in the way of expansion, as did part of Durham

SALISBURY HOUSE | 147

House, in which Raleigh's right to lodge was challenged on the death of the queen. Soon after the accession of James I in 1603, an order had been given for Raleigh to vacate the stables and garden immediately and his lodgings by midsummer (see Chapter Nine). The king then on Cecil's behalf acquired from Bishop Matthew the strip of land sixty feet wide that adjoined Ivy Lane, which faced the 1602 addition but was still part of the garden of Durham House.[37] By 1606, Cecil as Earl of Salisbury had also obtained the lease of that garden, followed by the freehold secured by Act of Parliament.[38] More property was bought from 1604 to 1606, including Vincent's House and Rutland House, the most westerly of Durham Rents, and in 1607 the gatehouse portion of the Durham estate, previously granted by the king to Dudley Carleton, reverted to Cecil.[39] By 1610, Ivy Lane had been moved further west, clearing the way for more building.[40] This is the last intervention related to the second stage of the enlargement of Salisbury House.

The last stage of construction began in 1611 when both Rutland House and Vincent's House were pulled down. Extensive works, described in the accounts as 'charges of enlarging the garden and the new intended building at Salisbury House', for which the hefty £1753 14s 4d was paid, continued right up to the eve of Salisbury's death on 24 May 1612.[41] Referred to as 'Little Salisbury House', the new range extended the main house west towards the new Ivy Lane and included a new kitchen and further 'lodgeings of the newe building gowing from the newe Kitchin to the laundry'. It also had a new turret.[42]

While affording a palatial scale to the whole complex, Little Salisbury House provided accommodation for the earl's son William. In this, the 1st Earl may have followed the example of his own father, who had built the annexe to Burghley House for him. Little Salisbury House could also provide income, or secure lodgings for female members of the family as well as widows, who customarily left after the death of their husbands.[43] Its construction had the effect of creating a new court abutting the street, with a central gateway opening on to the Strand. Either side of it was a Caen-stone screen of 'open finishing worke on the Topp of the Brickwall affront the new court' by John Benson the mason.[44] There was also a second porter's lodge.

There are no plans of Little Salisbury House but its south front bears some similarities with Basil's first series of designs of 1600: the two lower floors had six oriel windows, three per storey, each comprising ten lights, while on the top floor there were '2 french windows of 2 lights apiece with vauz + ornaments' (see figs 143 and 13).[45] According to Hollar's 'West Central District', Little Salisbury House was composed of two wings facing a courtyard open to the Strand, with 'gable ends, both on the front of the Court side, as that buildinge on the garden side' (see fig. 135).[46] The carpenter John Lovelidge undertook the internal work under the direction of Simon Basil. The house had three floors including the 'garrit flore', with a semi-basement level which contained the kitchen, cellars and other services. Conceived as an independent unit, it had its own Hall, Gallery, Great Chamber and all the other

154 John Osborne, elevational design for a 'porticus' in the garden of Salisbury House, 1605–10, as re-assembled by the author. Reproduced with permission of the Marquess of Salisbury, Hatfield House (Hatfield House MSS, CPM Supp. 89 London)

155 Reconstruction of the longitudinal section of (Great) Salisbury House as it stood in 1602, based on the plans by Simon Basil of 1600–02, with the reconstructed side elevation of the Porticus, based on the main elevation (see fig. 154) and John Osborne's own description, as it would have stood on the south end of the garden. © Manolo Guerci, 2004

156 Reconstruction of the plan and complete elevations of the Porticus, based on the main elevation (see fig. 154) and John Osborne's own description. © Manolo Guerci, 2004

157 Detailed reconstruction of the side elevation of the Porticus, based on the main elevation (see fig. 154) and John Osborne's own description. © Manolo Guerci, 2004

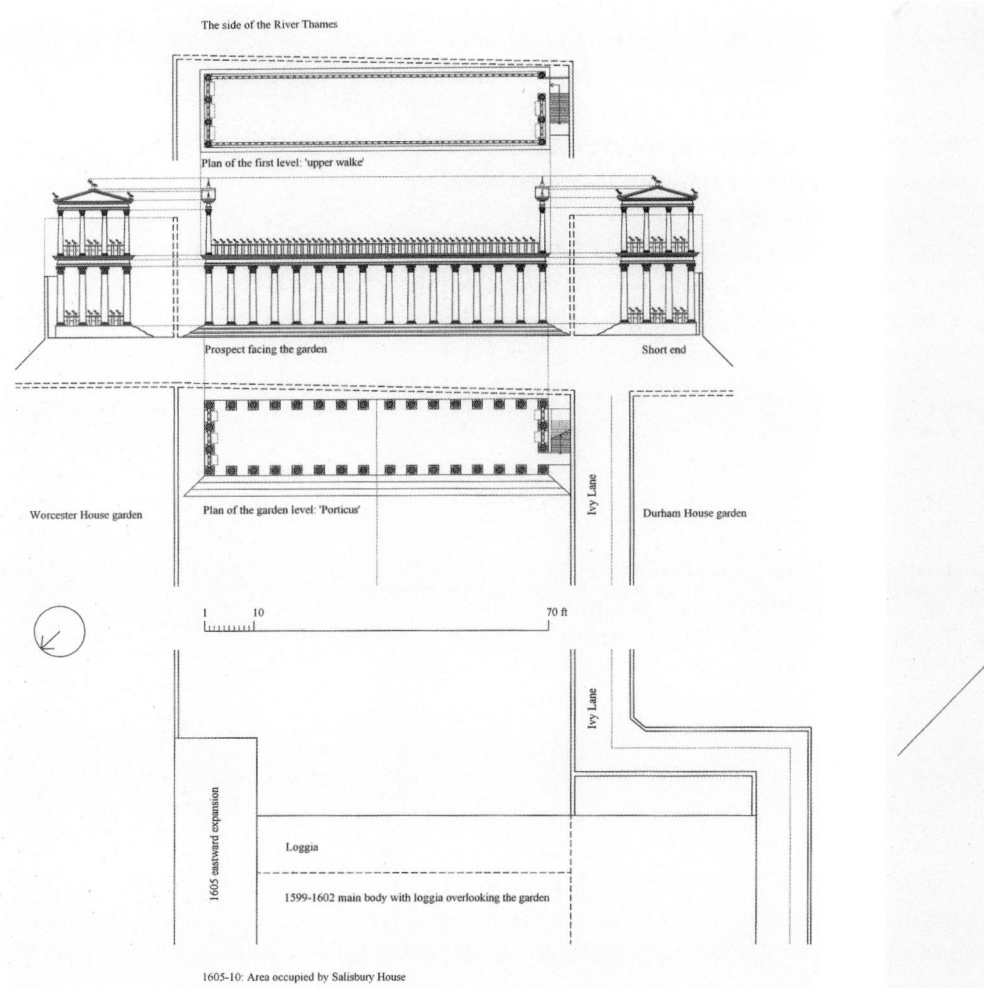

The side of the River Thames

Plan of the first level: 'upper walke'

Worcester House garden | Prospect facing the garden | Short end

Plan of the garden level: 'Porticus'

Ivy Lane | Durham House garden

1605 eastward expansion

Loggia

1599-1602 main body with loggia overlooking the garden

Ivy Lane

1605-10: Area occupied by Salisbury House

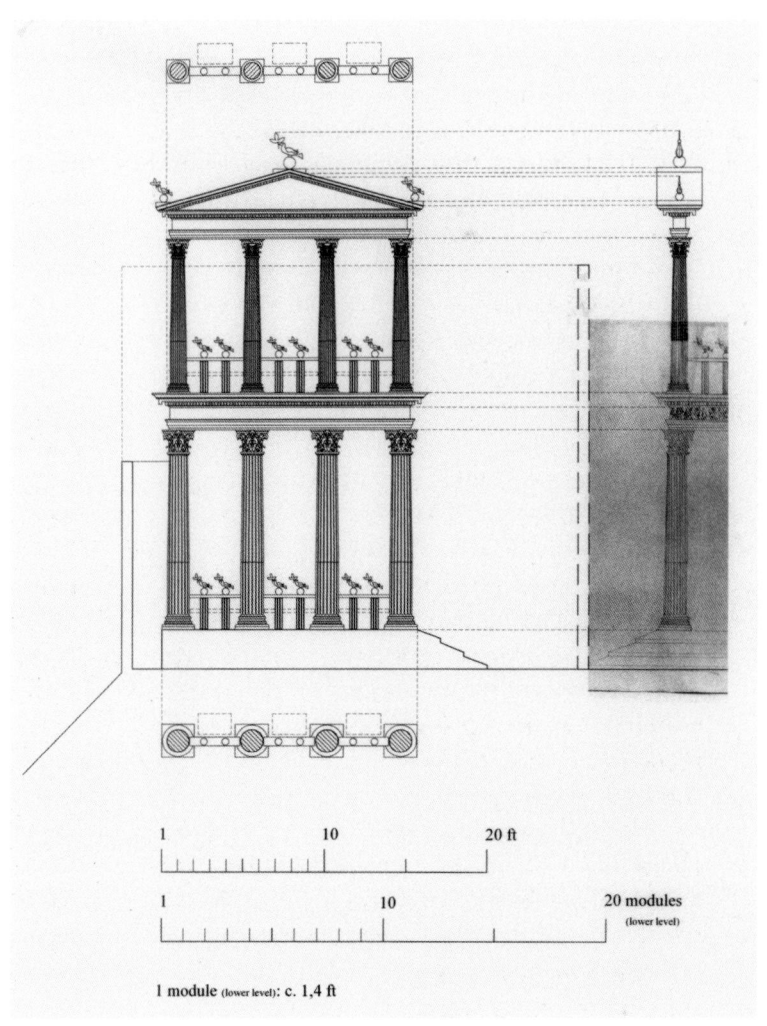

1 module (lower level): c. 1,4 ft

rooms that distinguished the main house. The great staircase was located in the west end of the range, near the new Ivy Lane, and had five half-paces 'with turned ballisters and railes of molding woorkes'.[47]

Like the 'old house at Ivy Bridge' (Great Salisbury House, as it was then beginning to be called), Little Salisbury House was adapted to a sloping site. On the south front, the basement was open to the garden and it is possible that an arcaded loggia featured in this part of the complex too. This hypothesis is supported by a reference in the accounts to 'the arches in the new terrace in the garden'.[48] '10 arches in the new court', recalling the 'stone gallery' in the courtyard at Great Salisbury House, are also mentioned.[49] It is possible to identify them with an arcaded porch running along the Strand front of the new house, similar to that of the inner court at Burghley House in Northamptonshire, as well as the one in Hatfield's south front.

The new development of 1611 necessitated extensive changes to the garden. The terrace of Great Salisbury House was extended west to run as far as the wall by the new Ivy Lane. A 'new stone walk in the garden', running parallel with the river along the south side of the property, was also built, no doubt embodying the same idea as the Porticus, though that unexecuted design had been conceived for a much smaller site. The 'stone gallery in the garden', or simply 'new stone walk', appears several times in the accounts until at least 1612.[50] It must have had some classical features, for the mason's work of 1612 included 'in the garden entering in to the new stone walk, removing the Cornish moulding of a pedestal + the base moulding of a flat pilaster'.[51] This bill also mentions carpentry works for 'an arched door case in the walk' and 'Turning two columns in the walk in the garden'. The suggestion that this new construction stood on the river front of the garden is given weight by bills for the demolition of a banqueting house 'pulled down by the water-side' to make way for the new walk.[52] One end terminated at the south-west corner of the garden where there was a small building called 'the S[ur]vaying place', shown by Hollar (see fig. 13) and familiar in a number of Tudor riverside palaces like Essex House (see Chapter One), whence the view of the river could be admired.[53] The stone walk did not, however, hamper access to the waterside, which was connected to the house via a series of steps to a private water gate.[54]

Ornamental works at both houses were carried out as late as 1613, well after Cecil's death the previous year, when the painter Roland Buckett was paid for 'colouring in oil 4 farne leteres that are in the front, + gilding 2 Sesturnes in the front with the date of Our Lord [Robert Cecil] + the Leteres for my Lord's name + other things', recalling those at the top of Northumberland House. At the same time, he painted '2 great beams that are over Ivy Lane, + 2 pillar', which provided decoration to the entrance into that lane.[55]

Stabling for Salisbury House was available at Somerset House and Durham House, only later somewhere within the complex itself. This brings us back to Inigo Jones, whose works for the Secretary remain clouded with uncertainty, as in many other cases. In 1608 and 1609, as noted, he had been employed for the masques at Salisbury House, for which he received £20.[56] He had also provided a design for the New Exchange, Cecil's commercial venture in the Strand, built on the western part of the former site of Durham Rents.[57] At the same time, after a visit to Hatfield House, Jones was paid £10 'for drawinge [or drawings?] of some Architecture', possibly related to the modification of the arcaded south front as well as to the design of the lantern.[58] This, however, may equally be linked to the proposal for a stable at Hatfield or London, where the accounts of 1609 register some 'works at the new stables', built for the Bishop of Durham in St Martin's Lane (fig. 158).[59] Seemingly sizeable stables for Salisbury House were also built at the northern end of the same lane near Long Acre, where two garden plots had been sold that year to Robert Cecil by the 3rd Earl of Bedford. Simon Basil certified one bill, Liminge designed at least part of the building, while the elder Richard Rider (or Ryder), later involved with Covent Garden, performed some of the carpentry work.[60]

Despite the existence of some views from the early seventeenth century – Norden's of 1600 and Vischer's of 1616 – the first complete depiction of the complex of Salisbury House was produced by Hollar in about 1630 (see fig. 13).[61] The complex then appears in his 'West Central District' (see fig. 135), the only surviving impression of his 'Great Map of London', prepared before the Great Fire of 1666.[62] Its riverfront was depicted once more in the early 1670s (fig. 159), so that, remarkably, we have three views of the complex from the same hand. These show the

158 Inigo Jones, elevation for an unidentified stable, c.1610. RIBA Collections (12970)

considerable differences in both scale and style between the two houses. Great Salisbury House appears as a turreted three-sided building round a courtyard screened from the Strand by a wall (or railing) with a central gateway surmounted by some form of pediment, possibly aligned with the entrance to the house. With three storeys and a crenellated top, hipped roofs and four-storey turrets at three corners, the house essentially followed a conventional model, apart from its seemingly open plan. Of French derivation, this typology had become increasingly popular in England after the publication of du Cerceau's volumes of *Les Plus Excellents Bâstiments de France* from 1576. But the house never had exactly that plan; instead, the construction of Little Salisbury House had resulted in a sort of – not the same – open plan (fig. 160), which Hollar, whose reliability has been questioned in this book, clearly reinterpreted.[63]

Newcourt and Faithorne's 1658 depiction is less carefully drawn than Hollar's and shows only Great Salisbury House and the New Exchange (fig. 161). It none the less appears as it truly was, a four-sided courtyard house, even if the garden elevation is characterised by two principal floors with large windows, instead of the three levels with mullioned windows shown by Hollar. Newcourt's features do not seem to be based on any known earlier view.[64] This is particularly interesting when his interpretation is compared with a later image of the house by William Morgan, published in 1682, which provides information about the development of London, including the changes at Salisbury House carried out in the 1670s (fig. 162). By comparing one of the plans for the construction of tenements on the western part of the property (fig. 163) with the elevation of the same tenements as depicted by Morgan, we realise that this view presents a certain fidelity to the documentary sources. If we then consider the way that Great Salisbury House is represented, we find considerable divergences from Hollar's depictions.

The interiors of Salisbury House were inventoried in 1612 and 1629. The first, dated 30 June,

SALISBURY HOUSE | 151

followed the death of Robert Cecil on 24 May and was outside the process of probate, hence does not indicate the value of items, which are listed by type, rather than by room.[65] Neither its title, 'An Inventorie of all houshold Stuffe att Salisbury house', nor the arrangement of its content makes any distinction between the goods in the main house and those in the smaller one, which confirms that the two were still used by a single family at that date.[66] Those contents were remarkable: there were 10 sets of 'Hangings of Tapestry', each containing several pieces, with 5 of 'Antick worke lined all with Damask'. These contrast with the 'Hangings of a Courser sort of tap' numbering 35 sets of multiple pieces, 'Nine peeces of Italian Hangings greene and painted wth borders and pillers', and a further 26 of different sorts, for a total well above 100. There were also 14 'Carpetts of Percia', all of large sizes, 29 'Turkey Karpetts', 23 'Nidle worke Carpetts', as well as more than 70 different kinds of window curtains and the like. Beds with a wealth of the usual accessories such as canopies and cushions, chairs and stools also featured prominently, while other furniture included some 67 pieces of inlaid, plain and 'Playinge tables', a 'Billiard Table covered wth grene velvet', as well as 46 cabinets full of all sorts of precious memorabilia.[67] At least one of these was effectively a room containing a 'picture of white marble of Aristotle' as well as 14 'Italian modells of white marble, wt[h] other piramides of porfery'.[68] The collection also featured 8 maps, one of England, one of Europe, one of the 'Habitt of all Cuntries' and another of 'Germany and the mother land', together with 'j Pedigree of all the Princes of England in a frame of wallnuttree inlayed'. There

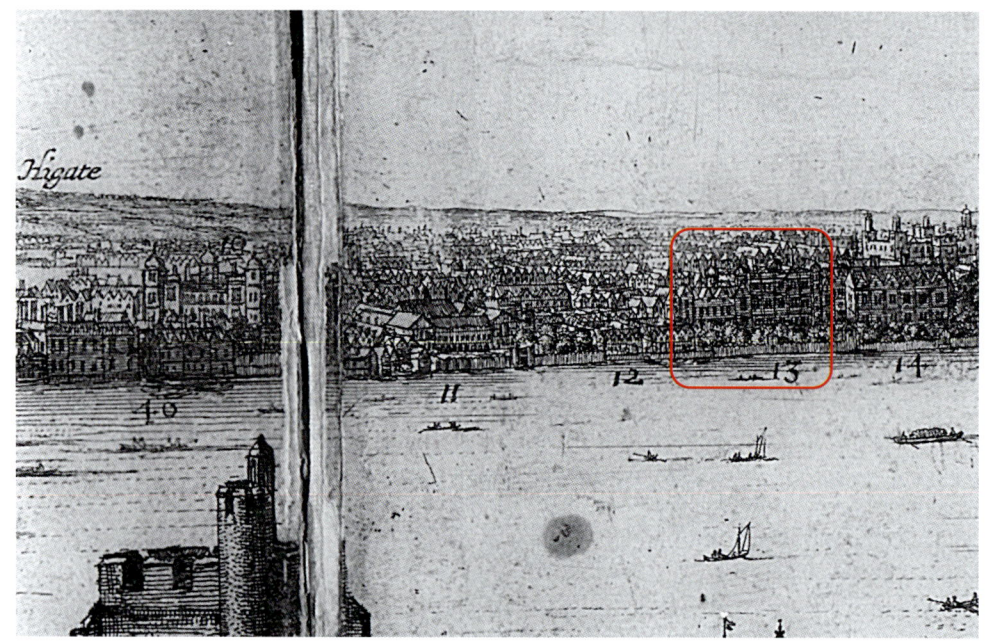

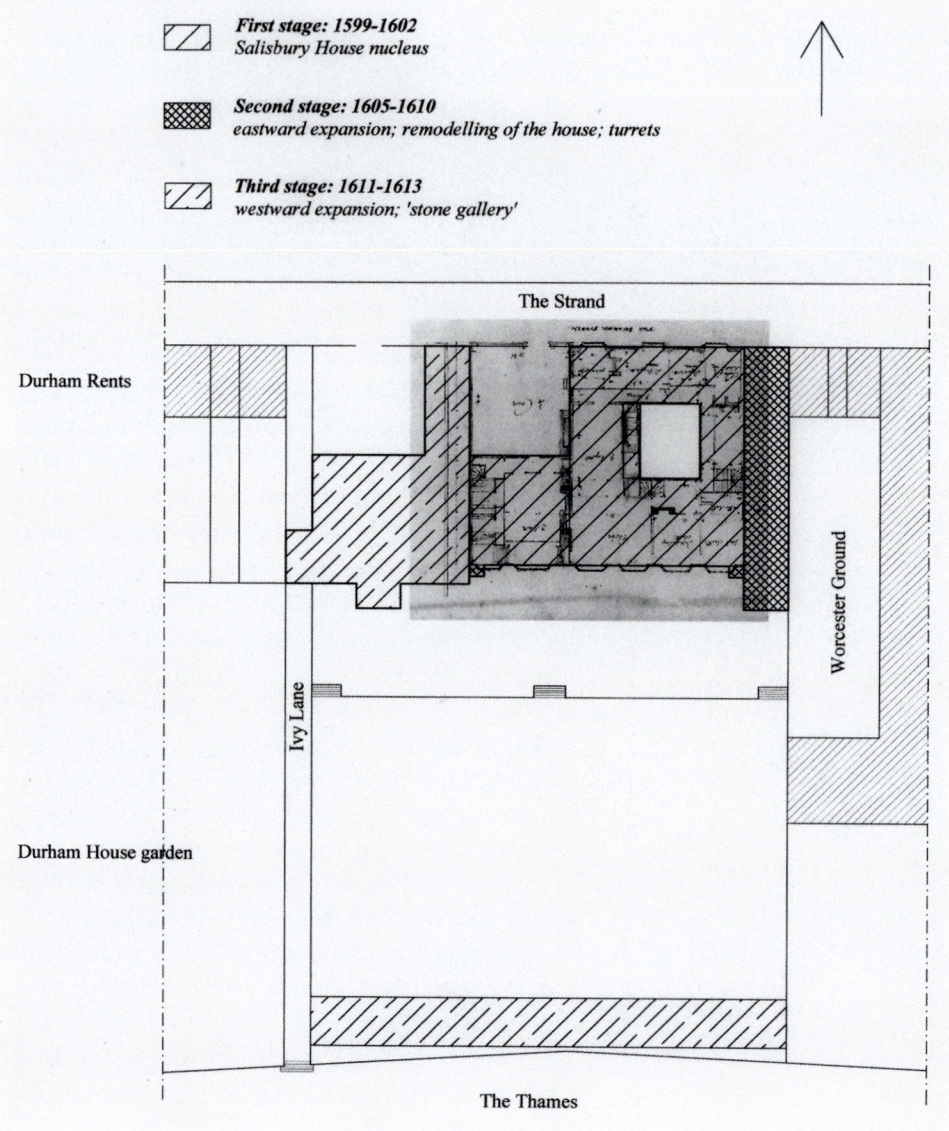

159 The complex of Salisbury House (13), detail of Wenceslaus Hollar, 'view of London extending eastwards from Peterborough House to Somerset House', early 1670s. By permission of the Pepys Library, Magdalene College, Cambridge ('London and Westminster', 1, 2972, 34–35)

160 Manolo Guerci, reconstruction, 2004, of the layout of the Salisbury House complex in 1612 based on Simon Basil's ground-floor plan of Great Salisbury House, 1600–02, and Hollar's 'West Central District'

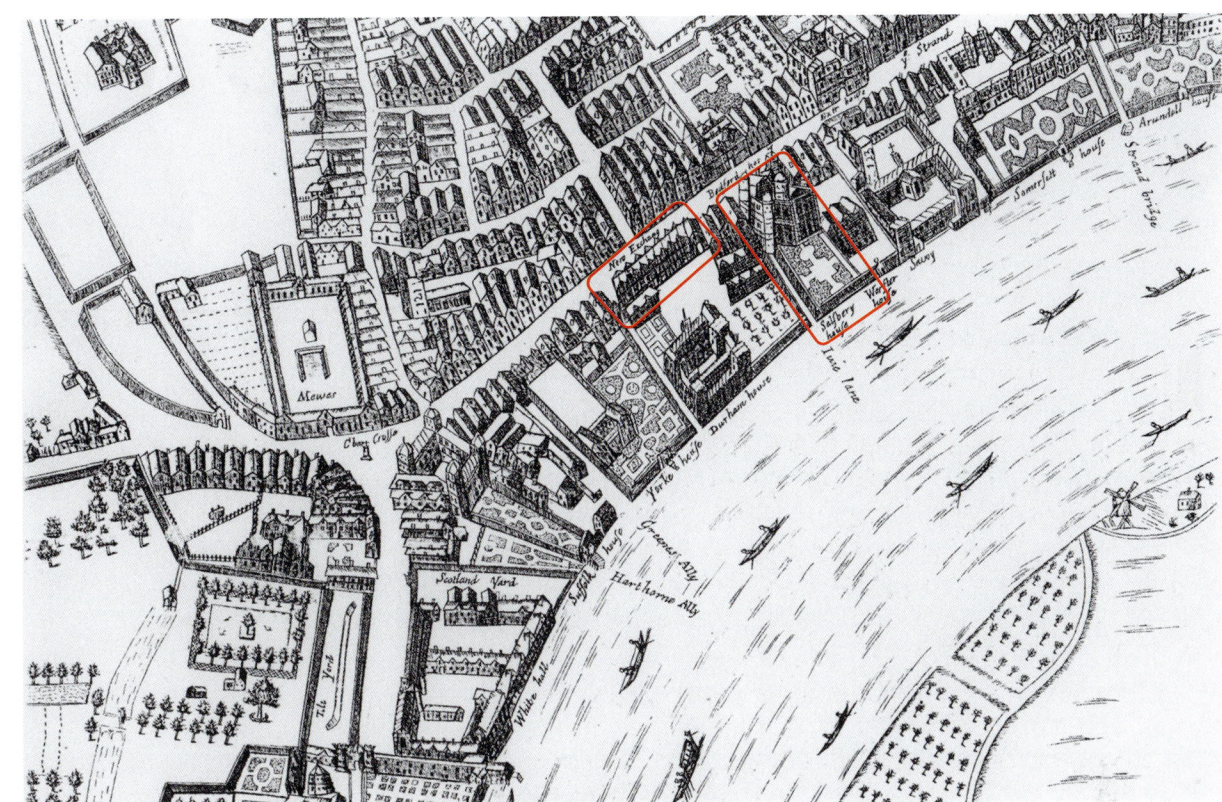

161 Great Salisbury House and the New Exchange, detail of Richard Newcourt and William Faithorne, 'An exact delineation of the City of London and Westminster', 1658. By kind permission of the Syndics of Cambridge University Library (Map Room, Maps BB.77.90.14)

162 Great Salisbury House and the adjoining tenements in the area formerly occupied by Little Salisbury House (see fig. 163), detail of William Morgan, *View of London and Westminster*, c.1682 (detail of images on pp. x and xi). By permission of the Pepys Library, Magdalene College, Cambridge ('London and Westminster', I, 2972, 38–39)

163 Layout of the new Salisbury Street with its tenements built on the site of Little Salisbury House, late 1670s. Reproduced with permission of the Marquess of Salisbury, Hatfield House (Hatfield House MSS, Drawer II/180

were also 4 'Looking Glasses' with 'j faire greate venetian lookinge glasse wth pillers of marble and the cover of agett [agate]' and 6 musical instruments including a 'greate Organ in a Case of Wainscott', a smaller one with a 'frame to stand upon', a 'greate Harpesicall virginall the Keys of mather of pearle' (a harpsicord with a portable keyboard instrument, the virginal, annexed to it) and a 'ffaire greate wynd Instrument the Case of Wallnuttree curiously inlayed'.[69] Paintings amounted to 72, of which 18 were of religious subjects, 19 of mythological and secular ones, while the rest were portraits of the Cecil family and of the royal family. Among the last were '1 picture of Henry the 7 and Henr[y] the 8 wth a curtaine of purple taffite fringed wth gould', which has been connected with Holbein's 'Chatsworth Cartoon' for the large dynastic mural at Whitehall Palace, destroyed by fire in 1698.[70] Sets of portraits of English and foreign monarchs were common to most collections of the period, not least given their significance in international diplomacy. That diplomacy played a vital role in most of the Strand palaces, as seen throughout this book. Salisbury had one such set at Hatfield House but it was in London that he chose to keep his most up-to-date paintings, which included four images of Mary Queen of Scots (appropriately under a Scottish monarch), one of Elizabeth, one of James I and his queen, Anne of Denmark, and a picture of 'the prince of Parma', perhaps Alessandro Farnese, Duke of Parma, whom Cecil had met in 1588 during his visits to the Low Countries.[71] Together with Walter Cope, Cecil was one of the most notable collectors of the early years of the seventeenth century and a major connoisseur, significantly antedating the better-known Earl of Arundel.[72] As such, Cecil had been asked to show his paintings to Henry Prince of Wales in March 1609.[73] Equally, his connoisseurship had been engaged in the collection of Persian, Ottoman and, pioneeringly, Chinese objects, which included a mixture of fabrics, porcelain, lacquerwork and larger objects systematically accrued from the late 1590s and substantially in place by the time of the housewarming festivities in 1602.[74]

As appears to have been customary when appraising a household of this high status, the inventory does not list books.[75] Yet we have a full description of these from their two libraries' catalogue of 1614–15, which features 1300 entries, ordered under the categories 'Divinitie', 'Historie', 'natuarall Philosophie & Phisice, &c.', 'Diverse sortes', 'Philoligie' and 'Lawe'.[76] Among the second and third categories are sixteen architectural books which include the 1607 edition of both volumes of du Cerceau's *Les Plus Excellents Bastiments de France*, the London 1612 edition of Salomon de Caus's *La Perspective* and three copies of Vitruvius, two in folio and one in quarto. While there is no further information about the first Vitruvius (as the catalogue states, it was 'given to my Lo[rd] of Arondell' and is no longer at Hatfield), the second is Cesare Cesariano's edition printed in Como in 1521, fully illustrated with reconstruction drawings of ancient Roman buildings. The third Vitruvius is the 1552 Jean de Tournes's Lyon edition, exquisitely illustrated by Bernard Salomon and with Guillaume Philander's commentaries, the most extensive at the time. Two thirds of this collection came from Burghley, whose passion for architecture Robert had clearly inherited.[77]

The second inventory was made on 20 June 1629 for no apparent reason but, again, not for probate.[78] Unlike the first, it is arranged by room and must relate to Great Salisbury House alone, for the main sets of rooms are not repeated twice. Indeed, Little Salisbury House had by then been leased to a separate household. Alhough of 1629, this inventory illustrates the interiors as Robert Cecil had left them, as nothing of relevance had happened since. It starts on the ground floor with the Hall, followed by the usual sequence of 'Parler', 'dyninge Chamber for my Lo.', 'with drawinge Roome adjoininge' and 'my Lords bedd chamber' on the garden side. The Bed Chamber was flanked by a Lobby, 'my Lords dressinge Chamber' and the 'Pallatt Chamber', while those rooms facing the Strand in the direction of the Porter's Lodge were for members of the household, as shown by the second series of Basil plans (see fig. 145). The next entry after the Porter's Lodge is the 'Withdrawinge Chamber to the Gallerie', which marks the shift between ground and first floors. That room was followed by the 'Gallarie', the 'Lobbie betweene the great Chamber and the Gallarie', the 'great Chamber' and the 'great with drawinge Chamber', with the 'Chapple above', as opposed to the one on the ground floor. There were also a number of lodgings for family members, among whom was Algernon Percy, 10th Earl of Northumberland, who had married Anne Cecil in 1626 and later gained possession of Northumberland House (see Chapter Eleven).[79] More chambers for household staff were recorded on the upper floors, while the basement included the Kitchen and related services.

Subsequent Years: 1612–1694

After Robert Cecil's death, the complex passed to his son William (1591–1668), 2nd Earl of Salisbury, who continued to live in both houses. From the early 1630s, however, Little Salisbury House was let and named after those families who occupied it: Lord Newport's House in 1630, Lord Cottington's in 1634 and Devonshire House from 1640 to 1647.[80] On 4 March 1639, William Cavendish, 3rd Earl of Devonshire (1617–1684), had married Elizabeth Cecil (1620–1689), the second daughter of the 2nd Earl. Little Salisbury House thus became the home of the philosopher Thomas Hobbes, Cavendish's former tutor, who lived with the couple. The Devonshires were to be followed in the tenancy by an unidentified 'Lord Howard', who seems to have been part of Salisbury's household.[81] In these circumstances, Little Salisbury House became completely detached from the main fabric, so much so that between 1637 and 1639 a commercial building known as the Middle Exchange was erected at the south end of its gallery (fig. 164).[82] Extended in 1670, it included shops and little dwellings facing onto a newly built lane which ran from the Strand to the Thames, where there was a public flight of steps for the use of passengers by water. Fifty years later Strype remarked that the Middle Exchange 'had the ill luck to have the nickname given it of the Whore's Nest, whereby, with the ill fate that attended it, few or no people took shops there, & those who did were soon weary and left them'.[83]

There is less information on the middle of the seventeenth century except for a curious proliferation of inventories, sometimes twice a year, which indicates a frequent and erratic change of occupants in both houses.[84] In 1639, however, the Strand front was redecorated with '2 new pedestal + 2 taffrails on them standing on the gable ends next the street', which was repaved in stone together with the courtyards. Other maintenance included the 'mending of the little clock + keeping of the great clock', which indicate the presence of two clock-houses, probably one for each building. By 1645 one of the two houses also had a 'pergulary next the garden' with a 'lower rail', which may be identified as the balcony on the first floor of Great Salisbury House, depicted by Morgan in 1682 (see fig. 162).[85] Perhaps it resembled a design by Inigo Jones of c.1618 with an iron-railed balcony over a rusticated arched entrance produced for Edward Cecil's Wimbledon House, annexed to Burghley House (see fig. 107). The 'floor in the portico where the arch was taken down' was also repaired in 1645, a clear reference to the 'stone walk' at the river end of the garden, which had survived despite the construction of the Middle Exchange.[86] In 1652 the property was damaged by a fire which nearly destroyed the Long Gallery and possibly

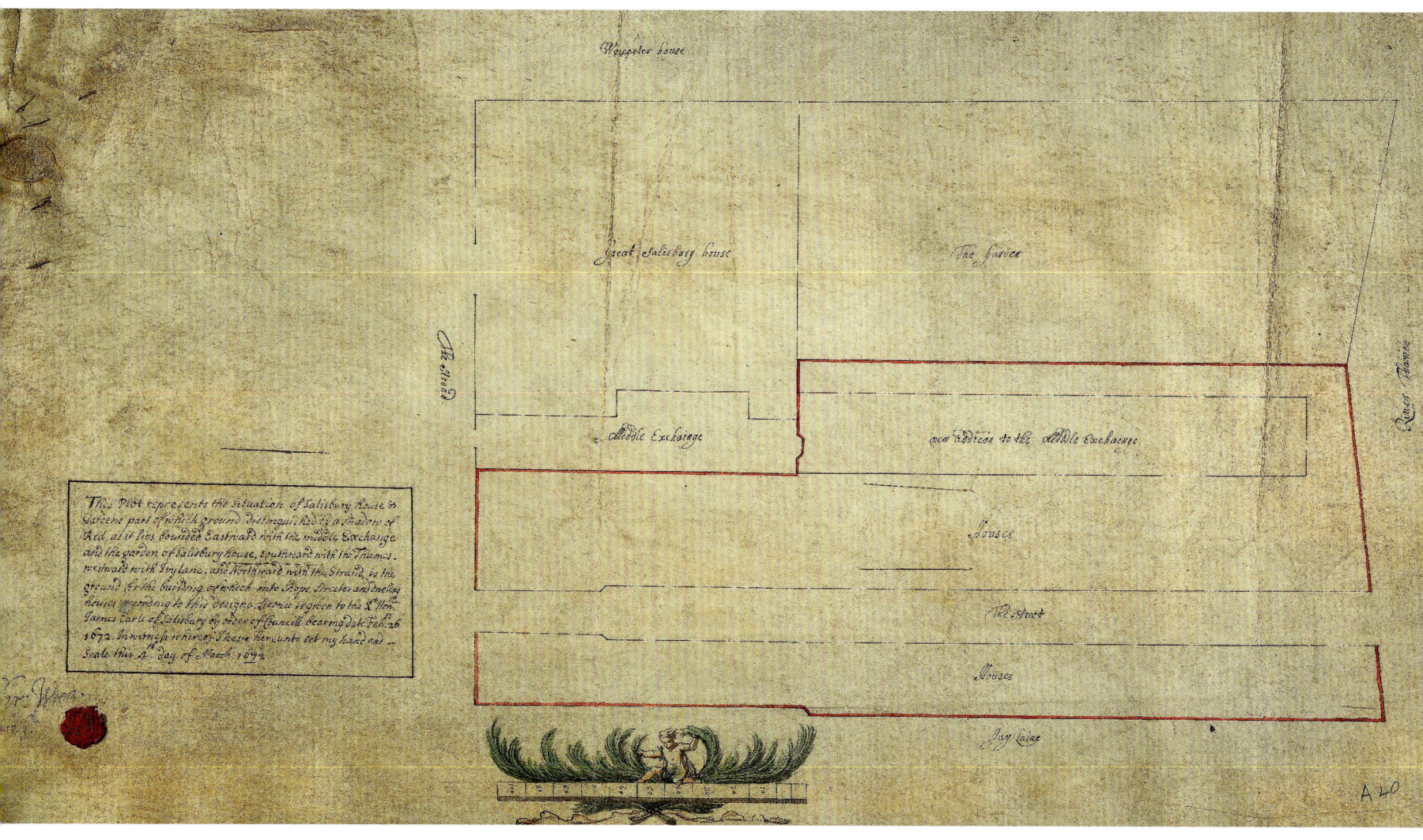

the Withdrawing Chamber of one of the two houses. Consequently, the 'wall in the Gallery' was consolidated, as also the 'new making all the wainscot that was burned and spoiled'.[87] The accounts of this year record that 'Bread [was] given to the poor who came to help when the fire was at S. House'.[88]

The 1670s mark a definitive decline in the complex, reflecting the financial situation of the Salisburys, which was at its lowest after the failure of both the New and Middle Exchanges.[89] Without capital for big new ventures, they opted to divide the ground floor of Great Salisbury House and transform it into shops and tenements, which were leased to the same merchants of the Middle Exchange.[90] We thus find a lease of a house with shops in the Strand, 'being part of Great Salisbury House as the same is now separated & divided with partitions from the rest of the house, & being the third house Eastward from Great Salisbury House gate'.[91]

On 25 June 1670 the greater part of the upper floors of Great Salisbury House and the whole of the Middle Exchange were leased to 'Laud' Doyley for a yearly rent of £300.[92] The 3rd Earl of Salisbury saved for himself and his family a few rooms in the western range of the house, where he must have lived in a rather different state from that of his grandfather Robert Cecil. Margaret, Countess of Salisbury, even expressed concern to her mother, the Countess of Rutland, on 'equall right to the garden, for we have no place els to dry cloathes in and therefore cannot be without'.[93] At the same time, considering their 'very low condition', she had turned into a 'dairy maid setting up a diary [sic] and little huswifries [housewiferies] about [the] house to imploy my self'.[94] The decision to lease Great Salisbury House, rather than redevelop the whole site, was put forward after a long debate in the family as to whether they could afford a new venture. In this regard, the Countess of

164 Christopher Wren, detail of map of site between the Strand and the River Thames, showing Great Salisbury House, the Middle Exchange and the new development on the site of Little Salisbury House, signed and sealed '4 March 1672', 1673. National Archives, Kew, MPA 1/40

Salisbury had anxiously sought her mother's help, writing that the earl

> *spoke himself to the King ... who most freely gave him liberty to make what improvement he can soe he is full of designes and we are advising the best way to advantage ourselves, god knows we need it, but complaints will not ease us, but I trust in his good time it will be better, though I feare to find the truth of the old proverb, whilst the grass grows &c.*[95]

This letter is part of a vivid correspondence between the two women and indicates the direct involvement of the Countess of Salisbury in most of the decisions regarding the future of her house.[96]

While Great Salisbury House, or whatever remained of it, was temporarily saved from demolition, the adjoining Little Salisbury House disappeared altogether. During 1672 and 1673 the 3rd Earl of Salisbury managed to secure an act of Parliament to build on the ground of both houses, having consistently bribed several government officials.[97] The patent was accompanied by a plan of the entire property by the Surveyor General, Sir Christopher Wren (see fig. 164), followed by various plans related to this development. They show two parallel rows of thirteen tenements each facing an internal street, with five more dwellings on the Strand side with shops at ground level. 'Being too narrow, and withal, the Descent to the Thames too uneasy', as Strype put it, the newly built Salisbury Street was not as successful as was expected, while the financial state of the Salisburys worsened further.[98] After the death of the 3rd Earl in 1683, James, 4th Earl of Salisbury, had thus no choice but to pull down the poor and incongruous remnants of Great Salisbury House and put up shops and tenements instead. The enabling act did not become law until his death in 1694, when the guardian of his infant son, the 5th Earl, also called James (d. 1728), carried out the long-dreaded finale and built Cecil Street, 'having very good houses fit for persons of repute'.[99] The plans of this campaign show a similar layout to that of the tenements built over the site of Little Salisbury House in 1673, with two rows of several dwellings opening onto a central street running from the Strand to the waterside. Of the two schemes, the second more elaborate one, with ten tenements on each side and six more facing the Strand (fig. 165), is likely to have been executed given that it is faithful to the actual shape of the site.

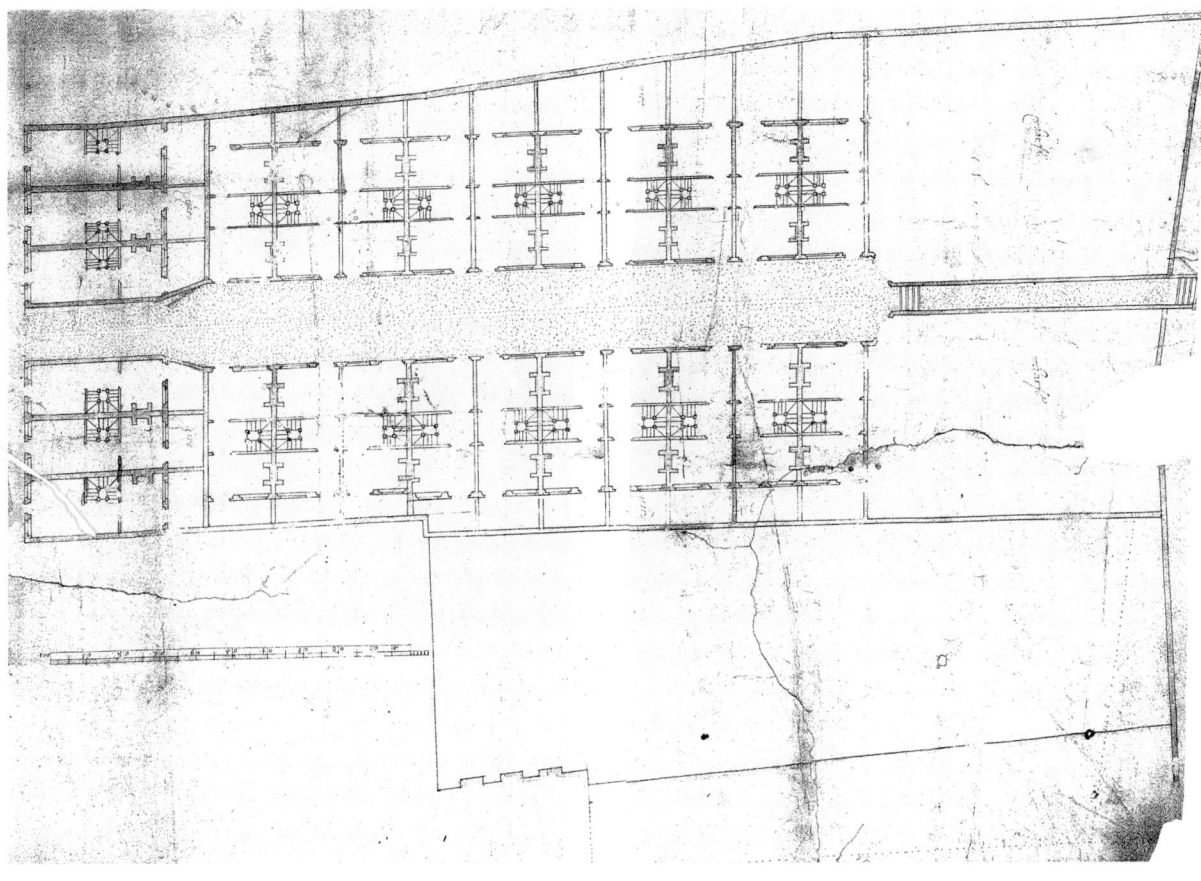

165 Ground-floor plan for the construction of new tenements on the site of Great Salisbury House, 1690s. Reproduced with permission of the Marquess of Salisbury, Hatfield House (Hatfield House MSS, General 63/5)

166 View, from left to right, of the Westminster Palace complex and Durham House (identified), followed by the Savoy with its imposing gatehouse (detail of fig. 9)

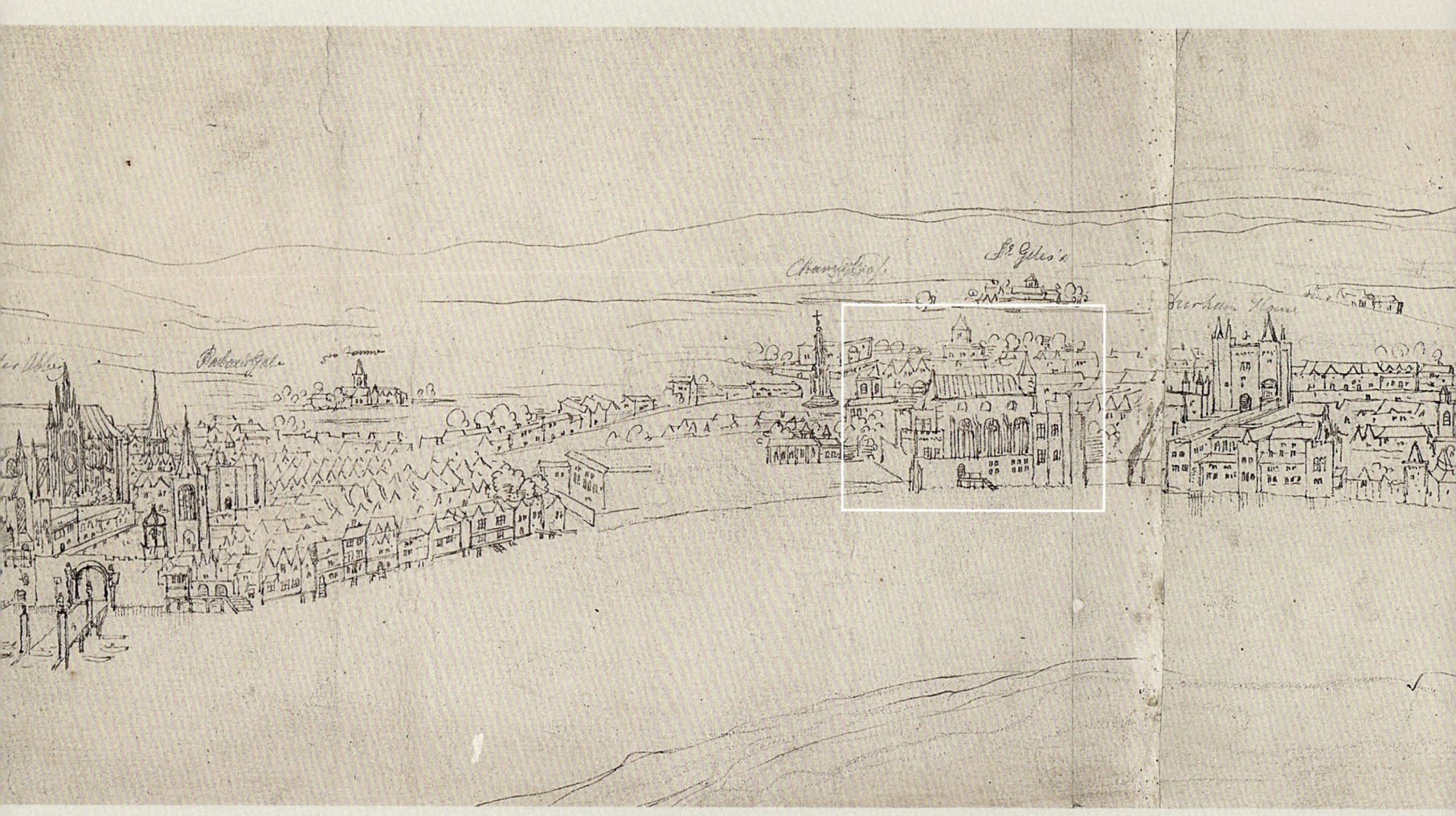

9 · DURHAM HOUSE

DURHAM HOUSE OR PLACE, RECORDED since at least 1238 when the papal legate Otto was lodged there, lay between Salisbury House and York House.[1] It stood right on the river edge with a heavily fortified appearance, first depicted by Wyngaerde in the 1540s as a complex with an imposing hall and chapel, enclosed by walls and towers on the Thames side and accessed by an equally imposing gatehouse on the Strand (fig. 166).

The Inn of the Bishops of Durham: 1230s–1536

It was probably Richard Poor, Bishop of Durham from 1228 to 1237 and a great builder, who first erected the London residence of that see but, as with every such old mansion, Durham House was the result of several additions and rebuilding, by Anthony Bek, bishop from 1284 to 1310, and Thomas Hatfield, bishop from 1345 to 1381.[2] The first available description of part of its interior dates to around the latter time, when Bishop Hatfield granted to William de Beverley and others, in charge of appointing twelve chaplains to celebrate services in Durham House,

> two chambers in the said manor, viz a vaulted chamber under the chapel and a sollar by the entrance of the chapel towards the north, and the vestibule of the chapel with two chambers adjoining, and the whole inn with houses on the east side of the north gate of the manor, inhabited by the said William de Beverley, and a quarter of a garden within the walls thereof, extending from the garden entrance northwards as far as the king's highway, 160 feet in length and 140 in breadth, and a waste without the manor opposite its north gate.[3]

Like all episcopal properties, Durham House was vast and could accommodate more than one household. This customarily included royals and guests of state, such Henry IV's son, Prince Henry, in 1412 and Katherine of Aragon in 1502. Between 1516 and 1518 Cardinal Wolsey probably lived there too while waiting for the completion of his own York Place. Then in 1528, when the Great Hall there was being rebuilt, he moved again to the Strand palace, this time as Bishop of Durham himself: in 1523 he had succeeded Thomas Ruthall, who had headed the see from 1509. In between, the house had accommodated Henry Fitzroy, Henry VIII's illegitimate son, then aged six, later the Duke of Richmond and Somerset.

Although Wolsey had purchased a great deal of furniture from Ruthall, more (mainly beds and household stuff) was brought from York Place and Hampton Court to provide for the his retinue. This occasioned what is to my knowledge the only existing inventory of Durham House, which lists objects associated with members of the household but also mentions a few rooms. These provide a glimpse into the whole spectrum of private, public and service functions: the Privy Chamber, the Great Chamber, the Hall, the Stable and Buttery.[4] After he resigned from the see in 1529, Wolsey was followed by Sir Thomas Boleyn, Anne's father, and by Anne herself, who appears to have been living there in May 1532.

Royal Owners, one Episcopal 'Come Back' and John Dudley, 1st Duke of Northumberland: 1536–1583

In 1536, as with all other episcopal palaces, Henry VIII took over the property 'comenly called Durham Place, with all Houses, Buyldings, Gardeyns, Orcheards, Pooles, fysshyngs, stables and all other commodytes'. He granted the bishop, Cuthbert Tunstall, a house called 'Cold Herbrow' in Thames Street, with five tenements in the parish of All Hallows.[5] Henry used Durham House for state entertainments and as a commodity to reward his associates. One such was Nicholas Fortescue, Groom Porter of his household, who was granted the twenty-two tenements along the Strand side of the complex known as Durham Rents (some of which later formed part of the Salisbury House site, as noted in Chapter Eight). Edward VI also resided at Durham House before ascending to the throne and in March 1550 he granted it to Princess Elizabeth, in fulfilment of their father's will. In the meantime, the building had been turned into a mint so Elizabeth was offered the use of Somerset House instead. The swap was engineered by John Dudley, 1st Duke of Northumberland, who had led the government of the young King Edward from 1550, after Edward Seymour's fall. As the historical residence of the prince bishops of Durham, the former episcopal palace was central to his ambitions of assembling a large landholding based on the great northern estates.[6] Dudley took possession of it early in 1553 and three weddings were celebrated there. These included that of Lady Jane Grey, the 'Nine Day Queen' from 10 to 19 July 1553, with Dudley's son Guilford, and of Jane's sister Catharine with Henry Herbert, the son of the 1st Earl of Pembroke (whose descendant, the 4th Earl, was granted Durham House in 1641). Neither union lasted, as is well-known, the first because Jane was executed, the second in consequence, since the Herberts soon distanced themselves from the disgraced Grey family by having the marriage annulled.

On Queen Mary's accession in 1553, the house was restored to Bishop Tunstall but not for long, as it went back to Elizabeth after her own accession in 1558. She held it for the next twenty-five years, during which time it continued as state lodgings for diplomats – the Spanish Ambassador Alvaro de La Quadra occupied it between 1559 and 1565 – and royal entertainments, including a supper with the queen and the Earl of Leicester

167 H. Flourit, *Sir Walter Ralegh at the age of thirty-four*, 1588. © National Portrait Gallery, London (7)

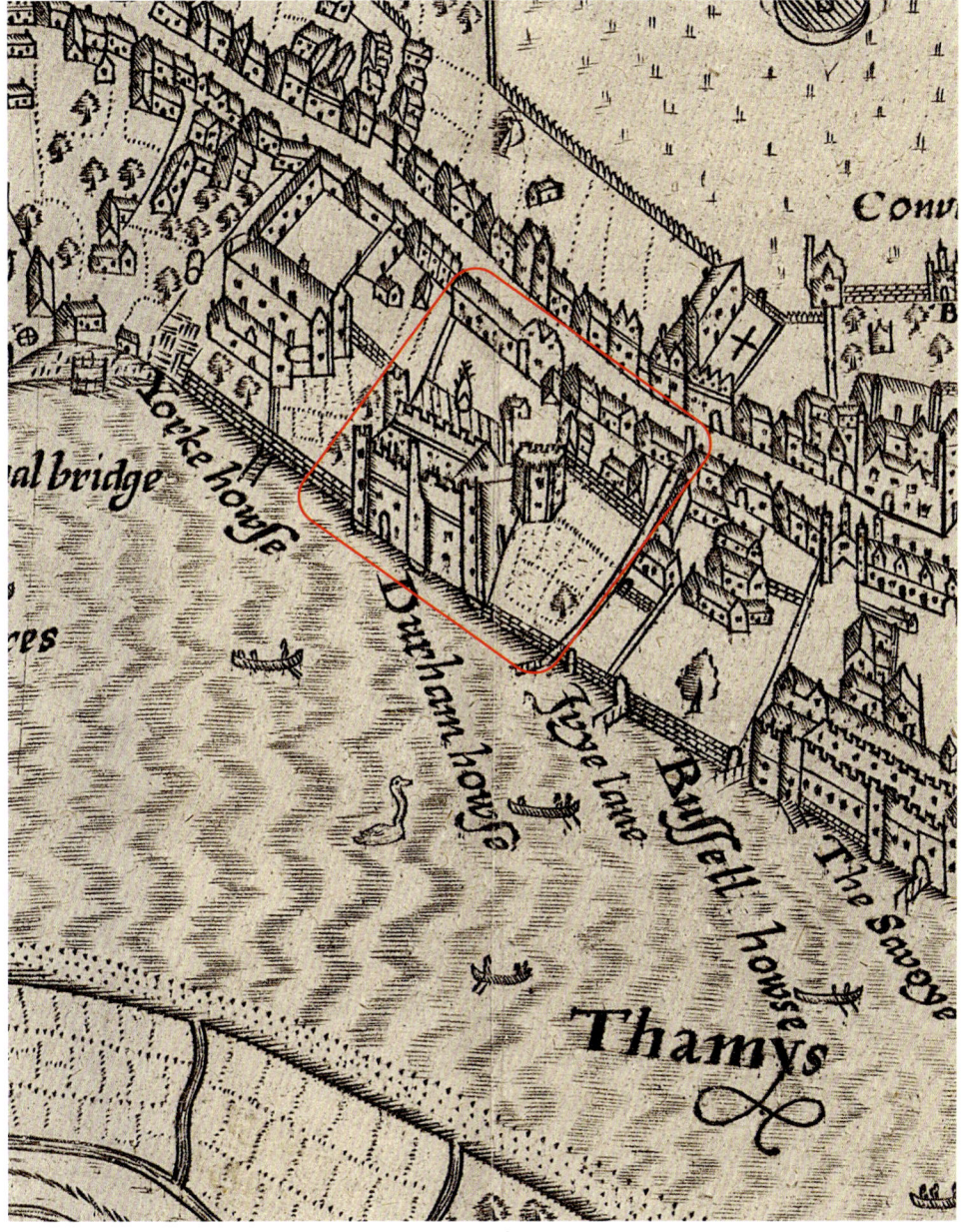

in 1566. Leicester in turn used the house between 1565 and 1568, until in 1569 he purchased the nearby Paget Place, renamed Leicester House (see Chapter One).[7] In the 1580s Durham House would then become associated with the fortunes of Sir Walter Ralegh.

The House of Sir Walter Ralegh: 1583–1603

Courtier, explorer and poet, Sir Walter Ralegh (1554–1618; fig. 167) is the resident perhaps most associated with Durham House: his occupancy was arguably the longest secular one and he was controversially evicted straight after the accession of James I.[8]

Notwithstanding this long tenure, evidence for it is scant as his archive has long been dispersed. In addition, Sherborne Castle and his Dorset estate took absolute priority, as the family's future lay there. Durham House meant status and convenience but it was essentially a grace and favour abode which 'never seemed to grab his heart'.[9] In effect, beyond costly repairs known to us via the correspondence of his wife, the formidable Bess Ralegh, and his own, little if anything of architectural relevance seems to have taken place.

Like its old episcopal neighbours, by 1600 Durham House was a 'rotten houes', as Lady Ralegh described it to Cecil, stressing that she knew 'none so un wies that will besto so mani hundred pounes as Sur Wattar hath dun, without fardar intrest or asurans of hit'.[10] Expenses amounted to about £2000 and had probably covered some kind of modernisation of the house in the form of glass or its replacement and the maintenance of freshwater conduits,[11] as well as wainscotting and panelling, as shown by a letter of 1603 to which I shall return. Could this expenditure also have covered some building? At Sherborne, Simon Basil, the Controller and later Surveyor of the King's Works (responsible for most of Robert Cecil's building campaigns, as seen in Chapter Eight), added polygonal corner towers from 1600.[12] One such tower appears conspicuously along the east side of Durham House as depicted by John Norden's 1593 view (fig. 168). By contrast, neither Wyngaerde's (see fig. 166) nor Braun and Hogenberg's (fig. 169) earlier views are revealing in this respect, as their angle is unfavourable. The Agas does show a tower in a comparable location, as well as one projecting out onto the Thames, but it is impossible to tell

168 The complex of Durham House, detail of John Norden, *Speculum Britanniae*, 1593. Folger Shakespeare Library, Washington DC. Licensed under Creative Commons Attribution-ShareAlike 4.0 International

169 The complex of Durham House, detail of Georg Braun and Frans Hogenberg, 'London' in *Civitates Orbis Terrarum*, 1572, derived from the lost 'Copperplate Map of London', 1553–9. University Library, Heidelberg. Wikipedia, Public Domain

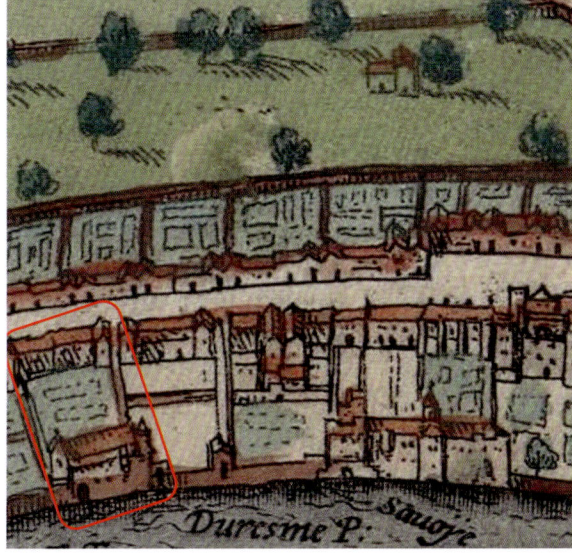

whether that on the inner eastern corner was actually polygonal (fig. 170). Therefore, whether such a feature was added from scratch or adapted, we cannot exclude the possibility that it was Ralegh's doing, as he is known to have been fond of his towers, where he retreated for contemplation. This was the case both at Sherborne, where a high attic room was used for that purpose, and in London, where his study was in 'a little turret that looked into and over the Thames, and had the prospect which is pleasant perhaps as any in the world, and which not only refreshes the eie-sight but cheeres the spirits, and (to speake my mind) I believe enlarges an ingeniose man's thoughts', as John Aubrey related in his *Brief Lives* (1696).[13] While this seems a perfect description of the projecting tower in the Agas view, no such feature can be clearly distinguished in Norden (see figs 170 and 168). An intriguing, if speculative, question is whether the study may have hosted the 'School of Night', so named in Edwardian times from a line in Shakespeare's *Love's Labour's Lost*. It describes one of English history's enigmatic intellectual circles, also known as the 'School of Atheism', centred on Sir Walter and Henry Percy, the Wizard (9th) Earl of Northumberland. Other supposed members included the scientist and writer Thomas Harriot, the occult poet George Chapman and Christopher Marlowe, whose tragedy *Tamburlaine the Great* (1587/88) had taken London by storm.[14] However, its very existence, let alone membership, is controversial and has been discredited in recent times.[15]

Apart from the topographical views already examined, a rough sketch plan of 1626, produced as evidence in a dispute, provides further clues

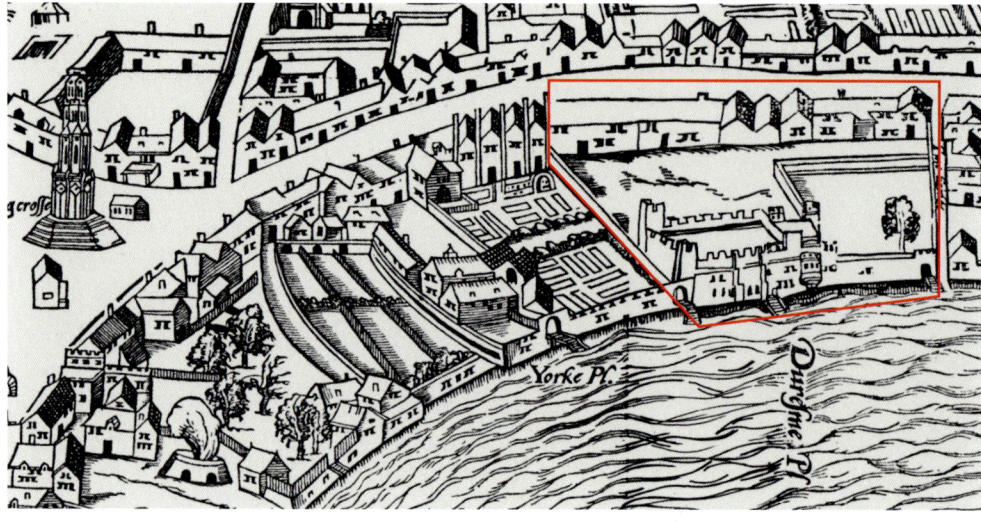

170 The complex of Durham House, detail of the *Woodcut Map of London*, 1561–70 ('Agas'), reprinted 1633, derived from the lost 'Copperplate Map of London', 1553–9. Mitton 1908. Wikimedia Commons Public Domain

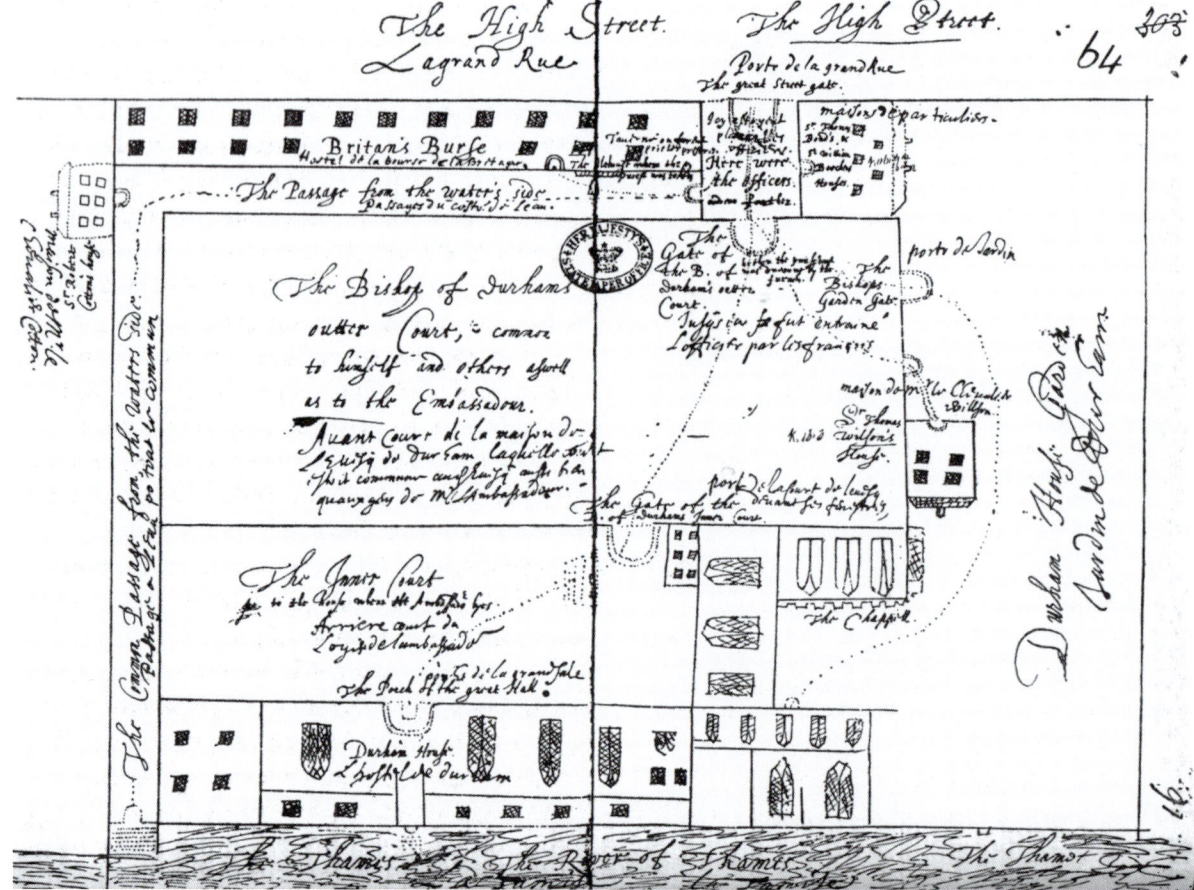

171 Rough sketch plan of Durham House, 1626. Gater and Godfrey 1937, 92

to the arrangement of Durham House, which it seems had not been altered since Ralegh's time (fig. 171). The Hall, described by Norden as 'stately and high, supported with loftie marble pillers' and standing 'upon the Thamise verye pleasantly', occupied the central part of the building immediately behind the river wall. Hollar's *c*.1630 depiction of the riverfront (see fig. 13) shows it as crenellated and with high Gothic windows, which are similarly highlighted in the sketch. The Chapel sat on the eastern edge of the house, with three tall nave windows and a marked apse. Hollar's viewpoint hides it but Wyngaerde shows it as extremely grand (see fig. 166). Just as grand was the Strand gatehouse (seen in Norden too, fig. 168), which must have been the main entrance to the complex for no formal water gate is depicted, just simple steps leading to the Hall. This was common in the episcopal palaces along the Strand, as they had been built at a time when river access was public but therefore open to attack. On both sides of the gatehouse stood Durham Rents, while a large court negotiated their relationship with the main house. At the same time, a garden separated the complex from its eastern neighbours across Ivy Lane.

Like other prominent residents before him, Ralegh occupied only one part, albeit possibly the greater, with a household of about forty people. The remainder was lived in by Sir Edward Darcy, a cousin of Lady Ralegh. Darcy's presence is first mentioned in her letter to Cecil of October 1600, apropos a fire which destroyed the stables: 'I am glad this mischans of feeiar cam not by ani neck-elegans of ani servant of mine, but by me cossin Darci's sarvant – a woman that delleth just under our loggong, and anoyeth ous infenitly'.[16] This event may eventually have procured new stables in St Martin's Lane, to which a design by Inigo Jones has been linked, billed in 1609 (see fig. 158). Lady Ralegh's letter also reveals that Cecil, who was building his own house next door, had already taken an interest in Ralegh's right to the property: she told him that 'Hit will be now a fit time for you to get sum intres in that rotten house for your selfe and your frind', clearly pointing at Cecil's attempt to expand his own estate in the Strand. This proved prophetic, as from then on events seems to have turned against the Raleghs.

To begin with, in 1601 Durham House was broken into, an event which sheds indirect light on its contents, of which we also have limited knowledge. Stolen objects included '"pillowbeeres … fitted with silke and golde" worth ten pounds, a linen "cushinge cloth" adorned with silke and gold worth five pounds, and a diaper tablecloth worth forty shillings'.[17] Another glimpse into Ralegh's lavish objects, including some exotics acquired on his journeys round the world, is provided by a request he made in 1601 to his nephew John Gilbert, whose privateer the *Refusal* had taken a Brazilian vessel laden with porcelain and silk. Sir Walter wanted a share of both, the first specifically requested by his wife, the second for 'pied silks for curtens', wall-hangings as well as 'a ce[rta]yne fine saddell, and silk stoc[kin]ges' for himself.[18] We can then resort to his will, drawn up in 1597, where the section on Durham House lists the contents bequeathed to his son among others. These included silver plate, porcelain 'sett in silver and gylt', 'one bed steede of mother [of] perele and one chyna bed of sylke ymbrodered with silke and china gold, with the bedsted guilte' and 'eight peeces of my richest hangings havinge my armes on them'.[19] Ralegh's library was inherited by Thomas Harriot (1560–1621), the astronomer, mathematician and translator who served both Sir Walter and the 9th Earl of Northumberland, dividing his time between Durham House and Syon throughout the 1590s. At the Strand palace he helped establish a kind of navy school, conducted measurements for astronomical observations from the lead roof and calculated the angle between the two abodes and their exact distance, Syon being eight miles west and 4¼ miles south. He also measured his chamber at Durham House, as 21½ by 12½ feet, spacious enough to conduct his classes and keep his instruments there. It was located, like Ralegh's (or his study, which may have joined Harriot's), on the top floor with access to the leads. This is known from a description of one of his mathematical quests, to estimate the volume of rain that would have occupied the chamber had it not been turned away by the leads and spouts.[20]

After the queen's death in March 1603, Ralegh was deprived of the Captaincy of the Guard and of his lucrative monopoly of the wine licences, followed, at the end of May, by a warrant signed by the new king to surrender Durham House to Bishop Tobias Matthew, in office since 1595. This had long been orchestrated by Robert Cecil, who clearly had an interest in the property, and Henry Howard, the builder of Northampton House (see Chapter Eleven), both of whom had blackened

Ralegh's name in the eye of James I while securing his accession, for they considered him inimical to the Stuarts.[21] It fell to Sir Thomas Egerton as Keeper of the Privy Seal, and therefore resident at the neighbouring York House, to execute the king's warrant, ordering both Ralegh and his kinsman Darcy 'to delyver quyet possession of the said house to the Bishop of Duresme'.[22] The bishop had been plotting to this end with Cecil and was so eager that on 7 June, barely a week after the warrant, urged Egerton to grant him early possession, for 'the supposed tenaunts [are] seeking nothing els but to gaine tyme to deface the house more than is justifiable by law'.[23]

Ralegh's response to the Keeper, produced about two days later on or before 9 June 1603, portrays the circumstances of the eviction while summing up his residency:

> *I received a warrant from your lordshipps, my Lord Keeper and my Lord Cheife Justice, and signed also by Master Aturney Generall, requiringe mee to deliver the possession of Derum Howse to the Byshope of Derum ... before the xxiiiith of June next ... and that the stabells and garden should be presently putt into his hands. And that I should not remove any seelinge [panelling], glass, iron, etc., without warrant from your lordships ... This letter seemeth to mee very strange seinge I have had the possession of the howse almost xx yeare and have bestowed well nire 2000li upon the same out of myne own purse. I am of opinion that if the Kings Majestye had recovered this howse or the like from the meanest gentleman and sarvant hee had in Inglande that His Majestye would have geven six moneaths tyme for the avoydance [vacating] and I do not know butt that the poorest artificer in Londun hath a quarters warni[n]ge geven hyme by his land lord ... I have made my provisions for 40 persons in the springe and I have a fa[m]yley of no less number [? in the howse] and the like for almost xx horse. Now to cast out my hay and oates into the streats att an howres warni[n]ge, and to remove my fa[m]yley and stuff in 14 dayes after is such a seveare expultion as hath not bynn offred to any man before this daye. But this I would have written to any that had not bynn of your lordships place and respect, that the cource taken with mee is bothe contrary to honor, to custome and to civillety, and therefore I pray your lordships to pardon mee till I have acquainted the Kings Majestye with this letter, and then if His Majestye shall thinck it reasonabell I will ob[e]y it. Butt for the cummandment sent mee for the wenscote and other things I do not finde that it pleased His Majestye to geve your lordships any such direction and if I do any thinge contrary to law the Byshope may take his remedy ...*[24]

Ralegh's appeal to James was to no avail for by July he was indeed out of the house. Barely three months later, Bishop Matthew leased a parcel of its garden to the king, who immediately granted it to Robert Cecil, squaring, one might say, the circle of those who had orchestrated the eviction. For this lease allowed not simply the westward expansion of Salisbury House, which culminated in its eventual doubling, but also the erection of the New Exchange, the first commercial venture in the Strand to rival its counterpart in the City, the Royal Exchange. By Cecil's death in 1612, much of the once massive site of Durham House, including the totality of Durham Rents, had been absorbed by these operations.

Ralegh's misfortunes did not cease with the surrender of Durham House: soon after that he gained another 'state' lodging, this time in the Tower, where he was kept fourteen years for alleged treasonable practices. His suspended death sentence issued in 1603 was eventually carried out in November 1618, after a short release followed by yet more misfortune including an unsuccessful attempt to secure help from George Villiers, James's new favourite (soon the owner of the neighbouring York House; see Chapter Ten). Ralegh's fiercest enemies, from Howard to Cecil, kept hounding him.

The House of Philip Herbert, 4th Earl of Pembroke: 1641–1650

Throughout the early decades of the seventeenth century Durham House continued to accommodate a large number of state guests and diplomats in its several apartments. Sir Thomas Wilson, one of Cecil's agents who himself had been living in the Durham precincts since 1600 (and had repeatedly interviewed Ralegh on behalf of the Privy Council), wrote in 1619 that it was occupied by three ambassadors: 'for France, the Count de Tilliers; for Savoy, Signor Gabellione ... for the States, Sir Noel Caron'. In addition, there were those 'that go by name of Agents': 'for Spayne, a Fryar, called Padre Maestro; for the Palsgrave now King of Bohemia, Mr. Abraham Williams; for the Archduke, Signor Van Male'. Last, there was also 'a Secretary for Venice in manner of an Agent', while 'Florence has had one of late'.[25]

Eleven). At the time the sketch of the property was produced in 1626 (see fig. 171), Durham House was occupied by the French ambassador, who may have moved there from Blackfriars in 1623. This followed the so-called 'Fatal Vespers', the death of ninety-eight persons including two priests who had attended a Catholic Mass at the ambassador's when the floor suddenly collapsed.[27] Ironically, the dispute that led to the sketch, attached to an account probably produced by Wilson, also described a gathering of Catholics among whom were English 'Papists' who attended Mass at Durham House. Rough though it is, the drawing offers a good idea of how the property had changed after Cecil's building campaigns: along the Strand, the New Exchange, or Britain's Burse, as James I had called it, replaced most of Durham Rents and included a long strip of land down to its own water gate, granted to Salisbury in 1609. The old gatehouse survived as the eastern boundary of the Exchange but it too had been acquired by Cecil in 1607. Wilson's house can be seen in the middle of the area next to the chapel and what remained of the garden. Only the main building, with its inner and outer courtyards separated by a wall, had seemingly withstood any alteration.

Some 240 feet of hangings were put up in the 'Dyning roome and presence' for the French ambassador, while his bedchamber was 'new matted with Bullrush matts'.[28] These were three of about thirty of the best rooms in the house granted at the king's request by the Bishop of Durham, who had consequently crowded 'himself and his whole family being great, into the worst and basest roomes of his house'.[29] Secretary Conway, who had received reports on the suitability of Durham House on the occasion of the Spanish match, also lodged there in 1632, followed by the Lord Keepers Coventry and Finch from 1625 to 1641, when it was granted to Philip Herbert, 1st Earl of Montgomery and 4th Earl of Pembroke (1584–1650; fig. 172).

A master of hunting and a great entertainer, Philip had enjoyed uninterrupted patronage as a favourite of both James I and Charles I, who had bestowed offices and titles on him.[30] It was Charles who suggested to the then bishop, Thomas Morton, that he should relinquish the house in return for an annual payment of £200, a small amount for Pembroke: his revenues after he had succeeded his brother to the title in 1630 were estimated at £30,000 a year. This allowed him to live lavishly, maintaining a household of eighty in

172 Philip Herbert, 4th Earl of Pembroke, in the robes of the Order of the Garter, c.1615. © National Portrait Gallery, London (5187)

In 1623, when preparations were being made to receive the Infanta following Prince Charles and Buckingham's marriage expedition to Spain, Durham House was again at the centre of discussion alongside St James's Palace and Somerset House, as 'the fittest for the grandees'.[26] Other Strand palaces reviewed for the Spanish delegation included Exeter (Burghley) House and Suffolk (Northampton) House (the latter surveyed by Inigo Jones perhaps for this purpose; see Chapter

DURHAM HOUSE | 165

London and twice as many at his ancestral seat, Wilton House, Wiltshire, where he regularly entertained the king. The latter took a great interest in Pembroke's rebuilding of that house: he employed Isaac de Caus to rebuild the south front and lay out an elaborate formal garden from the 1630s, but after a fire destroyed most of it in 1647 John Webb continued the works. Early in his career, Webb had assisted Inigo Jones in designing ceilings and doors there, executed by de Caus.[31] The latter was recommended by Jones, who gave him 'advice and approbation', as the Wiltshire antiquary John Aubrey noted, for the two had worked together at the Banqueting House and Covent Garden for the 4th Earl of Bedford.[32]

Even though he was a literary patron with more than forty dedications, including Shakespeare's first folio, Pembroke 'did not delight in books, or poetry: but', as Aubrey continues, 'exceedingly loved painting and building, in which he had singular judgement, and had the best collection of any peer in England, and was the great patron to Sir Anthony Van Dyck: and had most of his painting'.[33] When in January 1637 a consignment of pictures arrived in London as a present to Charles from Pope Urban VIII, Herbert was among a select group including the queen and Inigo Jones invited to view them.

The Pembroke collection known to scholars is the one restored and enlarged by Thomas Herbert, 8th Earl (1656/7–1733), who set about refilling Wilton after it had been denuded by enforced sales, both after the Civil Wars and on the death of his brother, the 7th Earl.[34] Its early stages, however, represent 'one of the big gaps in knowledge of Stuart collecting', as no documents survive.[35] The collection appears to have started at the beginning of James I's reign, when William, 3rd Earl of Pembroke and Philip's brother, was Lord Steward to the King. It is believed that the two brothers went on the Grand Tour and were greatly impressed by Italian, French, Dutch, Flemish and German paintings, some of which may well have found their way to England, for by James's death in 1625 they owned works of considerable interest.[36] Purchases and exchanges of pictures went on when Philip became 4th Earl in 1630 – he famously competed to acquire from under Arundel's nose the sculpture cargo assembled in about 1628 by Sir Thomas Roe for the disgraced Duke of Buckingham.[37]

Richard Symonds's early 1650s 'Observations concerning Pictures & paintings in England' includes the only account of what was on the walls at Durham House, namely works by Titian, Correggio, Giorgione, Andrea del Sarto, Jacopo Palma, Bassano, Tintoretto, other Italian artists and by Van Dyck:

a head of O[u]r Saviour bearing the crosse the haire mighty finely finisht by Correggio.
Danae naked & ye shower of gold al large by Titian originall.
Mars & Venus. A sbozzo by Titian. Mars is leaving of her.
A Head of an old man by Titian askes 35t.
A Head of a Woman by Andrea del Sarto never sfumd yet harsh.
4 or 5 demi figures by Giorgione.
A Black Red Satyre carrying away a fare woman & at bottome JACOB' *Palma*
4 seasons by Bassano large & the Entring into the arke.
A mighty large piece of the Ea:[rl] of Pembroke & all his family by Vandyke. Divers ladyes by Vandyke, many pieces having 2 ladyes in a piece.
A Ritratto of a man & written upon it: Roma 16.. by Angelo Caracelli. A most rare thing
The light of the field is very yellow & light on the shadow side of the face & dos admirably 5t askes.
A large story of St John Bapt. in the Wild by Palma il Giovane.
A Ritratto of a Venetian looking Sidewaise & showing a full body. by Tintoreto il filio
Picture of ye King of Spayne at length by Titian as big as the life.[38]

No stranger to the great collections of the Strand palaces, Symonds had also listed the paintings of the 10th Earl of Northumberland at his house (see Chapter Eleven). What he saw at Durham House, however, must have been a smaller number of the original paintings, as his note ends with 'others most or all to be sold & divers are already sold'. Indeed, the 4th Earl's executors' accounts, dated 1650 to 1655, record the sale of many pictures to various parties, including the Spanish ambassador, Alonso de Cárdenas, and David Teniers, who bought 'three or four paintings from the heirs of the Earl of Pembroke' on behalf of another Spanish official.[39] Don Luis de Haro, 'First Minister' of Spain, and Cárdenas, also made efforts to buy a Holy Family by Raphael 'from a member of parliament, who had taken it out of the sale in spite of claims against

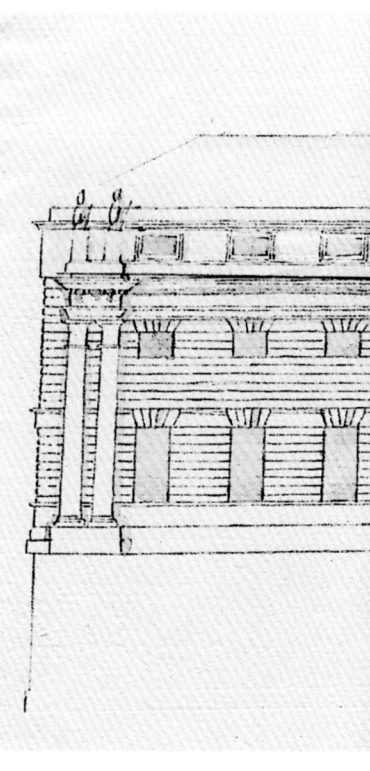

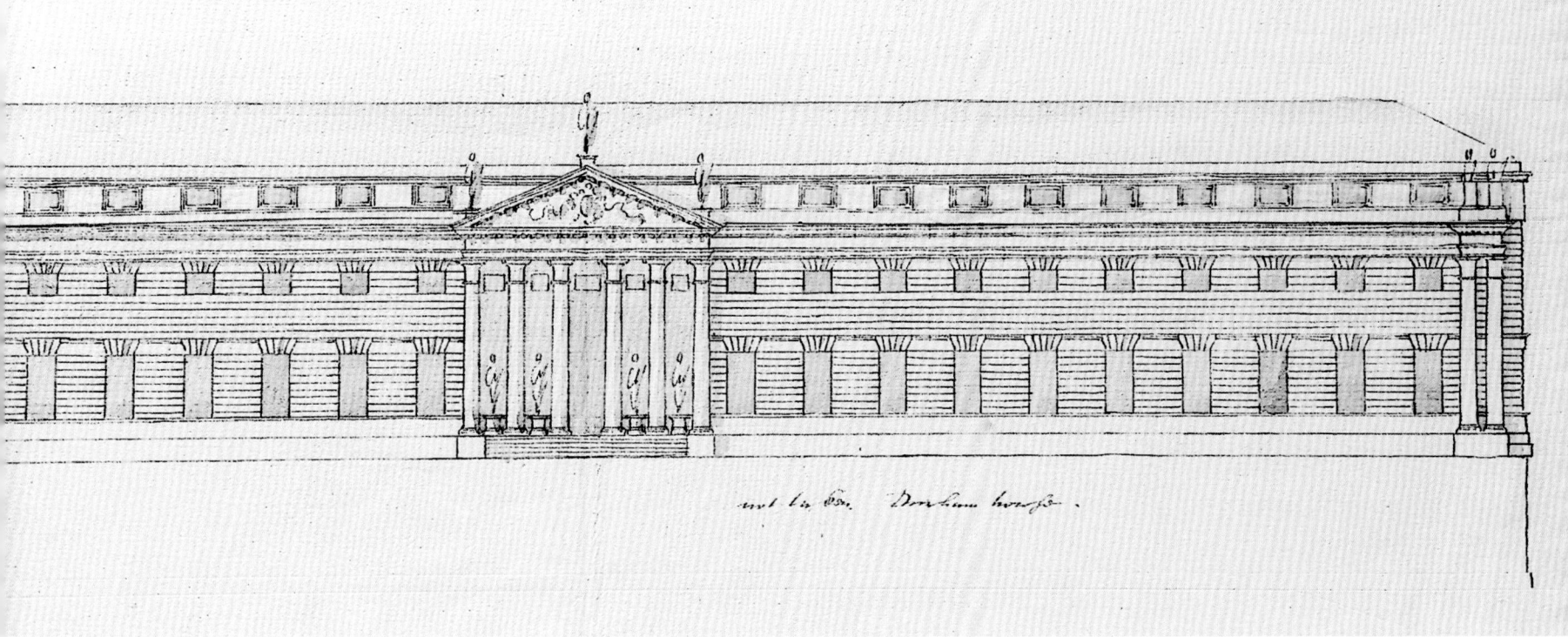

173 John Webb, proposal for the north elevation of Durham House, 1640s. The Provost and Fellows of Worcester College, Oxford (H&T 81)

it by the Earl of Pembroke'.[40] While quite a few pictures may have reached Spanish soil, those that remained were taken to Wilton after Webb's reconstruction of 1647.[41] Indeed, the Double Cube Room was expressly designed to receive the Van Dyck portraits, dominated by the famous group of the Herbert family, which contains ten life-size figures and measures eleven by seventeen feet. As Symonds's list testifies, this painting certainly hung at Durham House but it could not, as previously suggested, have been painted there because in 1636, when it was apparently finished, that house was not in the possession of the Earl of Pembroke.[42]

As far as the architectural history of Durham House is concerned, the Pembroke phase is certainly the most conspicuous: John Webb, following his work at Wilton, conceived a number of remarkable plans for its grandiose rebuilding, which would have turned the old rambling fabric into 'an aristocratic palace of monarchical intent'.[43] It could be argued that this had been the aim of most if not all the Strand magnates and Pembroke was merely following on. None of them, however, had quite managed that 'incomparable antique splendour'[44] – styles had changed by the 1640s but the primary reason was that the location of Durham House would have offered Webb's designs a unique platform. Indeed, the new Pembroke House would have risen 'like a palazzo on the Grand Canal, almost directly from the Thames'.[45] It would not, however, have stood right on the river, for close examination of the plans reveals the presence of a garden between the Thames and the house (see fig. 176). In all likelihood, this garden occupied the space between the hall and the old river-wall building, the foundations of which might perhaps have been used by Webb as the base of the new structure.

Consisting of two sets of plans, two elevations and one sheet of annotations preserved at Worcester College, Oxford, these drawings are uniquely important as they represent all we know about this period at Durham House.[46] The only surviving record among the Pembroke papers related to the palace is in fact of no relevance.[47] Except for the sheet of annotations, they were published and catalogued by John Harris and A. A. Tait in 1979, and subsequently discussed by John Bold in 1989, but have received little attention since.[48] I shall therefore analyse them afresh while also comparing them to one of the designs by Webb at Worcester College 'for a large country house or palace', still unidentified. For convenience, I use Harris and Tait's (hereafter, H&T) sequence and catalogue numbers, which follow the folio numbers in the Worcester College archives.

The first (fig. 173; H&T 81) shows a symmetrical, temple-fronted, rusticated elevation

DURHAM HOUSE | 167

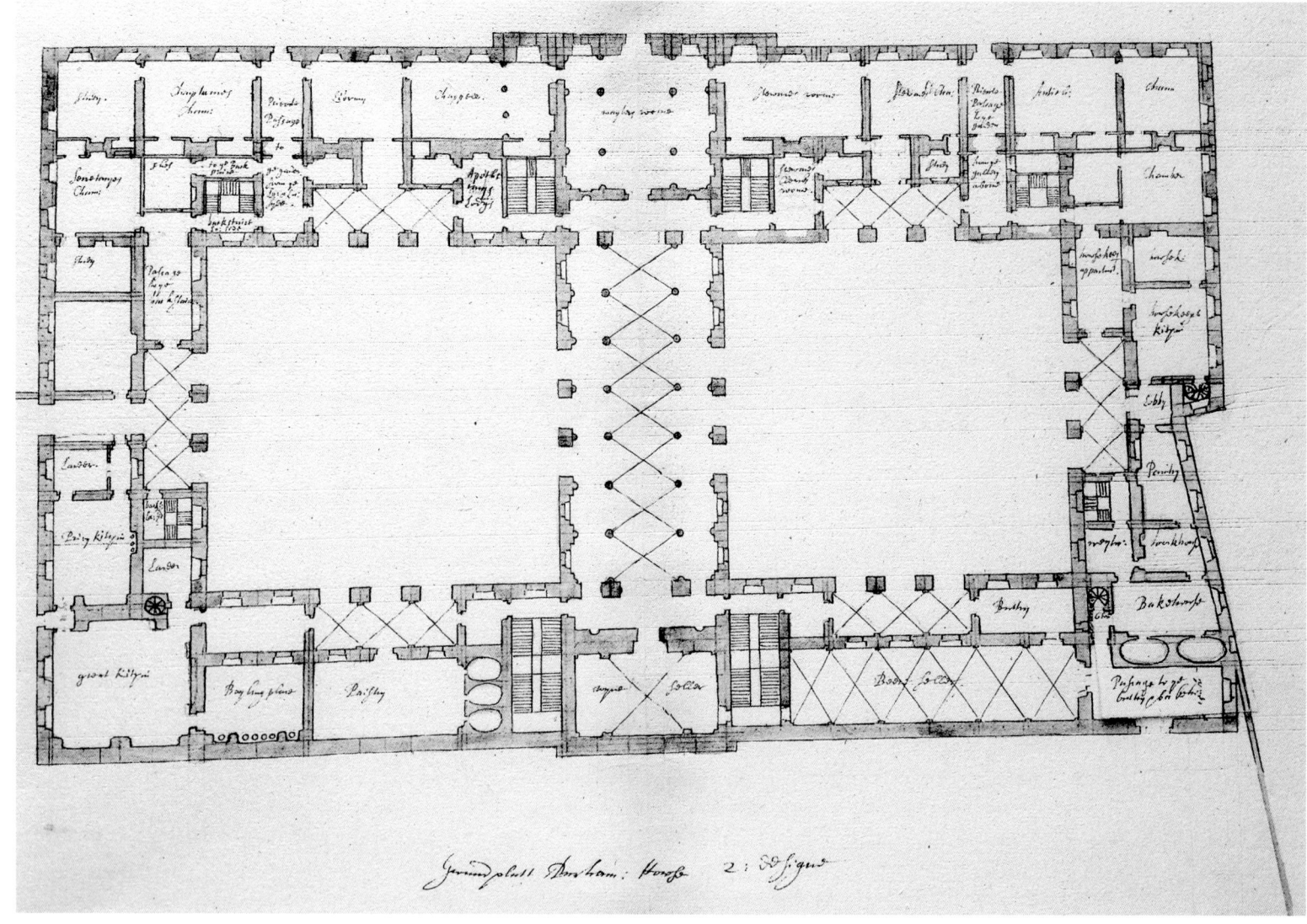

consisting of a raised ground floor, a mezzanine and an attic storey, with a double-height entrance. There is also a hint of a partly underground floor in the descending lines at either end. The only inscription, in Webb's hand, reads 'not taken Durham House' but there can be little doubt that this shows the north elevation facing the New Exchange. Firstly, the elevation corresponds but for the paired columns at either end to the plan of the 'second ffloor' of the first set of designs (fig. 175; H&T 83), that is, the second floor on the river side but ground floor on the Strand side. This plan reveals the irregularity of the western boundary with York House (right), as opposed to the straight-sided elevation on the east (left) which would have faced the garden. Secondly, the sheet of annotations (H&T 87 and 88) lists 'pillers of the front towards the Exchange', which can only refer to those of the central portico, since neither set of plans features columns along the south side. Hidden by the Exchange and the remaining Durham Rents, the north facade (H&T 81) would not have been visible from the Strand. As a result, its symmetry would have been lost as the entrance was to be approached at an angle. The lack of a working relationship with the site may be due to the fact that much of Webb's work on paper up to that time was theoretical, born out of reconstructions of ancient Roman houses and hence far removed from reality.[49] The amount and type of information found in these drawings is none the less such that the opposite seems to be the case. Harris and Tait catalogued the elevation as 'first design', presumably because it differs in its details from both sets of plans, marked by Webb himself as second and third designs. As just noted, however, the only difference between the elevation (H&T 81) and the ground floor of the second design (H&T 83) lies in the paired giant columns at the extremities. Apart from framing

174 John Webb, proposal for the ground-plan at river level of Durham House, 1640s. South at the top, north at the bottom. The Provost and Fellows of Worcester College, Oxford (H&T 82)

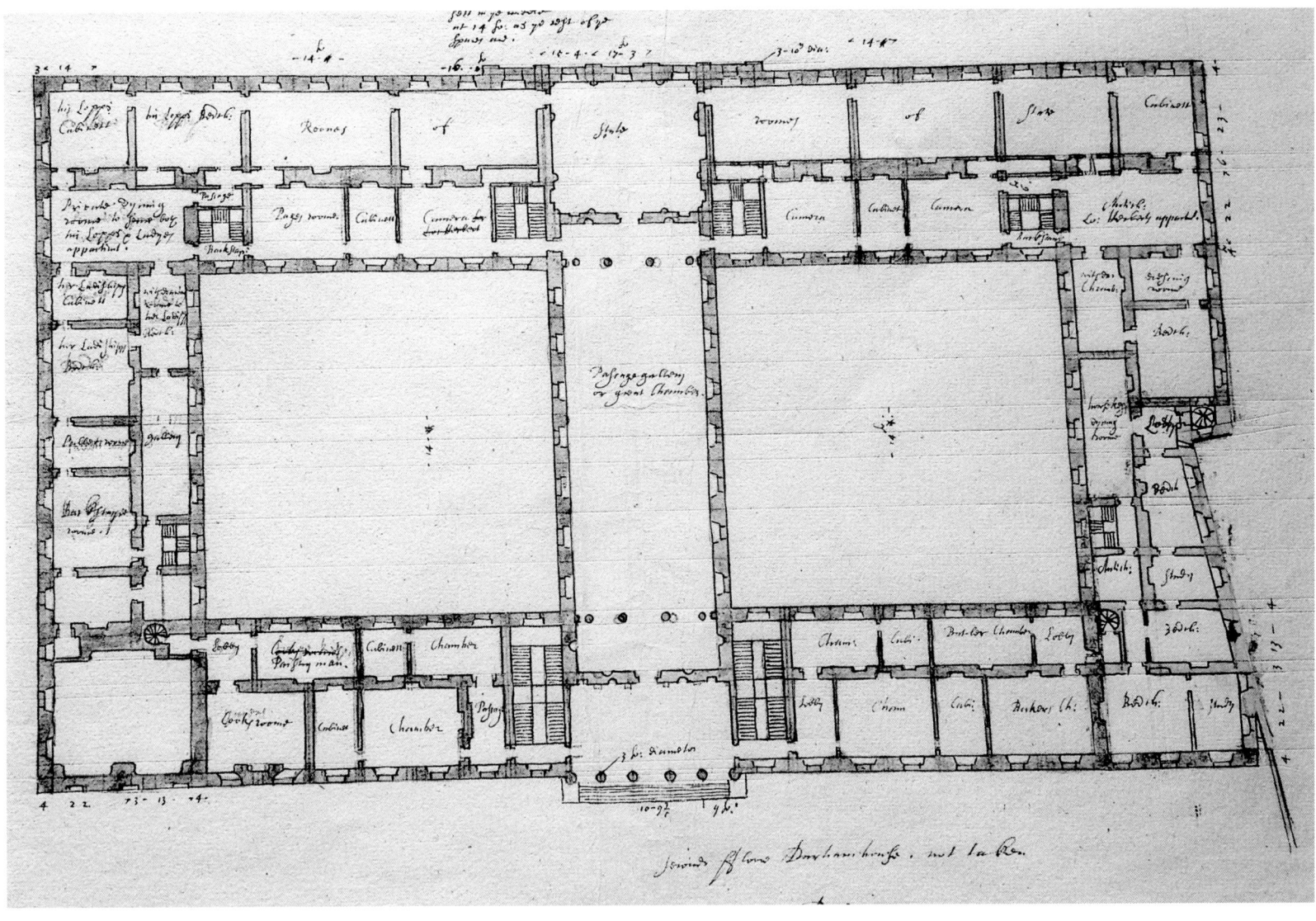

175 John Webb, proposal for the 'second ffloor' plan (raised ground level on the Strand side) of Durham House, 1640s. South at the top, north at the bottom. The Provost and Fellows of Worcester College, Oxford (H&T 83)

an otherwise bare facade, these were probably conceived to cover or regularise the odd angle at the north-western corner, occasioned by the existing boundary. If so, the elevation would follow rather than precede the plan, where the issue is unresolved.

The first set of plans (see figs 174 and 175; H&T 82 and 83) shows what Webb called the second design for the ground and first (or principal) floors of a massive, two-courtyard rectangular building over 300 feet long (as shown by the scale in the second set). Both drawings are inscribed with room functions, while that of the 'second ffloor' includes a number of annotations and calculations. Its title also specifies that the design was 'not taken'. The internal arrangement is clearly adapted to the actual site of Durham House, as all the services and least important rooms are placed in the northern, partly underground side of the basement plan towards the New Exchange. By contrast, the 'Roomes of State' on the 'second ffloor' face the Thames, whence they are accessed via grand staircases either side of a columned hall, spectacularly connected to an enormous vaulted vestibule (cross-vaults indicated by Xs). This was a double-height 'Passage gallery or great Chamber', aligned with both the entrance to the north and the biggest state room on the south in a majestic enfilade, whereby anyone going through the main access from the Strand would have seen the river. The earl and countess's lodgings were also prominently located in the south-east corner of the house, partly facing the Thames ('His Lo[rdshi]pps. Bedch:[amber]' and 'Cabinett'), partly the garden – namely the 'Private Dyning roome to serve both his Lo[rdshi]pps & Ladyes appartement', 'her Ladyshipp Cabinett' and 'withdrawing roome to her Ladyshipp bedch.[amber]', her Bed Chamber proper, a small Gallery and other ancillary rooms.

DURHAM HOUSE | 169

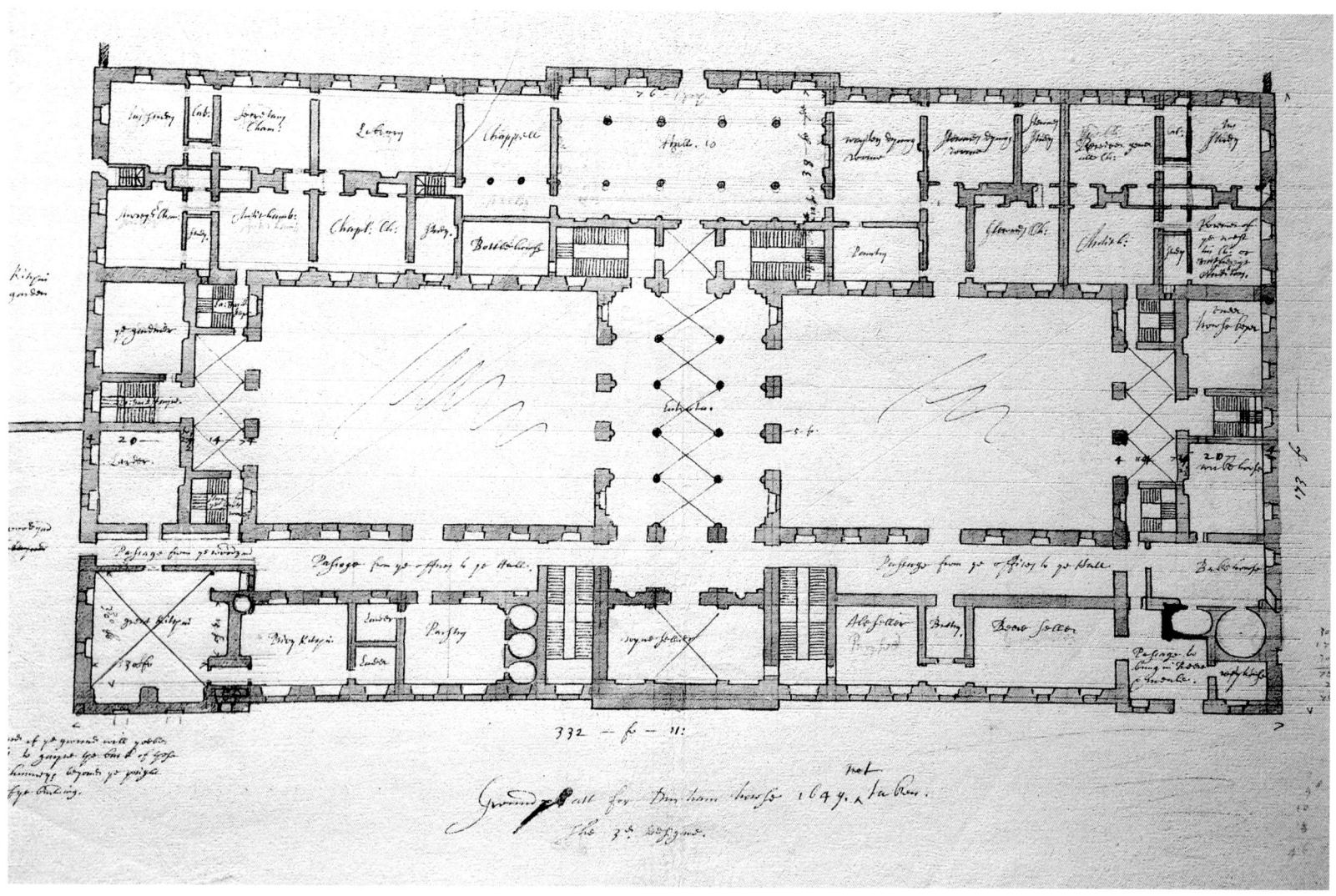

176 John Webb, proposal for the ground-plan at river level of Durham House, 1649. The Provost and Fellows of Worcester College, Oxford (H&T 84)

This arrangement was mirrored in the western wing by a similar set for 'Lo: Herbert', the son and heir, thus styled since 1636.[50] Below the state apartments would have been the Library and Chapel, connected by way of the main staircases as well as via a back staircase leading to a 'private passage to ye garden from y[ou]r Lo:[rdship] & La:[diship's] lod[gings]'. The ground-floor plan on the river side also features self-contained sets for the chaplain, secretary, steward and housekeeper, as well as a room for the apothecary, while the whole of the northern half would have been occupied by an impressive suite of service rooms which included a Privy and a Great double-height Kitchen, two Larders, two 'Pastries', a Wine and a Beer Cellar, a Buttery, a Bake House and a Cook House.

The second set of plans (figs 176 and 177; H&T 84 and 85) consists of a more elaborate version of the first.[51] The ground-plan at river level is dated 1649 and marked '3d designe', while the words 'not taken' ('not' was added later) appear on both drawings. That they were initially accepted is confirmed by the sheet of annotations (H&T 87 and 88), which refers to 'ye 3d designe taken' without the 'not': it must have escaped the correction.[52] The main difference with the previous plans lies in the treatment of the public side of the house, which appears altogether more palatial: the rooms would have been 'up to ye roofe', that is, double-height, either coved or vaulted and considerably bigger. The Great Chamber alone, for instance, is a double cube 40 by 40 by 80 feet, designed while Webb was working at the Double Room at Wilton – one even wonders whether some of the ceiling drawings for that room, could actually refer to Durham House, as suggested by John Martin Robinson. Either side of this impressive space, symmetrically disposed, would have been Presence Chambers the full depth of the range, with Privy Chambers next to them on the river

170 | LONDON'S 'GOLDEN MILE'

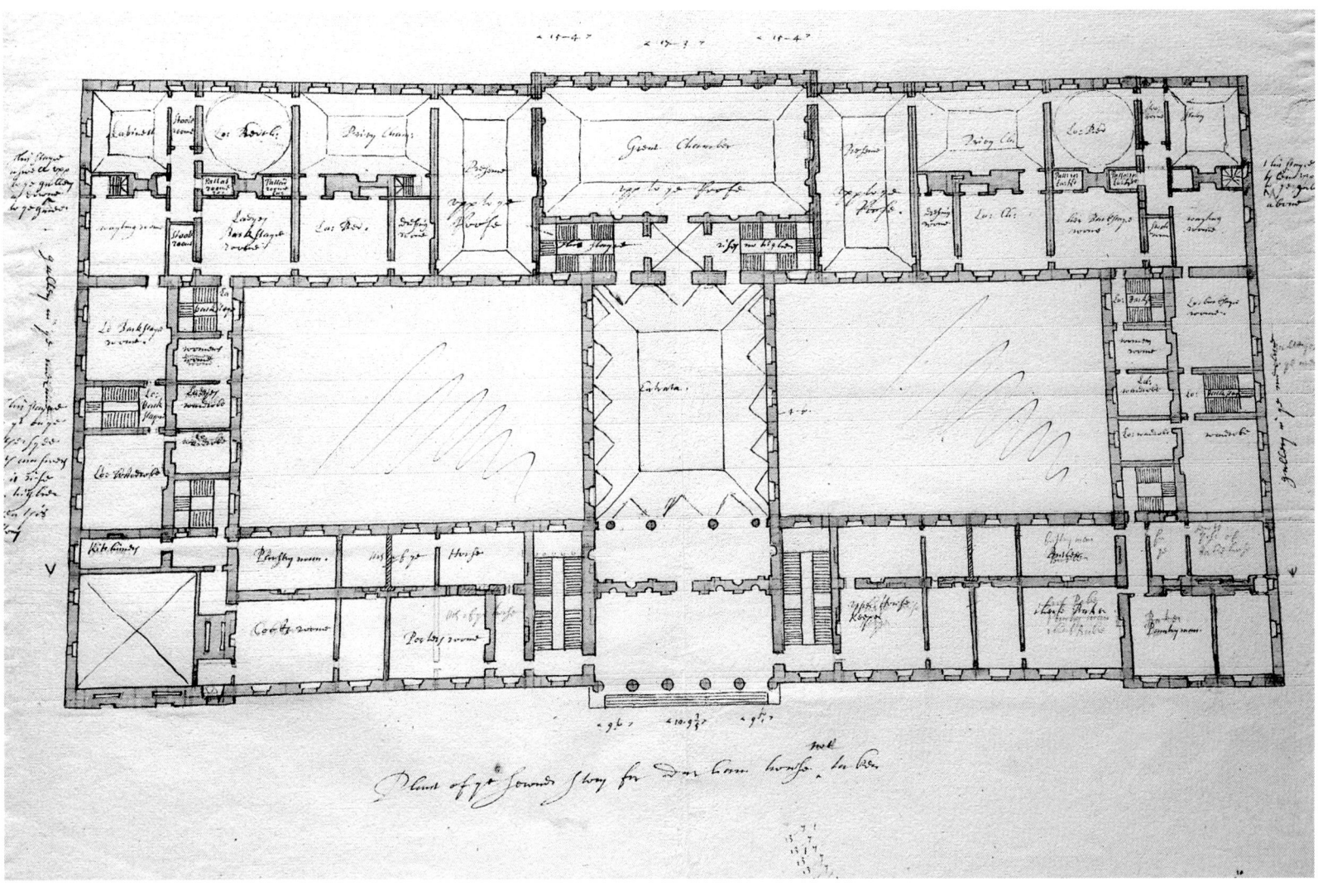

177 John Webb, 1640s, proposal for the 'Second story' plan (raised ground level on the Strand side) of Durham House, 1640s. The Provost and Fellows of Worcester College, Oxford (H&T 85)

front and State Bedrooms beyond (see fig. 177). Unlike the earlier design, the earl and countess's apartments are not specifically identified, for two identical sets for their use appear in the east and west corners of the south wing. Access to the ground floor was provided by an increased number of staircases, while the formal route from the water gate was still through the Hall underneath the Great Chamber, connected by the two main staircases that were realigned so as to mirror one another. As in the earlier design, this sequence included an impressive vestibule or 'Entrata', now featuring a coved ceiling, right above a vaulted and arcaded room of basilical proportions, which afforded an even more monumental entrance. Two galleries to house Pembroke's picture collection were then proposed for the second floor in the east and west ranges.

As well as catering for a large household in a very grand yet functional way, these designs are interesting from a planning point of view: they include such features as the chimneypieces combined with small recesses – variously used for service stairs, cupboards or as 'pallet roomes' (in the second set of drawings) – which, in turn, act as a central partition in the south wing, like a modern 'furbished wall'. It appears to be of English origin as a device to maximise the space in small double-pile town-houses, such as Sir Peter Killigrew's in Holborn, recorded by Webb, or comparable examples in John Thorpe's album.[53] A similar feature can also be found in the compact, medium-sized country houses of Peter Mills and Roger Pratt, which owed much to the town-house.[54] The sequence of loggias in the centre and along the sides in the Durham House plans also allows for circulation in between the courts and for separate access to the various parts of the house. Webb experimented with these features in his drawings for Whitehall Palace, and later applied them at Greenwich, and both can be found in a number of Webb's other designs.[55]

DURHAM HOUSE | 171

Before moving on to the last of the Durham House drawings, let us turn now to what Harris and Tait catalogued as the unidentified 'Design for a large country house or palace' (fig. 178; H&T 97).[56] This consists of two elevations of a symmetrical house of twenty-three bays with a temple front, two courtyards, sitting on a sloping site, which are remarkably close to the north elevation and plans for Durham House, particularly the second set (or 'third design'; H&T 81, 84 and 85). Indeed, the top elevation in H&T 97 could be used to illustrate what the missing south facade of the Strand palace could have looked like, were it not for the presence of part-basement windows, to which nothing at Durham House corresponds, as far as we know. In addition, the bottom elevation in H&T 97 indicates two, perhaps joined courtyards, contrary to H&T 82–5 where they are clearly separate. But this does not really make sense, as the temple front in the unidentified design does not seem to lead anywhere, unless the podium on which it sits was meant to indicate some kind of bridge. Once again, this drawing may be theoretical but its characteristics are comparable to the Durham House plans. By contrast, the last of Webb's drawings for Durham House (fig. 179; H&T 86) would hardly be identifiable as such were it not for his inscription on the verso: 'For ye Earle of Pembroke in Durham Yard'. This elevation for a temple-fronted house of nine bays and two main storeys was clearly conceived for a much reduced site, perhaps as a manageable alternative to the rejected third design. Durham Yard must have been the space between the New Exchange and Durham House but it is hard to imagine how such a building would have functioned between existing buildings, not least as its style and proportions, modelled on Scamozzi's Villa Verlato (1574), called for an adequate setting.[57]

Webb's drawings illustrate what a courtier at Pembroke's level could achieve or at least aspire to in the London of the 1640s, in spite of the outbreak of the Civil Wars. Yet the grandest of Webb's designs, however fully worked out as practical propositions, remained unexecuted. The elevation for the smaller house (H&T 86) is more puzzling, for the 1626 rough sketch of Durham House (see fig. 171) shows no apparent building in Durham Yard, while Newcourt's 1658 depiction (fig. 180) reveals a sizeable house with a formal garden towards the river. Could this refer to the smaller building designed by Webb? Or does it

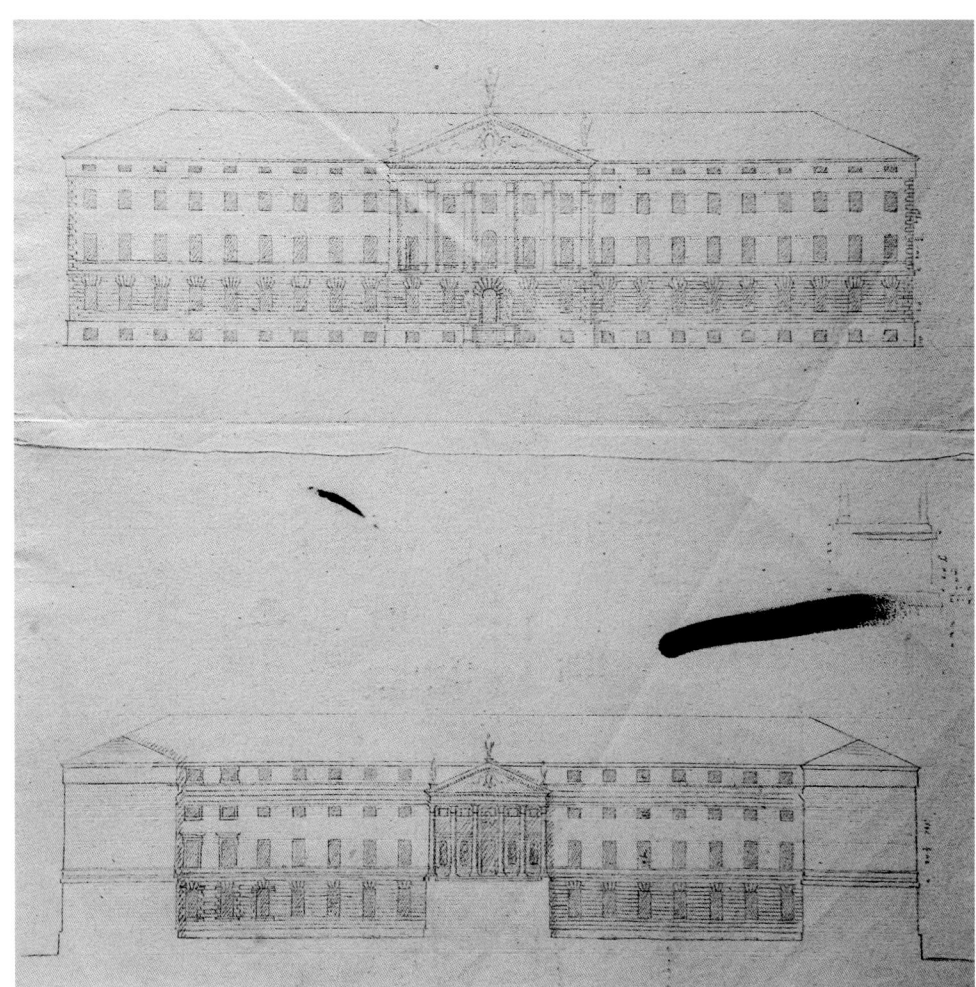

178 John Webb, unidentified designs for a large country house or palace. The Provost and Fellows of Worcester College, Oxford (H&T 97)

179 John Webb, design for elevation of Durham House, 1649. The Provost and Fellows of Worcester College, Oxford (H&T 86)

180 The complex of Durham House with the house in Durham Yard, detail of Richard Newcourt and William Faithorne, 'An exact delineation of the City of London and Westminster', 1658. By kind permission of the Syndics of Cambridge University Library (Map Room, Maps BB.77.90.14)

181 The area formerly occupied by Durham House (12), detail of Wenceslaus Hollar, 'view of London extending eastwards from Peterborough House to Somerset House', early 1670s. By permission of the Pepys Library, Magdalene College, Cambridge ('London and Westminster', I, 2972, 34–35)

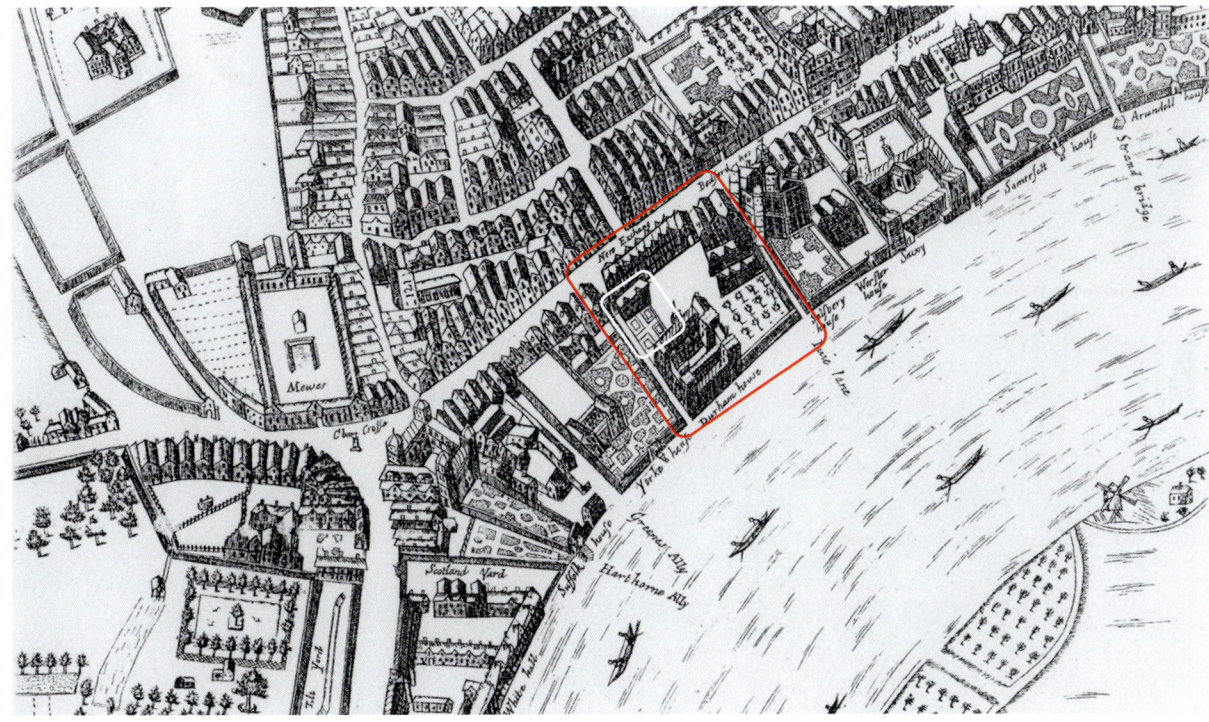

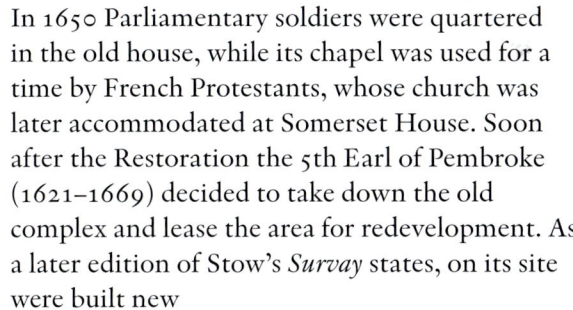

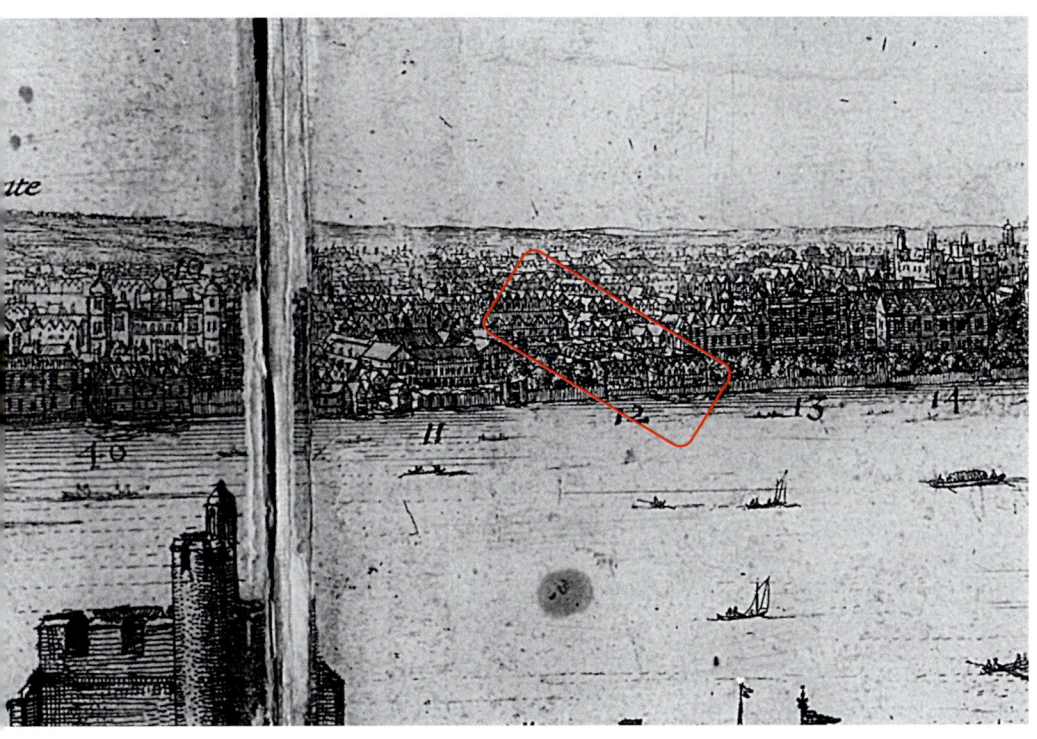

represent what is marked in the 1626 sketch as 'Sr Robert Cotton's house', a relatively small house in the eastern corner with the New Exchange but on the west side of the lane which connected it to the river, as opposed to what Newcourt shows? In any event, it seems likely that the 5th Earl would have been in charge by then, as the third design was produced in 1649 and the 4th Earl died on 23 January 1650, still 1649 in the old calendar.[58]

In 1650 Parliamentary soldiers were quartered in the old house, while its chapel was used for a time by French Protestants, whose church was later accommodated at Somerset House. Soon after the Restoration the 5th Earl of Pembroke (1621–1669) decided to take down the old complex and lease the area for redevelopment. As a later edition of Stow's *Survay* states, on its site were built new

> houses, as now they are standing, being a handsome Street, descending down out of the Strand, which falls into another, much better inhabited, especially on the South side, where there are Gardens fronting the Thames, very pleasant, with two Woodmongers Wharfs for the sale of Fuel. Beside, where the Dairy-house stood, now taken down, is a more open Passage to another Row of Houses, fronting the Backside of the New Exchange. And on the north side of the Street, near Ivy-bridge, is a pretty handsome Court, with a Freestone pavement, called Bishop's Court …[59]

Hollar's 1670s view of the riverside shows how the once majestic site had been filled by tenements (fig. 181). Given the commercial wharves, the remaining space was also soon occupied by traders and artisans and by the middle of the eighteenth century it had been transformed beyond recognition: 'Where the medieval bishops and Tudor statesmen had once dwelt in splendour, the outcasts and roughs of London found a squalid shelter.'[60]

DURHAM HOUSE | 173

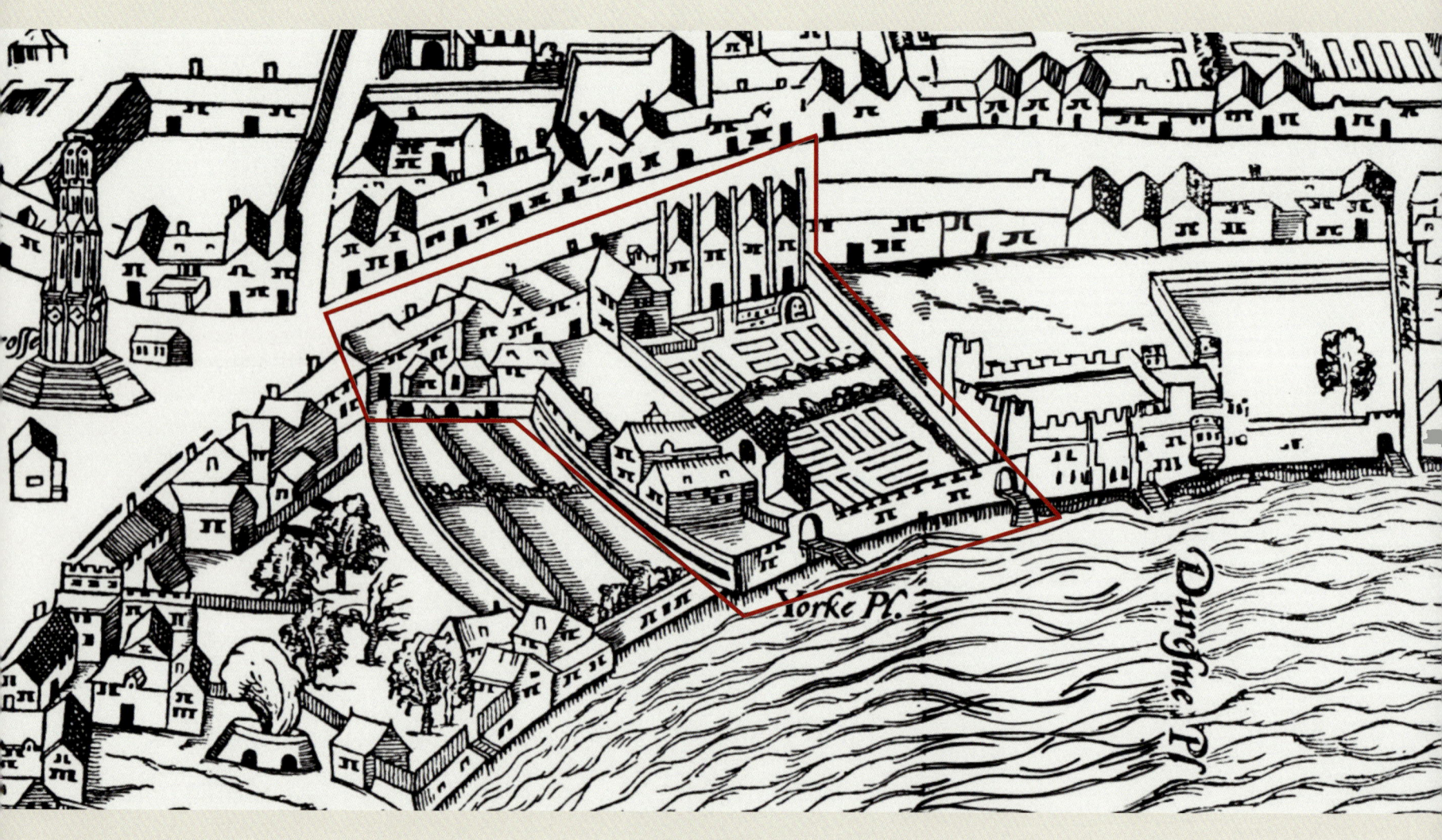

182 The complex of York House, detail of the *Woodcut Map of London*, 1561–70 ('Agas')

10 · YORK HOUSE

YORK HOUSE WAS BOUNDED BY DURHAM House on the east and it too was an episcopal palace belonging to the See of Norwich, hence its original name of Norwich Inn or Place. An early record of 1237 mentions repairs to its quay.[1] Like its neighbour and most of the bishops' inns along the Thames, Norwich Place was compact, with a somewhat fortified appearance, sitting nearly on the river's edge and surrounded by a number of plots and outbuildings, amounting to a sizeable area. The complex appears for the first time in the Woodcut Map of London (or 'Agas') of 1561–70 (fig. 182) and as Suffolk Place in Georg Braun and Frans Hogenberg's 'London' in their *Civitates Orbis Terrarum*, published in 1572. Both derive from the lost 'Copperplate Map of London' of 1553–9. It is, however, the better viewpoint in Norden's 1593 map of Westminster (fig. 183) that allows us to distinguish the main house as composed of two attached but different wings, of which the main one resembles a large hall with double turrets at either end that may originally have stood on its own. This prominence is clear in the 1600 version of Norden's view (fig. 184), which, by contrast, is quite vague about the surrounding buildings. In the 1593 map, on the north, west and east sides the main house is enclosed by three lower wings, which provide the traditional courtyard arrangement with a gateway onto the Strand. The street front existed from at least 1437, when the small houses there were mentioned in addition to the 'hospicium'. The gatehouse, roughly in the middle of that front, as Norden shows, probably contained servants' lodgings, while to its east were five tenements, leased out since the fifteenth century. In 1520 these were rebuilt as seven and twelve more were added eastward along the Strand edge of the property, no doubt to increase rent revenue. The resulting nineteen tenements became known as Norwich, later York, Rents. As noted throughout this book, this is typical of all the Strand palaces with episcopal roots. They were set in substantial plots that gave seclusion to the main house, which was often located away from the street. This was the case at Essex House and Arundel House (see Chapters One and Two). Somerset House was built from scratch by Seymour with a front on the Strand but even that was not extensive: instead, the house developed towards the river in order to retain a good number of letting properties along the highway (see Chapter Three).

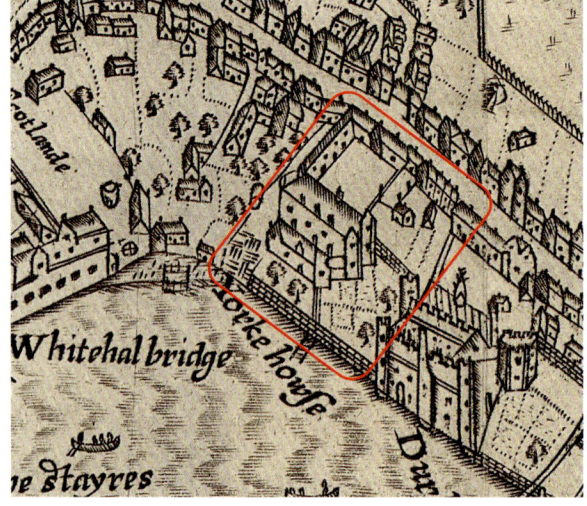
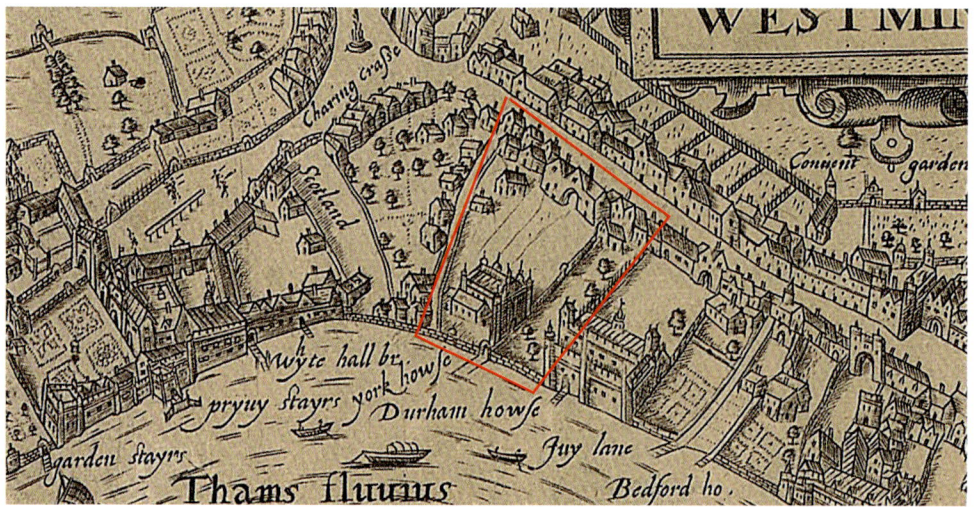

Norwich Place, again like its episcopal counterparts, was used to host dignitaries and courtiers throughout its history, as its scale and arrangement allowed for multiple occupancy. In 1528, for instance, it was suggested as a potential abode for Cardinal Campeggio (1474–1539), the last Cardinal Protector of England who was on the commission which excommunicated Henry VIII in 1535. Letters dated 1532 from the Duke of Norfolk and Sir Thomas Audley may suggest their residence there, while in 1534 the house appears as the Duke of Richmond's address. When the king took possession of it in 1536 and provided the Bishop of Norwich with a house in Cannon Row, Westminster, the keepers William Hale and Richard Hale and his wife reserved the right, due to their office, to keep Norwich Inn and the profits of its garden. This in turn implies that those plots to the east of the main house, demarcated by Norden as a series, would have been orchards put to profit. Henry VIII's exchange of the property may have originated in a wish to provide his former brother-in-law with a house in the Strand: Charles Brandon, 1st Duke of Suffolk and 1st Viscount Lille (c.1484–1545) in 1515 had married Mary Tudor, Queen Dowager of France, but in 1536 Mary died and the duke remarried. Either way, it was probably Brandon's house in Southwark that the king had sought from the start, for it was eventually exchanged with Norwich Inn, which was then renamed Suffolk Place after its first secular owner. Brandon, however, had another house in the Barbican and seems to have rarely used the Strand house, which by 1556 had been surrendered by his heirs to Queen Elizabeth. She in turn granted it to Nicholas Heath (c.1501–1578), Archbishop of York. It is at this point that the complex became known as York House, consisting, as the grant deed describes it for the first time, of 'the capital messuage commonly called Suffolke Place alias Norwiche place with the appurtenaces and 50 messuages, 10 cottages, 4 stables and 7 gardens in the parish of St. Martin in the Fields'.[2]

The Keepership of Sir Nicholas Bacon: 1558–1579

Since 1555 Archbishop Heath had been in charge of the Great Seal, an office which remained associated with York House for the following seventy years, till 1625. As a Catholic, Heath was forced to give up the Seal in 1558 in favour of the rising lawyer and administrator favoured by the queen, Sir Nicholas Bacon (1510–1579), who retained the Seal and York House for twenty-one years, until his death.[3] Sir Nicholas's second marriage to Anne Cooke in 1553 had brought him an exceptional set of marital connections: her four sisters had respectively married William Cecil, Lord Burghley (Mildred); the London goldsmith Ralph Rowlett (Margaret); the courtier and humanist Thomas Hoby and then John Russell, 2nd Earl of Bedford (Elizabeth); and the diplomat Henry Killigrew (Katherine).[4] By then, Bacon had already secured a sizeable landed estate, purchasing properties throughout the 1540s in and around his native Suffolk (such as the manor of Redgrave) and in western Norfolk, Essex and London. In 1560, when his career in London and Westminster made it difficult to spend time in Suffolk, he then purchased the Hertfordshire manor of Gorhambury, outside St Albans. The main construction of Gorhambury

183 The complex of York House, detail of John Norden, *Speculum Britanniae*, 1593. Folger Shakespeare Library, Washington DC. Licensed under Creative Commons Attribution-ShareAlike 4.0 International

184 The complex of York House, detail of John Norden, *Civitas Londini*, 1600. National Library of Sweden

Hall took place from 1563 to 1568, with a long gallery added about 1574 in the hope of a second royal visit. Redgrave and Gorhambury, the house at Stiffkey in Norfolk built for his son Nathaniel and the Chapel of Corpus Christi College, Cambridge, which he had sponsored as a former alumnus, gained Bacon a fair position among the architectural patrons of the day and a sharp eye for the subject. At Burghley's Strand palace, for instance, he found the privy too close to the larder and lodgings, commenting that 'you had bene better to have offendyd yor yey [eye] outwrds than yor nose inward' (see Chapter Five).[5] In effect, while Bacon's architectural vocabulary generally sits within the English medieval tradition, the porch he added at Gorhambury (fig. 185) stands out as a reminder of his humanistic inclinations, as well as being another instance of those early Renaissance experiments influenced by the circle around the Protector Somerset.

Bacon's building activities have been the subject of detailed investigation by Ernest R. Sandeen, who examined the Bacon Manuscripts held at the University of Chicago Library.[6] These came from Redgrave Hall and had been sold between 1919 and 1921 by George Holt Wilson, one of the Hall's late owners before its demolition soon after the Second World War. Unfortunately, the study of Bacon's London houses, including York House, had to be curtailed by Sandeen due to 'an almost complete lack of contemporary documentation',[7] a status confirmed by my own researches. A separate group of papers, those belonging to Anthony Bacon (1558–1601), the Keeper's first son from his second marriage, went to Lambeth Palace, but again no documents specifically on York House could be found, beyond mentions of it as the venue for theological meetings or as the address for correspondence.[8] Consequently, Sandeen's claim that Sir Nicholas did not do anything to York House could not be verified.[9] However, other buildings in London associated with Bacon were noticed by Stow, including the house in Noble Street called 'Bacon House, because the same was new builded by sir Nicholas Bacon'.[10] His name has also been associated with other buildings in the capital, such as the new hall at Gray's Inn, built between 1556 and 1560, or the offices for the Cursitors (clerks in the Chancery), which Stow again attributed to Sir Nicholas, describing them as 'the first faire building to be noted' in Chancery Lane.[11] Bacon is then tentatively linked to the repairs of St Paul's Cathedral after the fire of 1561, where his funeral monument was installed before his death in 1576.[12] This tomb was almost totally destroyed in the Great Fire of 1666 but can be assessed through an engraving that shows the effigies of Bacon and his wife framed by a two-bay temple front, yet another example of how much the *all'antica* taste had penetrated Elizabethan England.[13]

While none of this accounts for the lack of evidence for York House, we get a fair idea of the tenure of its resident, which is probably as far as one can go. The complex remained a dwelling tied to the office of Keeper, hence not worth spending one's own means on improving it. Therefore it is plausible that Bacon directed expenses towards his own properties, even if York House later fell into the hands of his second son with Anne Cooke, the celebrated philosopher and statesman Sir Francis Bacon (1561–1626; see fig. 186), who was born there. Sir Nicholas died on 20 February 1579 at York House, where he lay in state for nearly a fortnight. All 'intereste in Yorke House' (to be explained shortly) was left to his wife Anne.[14]

185 The porch at Gorhambury House, Hertfordshire, built by Sir Nicholas Bacon, 1563–8. Girouard 2009, 154, fig. 168

The Keepership of Sir Thomas Egerton, 1st Baron Ellesmere: 1596–1617

The years between Sir Nicholas's death in 1579 and the nomination to the Great Seal of Sir Thomas Egerton (1540–1617) in 1596 were covered by a succession of relatively brief tenures. It was held until 1587 by Sir Thomas Bromley (1530–1587), a lawyer and judge who famously presided over the trial of Mary, Queen of Scots, and then until 1591 by Sir Christopher Hatton (c.1540–1591), a commissioner for that trial but above all a favourite of Elizabeth I.[15] He was also the great builder of Holdenby in Northamptonshire, then the largest and most magnificent of the 'prodigy houses' conceived to host the entire court. In 1579, when an aged Lord Burghley visited it, he was so impressed that he forgot the 'infirmity of his legs' while he walked around.[16] Himself no stranger to the financial strain of such buildings, which eventually ruined Hatton, Burghley had written to him that 'God send us both long to enjoy her [Elizabeth I], for whom we both meant to exceed our purses in these [houses]', referring, of course, to his own Theobalds.[17]

Hatton was succeeded by Sir John Puckering (1544–1596), in the small pond of Tudor politics yet another of those involved in Mary's trial, as Queen's Sergeant. That position also saw him as the leader in the trial against Philip Howard, 13th Earl of Arundel (see Chapter Two). Puckering was no stranger to the Strand, as he had lived at Russell House near Ivy Bridge (later Worcester House; see Chapter Seven).

While York House remained the property of the office of Lord Keeper, it appears that on several occasions its lease was granted for short periods, as with Lady Bacon's interest in the house. According to John Norden's *Speculum Britanniae*, published in 1593, the queen had also given the house to Robert Devereux, 2nd Earl of Essex, whose tenure must have been short-lived, not least because at that time Essex had inherited his stepfather's Leicester House in the Strand (as seen in Chapter One).[18] In any case, at the end of 1594 it was Puckering who secured a lease for himself from the Archbishop of York, Matthew Hutton, claiming that he had not been 'a badd tenant … for I have in this litle time bestowed above 200*l* in reparations about the house'. His letter also informs us that the previous Lord Keeper (Hatton) had been granted such a request and that the petitioner would not only maintain the building 'in due reparations' but also gladly provide the archbishop with an alternative 'convenient house' for his stays in London.[19] This again is a reminder that these palaces were by then episcopal in name only. Puckering, whose keepership lasted until his death in 1596, left his interest in the house to his wife, for the archbishop wrote to his successor, Sir Thomas Egerton, that 'My Ladie Puckering hathe a state in it for one yeare after her husbands death'. This followed a previous letter in which Archbishop Hutton had been informed by Sir Thomas that he did not particularly wish to live at York House, as its position near the river made it 'somewhat rheumaticke'.[20] While Egerton did in fact move to the Strand palace, where he remained for two decades, remarks of this kind are not rare in his correspondence and point to the unfavourable condition of the complex. This, by the late 1500s, was nearly three centuries old and no doubt in considerable need of repair, in spite of what Puckering might have done to it. One such hint is provided by the Earl of Essex, Egerton's friend and as such put in his custody at York House in 1597 after the ill-fated expedition to Ireland: Essex needed to be 'removed to a better air, for he is somewhat straitly lodged in respect the Lord Keeper's household is not great'.[21] Egerton too complained again about the 'unsavory' nature of the house, begging Sir Robert Cecil to relieve him from the charge of Essex, so that he could presumably move back to the country 'to air both myself and my house', as he had remarked in an earlier letter to Essex himself.[22] As for Essex, his freedom was short-lived, for the Essex House Cabal early in 1601 cost him his head (as noted in Chapter One). Interestingly, later that summer the queen paid a visit to York House and was presented with several gifts in a 'Lottery'.[23]

After the accession of James I in 1603 Egerton was reappointed Lord Keeper, ennobled with the title of 1st Baron Ellesmere, and continued to preside over the Chancery and Star Chamber for fourteen more years, conducting a number of famous trials, from that of Sir Walter Ralegh in 1603, the Gunpowder Plotters' of 1605 and of Robert Carr and his wife Frances in 1616.[24] (As described in Chapter Nine, Ralegh's trial followed his eviction from Durham House, so that parts of it could be granted to Robert Cecil, while the main building later passed to one of James's favourites, the 4th Earl of Pembroke.)

186 John Vanderbank, *Francis Bacon, Viscount St Alban*, c.1731, after a portrait of c.1618 by an unknown artist. © National Portrait Gallery, London (520)

If Egerton's household was deemed 'not great' by Essex's followers, his household ordinances have come to symbolise how much the keeping of state was entrenched with ritual, following what has been described as the 'secularisation of liturgy'.²⁵ This definition seems most appropriate, for ritual was indeed followed in the former monastic properties on the Strand. York House was certainly the most important among its counterparts as the palace of one of the top offices of state. For instance, dining there occurred in the 'place of state', where, as related in the ordinances under 'the Office of a gent[leman] Usher', 'The Lord, who being an Earle or upwards, if he be served in state, he is to have in ye great Chamber a Cloth of State according to his place; under an Earle to the pommell of his Chaire, A Marquess to ye seate of his chaire A Duke wthin a foote of ye grounde'.²⁶ This precise categorisation describes a process whereby protocol and architecture had become so ingrained that every house of rank would need, *de rigueur*, a great chamber with a canopy or *baldacchino*, that 'Cloth of State' which identified the centrality of the space and the liturgical hierarchy, as in Baroque churches. In turn, the great chamber was part of a precise sequence of rooms for the keeping of state, as has been seen throughout this book. At 'diner or supper', Ellesmere continued, the '[Lord] is to have his seate in the middest of ye table a litle above ye salt his face being in ye whole veiwe of ye chamber', while guests of high rank were to be placed at the upper end of the table. As for serving, 'Cupbearers attend their places of their Lord and Ladys service and, when they call for wine or beare, to serve them wth takeing of steps on their knee in humble and dutifull sort'.²⁷ And so it continued, according to a procedure of Byzantine complexity.

Lord Ellesmere, created Viscount Brackley on 7 November 1616, retired from office shortly afterwards and died at York House on 15 March 1617. He was succeeded by Sir Francis Bacon, since 1596 the first Queen's Counsel Extraordinary, probably on Ellesmere's recommendation as they had worked together closely on matters of state and Bacon had become his particular protégé.

The Keepership of Sir Francis Bacon, 1st Viscount St Albans: 1617–1621

While Bacon's keepership of the Great Seal was one of the shortest in history, his link to York House dated back to 1561, when he was born there, as noted earlier.²⁸ Once in charge of the Great Seal, he had eagerly secured a lease of twenty-one years, like previous keepers but with a particular degree of attachment to the old palace, where he intended to spend his old age (fig. 186).²⁹ Hardly anything is known of what Bacon may have done to the palace except that he built an aviary, according to the long entry on him in Aubrey's *Brief Lives*.³⁰ Be that as it may, his sixtieth birthday on 22 January 1621, followed by his creation as Viscount St Albans five days later, was celebrated with a lavish banquet at York House, for which Ben Johnson composed verses beginning: 'Hail happy genius of this Ancient Pile, / How is it all things so about thee Smile?'³¹ That smile, alas, was soon to turn into grievance, for three months later Francis was impeached and his decline begun. The accusation originated in the attack on patents and monopolies (for which Bacon had acted as a legal referee), which disturbed the interests of many, including the king and his chief favourite, George Villiers, the future 1st Duke of Buckingham. As the scapegoat for such grievances, Bacon was fined the enormous sum of £40,000 and sent to the Tower at the king's pleasure, after a controversial admission of bribery. He was also barred from any office or employment in the state and forbidden to sit in Parliament or come within twelve miles of the court.[32] In fact the fine was never collected and his imprisonment lasted only three days, a turn of events again influenced by Buckingham, who managed his capture in order to gain the palace.

This period is characterised by intense correspondence between the king's favourite, who had taken it into his head to covet the exile's Strand palace, and the disgraced Bacon, who could not but still regard him as 'a good master, a good friend, and a good servant'.[33] Buckingham pretended that 'if your Lordship or your Lady find it inconvenient for you to part with the house, I would rather provide myself otherwise than any way incommodate you, but will never slack anything of my affection to do you service'.[34] Beyond the patina of courtly exchanges, the request had none the less been made and there would be no surrendering, even when Bacon asserted that 'no money or value shall make me part with it'. He offered instead Gorhambury House, inherited from his father and since extended, with a water garden featuring a Roman-style banqueting house as its centrepiece. Buckingham, in the meantime, had managed to secure Wallingford House near Whitehall from Lord and Lady Wallingford of the Howard family, negotiated against the creation of Sir Thomas Howard as Viscount Andover, as well as the release of Somerset and his wife. 'Now that I am provided with a house', he thus wrote to Bacon, 'I may no longer hang upon the treaty (…) touching York-house; [on] which I assured your Lordship, I never desired to put you to the least inconvenience.'[35] And so they went on with seemingly friendly correspondence until early 1622, when the remainder of Bacon's lease was given up for £1300 and a promise from Villiers to convince the king to reverse the ban.[36] Indeed, as laconically advised by Edward Sackville, 4th Earl of Dorset (whose Dorset House in Fleet Street Francis Bacon had rented prior to moving back to the Strand), 'if York-house were gone, the town were yours'.[37] As a last act in this cat-and-mouse game, the lessee was not the favourite himself but the new Lord Treasurer, Sir Lionel Cranfield, who replaced the other big casualty of the patents affair, Henry Montagu, 1st Earl of Manchester. As opposed to his active role in both Montague and Bacon's downfalls, Cranfield was no more than a mere name in this transaction. In spite of it all, Bacon then served Villiers in the purchase of New Hall in Essex, acquired from the Earl of Sussex in the autumn of 1622 for £22,000. But Bacon's decline was as fast as the ascent of the favourite. Buckingham's formal possession of York House finally came in May 1624, as the transfer of ownership required an Act of Parliament. The See of York, still the freeholder of the property, was given lands of 'greater profit', as the king remarked to Archbishop Tobias Matthew, noting that 'the house has not for a long time past been used as a bishop's residence'.[38]

The House of George Villiers,
1st Duke of Buckingham: 1622–1628

York House played a crucial role in Tudor and early Jacobean politics but Buckingham's brief ownership brought the house to the fore in architectural competition. It is not simply because this is the period best documented in the palace's history: it is primarily because of George's will to turn it into a residence that would match his extraordinary ambitions.

Another of those accomplished climbers of courtly ladders, George Villiers (1592–1628; fig. 187) had begun life as the anonymous son of a minor gentleman, Sir George Villiers, and his second wife Mary, who, widowed early, had educated him for courtly life. By his coming of age in 1614, the beautiful Villiers had managed to catch the king's eye, notoriously susceptible to the charm of young male courtiers, particularly those whose manners had been refined in France, as in George's case.[39] The time was also ripe for a change of favourite, as the incumbent, Robert Carr, Earl of Somerset, had married into the powerful philo-Catholic Howard family and his growing influence had attracted strong opposition. This concluded in the trial of Carr and his wife in spring 1616, managed by Egerton at York House (as noted earlier), after they had been accused of murdering Sir Thomas Overbury. That was a convoluted affair orchestrated by

187 Peter Paul Rubens, *George Villiers, 1st Duke of Buckingham*, 1625. Pollock House, National Trust. Wikimedia Commons Public Domain

Buckingham's hyperbolic ascent at court was matched by equally swift acquisitions of property in both town and country, the essential counterpart of political prominence and the establishment of a dynasty. In less than ten years, from 1618 to 1625, he gained three country houses: Wanstead House in Essex in 1618, Burley-on-the-Hill, Rutland, in 1621, and New Hall, again in Essex, in 1622, which replaced Wanstead which he had sold in 1619. In addition to lodgings assigned to him at Whitehall in 1616 and at Somerset House in 1619, he then secured the nearby Wallingford House in 1621, soon followed by the purchase of York House, as noted, at his disposal from 1622 though not officially his until 1624. Early in 1625 he also bought the suburban Chelsea House for his mother, who had been made Countess of Buckingham, thereby completing the family transformation. Alongside an increasingly active role as the king's representative, which saw him at Prince Charles's side in the Spanish expedition in 1623, Buckingham carried out extensive refurbishment at three of these properties (Burley, New Hall and York House), while also amassing an astonishing collection of works of art: 'For out of all the amateurs, and Princes and Kings', as Sir Balthasar Gerbier told him in 1625, 'there is not one who has collected in forty years as many pictures as your Excellency has collected in five!'[40] Courtier, diplomat, art adviser, miniaturist, architect and architectural writer, Gerbier (1592–1663) had entered Villiers's service in the mid-1610s as his 'Painter', travelling around Europe to collect on his behalf.[41] As the official Keeper of York House, he also supervised works in the Strand, turning the palace into a private museum of such quality and scale as to rival Arundel's.[42] Given the animosity between the duke and the collector earl, the 'museum' must have been conceived with gusto.[43]

The houses of the Duke of Buckingham have been the subject of a dissertation by Philip McEvansoneya, who has also published a number of related articles.[44] His study of York House is one of those dissertations produced between the 1980s and early 2000s under the supervision of John Newman at the Courtauld Institute of Art, which almost all concentrate on the wider patronage of an individual rather than on specific buildings.[45] What follows is based on a complete re-evaluation of the sources, beginning with Gerbier's correspondence with the duke[46] and includes references to the works at York House in

another notorious resident of the Strand, Lord Henry Howard, 1st Earl of Northampton, the builder of Northampton House next door (see Chapter Eleven). With Carr in the Tower, Villiers rapidly advanced. In 1615 he had been knighted as a Gentleman of the Bedchamber, followed a year later by his appointment as Master of the King's Horses, elevation to the peerage as Baron Whaddon, Viscount Villiers and the investiture of the Garter. In 1617 he was made an earl, then in 1618 Marquess of Buckingham and in 1619 the Admiral of the Fleet and Keeper of Somerset House after the death of Anne of Denmark (see Chapter Three). By 1623, aged thirty-one he had not only reached the highest rank as a duke but was also acting as the king's de facto adopted son, benefiting from privileges that continued under Charles I.

Gerbier's *Brief Discourse Concerning the Three Chief Principles of Magnificent Building*, first published in 1662.[47]

Unlike some of his neighbours', Buckingham's patronage and connoisseurship is thought to have concentrated on painting, not architecture, for his extraordinary collection has dominated studies on him. This, however, was not quite the case for it is certain that he was actively involved at York House. As McEvansoneya pointed out, a letter of 1624 from Sir Henry Wotton, Ambassador at Venice, to Sir Albert Morton, the Secretary of State, begins to shed some light.[48] It informs us of 'plant or ground-lines' and 'the reared work, in perspective with all the dimensions so exactly' of the Villa Farnese at Caprarola which Morton should pass on to the duke, 'as if it please him, he may easily have a model made thereof in pasteboard'.[49] As well as pointing to Buckingham's interest in the subject, one wonders whether it may reveal a wider agenda: perhaps Gerbier was attempting to use his fellow architectural scholar Wotton, whose *Elements of Architecture* had just appeared, to establish the credentials of the Italianate architectural aesthetic with which he was refurbishing the Strand house. The magnificent pentagonal Villa Farnese, a virtuoso semi-fortified palace with two levels of giant orders, had been designed for Cardinal Alessandro Farnese (later Pope Paul III) from 1515 and must have been familiar to Gerbier from his art-purchasing trips to Italy in 1621 and 1623. Whether or not such a reference was intended, the Italian style was still negotiating its way in early seventeenth-century London. In fact, in about 1622 Villiers had already instructed Inigo Jones to alter New Hall 'according to the modern fashion'.[50] Jones's Palladian statement, the Banqueting House, had only just been completed, while instances of a completely classical design, like that of the Porticus for the garden of Salisbury House (see figs 154–7), had remained academic endeavours. Indeed, that palace and Northampton House, the only other built in the Strand in the early 1600s, were essentially traditional in outlook. To a certain extent,

188 Jacob Esselens, 'Westminster and Lambeth from the New Exchange', 1665. Hulton 1959, pl. 28a

189 *opposite, above* Jacob Esselens, 'View of Westminster and the Thames', 1665. Albertina Museum, Vienna

190 *opposite, below* York House, detail of Wenceslaus Hollar, 'view of London extending eastwards from Peterborough House to Somerset House', early 1670s. By permission of the Pepys Library, Magdalene College, Cambridge ('London and Westminster', I, 2972, 34–35)

therefore, Gerbier's work at York House was ground-breaking, as innovative as his choice of pictures for it.[51]

In the absence of plans, Buckingham's changes to York House (by then also called Buckingham House), can be ascertained by comparing Norden's 1593 and 1600 views with Hollar's of the 1630s and 70s and Newcourt's of 1658. In addition, Jacob Esselens's 'View of Westminster and the Thames', both dated 1665, provide a rare insight into the new arrangement and architectural idioms of the house (figs 188 and 189).[52] Norden's 1593 view has already been described (see fig. 183). The main building is essentially the same, if more elaborate, in the 1600 view (see fig. 184), where the side wings no longer appear and the garden towards Durham House, subdivided into small plots in 1593, appears as a long undivided orchard in 1600. Hollar's depictions, by contrast, show a symmetrical and somewhat classical-looking building characterised by a central crenellated wing of fifteen bays, with a loggia on the ground floor and a tall *piano nobile* (fig. 190 and see fig. 15). This is flanked by taller wings slightly projecting out towards the river, which still feature a loggia at ground level but reveal a different window pattern, probably reflecting the hierarchy of the interiors, as will be seen. To the right of the house we can see a mature garden, while the elaborate water gate, off axis from the

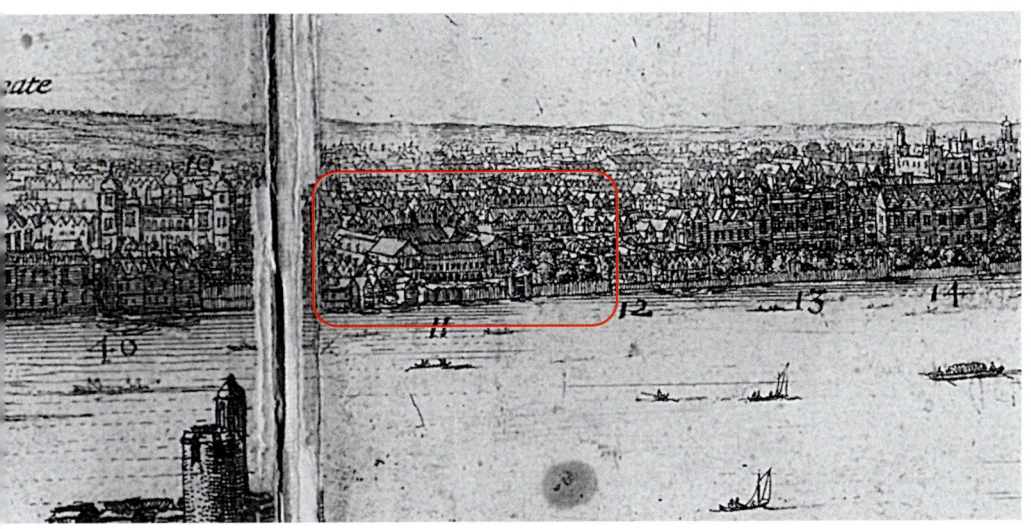

YORK HOUSE | 183

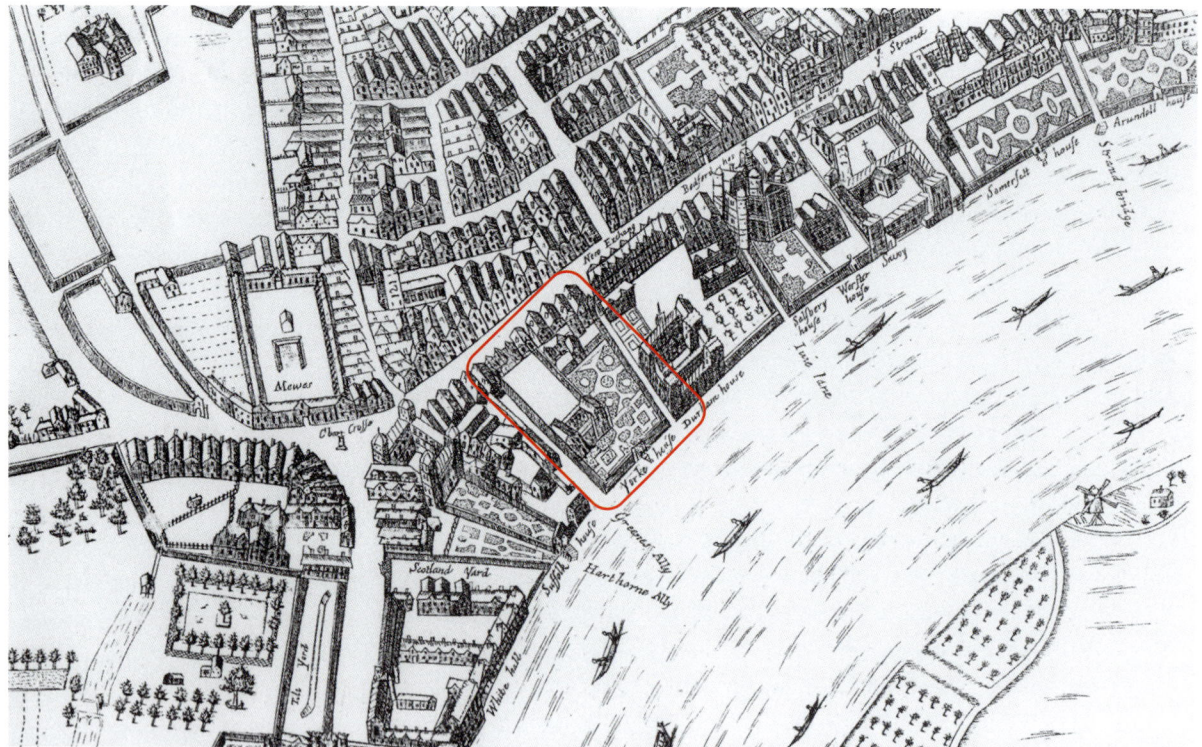

191 York House, detail of Richard Newcourt and William Faithorne, 'An exact delineation of the City of London and Westminster', 1658. By kind permission of the Syndics of Cambridge University Library (Map Room, Maps BB.77.90.14)

main building, stands in the centre of the river wall. Because of Hollar's viewpoint, we cannot clearly distinguish whether the new house had a courtyard arrangement as opposed to a semi-H shape, which in itself would have suggested how much reconstruction had actually taken place. Newcourt's 1658 view (fig. 191) shows the complex from above but is not as revelatory as it might have been due to its incorrect scale and poor representation. That said, the main building appears to be compact and the garden does indeed look highly elaborate.

While the difference between Norden's and Hollar's views is substantial, the evidence from Gerbier and others suggests that changes to the old York House, by then 'ruinous and ready to fall',[53] were swiftly carried out so as to provide Buckingham with an appropriate stage for state entertainment, for otherwise he continued to live at Wallingford House. In so far as comparison with the still-existing water gate's style, grandeur and even position is possible (see fig. 192), the changes have been judged in modern times as a short-term measure before Buckingham could begin work on a projected palace of colossal proportions, of which only that gate, marking the central axis of the new house, was completed before his death in 1628.[54] How promptly the rebuilding proceeded cannot be judged. The non-alignment of the gate, however, may not mean much, for the same happened at a number of other palaces, such as Arundel House or even Somerset House, both subject to piecemeal additions. One also wonders whether the economies of space and financial gain from letting parts of the complex, which had almost invariably dictated development along the Strand, would make a complete eastward reconstruction of York House at all worthwhile. Would it not be more plausible that the new gate simply replaced the old one, located in the middle of the property's waterside since at least the mid-sixteenth century but off-axis with the house because the site was at an angle? Equally, one needs to be cautious when assessing whether or not the much-noted stylistic differences between the gate (whose authorship is controversial) and the house as reworked (on which external evidence is limited to views) necessarily suggest a completely different project. Evidence from Gerbier, on which much of this interpretation relies, is not straightforward, while the information in Villiers's correspondence can be interpreted both ways, as will be discussed shortly.

As previously mentioned, Gerbier appears to have been in charge of all the works. This may seem a peculiarity in so far as the unwritten rules of high courtiers' building works were concerned, according to which materials were not only provided by the monarch but works were supervised by the royal surveyor of the moment (as at Salisbury House). Indeed, while Charles did indeed give Buckingham two thousand tons of Portland stone, Inigo Jones, who was simultaneously employed at New Hall, seems to have had no input at York House or if he did, as discussed later, it was limited to the water gate. Perhaps this is to do with a certain animosity between Jones and Gerbier (or the latter's jealousy as he had long coveted the former's position), who described Jones as 'surprised and abashed' when he visited the house in December 1624.[55] By then, works were fairly advanced, for Gerbier's *Brief Discourse* relates that Buckingham had begun building 'on a Ground before it be Purchased', hence around 1622.[56] Initially, he wrote, there had been 'much daubing and breaking through old rotten decayed Walls', which confirms the poor state of the house lamented by previous owners. This was 'first to make a Ladies Closet on the corner of a Wall where a Butteryses stood, and which was taken away for the Closet, intended only at first for a Closet of ease, and to serve untill the Archbishop of York could be perswaded to accept as good a Seat as that was, in liew of the same'. In May 1620 Villiers had married Lady Katherine Manners, reputedly the richest woman in the realm; she was the only daughter of Francis Manners, 6th Earl of Rutland, and his first wife, Frances Knyvet. Hence the necessity of a new lady's closet in a house which, albeit inhabited by a number of women before, had essentially remained a monastic establishment. But, Gerbier continued, a deal with the archbishop 'could not be so soon compassed, as the Duke of Buckingham had occasion to make use of Rooms, to entertain (according to the Dignity of a prime Minister of State) forreign Princes and Embassadors': that is, he had made full use of the house since the start, hindering progress of both legal and architectural matters, one might deduce. Consequently, 'as on a sudan, all the Butterises that upheld that rotten Wall were thrown down, the Seeling of Roomes supported with Iron bolts, Belconies clapt up in the old Wall, daubed over with finishing Morter, and all this (as the Toadestoole groweth in a night) to serve until a Model for a Solid Building (to stand even with the Street) were made, and to be built of such Stone as the Portico or Water Gate at the Riverside is'.[57] In other words, the house had been hastily consolidated and adapted for its owners before work could start on a new building 'even with Street' (presumably meaning a proper Strand front) and in tune with the more elaborate water gate. Gerbier's description confirms the provisional nature of this intervention, as proposed by previous scholars.

Much more insight into both building progress and Buckingham's involvement at York House (in itself further proof of his interest in architecture) comes from letters of 1624, clearly the year when works were at a climax. The first states that in May 'The duke', albeit 'verie sike still … both in bodie & mynd … was carried to York house to see them build there where he fell in a rage upon the sudden & sayd he would have the house pulled down & built anew after another fashion', perhaps because of the inevitably patchy nature of the works, in spite of the 'great cost'.[58] By June, however, the Earl of Strafford was reporting that

> My Lord of Buckingham returned to court yesternight, much discoloured and lean with Sickness, the Dearness bewixt the Prince and him still continuing, and outwardly all appearing very serene, yea not so much as York-House but goes on passing fast, another corner symmetrical now appearing answearable to that other raised before you went hence, beside a goodly Statue of Stone set out in the Garden before the new Building.[59]

The new 'corner' was probably the one side-wing yet to be completed, while the 'new Building' must be the central part of the house, by then well advanced. Not only does this point at substantial rebuilding but also that it must have been, after all, pleasing enough, for Buckingham was now taking 'great delight in his buildings at York House', as John Chamberlain reported shortly thereafter.[60] The works had no doubt gathered momentum from the king's gift of Portland stone at a cost of £1800, for which a warrant for payment was made on 19 July.[61] By September, the diplomat, politician and later Secretary of State Dudley Carleton reported that building at York House was almost complete but for the front facing the court, which was to be newly built. Might this have followed that 'Model for a Solid Building (to stand even with the Street) … to be built of such Stone as the Portico or Water Gate at the Riverside is'? Surely, the stone was no longer an issue, though Gerbier's account, which of course appeared forty years afterwards, leads us to believe otherwise. What Carleton was referring to appears to have been the north or Strand side of the central wing. If this is the case, the new complex consisted of the two side wings and the central block, which would confirm that York House as rebuilt was indeed H-shaped (on which more later). For that front towards the court Carleton (then in the Netherlands) had sent to England a marble gate which 'would be suitable there' and a chimney-piece, valued at £400, recommending his nephew to deliver them only if the duke 'admire[d] the design'.[62] This must have been the case as by January 1625 the marbles were 'in lighters at York House Stairs'.[63]

By Inigo Jones's visit in December 1624, the new interiors had also nearly been completed, as the 'grand chamber' was being paved and Gerbier had made a model for the somters 'which I have given to M. Olivier that he may send it to your Excellency' – another glimpse into the duke's involvement not just in the building works but in the furnishing of the house.[64] In this he was probably assisted, as at New Hall, by his wife, who 'will be pleased to furnish York House'.[65] 'I believe', Gerbier continued, that 'there is velvet enough to be had in London, and I have taken the size of the apartment; it will contain twelve somters, each of which will have seventeen ells of velvet. I have found so many things to employ me at York House that I could hardly get out of it.'[66] The last relevant reference among Gerbier's protracted letters to the duke is to be found in February 1625, by which date reconstruction must have neared the end: 'I wish your Excellency would decide about the water at York House, for it is time; you must resolve to expend four hundred pounds, and to do the whole with leaden pipes, not earthen ones, which are not so safe'.[67]

Whether for financial considerations or because the duke was actually content with what had been achieved, or possibly both, works seem to have halted after 1625.[68] As previously discussed, Hollar provides the most complete views, depicting a complex which must have gone some way towards fulfilling Gerbier's aspiration for a 'Solid Building', especially when compared with the old York House (see figs 15 and 190). The best glimpse of this attempt is in Esselens's two slightly different representations (see figs 188 and 189).[69] They show the house from the New Exchange, that is, the north-east, whence we can distinguish how the complex was not just a mixture of old and new but its very shape was probably more complicated than the seemingly regular form seen from the river. A tower, possibly containing a staircase, a classical hall, and a simple pitched-roof chapel appear to stand beside the east side wing, as close examination of Hollar's 1670s view shows (see fig. 190). In effect, Esselens's viewpoint would be somewhat unflattering, as it essentially shows a jumble of buildings, were it not for Westminster Hall and Abbey and Jones's Banqueting House in the background. A specific parallel with the latter, of which the York hall might seem designed by an amateur (although Esselens depicts the Banqueting House inaccurately), was indeed drawn by Gerbier when discussing the proportions of a 'Banquet Room' in his *Brief Discourse*. He maintained that 'as much as could be represented (as to Sceans) in the great Banqueting Room of Whitehall' had

been seen by the king 'close to the Gate at York House, in a Roome not above 35 foot Square' in 1628.[70] It was a five-bay, elevated building of two and a half storeys, with pedimented windows on the main floor surmounted by oculi and a central door flanked by giant pilasters (or three-quarter columns), repeated at the ends but not in between windows. The attic storey was framed by an order of fairly plain pilasters. One tends to attribute this amateurish appearance to Gerbier's supervision of the works, as also suggested by Vertue.[71] Both tower and chapel, in contrast, are

192 The York House water gate, *c*.1626. Photograph © Rowan Freeland

193 Thomas Wijck, view of Westminster and the York House water gate from the banks of the Thames, 1676. Gater and Godfrey 1937, pl. 30a

so strikingly different from the 'Banquet Room' that they were probably relics of the old house.

Another important piece of information gathered from Esselens is the presence of an elaborate series of garden walks and terraces adapted to the different levels of the site, descending from the Strand to the Thames. These enclose a geometric garden surrounding the house, seen also in Newcourt's 1658 depiction (see fig. 191), balanced by a wilder meadow towards its eastern boundary. Behind those trees the back of the water gate is clearly distinguishable, to which I now turn.

The water gate stands out as a powerful essay in using the motif of the triumphal arch (fig. 192). Crucial differences between the hall and this gate are that the latter still stands and a number of contemporary or near-contemporary drawings of it still exist, not just the topographical views. Its form is tripartite, with a central archway and two arched openings onto a terrace towards the river, one arch either side and three archways at the back. As the most important, its river front is the most elaborate, both in treatment and insignia: banded and rusticated three-quarter columns and backgrounds decorate the facades and an escutcheon is proudly placed in a broken arched pediment crowned by a scallop shell, a leitmotif on the gate that refers to Buckingham's position as Lord High Admiral. A lion and lioness couchant, holding further emblems of the Fleet, complete the composition like classical acroteria: the gate acted as a temple celebrating its owner. As depicted in several views (for example, Thomas Wijck's of 1676; fig. 193), it stood on a platform, preceded by a balustraded terrace up from the water stairs. Facing the house, by contrast, Villiers's motto, *Fidei Coticula Crux* ('the Cross is the touchstone of faith'), carved in the frieze would have saluted those going out, some of whom may have wondered about the relationship between this rather severe dictum and the extravagance of its owner.

The authorship of this theatrical piece has been widely debated by scholars. In the 1660s, Charles Stoke (or Stokes) attributed it to his great-uncle Nicholas Stone, Jones's sculptor at the Banqueting House and an architect in his own right from 1630. Colen Campbell, in his 1717 *Vitruvius Britannicus*, states that the gate had been erected in 1626 by Inigo Jones. Summerson ascribed it to Gerbier in 1963, reaffirmed by Colvin in 1978 on the basis of the well-known connection between the water gate and the Fontaine Médicis of c.1630 in Paris, as summarised by John Harris in 1989.[72] After re-examining that evidence and the plan, river and side elevations of 1641 by John Webb (figs 194 and 195), Harris affirmed Jones as the architect.[73] Colvin's last edition of the *Dictionary* (2008), however, kept the water gate among the unresolved attributions to both Jones and Stone.[74] They may well have shared the task, given their working relationship. This is substantiated by Gordon Higgott who, in his online catalogue of English Baroque drawings at Sir John Soane's Museum, London, examined with Adam White what Colvin described as 'the only surviving original drawing' for the structure (fig. 196).[75] This drawing is an incomplete proposal for the river front of the gate, which they convincingly attribute to Stone while granting Jones a role in revising the design for its execution. After all, Jones had already designed gates and a coffered ceiling for the Duke of Buckingham's New Hall in 1623. After comparing Gerbier's

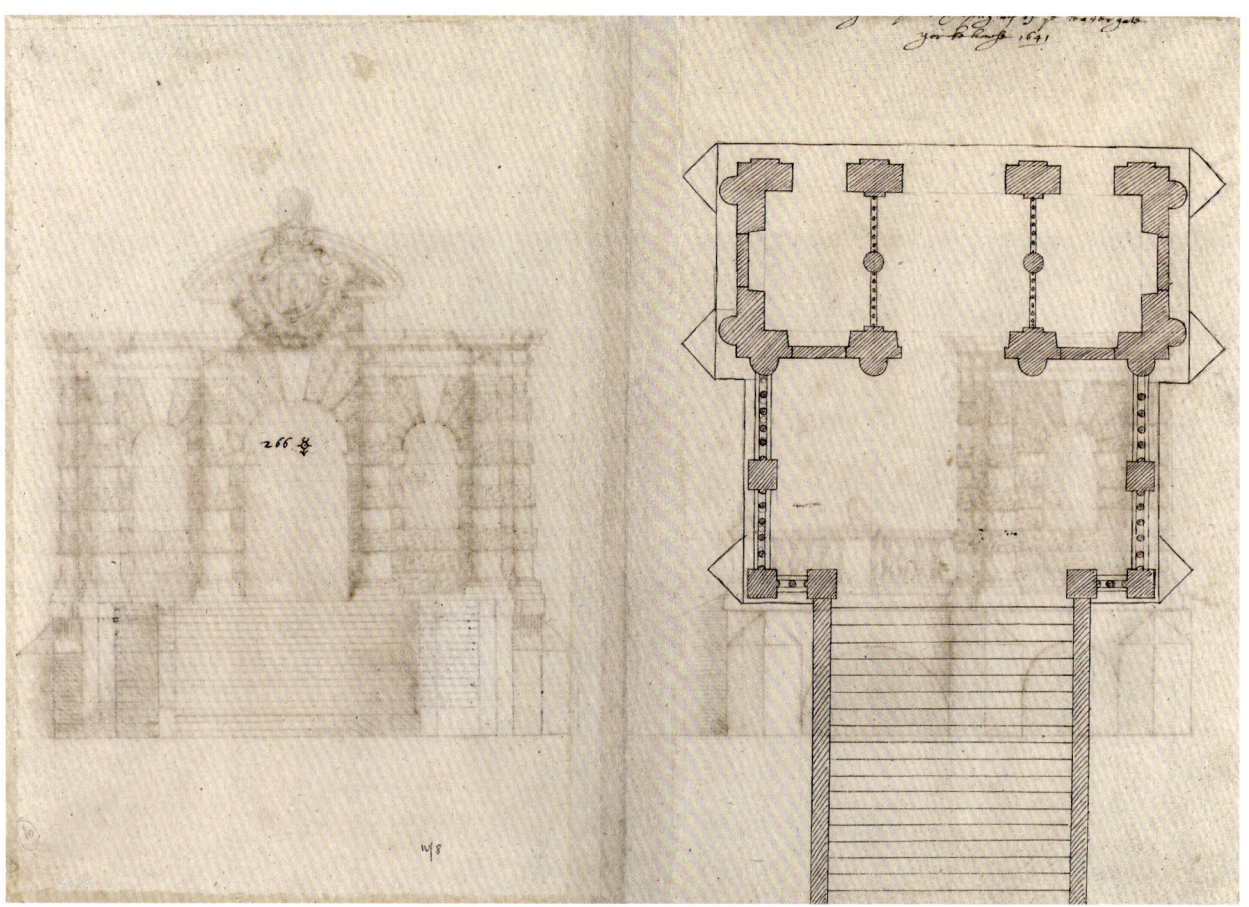

194 John Webb, survey plan of the York House water gate, 1641. RIBA Collections (84046)

195 John Webb, survey elevations of the York House water gate, 1641. RIBA Collections (22922)

196 Nicholas Stone, preparatory design for the York House water gate, c.1626–7. © Sir John Soane's Museum, London (vol. 148, no. 45, Fauntleroy Pennant, vol. III, fol. 64)

authenticated design for another gateway of c.1660, they exclude him, certainly as far as the drawing is concerned, noting that Gerbier never claimed that gate for himself when boasting of his works in the *Brief Discourse*.[76] He would not necessarily have boasted, however, for his *Discourse* only indirectly touches on authorship, let alone providing a clear chronology. In fact the date of the gate is also difficult to pin down. Gerbier stated that King Charles visited the York Banqueting Hall in 1628, remarking on its proximity to the water gate, thus attesting to its existence.[77] Campbell gave the year 1626, while Higgott and Adam's date for Stone's elevation is c.1626–7.

To turn to the contents of York House, its main rooms and Buckingham's extraordinary collection can be ascertained by analysing a probate inventory of 1635 and other miscellaneous sources. The inventory is a schedule of indenture of the Duke of Buckingham's property in the Strand and at Chelsea House, drawn up to secure the contents to the 2nd Duke, then aged seven, after his mother had remarried that year. (One of his two trustees was Philip Herbert, 4th Earl of Pembroke, just one of their connections; see Chapter Nine.) Although the inventory is arranged by room, it is not comprehensive because it lists only those rooms with, as its title indicates, 'Hangings of Arras Tapistry and other Hangings, Plate Jewells, Agatts, Pictures, Statues Household Stuffe, Goods, Chattells, Rings and other things'.[78] It thus illustrates only part of the interiors, albeit the most lavish, which makes it difficult to determine the exact arrangement (or provide reconstruction drawings). The appraisers must have omitted any room that did not fit their remit for the indenture. That said, the general location of most of the twenty rooms listed at York House can be identified.

The inventory begins with the 'Hall', where two paintings but no furniture were recorded. This could be the old hall of the house or the 'Banquet Room' or Banqueting Hall on its east side (see figs 188 and 189). The next entry is marked 'in the comeing in above', pointing at the possibility that the 'Hall' had an upper gallery, as twenty-two paintings but no furniture were recorded there. The 'Great Chamber' came next, with again twenty-two paintings including 'A great peice for the Ceiling of my Lords Closett' by Rubens, identified as the *Apotheosis of the Duke of Buckingham* later at Osterley, Middlesex, where it was inserted in the staircase ceiling by Robert Adam.[79] Its own ceiling featured the 'Nine Muses' by Orazio Gentileschi, by whom five more pictures hung in the duke's Withdrawing Room.[80] The Great Chamber had 'Two great Brasse Andirons' and 'Seaventeen Guilt Stooles and 4 Christall Candlesticks', while its floor, mentioned by Gerbier in the letter of 2 December 1624, was probably of marble.[81] This suggestion finds a possible reference in a poem entitled 'Upon some pieces of work in York House', attributed to William Lewis, Provost of Oriel College, Oxford, and published in 1656. It is a eulogy of Buckingham's 'large Gallery' and perhaps the Great Chamber, as towards the end one reads: 'Open the door and let my eyes come in, / A place that would entice a Saint to sin; / Almost too dear for a man to tread upon, / A floor all diapered with Marble stone'.[82] The question here is where the Great Chamber was situated and at which level, for McEvansoneya's suggestion that it was the new Banqueting Hall on account of its content is not actually supported by the inventory of York House.[83] Nevertheless, the poem does seem to refer to a room directly accessed from the garden, as it comes right after a description of the statuary there. In addition, the next entry is the 'Vaulted Roome', with ten paintings, which McEvansoneya rightly associated with Gerbier's statement in the *Brief Discourse* that 'first Stories ought rather to be vaulted than boarded, to prevent such accident as happened to Lewis 13th French King, (and his Queen at a Ball,) when the Floore of the Roome (with all the Company) fell down'.[84] Clearly, the vaults, or vaulted ceilings, belonged to ground-floor rooms in order to support those above, which would have had flat wooden ceilings (or false vaults) – the higher the building the lighter the structure. If one allows a direct sequence between the Great Chamber and the Vaulted Room (not a certainty given the nature of the inventory) and if Gerbier's 'paved' in relation to the 'Grand Chamber' refers to a solid material like marble, then that chamber might indeed have been the 'Banquet Room'. This suggests that a number of state apartments were located on the ground or raised floor, given the slope down to the Thames, as clearly depicted by Esselens (see figs 188 and 189). Further reference to 'vaulted apartments' is to be found in the memoir of the French ambassador, Bassompierre, who remarked that they contained 'five different collations [*sic*]' in November 1626, when he joined the king and queen at a supper at York House, which he judged 'extremely fine, and … the most richly fitted up than any other I saw'.[85]

Next in the list is the 'Sumpter Roome', which included fourteen paintings and no furniture, while the following, the 'Passage by my Ladyes Closett', had twenty-seven paintings and 'Two Guilt Stooles'. This must have been a relatively important passage, as on its walls hung the highest concentration of works by Rubens, 12, as opposed to 10 in the Great Chamber, out of 32 in the collection. Unsurprisingly, this space marks the separation between the state apartments and the king's own, to which it must have led, for the next three entries are marked: 'In the next Chamber to the King's withdrawing Chamber', with 12 paintings and 'Two Andirons and 4 Brasse Candlesticks'; 'In the Roome Call'd the King's Bedchambr.', with 13 paintings, 'hung wth. Green Embroider'd Velvett' and filled with tapestries and furniture which matched that decor, beginning with an elaborate French bed; and the 'Withdrawing Chamber next the King's Bed-Chamber', where the lack of paintings was balanced by an extremely lavish display of 'Crimson Velvet being Lac'd wth Gold and Silver' hung on its walls, and by 11 matching chairs among other precious objects. The next room is 'my Lord's Closett', with 25 paintings, 2 marble tables and other small objects, which separated the king's apartments from the duke's own. With the Rubens ceiling celebrating Buckingham in the Temple of Fame and Titian's *Ecce Homo* (fig. 197) among the paintings, this was much more than a simple closet. Indeed, as Mark Girouard has pointed out, 'it was not only a "cabinet de marbre" as at New Hall, but a "grand cabinet", designed for display, rather than retirement or study'. The

197 Titian, *Ecce Homo*, 1543, once 'In the Sumpter Room' at York House. Kunsthistorisches Museum, Vienna. © KHM-Museumsverband

marble closet at Bolsover is probably derived from this, while the source may well have come from the Continent via Gerbier.[86]

Between the king's and duke's apartments, as a mediating element – perhaps not just architecturally between James and the Favourite – was the Long Gallery, the next entry in the list. This room, probably facing the Thames, must have run the length of the first floor (from the river) in the central wing, seen in Hollar's views (see figs 15 and 190). It features 61 paintings, fewer than the 70 in 'my Ladyes Redd Closett' but the most impressive given that those in the duchess's closet were small works. The Long Gallery clearly caught Lewis's attention, as his poem begins thus: 'View this large Gallery faced with mats and / Is it not purer that Joves milky way? / Which should he know, mortals might justly fear say, / He would forsake his Heaven and sojourne here'.[87] The Gallery also featured 'An Organ & Harpsichord', 'Seven Italian Painted Chestes' and 'Twenty five Guilded Stooles'.[88] Proximity to the Gallery of both the king's and duke's private sets indicates that those rooms were located on the same floor, as one would expect. Each was probably in one of the side wings, as was customary in houses arranged to provide for royal visits.[89] James's must have been in the east wing, given its closeness to the Great Chamber, while George's lay in the west wing, arguably nearer to Whitehall and the king. The difference in height and elevations of those wings, as noted in Hollar's depictions, clearly reflected the status of their occupants. Buckingham's apartments consisted of four rooms, listed as the 'Dressing Roome', 'my Lords Bed Chamber', the 'Little Dressing Roome' and the 'Withdrawing Roome', each filled with paintings totalling forty-five but none furnished: the duke had been dead for seven years by the time the inventory was drawn up in 1635 and the set must either have been emptied or deliberately not appraised for the purpose of this indenture.

198 J. M. W. Turner, *York House Water-Gate, Westminster, with York Buildings Waterworks*, 1794–5. © Tate, London (D00684)

The following entry reads 'Upper Roomes', with only three paintings, attesting to another change of level, perhaps the garrets, while the next is the 'Vault', which may possibly be a storage space in the basement, where four paintings were registered. The last three rooms in the list are 'my Ladyes Redd Closett' with its concentration of 70 paintings and 3 ivory statues, 'my Ladyes Green Closett' with 19 paintings together with ivory, marble, gold and brass pieces among other objects and the 'Upper Closett' with 7 paintings. The duchess's set of rooms appears incomplete as there is no record of a bedroom or withdrawing room but, again, the inventory was partial.

What is clear from the inventory is that York House alone held a staggering number of paintings, believed to approach 400, including 22 Titians, 21 Bassanos (father and son), 17 Tintorettos, 16 Veroneses, 10 Palmas, 2 Leonardos, 2 Raphaels, one Michelangelo, 11 del Sartos, 5 Gentileschis and 32 Rubenses, among other celebrated artists.[90] Quite a few of those came from the collection of Rubens himself, who became a protégé of the duke, as did Gentileschi, who also kept lodgings at York House, like Gerbier.[91] Rubens had stayed at York House as a guest of Gerbier when he visited London in 1629–30 and Gerbier later supervised the importing and installing of the artist's paintings for the Whitehall Banqueting House in 1635–8.[92] Sculpture, in contrast, featured predominantly at Chelsea House where about a hundred pieces were recorded. One exception originally held at York House was Giambologna's celebrated *Cain and Abel*, now known as *Samson and the Philistine*, which Charles had received from the Spanish embassy and later donated to Buckingham.[93] It stood in the garden in front of the Long Gallery, with a Venus 'Under a tree whose arms were wide displayed / And broidered with blossoms', as recited by Lewis.[94] Overall, both paintings and furniture made for an astonishing display of

Italianate, French and Dutch interiors, unrivalled in paintings even by those of the great collector in the Strand, the Earl of Arundel. While Arundel's galleries provided the model for Buckingham, he was soon outdoing his rival: he even rejected Arundel's unheard-of offer of £7000 for a single painting by Titian, the *Ecce Homo* (see fig. 197), which Gerbier had bought for the duke for the already dear £275.[95] It was this painting that made Inigo Jones go down on his knees when he saw it at York House in December 1624.

Subsequent Years: 1628–1674

George Villiers was stabbed to death on 23 August 1628 at the Greyhound Pub in Portsmouth, where he had gone to organise yet another of the ill-fated military campaigns that had sealed a decline as swift as his ascent. The perpetrator was one of his army officers, John Felton, who became a hero, such was the unpopularity of the duke. His death put an end to whatever further development of York House there might have been and was followed by a period of no architectural interest and of neglect: in 1655 John Evelyn described the house and garden as 'much ruined'.[96] Buckingham was succeeded by his son, George (1628–1687), not yet seven months old, and the use of the Strand palace was left to his wife for life. It was she who tried to remove both Gentileschi and Gerbier from their lodgings on the east side of the gatehouse, 'for want whereof'; as she wrote in 1631, she was 'constrained to keep a family at Chelsea to look after her laundry'.[97] This indicates that even in such a big complex pressure on space was paramount, not least as most of the ancillary dwellings by the main house were let. The duchess remarried in 1635 and continued to live in the various Buckingham houses. Her new husband, Randall MacDonnell, 2nd Earl and 1st Marquess of Antrim, supported the Royalist cause in the Civil Wars and York House, which he held during his wife's lifetime, was sequestrated. The 2nd Duke regained possession for only two years, as the seizure was not fully revoked until October 1647 and the duchess died in October 1649.

From 1640 York House was rented by Algernon Percy, 10th Earl of Northumberland, while he was transforming his newly acquired Strand palace, the neighbouring Northumberland House (see Chapter Eleven).[98] Northumberland did little architecturally at York House, as his accounts document.[99] Instead, he was active in preserving its content, particularly the paintings, some of which ended up in his own collection.[100] In 1648, when the earl eventually moved next door, sixteen chests of pictures were sent to Holland, where the 2nd Duke of Buckingham escaped after renewed involvement in the Civil Wars.[101] York House was again sequestrated and granted to Fairfax for his services to Parliament. Buckingham, however, through a coup which would have pleased his father, returned to England in 1657 and managed to marry Fairfax's only daughter, Mary, thereby regaining the Strand palace. There he was allowed to live in confinement, as other more illustrious courtiers before him. His properties were fully restored by Charles II in 1662, after which the duke resumed his father's habit of living at Wallingford House, using the grander and impractical York House for ceremonial occasions.

In the 1670s the palace was rented in succession by the Spanish, Russian, Danish, French and Portuguese ambassadors for a substantial £450 per annum, but the maintenance of such a large and by then dilapidated place proved trying even for a man reputed to be the richest in the country. After all, as Gerbier had caustically noted in 1662, it was 'on a Moorish ground, whereon no New Building could stand any time without proppings which was contrary to the main Principle of good Building'.[102] A 'Pallace, like Cardinal Wolseyes ill-placed one (now called Whitehall) on a low ground by the Riverside', he continued, 'makes work for Physicttins, Apothecaries, Surgeons, Coffin and Gravemakers', summarising what one of York House's longest residents, Lord Chancellor Egerton, had often complained about.[103] Fashionable London had also moved westwards, making the Strand increasingly undesirable. Consequently, the 2nd Duke followed the redevelopment trend and divided his property into separate plots to be sold or leased to developers. Among those, Sir Philip Matthews, Matthias Bowman and Sir Anthony Dean appear to have purchased the largest shares, while Edward Christian was responsible for the erection of a large number of houses. By 1674, new streets were laid out, called after their most famous owner, George Villiers, 1st Duke of Buckingham.[104] The water gate was spared demolition and became part of a terraced walk depicted by a number of artists including Turner (fig. 198), until the creation of the Victoria Embankment from 1865, which retired it in earnest.[105]

199 Reconstruction of the elevation of the Strand front (north) of Northumberland House as originally built, with conjectural inscription on the roofline (detail of fig. 216)

11 · NORTHUMBERLAND HOUSE

NORTHUMBERLAND HOUSE IS THE WESTernmost of the Strand palaces, one of the last to be erected and the last to disappear, with a history that spans nearly three centuries. The many transformations it underwent illustrate the development of taste alongside the establishment of a British school of architecture, from the extravagant Jacobean of the original design (see fig. 16) to the grand Italian neo-Renaissance of the nineteenth century. Northumberland House has been extensively studied; while concentrating on the seventeenth century I shall also revisit the relevant parts of my previous work on this palace.[1]

Two great builders constructed the complex within a few decades: Henry Howard, 1st Earl of Northampton, who erected it from scratch between 1605 and 1614, and Algernon Percy, 10th Earl of Northumberland, who completely transformed it in the 1640s and '50s.

The House of Henry Howard, 1st Earl of Northampton: 1605–1614

'Sic transit gloria mundi', commented John Chamberlain on 9 June 1614, when the dying Northampton was rushed back to the Strand from Greenwich with a train of more than forty horses.[2] Six days later he had passed away, aged seventy-four, surrounded by tapestries, paintings and furniture which he had bought with extravagant liberality. His household goods and silver, gilt plate and jewels amounted to £8150, nearly half of what Algernon Percy paid in the 1640s to acquire the whole of Northampton House.[3]

Henry Howard (fig. 200) was the second son of the poet Henry Howard, Earl of Surrey, and was the younger brother of Thomas Howard, 4th Duke of Norfolk. He was born in 1540 at the zenith of his family's power but spent most of his adult life in the shadow of disgrace following his grandfather's imprisonment and both his father's and brother's executions in 1547 and 1572.[4] Norfolk had been plotting in favour of Mary Queen of Scots, while Henry himself was suspected of actively corresponding with her, even perhaps to become her husband.[5] His allegiance to Roman Catholicism, moreover, led to his imprisonment on five occasions, even though it was rumoured in 1570 that the influential See of York might fall to him.[6] Had that happened, he would have gained control of York House and the pages of this book would have told a different story.

200 Follower of H. Custodis, *Henry Howard*, 1594. Courtesy of the Mercers' Company, London

The Latin inscription underneath a small red or orange flower (a carnation?) to the left reads: 'Vt flosutus niue sic senectue iuventus' [or more probably 'Ut flosulus nive senectue inventus'], which can be translated: 'as snow is to small flowers so age is to youth'. Just as small flowers wilt under the weight of the snow, at 54 years of age Howard may be lamenting the loss of his youthful promise under the burdens and hardships of life.

'Inter Nobiles Literatissimus', the most learned among his peers, Howard was the only one to have studied at both Oxford and Cambridge (of the former he was High Steward, of the latter Chancellor); his body of writings, considered second only to Sir Francis Bacon's, was aimed at reinforcing his position at court.[7] That improved with the emergence of his cousin, Robert Devereux, 2nd Earl of Essex as Elizabeth's favourite but it was only after the accession of James VI of Scotland to the throne of England in 1603 that Howard's political career flourished. The king, grateful to him for having secured his succession, restored his properties and position and made him one of his most important ministers. This was followed by an accolade of titles and positions, from Constable of Dover Castle and Lord Warden of the Cinque Ports, to joint commissioner for the office of Earl Marshal, culminating in his creation as Baron of Marnhull and Earl of Northampton in 1604. A year later, he was installed as a Knight of the Garter, just after being made the Steward of Greenwich Park.

I have discussed elsewhere the contemporary perception of Henry Howard and how his building activities, at the Strand house, Greenwich Lodge, Audley End in Essex and Trinity Hospital at Greenwich, can be assessed against an obsession with self-representation and lineage, all in an age increasingly dominated by a new entrepreneurial elite. I have also expanded on his rivalry with the Cecils, particularly Sir Robert (whose uncontested position of Secretary of State was second to none among the council and courtiers), by way of comparing their architectural patronage. In effect, while the Cecils' houses combined stood unrivalled, not only did Howard's palace in the Strand recall great houses such as Hardwick but its scale was also such that its courtyard alone could have contained the whole of Salisbury House (see Chapter Eight).[8]

As soon as his restored position allowed it, Howard began amassing properties in the parish of St Martin-in-the-Fields, focusing on what was arguably the closest area to Whitehall. This extended south towards the Thames and was bounded by Charing Cross on the north, York House on the east and Scotland Yard on the west. In 1600, as Norden's map shows (fig. 201), the site consisted of different properties with buildings and gardens of various sizes, together with some land which had partly belonged to a monastic order.

The first indenture, dated 1 October 1605, was made between Henry and the family of Sir William Cooke, who appeared to have held several properties in the area from the mid-1500s. The earl paid £1500 for a large house with all its premises adjoining Scotland Yard on the Charing Cross side: its northern boundary was the Strand, the 'highe Streete there Leadinge from London towards westminster', while its east and west boundaries were two tenements in the tenure of Robert Scott and Richard Reed respectively.[9] A few months later, on 2 January 1606, he secured the whole of Scott's property for a further £1350. This included a house with its gardens and premises known as the 'Crosse Keys', together with five other dwellings and their respective yards and gardens.[10] The Cross Keys was an inn which appears in several contracts from at least 1572, a reminder of the old character of the Strand, lined with small tenements and inns of various sizes. As has been seen, these were retained whenever possible by their new landlords because of their profitable rental value. Northampton, however, was too eager to show off as much of his new palace as possible to hide it behind a mundane row of existing houses, whatever their worth. The site was also considerably narrower than its neighbour's, too narrow to allow an alternative to full clearance, despite continuing efforts to obtain more space: in 1606 he secured further leases of neighbouring dwellings and in 1608 he bought from Richard Cox three chambers or rooms with a parcel of ground 'of 12 foot Square', formerly part of a house known as St Mary Rounceval 'otherwise

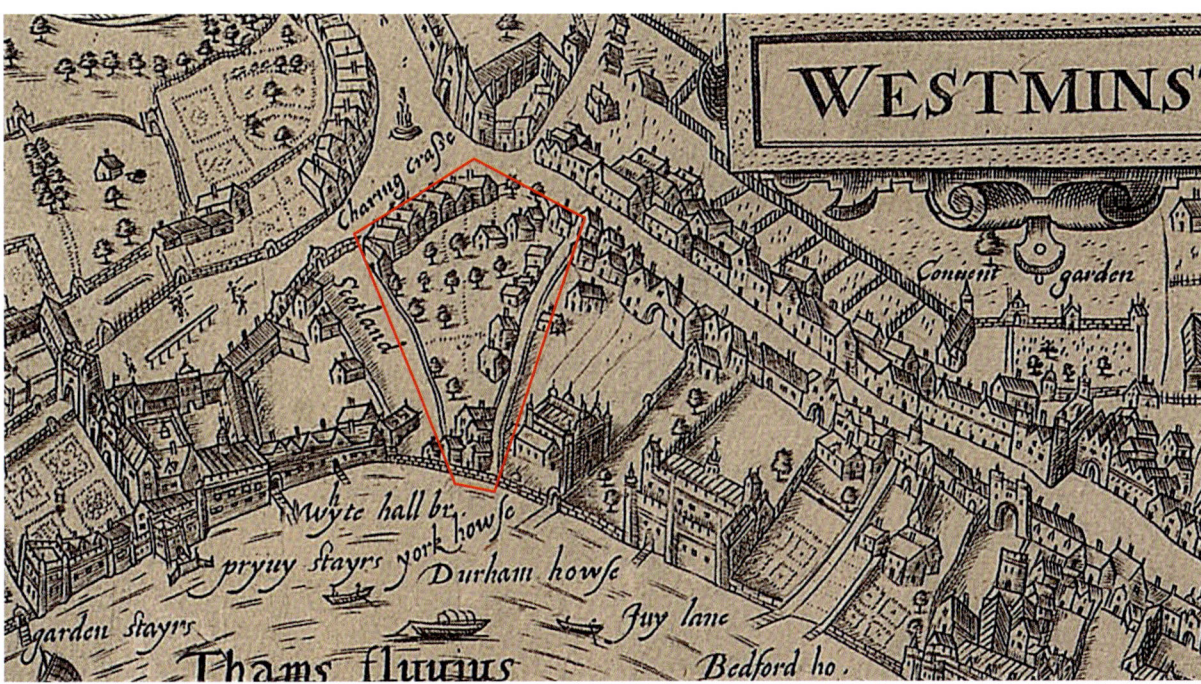

201 The site of Northampton House, detail of John Norden, *Civitas Londini*, 1600. National Library of Sweden

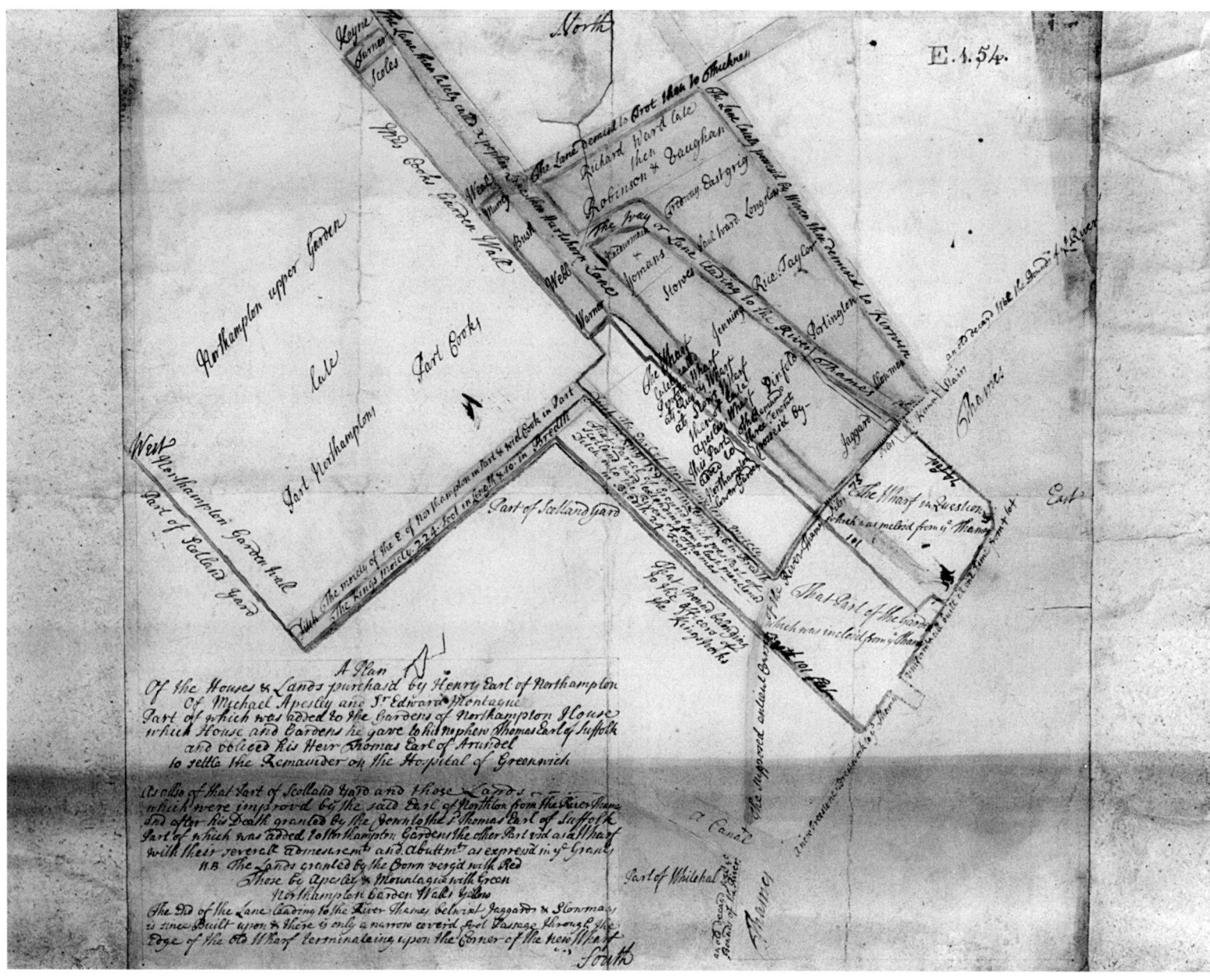

called the Angell'.[11] This belonged to the old Hospital of Roncesvalle, established by a foreign monastic house at Charing Cross, recorded since at least the thirteenth century, which had passed to secular ownership after the Dissolution.[12]

These acquisitions from 1605 to 1608 – eight tenements of different sizes with their premises – provided the site for the erection of Howard's new house, which must have been well under way by about 1608, for a year later it was recorded as the western boundary of the properties of Robert Reed, which Henry was about to acquire. The purchase deed, dated 6 June 1609, secured three further tenements with their shops and premises, two garden plots of considerable size and other connected properties 'adjoin[ing] next unto the house of the said Earle called North[ampt]on house near Charing Cross'.[13] Howard had thus managed to buy nearly everything that bounded his original acquisitions of 1605, with a substantial final disbursement, for he later claimed to be 'eaten up by debts incurred in building his new house'.[14]

The 1609 acquisition and further purchases in 1611 were connected to the enlargement of the garden, only the south-east end of which had a view of the river. This is evident from the earliest available plan of the property, produced by John Hutchinson in 1706 to indicate the 'Houses & Lanes purchas'd by Henry Earl of Northampton' (fig. 202), which shows that the main or 'upper Garden' was connected

202 John Hutchinson, 'Houses & Lanes purchas'd by Henry Earl of Northampton' by 1611, plan, 1706. Northumberland House would have been in the top left corner. Alnwick Castle, Sy: B.XV.1.d/3. Collection of the Duke of Northumberland

203 John Smythson, survey of the ground floor of Northampton House, c.1609. RIBA Collections (29112)

198 | LONDON'S 'GOLDEN MILE'

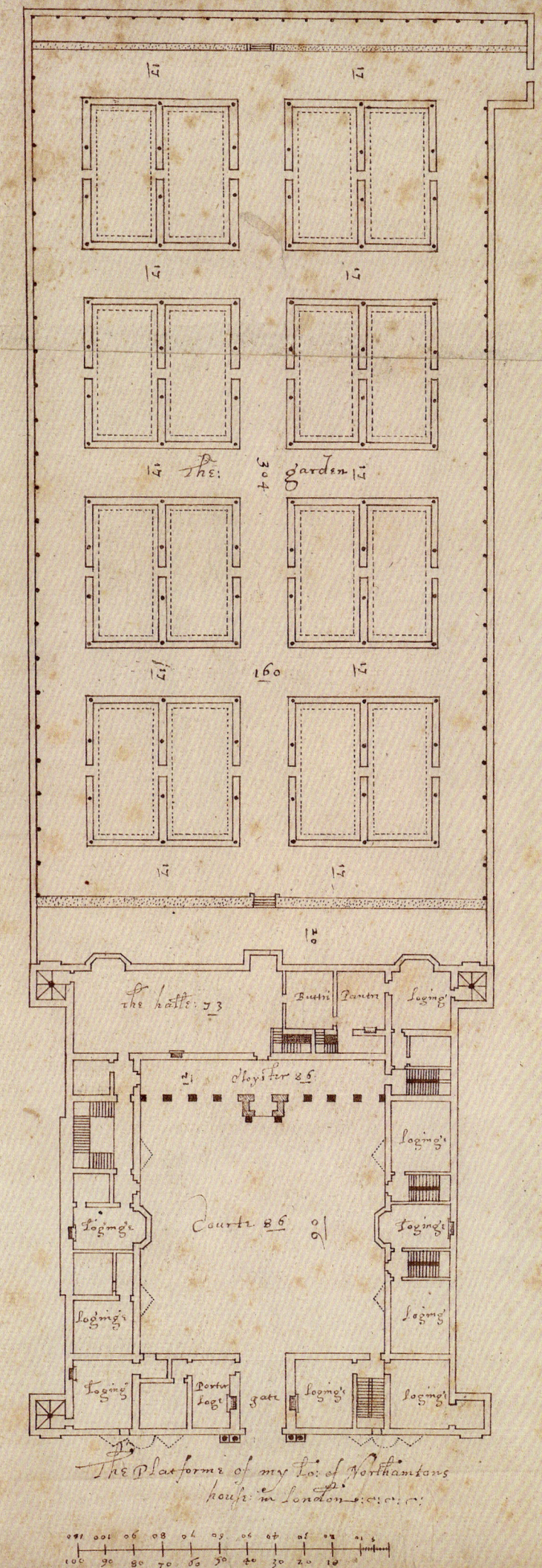

to a large rectangular addition overlooking the Thames, with a water gate towards its western corner.[15] The last purchase to be made by the Earl of Northampton is dated 6 July 1611 and was made through Robert Brett, a close ally and later witness to his will. It secured a portion of the 'Chappell of S.t Mary Rouncevall', which lay to the north-east of the garden wall of the newly built house and included further grounds.[16]

By around 1611, Northampton House had largely reached its final form, extending from Charing Cross towards the Thames, with an enclosed garden about 375 feet long. Its layout and plans are known from those by John Smythson and John Thorpe, while there exists a drawing of the Strand facade as built and one of its near-original south-west front with a layout of adjoining tenements, made in 1717 (figs 203–7). The house was also depicted in the canonical London views, that is Wenceslaus Hollar's in the 1640s and 1670s, Richard Newcourt and William Faithorne's in 1658 and William Morgan's in 1682 (figs 208–10 and see fig. 16).

Smythson's scaled survey depicts the ground floor as completed in around 1609 (fig. 203).[17] It was an almost perfect square of 162 feet, obtained by the introduction of corner turrets which made both north and south fronts equal the length of the side wings. Similarly, the courtyard was almost a square, 86 by 90 feet, with a loggia and central projection that not only marked the main entrance to the house but also contributed to the perception of a perfect square. These proportions attracted Inigo Jones, who included the house's court in a group of those of royal palaces (Windsor, Theobalds and Hampton Court) which he measured.[18] By the date of his first note, December 1619, Jones was rebuilding the Banqueting House, while the possibility of a great design for Whitehall Palace may indicate why he was establishing the dimensions of a typical royal court.[19] This, in turn, would have been the contemporary perception of Northampton House, well in tune with its builder's intentions. It followed a conventional arrangement, with the Hall (shown without a screen) asymmetrically placed on the south-east side of the building, followed by the standard set of service rooms on its south-west side.[20] Those rooms were flanked by two small staircases which led to the Kitchen and its ancillary spaces in the basement, given the southward slope of the site. The river front had a terrace at basement level the width of the

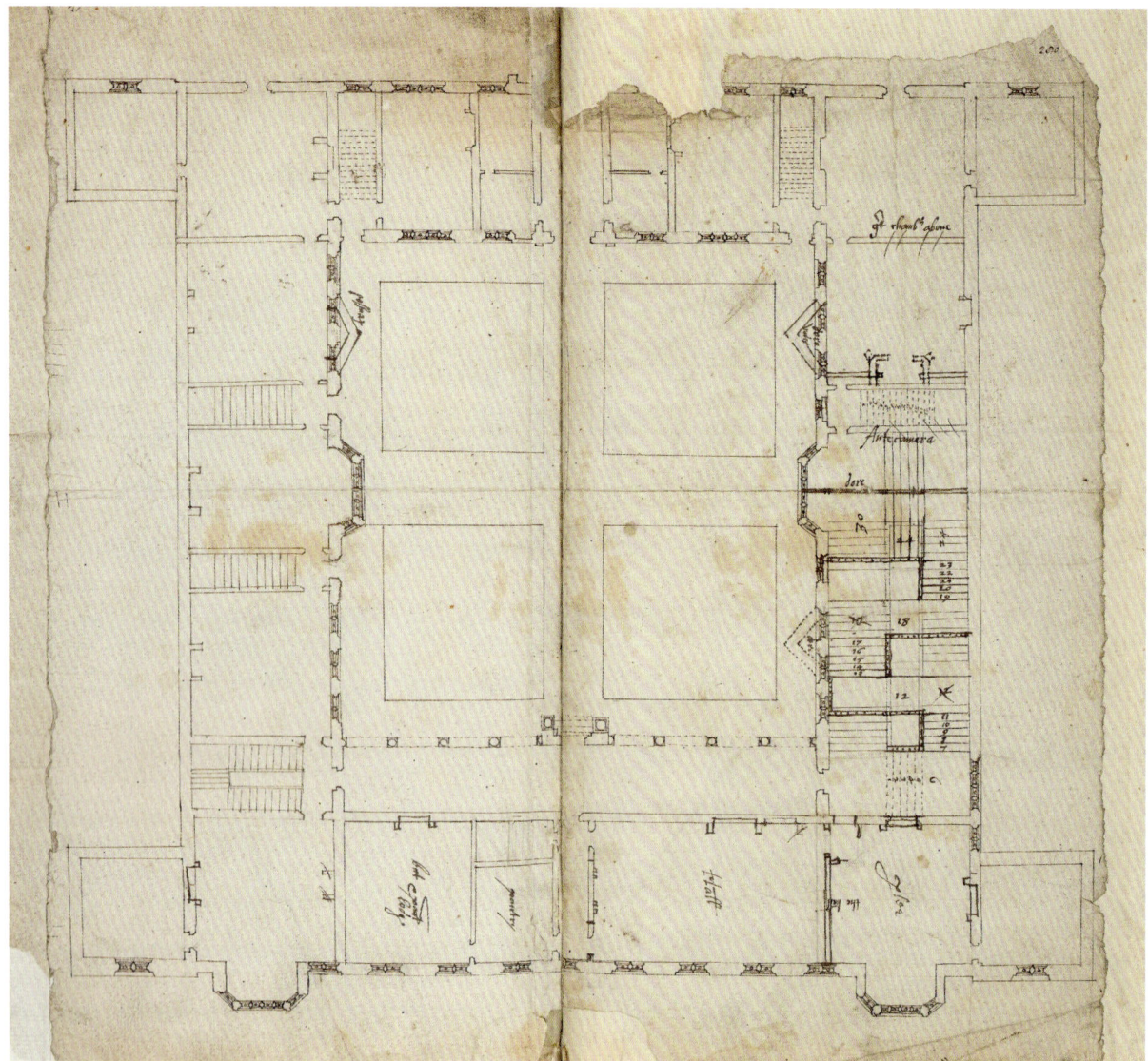

204 John Thorpe, survey of the ground floor of Northampton House, *c.*1614, with the Strand on the north (bottom), the garden on the south (top). © Sir John Soane's Museum, London (vol. 101, fols 279 and 280)

house, preceded by an arcaded loggia like at most of the Strand palaces. An elaborate formal garden extending 318 feet towards the Thames followed. It was accessed through the staircases in the turrets and, perhaps, by way of the basement, if the great staircase of three flights in the east wing went down to this floor (as at Hatfield House, for instance). The east and west wings contained lodgings and a series of staircases that led to the upper floors, while the Strand front on the north included the porters' lodge and one more lodging connected to a further staircase.

John Thorpe's working surveys, made no later than 1614, are more detailed and contain information about more than one floor on each plan (figs 204 and 205).[21] The modifications noted on the ground floor were largely aimed at creating an uninterrupted connection to the state apartments on the second (top) floor (see fig. 215). This was probably to adapt the house to the increasingly common trend of separating the public route from the more private ones. But it proved impossible, not only because the requisite number of treads could not be managed but also because a staircase leading directly to the top floor (as at Hardwick) would have split an otherwise continuous floor-plan. Nor does the other stair, on which Thorpe scribbled his more elaborate version (see fig. 204), make any sense as it too hinders circulation. Other intended alterations to the plan of the ground floor are more plausible. The Hall, which here features a screens passage, is divided in two to create a Parlour. Three sets of stairs in the north-west range also appear to have been modified from double to single flights, unless Thorpe was recording just one flight, for the number of treads is again insufficient. Finally, the rooms in the west wing are connected by a

200 | LONDON'S 'GOLDEN MILE'

205 John Thorpe, survey of the second floor of Northampton House, *c.*1614, with the Strand on the north (bottom), the garden on the south (top). © Sir John Soane's Museum, London (vol. 101, fols 275 and 276)

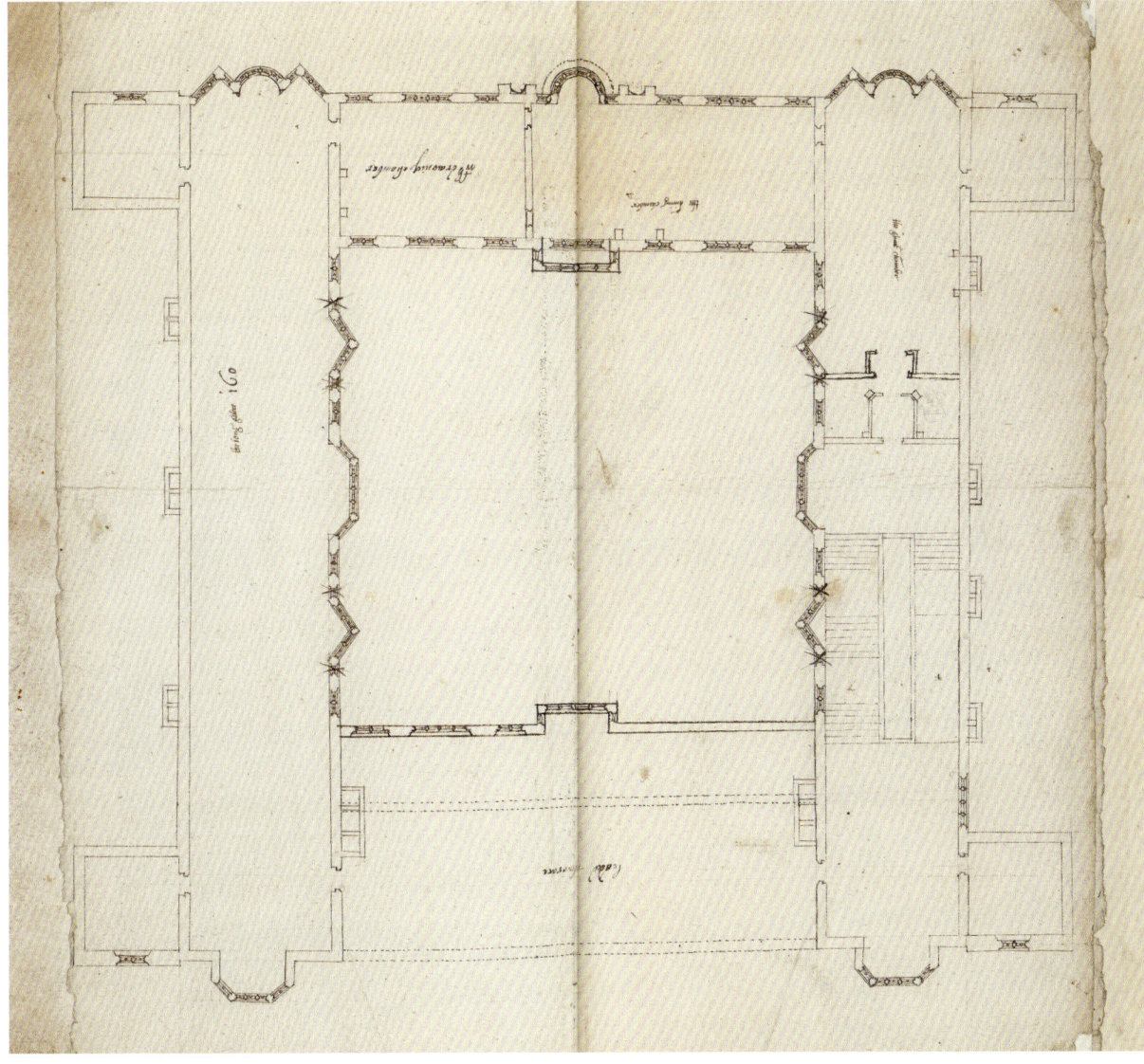

series of doors *en enfilade*. As for the exterior, the garden front no longer reveals a central projection, while the projecting part of the loggia in the courtyard, clearly marked by Smythson, is also reduced. A series of dotted steps here suggest a difference of levels between the court and the loggia but Thorpe is again inconsistent in not adding steps to the other entrances at court level. Along the east and west sides of the courtyard, the shape of those triangular windows outlined by Smythson is repeated in dotted lines. They are a hint of medievalism manifesting self-conscious continuity with the past, as well as a clear adaptation to the shortage of light in a northern climate. We see them continually used until at least the early 1600s, from the otherwise revolutionary Strand front of Somerset House (1547–52; see fig. 63) to lesser buildings such as Paul Pindar's House in London (*c.*1600).

Thorpe's plan of the second floor (third from the ground) shows the principal rooms of the house with their functions (see fig. 205) and is the earliest surviving source to depict this part of the building. The great staircase, even if half-drafted and unresolved, logically leads to the state rooms on the north side of the house via a space connected to the Great Chamber by a screen, of which Thorpe designs a second version. Here he repeats what he had drafted on the plan of the ground floor where the inscription 'gr[eat] chambr above' clearly refers to the top floor. The Great Chamber has an elaborate convex window projecting onto the Strand, while two others open onto the courtyard. It is followed by a large Dining Chamber with projecting windows on both street and courtyard sides, while the Withdrawing Chamber, also on the street front, leads to a Long Gallery which runs the entire

NORTHUMBERLAND HOUSE | 201

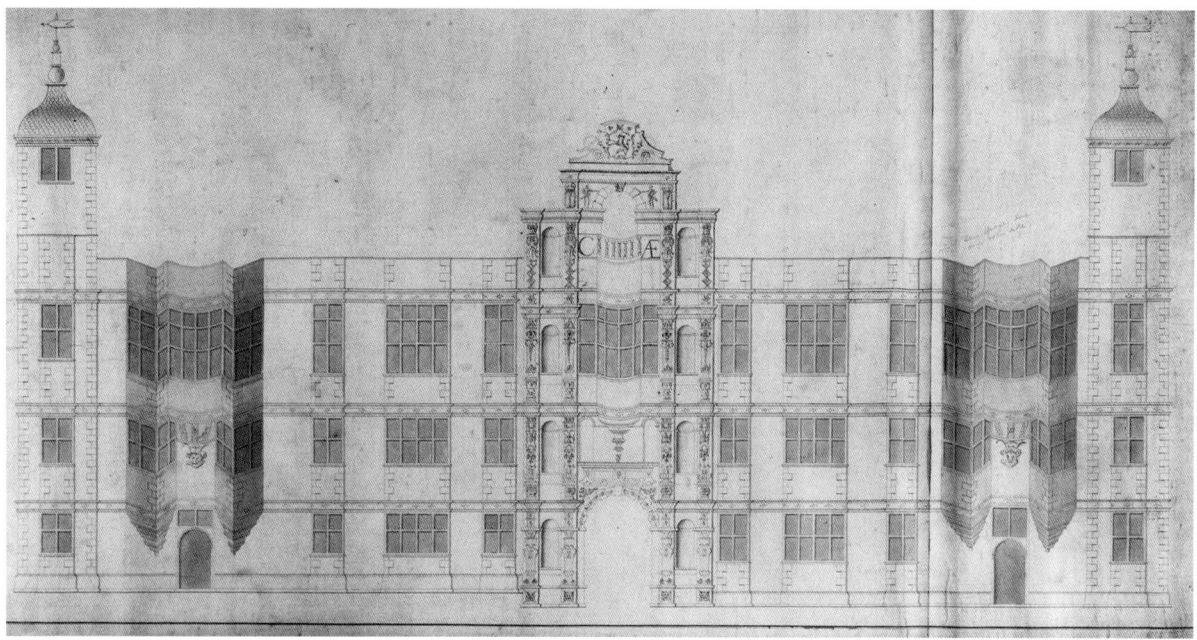

length of the west wing, 160 feet, with bay and flat windows on three sides. If the sequence of rooms followed an established pattern, the extent of the gallery was exceptional, especially in London, for it surpassed the otherwise unmatched Long Gallery at Leicester House (which, however, featured three such rooms; see Chapter One). Still, the contemporary Salisbury House's gallery at 84 feet long was about half that of Northampton's, while at Hardwick the famously extended gallery is only 7 feet longer. The roof of the south wing is inscribed as a

206 Elevational drawing of the Strand front (north) of Northumberland House, pre-1749. Alnwick Castle, Sy:B.xv.2. Collection of the Duke of Northumberland

207 'A view of the Southwest Front of his Grace the Duke of Somersets House at Charing Cross', 1717, the right-hand side when looking from the Strand. Alnwick Castle, Sy:B.xv.2.b/2. Collection of the Duke of Northumberland

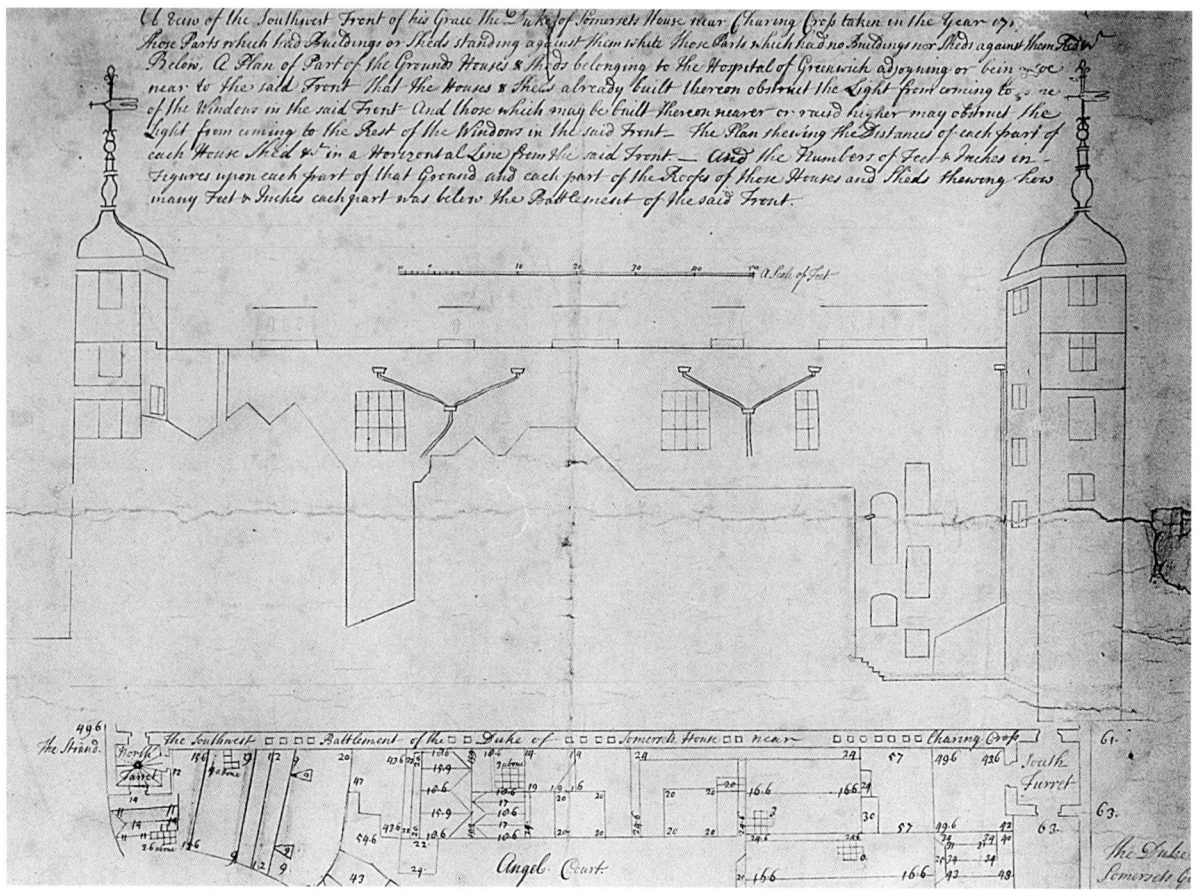

208 Northumberland House (10), detail of Wenceslaus Hollar, 'view of London extending eastwards from Peterborough House to Somerset House', early 1670s. By permission of the Pepys Library, Magdalene College, Cambridge ('London and Westminster', I, 2972, 34–35)

209 Northumberland House, detail of Richard Newcourt and William Faithorne, 'An exact delineation of the City of London and Westminster', 1658. By kind permission of the Syndics of Cambridge University Library (Map Room, Maps BB.77.90.14)

210 Northumberland House, detail of William Morgan, *View of London and Westminster*, c.1682 (detail of images on pp. x and xi). By permission of the Pepys Library, Magdalene College, Cambridge ('London and Westminster', I, 2972, 38–39)

202 | LONDON'S 'GOLDEN MILE'

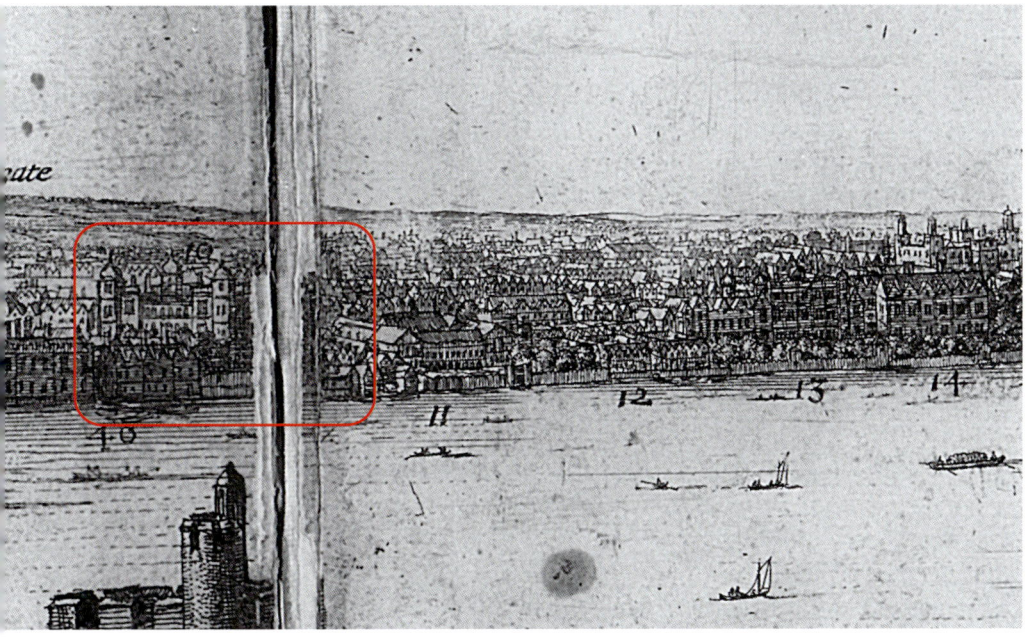

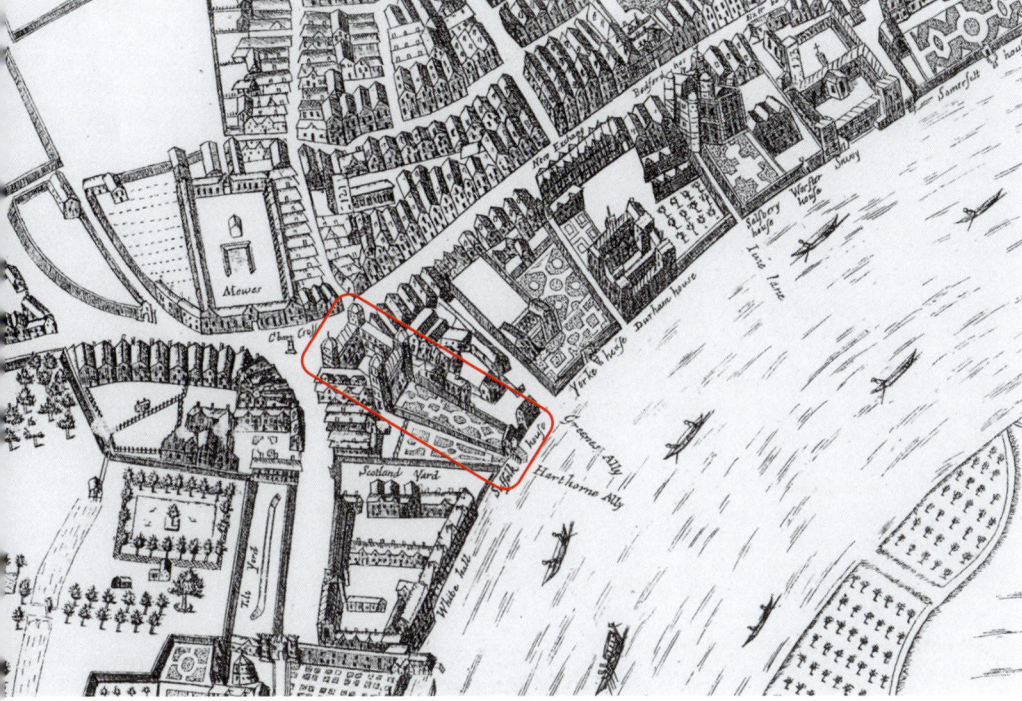

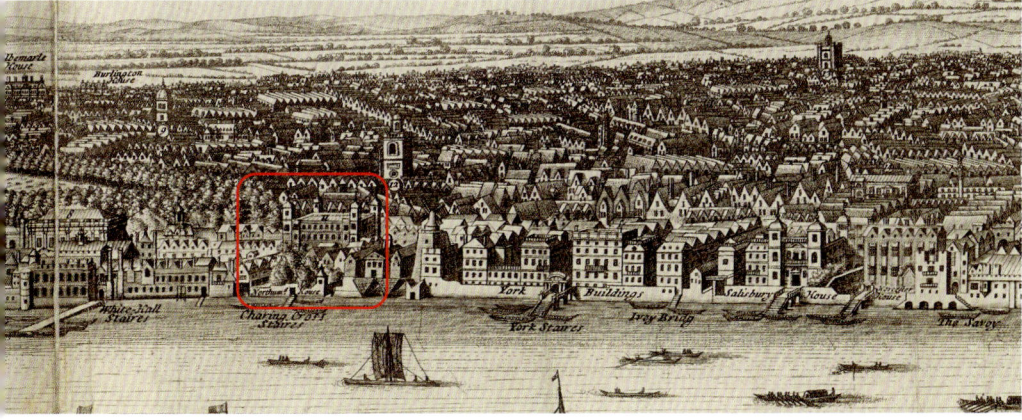

leaded terrace where the view over the garden towards the river could be appreciated. It was therefore one storey lower than the other ranges, as clearly depicted by Hollar and illustrated by my reconstruction elevations of both sides of that wing (figs 217 and 218 and see fig. 16). This arrangement had dictated the position of the *piano nobile*, which could only have been on the top floor, similar to the arrangement not just at Hardwick but at Chatsworth, Holdenby in Northamptonshire and Charlton House near Greenwich.[22]

The Strand front, as evidenced by an elevational drawing that predates the first changes to this side of the building carried out in 1749 (fig. 206),[23] was characterised by a central composition of superimposed terms crowned by a pediment with the Howards' lion and by virtuoso projecting windows in the centre and at either end. The frontispiece was a simplified version of the Tower of the Orders in the mould of Wendel Dietterlin, the sixteenth-century German architect who popularised Flemish Mannerist ornament through his *Architectura*, published in Nuremberg in 1598.[24] Its stone-mullioned windows, stringcourses and dressings, however, paid tribute to du Cerceau's *Les Plus Excellents Bastiments de France* (1576).[25] According to Vertue, the carver of the frontispiece was Gerard Christmas (1575/76–1633/34), a Northern European who had risen to become Carver of the Navy and had worked for Cecil at the New Exchange and Hatfield.[26] He and Bernard Janseen, a surveyor of Netherlandish origin associated with Audley End and with Sir Nicholas and Lady Bacon's altar tomb discussed in Chapter Ten, were credited with the design and construction of Northampton House.[27] Howard himself and John Thorpe, who collaborated at Audley End, may have played a role too, together with Miles or Moses Glover, the 'painter and architecter' later employed at Syon House.[28]

Notwithstanding the circumstantial nature of these attributions, the three letters 'C AE' shown as carved on top of the frontispiece did not stand for 'Christmas Aedificavit', as Vertue interpreted them: they were part of a larger inscription, as seen in my reconstruction elevation (fig. 216), stating the ownership and titles of the Earl of Northampton: 'h[enricus] howardius northamptoniae – c[omes] ae – dif[icavit] ad mdcv ii regis iacobi' (Henry Howard Earl of Northampton built [this house] in the year of our Lord 1605 the

NORTHUMBERLAND HOUSE | 203

second [year of the reign] of King James). The display of letters as balustrades of a parapet, seen in French architecture of the Renaissance, had found its way to the other side of the Channel in houses such as Audley End (unsurprisingly given its ties with Henry Howard), Temple Newsam and, more spectacularly, Castle Ashby.

Detailed information on the internal arrangement of Northampton House is provided by its first inventory, taken after Howard's death in 1614.[29] As illustrated in my reconstruction plans (figs 211–15), obtained by cross-referencing what has been described so far with the first complete set of plans executed *c*.1749, the top floor was almost exclusively devoted to public rooms (see fig. 214), above the simpler and more private rooms on the middle floor (see fig. 213). Both floors were richly furnished with contemporary European and Asian luxury objects, including Turkish carpets and wares from China, while Brussels tapestries mainly depicting biblical themes hung from their walls. Northampton's bedroom (room number 6 in fig. 213) contained a lavishly decorated bed of state and was hung with four of Cardinal Wolsey's tapestries, originally part of an outstanding collection of six hundred pieces commissioned and acquired by Wolsey for York House and Hampton Court from 1515. A large part of these hangings had been manufactured in the Netherlands and depicted religious, judicious or moral themes which no doubt attracted the earl.[30] He owned maps of Rome, Amsterdam and Antwerp, John Speed's large map of England, Scotland and Ireland, and a pair of Molineux globes of the world, one celestial, the other terrestrial. As for paintings, there were seventy-seven, principally portraits of family members and courtiers displayed in the two galleries (the Little Gallery was on the first floor above the loggia), though there were also several royal portraits, with a telling predominance of five of the Catholic Mary against one of Elizabeth. Northampton's religious outlook also determined the choice of the non-family or political pictures, which concentrated on a number of sacred subjects, mainly the Virgin and the Passion of Christ.[31]

Of Howard's striking collection of books and manuscripts only scant information has survived, as it was acquired by the Earl of Arundel in 1615 for £529. It may have required a separate appraisal, hence the library's absence from the general inventory.[32] By the time it was

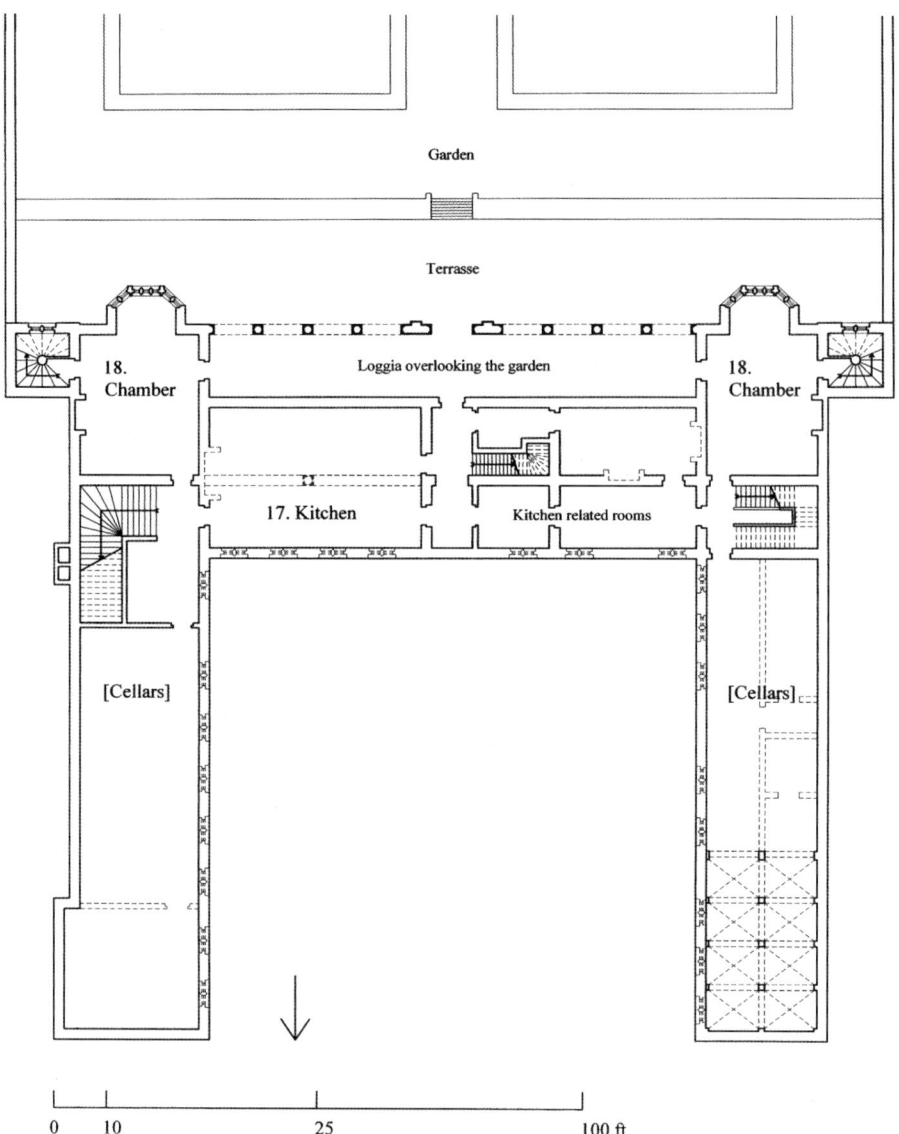

211 Reconstruction of the basement plan of Northumberland House as originally built, rooms identified as listed in the 1614 inventory. The main staircase in the east wing (left) is conjectural, while the service staircase next to the 'Kitchen related rooms' in the south wing (centre) is based on Thorpe's survey of the ground floor: see fig. 204. © Manolo Guerci, 2005

opposite

212 Reconstruction of the ground-floor plan of Northumberland House as originally built, room numbers as listed in the 1614 inventory. The main staircase in the east wing (left), and of the three staircases in the west wing (right), are based on Smythson's survey of the ground floor: see fig. 203. The two single-flight staircases in the north wing (bottom) are as Thorpe showed them: see fig. 204. © Manolo Guerci, 2005

213 Reconstruction of the middle-floor plan of Northumberland House as originally built, room numbers as listed in the 1614 inventory. © Manolo Guerci, 2005

214 Reconstruction of the second-floor plan of Northumberland House as originally built, room numbers as listed in the 1614 inventory. © Manolo Guerci, 2005

215 Reconstruction of the second-floor plan of Northumberland House as it would have been after Thorpe's hypothetical (and unresolved) alterations. © Manolo Guerci, 2005

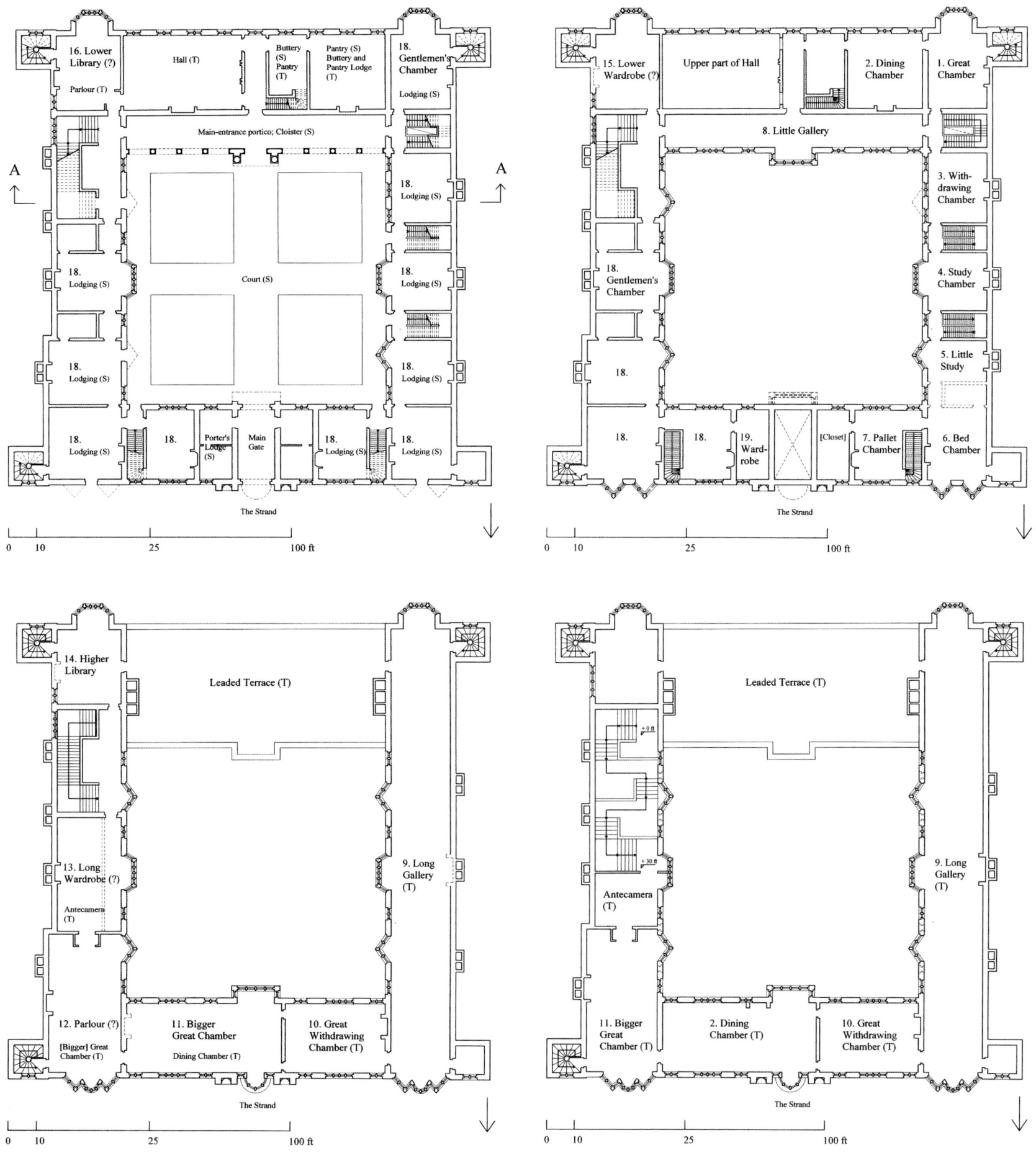

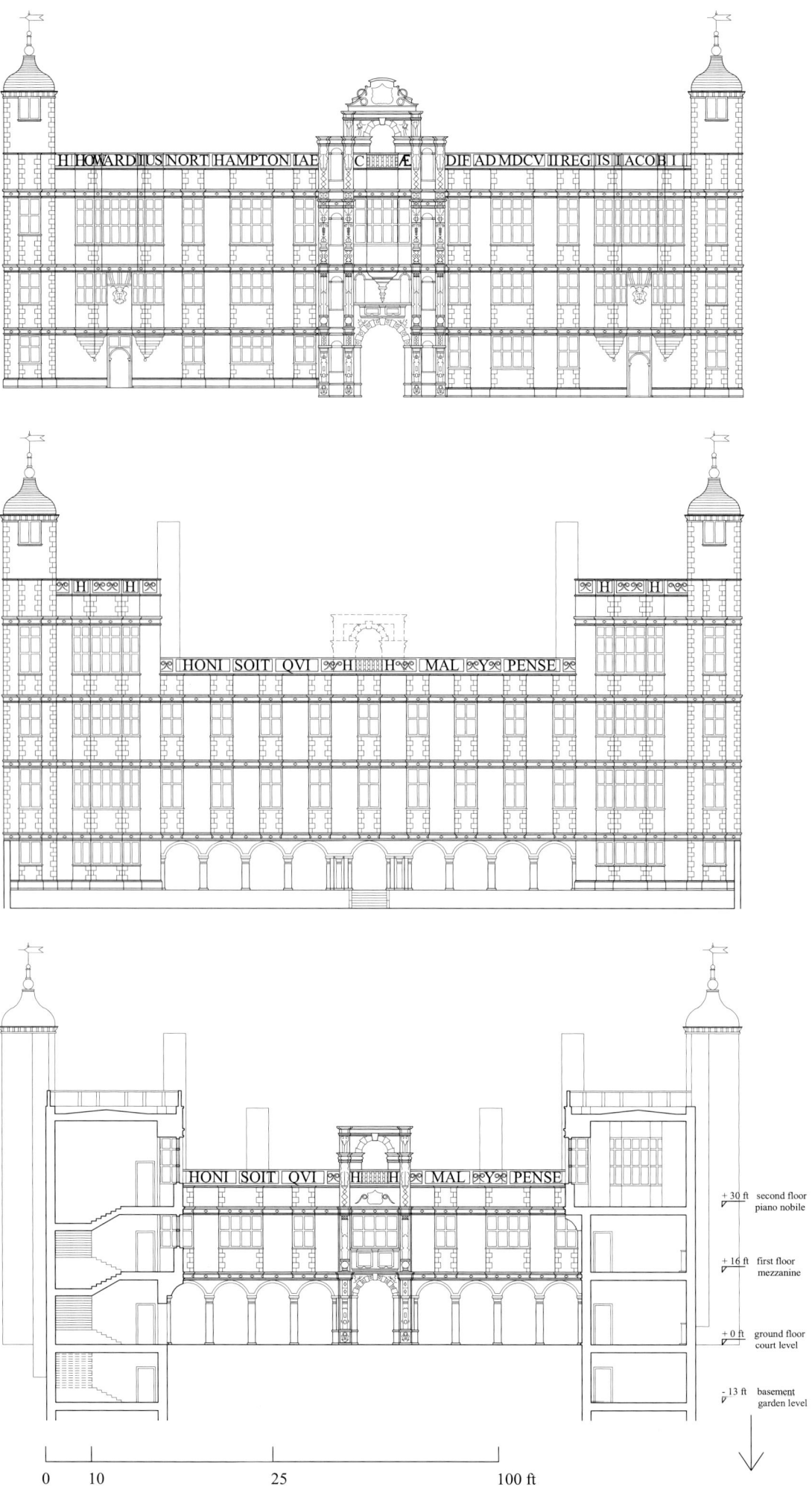

216 Reconstruction of the elevation of the Strand front (north) of Northumberland House as originally built, with conjectural inscription on the roofline. © Manolo Guerci, 2005

217 Reconstruction of the elevation of the south front of Northumberland House as originally built, facing the garden, with conjectural inscription on the roofline. © Manolo Guerci, 2005

218 Reconstruction of the elevation of the south front of Northumberland House as originally built, facing the court, with sections of the side wings and conjectural inscription on the roofline. © Manolo Guerci, 2005

donated to the Royal Society by the 6th Duke of Norfolk in 1667, the 'Bibliotheca Norfolciana' featured numerous books on art and architecture including volumes on most of the Renaissance masters.[33]

The Suffolk Period: 1614–1642

Whether or not Northampton's death was 'so hart whole and so little expected' as Chamberlain wrote,[34] the earl had long before disposed of the bulk of his estate. His will was mainly concerned with valuable 'leftovers', since he had previously made provision for the setting up of almshouses, while his buildings and lands had been dealt with through earlier conveyances.[35] Most of the land, with the greater part of Greenwich Lodge, had gone to Thomas Howard, 14th Earl of Arundel and Northampton's great-nephew,[36] while Northampton House, part of the East Anglia estate and some of his most precious possessions were left to another Thomas Howard (1561–1626), 1st Earl of Suffolk and Northampton's closest relation.[37] As early as 1611, his keepership of the Tower at Greenwich, which joined the Lodge there, had in fact reverted to Theophilus (d. 1640), Suffolk's son and heir.[38]

The career and fortunes of the 1st Earl of Suffolk, as well as his debts, rose dramatically until 1618. With Sir Thomas Knyvett, in November 1605 he discovered the Gunpowder Plot while searching the vaults under the House of Lords. As a result, he soon succeeded the disgraced 9th Earl of Northumberland, suspected of involvement in the plot, as Captain of the King's Band of Gentlemen Pensioners. (This position he kept until 1614, passing it to Theophilus after succeeding Northampton as Chancellor of the University of Cambridge.) The mighty families of Howard and Cecil were then officially linked by the marriage in 1608 of Salisbury's son and heir, William, to Suffolk's daughter Catherine. In the following year, Suffolk's eldest daughter, Frances, was divorced and took as her second husband the favourite Robert Carr, after intricate manoeuvres orchestrated by Henry Howard. The extended Suffolk clan thus dominated the court and when Northampton died in 1614 he had good reason to hold his nephew in high esteem, whose political dominance had re-established the position of the family. In effect, Northampton House had been bequeathed to Thomas Howard shortly after 1611 when his escalating debts had forced him to sell his own town-house in the City, Howard House, the former fourteenth-century Charterhouse (acquired by the 4th Duke of Norfolk in 1565 and re-granted to the Howards in 1601). As a result, the Suffolks took up residence at Durham House.[39]

The Earl of Northampton did not live to see the scandal and subsequent fall of his relatives, tried and imprisoned following impeachment after Suffolk had fallen from the pinnacle of his political career as Lord Treasurer (1614–19). Nor did he have to face the accusation of the murder of Sir Thomas Overbury in 1613, as it too came after Howard's death. Overbury had opposed the match between Frances Howard and Robert Carr, a short-lived success for the king's eye had quickly settled on a new favourite, George Villiers, whose tenure of York House was discussed in the previous chapter. Above all, perhaps, Henry Howard could not foresee that his Strand palace, renamed Suffolk House, would stay in that family no longer than twenty-eight years, for Thomas's grandson was also forced to sell because of his debts.

The chronic financial difficulties that beset the 1st and 2nd Earls of Suffolk have been put down to their 'excessive building and excessive children': indeed, the rebuilding and furnishing of Audley End alone was rumoured to have cost £200,000.[40] Salisbury's contemporary Hatfield House had cost him a fifth of that amount. This 'excessive building', however, did not include Northampton House, for the suggestion that Thomas Howard completed the quadrangle by adding the south wing is incorrect.[41] In effect, the only transaction related to the Strand palace was the acquisition of all Northampton's furniture for a hefty £5000 by the 1st Countess of Suffolk (she wrote that 'the like whereof then could not elsewhere be gotten'), who seems to have acted as the conduit of the Spanish pensions that allegedly funded Northampton House and Audley End (as also much of Hatfield House, then owned by her son-in-law).[42] Her family business included the transfer of the Suffolk estate to one of the cadets, Lord William Howard, when in 1620 the risk of seizure because of debts became a reality. On that occasion, Audley End and Suffolk House were stripped of all their precious movable possessions and Inigo Jones surveyed the Strand palace.[43] On 27 June 1616 Thomas Howard had bought a house and its premises which lay near, or were part of, the Cross Keys, previously acquired by Henry Howard. The 1706 layout of the 'Houses & Lanes' (see fig. 202) previously purchased by Northampton offers some clues as to the situation of that property, whose purchase may have been related to extending the south-east end of the garden. The year after, on 15 March 1617, Thomas Howard had also been granted the liberty of conveying water to Suffolk House by inserting a small pipe into the main one from Hyde Park to the Palace of Westminster.[44]

Throughout the 1620s, Suffolk House was used for political meetings and for hosting foreign ambassadors. In 1623 it was offered as a residence to Prince Charles on his return from Spain,[45] while in 1625, from 18 April to 11 May, it accommodated the ambassador extraordinary from France, the Comte de Tremes, and his train.[46] In 1626 a long list of residents who did not pay towards the mending of the highways of the parish of St Martin-in-the-Fields included the name of Inigo Jones, alongside the Salisburys and Suffolks.[47]

With the death of Thomas Howard in 1626, Suffolk House passed to Theophilus, together with his father's heavy debts. The 2nd Earl was married to Elizabeth, the heiress of another of the king's favourites, the Earl of Dunbar, with whom he had four sons and five daughters. He also had many brothers and sisters, whose fortunes depended solely on him.[48] In such circumstances, the estate became increasingly difficult to maintain and when Theophilus died in 1640 the young 3rd Earl, James Howard (d. 1689), was forced to part with Suffolk House. By that time, Algernon Percy, 10th Earl of Northumberland, had set his sights on the property, which he must have known well as he was related to those who built and owned it: his first wife was the daughter of William Cecil, 2nd Earl of Salisbury, and Catherine Howard of the Suffolk branch, while his mother, Dorothy Devereux, was Northampton's first cousin. No wonder, therefore, that after the death of his wife in 1637 he went so far as to remarry into the Suffolk family to get hold of their Strand palace, even if it meant renewed association with those who had been responsible for his father's fall.[49] This was indeed perfect for him in its proximity to Whitehall and to York House, the earl's rented residence since 1640 after he had left Salisbury House, where he had previously lived as the husband of Anne Cecil.

The House of Algernon Percy, 10th Earl of Northumberland: 1642–1668

On 1 October 1642 Algernon married Lady Elizabeth Howard (c.1608–1705), Theophilus's second daughter, whereby he came into possession of Suffolk House. By an article in the marriage settlement, it was in fact transferred to him on payment of £15,000, £5000 of that being remitted as Elizabeth's dowry.[50] He had been born at his maternal grandfather's Essex House on 29 September 1602 and his education had been supervised by the scholarly 9th Earl, who sent him on a six-year tour through the Netherlands, Italy and France.[51] By the 1630s, Algernon had ascended to the earldom and secured honours and offices as Master of the Horse to Charles I, Privy Councillor, Knight of the Garter and Lord Admiral of the Navy (fig. 219).

The decade before the king's break with Parliament in 1642 provided the 10th Earl with both the means and ambition to build on a significant scale, beyond merely continuing what his father had started at Petworth and Syon.[52] In effect, by the early 1640s he was so influential a figure that some considered him a potential Lord Protector after he had been given the charge of Charles's younger children, the Duke of Gloucester and Princess Elizabeth. Hence his quest for an appropriate residence, as well as its costly refurbishment, regardless of the financial difficulties experienced from the loan of huge sums to Parliament and the disruption of the northern rents. The earl had little choice, for Suffolk House, conceived for a bachelor and since unaltered, was virtually uninhabitable for a married household at the Percys' level.

Works were concentrated in two stages: the first, between 1642 and 1649, involved the reconstruction of the south front together with new decoration of the courtyard facades, at a total cost of £6570 18s 3d; the second, from 1655 to 1657, was devoted to the erection of an external staircase connecting the garden to the state rooms on the first floor, which were rearranged to receive it, for a further £1828 5s 8d.[53] The architect employed by Northumberland throughout the first stage was Edward Carter (d. 1663), who received £100 for 'his paines in this worke' in 1649.[54] Carter had worked with Inigo Jones for several patrons, including the 4th Earl of Bedford at Bedford House (see Chapter Six), but in 1643

219 Sir Anthony Van Dyck, *Algernon, 10th Earl of Northumberland*, c.1638. Alnwick Castle, 03518. Collection of the Duke of Northumberland

had managed to have the Surveyorship reverted to himself after skilfully denigrating Jones in the eyes of the Committee of Revenue and 'thrusting out Webb', whom Jones had nominated as his deputy in 1642.[55] Among the notable craftsmen employed by Carter were Thomas Steevens, Zachary Taylor, John Embree and Henry Stone. Steevens was the chief mason who had worked at St Paul's around 1640 and was employed at Syon in 1650–51 and again at Northumberland House in 1650 and 1654.[56] Taylor, a woodcarver, had executed a great deal of work at Somerset House in the mid-1630s, including the Queen's Chapel and Cabinet Room, as well as the Cross Gallery there, all designed by Jones. He had also carved picture frames and pedestals of statues for the royal collection and worked at St James's and Whitehall.[57] Embree, Sergeant Plumber as of 1639, superseded Carter as the Surveyor during the Protectorate (1653–60), while Stone, Nicholas Stone's eldest son, was the main stonecutter.

Work began with the demolition of the garden wing between the south ends of the east and west ranges, from the ground floor to the leaded terrace, while the basement was completely rearranged.[58] Externally, the new wing maintained its distinctive aspect, while inside it was occupied by two sets of lodgings on the ground and first floors, as can be seen in my reconstruction plans (figs 220–3). These are primarily based on the first complete series of plans executed *c*.1750 and on the inventory made in 1670 after the death of Josceline Percy, 11th Earl of Northumberland (1644–1670). The basement, from east to west, included a Waiters' Room in the south-east corner of the house next to the property of Sir Henry Vane, whence there was access to the 'Lower hall', a new, less significant version of the Great Hall and probably exclusively a servants' hall, which occupied the left-hand side of the former garden loggia and part of the old kitchen (fig. 220).[59] This was achieved by demolishing the wall formerly dividing the loggia from the kitchen and by erecting a new wall in the middle of the former kitchen, seemingly in lieu of some kind of timber-framed arch. The remaining half of the old kitchen probably became what is referred to as 'little Kitchen', in contrast with the new 'greate Kitchen' and related services which must have occupied the other half of this part of the basement.[60]

The right-hand side of the loggia was turned into the 'Orange house', among the earliest of its kind in the country, where exotic fruits could benefit from its southern aspect.[61] Thus, what had been an 'arched walk' open to the terrace became an integral part of a semi-public interior, while the new front no longer featured a loggia. Here, the columns were given new capitals of

Portland stone, while the arches were filled in with eight new windows, four on either side of a new elaborate doorway leading onto the terrace and accessible via a corridor between the lower hall and the orangery. This door was flanked by a pair of pilasters with rusticated quoins surmounted by an elaborate frontispiece bearing the Percy insignia. A portico framed the doorway, three feet six inches deep with two matching columns and balusters on either side, while its structure was also strengthened to bear the stonework of the corresponding doorway onto the 'purgola', or balcony, on the first floor, directly above the portico. Below the portico was a new vaulted space thirteen feet wide and twenty-eight feet long, that is the width of the terrace and former loggia together, which could be entered through a doorway in the middle of the terrace wall. The function of this new space is not clear: it could simply have acted as a large storeroom for the gardener, given the presence of a door, or it may have been a grotto. After all, other Strand palaces such as Bedford House had such grottos, with which Carter must have been familiar as he had worked there (see Chapter Six). As for the old terrace itself, running the length of the house a few steps above the garden, it was completely repaved. It was accessed via the portico and by two new doors at the base of the turrets, which replaced former windows. The south-west corner room of the basement seems to have been used as a closet, while on the north side the lowest floors of the east and west wings were kept as cellars for wine and beer. As before, the basement would have been reached from the great staircase in the east wing, from the staircase in the west wing, from the turrets at either corner and from one or perhaps two new stairs next to the great staircase, referred to as the 'new backstairs' and the 'stone staires next Sr Henry Vanes'. While the location of this new staircase remains tentative, it is clear that it was built to connect the Kitchen and Waiters' Room directly to the new Dining Room on the ground floor.

The ground floor or Strand level, which was the second level from the terrace on the garden side, contained the lodgings of the Earl of Northumberland (fig. 221). Access was still through the old frontispiece in the middle of the loggia on the courtyard side, which had been saved from demolition. It may, however, have been partitioned and part of it turned into the Lobby, described in the accounts as being near the back stair on the east side of the house.[62] This new space, which was given a chimneypiece of Portland stone with inlaid black marble and a hearth of black and white marble, probably acted as an antechamber, like its equivalent on the first floor, 'intended to be a waiting roome to the dining roome above stairs'.[63] The room in the south-east corner of the house, immediately above the Waiters' Room, appears to have been the new Dining Room. It led directly to the earl's Withdrawing Chamber, which replaced what had formerly been the Hall. A 'balcony roome', so called because of the newly created 'purgola' in the centre of the garden front, followed, while the earl's Bedchamber and Closet, the last rooms of this set, replaced the former Pantry and Gentlemen's Chamber.

Northumberland's new apartment was decorated with wainscot and classical mouldings by the carpenter Thomas Simson, while Zachary Taylor provided a series of rich carvings including 'string with Lillies' and 'Cherubins and festoones', which may have recalled the work he had carried out in the late 1620s and 30s at St James's Palace, Oatlands, Somerset House and Whitehall, often to Jones's designs.[64] In the earl's Bedchamber and Closet two elaborate chimneys in black and white marble were also set up by Thomas Steevens. Here Algernon took a personal interest and provided the marble for his two chimneys, while Henry Stone had reserved one of eight chimneypieces made of several marbles for 'his Lo.ps owne use where he shall appointe'. Northumberland's lodgings were also arranged to receive the paintings he had been actively collecting since he had succeeded to the earldom in 1632 and the carpenter provided several cases for 'his Lo.pps picktures' and new 'battens to keepe the hangings from the wall'. Likewise, a system of servants' bells, probably innovative for this date, was installed in both the earl and countess's lodgings. On the west side of the ground floor was a staircase which originally rose from the basement to the first floor, but not to the Long Gallery on the top floor: this was demolished and a new one built all the way to the top floor. This stair, referred to as 'little staires' to distinguish it from the old 'greate staires' on the east side of the house, was elaborately carved by Zachary Taylor and bore the emblems of the new owners. It had windows opening onto the courtyard as well as onto Angel Court along the

220 Reconstruction of the basement (garden level) plan of Northumberland House as altered in the 1640s. The highlighted walls indicate reconstructed areas; the arrangement of the new Great Kitchen and related spaces is tentative. © Manolo Guerci, 2005

221 Reconstruction of the ground-floor plan of Northumberland House as altered in the 1640s. The highlighted walls indicate reconstructed parts. © Manolo Guerci, 2005

222 Reconstruction of the first-floor plan of Northumberland House as altered in the 1640s. The highlighted walls indicate reconstructed parts. © Manolo Guerci, 2005

223 Reconstruction of the second- (top) floor plan of Northumberland House as altered in the 1640s. The highlighted walls indicate reconstructed parts. © Manolo Guerci, 2005

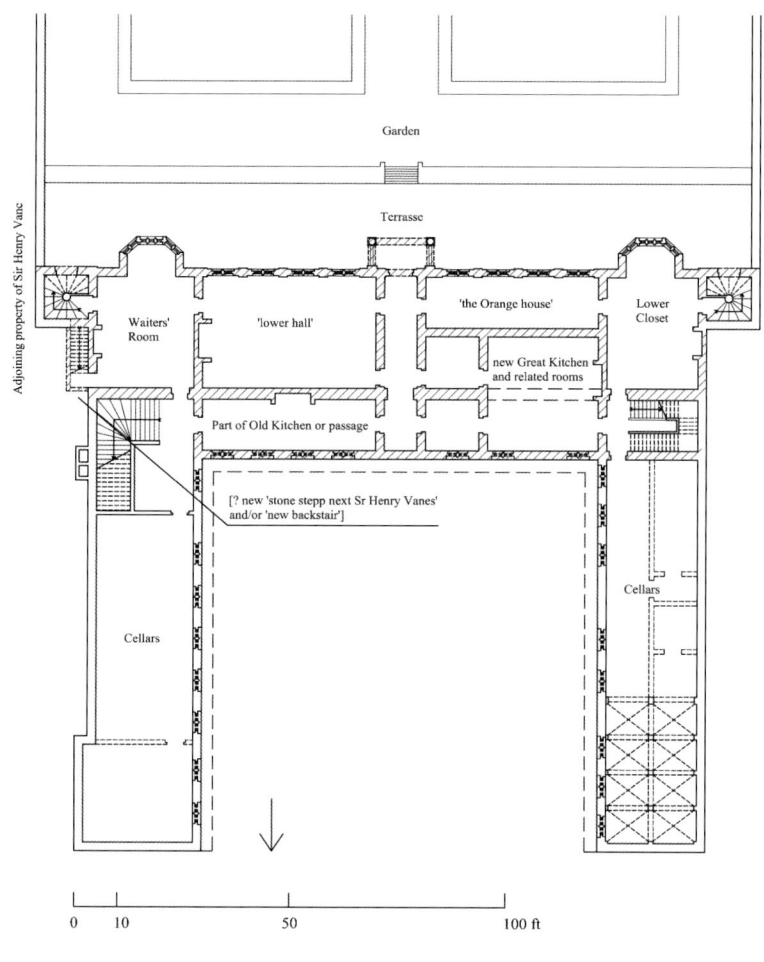
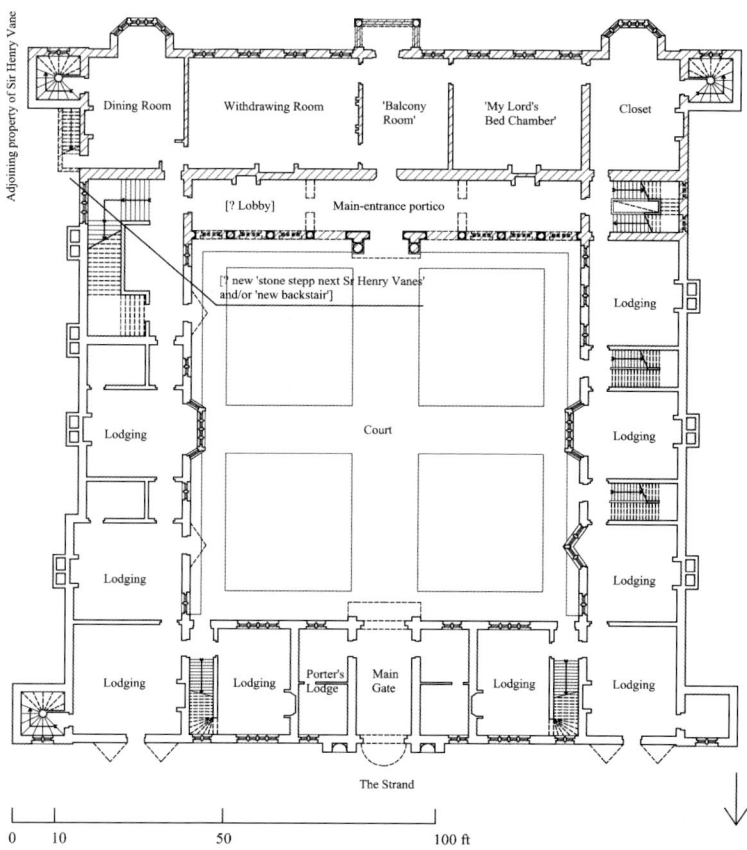
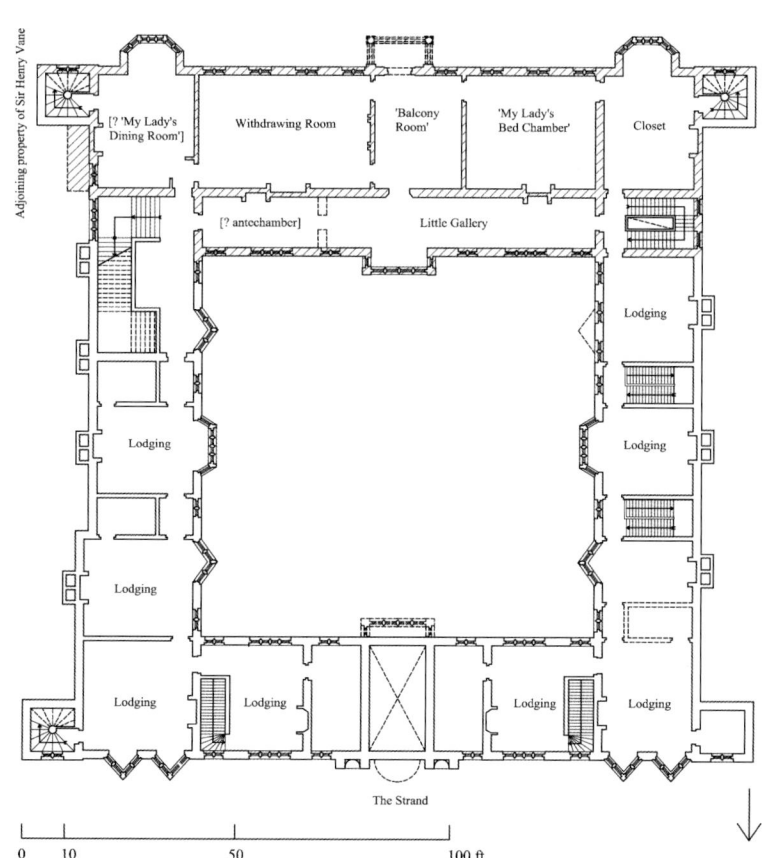
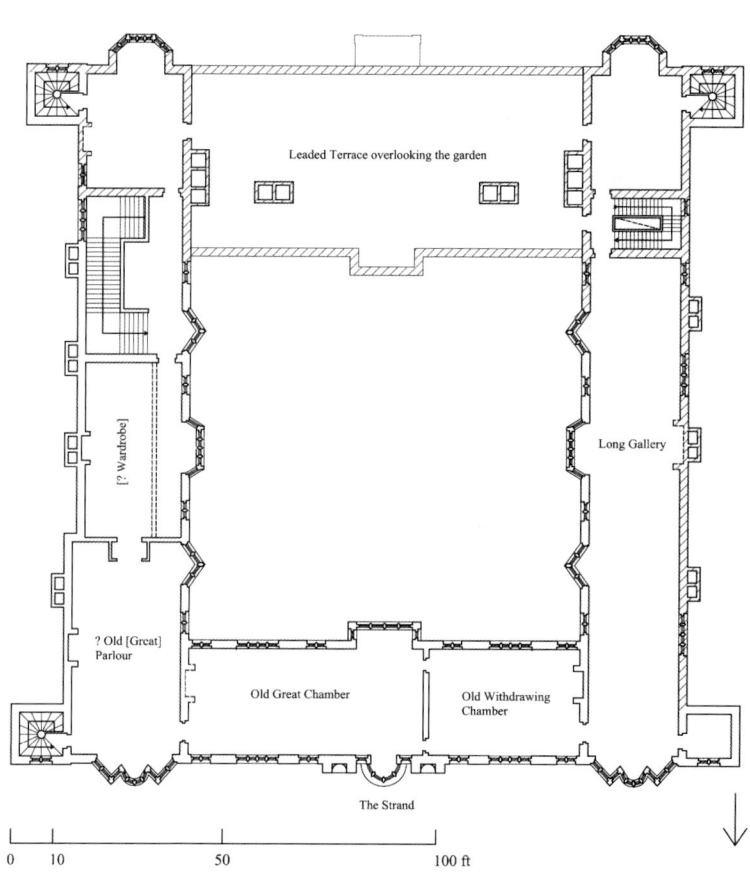

west wall, as can be seen in the 1717 elevation of this side of the house (see fig. 207).

The first floor (second floor on the garden side) was for the countess's use (fig. 222).[65] Her lodgings could be privately accessed via the reconstructed stair in the west wing, as well as by way of the great staircase on the east. The arrangement seems to have mirrored that of the earl's lodgings below, with a Dining Chamber in the south-east corner, followed by a Withdrawing Chamber and a passage or room which gave access to the countess's Bedchamber and Closet in the south-west corner. Their decoration may also have reflected that of the earl's, to which they were connected by an internal staircase, though only a small part of the countess's rooms, namely the Closet or Cabinet, appears to have been adorned. It is known, however, that the Little Gallery over the loggia on the courtyard side was given a new wainscot with architrave and cornice, while some internal partitioning may have divided the space.

The second floor of the house still acted as the *piano nobile*, its great public rooms created by Northampton and almost untouched during his ownership (fig. 223). Alterations there were concentrated on the south-west side of the Long Gallery for the new so-called 'little stair'. Thus the gallery's uninterrupted length of 160 feet was compromised. Perhaps Northumberland judged it too long and narrow, as well as probably too dark, and wanted to transform it into a more manageable space to be reached more conveniently than via the main staircase in the opposite wing or via the turrets. Other than covering the rearrangement and mending of various chimneys and alterations to the two turrets on the garden side, the accounts are silent about this floor, though they confirm the presence of a Wardrobe.

Apart from various repairs and rearrangements of chimneys and windows, the rest of the house was generally left undisturbed.[66] Expenses included new lead for the roofs and pipes and cisterns in the kitchen, the polishing of three thousand paving tiles around the house, as well as '3 daies hors[e]hire to Chersey', whence came some of the new tiles for the basement. A reference in the accounts to a 'p[ar]ticon in the garrett' is puzzling, considering that no such space is known to have existed in a house with nearly flat roofs. Neither is it clear, from later plans, whether such a level ever existed at all.[67] A major novelty for a former bachelor's house, as well as an indication of changing requirements, was the Nursery, which seems to have been on the first floor, not far from the countess's lodgings.[68] Other rooms, not listed in the inventory of 1614, included a Chapel, somewhere near the earl's apartment, for which one of the rooms must have been adapted, as a chapel proper never existed in the house.[69] Servants had their lodgings on either side of the ground floor, as well as in the north-east range of the first floor, following the arrangement of previous owners.

The altered version of the palace, renamed Northumberland House (with 221,200 new bricks), maintained the old courtyard structure. Externally, the only range to stand unaltered was the north one with its elaborate Jacobean frontispiece as a marker of lineage. There the canted windows were restored, while the courtyard elevations were completely redecorated in a more up-to-date style with a wealth of classical motifs. This included new architraves, cornices and mouldings, as well as the removal of all the letters from the top of the house. Instead, a new parapet with balusters was put up, in tune with the new classicism of the facades. As discussed, the porch supporting the Little Gallery on the north side of the garden wing survived, with some modifications, while its south side was given sixteen new windows with classical motifs, eight per floor, symmetrically arranged on either side of the central balcony. This acted as a frontispiece, recalling an original feature of the garden front recorded by Smythson in 1609 (see fig. 203). The balcony was supported by a portico of an unspecified order: it was probably Doric, for the two columns and pilasters above it were Ionic. It is unclear whether those columns supported a canopy or a second balcony, while a doorway, or French window, with composite capitals, brackets and drapery in the frieze certainly existed in the middle of the second floor (third level from the garden). An engraving after Simon Wale, published in 1761 and supposedly showing that part of the south front as left by Northumberland, reveals the presence of two balconies (fig. 224). This is in contrast with information provided by the *c.*1750 plans of the house, which, while showing the garden staircase, do not register a balcony or indeed a canopy on the second floor.[70] Either way, Carter's new facade established the use of the orders and reflected the work of Inigo Jones, even if little attempt had been made to harmonise these changes with the rest – the garden elevations

224 C. Grignon after Simon Wale, *South View of Northumberland House*, the garden front, 1761. Guildhall Library, London. Dodsley and Dodsley 1761, 59

of the east and west wings stood unaltered with their towers of canted windows.[71]

The end of the first series of alterations in 1649 coincided with, was perhaps determined by, the execution of Charles I at the beginning of that year.[72] This caused Northumberland's withdrawal from public life, while the palace he had acquired at the very peak of his political career, and where he had permanently moved in 1648 after the lease of York House expired, ironically became a place of enforced retreat. On two occasions, Northumberland House even became a potential prison for the earl, put under house arrest in the spring and summer of 1655. The relations between Algernon and Parliament had been difficult at times, though he seems to have had the better of it. This included his role in preventing the sale of that part of the Buckingham collection still at York House, a part of which ended up in his own collection.[73] Equally, an important group of antique statues and busts were bought in the late 1650s at the dispersal of the king's collection.[74] This leads us to the second stage of alterations, when arrangements were made to position these new statues so that they would coexist with sixteenth-century paintings.

Works began in 1655 when it was decided to build a great external staircase connecting the garden directly to the earl's apartment on the first floor, which was itself being turned into the new *piano nobile* of the house. Such a staircase was innovative among the Strand palaces and perhaps in an urban setting, where the descent from public rooms, traditionally located on an upper floor, to the garden, was invariably via small stairways often in cramped turrets. These would normally lead to a loggia preceding a terrace, which balanced the relation between inside and outside, whence access to the garden was reached at an axial point.[75] While it may be surprising that the state rooms were not more formally connected to the garden, viewing the garden from within was equally important, as epitomised in the portrait of the 14th Earl of Arundel showing the 'garden of antiquities' at Arundel House (see fig. 52). The new staircase at Northumberland House was built by Edward Marshall (c.1598–1675), a prominent London mason who became the Master Mason to the Crown (1660–73), and probably designed by John Webb.[76] The two had previously collaborated at The Vyne in 1654 and did so at Syon around 1656. It consisted of two flights descending either side of what had previously been the balcony on the first level but the result, in Evelyn's caustic judgement in 1658, was 'too massy and clumsy'.[77] It was made of Portland stone with iron rails and balusters gilded by John Walker and painted by Edward Peirce, while the younger Richard Rider (or Ryder) produced a timber centering for the mason in order to build the arch of the door underneath the stairway.[78] The size of this staircase is suggested by a payment of £42 for '63 foote of Rayle and Balister wrought compasse', which would have covered more than a third of the garden front, 162 feet long.

The construction of the new Dining Room in the middle of the south front, whence the new staircase descended, coincided with the transformation of the earl's lodgings, completed by Carter less than a decade earlier, into a new set of public rooms. As can be seen in my reconstruction (fig. 225), this provided a large Dining Room in lieu of the former earl's Withdrawing Chamber and part of the 'balcony room', and a new Withdrawing Chamber which occupied the other part of the balcony room and the whole of the former Bed Chamber on the right-hand side. The earl's Bed Chamber was probably moved to the next room, formerly the Lower Closet, while the old and rather small Dining Room in the south-east corner of the house may have become the 'gentlewomens dining roome', not before mentioned.[79] The internal alterations in these rooms can also be attributed to Webb. Four designs by him survive for two chimneypieces and overmantels dated 1657 and 1660, as well as for their fanciful composite capitals, with swans and lion masks pointing to the Percy heraldry instead of the top volutes (figs 226–9).[80] Webb specialised in emblematic inventive capitals, many versions of which were included in his 'Book of Capitols', for which he drew on Book I of Giovanni Battista Montano's *Cinque Libri di Architettura* (1636). According to Christopher Wren, Webb also drew on Pirro Ligorio, whose book of 1553 on Roman antiquities Wren had seen in the collection of Inigo Jones.[81] The 'Book of Capitols' featured capitals at various houses including Wilton, where the interiors were reconstructed by Webb for the 4th Earl of Pembroke in the late 1640s.[82] At the same time, Webb had produced several designs for a grandiose rebuilding of Durham House, granted to Pembroke in 1641 (see Chapter Nine).

Northumberland's decision to employ Webb at this stage came after seeing his work at Wilton; the earl and Pembroke had been politically allied at various stages and shared an enthusiasm for Van Dyck.[83] Northumberland may also have decided that Webb's classical scheme would provide a suitable setting for his antique statues, and in 1657 he bought five unspecified sculptures and a Bacchus from Emmanuel de Critz, the younger son of the Sergeant Painter John.[84] For these Marshall produced a 'greate Carved Pedistall' which was transported from his workshop in Fetter Lane, together with '4 stones provided for the bodies of the round pedistalles'.[85] Two further pedestals 'to raise the marble statue higher' were also made, while those statues formerly in the king's collection – ten marble heads, two figures of Bacchus, a 'Young Apollo' and a head of Jupiter – replaced five bronze statues which had been removed from the terrace.[86] Here, new stone balusters were also set up. In addition, a sketch by Webb for a pedestal of one such statue was to be built by Edward Marshall in 1658 (fig. 230), while Robert Cleare, the joiner, was paid for making nineteen pedestals, six of which were carved by Richard Cleare with 'fowleage shieldes and Corronettes, and the upper mouldings inriched with lace'. Of those, one was painted by John Peirce.[87]

Northumberland's patronage of the arts is well known. Unlike his father, who was more interested in the practice of science, he had begun collecting soon after he succeeded to the title in 1623, initiating a long-lasting relationship with Van Dyck.[88] Detailed information on the earl's collection is provided by the following: Richard Symonds's notes on the collection in 1652,[89] John Evelyn's account of 1658[90] and the list of pictures taken and appraised by Simon Stone, the keeper of the collection, in 1671, as part of the 1670 inventory of Northumberland House.[91] In 1652 there were thirty-six paintings in the house, displayed in the galleries and private lodgings, 'whereoff that of the Venetian Senator was one of the best of Titians', as Evelyn remarked a few years later, adding 'another of Andrea da Sarta, viz, a Madonna, Christ, St John & an old Woman & c: a St. Catharine of Da Vinci, with divers Portraits of V. Dyck, a Nativity of Georgioni:

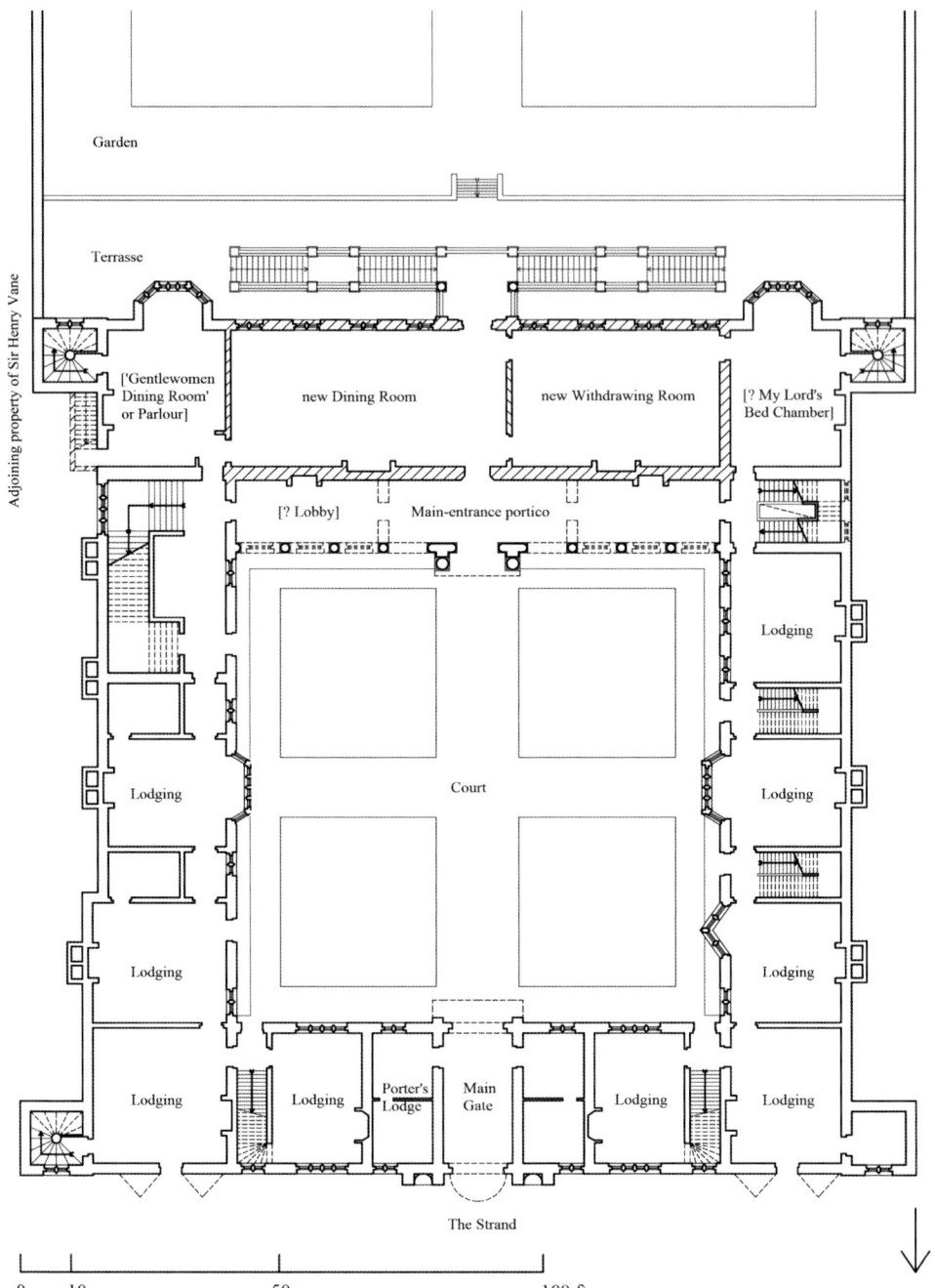

225 Reconstruction of the ground-floor plan of Northumberland House as altered in the 1650s. The highlighted walls indicate reconstructed parts.
© Manolo Guerci, 2005

214 | LONDON'S 'GOLDEN MILE'

226 John Webb, design for an overmantel in the Dining Room of Northumberland House, 1657. RIBA Collections (22926)

227 John Webb, design for a fanciful composite capital for the overmantel of the Dining Room, Northumberland House, 1657. 'Book of Capitols', formerly at Chatsworth, fol. 32. RIBA Collections (96666)

228 John Webb, design for a fanciful composite capital for the overmantel of the Withdrawing Room at Northumberland House, ?1660. 'Book of Capitols', formerly at Chatsworth, fol. 33. RIBA Collections (96667)

The last of our blessed Kings, & D: of Yorke by Lilly: A rosarie of flo[wers]: by the famous Jesuite of Bruxells & severall more'. But by 1671, only three years after the death of the 10th Earl, the number of paintings had nearly doubled to 66, while there were 55 at Petworth and 19 at Syon. Totalling 140, they were valued altogether at £4260 10s, a relatively low figure considering the number of masterpieces and the prices originally paid by Northumberland.[92] The collection included six Brussels tapestries of the Story of David acquired by the earl in the early 1630s and

NORTHUMBERLAND HOUSE | 215

still at Petworth in 1670, together with five more hangings of the Story of Vulcan, probably woven at Mortlake, which were later sold.[93] Eight tapestries of the Story of Esther, once in the 9th Earl's Closet and Bed Chamber at Petworth, had also left the collection during Algernon's lifetime.[94]

The contents of Northumberland House alone, with the exception of the sixty-six paintings, which were separately appraised, were worth more than £31,000 in 1670.[95] They included five coaches with twenty-six horses, jewellery and gold plate, fabrics bought in Venice, as well as 116 pieces of either tapestry or gilt leather hangings, old and new, with seven 'of the hunting Story 13 foot deepe with half Moones at the Corners'. The furniture was housed in some ninety rooms, not the total since the inventory is incomplete. It included 'Two new French Beds one of greene Damask with Gold & Silver Fringe … The other of Yellow Damask with Silk Fringe and Silk Buttons', valued at £800; a set of new and old French plates, including '14 Mazarene Plates', came to a further £3056 5s 11d.[96] To this collection must be added the group of antique statues and busts bought in the late 1650s from the king's collection, which were returned to the Crown in 1660.[97]

The Restoration of the Monarchy marked the end of the second and last series of works, and is referred to in the accounts as 'Railing the streete before the house when his Ma:tie came through the City to Whitehall', to protect the house from the masses.[98] The danger was real, since the 10th Earl had taken an active part in the very first discussions for the return of the king, known as the Suffolk House Cabal and held at Northumberland House. Clarendon labelled the earl as the 'proudest man alive', continuing that 'if he had thought the King as much above him as he thought himself above other considerable men, he would have been a good subject'.[99] But the earl was to rise once again, as Charles II made him a Privy Councillor, the Lord Lieutenant of Sussex and of Northumberland and Lord High Constable.

Subsequent Years: 1668–1874

Algernon Percy spent his last years at Petworth, where he died on 13 October 1668 aged sixty-five. He was succeeded by his son Josceline, 11th Earl (1644–1670), who died without a male heir two years later.[100] The estate, together with

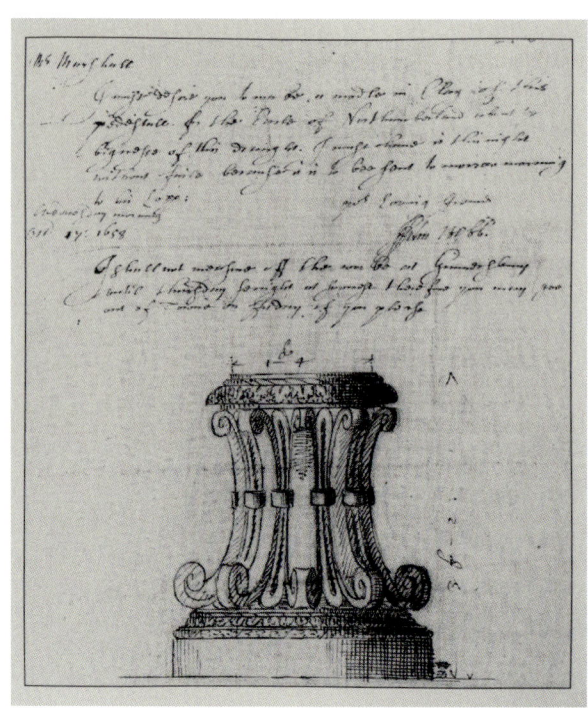

229 John Webb, design for a chimneypiece and overmantel, and plan of the overmantel, in the Withdrawing Room, Northumberland House, 1660. RIBA Collections (22927)

230 Letter from John Webb to Edward Marshall, with an elevation for a pedestal, 17 October 1658. RIBA Collections, Boy Collection 17. Reproduced by permission of Chatsworth Settlement Trustees

'Mr Marshall / I must desire you to make a modle in clay of this / pedestal for the Earle of Northumberland about ye bignesse of this draught. I must have it this night / without faile because it is to be gone tomorrow morning / to his Lopp, / your loving friend / John Webb/ Wednesday morning / Oct. 17, 1658 / I shall not measure off the [?] be at Gunnersbury / until Thursday sennight at [?] therefore you may goe / out of town on Friday if you please.'

Northumberland House, was inherited by his infant daughter, Lady Elizabeth Percy (1667–1722), who married Charles Seymour, 6th Duke of Somerset (1662–1748), in 1682.[101] Their son, Algernon, 7th Duke of Somerset (1684–1750), was created Earl of Northumberland in 1749 with special remainder to Sir Hugh Smithson, 4th Baronet (1714–1786), who in 1740 had become Seymour's son-in-law by marrying his daughter Elizabeth, Baroness Percy, his heiress and only surviving child. On the 7th Duke's death, Sir Hugh assumed the name and arms of the ancient house of Percy and was created 1st Duke of Northumberland of the third creation in 1766.[102]

Nothing of relevance seems to have happened at Northumberland House between 1668 and the late 1730s, when the 7th Duke of Somerset started updating the Jacobean house.[103] From then on, alterations were carried out almost without interruption, alongside building at Alnwick and Syon. In London, this outpouring of activity, made possible by the combination of Percy, Seymour and Smithson wealth, concentrated on the south front of Northumberland House, which increasingly became the heart of its public life.[104] During the course of the eighteenth and nineteenth centuries, the architects called in for advice or directly involved with alterations included leading professionals such as Daniel Garrett, James Paine, Robert Adam, C. R. Cockerell, Thomas Hardwick, Thomas Cundy and Sir Charles Barry.[105] Called in 1852, Barry's grand scheme of reconstruction was to link the outer wings by a continuous arcade to avoid the inconvenience of a single, narrow entrance from the street, thus effectively bypassing the old side of the house while giving the new one a proper approach from the garden, like a country house.[106] Furthermore, there was to be a new State Dining Room in the east wing, corresponding to the opposite Gallery or Ball Room created by Garrett a century earlier, which would have finalised the process of shifting the house's core, initiated by Algernon Percy. This was the last proposed improvement, for the amenities of the house were seriously affected by the building of Charing Cross Station in the 1860s, when the Metropolitan Board of Works began the process for the compulsory purchase of the complex. After years of litigation, the 5th Duke of Northumberland agreed to sell the house for £500,000 and from Tuesday–Thursday 8–10 September 1874 the greater part of the architectural fittings were sold in situ, while the remaining portion including the Strand front was sold on 10 November.[107] Each lot, as the sale catalogue specified, 'to be pulled down to the ground'.[108] In little less than three days, the last vestige of the Strand palaces was, tragically, stripped of its entire contents and subsequently demolished to make space for a new street connecting Trafalgar Square with the newly created Victoria Embankment.[109]

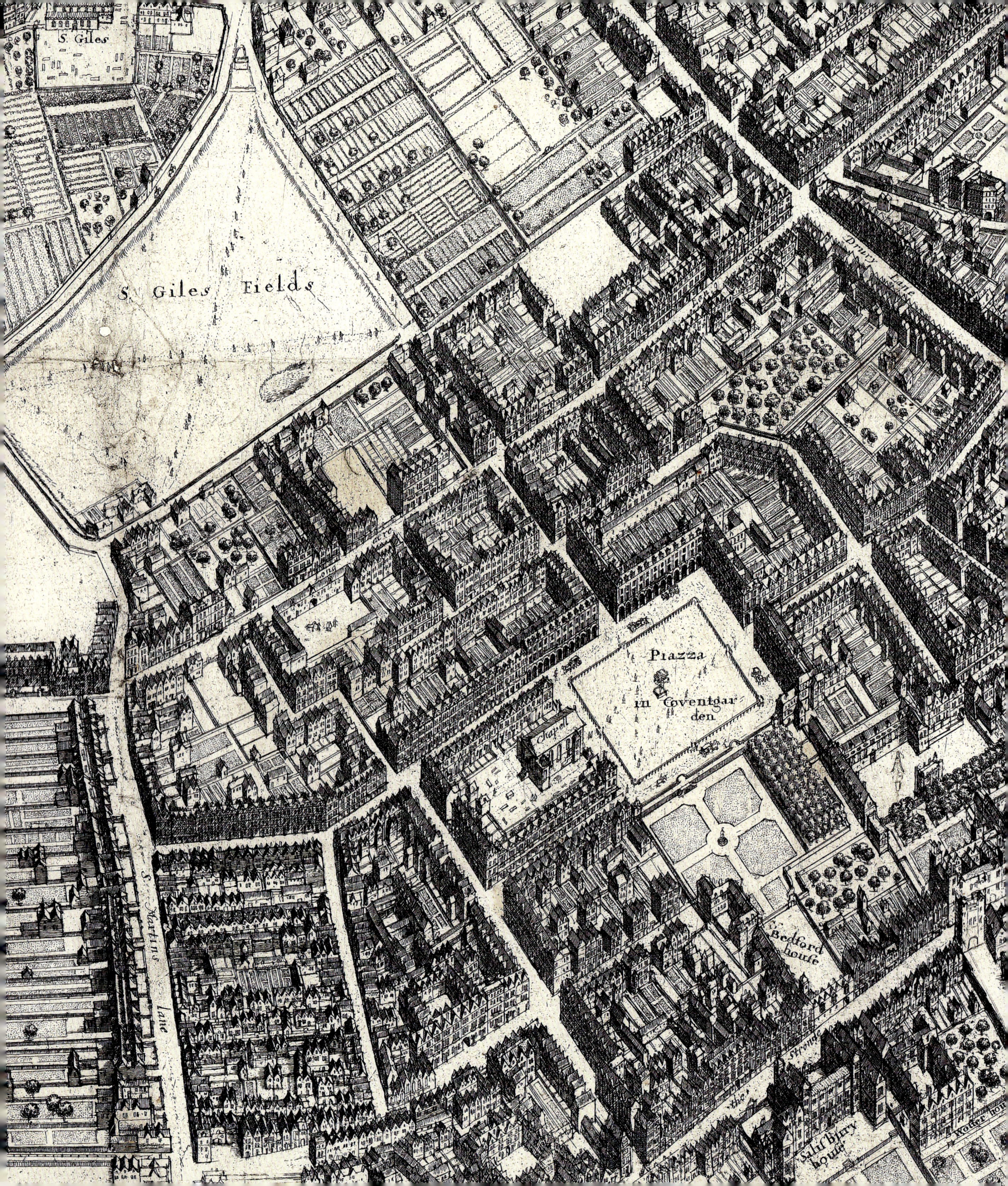

CONCLUSION

THE READER WHO HAS PROGRESSED THUS far may remember the promise made in the Preface that the Conclusion would highlight parallels and paint the broader picture. That, however, would be no small feat and would probably require another book, as is often the case in pioneering work. Two aspects, however, seem of particular importance here. The first concerns the architectural impact of the Strand palaces and their place in the wider history of Elizabethan and Jacobean architecture. The second is about their European significance. The first allows a useful discussion on similarities and innovations, peculiarities and differences, as well as rivalries, all displayed in the patterns of patronage by both men and women, artistic circles, long galleries and collections, gardens, size and style. These are the features that made these buildings startlingly modern or new, locating them historically as a unique group, while also revealing what each individual house represented in the complex and competitive galaxy of the Golden Mile.[1] This, in turn, leads to a core part of this conclusion, the Strand palaces in the context of the great country houses of the period.

Let me begin, therefore, with impact and significance. As noted at the outset, English architecture of the period has been contrasted with Inigo Jones's Italianate style and been found insular or backward. In this book, however, what I have argued is that each house fills a particular part of an elaborate, self-conscious and potent jigsaw, whereby London as the undisputed headquarters of architectural conspicuous consumption represented the nation's ascendancy over the world. That jigsaw was nationalistic but was equally forward-looking and international – just the right mixture for the sense of Englishness at that time. The Tudor and Jacobean court was striving to establish a new identity after the break with Rome, using trade and political alliances that went far beyond those just across the Channel, as Matt Dimmock brilliantly recounts in *Elizabethan Globalism* (2019).[2] It is ironic, given present politics, that English identity and the legacy of its principal architect, Henry VIII, is still in flux, and perhaps architecture can only achieve so much. But the Strand reached an unprecedented level of sophistication, to the extent that one might even say that it gave rise to a truly English style, exemplified at Hardwick Hall, Derbyshire. What, then, do we understand of each of the houses and how do they contribute to the jigsaw? Essex House, the most easterly, was very large and presented

231 Wenceslaus Hollar, bird's-eye view of the 'West Central District' (detail of fig. 8)

an entirely formal elaborate garden, which must have acted as the main public access from the river. Yet the palace was architecturally conventional and inconspicuous, accrued in a piecemeal fashion. Until, that is, you stepped inside and were confronted not just by three great chambers but three long galleries, one exceptionally located on the top floor.

Galleries had become established features by the mid-1570s but few contemporary palaces, whether in London or in the country, matched those at Essex House created by Robert Dudley, 1st Earl of Leicester, from 1569. One exception may have been the London house of his grandfather Edmund Dudley, which featured four galleries on different levels, in place by as early as 1509.[3] Early Tudor prototypes could be found at Richmond, Thornbury and Whitehall, though the first proper long gallery was the Queen's Gallery at Hampton Court, built between 1533 and 1537 and located on the first floor.[4] Putting a gallery on the top floor was probably in response to lack of ground space in dense urban environments, such as at Thomas Fowler's house in the 1560s or at Lord Shrewsbury's a decade later, both in London.[5]

In the Strand itself, the two long galleries of Somerset House as built by Edward Seymour in the mid-sixteenth century were on the first floor, one in the east wing of the main quadrangle, 100 feet across by 120 feet, while the other, on the east side of the inner courtyard, must have been about 120 feet long and 20 feet wide. These were of a comparable breadth to the High or top-floor Gallery at Essex House but may have been shorter than its Long Gallery, which does not appear in bills of the period. Equally, the Gallery at Burghley House, while chronologically earlier, could hardly have competed, not least in terms of position. It is clear that not just the breadth but the succession of galleries from top floor to bottom at Essex House set the pace in the Strand and beyond. Indeed, as far as top-floor galleries were concerned, the High Gallery with its barrel-vaulted ceiling was probably the first of its kind. The gallery at Chatsworth followed in 1575–8 and was seen by Dudley when it had just been completed, during his visit in June 1579.[6] Back on the Strand, at the neighbouring Arundel House the gallery wing, completed and perhaps conceived by Henry Fitzalan, 12th Earl of Arundel, in the second half of the sixteenth century, was remodelled by Inigo Jones in the mid-1610s as the highlight of the state rooms. About a decade earlier, Robert Cecil, 1st Earl of Salisbury, had also added a second gallery to his own Salisbury House, possibly in part to match that of his fellow architectural patron and rival at Northampton House, built between 1605 and 1614. With its 160 feet, this gallery occupied the whole top floor of the eastern wing and clearly epitomised how far the influence of Essex House had reached. Indeed, even Bess of Hardwick's celebrated top-floor gallery of 167 feet was built after those at Essex House, which she saw when she lodged there in June 1576.[7] Hardwick Hall may even have been influenced by what Leicester had done at Kenilworth, which set the model for the Elizabethan compact 'high house'.[8] In terms of content and display, almost every room at Essex House had tapestries on view, totalling 131 pieces predominantly 'ould', while 1348 items – pistols, muskets and other warfare memorabilia, including five complete sets of armour – decorated its interiors. Yet Leicester's interest in paintings, recorded at eighty-one, preceded the great aristocratic picture collections of seventeenth-century London, of which the next house became the embodiment.

Arundel House is a game of contrasts, from a piecemeal ensemble of the main buildings over an impressive site, to the novelty of galleries, gardens and water gate, all of which saw the virtuoso collaboration between the famous Earl Collector, Thomas Howard, and Inigo Jones. This is an important shift from the previous house, and follows what had begun at Somerset House: the use of the Italianate style to stress cultural lineage and distinction. After all, Jones largely owed his architectural career to Arundel, well known as the 'father of *virtu*' in England but equally conscious of his ancient ancestry. Others of newer ancestry, such as Seymour or the Cecils, could only pretend to such pride.

Arundel was not alone in this pursuit of architectural innovation, for his wife Aletheia Talbot, Bess of Hardwick's granddaughter, played an important role too. Indeed, scattered throughout the history, there are many women who took leading roles in the construction, development and the overall management of the Strand palaces. The obvious role model was that one woman at the top of the pyramid, Elizabeth I, who treated the Strand for what it was, an extension of Whitehall, beginning with her lover's nest at Essex House. Mildred

Cecil, for instance, wife to Lord Burghley, is well known for her part in his enterprises and success, while their son Robert Cecil's own wife Elizabeth had a similar role. But Countess Aletheia, as well as managing Jones's changes at Arundel House, was an architectural and artistic patroness in her own right. She was involved, for instance, with the purchase of the Gonzaga collection by Charles I.[9] Lucy Harrington, Countess of Bedford, the wife of the 2nd Earl, was a celebrated gardener, patroness and literary hostess too. There are leading women among the Worcesters who dared challenge Robert Cecil's expansion frenzy, while Bess Ralegh, the wife of Sir Walter, corresponded with him over another complex transaction, thereby providing us with the chief evidence on Durham House. Margaret, Countess of Salisbury, the wife of the 3rd Earl, took an active part at a difficult juncture for the family, while Percy women, especially Elizabeth, Duchess of Northumberland, made headlines in the later history of Northumberland House and in London's cultural scene more generally.[10] It is indeed through the writings of these figures that we often learn what happened to the Strand palaces, for their husbands, with some notable exceptions, were too busy to write. Equally, one gets the impression that these women were the ones left to disentangle various business matters, perhaps because their husbands were imprisoned or away or had died.

If the collection of the Earl and Countess of Arundel is shrouded in myth when it comes to numbers – paintings alone may have approached 700 – its quality and diversity clearly stood out, even when compared with that of the other great collector and rival in the Strand, the Duke of Buckingham, whose paintings may 'merely' have numbered some 400. Not only did the Arundel collection include the celebrated marbles which filled the earl's gallery and garden but it also featured some 200 books of drawings by the greatest Italian masters, for which Jones created a purpose-built design room, perhaps the first of its kind and certainly the first in the Strand. Then there was the famous library, furnished with globes and marble busts of Greek and Roman philosophers, which contained an impressive collection of books and manuscripts, including architectural treatises, some from Northampton House.

Somerset House is a special case. It was built largely from scratch and established a new type, that of an 'aristocratic palace of monarchical intent'.[11] This was to change the course of English architecture, in both town and country, beginning with the patrons in Edward Seymour's powerful inner circle. His steward, Sir John Thynne, built Longleat, Wiltshire (1567–75), one of those 'prodigy houses' which could offer hospitality to the entire court, and William Cecil, whose early career was spent in Seymour's service, created Burghley House, Northamptonshire (1558–87), Theobalds, Hertfordshire (1564–85) and his own Burghley House in the Strand (from 1559). Other houses such as Kirby Hall, Northamptonshire (1570–75), Wollaton, Nottinghamshire (1580–88) or again the splendid Hardwick Hall (1590–97) all paid tribute to the model set up by Seymour in the Strand. It is therefore not surprising that the typology of the stately town-house began to merge with that of the country house. The grand town-house was defined by a style but was also governed by precise ceremonial arrangements requiring a sequence of rooms for the so-called 'keeping of state' (Hall, Great Chamber, Withdrawing Chamber, Bedchamber and Long Gallery). Somerset House's role in the seventeenth century was no less important: like Theobalds, Audley End or even Northampton House in the Strand, all designed to attract royal attention, it officially became the residence of queens. As a royal palace, Somerset House was provided with a chapel, thereby establishing a new secular model of palace and church in London. Chapels within palace complexes were certainly a must in Renaissance and Baroque Italy and in London had previously characterised those with episcopal origins such as the Savoy and Durham House. The type was later reinterpreted at Bedford House with the construction of St Paul's Covent Garden. There too, as well as at Somerset House, Jones was the architect.

Bedford House and Burghley House were the only two palaces on the north side of the Strand. Without a riverfront, they developed towards Covent Garden and had magnificent gardens. This was perhaps their most distinctive attribute, though Bedford House was unique in having a Long Gallery entirely facing the Strand, with three large windows on both sides. Its garden featured a grotto and three banqueting houses attributed to Isaac de Caus, who had joined Edward Carter in the surveyorship of Jones's work at Covent Garden. De Caus was also responsible for the grottos at the Banqueting House

(1623), Somerset House (1630–33) and Woburn Abbey (1633–4), while Carter later worked at Northumberland House. As for Burghley House, its rather austere Strand facade contrasted sharply with its garden one, which had an open loggia overlooking a remarkable ensemble of garden features. This mirrored what one would expect in a large country estate, mixing formality with three banqueting houses (much bigger than Bedford's) and the utilitarian with orchards and kitchen gardens, and a mound such as those at Sir Thomas Gresham's Lyveden New Bield. Burghley House's mound may have provided an elevated viewing platform and perhaps a glimpse of the river (another banqueting house could even have sat on top of it, like that of Henry VIII at Hampton Court) and statues of twelve Roman emperors (sent from Venice in 1561) may also have decorated this garden of the 'Nestor of Britain', as Camden called Burghley. The poet also noted the presence there of an inscription from the Roman remains at Chichester, all of which preceded the museum gardens of Arundel, Buckingham or indeed Charles I.

Where the castle-like appearance of Burghley House reflected the ambition of its owner and creator – for William Cecil was the quintessential architectural patron of the day – the interiors, with two libraries and three studies where 'all evidences and rolls belonging to his pedigrees' as well as 'all writing concerning the Queen' were preserved,[12] remind us of the character of the man who had ruled the country (and thereby became extremely wealthy). Cecil's libraries are also a reminder that the Strand palaces were centres of administration, where all records were kept. Similarly, it was in London that the bulk of their collections were displayed: while ancestral roots lay deep in the country, political (and therefore material) fortunes were made in town.

Back on the riverside, the special character of the Savoy was as a place of lodging and reception, whereas that of its neighbouring Worcester House was about sequestration and the Civil Wars. Neither are architecturally particularly significant, the first as it never developed into a Strand palace (despite having begun as a royal palace), the second as it appears to have lost scope somewhat once the Russells had crossed the Strand to Bedford House: indeed, the Russells became key pioneering players in the area.[13] That said, Worcester House featured a 'Surveying Place', one of those buildings by the river's edge also to be found at Essex House and Salisbury House. Essex's was a fairly grand one, where the famous series of four tapestries adapted from plates by Jan Vredeman de Vries hung. De Vries was also one of the main sources of influence for the 'Porticus' at Salisbury House, a monument to Robert Cecil's scholarly reputation and a celebration of James I as the *Rex Pacificus*.[14] That palace was completed at remarkable speed thanks to an unprecedented level of what might be called indiscriminate state support, with not only materials but a royal surveyor and craftsmen fully deployed on it. Such haste was propelled by the advanced age of Queen Elizabeth, who attended the housewarming party in December 1602, barely three months before her death. It seems fitting that the event was the ultimate display of Elizabeth's globalism, such was the exoticism of Cecil's collection.

Durham House, in contrast, is an excellent example of how an important episcopal palace was repurposed, almost with no change. But for this book its interest lay in what was not built, what would have happened had Webb's plans for its grandiose rebuilding been executed. These illustrate a clear shift from the notion (and acceptability) of a complex defined by piecemeal additions to that of a majestic regularity hitherto unseen, embodying what a royal favourite at Pembroke's level could aspire to in the 1640s, despite the outbreak of the Civil Wars. After all, major Strand projects did indeed carry on regardless: Northumberland House was completely refurbished throughout the 1640s and '50s. York House is another exceptional case. Not only is it the palace where the secularisation of liturgy via the Ellesmere ordinances took root but it also became the epitome of extravagance of one of the most notorious courtiers of the Stuart era, the Duke of Buckingham. This is connected to the grandeur of Pembroke's plans, as both were royal favourites. But in Buckingham's case, the old episcopal palace linked to the country's highest office, that of the Privy Seal, was indeed transformed. Behind it all was Balthasar Gerbier, perhaps as extravagant as his patron, who filled the palace with the other great collection assembled in the Strand – hundreds of paintings and a range of furniture which made for astonishing Italianate, French and Dutch interiors, unrivalled in significance. After all, Rubens was among Buckingham's chief protégés, thirty-two of whose paintings hung at York House. The new interiors also included a 'grand cabinet de marbre' designed for display, from which the Marble Closet at Bolsover Castle is probably derived.

Last but not least, Northumberland House is primarily about scale and how northern European influences added to the eclecticism of the early Jacobean style. These reflect Northampton's own taste, apparently distinct from Jones's classicism. This take is in a way peculiar, as Northampton's design choices may seem unexpected given that all the Howards, including his great nephew the Earl of Arundel, were famously philo-Catholic. But one cannot connect style to religious affiliations in a simple way, for what mattered most of all was lineage and dynastic ambitions, which took different, individual paths. After all, Northampton was a bachelor in old age when he finally embarked on building works, like Bess of Hardwick, and was perhaps more interested in following tradition (say, of Perpendicular English Gothic) than being innovative via the Italianate. Indeed, given his ancient roots, he may have considered it as unnecessary. But this was not backwardness or lack of knowledge – Howard was the most learned among the nobles. Rather, it was a conscious iconography. His collection reflected his stature, an exotic mixture of contemporary European and Asian luxury objects, including Turkish carpets and wares from China, while some of Cardinal Wolsey's tapestries, commissioned for York House and Hampton Court from 1515, hung in his bedroom. His two libraries were also famed, later forming the bulk of the Bibliotheca Norfolciana at the Royal Society. From what might be thought an architecturally conservative start, Northumberland House then became a laboratory for architectural experimentation, beginning from the major refurbishments carried out by the Percys when they took it over in 1642, down to the many changes it underwent until its demolition in 1874. By then, almost every architect of standing, from the dominance of immigrant sculptor architects such as Bernard Janssen and Gerard Christmas in Jacobean times, to the great native-born designers of public buildings of the nineteenth century such as Sir Charles Barry, had passed through its doors.

What then can be inferrred about the relationship of the Strand palaces to their rural counterparts? First of all, the question of whether a model for the elite town-house existed independently from that of the country house (one which I explored elsewhere[15]) appears to be the wrong one. For they are not one versus the other, as one might deduce from the far more numerous studies on the country house (partly because country houses have generally survived). But they are in all respects two sides of the same coin, certainly in so far as the period of this book goes. One should therefore not fall into the trap of seeming to place the town palaces in temporal advance of the great country houses. For the question is actually what distinguishes them and the answer is scale and, most crucially, land.[16] In terms of style and fashion, however, London took the lead, as illustrated by the impact of Somerset House on an extensive list of country houses. This is not surprising or unique to England, for anyone wishing to establish a dynasty, especially in the Early Modern period, needed a palace in town and a base in the country (ideally, more than one!). Apart from town-houses being accessible and consequently influential, the deployment of the latest urban style was a strong indicator of the status of a magnate, especially on large and isolated rural estates, where comparison was nil. This was particularly the case when a new elite, alongside a new geo-political identity, was in the process of being established. To their subjects, great country houses such as Burghley or Longleat would have looked like a wave of new cathedrals celebrating new secular lords, as potent as those white villas of Palladio, used as tools in a programme of land restructuring (hence of the aristocracy connected to it) in the Veneto.

It is the interiors that illustrate more clearly the different functions of town and country. The most fashionable items, particularly paintings and particularly those of foreign monarchs and dignitaries, were kept in the Strand, for that was the site of politics and diplomacy. By contrast, the dynastic side of collections naturally found its place in the ancestral seats, for they represented roots, actual or invented. Country houses also enabled the erection of prominent chapels, not straightforward within urban confines. In addition, family chapels attached to country parish churches acted as dynastic mausolea, another fundamental tool in stressing the link between origins and land. And it is indeed land, hence space, which allowed the scale and development that was rarely affordable otherwise, and which gave rise to the prodigy house in which the entire court could be hosted during the summer progress. This was particularly the case with Elizabeth I, who treated both the Strand houses and their rural counterparts as an extension of Whitehall, an attitude that shaped both and continued to do so under the Stuarts. After all, the most prominent Strand palaces were themselves prodigy houses, while that idea of a 'royal palace with monarchical intent', perhaps first exercised by Wolsey at Hampton Court, had clearly taken root in the Strand.

While the Thames acted as a powerful backdrop for ceremonial access via imposing water gates, ample views of the river and city were commanded through loggias, surveying and banqueting houses, porticoes, towers and roof promenades. So from the roofs of country houses land could be seen as far as the horizon. At Burghley, once again, this is most emphatic, for its extraordinary chimneystacks devised as Doric columns act as powerful reminders of the might and scholarly nature of its builder. As a clear symbol of wealth, they can be seen from afar, like great cathedral spires, while all together they recreate an archaeological promenade, as if the viewer were in a Greek temple. Hardwick too, with its top-floor majestically tall state rooms, is an essay in English Perpendicular Gothic, while Wollaton, with its puzzling Great Hall at the top is reminiscent of the suspended and equally bewildering room at Ely Cathedral. As we observed, this eclecticism full of symbols was tried out in London and then amplified and re-interpreted in the country, at the behest of the same patrons and often using the same craftsmen. Outside London, patrons could generally build from scratch according to a chosen plan, an important by-product of space. It is not by chance that those Strand palaces built largely from scratch – Somerset House, Burghley House, Northampton (Northumberland) House – were in all respects smaller versions of country houses. Indeed, the 'Book of Architecture' of John Thorpe contains plans applicable to both town and country, including one for 'three houses for the city or for a country house': precisely as I argue, space alone made the difference.[17]

The difference in role between town and country is key to the European significance of the Strand palaces. In extent and nature their collections, for instance, were such that they acted as proto-academies at a time when dedicated institutions were being established on the Continent (such as the Académie de France à Rome);[18] they were, in all respects, the precursors of public museums. Apart from displaying conspicuous consumption, the long galleries acted as multinational assemblages of the material products of the known world (see Essex House), pioneering the museum. Another role of the town palace was its ceremonial one, which generated a typology for the keeping of state that provided the perfect stage for international diplomacy. As has been remarked, the Strand acted as an extension of the court, not only because royal construction had virtually halted after Henry VIII but perhaps because it actually made more sense to let courtiers undertake it. This is not, once again, an isolated phenomenon but can be seen throughout the great European courts, beginning with the popes in Rome – in the great projects of 1655–67 initiated and promoted by Fabio Chigi, Pope Alexander VII, he largely relied on the aristocracy to organise construction, mutually benefiting each other.[19]

Throughout this book the meanings of the term 'palace' and the implications for the way these houses were perceived have been discussed. Further discussion of whether the overall development of the Strand echoes, perhaps precedes or shows a different chronology from similar developments in other great European cities (such as Rome, Genoa or Antwerp) would compare aristocracies, courts and customs, which is outside the remit of this book. James Howell's *Londinopolis*, published in 1657, includes a fascinating chapter called 'A Parallel, By Way of Corollary, Betwixt London and Other great Cities in the World', where one reads of how Rome, though 'as big as London', may instead 'be called a Wilderness, in comparison of her'. While Howell's is a witty though biased comparison with what he described as 'Cities of the first Magnitude',[20] this book has shown how the prestige and the use and role of the Strand palaces in impressing visitors can be traced through those (perhaps less biased) foreigners who worked or lodged in them, or indeed visited, in great numbers and often from far away. Indeed, their comparisons with their own familiar towns and cities and what exactly impressed them about 'the palace' of the sovereign are one of the most telling sources we have to determine the European impact of the Strand houses.

The French ambassador Sully, who stayed at Arundel House in 1603, described it as 'one of the most beautiful and convenient lodgings with the most numerous rooms on one floor and all of one suite that I have ever seen'.[21] Its outstanding collection and splendour became famous and the palace was visited by artists up to royalty. These included Joachim von Sandrart,[22] Abram Booth of the Dutch East India Company[23] and Charles I.[24] Along similar lines, as discussed in Chapter Three, the Venetian ambassador described Somerset House in 1604 as 'the most splendid house in London after the royal palace'.[25] Indeed, it accommodated embassies in 1572 and 1578–9, the Prince Dauphin of France in 1581 and in 1604 the Spanish and Dutch delegations gathered there for the 'Somerset House Conference' (see fig. 7).[26] It was inspected in 1623 as a possible residence for the new queen but Durham House was judged the most suitable (as described in Chapter Three). The Spanish Ambassador Extraordinary was instead lodged at Burghley House, which had been used for such events as a magnificent state dinner for the French delegation in 1581, after a similar one at Essex House, when hopes to secure a marriage for Elizabeth I were still alive.

The Savoy was the most royal in origin of all the palaces within our period but among the first hospitals to be established in London, even drawing foreign visitors in the 1540s.[27] After the Restoration in 1660, it hosted the Savoy Conference in 1661, which led to the Act of Uniformity. Then in 1666 it was Bedford House that the Frenchman Samuel de Sorbière called a 'palais'.[28] And Salisbury House in 1602 had been the stage, as previously noted, for one of Elizabeth I's last public engagements, which turned out to be one of the most significant in terms of her international legacy. This house, alongside Somerset House, had also performed as the theatre for masques by Ben Jonson and Inigo Jones, another role that characterised the Strand palaces and their wider European significance. Robert Cecil's Exchange, or 'Britain Burse', was described as England's 'Venetian Rialto', an indication of the richness of its merchandise and how much London had become the centre of foreign luxuries.[29] Durham House, just behind it, was occupied by several embassies and agents in the 1620s, from France to Florence.[30]

York House, similarly to the others along the Strand, illustrates how English ambassadors had been involved in procuring architectural models, in this case of the Villa Farnese at Caprarola.[31] This was probably directed at Gerbier, who masterminded the reconstruction of York House while amassing its extraordinary collection. It is also Gerbier who informs us that Buckingham entertained 'forreign Princes and Embassadors'.[32] Its interiors were praised by the French ambassador in 1626 and in the 1670s it housed the Spanish, the Russian, the Danish, the French and the Portuguese ambassadors in succession.[33] As discussed in Chapter Ten, York House's water gate has also drawn the attention of many artists and architects and been compared to Paris's monumental arches.[34] Northumberland House too was used for political meetings and to host foreign ambassadors. In 1623 it was offered as a residence for Prince Charles and in 1625 it accommodated the French ambassador.[35] It was also here that the very first discussions for the return of the king after the Civil Wars took place. Indeed, by the end of its uniquely long history the house had come to signify both the peak and decline of the Strand's glory.

In conclusion, the Strand palaces stood as the epitome of a unique architectural and political epoch whereby an image of potency and influence was displayed both for internal and international consumption, so as to shape not just English but European identity. This followed the earthquakes of the Reformation and Calvinism, which forged new cultural, political and economic relations. And it is by emulating the polyglot nature and largesse of the great European courts, while still maintaining their own unique character, that these houses portrayed the image and power of Englishness to the world. What influence they had on the Continent is however hard to quantify and perhaps their uniqueness remains their most distinguishing trait. For, notwithstanding London's role in international diplomacy and the pivotal role of the Strand palaces which impressed visitors, it remains the case that English buildings were only rarely engraved (and building designs not at all), unlike those in France and Italy (less perhaps in Northern Europe). The wider circulation of all the views and maps at the core of this book forms another strand for future research but there is certainly no equivalent of de l'Orme, du Cerceau, de Vries, Serlio, Palladio, Scamozzi or indeed the architectural propaganda albums of the likes of Giovan Battista Falda's *Nuovo Teatro delle Fabbriche et Edificii in prospettiva di Roma moderna* (1665–99), widely distributed in Europe. Lack of images also means that there was no wider knowledge of what English buildings in the provinces looked like – no available images of Hardwick or Montacute, for instance. But, if anything, this reinforces my main point: the importance of the example of actual buildings in London and the crucial role played by its 'Golden Mile'.

Notes

Introduction

1 I am grateful to Maurice Howard for pointing this out to me and for his suggestions about the title of this book.

2 According to Google Maps, the length of the Strand from Temple Bar and Charing Cross is 0.8 miles. In 'Location, Location, Location! Cecil House in the Strand', *Architectural History*, 45 (2002), 159, Jill Husselby and Paula Henderson refer to it as the 'Golden three-quarter Mile'. This was picked up by Matthew Dimmock, *Elizabethan Globalism: England, China and the Rainbow Portrait* (New Haven and London, 2019), 31.

3 David Pearce, *London's Mansions: Private Palaces of the Nobility* (London, 1986), 13.

4 Of the nine palaces overlooking the Thames, all but Northumberland House had gardens right down to the river. Two of them, the Savoy and Durham House, featured buildings on the water's edge.

5 John Stow, *The Survay of London* (1598) (London, 1618), 14.

6 William Harrison, *Description of England*, 1577, quoted by Christopher Simon Sykes, *Private Palaces: Life in the Great London Houses* (London, 1985), 15.

7 I am grateful to Gordon Higgott for this suggestion, and for reading and commenting on a draft of this introduction.

8 Raphael Holinshed and William Harrison, *The first and second volumes of Chronicles, comprising 1 The description and historie of England, 2 The description and historie of Ireland, 3 The description and historie of Scotland: first collected and published by Raphaell Holinshed, William Harrison, and others: now newlie augmented and continued (with manifold matters of singular note and worthie memorie) to the yeare 1586* (London, 1587), bk II, ch. XII, 187. See also Georges Edelen, ed., *The Description of England: The Classic Contemporary Account of Tudor Social Life by William Harrison* (Ithaca, NY, 1968).

9 A pre-Roman track, later Romanised, the name 'Stronde' is found by 1185, at which date the road went along the river: see Gillian Bebbington, *London Street Names* (London, 1972), 312–13; Ben Weinreb and Christopher Hibbert, eds, *The London Encyclopaedia* (London, 1983), 852–3.

10 See Bruno Barber and Christopher Thomas, *The London Charterhouse* (London, 2002); Philip Temple, *The Charterhouse*, vol. 18 of *Survey of London* (New Haven and London, 2010).

11 See Phyllis Hembry, 'Episcopal Palaces, 1535 to 1660', in E. W. Ives, R. J. Knecht and J. J. Scarisbrick, eds, *Wealth and Power in Tudor England: Essays presented to S. T. Bindoff* (London, 1978), 146–66; Felicity Heal, *Of Prelates and Princes: A Study of the Economic and Social Position of the Tudor Episcopate* (Cambridge, 1980); Christopher Phillpotts, 'The Houses of Henry VIII's Courtiers in London', in David R. M. Gaimster and Roberta Gilchrist, eds, *The Archaeology of Reformation 1480–1580* (Leeds, 2003), 299–309. For most of the great monastic houses post-Dissolution see the monographs published by the Museum of London Archaeological Service (MOLAS).

12 Sometimes called Leicester House but I follow most of the literature in calling it Essex House.

13 Dimmock, *Elizabethan Globalism*, 31.

14 I am grateful to Mark Girouard for pointing out the lack of images and for reading and commenting on a draft of this introduction.

15 Artistic licence is clearly visible in Burghley and Salisbury House: see Chs 5 and 8. Nor has the date of Hollar's view been firmly set. See Richard T. Godfrey, *Wenceslaus Hollar: A Bohemian Artist in England* (New Haven and London, 1995), cat. 102; see also Ch. 1, n. 50.

16 See Howard Colvin and Susan Foister, eds, *The Panorama of London circa 1544 by Anthonis van den Wyngaerde* (London, 1996).

17 See Adrian Prockter and Robert Taylor, *A to Z of Elizabethan London* (London, 1979); Ann Saunders and John Schofield, eds, *Tudor London: A Map and a View* (London, 2001).

18 John Summerson, *Architecture in Britain: 1530–1830* (New Haven and London, 1993), 16.

19 See Chs 3, 8 and 11. The two palaces on the north side, Bedford House and Burghley House, did have Strand facades but of course lacked the more important river ones: see Chs 5 and 6.

20 See Susannah A. Bach, 'Courtier Classicism in the Reign of Edward VI: Protector Somerset and his Architectural Image', BA diss., University of Cambridge, 1995, 19–23.

21 François van der Delft quoted in Jennifer Loach, *Protector Somerset: A Reassessment* (Bangor, 1994), 38.

22 The phrase was aptly used in John Bold, *John Webb: Architectural Theory and Practice in the Seventeenth Century* (Oxford, 1989), 74, to define Webb's design for Durham House: see Ch. 9.

23 Christiane Hille, *Vision of the Courtly Body: The Patronage of George Villiers, First Duke of Buckingham, and the Triumph of Painting at the Stuart Court* (Berlin, 2012), 122.

24 Lord Howard to Viscount Rochester, 26 May 1612, CSP, *Domestic Series*, James I, *1611–18* (London, 1858), 133. See also Manolo Guerci, 'The Construction of Northumberland House and the Patronage of its Original Builder, Lord Henry Howard: 1603–14', *The Antiquaries Journal*, 90 (2010), 345–8.

25 See Stow, *Survay of London* (1598) (London, 1603); John Manningham, 'Diary of John Manningham ... 1602–1603', *Camden Society*, vol. 99 (1868); James Howell, *Londinopolis* (London, 1657); John Strype, *A Survey of the Cities of London and Westminster...* (London, 1720); Robert and James Dodsley, *London and its Environs Described*, 5 vols (London, 1761); William Harrison, *A New and Universal History...* (London, 1776); Thomas Pennant, *Some Account of London* (London, 1791); David Hughson, *A History and Description of London, Westminster and Southwark*, 4 vols (London,

n.d.), vol. 4; Robert Wilkinson, *Londina illustrata*, 2 vols (London, 1819–25); Thomas Allen, *History and Antiquities of London*, 4 vols (London, 1827–8); Walter Thornbury and Edward Walford, *Old and New London*, 6 vols (London, 1879–85); Edwin Beresford Chancellor, *The Private Palaces of London: Past and Present* (London, 1908); Beresford Chancellor, *Annals of the Strand …* (London, 1912); Alfred Clapham and Walter H. Godfrey, *Some Famous Buildings and their Story* (London, 1913); Greater London Council, *Survey of London* (London, 1900–); Henry Benjamin Wheatley, *London, Past and Present: A Dictionary of its History, Associations, and Traditions* (1891) (Cambridge, 2011); Hermione Hobhouse, *Lost London: A Century of Demolition and Decay* (London and Basingstoke, 1971); Weinreb and Hibbert, *London Encyclopaedia*; Pearce (1986); John Schofield, *Medieval London Houses* (New Haven and London, 1995, 2003), 212; Lena Cowen Orlin, ed., *Material London, ca 1600* (Philadelphia, Penn., 2000).
26 The Savoy (1878), Arundel House (1922) and Essex House (1923): see their respective chapters.
27 Salisbury House and Essex House (both 1981), York House (1985) and Bedford House (2001): see their respective chapters.
28 I owe this interesting description and some of these remarks to one of the anonymous peer reviewers, to whom I am most grateful for twice reviewing the manuscript of the book.

1 · Essex House

1 See Jane E. L. Clark, 'The Buildings and Art Collections of Robert Dudley, Earl of Leicester (with Notes on Portraits)', MA Report, Courtauld Institute of Art, University of London, 1981.
2 See Charles L. Kingsford, 'Essex House, formerly Leicester House and Exeter Inn', *Archaeologia*, 73 (1923), 1–54.
3 What follows is based on ibid. and Patricia E. C. Croot, Alan Thacker and Elizabeth Williamson, eds, *A History of the County of Middlesex*, vol. 13: *City of Westminster, Part 1* (London, 2009), 56–7, unless otherwise stated.
4 See M. C. Buck, 'Stapeldon, Walter', ODNB (Oxford, 2004), http://www.oxforddnb.com/view/article/26296, accessed 17 September 2016.
5 See A. Erskine, 'Grandison, John', ibid., http://www.oxforddnb.com/view/article/11238, accessed 17 September 2016.
6 John Stow, *The Survay of London: Containing, The Originall, Antiquitie, Encrease, and more Moderne Estate of the said Famous Citie* (London, 1598), vol. 2, 92, quoted by Kingsford, 'Essex House', 5; see also J. Howell, *Londinopolis: An Historicall Discourse …* (London, 1657), 348.
7 See Kingsford, 'Essex House', 6.
8 See M. A. R. Graves, 'Howard, Thomas, third duke of Norfolk', ODNB (Oxford, 2004), online edn., January 2008, http://www.oxforddnb.com/view/article/13940, accessed 4 October 2016.
9 Milford Lane, recorded by 1556, was probably named after William Milford, who had a ninety-year lease of a tenement on the western side of Exeter Inn from 1472: see Croot, Thacker and E. Williamson, *City of Westminster*, 57. The lane is clearly labelled in the Agas map of 1561–70 (see fig. 19).
10 See S. M. Jack, 'Paget, William, first Baron Paget', ODNB (Oxford, 2004), online edn., January 2008, http://www.oxforddnb.com/view/article/21121, accessed 4 October 2016.
11 Letters Patent, 19 July 1548, quoted in Kingsford, 'Essex House', 6.
12 See Ann Saunders and John Schofield, eds, *Tudor London: A Map and a View* (London, 2001).
13 TNA, C 54/818/32, deed of acquisition.
14 See Neville J. Williams, *All the Queen's Men: Elizabeth I and her Courtiers* (New York, 1972), 26.
15 See S. Adams, 'Dudley, Robert, earl of Leicester', ODNB (Oxford, 2004), online edn., May 2008, http://www.oxforddnb.com/view/article/8160, accessed 28 March 2017.
16 During the 1580s Dudley also used three other country houses: Grafton House in Northamptonshire, Benington in Hertfordshire and Langley in Oxfordshire.
17 As Master of the Horse, Dudley also had access to various royal palaces including Whitehall, where he entertained on a lavish scale in 1560. In 1588, the queen had granted him the old manor at Kew, which was his residence until he sold it in c.1563–4: see Simon Adams, 'Robert Dudley, Earl of Leicester, his Gardeners and Gardens', lecture at conference on Leicester and his gardeners, 2006 (related to English Heritage Kenilworth Garden Project); I am grateful to the author for kindly giving me a copy and for discussion on the subject. Where Dudley had lived before is unclear, though the household accounts suggest it may have been at Christchurch, or 'Cree Church', his brother and sister-in-law's London house, or at his uncle Sir Andrew Dudley's house in Holborn: Simon Adams, ed., *Household Accounts and Disbursement Books of Robert Dudley, Earl of Leicester, 1558–1561, 1584–1586*, Camden Society, 5th ser., vol. 6 (Cambridge, 1995), 25.
18 See Adams, *Household Accounts*, 25–7.
19 Clark, 'Buildings and Art Collections', 1981, 1.
20 Dudley quoted in HMC, *Calendar of the Manuscript of the Marquis of Bath Preserved at Longleat, Wiltshire*, vol. 2 (Dublin, 1907), 20–23 (1573–82): 'A note of things written in the glasse windowes at Buxtons': the adage was engraved in a window in the great guest hall at Buxton, Derbyshire; also quoted as 'proverbial' in Harrison's *Description of England* (London, 1577), 170.
21 Simon Adams's unrivalled knowledge of the subject he graciously shared with me on more than one occasion; see also Adams, *Household Accounts*; 'The Papers of Robert Dudley, Earl of Leicester I: The Browne–Evelyn Collection', *Archives*, 20, no. 87 (April 1992), 63–85; 'The Papers of Robert Dudley, Earl of Leicester II: The Atye–Cotton Collection', *Archives*, 20, no. 90 (October 1993), 131–44; 'The Papers of Robert Dudley, Earl of Leicester III: The Countess of Leicester's Collection', *Archives*, 22 (April 1996), 1–26.
22 TNA, Exchequer: King's Remembrancer: Memoranda Rolls and Enrolment Books, E 159/398.
23 John Norden, manuscript draft of *Speculum Britanniae*, BL, Harleian MS 570, fol. 39r, probably 1591–3, quoted in Elizabeth Goldring, *Robert Dudley, Earl of Leicester, and the World of Elizabethan Art* (New Haven and London, 2014), 213 and n. 45.
24 Stow, *Survay of London*, cited in John Strype, *A Survey of the Cities of London and Westminster: Containing the Origin …*, 2 vols (London, 1720), vol. 2, 105.
25 W. A. Oram et al., eds, *The Yale Edition of the Shorter Poems of Edmund Spenser* (New Haven and London, 1989), 'Prothalamion', 768. This is a marriage hymn for Elizabeth and Catherine Somerset, the daughters of the 4th Earl of Worcester, a close associate of Robert Devereux, 2nd Earl of Essex, in whose circle Spenser appears to have moved in the last years of his life. The joint marriage took place at Essex House on 8 November 1596, which Spenser could have attended; see Goldring, *Robert Dudley*, 213 and n. 44; A. Hadfield, 'Spenser, Edmund (1552?–1599)', ODNB (Oxford, 2004), online edn., January 2008, https://doi.org/10.1093/ref:odnb/26145, accessed 4 October 2019.
26 Robert Dudley to Lord Burghley, 17 May 1575, quoted in John Nichols, *The Progresses and Public Processions of Queen Elizabeth*, 3 vols (London, 1823), vol. 1, 524–5.
27 Clark, 'Buildings and Art Collections', 4, n. 19 refers to a temporary 'bankating house that must be made' for an entertainment at Kenilworth in the 1560s.
28 I am grateful to Mark Girouard for a discussion on the banqueting house and for raising the stone issue, and to Jennifer Alexander for information on Kenilworth's building material.
29 Rowland Whyte to Sir Robert Sidney, 21 August 1600, CKS, De L'Isle MS U1475, quoted by Goldring, *Robert Dudley*, 216 and n. 50. In a deed of 1676 there is reference to a 'stone building adjoining the Thames', which must be this banqueting house; Kingsford, 'Essex House', 19.
30 Henry Hawthorne also worked for Leicester at Windsor Castle, where he was the Constable and eventually the equivalent of Surveyor; see Howard Colvin, ed., *The History of the King's Works*, 6 vols (London, 1963–82), vol. 3, 85, 326.
31 Burghley to Dudley, 10 August 1571, LH, Dudley Papers II/47; see also HMC, *Calendar of the Manuscripts of the Most Honourable The Marquess of Bath Preserved at Longleat, Wiltshire*, vol. 5: *Talbot, Dudley and Devereux Papers 1533–1659*, ed. G. Dyfnallt Owen (London, 1980), 181.

32 HH, General 1, Bills 2/10: 'List of debts for household & works 6 Dec 1578'.
33 William Camden (Clarenceux King of Arms, author of *Britannia*, 1586), quoted by Clark, 'Buildings and Art Collections', 12; see also F. J. Furnivall, ed., *Robert Laneham's letter: describing a part of the entertainment unto Queen Elizabeth at the castle of Kenilworth in 1575* (London and New York, 1907).
34 Goldring, *Robert Dudley*, 34–40, 230–31.
35 See Adams, *Household Accounts*. In these accounts, Leicester House is clearly the centre of administration: there is hardly any reference to things done to it, while there are many bills for river traffic to and from the house, for card games lost by Leicester and for dignitaries' visits.
36 I owe this information to Simon Adams.
37 See Goldring, *Robert Dudley*, 167–83.
38 Ibid., 216.
39 See ibid., 227–36.
40 For all the inventories related to Dudley's tenure and beyond, see Adams, 'Papers of Robert Dudley, III', 23–4; Clark, 'Buildings and Art Collections', vii–x; Goldring, *Robert Dudley*, App. III, 283–5. Several appear in HMC, *Calendar of the Manuscripts of the Most Honourable The Marquess of Bath*, vol. 5, 202–4, 207, 208, 219, 221–2, 224. The other inventories are those of 1601 (TNA, E 178/1350, no mention of the hall or galleries) and of 1634 (printed in J. O. Halliwell, *Ancient Inventories …*, London, 1854, 43–50, similarly partial).
41 Dudley probate inventories, 1588, BL, Harley Roll, D. 35, fols 1r–24r; LH, Dudley Papers Xb, fols 1r–iiv, also in HMC, *Calendar of the Manuscripts of the Most Honourable The Marquess of Bath*, vol. 5, 208, probably the basis for or copy of the former. See Goldring, *Robert Dudley*, 283.
42 Leicester House inventory, 3 April 1590, TNA, E 177/1446.
43 Leicester House inventory, 21 November 1590, LH, Dudley Papers IV, fols 52r–61r; on microfilm, IHR, University of London.
44 Kingsford, 'Essex House', 28–54.
45 Ibid., 17–25.
46 'A Booke of Computations of buildings', c.1615–25, PHA, MS 1630; quotations by kind permission of the Duke of Egremont. I am grateful to Mark Girouard for bringing this source to my attention and for a discussion on it. The Booke includes information on a number of buildings, particularly those controlled by the 9th Earl of Northumberland (and a list of fourteen tennis courts in London). A note of similar date by Inigo Jones also gives measurements of royal palaces, including what was then Suffolk (later Northumberland) House: see Manolo Guerci, 'The Construction of Northumberland House and the Patronage of its Original Builder, Lord Henry Howard: 1603–14', *The Antiquaries Journal*, 90 (2010), 359–68.
47 This list in the 1588 inventory is preceded by four entries: 'In Mr Nevils Chamber', 'In the counting house', 'Mr Whites Chamber', and 'Mrs Lettis Garrettes Chamber'; Kingsford, 'Essex House', 28–9.
48 Kingsford, 'Essex House', 21 is contradictory in stating that the leads over the Hall were used for walking, while at the same time noting the existence of the Great Chamber over the Hall. It is probably the roof of the Great Chamber that was used for such purposes.
49 The difference in levels generally translated into a basement with services on the garden side, e.g. in Somerset House.
50 When Hollar's view is checked against documentary sources, one often finds discrepancies and, at times, a fair amount of artistic licence: see e.g. Chs 5, 6, 8. See Arthur M. Hind, *Wenceslaus Hollar and his Views of London and Windsor in the Seventeenth Century* (London, 1922); *Hollar's London: 37 Etchings of London Views (1636–1667)* (London, 1980); Graham Parry, *Hollar's England: A Mid-Seventeenth-Century View* (Salisbury, 1980); Richard Pennington, *A Descriptive Catalogue of the Etched Work of Wenceslaus Hollar 1607–1677* (Cambridge, 1982).
51 All quotations relating to the contents of the rooms come from the 1588 inventory as published in Kingsford, 'Essex House', unless otherwise stated.
52 In the 1639 lease, this room is described as 'being directly over the said great hall'. At its west end, it was adjoined by a 'little roome': ibid., 52.
53 Ibid.
54 While this room must have been sizeable, there is no reference to such a room in the Booke of Computations. In the 1639 lease, this is described as 'the chamber adioyning to the eastward end of the said great chamber, and there now called the Wthdrawing Chamber': ibid.
55 Ibid., 30, n. 3 suggested 'plush' for 'pillos'; see OED, 'plush, n.1 and adj.': 'rich fabric of silk, cotton, wool, or other material (or any of these combined), with a long soft nap, used esp. for upholstery, servants' livery, etc', OED online, June 2017, http://www.oed.com/view/Entry/146227?, accessed 29 June 2017.
56 LH, Dudley Papers IV, fols 52r–61r.
57 As the 1639 lease describes only those rooms in the part of the house that was being leased, it is not straightforward to distinguish between chambers mentioned at the start and then referred to as 'the said chamber[s]', and later-mentioned ones.
58 Kingsford, 'Essex House', 52–3, from which all quotations from the 1639 lease come.
59 Ibid.
60 These five rooms were the 'Ladye Garrettes Chambers', the 'Inner Chamber to that', the 'other Chamber to that', the 'Ladie Riches Chamber' and the 'Utter Chamber to that': ibid., 30–31.
61 These eleven rooms were 'The gentlewomens Chamber', 'My Ladyes Chamber', 'In the Wthdrawing Chamber next', 'The Earl of Essex Wthdrawing Chamber', 'In the L. of Essex bed Chamber', 'An Utter Chamber to the Same', 'The Embroderers prentise', 'Mr Sandes Chamber', 'In his Inner Chamber', 'Sr ffrauncis Knowles Chamber', 'The La. Shaundos Chamber': ibid., 32–4.
62 The link of Low Gallery to Long Gallery was made by ibid., 22.
63 LH, Dudley Papers IV, fols 52r–61r.
64 See Charles L. Kingsford, 'On some London Houses of the Early Tudor Period', *Archaeologia*, 71 (1921), 18–19, 42. A Low Gallery on the ground floor of Essex House would also chime with the sequence of rooms in the November 1590 inventory, where the Low Gallery appears before the Great or High Gallery, followed by the Armory Gallery: LH, Dudley Papers IV, fols 52r–61r.
65 Kingsford, 'Essex House', 35–6.
66 The apartment included 'The L. of Warwickes bedchamber' and 'his Closet', while the position of the service rooms is specified in the lease: ibid., 35–7, 53.
67 Ibid., 23–4.
68 LH, Dudley Papers IV, fols 52r–61r.
69 The probate inventory gives 52 rooms, the Commissioners' 47, the November 1590's 56.
70 PHA, MS 1630. It seems reasonable to locate this chamber on the first floor of the wing between the foreyard and the square Paved Court; a compass roof also indicates the first floor, which is where one would expect it.
71 Clark, 'Buildings and Art Collections', 10.
72 I am grateful to Mark Girouard for discussion on the reasons for building the galleries.
73 Goldring, *Robert Dudley*, esp. 217–27; my discussion here is based on this unless otherwise stated.
74 Leicester House, household inventory, 17 December 1588, LH, Dudley Papers XI, fols 59v–61v, transcribed by Goldring, *Robert Dudley*, 285–311; the inventory also lists many tapestries. I am grateful to Elizabeth Goldring for this information.
75 I am grateful to Elizabeth Goldring for these comments; see also Goldring, *Robert Dudley*, esp. chs 5 and 7.
76 See Goldring, 'A Portrait of Sir Philip Sidney by Veronese at Leicester House, London', *The Burlington Magazine*, 154 (August 2012), 548–54.
77 See Goldring, *Robert Dudley*, 118–21, 224.
78 See ibid., 70–71, 107–14; attribution to Zuccaro was challenged in reviews. The composition was never copied, which is unusual in images of Elizabeth: I owe this point to one of the anonymous peer reviewers.
79 Inventories of great households did not normally list books since their financial value was comparatively negligible (£10 here): see Guerci, 'Construction of Northumberland House', 391, and Ch. 8, 154–5.
80 See Jane E. L. Clark, 'A Set of Tapestries for Leicester House in the Strand: 1585', *The Burlington Magazine*, 125 (May 1983), 283–4; Anthony Wells-Cole, 'Some Design Sources

for the Earl of Leicester's Tapestries and other Contemporary Pieces', ibid., 284–5.
81 Adams, 'Dudley, his Gardeners and Gardens'.
82 Clark, 'Buildings and Art Collections', 15.
83 Kingsford, 'Essex House', 19.
84 Adams, 'Dudley, his Gardeners and Gardens'.
85 See Paula Henderson, 'The Evolution of the Early Gardens of the Inns of Court', in Jayne Elisabeth Archer, Elizabeth Goldring and Sarah Knight, *The Intellectual and Cultural World of the Early Modern Inns of Court* (Manchester and New York, 2011), 179–98, esp. 187–8.
86 Clark, 'Buildings and Art Collections', 15.
87 Other discrepancies between the plan and those of Hollar and Ogilby and Morgan are the stairs leading to a tunnel arbour on the east side and a platform and steps at the centre of the wall between the upper and lower terraces; nor is the Banqueting House shown. I am grateful to Paula Henderson for a discussion about this and for her observations.
88 See Adams, 'The Papers of Robert Dudley, III', 2–7.
89 See P. E. J. Hammer, 'Devereux, Robert, second earl of Essex', ODNB (Oxford, 2004), online edn., October 2008, http://www.oxforddnb.com/view/article/7565, accessed 25 July 2017.
90 I owe this information to Mark Girouard.
91 Adams, 'The Papers of Robert Dudley, III', 7.
92 Kingsford, 'Essex House', 12.
93 See J. Morrill, 'Devereux, Robert, third earl of Essex', ODNB (Oxford, 2004), online edn., January 2008, http://www.oxforddnb.com/view/article/7566, accessed 25 July 2017.
94 See Kingsford, 'Essex House', 14–15.
95 *The Diary of Samuel Pepys*, intro. G. Gregory Smith (London, 1905), x.
96 Arthur Capel, 1st Earl of Essex to his brother, Sir Henry Capel, 16 May 1674, part of a series of letters about selling or letting the house, in Osmund Airy, ed., *Essex Papers*, vol. 1: 1672–1679, *Camden Society*, n.s., vol. 47 (1890), 226–7, 309–13, 321–4.
97 Kingsford, 'Essex House', 16.
98 E. Beresford Chancellor, *The Private Palaces of London: Past and Present* (London, 1908), 30; Kingsford, 'Essex House', 16–17.

2 · ARUNDEL HOUSE

1 Charles L. Kingsford, 'Bath Inn or Arundel House', *Archaeologia*, 72 (1922), 243–77.
2 Ibid., 243.
3 Arthur Henry Johnson, *The History of the Worshipful Company of the Drapers of London: preceded by an introduction on London and her guilds up to the close of the xvth century by Rev. A. H. Johnson*, 5 vols (Oxford: Clarendon Press, 1914–22), vol. 2, 301; see Kingsford, 'Bath Inn', 244.
4 It is possible that originally the main house may have performed partly as a hospice (or been intended as one), but by the Reformation the term was probably a leftover. All translations mine unless otherwise specified.
5 John Sherren Brewer, ed., *Letters and Papers, Foreign and Domestic, of the reign Henry VIII, preserved in the Public Record Office, the British Museum, and elsewhere in England*, 21 vols (London: Longman, Green, Longman, & Roberts, 1862–1910), vol. 14, pt 1, 868, quoted in Kingsford, 'Bath Inn', 248–9.
6 AC, MXD1, printed in Heather M. Warne, ed., *The Duke of Norfolk's Deeds at Arundel Castle: Catalogue 2, Properties in London and Middlesex, 1154–1917* (Oving, Chichester, 2010), 2–4. The sale price is high compared to the £41-odd paid by his successor (see next section).
7 John Stow, *A Survey of London*, ed. Charles L. Kingsford, 2 vols (Oxford, 1908), vol. 2, 91, quoted in Patricia Croot, Alan Thacker and Elizabeth Williamson, eds, *A History of the County of Middlesex*, vol. 13: *City of Westminster, Part 1* (London, 2009), 44, n. 8; see also James Howell, *Londinopolis* (London, 1657), 348; John Strype, *A Survey of the Cities of London and Westminster*, 2 vols (London, 1720), vol. 2, 105.
8 Croot, Thacker and Williamson, *City of Westminster*, 44.
9 AC, MXD2: Warne, *Properties in London and Middlesex*, 4.
10 I am grateful to Mark Girouard for pointing out this Customs Account entry. See Ann Saunders, ed., *The Royal Exchange* (London Topographical Society Publication, 152, 1997), 39, n. 17, given as 'NA, PRO, Customs Accounts, E190.312'. However, the 312 sub-number does not seem to relate to 1565 but to various dates at the start of the seventeenth century. Customs accounts covering 1565 are numerous, and my attempt to clarify this reference (probably wrongly numbered) with Ann Saunders has proved inconclusive.
11 See ibid., 39, n. 17. On Theobalds see Emily Cole, 'Theobalds, Hertfordshire: The Plan and Interiors of an Elizabethan Country House', *Architectural History*, 60 (2017), 71–116.
12 Although the accounts' descriptions provoke speculation, it is unlikely that a gallery was transported wholesale: what was sent was probably no more than columns. I am grateful to Mark Girouard for a discussion over this.
13 See J. Lock, 'Fitzalan, Henry, twelfth earl of Arundel (1512–1580)', ODNB (Oxford, 2004), online edn., January 2008, http://www.oxforddnb.com/view/article/9530, accessed 28 May 2016; see also J. G. Nichols, 'Life of the last Fitz-Alan, earl of Arundel', *The Gentleman's Magazine*, 103, pt 2 (1833), 10–18, 118–24, 209–15.
14 Nichols, 'Life of the last Fitz-Alan', 122; Howard Colvin, ed., *The History of the King's Works*, 6 vols (London, 1963–82), vol. 4, pt 2, 202; Lock, 'Fitzalan, Henry'.
15 Quoted in Nichols, 'Life of the last Fitz-Alan', 122–3.
16 See J. G. Elzinga, 'Howard, Philip [St Philip Howard], thirteenth earl of Arundel (1557–1595)', ODNB (Oxford, 2004), http://www.oxforddnb.com/view/article/13929, accessed 2 June 2016; see also John Martin Robinson, *The Dukes of Norfolk* (Chichester, 1995), 68–79.
17 M. F. S. Hervey, *The Life, Correspondence and Collections of Thomas Howard, Earl of Arundel* (Cambridge, 1921), 10.
18 Ibid., Appendix 1.
19 See M. J. Hammerson, 'Excavations on the Site of Arundel House in the Strand, W.C.2., in 1972', *Transactions of the London and Middlesex Archaeological Society*, 26 (1975), 211, fig. 1.
20 Hervey, *Life, Correspondence and Collections*, 18; on the countess's circumstances after the attainder of her husband see 10–14.
21 HH, General 1, Bills 3. Three bills for work in the gardens at Arundel House were submitted by the gardener Munton (or Mountain) Jennings. The first (Bills 3/7) relates to a payment of £1.16.1 made on 7 June 1600, endorsed 'Jennings his bill of worke folks att arroundell howse in the garden & orchard' and headed 'for worke done at arrindell howse in ye gardyne for ye Ryght honorable Sure Robart sessell'. The second (Bills 3/6) is for a payment of £2.3.10 made on 19 June 1600, endorsed 'Jeninges his bill of worke donne att aroundell howse garden for one weeke ending the 19 of June 1600' and headed 'worke done at arrendell howse for the Ryghte honourable Sure Robarte sessell hyr maiestes Chefe Secretarye'. The third (Bills 3/2) is for a payment of £1.15.8, endorsed 'Jenings his bill of worke donne in Arundell gardene from the xxiijth of June to the iijth of Julij 1600' and headed 'worke done in ye gardine at arrendell howse ending ye 3th of Julye 1600'. While unambiguous in stating that Sir Robert Cecil was the customer, in what capacity he acted at Arundel House remains unclear, as detailed accounts of his household before 1608 do not survive. There is nothing at Hatfield to indicate whether or not Cecil was the tenant of Arundel House for a short period in 1600. I owe this information to Robin Harcourt-Williams, to whom I am grateful for his kind assistance.
22 AC, MXD6; see Warne, *Duke of Norfolk's Deeds*, 5.
23 See J. McDermott, 'Howard, Charles, second Baron Howard of Effingham and first earl of Nottingham (1536–1624)', ODNB (Oxford, 2004), online edn., January 2008, http://www.oxforddnb.com/view/article/13885, accessed 8 June 2016.
24 Grant to Thomas Howard dated 23 December 1607: CSP, James I, *Domestic*, 1603–10, vol. 8, 390, quoted by Hervey, *Life, Correspondence and Collections*, 41; letters patent, 6 January 1608, AC, MXD7; Warne, *Duke of Norfolk's Deeds*, 6–7. Correspondence from Arundel House was being sent from at least June 1607: Hervey, *Life, Correspondence and Collections*, 36–7.
25 Earl of Arundel to the Earl of Shrewsbury, 17 November 1607, quoted in Hervey, *Life, Correspondence and Collections*, 40. See

M. A. Tierney, *The History and Antiquities of the Castle and Town of Arundel* (London, 1834), 416; E. Lodge, *Illustrations of British History, Biography, and Manners, in the reigns of Henry VIII, Edward VI, Mary, Elizabeth, & James I*, 3 vols, 2nd edn. (London, 1838), vol. 2, 207–9.

26 See Hervey, *Life, Correspondence and Collections*, 20–23.

27 Duke of Sully quoted in Kingsford, 'Bath Inn', 252.

28 See R. M. Smuts, 'Howard, Thomas, fourteenth earl of Arundel, fourth earl of Surrey, and first earl of Norfolk (1585–1646)', ODNB (Oxford, 2004), online edn., May 2015, http://www.oxforddnb.com/view/article/13943, accessed 10 June 2016.

29 See M. DiMeo, 'Howard, Aletheia, countess of Arundel, of Surrey, and of Norfolk, and suo jure Baroness Furnivall, Baroness Talbot, and Baroness Strange of Blackmere (*d.* 1654)', ODNB (Oxford, 2006), online edn., January 2008, http://www.oxforddnb.com/view/article/94252, accessed 9 June 2016.

30 Arundel to Shrewsbury, 17 November 1607, quoted in Hervey, *Life, Correspondence and Collections*, 40.

31 See Elizabeth Angelicoussis, 'The Collection of Classical Sculptures of the Earl of Arundel', *Journal of the History of Collections*, 16, no. 2 (2004), 143–59. I am grateful to Elizabeth Angelicoussis for discussion on the subject and for kindly giving me all her material on Arundel House.

32 See Giles Worsley, *Inigo Jones and the European Classicist Tradition* (New Haven and London, 2007), 19–30.

33 See Percy Lovell and William McB. Marcham, eds, *Survey of London*, vol. 17: *The Parish of St Pancras Part 1: The Village of Highgate* (London, 1936), 46–53; see also David Howarth, 'The Patronage and Collecting of Aletheia, Countess of Arundel 1606–54', *Journal of the History of Collections*, 10, no. 2 (1998), 126.

34 Thomas Howard to Aletheia, his wife, n.d. [?1615], quoted by Tierney, *History and Antiquities of Arundel*, 426; see also 424; AC, Autographed Letters, 212.

35 See Manolo Guerci, 'The Construction of Northumberland House and the Patronage of its Original Builder, Lord Henry Howard, 1603–14', *The Antiquaries Journal*, 90 (2010), 351–4.

36 Aletheia to Thomas Howard, n.d. [?1615], AC, Autographed Letters, 207. The letter spells the place 'Gunborough' and was thus quoted by David Howarth, who suggested it might be a hamlet near Arundel Castle: *Lord Arundel and his Circle* (New Haven and London, 1985), 65. The letter is undated, with a possible date of 1615 added on the original and classified in a volume ending in 1617. Later, Howarth, 'Patronage and Collecting of Aletheia', 131, gave the date 1633. I am grateful to John Martin Robinson for pointing out the correct location to me.

37 Thomas to Aletheia Howard, 24 April 1615, AC, Autographed Letters, 194.

38 On Tart Hall see Diane Duggan, '"A Rather Fascinating Hybrid". Tart Hall: Lady Arundel's "Casino at Whitehall"', *The British Art Journal*, 4, no. 3 (Autumn 2003), 54–64; E. V. Chew, 'The Countess of Arundel and Tart Hall', in Edward Chaney, ed., *The Evolution of English Collecting: The Reception of Italian Art in the Tudor and Stuart Periods* (New Haven and London, 2003), 285–314. On Greenwich Lodge see Howarth, *Arundel and his Circle*, 57.

39 Thomas to Aletheia Howard, n.d. [? 1615/16], AC, Autographed Letters, 205, part of correspondence ending in October 1616.

40 Thomas to Aletheia Howard, 1618, AC, Autographed Letters, 236.

41 Thomas to Aletheia Howard, 1619, AC, Autographed Letters, 238.

42 Thomas to Aletheia Howard, October 1619, AC, Autographed Letters, 240; see also Tierney, *History and Antiquities of Arundel*, 489.

43 See Howarth, *Arundel and his Circle*, 57–64; Angelicoussis, 'Collection of Classical Sculptures'.

44 Howarth, *Arundel and his Circle*, 97–126.

45 Giles Worsley, *Inigo Jones*, 75–6, suggested that the stables seen in Hollar's view of Arundel House looking south (see fig. 35), clearly contrasting with the neighbouring structures and in the 'same language as the Clerk of Works building at Newmarket', may be part of Jones's remodelling of Arundel House.

46 Howarth, *Arundel and his Circle*, 102–4, 116.

47 See Mark Girouard, ed., 'The Smythson Collection of the Royal Institute of British Architects', *Architectural History*, vol. 5 (1962), III/7, 53, 142–3 and IV/11, 63, 178; John Harris and Gordon Higgott, *Inigo Jones: Complete Architectural Drawings* (London, 1989), 126–8, 308–9, 309 for a drawing by Jones which they identified as the eastern gateway.

48 Adam White, 'A Biographical Dictionary of London Tomb Sculptors c.1560–c.1660', *The Walpole Society*, vol. 61 (1998/99), 7.

49 See Angelicoussis, 'Collection of Classical Sculptures'.

50 Kingsford, 'Bath Inn', 254.

51 Bol's and Hollar's 'West Central District' views of the gallery include extrusions (or bows) every other window on both sides; Esselens's records one such feature towards the river end, while they do not appear at all in Hollar's riverfront view.

52 The view across the river in Mytens's painting is also fanciful as it would have been crowded with Southwark houses. Hollar's view from across the river equally depicts the south bank as an idealised Mediterranean hillside scattered with fallen antique columns. Fanciful though this was, Arundel did his best to make it a reality: in 1633 he purchased a three-acre property in the near vicinity, followed, in 1640, by the seven-acre Lumbards Garden nearby, now the Jubilee Gardens between the Royal Festival Hall and County Hall. See D. Sturdy and A. Brueggeman, 'British Gardens 1590–1740 and the Origins of the Museum', *Apollo*, 146 (September 1997), 6, n. 146.

53 The flat roof seen in Hollar's 'West Central District' view would not necessarily prohibit such a ceiling, contrary to what has been suggested, for a vault, especially in rooms on higher floors, could be a false one suspended from the main roof.

54 Sturdy and Brueggeman, 'British Gardens 1590–1740', 7.

55 The difference of levels between the two galleries is not clearly discernible in Mytens, though the floor tiles are different in the two portraits. Another reconstruction of the galleries is provided in Angelicoussis, 'Collection of Classical Sculptures', 152–3.

56 While the backgrounds of Mytens's paintings were often painted by others and followed a sort of invented pattern (e.g., the classical interiors in the portrait of William Herbert, 3rd Earl of Pembroke, NPG 5560), the Arundels' portraits are a special case, with the setting/background carefully selected and directed by the sitters, and largely executed by Mytens himself. I owe this information to Karen Hearn: I am grateful to her for a discussion on the matter. See Onno ter Kuile, 'Daniel Mijtens: "His Majesties Picture Drawer"', *Nederlands Kunsthistorisch Jaarboek*, 20 (1969), 1–106; Karen Hearn, ed., *Dynasties: Painting in Tudor and Jacobean England 1530–1630* (London, 1995).

57 See Sturdy and Brueggman, 'British Gardens 1590–1740', 3–8.

58 Angelicoussis, 'Collection of Classical Sculptures', 143.

59 See Hervey, *Life, Correspondence and Collections*, App. 5, 473–500.

60 See Christiane Hille, *Vision of the Courtly Body: The Patronage of George Villiers, First Duke of Buckingham, and the Triumph of Painting at the Stuart Court* (Berlin, 2012), 122.

61 Charlotte Bolland, '"Sat Super Est": A Portrait of Henry Howard, Earl of Surrey', in Tarnya Cooper et al., eds, *Painting in Britain 1500–1630: Production, Influences and Patronage* (Oxford, 2015), 352–61; see also Howarth, *Arundel and his Circle*, 101–2; for a different interpretation, Susan E. James, 'Edward Seymour, Duke of Somerset? Re-examining a Tudor Portrait', *The British Art Journal*, 2, no. 2 (Winter 2000/01), 14–21.

62 See Howarth, *Arundel and his Circle*, 116–17; J. Roberts, 'Thomas Howard, the Collector Earl of Arundel and Leonardo's Drawings', in Chaney, *Evolution of English Collecting*, 257–83.

63 See Nicolas Barker, 'The Books of Henry Howard', *Bodleian Library Record*, 13 (October 1990), 375–81; Linda Levy Peck, 'Uncovering the Arundel Library at the Royal Society', *Notes and Records of the Royal Society of London* (1998), 3–24. By the time it was donated to the Royal Society by the 6th Duke of Norfolk in 1667, the 'Bibliotheca Norfolciana' featured numerous books on

art and architecture including that of most of the Renaissance masters; see William Perry, *Bibliotheca Norfolciana* (London, 1681); *Catalogue of Manuscripts in the British Museum: The Arundel Manuscripts*, new series, 3 vols (London, 1834).
64 See Robinson, *Dukes of Norfolk*, 109–11.
65 Joachim von Sandrart quoted in Hervey, *Life, Correspondence and Collections*, 255–6.
66 Chew, 'Countess of Arundel', 290–91.
67 Hervey, *Life, Correspondence and Collections*, 264.
68 On the dating of the Hollar see Ch. 1, n. 50.
69 See G. Goodwin, 'Howard, Henry Frederick, fifteenth earl of Arundel, fifth earl of Surrey, and second earl of Norfolk (1608–1652)', rev. J. T. Peacey, ODNB (Oxford, 2004), online edn., October 2006, http://www.oxforddnb.com/view/article/13915, accessed 22 June 2016.
70 CSP, *Domestic Series, 1650* (London, 1876), 405; Kingsford, 'Bath Inn', 255.
71 CSP, *Domestic Series, 1656–7* (London, 1883), 110; Kingsford, 'Bath Inn', 255.
72 Robinson, *Dukes of Norfolk*, 119.
73 See J. Miller, 'Howard, Henry, sixth duke of Norfolk (1628–1684)', ODNB (Oxford, 2004), http://www.oxforddnb.com/view/article/13907, accessed 22 June 2016.
74 John Evelyn quoted in ibid.
75 Robinson, *Dukes of Norfolk*, 121–3.
76 Samuel Pepys quoted in Kingsford, 'Bath Inn', 255.
77 John Evelyn quoted in ibid., 255–6.
78 See Warne, *Duke of Norfolk's Deeds*, 31.
79 CSP, *Domestic: Charles II, 1676–7*, ed. F. H. Blackburne Daniell (London, 1909), 226, quoted in Kingsford, 'Bath Inn', 256.
80 Kingsford, 'Bath Inn', 256; Robinson, *Dukes of Norfolk*, 123.
81 Warne, *Duke of Norfolk's Deeds*, 32.
82 AC, IN. 52. I thank John Martin Robinson for alerting me to this inventory.
83 Angelicoussis, 'Collection of Classical Sculptures', 145.

3 · SOMERSET HOUSE

1 John Bold, *John Webb: Architectural Theory and Practice in the Seventeenth Century* (Oxford, 1989), 74, defining Webb's grand design for Durham House; see Ch. 9, n. 42 below.
2 See James Howell, *Londinopolis* (London, 1657), 349; John Strype, *A Survey of the Cities of London and Westminster* (London, 1720), vol. 2, 105–6; W. Maitland, *The History and Survey of London from its Foundations to the Present Time* (London, 1756), vol. 2, 1346; Robert and James Dodsley, *London and its Environs Described* (London, 1761), vol. 6, 41–3; Thomas Pennant, *Some Account of London*, 2nd edn. (London, 1791), 149–53; David Hughson, *A History and Description of London, Westminster and Southwark* (London, n.d. [19th c.]), vol. 4, 172; Hughson, *Walks through London, including Westminster and the Borough of Southwark*, 2 vols (London, 1817), vol. 1, 197–201; Robert Wilkinson, *Londina Illustrata* (London, 1819), vol. 1, intro.; Thomas Allen, *History and Antiquities of London, Westminster, Southwark, and parts adjacent* (London, 1827–8), vol. 4, 324–34; Walter H. Godfrey, 'The Strand in the 17th Century: Its River Front', *Transactions of the London and Middlesex Archaeological Society*, vol. 4, pt 1 (1918), 216–18; Howard Colvin, ed., *The History of the King's Works*, 6 vols (London, 1963–82); Raymond Needham and Alexander Webster, *Somerset House Past and Present* (London, 1905); Simon Thurley, ed., *Somerset House: The Palace of England's Queens 1551–1692* (London, 2009).
3 See Patricia Croot, 'The Strand before Somerset Place', in Thurley, *Somerset House*, 9–15, on which information in this section is based unless otherwise stated.
4 See B. L. Beer, 'Seymour, Edward, duke of Somerset (c.1500–1552)', ODNB (Oxford, 2004), online edn., January 2009, http://www.oxforddnb.com/view/article/25159, accessed 3 May 2016.
5 For a diagram of properties assembled by Seymour see Croot, 'The Strand', 12; see also Croot, Alan Thacker and Elizabeth Williamson, eds, *A History of the County of Middlesex*, vol. 13: *City of Westminster, Part 1* (London, 2009), 185–8.
6 Llandaff Inn from John Stow's *Survay of London* (1599) onwards; cited by Needham and Webster, *Somerset House*, 34.
7 See F. H. W. Sheppard, ed., *Survey of London*, vol. 36: *The Parish of St. Paul Covent Garden* (London, 1970), 19–21; see also Ch. 6.
8 Needham and Webster, *Somerset House*, 39–40.
9 See Thurley, *Somerset House*, 17–20.
10 See Colvin, *History of the King's Works*, vol. 3, 36–7, 61–85, 101, 330, 411.
11 See ibid., vol. 4, 194–6.
12 Howell, *Londinopolis*, 349.
13 See Needham and Webster, *Somerset House*, 54; Horace Walpole, *Anecdotes of painting* (London, 1849), vol. 1, 218. The list of Somerset's 'debts and chattels' includes information suggesting that the Great Hall was nearing completion: Thurley, *Somerset House*, 19–20.
14 The difference in height between this front and the opposite one facing the river can be accounted for by the slope of the site, which meant that the south front had an extra storey.
15 See Thurley, *Somerset House*, esp. 98–101; John Summerson, *The Book of Architecture of John Thorpe*, Walpole Society XL (London, 1966), 23, 69–70.
16 SP 14/62, no. 33, quoted by Thurley, *Somerset House*, 98.
17 SP 14/65, no. 61, quoted by Thurley, *Somerset House*, 99.
18 Thurley, *Somerset House*, 23, 100.
19 Summerson, *Book of Architecture*, 69–70; Colvin, *History of the King's Works*, vol. 4, 254, n. 5.
20 Thurley, *Somerset House*, 100. Mark Girouard told me that Thorpe is not known to have made designs on behalf of anyone, the only exception being Ampthill. I am grateful to him for a discussion on this.
21 Mark Girouard, *Elizabethan Architecture: Its Rise and Fall* (New Haven and London, 2009), 142.
22 I owe this information to Mark Girouard. See Vaughan Hart and Peter Hicks, eds, *Sebastiano Serlio on Architecture, Volume One: Books I–V* (New Haven and London, 1996), x. Apart from Somerset House and Burghley House, flaming grenades are seen on the monument to Dean Nicholas Wootton in Canterbury Cathedral (1567) and on the drawing of c.1568–70 by Robert Smythson linked to Longleat House; see Girouard, ed., 'The Smythson Collection of the Royal Institute of British Architects', *Architectural History*, vol. 5 (1962), 34, 77. As for the square with an inscribed circle, there is no direct evidence in Serlio, though his gates in Book VI, completed c.1553, hence after Seymour's tenure of Somerset House, reveal similar devices; see Vaughan Hart and Peter Hicks, eds, *Sebastiano Serlio on Architecture, Volume Two: Books VI and VII* (New Haven and London, 2001), x.
23 On Burghley see Girouard, *Elizabethan Architecture*, 185–8.
24 Thurley, *Somerset House*, 27.
25 Colvin, *History of the King's Works*, vol. 4, 253.
26 Thurley, *Somerset House*, 28.
27 Colvin, *History of the King's Works*, vol. 4, 254.
28 Thurley, *Somerset House*, 28–9.
29 Ibid., 31.
30 Colvin, *History of the King's Works*, vol. 4, 255; Thurley, *Somerset House*, 31.
31 Denmark House may have been its courtesy title since 1606: Colvin, *History of the King's Works*, vol. 4, 260.
32 Thurley, *Somerset House*, 93–6, cat. 4. Another version (National Maritime Museum, Greenwich, Caird Collection, BHC2787), is thought to be a contemporary copy of the NPG original; see https://collections.rmg.co.uk/collections/objects/14260.html, accessed 11 October 2019; see also Karen Hearn, *Talking Peace 1604: The Somerset House Conference Paintings*, exh. cat., Somerset House (London, 2004), whom I thank for giving me a copy.
33 See Charlotte Bolland, *Tudor and Jacobean Portraits* (London, 2019), 164.
34 Venetian ambassador quoted in Thurley, *Somerset House*, 31.
35 TNA, E317 Middlesex 82, cited by Thurley, *Somerset House*, 35, n. 167.
36 See Girouard, 'Smythson Collection', I/13, 33, 75; Colvin, *History of the King's Works*, vol. 4, 255; Thurley, *Somerset House*, 96–8.
37 Thurley, *Somerset House*, 98; see also Colvin, *History of the King's Works*, vol. 4, 269, where the grotto is linked to a fountain attributed to Salomon de Caus, as opposed to Isaac. This is reiterated in John Harris and Gordon Higgott, *Inigo Jones: Complete Architectural Drawings* (London, 1989), 193, but Colvin, *A Biographical Dictionary*

38 For a detailed reconstruction see Colvin, *History of the King's Works*, vol. 4, 255–8.
39 Ibid., 255.
40 Thurley, *Somerset House*, 100, cat. 7, mentions this payment of 1610–11 in relation to Thorpe's plan; see discussion above.
41 On the growing importance of roof walks see Gordon Higgott, 'Roof Walks and Roof Platforms on English Country Houses, *c*.1550 to *c*.1700', in Monique Chatenet and Alexandre Gady, eds, *Toits d'Europe: Formes, structures, décors et usages du toit à l'époque moderne (XVe–XVIIe siècle). Actes du huitièmes Rencontres d'architecture européenne, Paris, 12–14 juin 2013* (Paris, 2016), 185–98.
42 Smythson's plan shows a couple of paired columns either end of the Strand facade which do not correspond to the plans discussed here. But this may be due to the type and scale of the drawing, as the bay windows shown in both the *c*.1608–11 plan and Thorpe's were in fact in place. For a discussion of Thorpe's plan see Summerson, *Book of Architecture*, 69–70, and Thurley, *Somerset House*, 98–101, cat. 7.
43 The scale indicator in Smythson's plan is confusing. Thorpe, however, gives the north–south dimension as 120 while the opposite as 90, though he writes 'should be'. The 1775 survey of the house confirms the 120 if taken along the side wings, that is, without the recess created by the loggia, while the width appears as 100 feet; see Thurley, *Somerset House*, 127–8, cat. 33b.
44 As Thorpe makes clear in his annotations: 'And all the offices are under both sides [side wings] round about with kytchens & sellers'.
45 The new height is evidenced in the accounts and by later views of the house; see Colvin, *History of the King's Works*, vol. 4, 258; Thurley, *Somerset House*, 131–3, cat. 36.
46 The ceilings of the reconstructed wings were lower than those in the Strand front, which remained unaltered; see Thurley, *Somerset House*, 131–2, cat. 36 and 133–4, cat. 38. A plan indicating the various stages of works, from Protector Somerset's onwards, is included in Colvin, *History of the King's Works*, vol. 5, fig. 22.
47 Thurley, *Somerset House*, 22, fig. 5; 29–30, provides a reconstruction plan of the principal rooms of the house in *c*.1600, with no distinction as to their level. According to him, the west side of the court had remained incomplete throughout the Elizabethan era.
48 See ibid., 123, cat. 31; 25, 27–9.
49 Colvin, *History of the King's Works*, vol. 4, 260.
50 See Martin Butler, *The Stuart Court Masque and Political Culture* (Cambridge, 2008), esp. 128–43. For the masques in which Queen Anne was involved as a performer (1605–11) see Stephen Orgel and Roy Strong, *Inigo Jones: The Theatre of the Stuart Court*, 2 vols (London, Los Angeles and Berkeley, 1973), vol. 1, 85–237.

51 The contents of Denmark House were inventoried on 19 April 1619; see M. T. W. Payne, 'An Inventory of Queen Anna of Denmark's "Ornaments, furniture, household stuffe, and other parcels" at Denmark House, 1619', *Journal of the History of Collections*, 13, no. 1 (2001), 23–44.
52 Lord Chamberlain Pembroke to Secretary Conway, 23 March 1623, HMC, CSP, James I *Domestic*, 63, quoted by Thomas Nadauld Brushfield, *Raleghana … Reprinted from the Transactions of the Devonshire Association for the Advancement of Science, Literature, and Art*, 8 parts (London, 1896–1906), pt 5: *The History of Durham House*, 38.
53 See Harris and Higgott, *Inigo Jones*, 198–203. Because of its enclosed position, only part of the south end of the chapel can be seen in the various views of Denmark House, in e.g. Thurley, *Somerset House*, 101, 103, cat. 9.
54 Colvin, *History of the King's Works*, vol. 4, 266. The screen and reredos were drawn by Isaac Ware in *c*.1731, the coffered ceiling by Henry Flitcroft in the 1720s; see Harris and Higgott, *Inigo Jones*, 198–200.
55 Harris and Higgott, *Inigo Jones*, 196–7.
56 For a detailed discussion see Thurley, *Somerset House*, 45–9. Other rooms redesigned in this period are analysed by Colvin, *History of the King's Works*, vol. 4, 262–3.
57 Harris and Higgott, *Inigo Jones*, 212–13.
58 Ibid. For images of the gate see Thurley, *Somerset House*, 101, 103, cat. 9; 113–14, cat. 20.
59 Two more designs for chimneypieces, one from an unknown French designer, were also produced; Harris and Higgott, *Inigo Jones*, 206–11.
60 Ibid., 214–15.
61 See David Howarth, '"Mantua Peeces": Charles I and the Gonzaga Collections', in D. S. Chambers and J. T. Martineau, eds, *Splendours of the Gonzaga*, exh. cat., Victoria and Albert Museum, London, 1981–82, 95–100; Christina M. Anderson, *The Flemish Merchant of Venice: Daniel Nijs and the Sale of the Gonzaga Art Collection* (New Haven and London, 2015); Desmond Shawe-Taylor and Per Rumberg, eds, *Charles I: King and Collector*, exh. cat. (London, 2018).
62 Harris and Higgott, *Inigo Jones*, 204–5.
63 See John Harris and A. A. Tait, *Catalogue of the Drawings by Inigo Jones, John Webb and Isaac de Caus at Worcester College Oxford* (Oxford, 1979), 18–19, cat. 17–19, pls 16–18; Bold, *John Webb*, 103–7.
64 Colvin, *History of the King's Works*, vol. 4, 262–3.
65 For a view of the house during the Commonwealth see Hollar's bird's-eye 'West Central District' (see fig. 58), where the south front still appears as Henrietta had left it in the early 1640s. While this is certainly accurate of the elevation, the front seems to be composed of two attached wings, as one can recognise two distinct roofs. This further questions Hollar's reliability and the date of this view.
66 For a detailed account of these works see Colvin, *History of the King's Works*, vol. 5, 254–6.

67 This was a direct copy of French salons, which eventually developed into English drawing rooms; see Thurley, *Somerset House*, 65–9.
68 Colvin, *History of the King's Works*, vol. 5, 256; Bold, *John Webb*, 106; Thurley, *Somerset House*, 60–63.
69 For a detailed account of these works see Colvin, *History of the King's Works*, vol. 5, 256–8; for the stables see Thurley, *Somerset House*, 105, 107, cat. 13.
70 See Colvin, *History of the King's Works*, vol. 5, 258–62.
71 Dodsley, *London and its Environs*, vol. 6, 42–3.
72 See John Newman, *Somerset House: Splendour and Order* (London, 1990); John Martin Robinson, *Buckingham Palace: Official Guidebook* (London, 2004).

4 · THE SAVOY

1 John Norden, *Speculum Britanniae* (London, 1593), 46; James Howell, *Londinopolis* (London, 1657), 346–8; John Strype, *A Survey of the Cities of London and Westminster* (London, 1720), vol. 2, 106–8; Robert and James Dodsley, *London and its Environs Described*, 5 vols (London, 1761), vol. 5, 311–14; Walter Harrison, *A New and Universal History, Description and Survey of the Cities of London and Westminster* (London, 1776), 524; Thomas Pennant, *Some Account of London*, 2nd edn. (London, 1791), 146–8; David Hughson, *A History and Description of London, Westminster and Southwark*, 4 vols (London, n.d. [19th c.]), vol. 4, 199–202; Hughson, *Walks through London, including Westminster and the Borough of Southwark*, 2 vols (London, 1817), vol. 1, 205–9; Thomas Allen, *History and Antiquities of London, Westminster, Southwark, and parts adjacent*, 4 vols (London, 1827–8), vol. 4, 378–86; C. Knight, ed., *London*, 6 vols (London, 1842), vol. 2, 167–74; W. J. Loftie, *Memorials of the Savoy. The Palace: The Hospital: The Chapel* (London, 1878); Walter H. Godfrey, 'The Strand in the 17th Century: Its River Front', *Transactions of the London and Middlesex Archaeological Society*, 4, pt 1 (1918), 218–21.
2 See Loftie, *Memorials*.
3 Norden, *Speculum Britanniae*, 46.
4 Loftie, *Memorials*, 4–5.
5 Howell, *Londinopolis*, 347.
6 See N. Vincent, 'Savoy, Peter of, count of Savoy and de facto earl of Richmond (1203?–1268)', ODNB (Oxford, 2004), online edn., January 2008, http://www.oxforddnb.com/view/article/22016, accessed 1 March 2016.
7 See S. Lloyd, 'Edmund, first earl of Lancaster and first earl of Leicester (1245–1296)', ibid., http://www.oxforddnb.com/view/article/8504, accessed 3 March 2016.
8 Eleanor of Provence, grant to Edmund, 24 February 1284, in Loftie, *Memorials*, 24, Appendix A.
9 Ibid., 26–7.

10 See ibid., 25.
11 See J. R. Maddicott, 'Thomas of Lancaster, second earl of Lancaster, second earl of Leicester, and earl of Lincoln (c.1278–1322)', ODNB (Oxford, 2004), online edn., January 2008, http://www.oxforddnb.com/view/article/27195, accessed 3 March 2016.
12 Loftie, *Memorials*, 30.
13 See S. L. Waugh, 'Henry of Lancaster, third earl of Lancaster and third earl of Leicester (c.1280–1345)', ODNB (Oxford, 2004), online edn., May 2006, http://www.oxforddnb.com/view/article/12959, accessed 3 March 2016.
14 W. M. Ormrod, 'Henry of Lancaster, first duke of Lancaster (c.1310–1361)', ODNB (Oxford, 2004), online edn., January 2008, http://www.oxforddnb.com/view/article/12960, accessed 4 March 2016.
15 Loftie, *Memorials*, 41.
16 Harrison, *New and Universal History*, 524.
17 See Ormrod, 'Henry of Lancaster'.
18 For the origins of the Savoy Chapel see Loftie, *Memorials*, 64–6 and the chapters dedicated to it. During her residency at Somerset House, Elizabeth I's private services were held here; see Simon Thurley, *Somerset House: The Palace of England's Queens 1551–1692* (London, 2009), 29.
19 Howell, *Londinopolis*, 347.
20 S. Walker, 'John, duke of Aquitaine and duke of Lancaster, styled king of Castile and León (1340–1399)', ODNB (Oxford, 2004), online edn., May 2008, http://www.oxforddnb.com/view/article/14843, accessed 4 March 2016.
21 Loftie, *Memorials*, 57; see also 54–5.
22 Geoffrey Chaucer, 'Dream', quoted by ibid., 58–9.
23 See Loftie, *Memorials*, 59–62.
24 See ibid., 56–7.
25 Howell, *Londinopolis*, 347.
26 See Loftie, *Memorials*, 76–9.
27 See ibid., 82–5.
28 Extracts from Henry VII's will, quoted in ibid., 87–92.
29 See Hughson, *History and Description*, vol. 4, 199–200.
30 See Strype, *Survey of the Cities*, 110.
31 See Loftie, *Memorials*, 96–7, 100.
32 Norden, *Speculum Britanniae*, 46.
33 Lords of the Council to Cardinal Wolsey, 2 July 1520, quoted by Loftie, *Memorials*, 98–9.
34 See Loftie, *Memorials*, 106.
35 See ibid., 109–10.
36 Strype, *Survey of the Cities*, 107. William Cecil also supported twenty poor men lodging in the Savoy, to whom he donated 'Suytes of Apparell' every year; see F. Peck, *Desiderata Curiosa*, ed. T. Evans, 2 vols (London, 1732–5), vol. 1, 30.
37 Pennant, *Some Account*, 147; Harrison, *New and Universal History*, 524.
38 See Loftie, *Memorials*, 129–33.
39 See W. B. Patterson, 'Dominis, Marco Antonio de (1560–1624)', ODNB (Oxford, 2004), online edn., January 2008, http://www.oxforddnb.com/view/article/7788, accessed 9 March 2016.
40 See Loftie, *Memorials*, 142.
41 Pennant, *Some Account*, 147.
42 See Loftie, *Memorials*, 149–50.
43 See J. P. Vander Motten, 'Killigrew, Henry (1613–1700)', ODNB (Oxford, 2004), online edn., January 2008, http://www.oxforddnb.com/view/article/15534, accessed 11 March 2016; Motten, 'Killigrew, Thomas (1612–1683)', ibid., http://www.oxforddnb.com/view/article/15538, accessed 11 March 2016.
44 Thomas Babington Macaulay, *The History of England from the Accession of James the Second*, 5 vols (London, 1848), vol. 2, 79–80.
45 Loftie, *Memorials*, 155.
46 Strype, *Survey of the Cities*, 107.
47 Ibid.
48 Dodsley, *London and its Environs*, vol. 5, 313; Harrison, *New and Universal History*, 524.
49 Pennant, *Some Account*, 147.
50 Hughson, *Walks through London*, vol. 1, 207.

5 · Burghley House

1 See W. T. MacCaffrey, 'Cecil, William, first Baron Burghley (1520/21–1598)', ODNB (Oxford, 2004), http://www.oxforddnb.com/view/article/4983, accessed 4 August 2017; Stephen Alford, *Burghley: William Cecil at the Court of Elizabeth I* (New Haven and London, 2011). On his patronage see also Mark Girouard, *Elizabethan Architecture: Its Rise and Fall* (New Haven and London, 2009).
2 Jill Husselby and Paula Henderson, 'Location, Location, Location! Cecil House in the Strand', *Architectural History*, 45 (2002), 159–93.
3 While inventories could have been lost (or not found), their apparent lack seems peculiar in Burghley's highly organised household (and, by extension, muniments). By contrast, the Earls of Exeter who succeeded him appear to have been not particularly assiduous about their archives. Burghley's very organisation may also have ensured that his affairs had long been settled before his death, and that only the few items mentioned in his will (the only document, as we shall see, which provides some idea of both the arrangement and contents of Burghley House) were still to be allotted. I am grateful to Jon Culverhouse, Paula Henderson and Jill Husselby for a discussion on this.
4 BH, Exeter MSS 5/17.
5 John Stow, *The Survay of London: Contayning the Originall, Antiquity, Increase, Moderne estate and description of that Citie, written in the year 1598* (London, 1599), 370.
6 William Cecil licence to William Harward, 1560, BH, Exeter MSS 80/29.
7 William Cecil, conveyance with Lord Paget and Philip Cockeram, February 1560, BH, Exeter MSS 5/18.
8 Nicholas Bacon to William Cecil, 17 June 1560, quoted in Malcolm Airs, *The Making of the English Country House 1500–1640* (London, 1975), 2.
9 Queen Elizabeth, grant to Cecil, 20 February 1561, BH, Exeter MSS MC 2/3 (formerly 49/7).
10 Francis, 2nd Earl of Bedford, grant to Cecil, 24 January 1561, BH, Exeter MSS 5/21.
11 Florence Diaceto to Cecil, 25 May 1561, CSP, *Foreign Elizabeth 1561–62* (London, 1966), 125–6; see also 417. On Diaceto see E. J. B. Allen, *Post and Courier Service in the Diplomacy of Early Modern Europe* (The Hague, 1972), 113.
12 Cecil, diary entry, 14 July 1561, quoted by Husselby and Henderson, 'Location, Location, Location!', 161. See also CSP, *Foreign Elizabeth 1561–62*, 187, n. 8 (summary).
13 See Julia F. Merritt, 'The Cecils and Westminster 1558–1612: The Development of an Urban Power Base', in Pauline Croft, ed., *Patronage, Culture and Power: The Early Cecils, 1558–1612* (New Haven and London, 2002), 231–48.
14 Conveyance by Cuthbert to Sir William Cecil of a house in Milford Lane, 1561, BH, Exeter MS 5/25; grant by William Harward, rector of St Clement Danes to Richard Forsett and Roger Alford of the parsonage house and house adjoining, 1561, MS 5.26; feoffment of the same, 1561, MS 5.27; feoffment by Forsett and Alford to Sir William Cecil of the same, 1561, MS 5.28.
15 Richard Clough to Cecil, 28 January 1563, summarised in CSP, *Elizabeth 1563* (London, 1966), 82. On Clough see I. Blanchard, 'Clough, Richard (d. 1570)', ODNB (Oxford, 2004), online edn., January 2008, http://www.oxforddnb.com/view/article/5712, accessed 8 August 2017.
16 Thomas Gresham to Cecil, August 1561, cited in Husselby and Henderson, 'Location, Location, Location!', 174. The bill was from John Mounte, SP 12/20/43.
17 Conveyance by Earl of Bedford to Cecil, December 1563, BH, Exeter MSS 5/29; jury finding, November 1564, HMC, *Calendar of the Manuscripts of the Most Hon. the Marquess of Salisbury*, pt XIII (addenda) (London, 1915), 66.
18 I am grateful to Mark Girouard for this suggestion.
19 Earl of Bedford, grant to Cecil, 14 November 1565, BH, Exeter MSS 5/32.
20 Covenant to levy a fine to Sir William Cecil of soil of Earl of Bedford on which Cecil has built a wall and 3 houses, 1568, BH, Exeter MSS 5/35; Husselby and Henderson, 'Location, Location, Location!', 166.
21 Lease, Earl of Bedford to Sir William Cecil of 'a pice' of Covent Garden near the White Hart Inn in the Strand, 1570, BH, Exeter MSS 5/37.
22 See Gladys Scott-Thomson, MS notes on Covent Garden and Bedford House, LMA, E/BER/CG/E/11/3.
23 Burghley to Leicester, 10 August 1571, LH, Dudley Papers 11/47; see HMC, *Calendar of the Manuscripts of the Most Honourable The Marquess*

24 Accounts for 1567–72 are in Burghley's own hand and brief. They are followed by those of Thomas Billot, Burghley's Steward, for 1574–7, not relevant here; see HH, CP, Box G 16. The same is true for abbreviated and haphazard accounts for the years 1592–5, HH, CP A/c 27. For a discussion see C. Read, 'Lord Burghley's Household Accounts', *Economic History Review*, 2nd ser., 9 (1956), 343–8.

25 Estimate, 1577; bills, 1578, HH, General 1, Bills 2/8, 10.

26 For Norden see BL, Harleian MS 570 I, fol. 39r, quoted in Husselby and Henderson, 'Location, Location, Location!', 186; for the leases, HH, Estate and Private MS, Middlesex, London 1/52, 66, 78.

27 After 1572, works in London no longer feature in the Burghley general accounts. By contrast, those of 1574–7 regularly cover expenses at both Burghley House at Stamford and Theobalds; see HH, CP, Box G 16.

28 Conyers Read, *Lord Burghley and Queen Elizabeth* (London, 1960), 321. For Norden's comments see BL, Harleian MS 570 I, fol. 39r, quoted in Edwin Beresford Chancellor, *Annals of the Strand, Topographical and Historical* (London, 1912); Husselby and Henderson, 'Location, Location, Location!', 172.

29 Read, *Burghley and Elizabeth*, 320.

30 F. Peck, *Desiderata Curiosa*, ed. T. Evans, 2 vols (London, 1732), vol. 1, 33.

31 See Ch. 8 for further instances. Hollar's depiction of Burghley House is also problematic when it comes to the area to the west of the house, which appears considerably wider in both its plan and layout survey of 1673 (see figs 97 and 108).

32 Husselby and Henderson, 'Location, Location, Location!', 172.

33 See Husselby and Henderson, 'Location, Location, Location!', 168; Dorian Gerhold, *London Plotted: Plans of London Buildings c.1450–1720* (London, 2016), 43–4.

34 BL, Harleian MS 570 I, fol. 39r, quoted by Husselby and Henderson, 'Location, Location, Location!', 172.

35 For Winchester's comments see Husselby and Henderson, 'Location, Location, Location!', 173. Raphael Holinshed and William Harrison, *The first and second volumes of Chronicles* (London, 1587), bk II, ch. XII, 187; see also Georges Edelen, ed., *The Description of England: The Classic Contemporary Account of Tudor Social Life by William Harrison* (Ithaca, NY, 1968).

36 On Burghley's household staff see Peck, *Desiderata Curiosa*, vol. 1, 29; Read, 'Burghley's Household Accounts'; Husselby and Henderson, 'Location, Location, Location!', 182.

37 Peck, *Desiderata Curiosa*, vol. 1, 31–2.

38 A. Collins, *Life of William Cecil ... Lord Burghley* (London, 1732), 93; Peck, *Desiderata Curiosa*, vol. 1, 19.

39 Husselby and Henderson, 'Location, Location, Location!', 182–3; Collins, *Life of William Cecil*, 88, 91.

40 Husselby and Henderson, 'Location, Location, Location!', 183.

41 Burghley's banquet is also the best recorded: BL, Lansdowne MSS, xxxiii, fols 70–71; Richard Barnett, *Place, Profit, and Power: A Study of the Servants of William Cecil, Elizabethan Statesman*, James Sprunt Studies in History and Political Science 51 (Chapel Hill, 1969), 7–9.

42 See J. M. Sutton, *Materializing Space at an Early Modern Prodigy House: The Cecils at Theobalds, 1564–1607* (Aldershot, 2004), 30–78; Paula Henderson, *The Tudor House and Garden: Architecture and Landscape in the Sixteenth and Early Seventeenth Centuries* (New Haven and London, 2005), 46–8.

43 On the importance of Mildred Cecil see Pauline Croft, 'Mildred, Lady Burghley: The Matriarch', in Croft, *Patronage, Culture and Power*, 283–300; see also C. M. K. Bowden, 'Cecil [Cooke], Mildred, Lady Burghley (1526–1589)', ODNB (Oxford, 2004), online edn., May 2014, http://www.oxforddnb.com/view/article/46675, accessed 16 August 2017.

44 Collins, *Life of William Cecil*, 93.

45 Ibid.

46 Peck, *Desiderata Curiosa*, 1, 16; Camden quoted by Husselby and Henderson, 'Location, Location, Location!', 182.

47 This is clearly reflected in the two high viewing podia seen in the plan (see fig. 97) of Burghley House, which of course predate the construction of the banqueting houses. Apart from Norden's 1593 view, the rural nature of the area is confirmed by the addition of railings to protect the central Banqueting House from cows in 1607: see n. 54 below.

48 Husselby and Henderson, 'Location, Location, Location!', 177.

49 LMA, E/BER/CG/E8/1/1; E/BER/CG/E/11/3 for a full transcript of the letter.

50 For a full discussion on the garden and sporting facilities see Husselby and Henderson, 'Location, Location, Location!', 175–81; what follows derives from this. I am grateful to Mark Girouard for a discussion on how Burghley's role as Master of the Courts of Wards determined certain features in the garden.

51 Collins, *Life of William Cecil*, 84–5, 92. On Thomas Cecil see R. Milward, 'Cecil, Thomas, first earl of Exeter (1542–1623)', ODNB (Oxford, 2004), online edn., January 2008, http://www.oxforddnb.com/view/article/4981, accessed 17 August 2017.

52 See Howard Colvin, *A Biographical Dictionary of British Architects 1600–1840* (New Haven and London, 2008), 590; John Harris and Gordon Higgott, *Inigo Jones: Complete Architectural Drawings* (London, 1989), 90; Mark Girouard, ed., 'The Smythson Collection of the Royal Institute of British Architects', *Architectural History*, vol. 5 (1962), III/3, 52, 141.

53 Edwin Beresford-Chancellor, *The Private Palaces of London: Past and Present* (London, 1908), 48–9; what follows is based on this, unless otherwise indicated.

54 For the railings against cows see ACA, 'The Robert Scawen Papers', Sy:Y.III.2/1/3/1/1; for the 1622 grant, LMA E/BER/CG/T/11/E/6.

55 Christopher Wren, report on Exeter House, ordered 1 October 1671, TNA, PC/2/63.

56 See BH, Exeter MSS MC 1/2 (formerly 13/1).

57 John Strype, *A Survey of the Cities of London and Westminster* (London, 1720), 119.

58 See D. Hughson, *A History and Description of London*, 4 vols (London, n.d.), vol. 4, 199; M. Sorrell, 'Polito, Stephen (1763/4–1814)', ODNB (Oxford, 2004); online edn., January 2008, http://www.oxforddnb.com/view/article/73320; https://janeaustenslondon.com/tag/polito, both accessed 18 August 2017.

6 · BEDFORD HOUSE

1 John Lacy's map of Covent Garden, 1673, WA, BI-P73.

2 The northernmost part of the complex as depicted by Hollar does not tally with Lacy's or Crowle's later maps.

3 Edwin Beresford Chancellor, *The Private Palaces of London: Past and Present* (London, 1908), 50.

4 See F. H. W. Sheppard, ed., *Survey of London*, vol. 36: *The Parish of St. Paul Covent Garden* (London, 1970); Diane Duggan, 'London the Ring, Covent Garden the Jewell of That Ring: New Light on Covent Garden', *Architectural History*, 43 (2000), 140–61; Duggan, 'The Architectural Patronage of the 4th Earl of Bedford, 1587–1641', PhD diss., Courtauld Institute of Art, University of London 2001 (part of the group of studies on Tudor and Jacobean patrons supervised by John Newman, referred to in other chapters; I am grateful to the author for permission to quote from it); Duggan, 'The Fourth Side of Covent Garden Piazza: New Light on the History and Significance of Bedford House', *British Art Journal*, 3, no. 3 (Autumn 2002), 53–67; Duggan, 'Hale Church and St Paul's Church, Covent Garden', *Hampshire Studies: Proceedings of the Hampshire Field Club and Archaeological Society*, 58 (2003), 242–53; Duggan, 'Isaac de Caus, Nicholas Stone, and the Woburn Abbey Grotto', *Apollo*, 158, no. 498 (August 2003), 50–58; Duggan, 'Isaac de Caus: Surveyor, Grotto and Garden Designer', *Studies in the History of Gardens & Designed Landscapes: An International Quarterly*, 29, no. 3 (2009), 152–68.

5 For Gladys Scott-Thomson's works see below. Of her many publications, *Life in a Noble Household 1641–1700* (1937; London, 1950), is the most relevant here.

6 Papers at the LMA are fully catalogued but significant numbers of those at Woburn are not: I am grateful to Ann Mitchell, Nicola Allen and Andrew Mitchell for their assistance. The Bedfordshire Archives and Records Office, cited by Sheppard, *Survey of London*, held some material too but no longer. Their collection concerns the Bedfordshire and some of the Huntingdonshire estates up to 1910, while mention of issues outside these areas in the stewards' correspondence invariably dates from after 1748. I am grateful to Pamela Birch for this information.
7 Note of June 1970 with Covent Garden papers of 1593–1686, LMA, E/BER/CG/E/8/1/1.
8 I am grateful to Christopher Unwick at the ACA for this information. The dispute concerned an annuity of £40, which Bedford had apparently promised Scawen after the latter's marriage but failed to pay; ACA, 'The Robert Scawen Papers', AC, Sy: Y.III.2.
9 According to Sheppard, *Survey of London*, 205, the contents of Russell House were sold.
10 See ibid., 19–21; Patricia E. C. Croot, Alan Thacker and Elizabeth Williamson, eds, *A History of the County of Middlesex*, vol. 13: *City of Westminster, Part 1* (London, 2009), 69–71, 77, 100–02.
11 'Descriptive Plan Shewing the 3 Plots Granted by Henry 8th & Edward 6th to the Earl of Bedford', LMA, E/BER/CG/E5/1/21/1: reproduced in 1826 in relation to a scheme for widening the Strand, the plan also indicates the point where the 'Head of the Aqueduct' stood and may have been based on the ground-plan in fig. 115, produced for a dispute over water supply in the 1630s, discussed in Ch. 7; for the only other version see ACA, Sy: Y.III.2/5/2.
12 Curiously, the 1600 reprint of Norden's map is much less informative: it does not show the west wing but there appears to be a building on the east side of the property.
13 See notes of Gladys Scott-Thomson, 1930–40, LMA, E/BER/CG/E/11/3.
14 Notes by Gladys Scott-Thomson, WA, BE-AD2-GST121 (ii); see also WA, 3E 1–3.
15 P. Priestland, 'Russell [*née* Cooke], Elizabeth, Lady Russell [*other married name* Elizabeth Hoby, Lady Hoby] (1528–1609)', ODNB (Oxford, 2004), online edn., http://www.oxforddnb.com/view/10.1093/ref:odnb/978019861418.001.0001/odnb-9780198614128-e-13411, accessed 31 January 2018.
16 For the wardenship to the Earl and Countess of Warwick in 1586 see notes of Scott-Thomson, 1930–40, LMA, E/BER/CG/E/11/3; 'Copy of commission from Lord Burghley and others for ordering and letting estates during the 3rd Earl of Bedford's minority', WA, 3E-6.
17 Francis Russell, 2nd Earl of Bedford, to Lord Burghley, 16 July 1572, quoted by Duggan, 'Architectural Patronage', 28.
18 Rental (*sic*), 1592, quoted in Sheppard, *Survey of London*, 205.
19 See ibid.
20 Ibid.
21 Scott-Thomson, *Life in a Noble Household*, 37; see also notes by Scott-Thomson, 24 March 1937, WA, BE-AD2-GST 121 (i).
22 Croot, Thacker and Williamson, *History of the County of Middlesex*, 100.
23 Sheppard, *Survey of London*, 23.
24 Ibid., 205.
25 Duggan, 'Architectural Patronage', 82, states that 'the further-most northern point of the house on Norden's engraving – at the end of the long, narrow range', presumably the northernmost part of the west wing, 'was the original extent of the house'. But this goes against all available evidence: even if both the Agas and Braun and Hogenberg maps were derived from the Copperplate map of 1553–9, the chance that they missed the 'wooden mansion' erected by the 1st Earl by 1555 is slim, assuming that at least part of it was in the west wing.
26 Stow's *Survay*, transcr. Gladys Scott-Thomson, n.d., LMA, E/BER/CG/E/11/3.
27 John Stow, *The Survay of London: Contayning the Originall, Antiquity, Increase, Moderne estate and description of that Citie, written in the year 1598* (London, 1599), 370–71.
28 Stow's *Survay*, transcr. Scott-Thomson, n.d., LMA, E/BER/CG/E/11/3. For a similar version see David Hughson, *A History and Description of London, Westminster and Southwark*, 4 vols (London, n.d.), vol. 4, 221: 'a large old built house, having a great yard before it for the reception of carriages, and a spacious garden; behind which were coach houses, and stables, with a conveyance into Charles Street, through a large gate.' This is repeated by Beresford Chancellor, *Private Palaces*, 50, who cites William Strype's edition of the Survay, 1720, but that does not appear to contain this passage, which is not included in Stow's original version.
29 See Sheppard, *Survey of London*, 24; Duggan, 'Architectural Patronage', 83–4.
30 H. Payne, 'Russell [*née* Harington], Lucy, countess of Bedford (*bap*. 1581, *d*. 1627)', ODNB (Oxford, 2004), online edn., https://doi.org/10.1093/ref:odnb/24330, accessed 14 February 2018.
31 See Duggan, 'Architectural Patronage', 84–5; Paula Henderson, *The Tudor House and Garden* (New Haven and London, 2005), 99, 228.
32 See Barbara K. Lewalski, 'Lucy, Countess of Bedford: Images of a Jacobean Courtier and Patroness', in Kevin Sharpe and Steven N. Zwicker, eds, *Politics of Discourse: The Literature and History of Seventeenth-Century England* (Berkeley, Los Angeles and London, 1987), 52–77; Karen Hearn, 'Lucy Harington, Countess of Bedford as Art Patron and Collector', MA diss., Courtauld Institute of Art, University of London, 1990.
33 Robert Cecil quoted in Lewalski, 'Lucy, Countess of Bedford', 55.
34 See Sheppard, *Survey of London*, 24–5; Duggan, 'Architectural Patronage', 13–15; see also notes of Scott-Thomson, 1930–40, LMA, E/BER/CG/E/11/3.
35 For the mismanagement of the estate and the Rutland occupancy see Laurence Stone, *The Crisis of the Aristocracy, 1558–1641* (Oxford, 1965).
36 One of the Bedfords' nineteenth-century stewards quoted in Sheppard, *Survey of London*, 25; Conrad Russell, 'Russell, Francis, fourth earl of Bedford (*bap*. 1587, *d*. 1641)', ODNB (Oxford, 2004), online edn., https://doi.org/10.1093/ref:odnb/24307, accessed 17 February 2018.
37 On Woburn see Diane Duggan, 'Woburn Abbey: The First Episode of a Great Country House', *Architectural History*, 46 (2003), 57–80.
38 Stonemason 'Meller' (Hans Weller?), bill, 9 August 1628, WA, 4E-18.
39 Howard Colvin, *A Biographical Dictionary of British Architects 1600–1840* (New Haven and London, 2008), 229–30.
40 See Duggan, 'Architectural Patronage', 86, n. 27; ch. 2 for the funeral monuments.
41 Document signed by Nicholas Stone et al., WA, 4E-20. For a discussion of the other signatories see Duggan, 'Architectural Patronage', 92, footnote 40.
42 See Duggan, 'Architectural Patronage', 51–3.
43 Ibid., 110.
44 John Summerson, *Georgian London* (London, 1945), 14, as quoted and described in Sheppard, *Survey of London*, 25.
45 4th Earl of Bedford, Commonplace Book, vol. 1, WA, HMC11-V1 (1627–41).
46 Henry Howard, 1st Earl of Northampton, quoted in Russell, 'Russell, Francis, fourth earl'.
47 Duggan, 'Architectural Patronage', 87.
48 The church could also be part of the same complex, as in the fifteenth-century Palazzi Venezia and della Cancelleria, both in Rome. (Private chapels inside palaces could not, nor were they meant to, have the same function and impact.)
49 Plans of Covent Garden and Bedford House, ACA, Sy: Y.III.2/1/3/3/5–6.
50 See Duggan, 'Architectural Patronage', 88; Duggan, 'Fourth Side of Covent Garden Piazza', 61–4; Duggan, 'Isaac de Caus, Nicholas Stone'; Duggan, 'Isaac de Caus: Surveyor'.
51 See Sheppard, *Survey of London*, 28; Duggan, 'Architectural Patronage', 52.
52 Duggan, 'Architectural Patronage', 99. On the issue of sewage from Covent Garden see also notes by Scott-Thompson, LMA, E/BER/CG/E/11/3.
53 John Cornforth, 'The Earliest View of Covent Garden', *Country Life*, 13 May 1971, 1182.
54 See Duggan, 'Architectural Patronage', 88, 92–100.
55 Colvin, *Biographical Dictionary*, 306–8.
56 Sheppard, *Survey of London*, 207. The identification of the building as the Evidence House is based on later documents, particularly a carpenter's bill of 1671 (see n. 72 below).

57 Inventory, 1635, WA, 4E-27; on the verso of p. 27 is an architectural sketch showing a rectangular building with four small rooms, a single staircase, what appear as two windows at the front and a door up a couple of steps.

58 Duggan, 'Architectural Patronage', 100.

59 See Scott-Thomson, *Life in a Noble Household*, 246.

60 'Agreement with the Bishop of Durham', n.d., LMA, E/BER/CG/T/11/E/08.

61 Countess of Worcester to Francis, Earl of Bedford, 8 July [1634], ACA, Sy: Y.III.2/5/11 (whole dispute, Y.III.2/5/1–13), partly quoted by Russell, 'Russell, Francis, fourth earl of Bedford'.

62 Inventory, 12 September 1643, WA, MS 5E-I-1; referred to by Scott-Thomson, *Life in a Noble Household*; Sheppard, *Survey of London*, 205–6; and Duggan, 'Architectural Patronage', 81–2, but not published in full.

63 The total length of the west wing was about 140 feet (dimensions obtained via Lacy's and later maps).

64 While there is no indication that Bedford House had more than one gallery in 1643, 'towards the Streete' seems to suggest a distinction from another gallery.

65 Scott-Thomson, *Life in a Noble Household*, 38, mentions a 'Terrace Room' described as 'a long room running the entire length of the north wing, opened onto the terrace', hence its name. The content is similar to what was in the 'Terrett Roome', perhaps mistaken as 'Terrace Room', but such a room is impossible to identify in the available evidence.

66 The leads of Bedford House, perhaps at the base of the gables, were also accessible, for the bill of 1671 includes a 'new door to goe out upon ye leads'.

67 On the books of the 4th and 5th Earls of Bedford see Scott-Thomson, *Life in a Noble Household*, 262–79.

68 Ibid., 70–71.

69 For an idea of the paintings at the various Bedford residences see ibid., 280–301.

70 V. Stater, 'Russell, William, first duke of Bedford (1616–1700)', ODNB (Oxford, 2004); online edn., https://doi.org/10.1093/ref:odnb/24346, accessed 1 March 2018; Scott-Thomson, *Life in a Noble Household*, 69.

71 See Sheppard, *Survey of London*, 36.

72 Bills, 1657–94, LMA, E/BER/CG/E7/12/1; these bills cover all expenses in this period.

73 Duggan, 'Architectural Patronage', 91, ascribes new construction work to 1669 which, as will be shown, relates to new stables. Sheppard, *Survey of London*, 206–7, however, acknowledged some early rebuilding to the northern part of the house but referred to a 'New Building for the Earle of Bedford' paid for in 1680–82 as the culmination of works.

74 On the 5th Earl of Bedford's gardens see Scott-Thomson, *Life in a Noble Household*, 239–61. A bill of 1660 indicates the presence of 'the halfe mound', for which tiling was being made, while seats in the wilderness are documented by bills from 1678. There were five painted benches in 1692.

75 A bill of 1659 refers to the 'old stables', perhaps those which originally served Bedford House in Drury Lane.

76 Colvin, *Biographical Dictionary*, 891–3.

77 Works in 1669 include new chimneys and doors; LMA, E/BER/CG/E7/12/1.

78 This repair of the Evidence House has been taken as further support for a construction date under the 4th Earl, assuming a connection between stability and age of fabric; Duggan, 'Architectural Patronage', 91.

79 A further reference to the 'High old building' appears in 1681 in relation to digging a trench 'to remove the pipe that comes from the cisterne into the Kitchen'. A great cistern was located next to the Evidence House.

80 On Mandey see Colvin, *Biographical Dictionary*, 675.

81 Other names in later bills that clearly refer to the gallery along the Strand are 'long roome' or Long Gallery.

82 See Beresford Chancellor, *Private Palaces*, 50.

83 It is not clear what Hollar depicts as the northernmost part of Bedford House. While he could not have seen the new brick building of 1680–81 for he died in 1677, the scale of what he shows makes one wonder whether it could simply refer to the 1657 addition. For that to be the case, one would have to assume that this elaborate part was demolished to accommodate the later addition, since the plans from Lacy's onwards indicate a different arrangement.

84 'An Inventory of Goods, with Appraisement & Valuation at Bedford House in the Strand Appraised Oct. 6. 1700', WA, 5E-25.

85 For a study on the emerging cult of Japanese art in the seventeenth century see Tomiko Yoshida-Takeda, 'La collection intérieure du palais Mazarin et sa collection d'art décoratif de l'Extrême-Orient (Chine et Japon)', in Isabelle de Conihout and Patrick Michel, eds, *Mazarin: les lettres et les arts* (Paris, 2006), 189–95.

86 In 1673 Bedford was taxed for sixty hearths; Sheppard, *Survey of London*, 205.

87 See Gladys Scott-Thomson, *The Russells in Bloomsbury 1669–1771* (London, 1940).

88 For a detailed account of this development see Sheppard, *Survey of London*, 37–40.

89 See notes of Scott-Thomson, 1930–40, LMA, E/BER/CG/E/11/3.

7 · WORCESTER HOUSE

1 Boteler indentures, early 1400s, paraphrased from the original by Sidney J. Madge, 'Worcester House in the Strand', *Archaeologia*, 91 (1945), 159; information in this section is based on this source unless otherwise stated.

2 George Gater and Walter H. Godfrey, eds, *Survey of London*, vol. 18: *The Strand* (London, 1937), 120.

3 Direct analysis of the papers of the Herberts, Earls and Marquesses of Worcester, at Badminton House has not been possible; hence all references to that important collection are based on summaries provided by Gloucestershire County Council Archives' online catalogue, https://www.gloucestershire.gov.uk/archives, which lists documents deposited at Badminton. I am grateful to Andrew Parry at Gloucestershire County Council Archives and to John Harris for their assistance.

4 Thomas Fuller, *Church-History of Britain* (1655), quoted by Madge, 'Worcester House', 158.

5 Russell House at Chiswick was returned in 1542 to John Russell in exchange for another property at Southwark; see notes by Gladys Scott-Thomson (archivist at Woburn in the 1930s–50s; see Ch. 6 above), WA, BE-AD2-GST121 (ii).

6 See D. Willen, 'Russell, John, first earl of Bedford (c.1485–1555)', ODNB (Oxford, 2004), online edn., January 2008, http://www.oxforddnb.com/view/article/24319, accessed 3 February 2016.

7 The house is thus described in the 2nd Earl's will, made in the house; see notes by Gladys Scott-Thomson, LMA, E/BER/CG/E/11/3.

8 The 2nd Earl had a fourth son, William, 1st Baron of Thornhaugh, whose own son eventually became 4th Earl of Bedford; see Ch. 6 above. William did not inherit the title as the 2nd Earl had settled his estate on his eldest son and male heirs; see F. H. W. Sheppard, ed., *Survey of London*, vol. 36: *The Parish of St. Paul Covent Garden* (London, 1970), 24.

9 Ibid., 205.

10 Gladys Scott-Thomson to E. B. Goodsens, 24 March 1937, WA, BE-AD2-GST 121.

11 E. B. Goodsens to Gladys Scott-Thomson, 19 and 25 March 1937, ibid. The Derbys' tenure at Russell House is confirmed by a letter from Lady Russell to Robert Cecil of 1599; see n. 17 below; see also Madge, 'Worcester House', 161.

12 Gater and Godfrey, *Survey of London*, 120. The Russell–Somerset marriage had been long in the making; see Henry Dircks, *The Life, Times and Scientific Labours of the Second Marquis of Worcester* (London, 1865), 1–5.

13 Anne Russell and her sister Elizabeth, who died in June 1600, had been given the Manor of Chaldon Herring by the 2nd Earl of Bedford, 'in recompense for the capital messuage formerly called the Bishop of Carlisle's place, now Russell House … now settled on Bridget, Countess of Bedford, for life, then on his [the 2nd Earl's] heirs male'; BHA, D2700/NJ/1; see also n. 3 above.

14 See John Stow, *The Survay of London: Contayning the Originall, Antiquity, Increase, Moderne estate and description of that Citie, written in the year 1598* (London, 1599), 370–71.

15 Gater and Godfrey, *Survey of London*, 120.

16 Lady Russell to Robert Cecil, September 1599, HMC, *Salisbury MS*, part IX (1902), 358–61.

17 Ibid., 358.
18 With no direct access to the Badminton Collection, what follows is based on miscellaneous, limited evidence from contemporary sources.
19 J. Howell, *Londinopolis* (London, 1657), 349.
20 Timothy Willis to Robert Cecil, 11 August 1603, HMC, *Salisbury* MS, part XV (1930), 227–8.
21 Madge, 'Worcester House', 162.
22 'Deed executed by Edward, Earl of Worcester entailing on Henry, Lord Herbert … Worcester House (late Russell House) in St Clement Danes, London Settling them on the Earl for life, then Lord Herbert for life, then to Edward his eldest son for life … 1627/8', BHA, D2700/OA/9.
23 'Settlement before marriage of Edward, Lord Herbert and Elizabeth Dormer Includes … 16 messuages called Carlisle Rents, St Clemant Danes, Mddx (held by the Earl as lodgings, part and parcel of Worcester House) … 1628', BHA, D2700/OD/1.
24 On the water dispute see ACA, 'The Robert Scawen Papers', Sy:Y.III.2/5/1–13; on this collection see also Ch. 6 above.
25 Madge, 'Worcester House', 163.
26 'An Inventory of the goods of the Earle of Woster A delinquent', 21 July 1643, SP, 19, vol. 91, no. 1; for a full transcription see Madge, 'Worcester House', 170–80.
27 For the 1622 inventory see BHA, D2700/OC/2. The online catalogue summary shows that it features a detailed list of furniture and effects, including a 'great chest of viols and bows' (one now in the Ashmolean Museum, Oxford), of music, books in Greek, Latin, French and Italian and an inventory of plate.
28 See Madge, 'Worcester House', 162.
29 The servants named in the inventory are [Sarah] Watson, Robert and Hugh Owen, Morgan, James Redman 'the housekeeper' and John Smith 'constant Solicitor there'; ibid., 173.
30 Ibid., 166.
31 'Case papers, 1652–1657, and related papers in suit of "Henry Somerset, commonly called Lord Herbert" v. Lord and Lady Montague about the validity of the nuncupative will of Henry, 1st Marquess of Worcester … Includes deposition by Dr Thomas Bayly … 1631–1657', BHA, D2700/P4/3.
32 Madge, 'Worcester House', 164–5.
33 Survey, 23 March 1648, SP, Domestic, 23, vol. G 133, 341, quoted by Madge, 'Worcester House', 165, who also makes the association.
34 Petition for the return of Worcester House, 3 October 1653, BHA, D2700/QA5/1/19; online summary: 'Printed petitions from Margaret, Countess of Worcester, to Parliament, declaring that she is in great want and has received no relief from Lord Herbert, and asking for a fifth of the family estates for jointure, or an equivalent allowance (her portion in 1639 when she married the Earl was valued at £20,000), or Worcester House (as yet unsold)', c.1654.
35 Edwin Beresford Chancellor, *The Private Palaces of London: Past and Present* (London, 1908), 36.
36 House of Lords MSS, HMC, 7th Report, 80, 122, quoted in Madge, 'Worcester House', 147.
37 Samuel Pepys, diary entry, 20 August 1660, *The Diary of Samuel Pepys*, intro. G. Gregory Smith (London, 1905), 46.
38 John Evelyn, diary entry, 21 December 1660, in E. S. de Beer, ed., *The Diary of John Evelyn*, 6 vols (Oxford, 1951), vol. 3, 264.
39 Pepys, 19 August 1661, *Diary of Samuel Pepys*, 96.
40 Beresford Chancellor, *Private Palaces*, 36.
41 See Thomas Pennant, *Some Account of Old London*, 2nd edn. (London 1791), 145; Walter Thornbury and Edward Walford, *Old and New London*, 6 vols (London, 1879–85), vol. 3, p. 101.
42 John Strype, *A Survey of the Cities of London and Westminster*, 2 vols (London, 1720), vol. 2, 119.
43 Beresford Chancellor, *Private Palaces*, 38.
44 See miscellaneous papers, 1678–86, BHA, D2700/QA2/3/2, D2700/OF2/1; online summaries of these documents include 'removal of wainscot from Worcester House, 1681/2; building Beaufort Buildings, 1682–3; building at Beaufort House (Chelsea) by George Hall, 1682–3' and mention of the 'site of Worcester House "whereon the said house lately stood"; Carlisle Rents (now Worcester Rents) being 16 houses "between the Savoy and the next house to the gate of the said late house called Worcester House". 1682'.
45 Madge, 'Worcester House', 169.

8 · SALISBURY HOUSE

1 Manolo Guerci, 'Robert Cecil and his Strand Palace: Construction and Development', MPhil diss., University of Cambridge, 2004; Guerci, 'John Osborne, the Salisbury House "Porticus" and the "Haynes Grange Room"', *The Burlington Magazine*, 148 (January 2006), 15–24; Guerci, 'The Strand Palaces of the Early Seventeenth Century: Salisbury House and Northumberland House', 2 vols, PhD diss., University of Cambridge, 2007; Guerci, 'Salisbury House in London, 1599–1694: The Strand Palace of Sir Robert Cecil', *Architectural History*, 52 (2009), 31–78.
2 Nicolo Molin, Venetian ambassador, CSP, Venetian 10 (1603–07), 515, quoted by Susan Bracken, 'Robert Cecil as Art Collector', in Pauline Croft, ed., *Patronage, Culture and Power: The Early Cecils* (New Haven and London, 2002), 123.
3 See P. Croft, 'Cecil, Robert, first earl of Salisbury (1563–1612)', ODNB (Oxford, 2004), online edn., October 2008, http://www.oxforddnb.com/view/article/4980, accessed 18 December 2015; see also David Cecil, *The Cecils of Hatfield House* (London, 1973); Pauline Croft, 'The Religion of Robert Cecil', *Historical Journal*, 34 (1991), 773–96; Croft, 'The Reputation of Robert Cecil: Libels, Political Opinion and Popular Awareness in the Early Seventeenth Century', *Transactions of the Royal Historical Society*, 6th ser., 1 (1991), 46; Croft, 'Robert Cecil and the Early Jacobean Court', in Linda Levy Peck, ed., *The Mental World of the Jacobean Court* (1999; Cambridge, 2005), 134–47.
4 Deed granting Dacre House to Robert Cecil, Chancery roll, TNA, C 54/17/13; see George Gater and Walter H. Godfrey, *Survey of London*, vol. 18: *The Strand* (London, 1937), 120.
5 Lady Russell to Robert Cecil, September 1599, HMC, *Salisbury* MS, part IX, 358–61.
6 See HMC, *Egremont I*, 488, quoted in Anthony P. Baggs, 'Two Designs by Simon Basil', *Architectural History*, 27 (1984), 104.
7 Simon Basil to Robert Cecil, 14 August 1601, CP 87/112; see Howard Colvin, ed., *The History of the King's Works*, 6 vols (London, 1963–82), vol. 3, 105–7, 108–20; Colvin, *A Biographical Dictionary of British Architects 1600–1840* (New Haven and London, 2008), 105–6.
8 Basil to Cecil, 14 August 1601, CP 87/112.
9 On Cecil's architectural patronage see Guerci, 'Salisbury House in London', 32–6. Thirty tons of stone from Oxford, in addition to a large quantity that 'we will borrow here that is the Queen's', had been provided for 'tables crest and piers'; Basil to Cecil, 14 August 1601, CP 183/7. More was taken from Lady Sidney; B. Sidney to Cecil, 24 August 1601, HMC, *Salisbury* MS, part XI, 1906, 358, who had offered 'a choice of wrought stone as he found fit', though Basil reported a problem with the 'lights' from Kent because they were unsuitable for clerestories, canted or square windows; Basil to Cecil, 7 September 1601, FP 2/173–4. Richard Bancroft, Bishop of London, gave Cecil the remainder of the Caen stone bought 'to repair the Church of St. Paul's'; Bancroft to Cecil, 26 August 1601, HMC, *Salisbury* MS, part XI, 362; FP 2/172; CP 183/24.
10 Basil to Cecil, 18 August 1601, CP 87/112; see also *A book conteyning the evidences of a capitall messuage now called Salisbury House … being collected … by Richard Langley of Lincolnes Inne Anno Domini 1606*, AT, MS.2003.7.22, 6 April 44 Eliz. [1602], p. 26; 'Grant of licence to Sir Robert Cecil to enclose ground before his house in the Strand … ', HH Deeds 131/4.
11 Cope quoted in Basil to Cecil, 14 August 1601, CP 183/7.
12 Walter Cope to Cecil, 28 September 1601, HMC, *Salisbury* MS, part XI, 396–7.
13 Robert Johnson to Cope, 10 January 1602, ibid., part XII, 1910, 597–8.
14 Richard Percival to Cecil, 17 September 1602, ibid., 375.
15 John Haryngton (*sic*) to Cecil, 22 June 1602, ibid., 199.
16 John Chamberlain to Dudley Carleton, 6 December 1602: 'The Quene dined this day at Master Secretaries, where they say there is

great varietie of entertainment prepared for her, and many rich jewells and presents'; Norman E. McClure, ed., *The Letters of John Chamberlain*, 2 vols (Philadelphia, 1939), vol. 1, 174–6; see FP 2/207; John Nichols, *The Progresses and Public Processions of Queen Elizabeth*, 3 vols (London, 1823), vol. 3, 600–01. Matthew Dimmock, *Elizabethan Globalism: England, China and the Rainbow Portrait* (New Haven and London, 2019) sets a clear picture of the whole event, discussing its broader significance within Elizabethan England's global ambitions.

17 John Stow, *The Survay of London* (1603; London, 1956), 397.

18 John Manningham, *Diary of John Manningham of the Middle Temple and of Bradbourne, Kent, barrister-at-law, 1602–1603*, ed. John Bruce, Camden Society 99 (1868), 100; Cope to Cecil, 28 September 1601, HMC, *Salisbury* MS, part XI, 396–7: 'I cannot imagine, except you will use gilt hangings for your gallery, how you can possibly furnish it. To have one suit or two that will supply that compass will be hard to find, and to have them of one work will be impossible. Good you resolve before the term, for there are not many suits in London, and against the Parliament they will soon be bought up'.

19 Sir Arthur Gorges to Cecil, 1 January 1603, HMC, *Salisbury* MS, part XII, 582, quoted in Susan Bracken, 'The Early Cecils and Italianate Taste', in Edward Chaney, ed., *The Evolution of English Collecting: The Reception of Italian Art in the Tudor and Stuart Periods* (New Haven and London, 2003), n. 125.

20 For a full discussion of Basil's designs see Guerci, 'Salisbury House in London', 40–50.

21 See John Summerson, *Architecture in Britain: 1530–1830* (1953; London, 1970), 97–102.

22 Thomas Wilson to Cecil, 9 August 1605, HMC, *Salisbury* MS, part XVII, 1938, 358–9; 'Charges of the King's dinner at S. House', 27 May 1605, FP 3/27; also in Richard T. Gunton, 'Properties: London, Quixwood, Theobalds 1509–1891', HH MSS Catalogue, 1900, under 'Summary of Documents concerning Salisbury House, Strand, afterward divided into Great Salisbury House & Little Salisbury House'. On Wilson see A. F. Pollard, 'Wilson, Sir Thomas (d. 1629)', rev. Sean Kelsey, ODNB (Oxford, 2004), online edn., January 2008, http://www.oxforddnb.com/view/article/29690, accessed 18 December 2015.

23 FP2S 1/85–89, Bills 28, 1608.

24 'Entertainment to the King and Queen in the Library of Salisbury House, may 6th, 1608': 'Inigo Jones his Accounte for the workes donn for the Right Honourable the Lo. Treasurer 1608 … for Glasses for the Rokks 3/8', FP 3/246, Bills 22. See also Ben Jonson, 'The Entertainment at Salisbury House', ed. James Knowles, in David Bevington, Martin Butler and Ian Donaldson, eds, *The Cambridge Edition of the Works of Ben Jonson*, 7 vols (Cambridge, 2010), vol. 3, 276–9.

25 See Stephen Orgel and Roy Strong, *Inigo Jones: The Theatre of the Stuart Court*, 2 vols (London and Berkeley and Los Angeles, 1973); John Harris and Gordon Higgott, *Inigo Jones: Complete Architectural Drawings* (London, 1989), 30–31.

26 The accounts of 1605 include joiners' bills 'for wainscot in the gallery of the Earle's house in the Strand', FP Bills 8, 9; this must have been for the new gallery since the older had been finished and decorated in 1602.

27 'Details of extensive works at S. House', FP2S 1/56–59, Bills 16, 1607.

28 For Liminge and Basil working together see FP2S 1/56, Bills 16, 1607. Liminge also carried out some carpentry work at Theobalds in 1607 and in 1616–17 provided the design for Blickling Hall, Norfolk, built by Sir Henry Hobart; see Colvin, *Biographical Dictionary*, 642.

29 See 'Account of all such works as hath been done by John Decretts for the Earl of Salisbury, 1606', FP2S 1/37–38, General 17/20, 1606; 1/56–59, Bills 16, 1607. 'Tafferel', of Dutch origin, indicates here a kind of cornice crowning the upper part of the window; its old meanings include 'panel' and 'carved panel', suggesting that the tafferel might be elaborate; in common use in seventeenth-century accounts after Dutch carvers became established in England.

30 'Details of extensive works at S. House', FP2S 1/85–89, Bills 28, 1608; on Buckett see Edward Town, 'A Biographical Dictionary of London Painters 1547–1625', *Walpole Society*, 76 (2014), ad vocem.

31 'Glazing the upper part of 2 turrets', FP2S 1/56–59, Bills 16, 1607; a bill of 1606, FP2S 1/37–38, General 17/20, 1606, mentions 'the Cornish under the Torris'.

32 'Details of extensive works at S. House', FP2S 1/85–89, Bills 28, 1608.

33 'Payment for works at S. House', 'Charges of keeping pheasants there. Charges of repairs & building there', FP 3/263, 3/287, Accounts 160/1, 1609.

34 On the 'porticus' see Guerci, 'John Osborne'; John Harris, *A Passion for Building: The Amateur Architect in England 1650–1850*, exh. cat. (London: Sir John Soane's Museum, 2007), 26–8; Colvin, *Biographical Dictionary*, 760–61.

35 See Jules Lubbock, *The Tyranny of Taste: The Politics of Architecture and Design in Britain 1550–1960* (New Haven and London, 1995), 147–66.

36 Richard Percival to Cecil, 19 April 1603, HMC, *Salisbury* MS, part XV, 1930, 54.

37 Land adjoining Ivy Lane obtained October 1603 but reverted to Cecil January 1604; see T. N. Brushfield, 'Raleghana, Part V: The History of Durham House', 27, apps C and D, repr. from *Transactions of the Devonshire Association for the Advancement of Science, Literature, and Art*, 35 ([Plymouth] 1903).

38 James I, Private Acts, ch. 1; see Gater and Godfrey, *Survey of London*, 121.

39 Percival to Cecil, 20 and 26 September 1605, HMC, *Salisbury* MS, part XVII, 426, 433–4: 'you must of necessity have Vincent's House which is next the Cutlers, else the way will not range directly with Durham wall, but will come upon the wall which now cants out, where the outhouses and houses of office are'. On the gatehouse see Brushfield, 'Raleghana', 27–8.

40 Documents covering moving Ivy Lane, FP2S 1/135–37, Bills 51, 1610.

41 'Charges of enlarging the garden and the new intended building at Salisbury House', FP 4/67, Accounts 160/1, 1611.

42 'Upholster's bill for S. House, for furniture & works. Rent for the passage into "Common [*sic*] Garden"', FP 1/171–76, Bills 59, 1611.

43 Accommodation for widows evidenced by the inventory of 1629, EP, Box C/8.

44 'Charges of buildings at S. House', FP 4/241, Box G 13, 1612.

45 'Details of extensive works at S. House', FP2S 1/171–76, Bills 59, 1611.

46 Ibid., 4 July 1611.

47 'Details of extensive works at S. House', FP2S 1/171–76, Bills 59, 1611.

48 Ibid.

49 'Charges of the "last new building" at S. House' and for repairs, FP 4/135–36, Box G 13, 1612.

50 'Details of extensive works at S. House', FP2S 1/171–76, Bills 59, 1611; FP2S 1/223–27, Bills 70, 1612; 'Charges of the "last new building" at S. House', FP 4/135–36, Box G 13, 1612.

51 'Details of extensive works at S. House', FP2S 1/223–27, Bills 70, 1612.

52 'Details of extensive works at S. House', FP2S 1/171–76, Bills 59, 1611.

53 See John Adamson, 'Rough notes for a study of the building history of Salisbury House, London, under the First and Second Earls of Salisbury', notes for 1607–11. I am grateful to the author for kindly providing me with a copy.

54 The 'mending of the water stairs' is a frequent entry in the accounts from 1606, e.g. FP2S 1/85–89, Bills 28, 1608: payment for 'cramp staple for the water gate'; FP2S 214, Accounts 148/15, 1650: 'mending the stairs at the water side + repairing the rails + balusters, new setting up the same stairs which fell down by a great wind in Dec 1649'.

55 'Details of works there', FP2S 1/265–66, Bills 77, 1613. The 'Sesturne' was a cistern or a water-pipe gilded with Salisbury's dates.

56 'Bills for work at S. House', FP 3/246, Bills 22.

57 See Gater and Godfrey, *Survey of London*, 94–8; Harris and Higgott, *Inigo Jones*, 30; Laurence Stone, *Family and Fortune: Studies in Aristocratic Finance in the Sixteenth and Seventeenth Centuries* (Oxford, 1973), 95–113; Guerci, 'Strand Palaces', vol. 1, 27–8.

58 Colvin, *Biographical Dictionary*, 592.

59 For 'works at the new stables' see FP 3/287, Accounts 160/1, 1609; see Harris and Higgott, *Inigo Jones*, 48–9.

60 F. H. W. Sheppard, ed., *Survey of London*, vol. 36: *The Parish of St. Paul Covent Garden* (London, 1970), 29, 267.
61 See Robert Latham, ed., *Catalogue of the Pepys Library at Magdalene College, Cambridge*, 7 vols (Woodbridge, 1970–94), vol. 3: *Prints and Drawings*, pl. 237c.
62 Richard T. Godfrey, *Wenceslaus Hollar: A Bohemian Artist in England* (New Haven and London, 1995), cat. 102.
63 See Guerci, 'Salisbury House in London', 50–58.
64 The only possible source for Newcourt might have been the riverfront view of Salisbury House by Hollar, controversially dated to the 1630s; see Arthur M. Hind, *Wenceslaus Hollar and his Views of London and Windsor in the Seventeenth Century* (London, 1922); *Hollar's London: 37 Etchings of London Views (1636–1667)* (London, 1980); Graham Parry, *Hollar's England: A Mid-Seventeenth-Century View* (Salisbury, 1980); Richard Pennington, *A Descriptive Catalogue of the Etched Work of Wenceslaus Hollar 1607–1677* (Cambridge, 1982). Newcourt's design can reasonably be dated to the early 1650s, thus earlier than 1658–66 when Hollar's 'West Central District' is supposed to have been produced.
65 'An Inventorie of all houshold Stuffe att Salisbury house', 30 June 1612, HH Box C/40.
66 See Susan Bracken, 'Holbein's "Chatsworth Cartoon": Its Possible Location in the 17th Century', *British Art Journal*, 1 (Autumn 1999), 14–15.
67 'A note of divers things wch were in the Cabenetts', HH Box C/40.
68 Description of cabinet room quoted in Bracken, 'Early Cecils and Italianate Taste', 212.
69 The Venetian mirror, and perhaps a good part of the Italian items at Salisbury House, may have been brought back by William Cecil, Salisbury's first son, who travelled in Italy in 1610. William's step-cousins from the Exeter line had also paid several visits there and may also have imported goods; Robert Cecil himself never travelled to Italy; see ibid., 201–19.
70 Bracken, 'Holbein's "Chatsworth Cartoon"', 14.
71 A portrait of the Duke of Parma is recorded in the Hatfield collection from 1868; see Erna Auerbach and C. Kingley Adams, *Paintings and Sculpture at Hatfield House* (London, 1971), 64, 134.
72 See Bracken, 'Robert Cecil'; 'Holbein's "Chatsworth Cartoon"'.
73 Henry Peacham described Cecil as the 'principall patrone' of the visual arts: *The Compleat Gentleman* (London, 1612), 7–8, quoted in Edward Chaney, 'The Italianate Evolution of English Collecting', in Chaney, *Evolution of English Collecting*, 107, n. 311.
74 See Dimmock, *Elizabethan Globalism*, 129–51.
75 See Maurice Howard, 'Inventories, Surveys and Histories of Great Houses', *Architectural History*, 41 (1998), 14–29; Joan Dils, 'The Books of the Clergy in Elizabethan and Early Stuart Berkshire', *The Local Historian*, 36, no. 2 (May 2006), 92–105.
76 HH, 'A Cattalogge of all your Lordships printed Bookes as they are nowe disposed in your Lordships Librarie [at Salisbury House] taken this 26th of Januarie 1614 [i.e. 1615]'.
77 Of the architectural books only the du Cerceau and de Caus were added by Robert Cecil (I owe this information to Robin Harcourt-Williams). For a list of the other architectural books see Guerci, 'Salisbury House in London', 69, n. 16.
78 Inventory, 20 June 1629, EP Box C/8.
79 Ibid., listing 'my Lord Peircies Chamber', 'lodginge Chamber, and mens Chamber'.
80 Little Salisbury House leases, 1630, 1634, 1640 to 1647, FP 3/36, 36a, Estate Papers, Accounts 28/16; FP 6/98, Strafford Letters, vol. 1, 207, 227; FPS 2/36, Bills 196, 1640; FPS 2/68–71, Bills 211, 1645.
81 For the unidentified Lord Howard see FPS 1/354, Bills 181, 1636; FP 7/119, Box L, 2, 1647; FPS 2/90, Bills 242, 1649.
82 Middle Exchange built, FP 6/148–53; 6/157, Box 1, 4, 1637 and 1638; 6/187; 6/157, 1637.
83 John Strype, *A Survey of the Cities of London and Westminster*, 2 vols (London, 1720), vol. 2, 120.
84 After 1612, Salisbury House was inventoried in 1618 (perhaps lost); 1629, EP Box C/8; 1639/40, EP Box C/9; 1646, EP Box C/4; twice in 1647, EP Box C/5–6; 1657, EP Box C/6; 1685, FP 10/113a; 1686/7, FP 9/169; 1688/9, FP 2/264; 1692, FP 2/268. Most of these are labelled 'inventory of goods' and are not ordered by room.
85 FPS 2/23, Bills 193, 1639; FP2S 2/148, Accounts 148/11, 1640; 'Salisbury House, repairs to the lower rail on the "pergulary" next the garden', FPS 2/68–71, Bills 211, 1645.
86 Bill for repairs to 'floor in the portico', FPS 2/68–71, Bills 211, 1645.
87 Bills for 'work at S. House', FP 7/227–8, Box M 2, 1652.
88 Accounts, bread for poor helpers, FP2S 2/29, 221, Bills 255, 1652.
89 When the New Exchange opened in 1609 shops were offered on eleven-year leases. The expiry of the leases coincided with the most serious trade depression of the century, so that a large portion of the exchange remained untenanted during the 1620s. In 1623 it was reported that the 2nd Earl of Salisbury had sold for £6000 the whole of its first floor to Lady Hatton, the wife of Sir Edward Coke, to be converted into her own town-house; see Stone, *Family and Fortune*, 106. However, the project fell through and in 1627 the first floor was transformed into sixteen small tenements to be let on 21-year leases at £12–£15 per year. This did not work well either, for in 1635 the tenements were pulled down and the shops restored. For the designs of this transformation, made by the carpenter architect Thomas Avys and carried out under Francis Carter, senior officer in the Royal Works when Inigo Jones was the Surveyor, see Hatfield MS, General 57/19, 22; Guerci, 'Strand Palaces', vol. 2, cats ix, x, 263–6.
90 'Lease by L Doyley to R Cordwell of shop as the same is now lately built & made in the Hall & cloister & part of the passage belonging to Great Salisbury House. (Salisbury Hall, or Middle Exchange)'; 'Lease by the same to H Allen, of shop, adjoining a messuage & shop near Worcester House Gate, being part of the east end of Great Salisbury House'; 'Agreement for lease to J staples, of part of a courtyard, certain rooms &c (part of Salisbury House)'; HH, Deeds 125/3, 1670; Deeds 125/5, 1670; EPM, London 2/121, Legal 110/2, 1670.
91 EPM, Herts., 1/145, Legal 2, 1670.
92 EPM, London 2/113, 118, Deeds 125/4, 1670; see Guerci, 'Salisbury House in London', 78, nn. 180, 181.
93 Countess of Salisbury to Countess of Rutland, 4 June 1670, FP 8/211, Rutland Letters 66.
94 Ibid., before 1671, FP 8/208, Rutland Letters 63.
95 Ibid., before 1671, FP 8/201, Rutland Letters 57.
96 See the same to the same, FP 8/204, Rutland Letters 59; FP 8/208, Rutland Letters 63; FP, 8/209, Rutland Letters 64, copied in Guerci, 'Salisbury House in London', footnote 185.
97 'Provise to an act enabling Earl of Salisbury to build on the grounds of Great + Little Salisbury House in the Strand, by licence under the great seal to be obtained before the 24th of June next. Offered by the Earl of Salisbury this day', EPM, London, 2/144, Act 57/5, 1672/3; Earl of Salisbury to 'Mr Churchill', 21 February 1673, FPS 2/229, Bills 298, 298a: 'Mr Churchill, I desire you to let Batison have £26.3.6 towards the passing of my bill, + this shall be your sufficient discharge. Salisbury'. Endorsed: 'passing the Act of Parliament.'; various payments to Mr Corke, March 1672/3, 'towards your patent to build', also described as 'to pay the fees at the house of Commons for my bill for liberty to let leases for [blank] years; also to pay for the order upon my petition for building.'
98 Strype, *Survey of the Cities*, vol. 1, 122.
99 Ibid., vol. 2, p. 120.

9 · DURHAM HOUSE

1 See George Gater and Walter H. Godfrey, *Survey of London*, vol. 18: *The Strand* (London, 1937), 84–94, on which the information in this section is based unless otherwise stated. Beyond this, the only dedicated account of Durham House is Thomas Nadauld Brushfield, *Raleghana … Reprinted from the Transactions of the Devonshire Association for the Advancement of Science, Literature, and Art*, 8 pts (London, 1896–1906), pt 5: *The History of Durham House*, 1–44.
2 On Richard Poor see P. Hoskin, 'Poor, Richard (d. 1237)', ODNB (Oxford, 2004), online edn.,

October 2009, http://www.oxforddnb.com/view/article/22525, accessed 8 January 2016.
3 Bishop Hatfield grant to William de Beverley et al., 1380s, Calendar of Patent Rolls, quoted by Gater and Godfrey, *Survey of London*, 85.
4 'Inventory of Property at Durham Place', September 1528, LMA, MS 231.
5 See Brushfield, *Raleghana*, 5–6; Gater and Godfrey, *Survey of London*, 87; both quote only part of the deeds copied here.
6 Simon Thurley, *Somerset House: The Palace of England's Queens 1551–1692* (London, 2009), 27.
7 See Elizabeth Goldring, *Robert Dudley, Earl of Leicester, and the World of Elizabethan Art* (New Haven and London, 2014), 320 n. 55.
8 See M. Nicholls and P. Williams, 'Ralegh, Sir Walter (1554–1618)', ODNB (Oxford, 2004), online edn., September 2015, http://www.oxforddnb.com/view/article/23039, accessed 9 January 2016; see also Mark Nicholls and Penry Williams, *Sir Walter Raleigh in Life and Legend* (London, 2011).
9 Mark Nicholls put it thus to me; I am grateful for his suggestions.
10 Lady Ralegh to Robert Cecil, October 1600, CP, in Brushfield, *Raleghana*, 19–20. On Elizabeth Ralegh see Anna Beer, *Bess: The Life of Lady Ralegh, Wife to Sir Walter* (London, 2004).
11 Water to Durham House came from a spring in Covent Garden, the use of which had long been granted to the See of Durham; 'Agreement with the Bishop of Durham that water should run from a conduit in Covent Garden to Durham House in the Strand, and to repair and preserve the water course existing from time immemorial, n.d.', LMA, E/BER/CG/T/II/E/08; see also Brushfield, *Raleghana*, 14–15.
12 Howard Colvin, *A Biographical Dictionary of British Architects 1600–1840* (New Haven and London, 2008), 105–6.
13 John Aubrey, *Brief lives: chiefly of contemporaries, set down by John Aubrey between the years 1669 and 1696*, ed. Andrew Clark, 2 vols (Oxford, 1898), vol. 2, 183, in Brushfield, *Raleghana*, 14. For Sherborne see Nicholls and Williams, 'Ralegh, Sir Walter'.
14 See Frances Yates, *A Study of Love's Labour's Lost* (Cambridge, 1936); http://www.marlowe-society.org/christopher-marlowe/life/the-free-thinkers/ and Neal McDevitt, https://poetopography.wordpress.com/2017/01/30/durham-house/, both accessed 2 October 2020; McDevitt conducted research on Marlowe and his relationship with Ralegh. I am grateful to Alan Cox, formerly at the Royal Shakespeare Company, for pointing this out to me and for discussion on the matter.
15 I am also grateful to Mark Nicholls for discussion on the 'School of Atheism' and for a critical appraisal.
16 Lady Ralegh to Cecil, in Brushfield, *Raleghana*, 19–20.
17 Middlesex County Records, 1602, in ibid., 22.
18 Walter Ralegh to John Gilbert, 1601, quoted in Beer, *Bess: Life of Lady Ralegh*, 123; Nicholls and Williams, *Sir Walter Raleigh in Life*, 136–7; see also Agnes Latham and Joyce Youings, eds, *The Letters of Sir Walter Ralegh* (Exeter, 1999), 223–5.
19 Sir Walter Ralegh's Will, 8–10 July 1597, Sherborne Castle Archives, transcr. Latham and Youings, *Letters of Ralegh*, app. 2, p. 383.
20 On Harriot and Ralegh see J. W. Shirley, *Thomas Harriot: A Biography* (Oxford, 1983). I am grateful to Andrew Lawler for pointing this out to me.
21 See Nicholls and Williams, 'Ralegh, Sir Walter'.
22 King's warrant, 31 May 1603, Egerton Papers, 377, in Brushfield, *Raleghana*, 25–6.
23 Bishop of Durham to Thomas Egerton, 7 June 1603, in ibid., 26.
24 Ralegh to Egerton, 9 June 1603, HL, Ellesmere Papers 6231, transcr. Latham and Youings, *Letters of Ralegh*, 245–6.
25 Thomas Wilson to Richard Willis, 1619, CSP, *Domestic Series*, James I, *1619–23* (London, 1858), Appendix to the 4th Report, 284, in Brushfield, *Raleghana*, 37.
26 Lord Chamberlain Pembroke to Secretary Conway, 23 March 1623, ibid., 38.
27 For the 'Fatal Vespers' see Brushfield, *Raleghana*, 38.
28 Gater and Godfrey, *Survey of London*, 92–3.
29 Ibid., 93.
30 See D. L. Smith, 'Herbert, Philip, first earl of Montgomery and fourth earl of Pembroke (1584–1650)', ODNB (Oxford, 2004), online edn., January 2016 http://www.oxforddnb.com/view/article/13042, accessed 15 January 2016.
31 On Wilton see John Bold, *John Webb: Architectural Theory and Practice in the Seventeenth Century* (Oxford, 1989), 57–69; John Heward, 'The Restoration of the South Front of Wilton House: The Development of the House Reconsidered', *Architectural History*, 35 (1992), 78–117; Howard Colvin, 'The South Front of Wilton House', *Essays in English Architectural History* (New Haven and London, 1999), 136–57; Dianne Duggan, 'Pembroke's Arcadia: "Delicious Wilton … that Arbour of the Muses"', *The British Art Journal*, 14, no. 3 (2013/14), 9–20.
32 Aubrey quoted by Colvin, *Biographical Dictionary*, 306–8.
33 Aubrey, *Brief lives*, quoted by Smith, 'Herbert, Philip'. On Pembroke's literary patronage see Michael Brennan, *Literary Patronage in the English Renaissance: The Pembroke Family* (London and New York, 1988).
34 See Ruth Guilding, *Owning the Past: Why the English collected Antique Sculpture, 1640–1840* (New Haven and London, 2014), 50–65. I am grateful to the author for discussion on the subject.
35 Thus described to me by Jeremy Wood, who also generously provided most of the limited references on the topic. I am grateful to him and John Martin Robinson for discussion on this.
36 Sidney Herbert, 16th Earl of Pembroke, *A Catalogue of the Paintings and Drawings in the Collection at Wilton House* (London and New York, 1968), 1–9.
37 Guilding, *Owning the Past*, 50.
38 Richard Symonds, 'Observations concerning Pictures & paintings in England', early 1650s, BL, Egerton MS 1636, transcr. Mary Beal, *A Study of Richard Symonds: His Italian Notebooks and their Relevance to Seventeenth-Century Painting Techniques* (New York and London, 1984), 305–13.
39 See Herbert, *Catalogue of the Paintings*, 3; Alexander W. Vergara, 'The Count of Fuensaldana and David Teniers: Their Purchases in London after the Civil War', *The Burlington Magazine*, 131 (February 1989), 127–32; Jonathan Brown, 'Artistic Relations between Spain and England 1604–1655', in Jonathan Brown and John Elliott, eds, *The Sale of the Century: Artistic Relations between Spain and Great Britain, 1604–1655* (New Haven and London, 2002), 65.
40 Marcus Burke, 'Louis de Haro as Minister, Patron and Collector of Art', in Brown and Elliot, *Sale of the Century*, 95.
41 As Jeremy Wood pointed out to me, 'there may be more to be found out about Pembroke pictures in the Spanish sources. Apart from the inventories published by Marcus Burke in his 1984 thesis, there's a huge amount of very diverse material in José Juan Pérez Preciado, "El marqués de Leganés y las artes", PhD Universidad Complutense de Madrid, 2010, which is available online, and there's also scattered new information on the arrival in Spain of paintings from England in Matías Díaz Padrón's erratic and unreliable *Van Dyck en España* (2012).'
42 See Herbert, *Catalogue of the Paintings*, 2.
43 Bold, *John Webb*, 74.
44 Ibid.
45 John Adamson, 'Architecture and the English Court: The Town Houses of the English Nobility in London and Westminster, 1590–1660', paper delivered at the Huntington Library, San Marino, California, 2000, 21. I am grateful to the author for providing me with a copy of this paper.
46 WC, folios 81–5, 87–8.
47 The Pembroke papers are preserved in WSHC; for the the only document on Durham House see http://discovery.nationalarchives.gov.uk/results/r?_st=adv&_ep=durham%20house&_dss=range&_hb=oth&_nrar=190.
48 John Harris and A. A. Tait, *Catalogue of the Drawings by Inigo Jones, John Webb and Isaac de Caus at Worcester College Oxford* (Oxford, 1979), 36–7, cats 81–8, pls 63–8; Bold, *John Webb*, 69–74.
49 I owe this information to Gordon Higgott.
50 See Smith, 'Herbert, Philip'.
51 Bold, *John Webb*, figs 2 and 3 redrew these plans with a transcription of the rooms' functions.
52 Harris and Tait's suggestion, *Catalogue of the Drawings*, 37, that it refers to the second design is incorrect.
53 See ibid., cat. 181A, pl. 117; John Harris and Gordon Higgott, *Inigo Jones: Complete Architectural Drawings* (London, 1989), cat. 118; John

Summerson, ed., *The Book of Architecture of John Thorpe in Sir John Soane's Museum*, Walpole Society XL (Glasgow, 1966), T18, 28, 43, 79, 98, 132, 176, 225–6. I am grateful to Gordon Higgot for discussion on the subject.
54 See Nicholas Cooper, *Houses of the Gentry, 1480–1680* (New Haven and London, 1999). On Webb's country-house planning see Kimberley Skelton, 'At once National and International: John Webb and the 1650s Country House', in Barbara Arciszewska, ed., *The Baroque Villa: Suburban and Country Residences c.1600–c.1800* (Warsaw, 2009), 229–44.
55 See e.g. Harris and Tait, *Catalogue of the Drawings*, pls 33, 37, 56, 73.
56 Ibid., 40, pl. 78.
57 I am grateful to Gordon Higgot, who pointed out to me the model for this design; see Giles Worsley, 'Scamozzi's Influence on English Seventeenth-Century Architecture', *Annali di architettura*, 18–19 (2006–7), 230; Vincenzo Scamozzi, *L'Idea dell'Architettura Universale*, 2 vols (Venice, 1615), vol. 1, 287.
58 Harris and Tait, *Catalogue of the Drawings*, 37.
59 Stow, *Survay* (1755), quoted by Brushfield, *Raleghana*, 40.
60 Ibid.

10 · YORK HOUSE

1 George Gater and Walter H. Godfrey, *Survey of London*, vol. 18: *The Strand* (London, 1937), 51, on which information in this section is based unless otherwise stated.
2 Queen's grant to Nicholas Heath, TNA, C 82/1026, quoted in Gater and Godfrey, *Survey of London*, 51.
3 See e.g. Nicholas Bacon to Robert Dudley, 1st Earl of Leicester, 27 March 1573, 'From my house beside Charing Cross', HMC, *Calendar of the Manuscripts of the Most Honourable The Marquess of Bath Preserved at Longleat, Wiltshire*, vol. 5: *Talbot, Dudley and Devereux Papers 1533–1659*, ed. G. Dyfnallt Owen (London, 1980), 194.
4 See R. Tittler, 'Bacon, Sir Nicholas (1510–1579)', ODNB (Oxford, 2004), online edn., January 2011, http://www.oxforddnb.com/view/article/1002, accessed 6 November 2015.
5 Bacon to Lord Burghley, 17 June 1560, CSP, *Scotland, vol. 1 (1509–1589)* (London, 1858), 426, quoted by Malcolm Airs, *The Making of the English Country House 1500–1640* (London, 1975), 2, and Jill Husselby and Paula Henderson, 'Location, Location, Location! Cecil House in the Strand', *Architectural History*, 45 (2002), 166.
6 Ernest R. Sandeen, 'The Building Activities of Sir Nicholas Bacon', PhD diss., University of Chicago, 1959.
7 Ibid., 267.
8 Anthony Bacon MSS 647–662, Lambeth Palace Library, London; I am grateful to the archivist Clare Brown for her assistance.
9 See Sandeen, 'Building Activities', 267.
10 John Stow, *A Survey of London*, ed. Charles L. Kingsford, 2 vols (Oxford, 1908), vol. 1, 339, quoted by Sandeen, 'Building Activities', 268, n. 1; see 267–8 for another, described by Stow as a 'great house built of stone and timber' near St Paul's, where Bacon resided before moving to York House.
11 Stow, *Survey*, vol. 2, p. 88, quoted by Sandeen, 'Building Activities', 269, who also appraises the association with the new hall at Gray's Inn.
12 See Gordon Higgott, 'The Fabric in 1670', in Derek Keene, Arthur Burns and Andrew Saint, eds, *St Paul's: The Cathedral Church of London 604–2004* (New Haven and London, 2004), 170–89.
13 For the engraving of Bacon's tomb see Sandeen, 'Building Activities', 275.
14 Gater and Godfrey, *Survey of London*, 52.
15 See W. T. MacCaffrey, 'Hatton, Sir Christopher (c.1540–1591)', ODNB (Oxford, 2004), online edn., January 2015, http://www.oxforddnb.com/view/article/12605, accessed 6 November 2015.
16 Burghley to Christopher Hatton, 1579, in Nicholas Harris Nicolas, *Memoirs of the Life and Times of Sir Christopher Hatton* (London, 1847), 126, quoted by J. M. Sutton, *Materializing Space at an Early Modern Prodigy House: The Cecils at Theobalds, 1564–1607* (Aldershot, 2004), 16. On Holdenby see Mark Girouard, *Town and Country* (New Haven and London, 1992), 197–210; Girouard, *Elizabethan Architecture: Its Rise and Fall, 1540–1640* (New Haven and London, 2009), 191–4.
17 Burghley to Hatton, 1579, in Sutton, *Materializing Space*, 16.
18 Essex's tenure is confirmed by correspondence between him and Leicester from York House: Essex to Leicester, dated thence 28 August 1588, shortly before Leicester's death that September; HMC, *Calendar of the Manuscripts of the Most Honourable The Marquess of Bath Preserved at Longleat, Wiltshire*, vol. 5: *Talbot, Dudley and Devereux Papers 1533–1659*, ed. G. Dyfnallt Owen (London, 1980), 216.
19 Sir John Puckering to Matthew Hutton, Archbishop of York, 2 December 1594, quoted by Gater and Godfrey, *Survey of London*, 52.
20 Sir Thomas Egerton to Archbishop Hutton, 1596; Hutton to Egerton 1596, quoted by ibid.
21 Letter, 1597, quoted by ibid., 53.
22 Egerton to Sir Robert Cecil, March 1600; and Egerton to Essex, January 1597, quoted by ibid., 52–3.
23 John Nichols, *The Progresses and Public Processions of Queen Elizabeth*, 3 vols (London, 1823), vol. 3, 570–75.
24 J. H. Baker, 'Egerton, Thomas, first Viscount Brackley (1540–1617)', ODNB (Oxford, 2004), online edn., May 2015, http://www.oxforddnb.com/view/article/8594, accessed 6 November 2015.
25 John Adamson, 'Architecture and the English Court: The Town Houses of the English Nobility in London and Westminster, 1590–1660', paper delivered at the Huntington Library, San Marino, California, 2000, 7; I am grateful to the author for kindly providing me with a copy. See also Adamson, *Princely Courts of Europe* (London, 2000). Adamson suggests a date for Egerton's ordinances of c.1610; HL, Ellesmere Papers, MS 1179 is an undated MS copy; for another version, dated 1605, see 'Copy of an Original Manuscript entitled "A Breviate touching the Order and Goverment of a Nobleman's House, &c."', *Archeologia*, vol. 13 (London: T. Bensley, 1800), 315–83.
26 HL, Ellesmere Papers, MS 1179.
27 Ibid.
28 The dispersal of the Bacon papers makes it impossible to ascertain whether Sir Francis did anything at all to York House.
29 Bacon to Duke of Lennox, 1621, quoted by Roger Lockyer, *Buckingham: The Life and Political Career of George Villiers, First Duke of Buckingham, 1592–1628* (London, 1981), 118.
30 I am grateful to Mark Girouard for pointing out Aubrey's mention of the aviary to me.
31 Bernard H. Newdigate, ed., *The Poems of Ben Jonson* (Oxford, 1936), 136.
32 M. Peltonen, 'Bacon, Francis, Viscount St Alban (1561–1626)', ODNB (Oxford, 2004), online edn., October 2007, http://www.oxforddnb.com/view/article/990, accessed 5 November 2015.
33 Francis Bacon to George Villiers, Marquess of Buckingham, [June] 1621, quoted in Philip Gibbs, *The Romance of George Villiers, First Duke of Buckingham, and some Men and Women of the Stuart Court* (London, 1908), 118.
34 Buckingham to Bacon, 1621, quoted in ibid., 119.
35 Ibid., 1621, 121.
36 Philip McEvansoneya, 'The Houses of the Duke of Buckingham', MA diss., Courtauld Institute of Art, University of London, 1985, 14; see also n. 44 below.
37 Edward Sackville, ?1622, quoted by Peltonen, 'Bacon, Francis'.
38 James I to Archbishop Tobias Matthew, 30 March 1624, CSP, *Domestic Series, James I, 1623–1625* (London, 1859), 302; see also 254 (24 May), 260 (29 May), 266 (2 June), 301 (14 July). It was James I who apparently pressed his favourite to get the house and who provided the See of York with Crown land. The exchange, as the king reassured the Lords, would be beneficial since rent from York House came to no more than £11 a year, while what he offered could be worth £700; see Lockyer, *Buckingham*, 213.
39 R. Lockyer, 'Villiers, George, first duke of Buckingham (1592–1628)', ODNB (Oxford, 2004), online edn., May 2011, http://www.oxforddnb.com/view/article/28293, accessed 12 November 2015. Villiers's life has attracted attention from

many scholars; see Gibbs, *Romance of George Villiers*.

40 Sir Balthasar Gerbier to Duke of Buckingham, 1625, quoted by Godfrey Goodman, *The Court of King James the First*, 2 vols (London, 1839), vol. 2, 369–70.

41 According to McEvansoneya, 'Houses of the Duke of Buckingham', 4, Gerbier entered Buckingham's service in 1619, while Adamson, 'Architecture and the English Court', 14, suggests 1616, pointing to a letter from Gerbier to Dudley Carleton, Viscount Dorchester, of 3 July 1629 which states that the architect had worked twelve years for the duke. Considering that the duke died in 1628, when presumably Gerbier's services ended, 1616 appears correct; see CSP, *Domestic Series*, Charles I, *1629–1631* (London, 1859), 4. That is also the year Gerbier came to England; Howard Colvin, *Biographical Dictionary of British Architects 1600–1840* (New Haven and London, 2008), 414–16.

42 See L. R. Betcherman, 'The York House Collection and its Keeper', *Apollo*, 92 (October 1970), 250–59.

43 See Kevin Sharpe, 'The Earl of Arundel, his Circle and the Opposition to the Duke of Buckingham, 1618–1628', in Sharpe, ed., *Faction and Parliament: Essays on Early Stuart History* (Oxford, 1978), 1–42.

44 McEvansoneya, 'Houses of the Duke of Buckingham', to whom I am grateful for permission to quote from this and for corresponding on the subject of York House; for the articles see below.

45 Another work, not supervised by Newman or dealing with York House but interesting for Villiers's profile, is Brigit Gebhart, 'George Villiers, First Duke of Buckingham: Clothes, Jewels, Portraits and Courtly Manners of a Royal Favourite', MA diss., Courtauld Institute of Art, University of London, 1997.

46 Buckingham–Gerbier correspondence, BOD, Tanner MS 73, fols 491–510v. For translations from French of several of these letters see Goodman, *Court of King James*, vol. 2, 238–40, 260–67, 326–45, 356–97.

47 Balthasar Gerbier, *A Brief Discourse Concerning the Three Chief Principles of Magnificent Building: viz. Solidity, Conveniency, and Ornament* (London, 1662). His account book for 1622–8, BL Add. MS 12528, compiled posthumously to sort out his debts, is of little use here.

48 McEvansoneya, 'Houses of the Duke of Buckingham', 6–7.

49 Sir Henry Wotton to Sir Albert Morton, December 1624, quoted by Logan Pearsall Smith, *The Life and Letters of Sir Henry Wotton*, 2 vols (Oxford, 1907), vol. 2, 286, n. 408.

50 As reported by John Chamberlain, c.1622, quoted by Lockyer, *Buckingham*, p. 120. Jones had also designed lodgings for Villiers and his wife in 1619–20 at Whitehall Palace and probably designed the stables at Burley later; see Colvin, *Biographical Dictionary*, 584–93.

51 Betcherman, 'York House Collection', 250–59.

52 The date 1665 was suggested in John Harris, 'Who designed the York Water-Gate?', *Country Life*, 2 November 1989, 151. P. H. Hulton, 'Drawings of England in the Seventeenth Century by Willem Schellinks Jacob Esselens and Lambert Doomer from the Van der Hem Atlas of the National Library, Vienna', *Walpole Society*, 35, pt 1, 1954–56 (1959), xvii, dates the drawing to the 1660s. Little is known of Esselens's life.

53 Secretary Williams, speech to the Lords, 1624, quoted by McEvansoneya, 'Houses of the Duke of Buckingham', 15.

54 The short-term idea was suggested in Hulton, 'Drawings of England', 32; McEvansoneya, 'Houses of the Duke of Buckingham', 20–21, and Adamson, 'Architecture and the English Court', 14, take a similar stance.

55 Gerbier to Buckingham, 2 December 1624, quoted by Goodman, *Court of King James*, vol. 2, 360.

56 Gerbier, *Brief Discourse*, 27.

57 Ibid., 27–8.

58 Owen Wynne to his father, Sir John Wynne, 24 May 1624, quoted in *Archaeologia Cambrensis: A Record of the Antiquities of Wales and its Marshes, and the Journal of the Cambrian Archaeological Association*, vol. 2 (London, 1847), 15–17; Sir Francis Nethersole to Dudley Carleton, 24 May 1624, CSP, *Domestic Series*, James I, *1623–1625* (London, 1859), 254–5, noted the 'great cost'.

59 Sir Thomas Wentworth, Earl of Strafford, to Christopher Wanderword, 17 June 1624, in W. Knowler, *The Earl of Strafforde's Letters and Dispatches* (Dublin, 1740), vol. 1, 21–3.

60 Chamberlain to Carleton, 19 June 1624, CSP, *Domestic Series*, James I, *1623–1625*, 278.

61 Warrant for £1800 for Portland stone, 19 July 1624, ibid., 307.

62 Carleton to his nephew Sir Dudley Carleton, 26 and 30 September 1624, ibid., 344–6.

63 Carleton to Sir Dudley Carleton, 24 January 1625, ibid., 457.

64 Gerbier to Buckingham, 2 December 1624, in Goodman, *Court of King James*, vol. 2, 359.

65 Gerbier to Buckingham, 17 November 1624; for the duchess's involvement at New Hall see Gerbier to Buckingham, 8 February 1625, both in Goodman, *Court of King James*, vol. 2, 342, 374.

66 Gerbier to Buckingham, 2 December 1624, in Goodman, *Court of King James*, vol. 2, 360.

67 Ibid., 375–6.

68 On Buckingham's finances see Lockyer, *Buckingham*, 212–13.

69 See Hulton, 'Drawings of England', 31, listing both versions in the Van der Hen Atlas, National Library, Vienna; one is now in the Albertina, http://sammlungenonline.albertina.at/default.aspx?lng=english2#1754677e-a8e7-4c64-9867-991e8fa51f98.

70 Gerbier, *Brief Discourse*, 42.

71 George Vertue, 'Vertue Note Book II', ed. A. J. Finberg, *Walpole Society*, 20, 1931–32 (Oxford, 1932), 49.

72 Harris, 'Who Designed the York Water-Gate?'.

73 RIBA, London, Collections, SC206/Jol&WeJ[170]; both sides of the sheet illustrated on www.ribapix.com, RIBA 22922 and RIBA 84046. I am grateful to Charles Hind for his suggestions and assistance and to Gordon Higgott, who told me that around 1641 Webb was recording examples of good practice, perhaps with a treatise in mind, and that a manuscript by Webb, 'Notes of practise upon the gate at Temple Barr: 1638', BL, confirms the purpose of the drawing; see John Peacock and Christy Anderson, 'Inigo Jones, John Webb and Temple Bar', *Architectural History*, 44 (2001), 29–38.

74 Colvin, *Biographical Dictionary*, 592, 991.

75 SM, Fauntleroy Pennant, vol. III, fol. 64, http://collections.soane.org/OBJECT1933. I am grateful to Gordon Higgott for discussion on this.

76 Gordon Higgott and Adam White in http://collections.soane.org/OBJECT1933, accessed 11 November 2015.

77 Gerbier, *Brief Discourse*, 42.

78 Duke of Buckingham inventory, 1635, BOD, MS Rawlinson A341, fols 30–41, or BL, Add. MS 18914; first but only partly published in Randall Davies, 'An Inventory of the Duke of Buckingham's Pictures, etc. at York House', *The Burlington Magazine*, 10 (1906–7), 376–82; full transcription in Simon Jervis, 'Furniture of the First Duke of Buckingham', *Furniture History*, 33 (1997), 57–74. For the manuscript see Philip McEvansoneya, 'Vertue, Walpole and the Documentation of the Buckingham Collection', *Journal of the History of Collections*, 8, no. 1 (1996), 1–14. A subsequent catalogue of 1648 of Buckingham's pictures sold by the 2nd Duke at Antwerp was published in Brian Fairfax, *A catalogue of the curious collection of pictures of George Villiers, Duke of Buckingham* (London, 1758); it is therefore not relevant for the sequence of interiors at York House.

79 Rubens's *Apotheosis of the Duke of Buckingham* had probably been commissioned by the Duchess of Buckingham as a memorial to her husband after his death in 1628; see Edward Croft-Murray, *Decorative Painting in England 1537–1837*, 2 vols (London, 1962), vol. 1, 35 and fig. 63; Christiane Hille, *Visions of the Courtly Body: The Patronage of George Villiers, First Duke of Buckingham, and the Triumph of Painting at the Stuart Court* (Berlin, 2012), 207–26. According to Mark Girouard on Gerbier in *A Biographical Dictionary of English Architecture 1540–1640* (New Haven and London, 2021), it was commissioned by Gerbier in 1625 but completed only shortly before Buckingham was assassinated in 1628. See Eileen Harris, *Osterley Park, Middlesex* (National Trust, 1994), 44, and *The Genius of Robert Adam: His Interiors* (New Haven and London, 2001), 169. The painting was destroyed by fire in 1949 but Rubens's sketch for it survives in the National Gallery, London.

80 Betcherman, 'York House Collection', 255.

81 For the marble see McEvansoneya, 'Houses of the Duke of Buckingham', 25, suggested in relation to Gerbier's selection of it for rooms on 'moist ground' on the ground floor, as in his *Counsel and Advise to All Builders* (London, 1663), 22.

82 G. Thorn-Drury, ed., *Parnassus Biceps or Several Choice Pieces of Poetry* (1656; London, 1927), 33; see also 127. I am grateful to Paul Hartle for discussion on this.

83 McEvansoneya, 'Houses of the Duke of Buckingham', 24. His identification refers to statues above two chapel doors, hence the link to the chapel and the neighbouring hall seen in Esselens's view. However, these statues feature in the Great Chamber at Chelsea, not York House; see Jervis, 'Furniture of the First Duke', 68.

84 Gerbier, *Brief Discourse*, 29; McEvansoneya, 'Houses of the Duke of Buckingham', 22.

85 François de Bassompierre, *Memoirs of the Embassy of the Marshal de Bassompierre to the Court of England in 1626* (London, 1819), 24–5.

86 I owe this information to Mark Girouard, who kindly showed me the draft entry on Gerbier in his *Biographical Dictionary*. On the Duke's Closet see Gerbier, *Brief Discourse*.

87 Thorn-Drury, *Parnassus Biceps*, 32.

88 See Jervis, 'Furniture of the First Duke', 52–3.

89 An 'open gallery', or 'galerie ouverte', 'which leads from your Excellency's chamber to the palace on the Thames' is noted by the Spanish ambassador, Count Gondomar, to Buckingham, 10 September 1622, quoted in Goodman, *Court of King James*, 238–9. However, it seems to refer to the loggia on the ground floor, rather than the Long Gallery, attesting that a link of some kind existed between the former and the duke's room.

90 The number of paintings in Buckingham's well-studied collection is disputed; see Betcherman, 'York House Collection'; Philip McEvansoneya, 'A Note on the Duke of Buckingham's Inventory', *The Burlington Magazine*, 128, no. 1001 (1986), 607; McEvansoneya, 'Some Documents concerning the Patronage and Collections of the Duke of Buckingham', *Rutgers Art Review*, 8 (1987), 27–38; McEvansoneya, 'An Unpublished Inventory of the Hamilton Collection in the 1620s and the Duke of Buckingham's Pictures', *The Burlington Magazine*, 134, no. 1073 (1992), 524–6; McEvansoneya, 'Van Dyck and the Duchess of Buckingham's Collection: New Documents relating to York House', *Apollo*, 140 (1994), 30–32; McEvansoneya, 'Italian Paintings in the Buckingham Collection', in Edward Chaney, ed., *The Evolution of English Collecting: The Reception of Italian Art in Tudor and Stuart Periods* (New Haven and London, 2003), 315–36; Hille, *Visions of the Courtly Body*, 23–4.

91 See Gerbier to Dorchester, 3 July 1629, CSP, *Domestic Series*, Charles I, *1629–1631* (London, 1859), 4; Duchess of Buckingham to Dorchester, 28 July 1631, ibid., *1631–1633* (London, 1862), 123.

92 I owe this information to Mark Girouard; see also n. 86 above.

93 See Betcherman, 'York House Collection', 252, fig. 8.

94 See Knowler, *Earl of Strafforde's Letters*, vol. 1, 21–3; Thorn-Drury, *Parnassus Biceps*, 33. By 1635 Giambologna's piece had been moved to Chelsea House, located 'On the Mount in the Garden' there; Jervis, 'Furniture of the First Duke', 68.

95 See Hille, *Visions of the Courtly Body*, 122.

96 John Evelyn, diary entry, 27 November 1655, in E. S. de Beer, ed., *The Diary of John Evelyn*, 6 vols (Oxford, 1955), vol. 3, 162.

97 Duchess of Buckingham to Dorchester, 28 July 1631, CSP, *Domestic Series*, Charles I, *1631–1633*, 123; see also Gater and Godfrey, *Survey of London*, 56. For a cultural history of Katherine Villiers see Megan Shaw, 'A Female Favourite: Katherine Villiers, Duchess of Buckingham (1603–1649)', PhD Thesis, University of Auckland, forthcoming 2023.

98 For the year 1641 the rent for York House was £350; ACA, Syon MS U.I.6/1 (Accounts of Thomas Cartwright).

99 ACA, Syon MS U.I.5/63, U.I.6/1, 3, 20, 27, 33 (Accounts of Thomas Cartwright, 1639–45); U.I.6/35 (Accounts of Henry Tayler, 1645–6); U.I.6/36, 44, 49, 52, 54 (Accounts of Robert Scawen, 1645–8).

100 See Philip McEvansoneya, 'The Sequestration and Dispersal of the Buckingham Collection', *Journal of the History of Collections*, 8, no. 2 (1996), 133–54; Jeremy Wood, 'Van Dyck and the Earl of Northumberland: Taste and Collecting in Stuart England', in Susan J. Barnes and Arthur K. Wheelock Jr., eds, *Van Dyck 350* (Washington DC, 1994), 281–326.

101 See B. Yardley, 'Villiers, George, second duke of Buckingham (1628–1687)', ODNB (Oxford, 2004), online edn., May 2009, http://www.oxforddnb.com/view/article/28294, accessed 3 December 2015.

102 Gerbier, *Brief Discourse*, 28.

103 Ibid., 14.

104 Gater and Godfrey, *Survey of London*, 57.

105 The water gate has fascinated many artists and architects; it was depicted for Sir John Soane's Royal Academy Lectures in which he compared it to the great monumental arches of Paris; SM, Drawers 24/3/2, 22/7/5, 22/7/6.

11 · NORTHUMBERLAND HOUSE

1 See Manolo Guerci, 'The Strand Palaces of the Early Seventeenth Century: Salisbury House and Northumberland House', 2 vols, PhD diss., University of Cambridge, 2007, vol. 1, pt II, 87–161; vol. 2, app. 18, 227–31; Guerci, 'Charles Barry's Designs for Northumberland House, 1852–55', in Frank Salmon, ed., *The Persistence of the Classical: Essays on Architecture presented to David Watkin* (London, 2008), 136–50; Guerci, 'The Construction of Northumberland House and the Patronage of its Original Builder, Lord Henry Howard, 1603–14', *The Antiquaries Journal*, 90 (2010), 341–400; Guerci, 'From Northampton to Northumberland: The Strand Palace during the Suffolk Ownership and the Transformations of Algernon Percy, Tenth Earl of Northumberland, 1614–68', *The Antiquaries Journal*, 94 (2014), 211–51; Guerci with Adrian Aymonino, 'The Architectural Transformation of Northumberland House under the 7th Duke of Somerset and the 1st Duke and Duchess of Northumberland, 1748–86', *The Antiquaries Journal*, 96 (2016), 315–61; Aymonino and Guerci, 'The Refurbishment of Northumberland House: Craftsmen and Interior Decoration in Mid-Eighteenth-Century London Town Houses', in Susanna Avery-Quash and Kate Retford, eds, *The Georgian London Town House: Building, Collecting and Display* (New York and London, 2019), 71–98.

2 John Chamberlain to Dudley Carleton, 9 June 1614, in Norman E. McClure, ed., *The Letters of John Chamberlain* (Philadelphia, 1939), vol. 1, 539.

3 The sum of £8150 was obtained by adding up the value of every single item appraised in the inventory, both in London and Greenwich; jewellery, gilt plates and silver vessels amounted to £4925, while the household goods in London alone were worth £2507 (against £718 at Greenwich Lodge); transcr. Evelyn Philip Shirley, 'An Inventory of the Effects of Henry Howard, K.G., Earl of Northampton … with a transcript of his Will … ', *Archaeologia*, 42 (1869), 347–78; Guerci, 'Construction of Northumberland House', 393–7.

4 See Linda Levy Peck, *Northampton: Patronage and Policy at the Court of James I* (London, 1982); P. Croft, 'Henry Howard', ODNB (Oxford, 2004), vol. 28, 366–74; Daniel C. Andersson, 'Studies in the Early Elizabethan Life and Works of Lord Henry Howard, later Earl of Northampton (1540–1614)', PhD diss., Warburg Institute, University of London, 2006.

5 See John Bossy, *Under the Molehill: An Elizabethan Spy Story* (New Haven and London, 2001).

6 See Andersson, 'Studies in the Early Elizabethan Life and Works', 47 and n. 151.

7 See Linda Levy Peck, 'The Mentality of a Jacobean Grandee', in Levy Peck, ed., *The Mental World of the Jacobean Court* (Cambridge, 2005), 149–67; Andersson, 'Studies in the Early Elizabethan Life and Works'.

8 See Guerci, 'Construction of Northumberland House', 342–54.

9 Indenture between Henry Howard and the Cooke family, 1 October 1605, ACA, Deeds, D.XVII.IIa.

10 Indenture between Howard and Robert Scott, 2 January 1606, ACA, Deeds, D.XVII.IIb.

11 Lease, 1606; purchase of portion of St Mary Rounceval, 1608, ACA, Deeds, D.XVII.II; D.XVII.IIc.

12 George Gater and Walter H. Godfrey, *Survey of London*, vol. 18: *The Strand* (London, 1937), 1–9.
13 Deed between Howard and Robert Reed, 6 June 1609, ACA, Deeds, D.XVII.IIC.
14 Howard to Robert Carr, Viscount Rochester, 20 August 1612, CSP, *Domestic Series*, James I, 1611–18 (London, 1858), 145.
15 This is confirmed by later plans of London, e.g. John Rocque, *Plan of the Cities of London and Westminster* (1746), facsimile edn. *The A to Z of Georgian London*, intro. Ralph Hyde (London, 1981), pl. 11; Richard Horwood, *Map and face of London* (1799–1819), facsimile edn. *The A to Z of Regency London* (1985), pl. 23.
16 Robert Brett for Howard, purchase of portion of St Mary Rounceval, 6 July 1611, ACA, Deeds, D.XVII.IIC.
17 For discussion on the date and authorship of the Smythson plan see Guerci, 'Construction of Northumberland House', 373–4.
18 See Inigo Jones, *Inigo Jones on Palladio*, ed. Bruce Allsopp, 2 vols (Newcastle upon Tyne, 1970), vol. 1, 1.
19 See Guerci, 'Construction of Northumberland House', 359–68.
20 On account of the difference in level between Hall and terrace a true screen passage was not possible but its presence was registered by Thorpe.
21 See Guerci, 'Construction of Northumberland House', 374, 380–82.
22 With the Hall as well as the Strand entrance porch occupying the first two levels of the house, the only way to have an uninterrupted sequence of state rooms was to place them at the top of the house, whence there would also be access to the terrace. On Hardwick see Mark Girouard, *Town and Country* (New Haven and London, 1992), 212; on Charlton see Nicholas Cooper, *The Jacobean Country House: From the Archives of Country Life* (London, 2006), 52–7.
23 For the 1748–50 phase see Guerci and Aymonino, 'Architectural Transformation', 318–29.
24 Wendel Dietterlin, *The Fantastic Engravings of Wendel Dietterlin: A Facsimile of the 1598 Edition of his Architectura* (New York, 1968).
25 See Jacques A. du Cerceau, *Les Plus Excellents Bastiments de France* (1576, 1607, facsimile edn., 1972).
26 George Vertue, 'Vertue Notebook II', *Walpole Society* 20 (1931/2; Oxford, 1932), 49; Adam White, *A Biographical Dictionary of London Tomb Sculptors c.1560–c.1660*, Walpole Society 61 (1998/9), 18–20.
27 Vertue, 'Vertue Notebook II', 49; later studies on the attribution of Northampton House are all based on Vertue's conclusions. On Janseen see White, *Biographical Dictionary*, 63–4; Howard Colvin, *A Biographical Dictionary of British Architects 1600–1840* (New Haven and London, 2008), 990–91.
28 For full discussion see Guerci, 'Construction of Northumberland House', 384–8.
29 See Evelyn Philip Shirley, 'An Inventory of the Effects of Henry Howard, K.G., Earl of Northampton … with a transcript of his Will …', *Archaeologia*, 42 (1869), 347–78, esp. 353–69.
30 Wolsey's tapestries included a set depicting the Acts of the Apostles after Raphael's cartoons, woven in gold and silver thread; see Edward Chaney, ed., *The Evolution of English Collecting: The Reception of Italian Art in the Tudor and Stuart Periods* (New Haven and London, 2003), 32; see also Simon Thurley, *Hampton Court* (New Haven and London, 2003), 26–7; Linda Levy Peck, *Consuming Splendour: Society and Culture in Seventeenth-Century England* (Cambridge, 2005), 80–85.
31 On Northampton's collection see Edward Chaney, 'The Italianate Evolution of English Collecting', in Chaney, *Evolution of English Collecting*, 48, n. 310; Levy Peck, *Mental World of the Jacobean Court*, 161–6; Levy Peck, *Consuming Splendour*, 80, 164, 215–18.
32 See Nicholas Barker, 'The Books of Henry Howard', *Bodleian Library Record*, 13 (October 1990), 375–81; Linda Levy Peck, 'Uncovering the Arundel Library at the Royal Society', *Notes and Records of the Royal Society of London* (1998), 3–24.
33 See William Perry, *Bibliotheca Norfolciana* (London, 1681); *Catalogue of Manuscripts in the British Museum: The Arundel Manuscripts*, new series, 3 vols (London, 1834).
34 Chamberlain to Carleton, 9 June 1614, in McClure, *Letters of John Chamberlain*, vol. 1, 539.
35 See Shirley, 'Inventory of the Effects', 376.
36 Chamberlain to Carleton, 30 June 1614 and 4 January 1617, in McClure, *Letters of John Chamberlain*, vol. 1, 541; vol. 2, 47; M. F. S. Hervey, *The Life, Correspondence and Collections of Thomas Howard, Earl of Arundel* (Cambridge, 1921), 91, 93, 119; Laurence Stone, *Family and Fortunes: Studies in Aristocratic Finance in the Sixteenth and Seventeenth Centuries* (Oxford, 1973), 274. Since there is no mention of the land and Greenwich Lodge in the will, it must be assumed that they were bequeathed to Arundel by other means.
37 Copies of the Conveyance of Northampton House to the Earl of Suffolk, 12 June 1612, ACA, Deeds, D.XVII.IIe; see Stone, *Family and Fortunes*, 268–94; P. Croft, 'Thomas Howard', ODNB (Oxford, 2004), vol. 28, 436–9.
38 Tower at Greenwich reverted to Theophilus Howard, 1611, CSP, *Domestic Series*, James I, 1611–18 (London, 1858), 145.
39 Chamberlain to Carleton, 5 October and 27 November 1611, in McClure, *Letters of John Chamberlain*, vol. 1, 306, 319. The Charterhouse was bought by Thomas Sutton for £13,000 as a school for 44 poor boys and a hospital for 80 poor gentlemen, parts of it surviving to this day; see Philip Temple, *Survey of London: The Charterhouse* (New Haven and London, 2010).
40 Stone, *Family and Fortunes*, 282–3.
41 See Robert and James Dodsley, *London and its Environs Described*, 5 vols (London, 1761), vol. 3, 50; *The History of Northumberland House* (London, 1866); Edwin Beresford Chancellor, *The Private Palaces of London: Past and Present* (London, 1908), 51; Christopher Simon Sykes, *Private Palaces: Life in the Great London Houses* (London, 1985), 147–8; Croft, 'Thomas Howard', 439.
42 See Chaney, 'Italianate Evolution of English Collecting', 48–9.
43 Chamberlain to Dudley Carleton, 8 January 1620, in McClure, *Letters of John Chamberlain*, vol. 2, 281; for Jones's surveying see also Ch. 9.
44 Grant of water to Suffolk House, 15 March 1617, CSP, *Domestic Series*, James I, 1611–18, 447.
45 Secretary Conway to Lord Treasurer [Thomas Howard], 23 April 1623, CSP, *Domestic Series*, James I, 1619–23 (London, 1858), 567.
46 Warrant to pay Thomas Mynne, Knight-harbinger, £72 2s for attendance with two Yeomen-harbingers at Suffolk House, 20 July 1625, CSP, *Domestic Series*, 1625–26 (London, 1858), 67.
47 List of 1626, ibid., 590.
48 See Stone, *Family and Fortunes*, 283.
49 See Gerald Brenan, *A History of the House of Percy, from the Earliest Times down to the Present Century by Gerald Brenan*, ed. William A. Lindsay, 2 vols (London, 1902), vol. 2, 255–6.
50 The house seems to have been bought in three annual instalments from 1642, the first of which came to c. £5000; General Household Accounts by Henry Tayler, 1642–1643, ACA, Syon MS, U.I.6, BL Microfilm 391.
51 See E. B. de Fontblanque, *Annals of the House of Percy, from the Conquest to the Opening of the Nineteenth Century*, 3 vols (London, 1887), vol. 2, 366–486; Lindsay, *History of the House of Percy*; G. A. Drake, 'Percy, Algernon, tenth earl of Northumberland (1602–1668)', ODNB (Oxford, 2004), online edn., January 2008, http://www.oxforddnb.com/view/article/21923, accessed 11 December 2015.
52 See Jeremy Wood, 'The Architectural Patronage of the 10th Earl of Northumberland', in John Bold and Edward Chaney, eds, *English Architecture Public and Private: Essays for Kerry Downes* (London, 1993), 56–8, 74–80.
53 Expenditure between these two stages, and in the decade that followed, was mainly for routine maintenance and reparations, though there were payments as late as 1660 for the redecoration of the state rooms altered for the garden staircase.
54 Payment to Edward Carter, 1649, Building Accounts up to 1649, ACA, Syon MS, U.III.2.
55 Howard Colvin, ed., *The History of the King's Works*, 6 vols (London, 1963–82), vol. 3, 156, 161.
56 See ibid., 151; for works at Syon see Accounts of Robert Scawen 1651–52, ACA, Syon MS, U.I.6.
57 For Zachary Taylor see Colvin, *History of King's Works* (1982), vol. 4, 39, 121, 259, 262–3, 265–8.
58 Building Accounts up to 1649, ACA, Syon MS, U.III.2.
59 Ibid.; these accounts provide the evidence for all works described hereafter unless otherwise

stated. For detailed description see Guerci, 'From Northampton to Northumberland'.

60 The presence of a little kitchen is first mentioned in accounts of 1654, PH, 5865; earlier records reveal the presence of a new, larger kitchen; Building Accounts up to 1649, ACA, Syon MS, U.III.2.

61 See Paula Henderson, 'The Loggia in Tudor and Early Stuart England: The Adaptation and Function of Classical Form', in Lucy Gent, ed., *Albion's Classicism: The Visual Arts in Britain, 1550–1600* (New Haven and London, 1995), 109–45; Henderson, *The Tudor House and Garden: Architecture and Landscape in the Sixteenth and Early Seventeenth Centuries* (New Haven and London, 2005).

62 The location of the Lobby remains uncertain, though it would be logical to find it next to the entrance.

63 Since the Little Gallery over the porch on the courtyard side was partitioned, the same is likely to have happened to the porch below, as seen in *c*.1750 plans which partly show the house as left by Algernon Percy; see Guerci, 'Strand Palaces', vol. 2, app. XXXIII c, 285; Guerci, 'From Northampton to Northumberland', 239.

64 Wood, 'Architectural Patronage', 68.

65 This is evident from a number of references in the accounts up to 1649, which describe the countess's rooms as above the 'stone arches' on the ground floor on the courtyard side.

66 Works included new partitions in two ground-floor lodgings on the west side of the house, one of which was occupied by Robert Scawen, Northumberland's paymaster and chair of the Parliament's Army Committee.

67 A space called 'the Garretts' features in the inventory of 1670, ACA, 107, GC 26; BL, Microfilm 351; transcr. in Jeremy Wood, 'Van Dyck and the Earl of Northumberland: Taste and Collecting in Stuart England', in Susan J. Barnes and Arthur K. Wheelock Jr., eds, *Van Dyck 350* (Washington DC, 1994), app. II, 304–8. It may have been a new room created at the top of one of the wings, though there is no clue as to its exact location.

68 The Nursery appears several times in the building accounts up to 1649; it had a large window of eight lights and apparently four chimneys of Portland stone, though this particular entry refers to 'nurceries' rather than to a single one.

69 See Guerci, 'From Northampton to Northumberland', 233.

70 See ibid., 234; Guerci, 'Strand Palaces', vol. 2, app. XXXIII, 284–5.

71 See Wood, 'Architectural Patronage', 63; the canted windows no longer existed by the time the facade was depicted by Wale.

72 Some internal decoration was still going on in 1652; PH 5848 (1652).

73 See Patrick McEvansoneya, 'The Sequestration and Dispersal of the Buckingham Collection', *Journal of the History of Collections*, 8, no. 2 (1996), 133–54; Wood, 'Van Dyck and the Earl of Northumberland', 281.

74 Accounts of Orlando Gee, foreign payments, 'for removing pictures and statues to Whitehall', PH 5931 (1660).

75 See Henderson, *Tudor House and Garden*.

76 Building Accounts 1655–57, ACA, Syon MS, U.III.3; see Colvin, *Biographical Dictionary*, 679–80; John Bold, *John Webb: Architectural Theory and Practice in the Seventeenth Century* (Oxford, 1989), 162–6; Wood, 'Architectural Patronage', 72.

77 John Evelyn, diary entry, June 1658, in E. S. de Beer, ed., *The Diary of John Evelyn*, 6 vols (Oxford, 1955), vol. 3, 216.

78 Building Accounts 1655–57, ACA, Syon MS, U.III.3; these accounts provide the evidence for all works described hereafter unless otherwise stated; for detailed description see Guerci, 'From Northampton to Northumberland', 237–46.

79 PH 5896 (1657). The 'gentlewomens dining roome' is confirmed by the inventory of 1670, ACA, 107, GC 26, BL Microfilm 351, in Wood, 'Van Dyck and the Earl of Northumberland', app. II, 304–8.

80 Bold, *John Webb*, 162–4.

81 Ibid., 32–3.

82 Ibid., 57–68.

83 See Fiona Allardyce, 'The Patronage of the 9th and 10th Earls of Northumberland', MA diss., Courtauld Institute of Art, University of London, 1987.

84 Accounts of Orlando Gee, PH 5893 (1657).

85 Ibid.

86 Ibid., PH 5903 (1658); see Wood, 'Architectural Patronage', 73.

87 Accounts of Orlando Gee, pedestal painted by John Peirce, PH 5915 (1659).

88 See Wood, 'Van Dyck and the Earl of Northumberland'.

89 Richard Symonds, notes on Northumberland collection, 1652, BL, Egerton MS 1636, transcr. in Wood, 'Van Dyck and the Earl of Northumberland', app. I, 303. For a transcription of the whole MS see Mary Beal, *A Study of Richard Symonds: His Italian Notebooks and their Relevance to Seventeenth-Century Painting Techniques* (New York and London, 1984), 214–313. I am grateful to Jeremy Wood for pointing this out to me.

90 De Beer, *Diary of John Evelyn*, vol. 3, 216.

91 Simon Stone, appraisal in 1671, ACA, 107, GC 26, in Wood, 'Van Dyck and the Earl of Northumberland', app. II, 304–8.

92 For full discussion of the paintings see Wood, 'Van Dyck and the Earl of Northumberland', 281–302.

93 The tapestries in the wardrobe appear in the 1670 inventory as 'in the Wardrobe at Petworth'; ACA, 107, GC 26, in Wood, 'Van Dyck and the Earl of Northumberland', 304–8. For the sale see Accounts of Peter Dodesworth for foreign payments, 1632/3–1633/4, 1648/9–1649/50, ACA, Syon MS, U.I.5, BL Microfilm 390; ACA, 72, MS 107, GC 26.

94 Document mentioning the sale of the Esther tapestries, ACA, Syon MS, H.II.1b; see Gordon R. Batho, ed., *The Household Papers of Henry Percy, Ninth Earl of Northumberland, 1564–1632*, Camden 3rd series, vol. 93 (London, 1962), 113, 116.

95 See 1670 inventory, ACA, 107, GC 26, in Wood, 'Van Dyck and the Earl of Northumberland', 304–8. The arrears of fines and rents of the estate, amounting to £10,742 1s 11d and included in the section on Northumberland House, have been deducted from the total value given here.

96 Mazarene plates were silver serving dishes fashionable at the time, thought to have been named after the celebrated niece of Cardinal Mazarin, Hortense Mancini, who as Duchesse de Mazarin settled in London and died at Chelsea in 1699; see John Nott, *The cooks and confectioners dictionary: or, The accomplish'd housewives companion* (1726). The duchess, however, came to England in the mid-1670s, so the dishes are more likely to have been named after the cardinal himself. On Mancini see Guerci, *Palazzo Mancini* (Rome, 2011), 191–2; on Mazarin's collection see Patrick Michel, *Mazarin, prince des collectionneurs* (Paris, 1999).

97 Accounts of Gee, foreign payments, PH 5931 (1660).

98 Payment for 'Railing the streete', PH 5943 (1661).

99 E. H. Clarendon, *The History of Rebellion and Civil Wars in England* (1702–4; 1826), quoted by Drake, 'Algernon Percy'.

100 See de Fontblanque, *Annals of the House of Percy*, vol. 2, 447–90.

101 Ibid., 491–512; R. O. Bucholz, 'Seymour, Charles (1662–1748)', ODNB (Oxford, 2004).

102 See de Fontblanque, *Annals of the House of Percy*, vol. 2, 513–46.

103 In 1738 Sir Thomas Bootle and the architect Robert Morris advised the duke on the conditions of the turrets, believed to be unsafe. In 1742–3 Somerset obtained powers by Act of Parliament to purchase an adjoining house to make way for repairs to Northumberland House; see Gater and Godfrey, *Survey of London*, 13–15.

104 See Guerci and Aymonino, 'Architectural Transformation'.

105 For the extensive literature on this period see Guerci, 'From Northampton to Northumberland', 246, n. 187.

106 See Guerci, 'Charles Barry's Designs', 136–50.

107 Beresford Chancellor, *Private Palaces*, 57.

108 *Northumberland House: A Catalogue of the First Portion of the Valuable Building Materials, Fixtures & Fittings…* (London, 1874).

109 For plans and images related to the demolition see HE (former National Monuments Record), AQ/06/014; for a record of what was salvaged see Guerci and Aymonino, 'Architectural Transformation', 353–5.

CONCLUSION

1 I am grateful to Mark Girouard, Maurice Howard and Gordon Higgott for their suggestions and comments on this chapter.
2 Matthew Dimmock, *Elizabethan Globalism: England, China and the Rainbow Portrait* (New Haven and London, 2019).
3 Of Edmund Dudley's galleries, 'The Long Galerre agayn[st] the gardynne' and the 'Galarre next the Great Chambre' were on the first or upper floor, while the 'Lowe Galare by the Gardeyn' and the 'Great Galare at thende of that' were probably on the ground floor; see Charles L. Kingsford, 'On some London Houses of the Early Tudor Period', *Archaeologia*, 71 (1921), 17–54, esp. 18–19, 39–42.
4 On the development of galleries see Rosalind Coope, 'The Gallery in England: Names and Meanings', in *Design and Practice in British Architecture: Studies in Architectural History presented to Howard Colvin*, *Architectural History*, 27 (1984), 446–55; Coope, 'The "Long Gallery": Its Origins, Development, Use and Decoration', *Architectural History*, 29 (1986), 43–84; Mark Girouard, *Elizabethan Architecture: Its Rise and Fall, 1540–1640* (New Haven and London, 2009), 69–71.
5 Fowler's house was recorded by John Thorpe and occupied 'the breadth of three ordinary tenements'; see John Summerson, *The Book of Architecture of John Thorpe*, Walpole Society 40 (Glasgow, 1966), pl. 61.
6 See Basil Stallybrass, 'Bess of Hardwick's Buildings and Building Accounts', *Archaeologia*, 64 (1913), 365–6.
7 I owe the information about Bess of Hardwick's visit to Essex House to Mark Girouard; see David N. Durant, *Bess of Hardwick: Portrait of an Elizabethan Dynast* (1977; London, 2008), 94.
8 See Elizabeth Goldring, *Robert Dudley, Earl of Leicester, and the World of Elizabethan Art* (New Haven and London, 2014), 174.
9 See Christina M. Anderson, *The Merchant of Venice: Daniel Nijs and the Sale of the Gonzaga Art Collection* (New Haven and London, 2015).
10 See Manolo Guerci with Adrian Aymonino, 'The Architectural Transformation of Northumberland House under the 7th Duke of Somerset and the 1st Duke and Duchess of Northumberland, 1748–86', *The Antiquaries Journal*, 96 (2016), 315–61.
11 John Bold, *John Webb: Architectural Theory and Practice in the Seventeenth Century* (Oxford, 1989), 74.
12 A. Collins, *Life of William Cecil … Lord Burghley* (London, 1732), 93.
13 Any judgement of Bedford House has to acknowledge the fact that direct access to primary sources was not possible.
14 See Manolo Guerci, 'John Osborne, the Salisbury House "Porticus" and the "Haynes Grange Room"', *The Burlington Magazine*, 148 (January 2006), 15–24.
15 See Manolo Guerci, 'The Construction of Northumberland House and the Patronage of its Original Builder, Lord Henry Howard: 1603–14', *The Antiquaries Journal*, 90 (2010), 392–3.
16 The role of land was discussed by Joseph Friedman at the Georgian Town House symposium at the Paul Mellon Centre, London, 2018. Friedman has explored the relationship between town and country in the Georgian Period in 'Town and Country: The Spencers of Althorp', in Susanna Avery-Quash and Kate Retford, eds, *The Georgian London Town House: Building, Collecting and Display* (New York and London, 2019), 99–118.
17 Summerson, *Book of Architecture of John Thorpe*, 26–7, 46, pl. 6.
18 See Manolo Guerci, *Palazzo Mancini* (Rome, 2011), 21–48.
19 See Dorothy Metzger Habel, *The Urban Development of Rome in the Age of Alexander VII* (Cambridge, 2002).
20 James Howell, *Londinopolis: An Historicall Discourse; or, Perlustration of the City of London, the Imperial Chamber, and Chief Emporium of Great Britain whereunto is added another of the City of Westminster, with the Courts of Justice, Antiquities, and New Buildings thereunto belonging* (London, 1657), 386.
21 Ambassador Sully, 1603, quoted in Charles L. Kingsford, 'Bath Inn or Arundel House', *Archaeologia*, 72 (1922), 252.
22 M. F. S. Hervey, *The Life, Correspondence and Collections of Thomas Howard, Earl of Arundel* (Cambridge, 1921), 255–6.
23 E. V. Chew, 'The Countess of Arundel and Tart Hall', in Edward Chaney (ed.), *The Evolution of English Collecting: Receptions of Italian Art in the Tudor and Stuart Periods* (New Haven and London, 2003), 290–91.
24 Hervey (1921), 264.
25 See Ch. 3, n. 34 above. The Venetian merchant Alessandro Magno also provides a fascinating description of London *c*.1560: 'Account of his Journeys to Cyprus, Egypt, Spain, England, Flanders and Germany, and of Brescia, 1557–1565', Folger Shakespeare Library, Washington DC, MS V.A. 259, published as Alessandro Magno, *Voyages (1557–1565)*, trans. and ed. W. Naar (Fasano and Paris, 2002), 692–706. I am grateful to one of the anonymous reviewers for pointing this out to me.
26 See Ch. 3, nn. 25 and 32 above.
27 See Ch. 4, n. 33 above.
28 See Ch. 6, n. 82 above.
29 See Dimmock, *Elizabethan Globalism*, 144.
30 See Ch. 9, n. 25 above.
31 See Ch. 10, n. 49 above.
32 See ibid., n. 57 above.
33 See ibid., n. 89 above.
34 See ibid., n. 105 above.
35 See Ch. 11, nn. 46 and 47 above.

Bibliography

Primary Sources

Alnwick Castle, Northumberland
72, MS 107, GC 26
107, GC 26
Deeds, D.XVII.11
Deeds, D.XVII.11a
Deeds, D.XVII.11b
Deeds, D.XVII.11c
Deeds, D.XVII.11e
Syon MS H.II.Ib
Syon MS U.I.5
Syon MS U.I.5/63
Syon MS U.I.6
Syon MS U.I.6/1, 3, 20, 27, 33, 35, 36, 44, 49, 52, 54
Syon MS U.III.2
Syon MS U.III.3
Sy: Y.III.2/1/3/1/1
Sy: Y.III.2/1/3/3/5–6
Sy: Y.III.2/5/1–13
Sy: Y.III.2/5/2

Arundel Castle, West Sussex
Autographed letters, 194, 205, 207, 212, 236, 238, 240
IN. 52
MXD1
MXD2
MXD6
MXD7

Badminton House Archives, Gloucestershire
D2700/NJ/1
D2700/OA/9
D2700/OC/2
D2700/OD/1
D2700/OF2/1
D2700/P4/3
D2700/QA2/3/2
D2700/QA5/1/19

Bodleian Library, Oxford
Rawlison MS A341
Tanner MS 73, fols 491v, 510v

British Library, London
Add. MS 12528
Add. MS 18914
Egerton MS 1636
Harleian MS 570, fol. 39r
Harley Roll, D. 35, fols 1r–24r
Lansdowne MSS, xxxiii, fols 70–71
Microfilm 351
Microfilm 390
Microfilm 391

Burghley House, Lincolnshire
Exeter MSS 5/17
Exeter MSS 5/18
Exeter MSS 80/29
Exeter MSS MC 1/2 (formerly 13/1)
Exeter MSS MC 2/3 (formerly 49/7)
Exeter MSS 5/21
Exeter MSS 5/25–8
Exeter MSS 5/32
Exeter MSS 5/33
Exeter MSS 5/35
Exeter MSS 5/37

Centre for Kentish Studies, Maidstone
De L'Isle MS U1475

Gloucestershire County Council Archives, Gloucester
https://www.gloucestershire.gov.uk/archives

Hatfield House, Hertfordshire
'A Cattalogge of all your Lordships printed Bookes as they are nowe disposed in your Lordships Librarie [at Salisbury House] taken this 26th of Januarie 1614 [1615]'
Box C/8
Box C/40
CP 87/112
CP 183/7
CP 183/24
CP A/c 27
CP Box G 16
Deeds 131/4
Deeds 125/3, 1670
Deeds 125/5, 1670
EP Box C/4
EP Box C/5–6
EP Box C/6
EP Box C/8
EP Box C/9
EPM, Herts, 1/145 (Legal 2, 1670)
   London 2/113, 118 (Deeds 125/4, 1670)
   London 2/144 (Act 57/5, 1672/3)
   London 2/121 (Legal 110/2, 1670)
   Middlesex, London 1 to 1650: London 1/52, 66, 78
FP 1/171–76 (Bills 59, 4 July 1611)
FP 2/172
FP 2/173–4
FP 2/207
FP 2/264
FP 2/268

FP 3/27
FP 3/36, 36a (Estate Papers, Accounts 28/16)
FP 3/246 (Bills 22–34)
FP 3/263 (Accounts 160/1, 1609)
FP 3/287 (Accounts 160/1, 1609)
FP 4/67 (Accounts 160/1, 1611)
FP 4/135–36 (Box G 13, 1612)
FP 4/241 (Box G 13, 1612)
FP 6/98 (Strafford Letters, vol. 1, 207, 227)
FP 6/148–53
FP 6/157 (Box 1, 4, 1637)
FP 6/157 (Box 1, 4, 1638)
FP 6/187
FP 7/119 (Box L, 2, 1647)
FP 7/227–8 (Box M, 2, 1652)
FP 8/201 (Rutland Letters 57)
FP 8/204 (Rutland Letters 59)
FP 8/208 (Rutland Letters 63)
FP 8/209 (Rutland Letters 64)
FP 8/211 (Rutland Letters 66)
FP 9/169
FP 10/113a
FP Bills 8, 9
FPS 1/354 (Estate Papers, Bills 181, 1636)
FPS 2/23 (Bills 193, 1639)
FPS 2/36 (Bills 196, 1640)
FPS 2/68–71 (Bills 211, 1645)
FPS 2/90 (Bills 242, 1649)
FPS 2/229, Bills 298, 298a
FP2S 1/37–38 (General 17/20, 1606)
FP2S 1/56–59 (Bills 16, 1607)
FP2S 1/85–89 (Bills 28, 1608)
FP2S 1/135–37 (Bills 51, 1610)
FP2S 1/171–76, Bills 59, 1611
FP2S 1/223–27 (Bills 70, 1612)
FP2S 1/265–66 (Bills 77, 1613)
FP2S 2/29, 221 (Bills 255, 1652)
FP2S 2/148 (Accounts 148/11, 1640)
FP2S 214 (Accounts 148/15, 1650)
General 1, Bills 2/8
General 1, Bills 2/10
General 1, Bills 3
General 57/19
Gunton, Richard T., 'Properties: London, Quixwood, Theobalds 1509–1891', MSS Catalogue, 1900

HISTORIC ENGLAND ARCHIVE, SWINDON
AQ/06/014

HUNTINGTON LIBRARY, SAN MARINO, CALIFORNIA
Ellesmere Papers, MS 1179

LAMBETH PALACE LIBRARY, LONDON
Anthony Bacon MSS 647–662

LONDON METROPOLITAN ARCHIVES
BE-AD2-GST 121
E/BER/CG/E5/1/21/1
E/BER/CG/E7/12/1
E/BER/CG/E8/1/1
E/BER/CG/E/11/3
E/BER/CG/T/11/E/6
E/BER/CG/T/11/E/08
MS 231

LONGLEAT HOUSE, WILTSHIRE
Dudley Papers II/47
Dudley Papers Xb, fols ir– iiv
Dudley Papers IV, fols 52r–61r
Dudley Papers vx

MAGDALENE COLLEGE, CAMBRIDGE
Pepys Library
Samuel Pepys, 'London and Westminster', album

THE NATIONAL ARCHIVES, KEW
C 54/17/13
C 54/818/32
Customs Accounts, E190.312
E 159/398
E 177/1446
E 178/1350
PC/2/63
SP 12/20/43
SP 14/62, no. 33
SP 14/65, no. 61
SP 19, vol. 91, no. 1
SP Domestic, 23, vol. G 133, 341

PETWORTH HOUSE ARCHIVES (WEST SUSSEX RECORD OFFICE), CHICHESTER
MS 1630
5848
5865
5893
5896
5903
5915
5931
5943

ROYAL INSTITUTE OF BRITISH ARCHITECTS, LONDON
Drawing Collection, SC206/Jol&WeJ[170]

SIR JOHN SOANE'S MUSEUM, LONDON
Drawers 24/3/2, 22/7/5, 22/7/6
Fauntleroy Pennant, vol. III, f. 64

ANTONY TAUSSIG'S PRIVATE ARCHIVES, LONDON
MS.2003.7.22

WILTSHIRE AND SWINDON HISTORY CENTRE
546/225

WOBURN ABBEY, BEDFORDSHIRE
BE-AD2-GST 121 (i)
BE-AD2-GST 121 (ii)
BI-P73
HMC11-V1 (1627–41)
MS 5E-I-1
3E-1–3
3E-6
4E-18
4E-20
4E-27
5E-25

WORCESTER COLLEGE, OXFORD
John Webb's plans, fols 81–5, 87, 88

EARLY PRINTED BOOKS AND MAPS

Bassompierre, François de, *Memoirs of the Embassy of the Marshal de Bassompierre to the Court of England in 1626*. London: John Murray, 1819

Braun, Georg, and Frans Hogenberg, *Civitates Orbis Terrarum*. 6 parts. Cologne, 1572–1617

Cerceau, Jacques A. du, *Les Plus Excellents Bastiments de France* (1576, 1607). Facsimile edn. 1972

Collins, A., *Life of William Cecil ... Lord Burghley*. London, 1732

'Copy of an Original Manuscript entitled "A Breviate touching the Order and Governmente of a Nobleman's House, &c."', *Archaeologia*, 13. London: T. Bensley, 1800, 315–83

Dodsley, Robert and James, *London and its Environs Described*, 5 vols, London: printed for Robert and James Dodsley, 1761

Dietterlin, Wendel, *The Fantastic Engravings of Wendel Dietterlin: A Facsimile of the 1598 Edition of his Architectura*. New York: Dover Publications, 1968

Fairfax, Brian, *A catalogue of the curious collection of pictures of George Villiers, Duke of Buckingham*. London: printed for W. Bathoe, 1758

Gerbier, Balthasar, *A Brief Discourse Concerning the Three Chief Principles of Magnificent Building: viz. Solidity, Conveniency, and Ornament*. London, 1662

———, *Counsel and Advise to All Builders*. London, 1663

Harrison, Walter, *A New and Universal History, Description and Survey of the Cities of London and*

Westminster, the Borough of Southwark … London: J. Cooke, 1776

Harrison, William, *Description of England*. London, 1577

Holinshed, Raphael, and William Harrison, *The first and second volumes of Chronicles, comprising 1 The description and historie of England, 2 The description and historie of Ireland, 3 The description and historie of Scotland: first collected and published by Raphaell Holinshed, William Harrison, and others: now newlie augmented and continued (with manifold matters of singular note and worthie memorie) to the yeare 1586.* London: Henry Denham, 1587

Horwood, Richard, *Map and face of London* (1799–1819), facsimile edn. *The A to Z of Regency London*, intro. Paul Laxton. Lympne Castle, Kent: Harry Margary with the Guildhall Library, 1985

Howell, James, *Londinopolis: An Historicall Discourse; or, Perlustration of the City of London, the Imperial Chamber, and Chief Emporium of Great Britain whereunto is added another of the City of Westminster, with the Courts of Justice, Antiquities, and New Buildings thereunto belonging.* London: printed by J. Streater for Henry Twiford, 1657

Knowler, W., *The Earl of Strafforde's Letters and Dispatches*, 2 vols. Dublin: Robert Owen, 1740

Knyff, Leonard, and Jan Kip, *Britannia Illustrata or Views of Several of the Queen's Palaces also of the Principal Seats of the Nobility and Gentry of Great Britain.* London, 1707

Magno, Alessandro, *Voyages (1577–1565)*, trans. and ed. W. Naar. Fasano: Schena, and Paris: Sorbonne, 2002

Maitland, W., *The History and Survey of London from its Foundations to the Present Time*, 2 vols. London, 1756

Manningham, John, *Diary of John Manningham of the Middle Temple and of Bradbourne, Kent, barrister-at-law, 1602–1603*, ed. John Bruce, Camden Society 99. London, 1868

Norden, John, *Speculum Britanniae*. London, 1593; 1600

Nott, John, *The cooks and confectioners dictionary: or, The accomplish'd housewives companion …* 1726

Ogilby, John, and William Morgan, *Map of London*. London, 1677

Peacham, Henry, *The Compleat Gentleman*. London, 1612

Peck, F., *Desiderata Curiosa*, ed. T. Evans, 2 vols. London, 1732–5

Pennant, Thomas, *Some Account of London*, 2nd edn. London: Robert Faulder, 1791

Perry, William, *Bibliotheca Norfolciana*. London: Royal Society, 1681

Rocque, John, *Plan of the Cities of London and Westminster* (1746), facsimile edn. *The A to Z of Georgian London*, intro. Ralph Hyde. London: Harry Margary and the Guildhall Library, 1981

Scamozzi, Vincenzo, *L'Idea dell'Architettura Universale*, 2 vols (Venice, 1615), facsimile edn. Centro Internazionale di Studi Andrea Palladio, Vincenza. Vicenza: Tipolitografia Pavan, 1997

Serlio, Sebastiano, *Regole Generali di Architettura* … Venice: F. Marcolini, 1537

Stow, John, *The Survay of London: Containing, The Originall, Antiquitie, Encrease, and more Moderne Estate of the said Famous Citie.* London: John Wolfe, 1598

——, *The Survay of London: Contayning the Originall, Antiquity, Increase, Moderne estate and description of that Citie, written in the year 1598.* London: John Wolfe, 1599

——, *The Survay of London: Containing, The Originall, Antiquitie, Encrease, and more Moderne Estate of the said Famous Citie.* London, 1603

——, *The Survay of London*. London, 1618

——, *A Survey of London*, ed. Charles L. Kingsford, 2 vols. Oxford: Clarendon Press, 1908

Strype, John, *A Survey of the Cities of London and Westminster: Containing the Origin, Antiquity, Increase, Modern Estate and Government of those Cities written at first in the year* MDXCVIII *by John Stowe, Citizen and Native of London..*, 2 vols. London: A. Churchill et al., 1720

Thorn-Drury, G., ed., *Parnassus Biceps or Several Choice Pieces of Poetry (1656)*. London, 1927

The Woodcut Map of London ('Agas'). 1561–70

Wyngaerde, Anthonis van den, *Panorama of London from the River*. c.1544

Published Calendars

Calendar of State Papers, *British History Online*, http://www.british-history.ac.uk/cal-state-papers

Foreign: Elizabeth, Volume 4, 1561–62, ed. Joseph Stevenson. London, 1866

Foreign: Elizabeth, Volume 6, 1563, ed. Joseph Stevenson. London, 1869

Domestic: James I, 1603–10, ed. Mary Anne Everett Green. London, 1857

Domestic: James I, 1611–18, ed. Mary Anne Everett Green. London, 1858

Domestic: James I, 1619–23, ed. Mary Anne Everett Green. London, 1858

Domestic: James I, 1623–1625. London: Longman, Brown, Green, Longmans, & Roberts, 1859

Domestic: Charles I, 1625–6, ed. John Bruce. London, 1858

Domestic: Charles I, 1629–1631. London: Longman, Brown, Green, Longmans, & Roberts, 1859

Domestic: Charles I, 1631–3, ed. John Bruce. London, 1862

Domestic: 1650. London, 1876

Domestic: 1656–7. London, 1883

Domestic: Charles II, 1676–7, ed. F. H. Blackburne Daniell. London, 1909

Scotland, vol. 1 (1509–89). London: Longman, Brown, Green, Longmans, & Roberts, 1858

Venice, Volume 10, 1603–1607, ed. Horatio F. Brown. London, 1900

HMC, *Calendar of the Manuscript of the Marquis of Bath Preserved at Longleat, Wiltshire*, vol. 2. Dublin, 1907

——, *Calendar of the Manuscripts of the Most Honourable The Marquess of Bath Preserved at Longleat, Wiltshire*, vol. 5: *Talbot, Dudley and Devereux Papers 1533–1659*, ed. G. Dyfnallt Owen. London, 1980

HMC, *Calendar of the Manuscripts of the Most Hon. the Marquess of Salisbury*, pt XIII (addenda). London, 1915

HMC, Egremont I

HMC, *Salisbury MS*, part IX, 1902

——, *Salisbury MS*, part XI, 1906

——, *Salisbury MS*, part XII, 1910

——, *Salisbury MS*, part XV, 1930

——, *Salisbury MS*, part XVII, 1938

Secondary Sources

Adams, Simon, 'Dudley, Robert, earl of Leicester (1532/3–1588)', ODNB. Oxford University Press, 2004, online edn., May 2008, http://www.oxforddnb.com/view/article/8160

——, 'Robert Dudley, Earl of Leicester, his Gardeners and Gardens'. Paper delivered at conference on Leicester and his gardeners, 2006

——, 'The Papers of Robert Dudley, Earl of Leicester I: The Browne-Evelyn Collection', *Archives*, 20, no. 87 (April 1992), 63–85

——, 'The Papers of Robert Dudley, Earl of Leicester II: The Atye-Cotton Collection', *Archives*, 20, no. 90 (October 1993), 131–44

——, 'The Papers of Robert Dudley, Earl of Leicester III: The Countess of Leicester's Collection', *Archives*, 2 (April 1996), 1–26

——, ed., *Household Accounts and Disbursement Books of Robert Dudley, Earl of Leicester, 1558–1561, 1584–1586*, Camden Society, 5th series, vol. 6, Cambridge: Cambridge University Press, 1995

Adamson, John, *Princely Courts of Europe*. London: Lawrence King, 2000

——, 'Architecture and the English Court: The Town Houses of the English Nobility in London and Westminster, 1590–1660'. Paper delivered at the Huntington Library, San Marino, California, 2000

——, 'Rough Notes for a Study of the Building History of Salisbury House, London, under the First and Second Earls of Salisbury' (for the years 1607–11). Private archive

Airs, Malcolm, *The Making of the English Country House 1500–1640*. London, 1975

Airy, Osmund, ed., *Essex Papers*, vol. 1: 1672–1679, *Camden Society*, n.s., vol. 47 (1890)

Allardyce, Fiona, 'The Patronage of the 9th and 10th Earls of Northumberland'. MA diss., Courtauld Institute of Art, University of London, 1987

Allen, E. J. B., *Post and Courier Service in the Diplomacy of Early Modern Europe*. The Hague: Martinus Nijhoff, 1972

Allen, Thomas, *History and Antiquities of London, Westminster, Southwark, and parts adjacent*, 4 vols. London: Jacques and Wright, 1827–8

Alford, Stephen, *Burghley: William Cecil at the Court of Elizabeth I*. New Haven and London: Yale University Press, 2011

Anderson, Christina M., *The Flemish Merchant of Venice: Daniel Nijs and the Sale of the Gonzaga Art Collection*. New Haven and London: Yale University Press, 2015

Anderson, Christy, *Inigo Jones and the Classical Tradition*. Cambridge: Cambridge University Press, 2007

Andersson, Daniel C., 'Studies in the Early Elizabethan Life and Works of Lord Henry Howard, later Earl of Northampton (1540–1614)'. PhD diss., Warburg Institute, University of London, 2006

Angelicoussis, Elizabeth, 'The Collection of Classical Sculptures of the Earl of Arundel', *Journal of the History of Collections*, 16, no. 2 (2004), 143–59

Archaeologia Cambrensis: A Record of the Antiquities of Wales and its Marshes, and the Journal of the Cambrian Archaeological Association, vol. 2. London: Pickering, 1847

Aubrey, John, *Brief lives: chiefly of contemporaries, set down by John Aubrey between the years 1669 and 1696*, ed. Andrew Clark, 2 vols. Oxford: Clarendon Press, 1898

Auerbach, Erna, and C. Kingley Adams, *Paintings and Sculpture at Hatfield House*. London, 1971

Aymonino, Adriano, and Manolo Guerci, 'The Architectural Transformation of Northumberland House under the 7th Duke of Somerset and the 1st Duke and Duchess of Northumberland, 1748–86', *The Antiquaries Journal*, 96 (2016), 315–61

——and ——, 'The Refurbishment of Northumberland House: Craftsmen and Interior Decoration in Mid-Eighteenth-Century London Town Houses', in Susanna Avery-Quash and Kate Retford, eds, *The Georgian London Town House: Building, Collecting and Display*. New York and London: Bloomsbury, 2019, 71–98

Bach, Susannah A., 'Courtier Classicism in the Reign of Edward VI: Protector Somerset and his Architectural Image'. BA diss., University of Cambridge, 1995

Baggs, Anthony P., 'Two Designs by Simon Basil', *Architectural History*, 27 (1984), 104–10

Baker, J. H., 'Egerton, Thomas, first Viscount Brackley (1540–1617)', ODNB. Oxford University Press, 2004, online edn., May 2015, http://www.oxforddnb.com/view/article/8594

Barber, Bruno, and Christopher Thomas, *The London Charterhouse*. London, MOLAS, 2002

Barker, Nicholas, 'The Books of Henry Howard', *Bodleian Library Record*, 13 (October 1990), 375–81

Barnett, Richard, *Place, Profit, and Power: A Study of the Servants of William Cecil, Elizabethan Statesman*, James Sprunt Studies in History and Political Science 51. Chapel Hill: University of North Carolina Press, 1969

Batho, Gordon R., ed., *The Household Papers of Henry Percy, Ninth Earl of Northumberland, 1564–1632*, Camden 3rd series, vol. 93. London: Royal Historical Society, 1962

Beal, Mary, *A Study of Richard Symonds: His Italian Notebooks and their Relevance to Seventeenth-Century Painting Techniques*. New York and London: Garland Publishing, 1984

Bebbington, Gillian, *London Street Names*. London: Batsford, 1972

Beer, Anna, *Bess: The Life of Lady Ralegh, Wife to Sir Walter*. London: Constable, 2004

Beer, B. L., 'Seymour, Edward, duke of Somerset (c.1500–1552)', ODNB. Oxford University Press, 2004, online edn., January 2009, http://www.oxforddnb.com/view/article/25159

Beer, E. S. de, ed., *The Diary of John Evelyn*, 6 vols. Oxford: Clarendon Press, 1955

Benham, William, and Charles Welch, *Medieval London*. London: Seeley, 1901

Beresford Chancellor, Edwin, *The Private Palaces of London: Past and Present*. London: Kegan Paul, Trench, Turner & Co., 1908

——, *Annals of the Strand, Topographical and Historical*. London: Chapman & Hall, 1912

Betcherman, L. R., 'The York House Collection and its Keeper', *Apollo*, 92 (October 1970), 250–59

Blanchard, I., 'Clough, Richard (d. 1570)', ODNB. Oxford University Press, 2004, online edn., January 2008, http://www.oxforddnb.com/view/article/5712

Bold, John, *John Webb: Architectural Theory and Practice in the Seventeenth Century*. Oxford: Clarendon Press, 1989

Bolland, Charlotte, *Tudor and Jacobean Portraits*. London: National Portrait Gallery Publications, 2019

——, '"Sat Super Est": A Portrait of Henry Howard, Earl of Surrey', in Tarnya Cooper et al., eds, *Painting in Britain 1500–1630: Production, Influences and Patronage*. Oxford: Oxford University Press, 2015, 352–61

Bossy, John, *Under the Molehill: An Elizabethan Spy Story*. New Haven and London: Yale University Press, 2001

Bowden, C. M. K., 'Cecil [Cooke], Mildred, Lady Burghley (1526–1589)', ODNB. Oxford University Press, 2004, online edn., May 2014, http://www.oxforddnb.com/view/article/46675

Bracken, Susan, 'Robert Cecil as Art Collector', in Croft, *Patronage, Culture and Power*, 121–37

——, 'The Early Cecils and Italianate Taste', in Edward Chaney, ed., *The Evolution of English Collecting: Reception of Italian Art in Tudor and Stuart Periods*. New Haven and London: Yale University Press, 2003, 201–19

——, 'Holbein's "Chatsworth Cartoon": Its Possible Location in the 17th Century', *The British Art Journal*, 1 (Autumn 1999), 14–15

Brenan, Gerald, *A History of the House of Percy, from the earliest times down to the present century by Gerald Brenan*, ed. William A. Lindsay, 2 vols. London: Fremantle, 1902

Brennan, Michael, *Literary Patronage in the English Renaissance: The Pembroke Family*. London and New York: Routledge, 1988

Brewer, John Sherren, ed., *Letters and Papers, Foreign and Domestic, of the reign of Henry VIII, preserved in the Public Record Office, the British Museum, and elsewhere in England*, 21 vols. London: Longman, Green, Longman, & Roberts, 1862–1910

Brown, Jonathan, 'Artistic Relations between Spain and England 1604–1655', in Jonathan Brown and John Elliott, eds, *The Sale of the Century: Artistic Relations between Spain and Great Britain, 1604–1655*. New Haven and London: Yale University Press, 2002, 41–68

Brushfield, Thomas Nadauld, *Raleghana … Reprinted from the Transactions of the Devonshire Association for the Advancement of Science, Literature, and Art*, 8 pts (London, 1896–1906), pt 5: *The History of Durham House*, 1–44

Buck, M. C. 'Stapeldon, Walter (b. in or before 1265, d. 1326)', ODNB. Oxford University Press, 2004, http://www.oxforddnb.com/view/article/26296

Bucholz, R. O., 'Seymour, Charles (1662–1748)', ODNB. Oxford: Oxford University Press, 2004

Burke, Marcus, 'Louis de Haro as Minister, Patron and Collector of Art', in Jonathan Brown and John Elliott, eds, *The Sale of the Century: Artistic Relations between Spain and Great Britain, 1604–1655*. New Haven and London: Yale University Press, 2002, 87–105

Butler, Martin, *The Stuart Court Masque and Political Culture*. Cambridge: Cambridge University Press, 2008

Catalogue of Manuscripts in the British Museum: The Arundel Manuscripts, new series, 3 vols. London: British Museum, 1834

Cecil, David, *The Cecils of Hatfield House*. London: Constable, 1973

Chaney, Edward, 'The Italianate Evolution of English Collecting', in Chaney, *Evolution of English Collecting*, 1–124

——, ed., *The Evolution of English Collecting: The Reception of Italian Art in the Tudor and Stuart Periods*. New Haven and London: Yale University Press, 2003

Chew, E. V., 'The Countess of Arundel and Tart Hall', in Chaney, *Evolution of English Collecting*, 285–314

Clapham, Alfred, and Walter H. Godfrey, *Some Famous Buildings and their Story; being the research of recent research in London and elsewhere*. London: Technical Journals, 1913

Clarendon, E. H., *The History of Rebellion and Civil Wars in England*. 1702–4; 1826

Clark, Jane E. L., 'The Buildings and Art Collections of Robert Dudley, Earl of Leicester (with Notes on Portraits)'. MA Report, Courtauld Institute of Art, University of London, 1981

——, 'A Set of Tapestries for Leicester House in the Strand: 1585', *The Burlington Magazine*, 125 (May 1983), 283–4

Cole, Emily, 'Theobalds, Hertfordshire: The Plan and Interiors of an Elizabethan Country House', *Architectural History*, 60 (2017), 71–116

Colvin, Howard, *A Biographical Dictionary of British Architects 1600–1840*. New Haven and London: Yale University Press, 2008

——, 'The South Front of Wilton House', *Essays in English Architectural History*. New Haven and London: Yale University Press, 1999, 136–57

——, ed., *The History of the King's Works*, 6 vols, London: HMSO, 1963–82

——, and Susan Foister, eds, *The Panorama of London circa 1544 by Anthonis van den Wyngaerde*. London: London Topographical Society, 1996

Coope, Rosalind, 'The Gallery in England: Names and Meanings', *Design and Practice in British Architecture: Studies in Architectural History presented to Howard Colvin, Architectural History*, 27 (1984), 446–55

——, 'The "Long Gallery": Its Origins, Development, Use and Decoration', *Architectural History*, 29 (1986), 43–84

Cooper, Nicholas, *Houses of the Gentry, 1480–1680*. New Haven and London: Yale University Press, 1999

——, *The Jacobean Country House: From the Archives of Country Life*. London: Aurum Press, 2006

Cornforth, John, 'The Earliest View of Covent Garden', *Country Life*, 149, no. 3857 (13 May 1971), 1182

Cowen Orlin, Lena, ed., *Material London, ca 1600*. Philadelphia: University of Pennsylvania Press, 2000

Croft, Pauline, *Patronage, Culture and Power: The Early Cecils, 1558–1612*. New Haven and London: Yale University Press, 2002

——, 'Mildred, Lady Burghley: The Matriarch', in Croft, *Patronage, Culture and Power*, 283–300

——, 'Robert Cecil and the Early Jacobean Court', in Linda Levy Peck, ed., *The Mental World of the Jacobean Court* (1999). Cambridge: Cambridge University Press, 2005, 134–47

——, 'Cecil, Robert, first earl of Salisbury (1563–1612)', ODNB. Oxford University Press, 2004, online edn., October 2008, http://www.oxforddnb.com/view/article/4980

——, 'Henry Howard', ODNB. Oxford: Oxford University Press, 2004, vol. 28, 366–74

——, 'Thomas Howard', ODNB. Oxford: University Press, 2004, vol. 28, 436–9

——, 'The Religion of Robert Cecil', *Historical Journal*, 34 (1991), 773–96

——, 'The Reputation of Robert Cecil: Libels, Political Opinion and Popular Awareness in the Early Seventeenth Century', *Transactions of the Royal Historical Society*, 6th series, 1 (1991), 43–69

Croft-Murray, Edward, *Decorative Painting in England 1537–1837*, 2 vols, London: Country Life, 1962

Croot, Patricia, 'The Strand before Somerset Place', in Simon Thurley, ed., *Somerset House: The Palace of England's Queens 1551–1692*. London: London Topographical Society, 2009, 9–15

——, Alan Thacker and Elizabeth Williamson, eds, *A History of the County of Middlesex*, vol. 13: *City of Westminster, Part 1*. London: Boydell & Brewer, 2009

Davies, Randall, 'An Inventory of the Duke of Buckingham's Pictures, etc. at York House', *The Burlington Magazine*, 10 (1906–7), 376–82

The Diary of Samuel Pepys, intro. G. Gregory Smith. London: Macmillan, 1905

Dils, Joan, 'The Books of the Clergy in Elizabethan and Early Stuart Berkshire', *The Local Historian*, 36, no. 2 (May 2006), 92–105

DiMeo, M., 'Howard, Aletheia, countess of Arundel, of Surrey, and of Norfolk, and suo jure Baroness Furnivall, Baroness Talbot, and Baroness Strange of Blackmere (d. 1654)', ODNB. Oxford University Press, October 2006, online edn., January 2008, http://www.oxforddnb.com/view/article/94252

Dimmock, Matthew, *Elizabethan Globalism: England, China and the Rainbow Portrait*. New Haven and London: Yale University Press, 2019

Dircks, Henry, *The Life, Times and Scientific Labours of the Second Marquis of Worcester*. London: Quaritch, 1865

Drake, G. A., 'Percy, Algernon, tenth earl of Northumberland (1602–1668)', ODNB. Oxford University Press, 2004, online edn., January 2008, http://www.oxforddnb.com/view/article/21923

Duggan, Diane, 'The Architectural Patronage of the 4th Earl of Bedford, 1587–1641'. PhD diss., Courtauld Institute of Art, University of London, 2001

——, 'Isaac de Caus, Nicholas Stone, and the Woburn Abbey Grotto', *Apollo*, 158, no. 498 (August 2003), 50–58

——, 'Isaac de Caus: Surveyor, Grotto and Garden Designer', *Studies in the History of Gardens & Designed Landscapes: An International Quarterly*, 29, no. 3 (2009), 152–68

——, 'The Fourth Side of Covent Garden Piazza: New Light on the History and Significance of Bedford House', *The British Art Journal*, 3, no. 3 (Autumn 2002), 53–67

——, 'Hale Church and St Paul's Church, Covent Garden', *Hampshire Studies: Proceedings of the Hampshire Field Club and Archaeological Society*, 58 (2003), 242–53

——, 'London the Ring, Covent Garden the Jewell of That Ring: New Light on Covent Garden', *Architectural History*, 43 (2000), 140–61

——, 'Pembroke's Arcadia: "Delicious Wilton … that Arbour of the Muses"', *The British Art Journal*, 14, no. 3 (2013/14), 9–20

——, '"A Rather Fascinating Hybrid". Tart Hall: Lady Arundel's "Casino at Whitehall"', *The British Art Journal*, 4, no. 3 (Autumn 2003), 54–64

——, 'Woburn Abbey: The First Episode of a Great Country House', *Architectural History*, 46 (2003), 57–80

Durant, David N., *Bess of Hardwick: Portrait of an Elizabethan Dynast* (1977). London: Peter Owen Publishers, 2008

Edelen, Georges, ed., *The Description of England: The Classic Contemporary Account of Tudor Social Life by William Harrison*. Folger Shakespeare Library. Ithaca, NY: Cornell University Press, 1968

Elzinga, J. G., 'Howard, Philip [St Philip Howard], thirteenth earl of Arundel (1557–1595)', ODNB. Oxford University Press, 2004, http://www.oxforddnb.com/view/article/13929

Erskine, A., 'Grandison, John (1292–1369)', ODNB. Oxford University Press, 2004, http://www.oxforddnb.com/view/article/11238

Fontblanque, E. B. de, *Annals of the House of Percy, from the Conquest to the Opening of the Nineteenth Century*, 3 vols. London, 1887

Friedman, Joseph, 'Town and Country: The Spencers of Althorp', in Susanna Avery-Quash and Kate Retford, eds, *The Georgian London Town House: Building, Collecting and Display* (New York and London: Bloomsbury, 2019), 99–118.

Furnivall, F. J., ed., *Robert Laneham's letter: describing a part of the entertainment unto Queen Elizabeth at the castle of Kenilworth in 1575*. London and New York: Chatto and Windus, 1907

Gater, George, and Walter H. Godfrey, eds, *Survey of London*, vol. 18: *The Strand*. London: London County Council, 1937

Gebhart, Brigit, 'George Villiers, First Duke of Buckingham: Clothes, Jewels, Portraits and Courtly Manners of a Royal Favourite'. MA diss., Courtauld Institute of Art, University of London, 1997

Gerhold, Dorian, *London Plotted: Plans of London Buildings c.1450–1720*. London: London Topographical Society, 2016

Gibbs, Philip, *The Romance of George Villiers, First Duke of Buckingham, and Some Men and Women of the Stuart Court*. London: Methuen & Co, 1908

Girouard, Mark, *A Biographical Dictionary of English Architecture 1540–1640*. New Haven and London: Yale University Press, 2021

——, *Elizabethan Architecture: Its Rise and Fall, 1540–1640*. New Haven and London: Yale University Press, 2009

——, *Town and Country*. New Haven and London: Yale University Press, 1992

——, ed., 'The Smythson Collection of the Royal Institute of British Architects', *Architectural History*, vol. 5 (1962), 21–184

Godfrey, Richard T., *Wenceslaus Hollar: A Bohemian Artist in England*. New Haven and London: Yale University Press, 1995

Godfrey, Walter H., 'The Strand in the 17th Century: Its River Front', *Transactions of the London and Middlesex Archaeological Society*, 4, pt 1 (1918), 216–18

Goldring, Elizabeth, *Robert Dudley, Earl of Leicester, and the World of Elizabethan Art*. New Haven and London: Yale University Press, 2014

——, 'A Portrait of Sir Philip Sidney by Veronese at Leicester House, London', *The Burlington Magazine*, 154 (August 2012), 548–54

Goodman, Godfrey, *The Court of King James the First*, 2 vols. London: Richard Bentley, 1839

Goodwin, G., 'Howard, Henry Frederick, fifteenth earl of Arundel, fifth earl of Surrey, and second earl of Norfolk (1608–1652)', rev. J. T. Peacey, ODNB. Oxford University Press, 2004, online edn., October 2006, http://www.oxforddnb.com/view/article/13915

Graves, M. A. R., 'Howard, Thomas, third duke of Norfolk (1473–1554)', ODNB. Oxford University Press, 2004, online edn., January 2008, http://www.oxforddnb.com/view/article/13940

Guerci, Manolo, *Palazzo Mancini*. Rome: Istituto Poligrafico e Zecca dello Stato, 2011

——, 'Charles Barry's Designs for Northumberland House, 1852–55', in Frank Salmon, ed., *The Persistence of the Classical: Essays on Architecture presented to David Watkin*, London: Philip Wilson, 2008, 136–50

——, 'Robert Cecil and his Strand Palace: Construction and Development'. MPhil diss., University of Cambridge, 2004

——, 'The Construction of Northumberland House and the Patronage of its Original Builder, Lord Henry Howard: 1603–14', *The Antiquaries Journal*, 90 (2010), 341–400

——, 'From Northampton to Northumberland: The Strand Palace during the Suffolk Ownership and the Transformations of Algernon Percy, Tenth Earl of Northumberland, 1614–68', *The Antiquaries Journal*, 94 (2014), 211–51

——, 'John Osborne, the Salisbury House "Porticus" and the "Haynes Grange Room"', *The Burlington Magazine*, 148 (January 2006), 15–24

——, 'Salisbury House in London, 1599–1694: The Strand Palace of Sir Robert Cecil', *Architectural History*, 52 (2009), 31–78

——, 'The Strand Palaces of the Early Seventeenth Century: Salisbury House and Northumberland House', 2 vols. PhD diss., University of Cambridge, 2007

Guilding, Ruth, *Owning the Past: Why the English collected Antique Sculpture, 1640–1840*. New Haven and London: Yale University Press, 2014

Hadfield, A., 'Spenser, Edmund (1552?–1599), ODNB. Oxford University Press, 2004, online edn., January 2008, https://doi.org/10.1093/ref:odnb/26145

Halliwell, J. O., *Ancient Inventories … illustrative of the Domestic Manners of the English in the Sixteenth and Seventeenth Centuries*. London, 1854

Hammer, P. E. J., 'Devereux, Robert, second earl of Essex (1565–1601)', ODNB. Oxford University Press, 2004, online edn., October 2008, http://www.oxforddnb.com/view/article/7565

Hammerson, M. J., 'Excavations on the Site of Arundel House in the Strand, W.C.2., in 1972', *Transactions of the London and Middlesex Archaeological Society*, 26 (1975), 209–51

Harris, Eileen, *Osterley Park, Middlesex*. National Trust, 1994

——, *The Genius of Robert Adam: His Interiors*. New Haven and London: Yale University Press, 2001

Harris, John, *A Passion for Building: The Amateur Architect in England 1650–1850*, exh. cat., Sir John Soane's Museum, London, 2007

——, 'Who Designed the York Water-Gate?', *Country Life*, 2 November 1989, 150–51

——, and Gordon Higgott, *Inigo Jones: Complete Architectural Drawings*. London: Philip Wilson, 1989

——, and A. A. Tait, *Catalogue of the Drawings by Inigo Jones, John Webb and Isaac de Caus at Worcester College Oxford*. Oxford: Clarendon Press, 1979

Harris Nicolas, Nicholas, *Memoirs of the Life and Times of Sir Christopher Hatton*. London: Richard Bentley, 1847

Hart, Vaughan, and Peter Hicks, eds, *Sebastiano Serlio on Architecture, Volume One: Books I–V of 'Tutte L'Opere d'Architettura et Prospetiva'*. New Haven and London: Yale University Press, 1996

—— and ——, *Sebastiano Serlio on Architecture, Volume Two: Books VI and VII of 'Tutte L'Opere d'Architettura et Prospetiva'*, with 'Castrametation of the Romans' and 'The Extraordinary Book of Doors'. New Haven and London: Yale University Press, 2001

Heal, Felicity, *Of Prelates and Princes: A Study of the Economic and Social Position of the Tudor Episcopate*. Cambridge: Cambridge University Press, 1980

Hearn, Karen, *Talking Peace 1604: The Somerset House Conference Paintings*, exh. cat., Somerset House. London, 2004

——, 'Lucy Harington, Countess of Bedford as Art Patron and Collector'. MA diss., Courtauld Institute of Art, University of London, 1990

——, ed., *Dynasties: Painting in Tudor and Jacobean England 1530–1630*. London: Tate, 1995

Hembry, Phyllis, 'Episcopal Palaces, 1535 to 1660', in E. W. Ives, R. J. Knecht and J. J. Scarisbrick, eds, *Wealth and Power in Tudor England: Essays presented to S. T. Bindoff*. London: Athlone Press, 1978, 146–66

Henderson, Paula, *The Tudor House and Garden: Architecture and Landscape in the Sixteenth and Early Seventeenth Centuries*. New Haven and London: Yale University Press, 2005

——, 'The Evolution of the Early Gardens of the Inns of Court', in Jayne Elisabeth Archer, Elizabeth Goldring and Sarah Knight, *The Intellectual and Cultural World of the Early Modern Inns of Court*. Manchester and New York: Manchester University Press, 2011, 179–98

——, 'The Loggia in Tudor and Early Stuart England: The Adaptation and Function of Classical Form', in Lucy Gent, ed., *Albion's Classicism: The Visual Arts in Britain, 1550–1600*. New Haven and London: Yale University Press, 1995, 109–45

Herbert, Sidney, 16th Earl of Pembroke, *A Catalogue of the Paintings and Drawings in the Collection at Wilton House*. London and New York: Phaidon, 1968

Hervey, M. F. S., *The Life, Correspondence and Collections of Thomas Howard, Earl of Arundel*. Cambridge: Cambridge University Press, 1921

Heward, John, 'The Restoration of the South Front of Wilton House: The Development of the House Reconsidered', *Architectural History*, 35 (1992), 78–117

Higgott, Gordon, 'The Fabric in 1670', in Derek Keene, Arthur Burns and Andrew Saint, eds, *St Paul's: The Cathedral Church of London 604–2004*. New Haven and London: Yale University Press, 2004, 170–89

——, 'Roof Walks and Roof Platforms on English Country Houses [apart from English the original title does not capitalise words], *c.*1550 to *c.*1700', in M. Chatenet and A. Gady, eds, *Toits d'Europe: Formes, structures, décors et usages du toit à l'époque moderne (XVe–XVIIe siècle). Actes du huitièmes*

Rencontres d'architecture européenne, Paris, 12–14 juin 2013. Paris: Picard, 2016, 185–98

——, and Adam White, 'York Water Gate, Westminster, London (Nicholas Stone)', http://collections.soane.org/OBJECT1933

Hille, Christiane, *Visions of the Courtly Body: The Patronage of George Villiers, First Duke of Buckingham, and the Triumph of Painting at the Stuart Court.* Berlin: Akademie Verlag, 2012

Hind, Arthur M., *Wenceslaus Hollar and his Views of London and Windsor in the Seventeenth Century.* London: Bodley Head, 1922

History of Northumberland House, The. London: Bell, Steward & Lloyd, 1866

Hobhouse, Hermione, *Lost London: A Century of Demolition and Decay.* London and Basingstoke: Macmillan, 1971

Hollar's London: 37 Etchings of London Views (1636–1667). London: Edgeworth Press and British Museum, 1980

Hoskin, P., 'Poor, Richard (d. 1237)', ODNB. Oxford University Press, 2004, online edn., October 2009, http://www.oxforddnb.com/view/article/22525

Howard, Maurice, 'Inventories, Surveys and Histories of Great Houses', *Architectural History*, 41 (1998), 14–29

Howarth, David, *Lord Arundel and his Circle.* New Haven and London: Yale University Press, 1985

——, '"Mantua Peeces": Charles I and the Gonzaga Collections', in D. S. Chambers and J. T. Martineau, eds, *Splendours of the Gonzaga*, exh. cat., Victoria and Albert Museum, London, 1981, 95–100

——, 'The Patronage and Collecting of Aletheia, Countess of Arundel 1606–54', *Journal of the History of Collections*, 10, no. 2 (1998), 125–37

Hughson, David, *A History and Description of London, Westminster and Southwark*, 4 vols, London, n.d.

——, *Walks through London, including Westminster and the Borough of Southwark*, 2 vols. London: Sherwood, Neely and Jones, 1817

Hulton, P. H., 'Drawings of England in the Seventeenth Century by Willem Schellinks Jacob Esselens and Lambert Doomer from the Van der Hem Atlas of the National Library, Vienna', *Walpole Society*, vol. 35, pt 1, 1954–6 (1959), iii–64

Husselby, Jill, and Paula Henderson, 'Location, Location, Location! Cecil House in the Strand', *Architectural History*, 45 (2002), 159–93

Jack, S. M., 'Paget, William, first Baron Paget (1505/6–1563)', ODNB. Oxford University Press, 2004, online edn., January 2008, http://www.oxforddnb.com/view/article/21121

James, Susan E., 'Edward Seymour, Duke of Somerset? Re-examining a Tudor Portrait', *The British Art Journal*, 2, no. 2 (Winter 2000/01), 14–21

Jervis, Simon, 'Furniture of the First Duke of Buckingham', *Furniture History*, 33 (1997), 57–74

Johnson, Arthur Henry, *The History of the Worshipful Company of the Drapers of London: preceded by an introduction on London and her guilds up to the close of the XVth century by Rev. A. H. Johnson*, 5 vols. Oxford: Clarendon Press, 1914–22

Jones, Inigo, *Inigo Jones on Palladio*, ed. Bruce Allsopp. 2 vols. Newcastle upon Tyne: Oriel Press, 1970

Jonson, Ben, 'The Entertainment at Salisbury House', ed. James Knowles, in David Bevington, Martin Butler and Ian Donaldson, eds, *The Cambridge Edition of the Works of Ben Jonson*, 7 vols. Cambridge: Cambridge University Press, 2010, vol. 3, 276–9

Kingsford, Charles L., 'Bath Inn or Arundel House', *Archaeologia*, 72 (1922), 243–77

——, 'Essex House, formerly Leicester House and Exeter Inn', *Archaeologia*, 73 (1923), 1–54

——, 'On some London Houses of the Early Tudor Period', *Archaeologia*, 71 (1921), 17–54

Knight, C., ed., *London*, 6 vols. London, 1842

Kuile, Onno ter, 'Daniel Mijtens: "His Majesties Picture Drawer"', *Nederlands Kunsthistorisch Jaarboek*, 20 (1969), 1–106

Latham, Agnes, and Joyce Youings, eds, *The Letters of Sir Walter Ralegh.* Exeter: University of Exeter Press, 1999

Latham, Robert, ed., *Catalogue of the Pepys Library at Magdalene College, Cambridge*, 7 vols. Woodbridge: Boydell & Brewer, 1970–94

Lewalski, Barbara K., 'Lucy, Countess of Bedford: Images of a Jacobean Courtier and Patroness', in Kevin Sharpe and Steven N. Zwicker, eds, *Politics of Discourse: The Literature and History of Seventeenth-Century England.* Berkeley, Los Angeles and London: University of California Press, 1987, 52–77

Levy Peck, Linda, *Consuming Splendour: Society and Culture in Seventeenth-Century England.* Cambridge: Cambridge University Press, 2005

——, *Northampton: Patronage and Policy at the Court of James I.* London: Allen & Unwin, 1982

——, 'The Mentality of a Jacobean Grandee', in Levy Peck, ed., *The Mental World of the Jacobean Court* (1991). Cambridge: Cambridge University Press, 2005, 149–67

——, 'Uncovering the Arundel Library at the Royal Society', *Notes and Records of the Royal Society of London* (1998), 3–24

Loach, Jennifer, *Protector Somerset: A Reassessment.* Bangor: Headstart History, 1994

Lock, J., 'Fitzalan, Henry, twelfth earl of Arundel (1512–1580)', ODNB. Oxford University Press, 2004, online edn., January 2008 http://www.oxforddnb.com/view/article/9530

Lockyer, Roger, *Buckingham: The Life and Political Career of George Villiers, First Duke of Buckingham, 1592–1628.* London: Longman, 1981

——, 'Villiers, George, first duke of Buckingham (1592–1628)', ODNB. Oxford University Press, 2004, online edn., May 2011, http://www.oxforddnb.com/view/article/28293

Lodge, E., *Illustrations of British History, Biography, and Manners, in the reigns of Henry VIII, Edward VI, Mary, Elizabeth, & James I*, 3 vols. 2nd edn., London: John Chidley, 1838

Loftie, W. J., *Memorials of the Savoy. The Palace: The Hospital: The Chapel.* London: Macmillan, 1878

Lloyd, S., 'Edmund, first earl of Lancaster and first earl of Leicester (1245–1296)', ODNB. Oxford University Press, 2004, online edn., January 2008, http://www.oxforddnb.com/view/article/8504

Lovell, Percy, and William McB. Marcham, eds, *Survey of London*, vol. 17: *The Parish of St Pancras Part 1: The Village of Highgate.* London: London County Council, 1936

Lubbock, Jules, *The Tyranny of Taste: The Politics of Architecture and Design in Britain 1550–1960.* New Haven and London: Yale University Press, 1995

Macaulay, Thomas Babington, *The History of England from the Accession of James the Second*, 5 vols. London, 1848

MacCaffrey, W. T., 'Cecil, William, first Baron Burghley (1520/21–1598)', ODNB. Oxford University Press, 2004, http://www.oxforddnb.com/view/article/4983

——, 'Hatton, Sir Christopher (c.1540–1591)', ODNB. Oxford University Press, 2004, online edn., January 2015, http://www.oxforddnb.com/view/article/12605

Maddicott, J. R., 'Thomas of Lancaster, second earl of Lancaster, second earl of Leicester, and earl of Lincoln (c.1278–1322)', ODNB. Oxford University Press, 2004, online edn., January 2008, http://www.oxforddnb.com/view/article/27195

Madge, Sidney J., 'Worcester House in the Strand', *Archaeologia*, 91 (1945), 157–80

McClure, Norman E., ed., *The Letters of John Chamberlain*, 2 vols, Philadelphia: American Philosophical Society, 1939

McDermott, J., 'Howard, Charles, second Baron Howard of Effingham and first earl of Nottingham (1536–1624)', ODNB. Oxford University Press, 2004, online edn., January 2008, http://www.oxforddnb.com/view/article/13885

McEvansoneya, Philip, 'The Houses of the Duke of Buckingham'. MA diss., Courtauld Institute of Art, University of London, 1985

——, 'Italian Paintings in the Buckingham Collection', in Chaney, *Evolution of English Collecting*, 315–36

——, 'A Note on the Duke of Buckingham's Inventory', *The Burlington Magazine*, 128, no. 1001 (1986), 607

———, 'The Sequestration and Dispersal of the Buckingham Collection', *Journal of the History of Collections*, 8, no. 2 (1996), 133–54

———, 'Some Documents concerning the Patronage and Collections of the Duke of Buckingham', *Rutgers Art Review*, 8 (1987), 27–38

———, 'An Unpublished Inventory of the Hamilton Collection in the 1620s and the Duke of Buckingham's Pictures', *The Burlington Magazine*, 134, no. 1073 (1992), 524–6

———, 'Van Dyck and the Duchess of Buckingham's Collection: New Documents relating to York House', *Apollo*, 140 (1994), 30–32

———, 'Vertue, Walpole and the Documentation of the Buckingham Collection', *Journal of the History of Collections*, 8, no. 1 (1996), 1–14

Merritt, Julia F., *The Social World of Early Modern Westminster: Abbey, Court and Community, 1525–1640*. Manchester: Manchester University Press, 2005

———, 'The Cecils and Westminster 1558–1612: The Development of an Urban Power Base', in Croft, *Patronage, Culture and Power*, 231–48

———, ed., *Imagining Early Modern London: Perceptions and Portrayals of the City from Stow to Strype, 1598–1720*. Cambridge: Cambridge University Press, 2001

Metzger Habel, Dorothy, *The Urban Development of Rome in the Age of Alexander VII*. Cambridge: Cambridge University Press, 2002

Michel, Patrick, *Mazarin, Prince des Collectionneurs*. Paris: Réunion ds Musées Nationaux, 1999

Miller, J., 'Howard, Henry, sixth duke of Norfolk (1628–1684)', ODNB. Oxford University Press, 2004, http://www.oxforddnb.com/view/article/13907

Milward, R., 'Cecil, Thomas, first earl of Exeter (1542–1623)', ODNB. Oxford University Press, 2004, online edn., January 2008, http://www.oxforddnb.com/view/article/4981

Mitton, G. E., ed., *Maps of Old London*. London: Adam and Charles Black, 1908

Morrill, J., 'Devereux, Robert, third earl of Essex (1591–1646)', ODNB. Oxford University Press, 2004, online edn., January 2008, http://www.oxforddnb.com/view/article/7566

Morrison, Kathryn, et al., *Apethorpe: The Story of an English Country House*. New Haven and London: Yale University Press, 2016

Needham, Raymond, and Alexander Webster, *Somerset House Past and Present*. London: T. Fisher Unwin, 1905

Newdigate, Bernard H., ed., *The Poems of Ben Jonson*. Oxford: Basil Blackwell, 1936

Newman, John, *Somerset House: Splendour and Order*. London: Scala Books, 1990

Nichols, John, *The Progresses and Public Processions of Queen Elizabeth*, 3 vols. London: Society of Antiquaries, 1823

Nichols, J. G., 'Life of the last Fitz-Alan, earl of Arundel', *The Gentleman's Magazine*, 103, pt 2 (1833), 10–18, 118–24, 209–15

Nicholls, Mark, and Penry Williams, *Sir Walter Raleigh in Life and Legend*. London: Continuum, 2011

———, and ———, 'Ralegh, Sir Walter (1554–1618)', ODNB. Oxford University Press, 2004, online edn., September 2015, http://www.oxforddnb.com/view/article/23039

Northumberland House: A Catalogue of the First Portion of the Valuable Building Materials, Fixtures & Fittings … London: Horne, Eversfield & Co., 1874

Oram, W. A., et al., eds, *The Yale Edition of the Shorter Poems of Edmund Spenser*. New Haven and London: Yale University Press, 1989

Orgel, Stephen, and Roy Strong, *Inigo Jones: The Theatre of the Stuart Court*, 2 vols, London: Sotheby Park Bernet, and Berkeley and Los Angeles: University of California Press, 1973

Ormrod, W. M., 'Henry of Lancaster, first duke of Lancaster (c.1310–1361)', ODNB. Oxford University Press, 2004, online edn., January 2008, http://www.oxforddnb.com/view/article/12960

Parry, Graham, *Hollar's England: A Mid-Seventeenth-Century View*. Salisbury: Michael Russell Publishing, 1980

Patterson, W. B., 'Dominis, Marco Antonio de (1560–1624)', ODNB. Oxford University Press, 2004, online edn., January 2008, http://www.oxforddnb.com/view/article/7788

Payne, H. 'Russell [née Harington], Lucy, countess of Bedford (bap. 1581, d. 1627)', ODNB. Oxford University Press, 2004, online edn., https://doi.org/10.1093/ref:odnb/24330

Payne, M. T. W., 'An Inventory of Queen Anna of Denmark's "Ornaments, furniture, household stuffe, and other parcels" at Denmark House, 1619', *Journal of the History of Collections*, 13, no. 1 (2001), 23–44

Peacock, John, and Christy Anderson, 'Inigo Jones, John Webb and Temple Bar', *Architectural History*, 44 (2001), 29–38

Pearce, David, *London's Mansions: Private Palaces of the Nobility*. London: Batsford, 1986

Pearsall Smith, Logan, *The Life and Letters of Sir Henry Wotton*, 2 vols. Oxford: Clarendon Press, 1907

Peltonen, M., 'Bacon, Francis, Viscount St Alban (1561–1626)', ODNB. Oxford University Press, 2004, online edn., October 2007, http://www.oxforddnb.com/view/article/990

Pennington, Richard, *A Descriptive Catalogue of the Etched Work of Wenceslaus Hollar 1607–1677*. Cambridge: Cambridge University Press, 1982

Phillpotts, Christopher, 'The Houses of Henry VIII's Courtiers in London', in David R. M. Gaimster and Roberta Gilchrist, eds, *The Archaeology of Reformation 1480–1580*. Leeds: Maney Publishing, 2003, 299–309

Pollard, A. F., 'Wilson, Sir Thomas (d. 1629)', rev. Sean Kelsey, ODNB. Oxford University Press, 2004, online edn., January 2008, http://www.oxforddnb.com/view/article/29690

Priestland, P., 'Russell [née Cooke], Elizabeth, Lady Russell [other married name Elizabeth Hoby, Lady Hoby] (1528–1609)', ODNB. Oxford University Press, 2004, online edn., http://www.oxforddnb.com/view/10.1093/ref:odnb-9780198614128-e-13411

Prockter, Adrian, and Robert Taylor, *A to Z of Elizabethan London*. London: Harry Margary, 1979

Read, Conyers, *Lord Burghley and Queen Elizabeth*. London: Jonathan Cape, 1960

———, 'Lord Burghley's Household Accounts', *Economic History Review*, 2nd series, 9 (1956), 343–8

Roberts, J., 'Thomas Howard, the Collector Earl of Arundel and Leonardo's Drawings', in Chaney, *Evolution of English Collecting*, 257–83

Robinson, John Martin, *Buckingham Palace: Official Guidebook*. London: Royal Collection Enterprises, 2004

———, *The Dukes of Norfolk*. Chichester: Phillimore, 1995

Russell, Conrad, 'Russell, Francis, fourth earl of Bedford (bap. 1587, d. 1641)', ODNB. Oxford University Press, 2004, online edn., https://doi.org/10.1093/ref:odnb/24307

Sandeen, Ernest R., 'The Building Activities of Sir Nicholas Bacon', PhD diss., University of Chicago, 1959

Saunders, Ann, ed., *The Royal Exchange*. London: London Topographical Society, 1997

———, and John Schofield, eds, *Tudor London: A Map and a View*. London: London Topographical Society, 2001

Schofield, John, *Medieval London Houses*. New Haven and London: Yale University Press, 1995; 2003

Scott-Thomson, Gladys, *Life in a Noble Household 1641–1700* (1937). 5th edn. London: Jonathan Cape, 1950

———, *The Russells in Bloomsbury 1669–1771*. London: Jonathan Cape, 1940

Sharpe, Kevin, 'The Earl of Arundel, his Circle and the Opposition to the Duke of Buckingham, 1618–1628', in Sharpe, ed., *Faction and Parliament: Essays on Early Stuart History*. Oxford: Clarendon Press, 1978, 1–42

Shawe-Taylor, Desmond, and Per Rumberg, eds, *Charles I: King and Collector*, exh. cat. London: Royal Academy Publications, 2018

Sheppard, F. H. W., ed., *Survey of London*, vol. 36: *The Parish of St. Paul Covent Garden*. London: Athlone Press and University of London for the Greater London Council, 1970

Shirley, Evelyn Philip, 'An Inventory of the Effects of Henry Howard, K.G., Earl of Northampton … with a transcript of his Will … ', *Archaeologia*, 42 (1869), 347–78

Shirley, J. W., *Thomas Harriot: A Biography*. Oxford: Clarendon Press, 1983

Skelton, Kimberley, 'At once National and International: John Webb and the 1650s Country House', in Barbara Arciszewska, ed., *The Baroque Villa: Suburban and Country Residences c.1600–c.1800*. Warsaw: Wilanów Palace Museum, 2009, 229–44

Smith, D. L., 'Herbert, Philip, first earl of Montgomery and fourth earl of Pembroke (1584–1650)', ODNB. Oxford University Press, 2004, online edn., January 2016, http://www.oxforddnb.com/view/article/13042

Smuts, R. M., 'Howard, Thomas, fourteenth earl of Arundel, fourth earl of Surrey, and first earl of Norfolk (1585–1646)', ODNB. Oxford University Press, 2004, online edn., May 2015, http://www.oxforddnb.com/view/article/13943

Sorrell, M., 'Polito, Stephen (1763/4–1814)', ODNB. Oxford University Press, 2004, online edn., January 2008, http://www.oxforddnb.com/view/article/73320

Stallybrass, Basil, 'Bess of Hardwick's Buildings and Building Accounts', *Archaeologia*, 64 (1913), 347–98

Stater, V., 'Russell, William, first duke of Bedford (1616–1700)', ODNB. Oxford University Press, 2004, online edn., https://doi.org/10.1093/ref:odnb/24346

Stone, Laurence, *The Crisis of the Aristocracy, 1558–1641*. Oxford: Clarendon Press, 1965

——, *Family and Fortune: Studies in Aristocratic Finance in the Sixteenth and Seventeenth Centuries*. Oxford, 1973

Strong, Roy, *The Renaissance Garden in England*. London: Thames and Hudson, 1979

Sturdy, D., and A. Brueggeman, 'British Gardens 1590–1740 and the Origins of the Museum', *Apollo*, 146 (September 1997), 3–8

Summerson, John, *Architecture in Britain: 1530–1830* (1970). New Haven and London: Yale University Press, 1993

——, *The Book of Architecture of John Thorpe*, Walpole Society 40. Glasgow: Walpole Society, 1966

——, *Georgian London*. London: Pleiades Books, 1945

Sutton, J. M., *Materializing Space at an Early Modern Prodigy House: The Cecils at Theobalds, 1564–1607*. Aldershot: Ashgate, 2004

Sykes, Christopher Simon, *Private Palaces: Life in the Great London Houses*. London: Viking, 1985

Temple, Philip, *Survey of London: The Charterhouse*. New Haven and London: Yale University Press, 2010

Thornbury, Walter, and Edward Walford, *Old and New London*, 6 vols, London: Cassell, Petter & Galpin, 1879–85

Thurley, Simon, *Hampton Court*. New Haven and London: Yale University Press, 2003

——, *Somerset House: The Palace of England's Queens 1551–1692*. London: London Topographical Society, 2009

Tierney, M. A., *The History and Antiquities of the Castle and Town of Arundel; including the Biography of its Earls, from the Conquest to the Present Time*. London: G. and W. Nicol, 1834

Tittler, R., 'Bacon, Sir Nicholas (1510–1579)', ODNB. Oxford University Press, 2004, online edn., January 2011, http://www.oxforddnb.com/view/article/1002

Town, Edward, 'A Biographical Dictionary of London Painters 1547–1625', *Walpole Society*, 76 (2014), 1–235

Vander Motten, J. P., 'Killigrew, Henry (1613–1700)', ODNB. Oxford University Press, 2004, online edn., January 2008, http://www.oxforddnb.com/view/article/15534

——, 'Killigrew, Thomas (1612–1683)', ODNB. Oxford University Press, 2004, online edn., January 2008, http://www.oxforddnb.com/view/article/15538

Vergara, Alexander W., 'The Count of Fuensaldana and David Teniers: Their Purchases in London after the Civil War', *The Burlington Magazine*, 131 (February 1989), 127–32

Vertue, George, 'Vertue Note Book II', ed. A. J. Finberg, *Walpole Society* 20 (1931/2). Oxford: Oxford University Press, 1932

Vincent, N., 'Savoy, Peter of, count of Savoy and de facto earl of Richmond (1203?–1268)', ODNB. Oxford University Press, 2004, online edn., January 2008, http://www.oxforddnb.com/view/article/22016

Walker, S., 'John, duke of Aquitaine and duke of Lancaster, styled king of Castile and León (1340–1399)', ODNB. Oxford University Press, 2004, online edn., May 2008, http://www.oxforddnb.com/view/article/14843

Walpole, Horace, *Anecdotes of painting in England: with some account of the principal artists, and incidental notes on other arts. Also, a catalogue of engravers who have been born or resided in England collected by the late George Vertue; digested and published from his original mss. by Horace Walpole; with additions by … James Dallaway*, 3 vols. London: H. G. Bohn, 1849

Warne, Heather M., ed., *The Duke of Norfolk's Deeds at Arundel Castle: Catalogue 2, Properties in London and Middlesex, 1154–1917*. Oving, Chichester: Phillimore, 2010

Waugh, S. L., 'Henry of Lancaster, third earl of Lancaster and third earl of Leicester (c.1280–1345)', ODNB. Oxford University Press, 2004, online edn., May 2006, http://www.oxforddnb.com/view/article/12959

Wells-Cole, Anthony, 'Some Design Sources for the Earl of Leicester's Tapestries and other Contemporary Pieces', *The Burlington Magazine*, 125 (May 1983), 284–5

Weinreb, Ben, and Christopher Hibbert, eds, *The London Encyclopaedia*. London: Macmillan, 1983

Wheatley, Henry Benjamin, *London, Past and Present: A Dictionary of its History, Associations, and Traditions*, 3 vols (1891). Cambridge: Cambridge University Press, 2011

White, Adam, *A Biographical Dictionary of London Tomb Sculptors c.1560–c.1660*, Walpole Society 61 (1998/9)

Wilkinson, Robert, *Londina illustrata. Graphic and historic memorials of monasteries, churches, chapels, schools, charitable foundations, palaces, halls, courts, processions … in the cities and suburbs of London & Westminster*, 2 vols. London: R. Wilkinson, 1819–25

Willen, D., 'Russell, John, first earl of Bedford (c.1485–1555)', ODNB. Oxford University Press, 2004, online edn., January 2008 http://www.oxforddnb.com/view/article/24319

Williams, Neville J., *All the Queen's Men: Elizabeth I and Her Courtiers*. New York: Macmillan, 1972

Wilson, Francesca, *Strange Island: Britain through Foreign Eyes, 1390–1940*. London and New York: Longmans Green, 1955

Wood, Jeremy, 'The Architectural Patronage of the 10th Earl of Northumberland', in John Bold and Edward Chaney, eds, *English Architecture Public and Private: Essays for Kerry Downes*. London: Hambledon Press, 1993, 55–80

——,'Van Dyck and the Earl of Northumberland: Taste and Collecting in Stuart England', in Susan J. Barnes and Arthur K. Wheelock Jr., eds, *Van Dyck 350*. Washington DC: National Gallery of Art, 1994, 281–326

Worsley, Giles, *Inigo Jones and the European Classicist Tradition*. New Haven and London: Yale University Press, 2007

——, 'Scamozzi's Influence on English Seventeenth-Century Architecture', *Annali di architettura*, 18–19 (2006–7), 225–34

Yardley, B., 'Villiers, George, second duke of Buckingham (1628–1687)', ODNB. Oxford University Press, 2004, online edn., May 2009, http://www.oxforddnb.com/view/article/28294

Yates, Frances, *A Study of Love's Labour's Lost*. Cambridge: University Press, 1936

Yoshida-Takeda, Tomiko, 'La collection intérieure du palais Mazarin et sa collection d'art décorative de l'Extrême-Orient (Chine et Japon)', in Isabelle de Conihout and Patrick Michel, eds, *Mazarin: les lettres et les arts*. Paris: Editions Monelle Hayot and Bibliothèque Mazarine, 2006, 189–95

Index

Note: page numbers in italics refer to illustrations.

A

Adam, Robert 190
Adams, Robert 29
Adams, Simon 20
'Agas', *Woodcut Map of London* 20, 35, 57, 82, 91, 109, *128*, *162*, *174*
Albury, Surrey 50
Aldrich, Robert 129
Alexander III, King of Scotland 78
Alienation Office Garden 29
Alnwick Castle 107, 217
Anne, Queen 74
Anne of Denmark 61–5
Appleby, Thomas de 129
Arundel Castle 37
Arundel House 10, 33–53, 220, 221, 224
  antique sculpture 46–7, 49, 50, 52–3
  during the Civil War 49, 50
  during the Commonwealth 52
  galleries 37, 40–44, *42*, *43*, 44, 45, 45–6, *46*, 47, 220
  garden of antiquities 10, 46, 47, 49, 53, 213
  gardens 38, 41, *41*, 45, 50, 51
  inventories 45, 47, 49–50, 52
  'Italyan' gate 41, *41*, 44, *44*, 47
  library 47, 49, 50
  painting and drawing collection 47, 49–50
  stables 52
  tenements 33, 34
Arundel Place 35
Ashby, Thomas 44
Aubrey, John 162, 166, 179
Audley End 203, 204, 207
Austin, Jane 102
Austin Friars 4

B

Bacon, Anthony 177
Bacon, Nathaniel 177
Bacon, Sir Francis, 1st Viscount St Albans 98, 177, *179*, 179–80
Bacon, Sir Nicholas 92, 176–7, 203
Bacon House 177
Balcanquall, Walter 83
Banqueting House 19, 113, 114, 166, 182, 187, 192
Barbon, Nicholas 31
Barry, Sir Charles 217, 223
Basil, Edward 60
Basil, Simon
  Salisbury House 138–9, *140*, *141*, *142*, *143*, *144*, *145*, 148, 150, *152*
  Sherborne Castle 161
  Somerset House 63
Basset, James 91
Bath and Wells, Bishops of 33
Bath Inn (or Place) *8*, 19, 33, *34*, 56–7
Bayly, Dr Thomas 133
Beaufort Buildings *135*, 135
Beaufort (former Worcester) House 127, 134, *135*
Bedford Estates 3, 6, 106, 108, 111, 116, 120
Bedford House 12, 105–25, 127, 221, 225
  banqueting houses 116–17, 121, 122, 123
  Evidence House 116, 122, 123, 125
  galleries 119, 122, 124
  garden 105, 113, 116–17, 121
  garden grotto 114, *114*, *115*, 115–16, 125
  Great Chamber 119, 121, 124
  inventories 118–20, 123–4
  shared cistern 118
  stables 110, 111, 113, 121
  Strand front 105, 110, 119, 122
  wall fountain 116, *116*, 117
Bek, Anthony, Bishop of Durham 159
Bellini, Nicola 57
Benson, John 148
Beresford Chancellor, Edwin 15, 105, 135
Berkeley, James 18
Berkshire House, St James's 134
Béthune, Maximilien de, Duke of Sully 39, 224
Beverley, William de 159
Blanche, Duchess of Lancaster 79, 80
Blome, Richard 102, 103, 119, 121, 123, *124*
Blount, Sir Christopher 30
Bol, Cornelis 37, 45
Bold, John 167
Boleyn, Anne 129, 160
Boleyn, Sir Thomas 160
Bolsover Castle 223
Bond, John 83
Book of Common Prayer 83
Booke of Computations 24, 25, 26
Booth, Abram 49, 224
Boteler, John, Julien and William 127
Bowman, Matthias 193
Bradshaw, Lawrence 96
Brandon, Charles, 1st Duke of Suffolk 176
Braun, Georg, *Civitates Orbis Terrarum* 3, 20, 35, 57, *161*
Brett, Robert 198
Bridgeman, Sir Orlando 31
Bridges, Giles, 3rd Baron Chandos 113
Bromley, Sir Thomas 178
Brueggeman, A. 45, 47
Buckett, Roland 150
Buckingham House 74
Burghley House (also known as Cecil or Exeter House) 12, 89–103, 222
  Banqueting Houses 92, 93, *94*, 95, 96, 101
  during the Commonwealth 101
  courtyards 95–6
  galleries 93, 98, 220
  garden 91, 92, 93, 99–100
  garden gallery 98, *98*
  Great Chamber 97, 98
  Great Hall 97
  marble 92, 93, 98
  Strand front 93, 95, 96
Burghley House, Stamford 35, 58, 60, 93, 150, 221, 223, 224
Burghley Street 103
Burley-on-the-Hill, Rutland 181
Byrd, William 132

C

Callot, Jacques 116
Camden, William 99
Campbell, Colen 73, 187, 189
Campeggio, Cardinal Lorenzo 34, 176
Canaletto 69
Capel, Arthur, 1st Earl of Essex of the new creation 31
Cárdenas, Alonso de 166
Carew, Lord 83
Carey, Henry, Lord Hudson 39, 60–61
Carleton, Dudley 148, 185, 186
Carlisle, Bishops of 78, 129
Carlisle House 129
Carlisle Inn (or Place) 127, *128*, 129
Carlisle Rents 127, 131, 133, 134
Caroline, Queen 74
Carr, Frances, Duchess of Richmond (née Howard) 101, 178, 207
Carr, Robert, Earl of Somerset 30, 178, 180, 207
Carter, Edward 113, 116, 208–9, 213, 221–2
Casimir, John 60
Castello (or Castellesi), Adriano da 34
Castle Ashby 204
Catherine of Braganza 73–4
Catholicism
  and Burghley House 101
  and Durham House 165
  Henrietta Maria 66, 70
  Howard family 38, 195, 223
  and the Savoy 83
  and Somerset House 73
Caus, Isaac de 63, 114, *114*, 115, *115*, *116*, *117*, 166, 221–2
Caus, Salomon de 154
Cavendish, William, 3rd Earl of Devonshire 155
Cecil, Anne 155, 208
Cecil, Edward, Viscount Wimbledon 100
Cecil, Elizabeth (Burghley's daughter) 98
Cecil, Elizabeth (daughter of the 2nd Earl of Salisbury) 155
Cecil, Elizabeth (Exeter's daughter) 100
Cecil, Elizabeth (wife of Robert Cecil) 221
Cecil, Lady Elizabeth (née Manners) 83
Cecil, Francis (daughter of the 3rd Earl of Exeter) 103
Cecil, James, 3rd Earl of Salisbury 156, 157
Cecil, James, 4th Earl of Salisbury 157
Cecil, James, 5th Earl of Salisbury 157
Cecil, John, 4th Earl of Exeter 103
Cecil, Margaret, (wife of the 3rd Earl of Salisbury) 156–7, 221
Cecil, Mildred, Lady Burghley 98, 110, 220–21
Cecil, Robert, 1st Earl of Salisbury 6, 7, 13, 14, 22–3, 39, 49, 61, 137–55
  Burghley House annex 12, 95, 100
  civic concerns 79
  collection 152, 154
  and Durham House 163–4
  and Henry Howard 197
  and Lucy Harrington 112
  portrait *138*
  and the Savoy 80
  and Somerset House 63–4
Cecil, Thomas, 1st Earl of Exeter 83, 98, 100, 130
Cecil, William, 2nd Earl of Exeter 101
Cecil, William, 2nd Earl of Salisbury 133, 148, 155, 207
Cecil, William, Lord Burghley 6, 12, 22–3
  antiquarian collection 99, 100
  Burghley House 89–100
  civic concerns 79, 99
  and Edward Russell, 3rd Earl of Bedford 110
  portrait *138*
  and the Savoy 80, 81
  and York House 178
Cecil House *see* Burghley House
Cecil Street 157
Chamberlain, John 185, 195, 207
Chancery Lane 177
Channell, John 122
Chapman, George 162
Charles, Prince of Wales (son of James I) 65
Charles I 83, 224–5
  and Arundel House 49, 213
  and Covent Garden piazza 113
  and Durham House 13, 165
  and Somerset House 69
  and St James's Palace 46
Charles II 73
  and Burghley House 103
  and Essex House 31
  and Worcester House 134
  and York House 193
Charles Street 103
Charlton House, Greenwich 203
Charterhouse 4, 5, 207
Château d'Anet 29
Chatsworth 203, 220
Chaucer, Geoffrey 12, 80
Chelsea House 181, 189, 192
Chester Inn 55, 56, 58
Chester Place 55
Chester Rents 55
Chichester, Bishop of 78
Christian, Edward 193
Christmas, Gerard 203, 223
Clarendon, E. H. 216
'Clarendon Code' 83–4
Clarendon House, Piccadilly 134
Clark, Jane 17
Cleare, Richard 214
Cleare, Robert 214
Cleare, William 122
Clerk, Bishop John 34
Clough, Richard 92, 95
Cockeram, Philip 91
Cole, John 132
Colepeper, Thomas *114*, 115
Colvin, Howard 55, 60, 187
Cook, Humphrey 81
Cooke, Anne 176, 177
Cooke, Elizabeth 110, 176
Cooke, George 103
Cooke, Katherine 176
Cooke, Margaret 176
Cooke, Sir William 197
Cooper, Anthony Ashley, 1st Earl of Shaftesbury 103
Cope, Walter 139, 154
Cornwallis, Sir William 40
Cotton Library 31
Covent Garden 3, 6, 7, 12, 56, 113, 120
  archives 107
  and Bedford House *108*, *111*, 111–12
  and Burghley House 91, 92, 93, 101
  map *106–7*
  market 120, 125
  piazza 12, 101, *102*, 113, *115*
  plans of *114*
Cox, Richard 197
Coxe, Robert 23
Cranfield, Sir Lionel 180
Critz, Emmanuel de 214
Crompton, George 118
Cromwell, Thomas 4, 86
Cross Keys 197, 208
Crouchback, Edmund, 1st Earl of Leicester and Lancaster 18, 21, 56, 78–9
Crowle's plan of Bedford House 116, *117*, 122
Cumberland, Earl of 83
Cure, William 57
Custodis, H. *196*

D

Dacre, Anne 39
Dacre, Thomas, 2nd Lord Dacre 127
Dacre, William, 3rd Lord Dacre 127
Dacre House 130, 137, *139*
Darcy, Sir Edward 163, 164
Davenport, John 121
De Beresford, William 18
De Breuse, William, Bishop of Llandaff 18
De Buck, John 146
De La Quadra, Alvaro 160
De l'Orme, Philibert 29
De Vries, Jan Vredeman 28, 222
Dean, Sir Anthony 193
Deeble, W. 87
Denham, Sir John 73
Denmark House 61, 65, 66
Devereux, Dorothy 30, 31
Devereux, Lady Frances (wife of William Seymour) 31
Devereux, Robert, 2nd Earl of Essex 9, 29, 178, 196
Devereux, Robert, 3rd Earl of Essex 29, 30, 31
Devereux, Robert (brother of 3rd Earl of Essex) 31
Devonshire House 155
Diaceto, Florence 92
Dietterlin, Wendel 203
Dimmock, Matthew 139, 219
Dodsley, Robert and James 74, 87
Dominis, Marco Antonio de 83
Dormer, Elizabeth 131
Drake, Robert 52

Drapers Company 33
Du Cerceau, Jacques Androuet 29, 151, 154, 203
Dudley, Ambrose, Earl of Warwick 110
Dudley, Edmund 24–7
Dudley, Guilford 160
Dudley, John, 1st Duke of Northumberland 20, 21, 60, 91, 160
Dudley, Robert, 1st Earl of Leicester 9, 17, 20–21, 22, 26, 30, 60, 61
    collection 26–7, 220
    and Durham House 160–61
    portrait 27
Dudley, Robert, son of 1st Earl of Leicester 29
Duggan, Diane 106, 113, *114*, 115, 116
Durham House 6, *12*, 13, 159–73, 222, 225
    and Cardinal Wolsey 34
    during the Civil War 173
    contents 163
    inventory 160
    John Dudley and 21
    'navy school' 163
    and Princess Elizabeth 60–61
    and the Suffolks 207
    tenements 160, 173
    wall fountain 115
    water supply 118–19
Durham Rents 40, 138, 143, 148, 150, 160, 163, 164, 165
Dyer, Edward 23

Edmonds, Sir Thomas 101
Edward II 79
Edward III 80
Edward VI 81, 160
Egerton, Sir Thomas, 1st Baron Ellesmere 6, 14, 164, 178–9, 193
Eleanor of Castile 78
Eleanor of Provence 77, 78
Elizabeth I 220, 222
    and Burghley House 92
    and Durham House 21, 60, 61, 160
    portrait 27
    and Robert Devereux 29
    and Salisbury House 139, 143
    and Somerset House 21, 60
    and Woburn Abbey 110
Embree, John 209
Esselens, Jacob 41, 45, *46*, 182, *183*
Essex House *16*, 17–31; *see also* Leicester House
    banqueting house 19, 22
    during the Civil War 31
    galleries 24–7, 219–20
    gardens 18, 19, 28–9, *30*
    inventories 21, 23–6
    tenements 17, 18, 21
Essex House Cabal 178
Essex Rebellion 29, 112
Evelyn, John 50, 51, 101, 193, 213, 214
Exeter, Bishops of 17–19
Exeter Change *102*, 103, *103*
    menagerie *102*, 102

Exeter House *see* Burghley House
Exeter Street 103

Fairfax, Mary 193
Fairfax, Thomas, 3rd Lord Fairfax 133, 193
Faithorne, William *84*, 151, *153*, *173*, *184*, 203
Falda, Giovan Battista 225
Fane, Sir Francis 83
Farnese, Alessandro 154, 182
'Fatal Vespers' 165
Fauconberg, Eustace de 33
Felton, John 193
Fitzalan, Henry, 12th Earl of Arundel 10, 19, 35, 37–8, 39, 40
Fitzalan, Mary 38
Fitzroy, Henry 159, 176
Fitzwilliam, William, 1st Earl of Southampton 34
Flourit, H. 160
Foix, Paul de 92
Fortescue, Sir Nicholas 138, 160
Fortescue, William 138
Fowler, Thomas 220
Fracart, Jacques 100
Friars Pyes 3, 109, 110
Fuller, Thomas 129

Galloway, Stephen 52
Gentileschi, Orazio 190, 192, 193
George, Lord Carew 83
George III 74
Gerbier, Sir Balthasar 14, 47, 181, 182, 183, 184–5, 186, 189, 190, 192, 193, 225
Gering, Giles 57
Gheeraerts, Marcus, the younger 96
Giambologna 192
Gilbert, John 163
Gillet, Edward 122
Girouard, Mark 60, 190
Glover, Miles (or Moses) 203
Goat Inn 56
Godeley, John 18
Goldring, Elizabeth 17, 26
Gonzaga collection 221
Goodrowse, William 63
Gorges, Sir Arthur 139
Gorhambury House 176–7, *177*, 180
Gowbarrow Park 40
Grandison, John 18
Gray's Inn 177
Greenwich Lodge 40, 207
Greenwich Palace 2, 171
Gresham, Sir Thomas 35, 92–3, 222
Grey, Catharine 160
Grey, Lady Jane 61, 91, 160

Hale, Richard 176
Hale, William 176

Hampton Court 204, 220, 224
Hampton Place 34
Hardwick Hall 15, 64, 202, 203, 219, 220, 221, 224
Harington, John 112
Harington House, Bishopsgate 112
Haro, Don Luis de 166
Harrington, Sir John 139
Harrington, Lucy, Countess of Bedford 112, 221
Harriot, Thomas 162, 163
Harris, John 167, 168, 172, 187
Harrison, Walter 79, 83, 87
Harrison, William 2, 3–4, 96
Harvey, Gabriel 23
Harward, William 91
Hatfield, Thomas, Bishop of Durham 159
Hatfield House 60, 143, 150, 154, 207
Hatton, Sir Christopher 178
Hatton, Sir William 100
Hawthorne, Henry 22, 23, 96
Hay, James, 1st Earl of Carlisle 30
Heath, Nicholas, Archbishop of York 176
Heath, Richard 121
Henderson, Paula 15, 89, 96
Heneage, Sir Thomas 39
Henrietta Maria (wife of Charles I) 46, 49, 65–73, 101
Henry, 3rd Earl of Lancaster 79
Henry, 4th Earl of Lancaster, later 1st Duke of Lancaster 79
Henry, Prince (son of Henry IV) 159
Henry III 33, 77
Henry IV 80
Henry VII 81
Henry VIII 55
    and Bath Place 34
    and Bedford House 108, 109
    and Durham House 21, 160
    and Greenwich Palace 2
    and Somerset House 56
    and Whitehall 4
    and Worcester House 129
    and York House 176
Herbert, Henry (son of the 1st Earl of Pembroke) 160
Herbert, Philip, 4th Earl of Pembroke 6, 13, 160, 164–73, *165*, 189, 214
Herbert, Philip, 5th Earl of Pembroke 173
Herbert, Thomas, 8th Earl of Pembroke 166
Herbert, William, 3rd Earl of Pembroke 166
Herbert House 127
Hervey, Sir William 39
Hickes, Richard 28
Higgott, Gordon 187, 189
Hill Hall, Essex 58
Hippesley, Sir John 131
Hobbes, Thomas 155
Hoby, Thomas 176
Hogenberg, Frans, *Civitates Orbis Terrarum* 3, 20, 35, 57, *161*
Holbein, Hans, the Younger 154
Holdenby, Northamptonshire 178, 203
Holgil, William 81

Hollar, Wenceslaus
　engraving of Lord Arundel as antiquarian 34
　forecourt of Arundel House 36
　riverfront view of Arundel House 10, *44*
　riverfront view of Durham House, Salisbury House and Worcester House 12
　riverfront view of Northumberland House 15
　riverfront view of Somerset House 11
　riverfront view of the Savoy 11
　riverfront view of York House 14
　view of Covent Garden piazza 118
　'view of London extending eastwards from Peterborough House to Somerset House' *134, 152, 173, 183, 203*
　'West Central District' *8, 16, 32, 45, 49, 76, 104, 126, 152*
Hooke, Robert 51
Howard, Lady Aletheia (née Talbot) *see* Talbot, Aletheia, Countess of Arundel
Howard, Lady Anne (née Somerset) 50
Howard, Catherine (daughter of Thomas, 1st Earl of Suffolk) 207
Howard, Charles, 1st Earl of Nottingham 30, 39
Howard, Elizabeth (wife of Algernon Percy) 208, 212, 221
Howard, Elizabeth (wife of Theophilus, 2nd Earl of Suffolk) 208
Howard, Frances, Duchess of Richmond (wife of Robert Carr) 30, 101, 178, 207
Howard, Henry, 1st Earl of Northampton 6, 7, 14–15, 19, 30, 39, 40, 49, 113, 163–4, 181, 207
　collection 204, 207, 223
　Northumberland House 195–207, 223
　portrait *196*
　and Robert Cecil 197
　Somerset House Conference 61
Howard, Henry, 6th Duke of Norfolk 50–51, 52, 207
Howard, Henry, 7th Duke of Norfolk 52
Howard, Henry, Earl of Surrey *47, 49,* 195
Howard, Henry Frederick, 15th Earl of Arundel 49, 50
Howard, James, 3rd Earl of Suffolk 208
Howard, Katherine, 1st Countess of Suffolk 207
Howard, Lady Mary (née Fitzalan) 38
Howard, Philip, 13th Earl of Arundel 19, 38, 178
Howard, Theophilus, 2nd Earl of Suffolk 207, 208
Howard, Thomas, 3rd Duke of Norfolk 19
Howard, Thomas, 4th Duke of Norfolk 4, 38, 195, 207
Howard, Thomas, 14th Earl of Arundel 6, 10, *34,* 50, 193
　Arundel House 39–49
　collection 39, 46–7, 49, 50, 221
　and Northumberland House 204, 207
　portrait *42, 48,* 213
Howard, Thomas, 16th Earl of Arundel 50
Howard, Thomas, 1st Earl of Suffolk 4, 30, 39, 42, *48,* 207, 208
Howard, William 130
Howard House 4, 207

Howell, James 131, 224
Hughson, David 87
Husselby, Jill 15, 89, 96
Hutchinson, John 198
Hutton, Matthew, Archbishop of York 178
Hyde, Anne 134
Hyde, Edward, 1st Earl of Clarendon 84, 134
Hyde, Henry, 2nd Earl of Clarendon 74

I

Inner Temple 29
Innocents, Church of the 78
Ivy Lane 139, 147, 148, 150

J

Jackson, John 118
James, Isaac 40
James I of England (and James VI of Scotland) 6, 13, 14
　and Arundel House 39
　and Burghley House 96, 100
　and Northumberland House 222
　and Somerset House 61, 65
James II 74
　and the Savoy 86
　and Worcester House 134
Janseen, Bernard 203, 223
Jesuits 86
Jocelyn, Bishop of Bath and Wells 33
John, King of France 79
John of Gaunt, 1st Duke of Lancaster 12, 79–80
John of St Paul (or Pol) 18
Johnson, Ben 179
Jolly, John 122
Jones, Inigo 221
　Arundel House 10, 39, 40, *41, 41,* 44, 45–6, *47, 47,* 220
　Banqueting House 166, 182
　Covent Garden piazza 113, 166
　design for a 'pergular' 100, *100,* 155
　design for a stable 150, *151,* 163
　Henry Howard, Earl of Surrey 49
　New Hall, Essex 182
　and Northumberland House 199, 209, 212
　Salisbury House 147, 150, *151*
　Salisbury House masque 143, 150
　Somerset House 65, *66, 66*–70, *70*
　Somerset House masques 65, 225
　St Paul's, Covent Garden 221
　and Titian's *Ecce Homo* 47, 193
　York House 185, 186, 187
Jonson, Ben 143, 225
Joyner, Thomas 122
Junius, Francis 49

K

Katherine of Aragon 34, 129, 159
Kenilworth Castle 20, 22, 23, 28, 220
Killigrew, Henry 86, 176
Killigrew, Sir Peter 171

Killigrew, Thomas 92
Kingsford, Charles 17, 23, 24, *24,* 33
Kip, Jan 72
Kirby Hall, Northamptonshire 221
Knights of St John 18
Knights Templar 17
Knollys, Lettice, Countess of Essex 21, 23, 25, 29, 30
Knyff, Leonard 72
Knyvet, Frances 185
Knyvett, Sir Thomas 207
Kyte, Bishop John 127, 129

L

Lacy, Edmund 18–19, 22
Lacy, John 106, 116, 117, 121
Langton, Walter 55
Le Scrop (Scrope), Sir Henry 79
Le Sueur, Hubert 69
Lea, Philip 51, *52, 74*
Lee, Rowland 56
Leicester House 20, *21,* 21–3, 161, 178, 202; *see also* Essex House
　armour and other military items 27
　Banqueting House 19, 22, 26, *28, 28, 29, 29*
　books 'great and small' 28
　galleries 24–6, 27, 29
　gardens 28–9
　inventories 21, 23–6, 28
　picture collection 26, 27
　plan 23, *24, 24*
　sculpture 27
　tapestries 26–7, *28, 28, 29*
Lewis, William 190, 191, 192
Libaerts, Eliseus 27
Ligorio, Pirro 214
Liminge, Robert 143, 150
Lisle, Brian 78
Llandaff, Bishop of 79
Llandaff Inn 56
Locke, John 103
Loftie, Rev. William John 77, 80
Long Acre 3, 109, 112, 150
Longleat, Wiltshire 58, 221, 223
Lovelidge, John 148
Lovell, Humphrey 57
Ludlow, Edmund 49
Lyveden New Bield 100, 222

M

MacDonnell, Randall, 2nd Earl and 1st Marquess of Antrim 193
Madge, Sidney J. 128–9
Maltravers, Lord 41
Mandey, Venterus 122
Manners, Elizabeth (wife of Thomas Cecil, 1st Earl of Exeter) 83
Manners, Francis, 6th Earl of Rutland 185
Manners, Sir George, 7th Earl of Rutland 83
Manners, Henry, 2nd Earl of Rutland 112, 129
Manners, Lady Katherine 185

INDEX | 259

Manners, Roger 83
Manningham, John 139
Marlowe, Christopher 162
Marshall, Edward 213, 214, *216*
Mary, Queen of Scots 178
Mary I (Mary Tudor) 81, 82, 160
Matilda (or Maud), Countess of Lancaster 79
Matthew, Tobias, Bishop of Durham 148, 163, 164, 180
Matthews, Sir Philip 193
Mauclerk, Walter 129
Maximilien de Béthune, Duke of Sully 39
May, Hugh 73
McEvansoneya, Philip 181, 182, 190
Merks, Thomas 129
Middle Exchange 155, *156*, 156
Middle Temple 19, 31
Milford Lane 17, 19, 20, 32, 33, 92
Milford Stairs 33, 38
Mills, Peter 171
Milner, Richard 131
Minories 34
Montagu, Henry, 1st Earl of Manchester 180
Montaigne, George 82, 83
Montano, Giovanni Battista 214
Montmorency, Duc de 60
Moor Park, Hertfordshire 112
Morden, Robert 51, *52*, 74
Morgan, Sir Thomas 131
Morgan, William
   Map of London 23, 38, 50, 102
   View of London and Westminster 51, 73, 86, *135*, 153, 203
Morrison, Sir Richard 129
Morton, Sir Albert 182
Morton, Thomas 121, 165
Mount, William 82
Murray, Sir David 82
Mytens, Daniel 41, *42, 43, 45*, 46

Neale, Richard 82
Needham, Raymond 55
Nethersole, Sir Francis 30
New Exchange *13*, 13, *102*, 102, 121, 150, *153*, 164, 165, 225
New Hall, Essex 180, 181, 187
Newcourt, Richard 83, *84*, 151, *153*, 173, *184*, 203
Newman, John 15, 17, 181
Nonsuch Palace 37
Norden, John 21
   Civitas Londini 61, 82, *130*, 176, 197
   Speculum Britanniae 21, 37, 58, 78, 95, 109, 128, 139, *161*, 178
North, Sir Edward 4
Northampton House 4, 14, *15*, 15, 39, 195-208, 207; *see also* Northumberland House
   gallery 201-2, 220
   and Somerset House similarities 64
Northumberland House 15, 195-217, 223, 225; *see also* Northampton House
   antique statues 214
   garden 200
   inventories 204, 214-16
   Strand front *194*, 203, *203*
   tenements 197, 198
Norwich (later York) Rents 175
Norwich Inn (or Place) 13-14, 175-6

Oatlands 210
Ogilby, John
   Map of London 23, 38, 50, 102
Oram, William 122
Osborne, John 13, 147, *148*
Overbury, Sir Thomas 30, 180, 207

Paget, Henry 20
Paget, William 19, 20, 91
Paget Place (later Leicester House) 19, 20, *20*, 91, 93, 161
Palazzo Farnese 10, 46
Palladio 113, 223
Palmer House 91, *91*, 109
Palmer Knight, Sir Thomas 91
Parker, William 131
Parsones, John 122
Paulet, William, 1st Marquess of Winchester 96
Pawlett, Elizabeth 30-31
Pawlett, Sir William 31
Peirce, Edward 213
Peirce, John 214
Pembroke collection 166-7
Pennant, Thomas 83, 87
Pepys, Samuel 31, 50, 134
Percival, Richard 137-8, 139, 147
Percy, Algernon, 10th Earl of Northumberland 6, 14, 30, 133, 155, 193, 207
   collection 213, 214-16
   Northumberland House 208-16, 223
Percy, Sir Allan 30
Percy, Elizabeth, Duchess of Northumberland (née Howard) 208, 212, 221
Percy, Lady Elizabeth 217
Percy, Henry, the Wizard (9th) Earl of Northumberland 30, 162, 207
Percy, Hugh, 1st Duke of Northumberland 217
Percy, Josceline, 11th Earl of Northumberland 30, 209, 216
Percy, Lucy 30
Petworth 215, 216
Pikarell, John 57
Pindar, Paul 201
Pinke, John 123
Pirckheimer, Willibald 49
Polito, Stefano 102
Poor, Richard, Bishop of Durham 159
Pratt, Roger 171
Prideaux, Humphrey 50
Puckering, Lady 178
Puckering, Sir John 178
Puncherdown, John 57

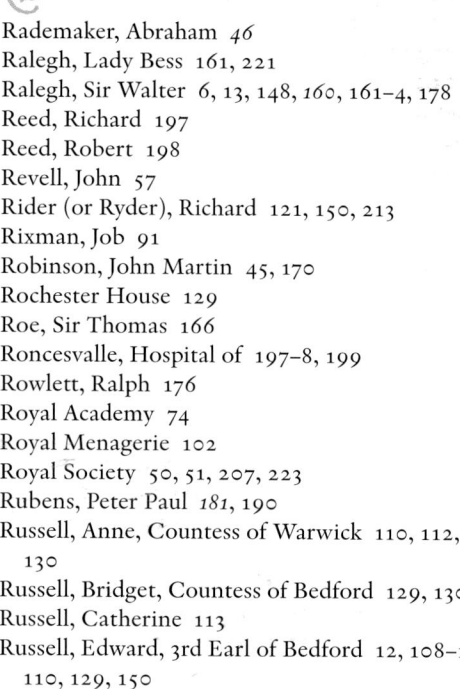

Rademaker, Abraham *46*
Ralegh, Lady Bess 161, 221
Ralegh, Sir Walter 6, 13, 148, *160*, 161-4, 178
Reed, Richard 197
Reed, Robert 198
Revell, John 57
Rider (or Ryder), Richard 121, 150, 213
Rixman, Job 91
Robinson, John Martin 45, 170
Rochester House 129
Roe, Sir Thomas 166
Roncesvalle, Hospital of 197-8, 199
Rowlett, Ralph 176
Royal Academy 74
Royal Menagerie 102
Royal Society 50, 51, 207, 223
Rubens, Peter Paul *181*, 190
Russell, Anne, Countess of Warwick 110, 112, 130
Russell, Bridget, Countess of Bedford 129, 130
Russell, Catherine 113
Russell, Edward, 3rd Earl of Bedford 12, 108-12, 110, 129, 150
Russell, Lady Elizabeth 130, 137
Russell, Francis, 2nd Earl of Bedford 92, 93, 108, 110, 112, 129
Russell, Francis, 4th Earl of Bedford 101, 107, 112-20, 131
Russell, John, 1st Earl of Bedford 108, 129
Russell, Lucy, Countess of Bedford (née Harrington) 112, 221
Russell, William, 5th Earl and 1st Duke of Bedford 108, 110, 117, 118, 120-25
Russell, William, Lord Russell of Thornhaugh 110, 112
Russell, Wriothesley, 2nd Duke of Bedford 125
Russell House 108, 127, *128*, 129, 178; *see also* Worcester House
Russell House, Chiswick 129
Ruthall, Thomas, Bishop of Durham 159
Rutland House 148
Rye House Plot 125

Sackville, Edward, 4th Earl of Dorset 180
Salisbury House 12, 13, 137-57, 222, 225
   and Durham House 147-8
   galleries 139, 142, *143*, 220
   garden 147, *148*, 150
   inventories 151-2, 154-5
   Little Salisbury House 13, 148, 150, 151, 155, 157
   'Porticus' (loggia) 147, 222
   portrait collection 154
   stables 150, *151*
   Strand front 142, *146*, 146, 150, 151, 155
   tenements 156, 157
Salisbury Street *154*, 157
Sandeen, Ernest R. 177
Sandrart, Joachim von 49, 224
Savoy, Peter, Count of 12, 33, 77-8

Savoy, the 12, 77–87, 222, 225
    Chapel 61, 79
    during the Civil War 83
    during the Commonwealth 84, 86
    Hospital 81–7
    tenements 82, 83
Savoy Conference (1661) 83, 225
Savoy Theatre 135
Scamozzi, Vincenzo 172
Scawen, Robert 107
'School of Night/Atheism' 162
Scott, Robert 197
Scott-Thomson, Gladys 106
Scrots, William 49
Seale, Humphrey 132
Serlio, Sebastiano 60, 73, 113
Seymour, Algernon, 7th Duke of Somerset 217
Seymour, Charles, 6th Duke of Somerset 217
Seymour, Edward, 1st Duke of Somerset 6, 6, 55–61, 91, 109
Seymour, Lady Elizabeth (née Percy) 217
Seymour, Jane (wife of Henry VIII) 55
Seymour, Thomas, 1st Baron Seymour of Sudeley 10, 34–5, 56–7
Seymour, William, 1st Marquess of Hertford and 2nd Duke of Somerset 31
Seymour Place 35
Sheldon, Gilbert 83
Sherborne Castle 161, 162
Shirley, Sir Charles 31
Shute, John 23
Sidney, Mary 112
Sidney, Sir Philip 23, 30, 112
Sidney, Robert and Dorothy, 2nd Earl and Countess of Leicester 30
Simson, Thomas 210
Smithson, Sir Hugh 217
Smythson (or Smithson), John 41, 44, 44, 45, 62, 100, 199
Smythson (or Smithson), Robert 62, 63
Somerset, Anne (née Russell) 130
Somerset, Lady Anne (daughter of 2nd Marquess of Worcester) 50
Somerset, Edward, 2nd Marquess of Worcester 50, 132, 133, 134
Somerset, Edward, 4th Earl of Worcester 130, 131
Somerset, Edward, son of Henry, Lord Herbert 131
Somerset, Elizabeth, Lady Montagu 133
Somerset, Henry, 3rd Marquess and 1st Duke of Beaufort 134
Somerset, Henry, Lord Herbert, later 5th Earl and 1st Marquess of Worcester 130, 131
Somerset, Margaret, Countess of Worcester, second wife of Edward Somerset 133–4
Somerset, Thomas (son of Henry, 5th Earl of Somerset) 132
Somerset House 4, 10–11, 55–74, 210, 221
    Cabinet Room 68, 68
    Chapel 66, 66, 67, 70, 73, 74, 221
    cistern house 68, 69
    during the Commonwealth 70, 72
    Council Chamber 61, 63, 65
    courtyards 57, 63, 64, 65
    galleries 63–4, 220
    garden front 65
    gardens 63, 69, 73
    Hall 64, 65, 72
    paintings 69
    Privy Lodgings 63, 65
    Robert Dudley and 21
    state rooms 63–4, 65, 72
    statues 69–70, 72
    Strand front 58, 59, 60, 64, 65, 70, 71, 72–3, 74
    tenements 55, 56, 65, 70
    tennis court 69
    theatre 70
    water gate 68, 68–9, 69
    and Zachary Taylor 209, 210
Somerset House Conference 7, 61, 65, 225
Sorbière, Samuel de 123, 225
Southampton House 125
Southampton Street 125
Spenser, Edmund 22, 23
Spicer, William 23
Spinelli, Giulio 23
St Bernard the Great 78
St Clement Danes 12, 17–18, 19, 20, 33, 89
St James, Hospital of 78
St James's Palace 65, 74, 210
St Martin-in-the-Fields 208
St Martin's Lane 112, 163
St Mary of Strand 56
St Mary-le-Strand 78, 79
St Paul's Cathedral 113, 177
St Paul's, Covent Garden 116, 221
Stanley, Elizabeth, Lady Derby 130
Stanley, William, 6th Earl of Derby 98, 129
Stapledon (Stapeldon), Walter de 17, 18, 19
Steevens, Thomas 209, 210
Stockett, Lewis 57
Stoke (or Stokes), Charles 187
Stone, Henry 209, 210
Stone, Nicholas 40, 113, 116, 187, 189, 189
Stone, Simon 214
Story, Edward 129
Stow, John 15, 18, 22, 35, 56, 58, 91, 111, 139, 173, 177
Strand Bridge Lane 35
Strand Inn 35, 56
Strickland, William, Bishop 127
Strype, John 15
    on Beaufort House 134–5
    on Burghley House 102
    on Middle Exchange 155
    on Salisbury Street 157
    on the Savoy 86–7
    A Survey of the Cities of London and Westminster 52, 75, 87, 135
    on Wimbledon House 100
Sturdy, D. 45, 47
Suffolk House 6, 207–8
Suffolk House Cabal 216
Summerson, John 58, 60, 107, 113, 187
Surrey Street 51
Sydney, Sir Philip 27
Symonds, Richard 166, 214
Syon House 203, 209, 213, 215, 217

T

Tait, A. A. 167, 168, 172
Talbot, Aletheia, Countess of Arundel 39, 40, 43, 220, 221
Talbot, Gilbert, 7th Earl of Shrewsbury 39
Tart Hall, St James's Park 40
Tavistock Street 125
Taylor, Zachary 209, 210
Temple Church 19
Temple Newsam 204
Teniers, David 166
Thanet House 103
Theobalds 35, 96, 98, 98, 99, 100, 178, 221
Thinne, Thomas 31
Thomas, 2nd Earl of Leicester and Lancaster 56, 79
Thorpe, John 58, 59, 60, 64–5, 171, 200, 200–01, 201, 203, 224
Throckmorton, Nicholas 92
Thurland, Thomas 81–2
Thurley, Simon 15, 55, 58, 60
Thynne, Sir John 23, 58, 60, 221
Tisser, Anne 134
Titian 14, 47, 191, 193, 214
Tremes, Comte de 208
Tresham, Sir Thomas 100
Trunquet (or Trunckey), Robert 23
Tunstall, Cuthbert, Bishop of Durham 160
Turner, J. M. W. 192
Twickenham Park 112

V

Valence, Aymer de, Earl of Pembroke 18
Van Dyck, Sir Anthony 166, 209, 214
Van Somer, Paul 47
Vanderbank, John 179
Vane, Sir Henry 209, 210
Venyt, Bartholomew de 78
Veronese 27
Vertue, George 79, 83, 84, 85, 87, 186, 203
Vesey, Bishop John 19
Villa Farnese 182, 225
Villiers, Charles, ?? 63
Villiers, George, 1st Duke of Buckingham 6
    collection 47, 182, 189–91, 192, 193, 213
    portrait 181
    and Somerset House 65
    York House 180–93
Villiers, George, 2nd Duke of Buckingham 193
Villiers, John, Viscount Purbeck 63, 65
Villiers, Katherine (née Manners) 193
Villiers, Lady Mary 180
Villiers Street 193
Vincent's House 148
Vitruvius 154–5
The Vyne 116, 213

W

Wale, Simon 212, *213*
Walker, John 213
Waller, Sir William 118
Wallingford House 180, 181, 184, 193
Walpole, Horace 58
Walsingham, Frances 30
Wanstead House, Essex 181
Wanstead Manor 20, 22, 28, 29
Webb, John 13, 69, 70, *71*, 73
    Durham House 166, *166–7*, 167–72, *168*, *169*, *170*, *171*, *172*
    Northumberland House 213, 214, *215*, *216*
    York House 187, *188*
Webster, Alexander 55
Weller, Hans 113
Wentworth, Sir Thomas, Earl of Strafford 185
Westcott, John 132
White, Adam 187, 189
White Friars 129
White Hart Inn 93
Whitehall Palace 4, 5, 171, 193, 199, 210
Wijck, Thomas 187
William III and Mary II 74, 86
Wilson, Sir Thomas 40, 142, 143, 164, 165
Wilton House, Wiltshire 116, 166, 167, 214
Wimbledon House 100, 101
Woburn Abbey 106, 110, 112, 113, 114, 115, 116, 117
Wollaton, Nottinghamshire 29, 221, 224
Wolsey, Cardinal 4, 34, 81, 129, 159, 160, 204, 223, 224
Wood, William 143
Worcester House 12, *12*, 108, *108*, 127–35, 222; *see also* Russell House
    during the Civil War 131
    garden 133
    inventory 131–3
    and Russell family 128
    shared cistern 131
    Surveying Place 131, 222
    tenements 127
Worcester Inn 56
Wotton, Sir Henry 182
Wren, Sir Christopher 51, *101*, 103, *156*, 157, 214
Wriothesley, Mary, Countess of Southampton 39
Wriothesley, Thomas, 4th Earl of Southampton 125
Wyngaerde, Anthonis van den 34
    Panorama of London from the River 8, 18, 19, 34, 57, 78, 79, 158
    view of Greenwich Palace from the river 2
    view of Whitehall Palace from the river 5

Y

York House 6, 13–14, *14*, 63, 116, 133, 175–94, 222–3, 225
    and Cardinal Wolsey 34
    garden 187
    inventory 189–92
    museum 181
    and Sir Thomas Egerton 164
    tenements 175
    water gate 183–4, 185, *186*, *187*, 187, *189*, 189, 192, 193, 225
York Place 34
York Rents 175

Z

Zuccaro, Federico 27